Media & Culture respects students' opinions, while challenging them to take more responsibility and to be accountable for their media choices. This text is essential for professors who are truly committed to teaching students how to understand the media.

DREW JACOBS,
CAMDEN COUNTY COLLEGE

The critical perspective has enlightened the perspective of all of us who study media, and Campbell has the power to infect students with his love of the subject.

ROGER DESMOND,
UNIVERSITY OF HARTFORD

I will switch to Campbell because it is a tour de force of coverage and interpretation, it is the best survey text in the field hands down, and it challenges students. Campbell's text is the most thorough and complete in the field. . . . No other text is even close.

RUSSELL BARCLAY,
QUINNIPIAC UNIVERSITY

The feature boxes are excellent and are indispensable to any classroom.

MARVIN WILLIAMS,
KINGSBOROUGH
COMMUNITY COLLEGE

I love *Media & Culture*! I have used it since the first edition. *Media & Culture* integrates the history of a particular medium or media concept with the culture, economics, and the technological advances of the time. But more than that, the authors are explicit in their philosophy that media and culture cannot be separated.

DEBORAH LARSON,
MISSOURI STATE UNIVERSITY

Media & Culture

Mass Communication in a Digital Age

Ninth Edition

Richard Campbell
Miami University

Christopher R. Martin
University of Northern Iowa

Bettina Fabos
University of Northern Iowa

BEDFORD/ST. MARTIN'S
Boston • New York

"WE ARE NOT ALONE."
For my family — Chris, Caitlin, and Dianna

"YOU MAY SAY I'M A DREAMER, BUT I'M NOT THE ONLY ONE."
For our daughters — Olivia and Sabine

For Bedford/St. Martin's

Publisher for Communication: Erika Gutierrez
Developmental Editor: Jesse Hassenger
Senior Production Editor: Bill Imbornoni
Senior Production Supervisor: Dennis J. Conroy
Marketing Manager: Stacey Propps
Copy Editor: Denise Quirk
Indexer: Melanie Belkin
Photo Researcher: Sue McDermott Barlow
Permissions Manager: Kalina K. Ingham
Art Director: Lucy Krikorian
Text: TODA (The Office of Design and Architecture)
Cover Design: Donna Lee Dennison
Cover Photo: Light Stage 6, USC Institute for Creative Technologies
Composition: Cenveo® Publisher Services
Printing and Binding: RR Donnelley and Sons

President, Bedford/St. Martin's: Denise B. Wydra
Presidents, Macmillan Higher Education: Joan E. Feinberg and Tom Scotty
Director of Development: Erica T. Appel
Director of Marketing: Karen R. Soeltz
Production Director: Susan W. Brown
Associate Production Director: Elise S. Kaiser
Managing Editor: Shuli Traub

Manufactured in the United States of America.

8 7 6 5 4 3
f e d c b a

For information, write: Bedford/St. Martin's, 75 Arlington Street,
Boston, MA 02116   (617-399-4000)

ISBN: 978-1-4576-2831-3

About the Authors

Richard Campbell, director of the journalism program at Miami University, is the author of *"60 Minutes" and the News: A Mythology for Middle America* (1991) and coauthor of *Cracked Coverage: Television News, the Anti-Cocaine Crusade, and the Reagan Legacy* (1994). Campbell has written for numerous publications, including *Columbia Journalism Review, Journal of Communication,* and *Media Studies Journal,* and he is on the editorial boards of *Critical Studies in Mass Communication* and *Television Quarterly.* He also serves on the board of directors for Cincinnati Public Radio. He holds a Ph.D. from Northwestern University and has also taught at the University of Wisconsin–Milwaukee, Mount Mary College, the University of Michigan, and Middle Tennessee State University.

Christopher R. Martin is a professor of journalism at the University of Northern Iowa and author of *Framed! Labor and the Corporate Media* (2003). He has written articles and reviews on journalism, televised sports, the Internet, and labor for several publications, including *Communication Research, Journal of Communication, Journal of Communication Inquiry, Labor Studies Journal,* and *Culture, Sport, and Society.* He is also on the editorial board of the *Journal of Communication Inquiry.* Martin holds a Ph.D. from the University of Michigan and has also taught at Miami University.

Bettina Fabos, an award-winning video maker and former print reporter, is an associate professor of visual communication and interactive media studies at the University of Northern Iowa. She is the author of *Wrong Turn on the Information Superhighway: Education and the Commercialized Internet* (2004). Her areas of expertise include critical media literacy, Internet commercialization, the role of the Internet in education, and media representations of popular culture. Her work has been published in *Library Trends, Review of Educational Research,* and *Harvard Educational Review.* Fabos has also taught at Miami University and has a Ph.D. from the University of Iowa.

Brief Contents

Preface

The media are in a constant state of change, but in recent years, a larger shift has become visible. E-books are outselling print books on Amazon; digital album sales have shot up as CD sales decline; and social networking sites like Facebook and Twitter reach hundreds of millions of users worldwide. As mass media converge, the newest devices multitask as e-readers, music players, Web browsers, TV and movie screens, gaming systems, and phones. In other words, the mass media world has *really* made the turn into digital technology.

Today's students are experiencing the digital turn firsthand. Many now watch television shows on their own schedule rather than when they are broadcast on TV, stream hit singles rather than purchase full albums, and use their videogame consoles to watch movies and socialize with friends. But while students are familiar with the newest products and latest formats, they may not understand how the media evolved to this point; how technology converges text, audio, and visual media; what all these developments mean; and how they have transformed our lives. This is why we believe the critical and cultural perspectives at the core of *Media and Culture*'s approach are more important than ever. *Media and Culture* pulls back the curtain to show students how the media really work—from the historical roots and economics of each media industry to the implications of today's consolidated media ownership to the details of their turn into the digital world. And by learning to look at the media—whether analog past, digital present, or converged future—through a critical lens, students will better understand the complex relationship between the mass media and our shared culture.

The ninth edition of *Media and Culture* confronts the digital realities of how we consume media *now.* To tie these developments together, new part openers offer an overview of the issues raised by converging media, accompanied by infographics with eye-catching statistics about how media consumption has changed in recent years, reflecting the power of technologies like DVRs, streaming radio, e-readers and digital companies like Amazon, Apple, and Google. New Past-Present-Future boxes offer perspective on where the media industries began, how they've evolved to where they are today, and where they might be headed next. And a brand-new Chapter 3, "Digital Gaming and the Media Playground," addresses gaming's newfound role as a mass medium.

Increased video game coverage is just one example of how *Media and Culture* addresses the way mass media are converging and changing: Consoles can play not just video games but movies, music, and streaming video; streaming music continues to impact the record industry's profits; magazines and books have evolved for e-readers. *Media and Culture* tells all of these stories and more. Convergence happens even within *Media and Culture* itself; the ninth edition combines print and digital media into a single accessible package: We have expanded the book beyond the printed page with videos offering vivid insider perspectives on the mass media industries. These fully integrated videos from *VideoCentral: Mass Communication,* featured in the text and accompanied by discussion questions, offer additional material that expands on the print portion of the text.

Of course, *Media and Culture* retains its well-loved and teachable organization that gives students a clear understanding of the historical and cultural contexts for each media industry. Our signature approach to studying the media has struck a chord with hundreds of instructors and thousands of students across the United States and North America. We continue to be enthusiastic about—and humbled by—the chance to work with the amazing community of teachers that has developed around *Media and Culture.* We hope the text enables students to become more knowledgeable media consumers and engaged, media-literate citizens with a critical stake in shaping our dynamic world.

The Ninth Edition

The ninth edition of *Media and Culture* takes the digital turn, keeping pace with the technological, economic, and social effects of today's rapidly changing media landscape.

- **Part openers show how convergence shapes our media experience.** Each of the book's five parts opens with a new overview offering broad, cross-medium context for the chapters that follow and draws connections to other sections of the book. Each part opener also includes an eye-catching infographic full of facts and figures related to how we consume media, in their various forms, right now.

- **New Chapter 3 recognizes and explains video games as a mass medium.** This comprehensive new chapter, "Digital Gaming and the Media Playground," explores the gaming industry's journey from diversion to full-fledged mass medium—a transition that would not have been possible without convergence and the digital turn. In addition to covering the history, economics, and technology behind the industry, Chapter 3 also examines how gaming consoles function as an epicenter of media convergence.

- **New Past-Present-Future boxes explore where the media have been, how they have converged, and where they're headed.** *Media and Culture* goes beyond simply telling students about the latest media technologies. The ninth edition analyzes the social and economic impact of these developments—from how the publishing industry is adapting to e-books and digital readers to how filmmakers are harnessing the power of social media to promote their movies.

- **Print and media converge with fully integrated VideoCentral clips.** The new VideoCentral feature merges and converges *Media and Culture* with the Web. Video clips, added to every chapter, get students to think critically about the text and the media by giving them an insider's look at the media industries through the eyes of leading professionals, including Noam Chomsky, Amy Goodman, and Junot Díaz, addressing topics like net neutrality, the future of print media, media ownership, and more. These clips are showcased throughout the book and easily accessible online, where accompanying questions make them perfect for media response papers and class discussions. For more ideas on how using VideoCentral can enhance your course, see the Instructor's Resource Manual. For a complete list of available clips and access information, see the inside back cover or **bedfordstmartins.com/mediaculture.**

The Best and Broadest Introduction to the Mass Media

- **A critical approach to media literacy.** *Media and Culture* introduces students to five stages of the critical thinking and writing process—description, analysis, interpretation, evaluation, and engagement. The text uses these stages as a lens for examining the historical context and current processes that shape mass media as part of our culture. This framework informs the writing throughout, including the Media Literacy and the Critical Process boxes in each chapter.

- **A cultural perspective.** The text consistently focuses on the vital relationship between mass media and our shared culture—how cultural trends influence the mass media and how specific historical developments, technical innovations, and key decision makers in the history of the media have affected the ways our democracy and society have evolved.

- **Comprehensive coverage.** The text gives students the nuts-and-bolts content they need to understand each media industry's history, organizational structure, economic models, and market statistics.

- **An exploration of media economics and democracy.** To become more engaged in our society and more discerning as consumers, students must pay attention to the complex relationship between democracy and capitalism. To that end, *Media and Culture* spotlights the significance and impact of multinational media systems throughout the text, including the media ownership snapshots in each of the industry chapters. It also invites students to explore the implications of the Telecommunications Act of 1996 and other deregulation resolutions. Additionally, each chapter ends with a discussion of the effects of various mass media on the nature of democratic life.

- **Compelling storytelling.** Most mass media make use of storytelling to tap into our shared beliefs and values, and so does *Media and Culture*. Each chapter presents the events and issues surrounding media culture as intriguing and informative narratives, rather than as a series of unconnected facts and feats, and maps the uneasy and parallel changes in consumer culture and democratic society.
- **The most accessible book available.** Learning tools in every chapter help students find and remember the information they need to know. Bulleted lists at the beginning of every chapter give students a road map to key concepts; annotated timelines offer powerful visual guides that highlight key events and refer to more coverage in the chapter, Media Literacy and the Critical Process boxes model the five-step process, and the Chapter Reviews help students study and review.

Student Resources

For more information on student resources or to learn about package options, please visit the online catalog at **bedfordstmartins.com/mediaculture/catalog**.

New! Bedford *x-Book for Media & Culture*

Make it easy to get on the same page with your class. Add your own pages, documents, links, and assignments; and drag and drop the contents to match the way you teach your course. Give your students video, audio, and activities–content that can't be delivered on the printed page. And get your class talking–in the book itself. With the x-Book, students can read, watch, reflect, and share in the pages, providing a new kind of social learning experience, and instructors can see and respond to student work. What do you want *your* x-Book to be?

Your e-book. Your way

A variety of other e-book formats are available for use on computers, tablets, and e-readers. For more information see **bedfordstmartins.com/ebooks**.

Expanded! *MassCommClass* at yourmasscommclass.com

MassCommClass is designed to support students in all aspects of the introduction to mass communication course. It's fully loaded with videos from *VideoCentral: Mass Communication*, the Online Image Library, the *Media Career Guide*, and multiple study aids. Even better, new functionality makes it easy to upload and annotate video, embed YouTube clips, and create video assignments for individual students, groups, or the whole class. Adopt *MassCommClass* and get all the premium content and tools in one fully customizable course space; then assign, rearrange, and mix our resources with yours. *MassCommClass* requires an activation code.

Book Companion Site at bedfordstmartins.com/mediaculture

Free study aids on the book's Web site help students gauge their understanding of the text material through concise chapter summaries with study questions, visual activities that combine images and critical-thinking analysis, and pre- and post-chapter quizzes to help students assess their strengths and weaknesses and focus their studying. Students can also keep current on media news with streaming headlines from a variety of news sources and can use the Media Portal to find the best media-related Web sites. In addition, students can access other online resources such as *VideoCentral: Mass Communication*. For more information, see **bedfordstmartins.com/ebooks**.

Media Career Guide: Preparing for Jobs in the 21st Century, Ninth Edition
Sherri Hope Culver, *Temple University*; James Seguin, *Robert Morris College*;
ISBN: 978-1-4576-4163-3

Practical, student-friendly, and revised with recent trends in the job market (like the role of social media in a job search), this guide includes a comprehensive directory of media jobs, practical tips, and career guidance for students who are considering a major in the media industries. *Media Career Guide* can also be packaged for free with the print book.

Instructor Resources

For more information or to order or download the instructor resources, please visit the online catalog at **bedfordstmartins.com/mediaculture/catalog**.

Instructor's Resource Manual
Bettina Fabos, *University of Northern Iowa*; Christopher R. Martin, *University of Northern Iowa*; and Marilda Oviedo, *University of Iowa*

This downloadable manual improves on what has always been the best and most comprehensive instructor teaching tool available for introduction to mass communication courses. This extensive resource provides a range of teaching approaches, tips for facilitating in-class discussions, writing assignments, outlines, lecture topics, lecture spin-offs, critical-process exercises, classroom media resources, and an annotated list of more than two hundred video resources.

Test Bank
Christopher R. Martin, *University of Northern Iowa*; Bettina Fabos, *University of Northern Iowa*; and Marilda Oviedo, *University of Iowa*

Available both in print and as software formatted for Windows and Macintosh, the Test Bank includes multiple choice, true/false, matching, fill-in-the-blank, and short and long essay questions for every chapter in *Media and Culture*.

PowerPoint Slides
PowerPoint presentations to help guide your lecture are available for downloading for each chapter in *Media and Culture*.

The Online Image Library for *Media and Culture*
This free instructor resource provides access to hundreds of dynamic images from the pages of *Media and Culture*. These images can be easily incorporated into lectures or used to spark in-class discussion.

VideoCentral: Mass Communication DVD
The instructor DVD for *VideoCentral: Mass Communication* gives you another convenient way to access the collection of over forty short video clips from leading media professionals. The DVD is available upon adoption of *VideoCentral: Mass Communication*; please contact your local sales representative.

About the Media: Video Clips DVD to Accompany Media and Culture
This free instructor resource includes over fifty media-related clips, keyed to every chapter in *Media and Culture*. Designed to be used as a discussion starter in the classroom or to

illustrate examples from the textbook, this DVD provides the widest array of clips available for introduction to mass communication courses in a single resource. Selections include historical footage of the radio, television, and advertising industries; film from the Media Education Foundation; and other private and public domain materials. The DVD is available upon adoption of *Media and Culture;* please contact your local sales representative.

Questions for Classroom Response Systems

Questions for every chapter in *Media and Culture* help integrate the latest classroom response systems (such as i>clicker) into your lecture to get instant feedback on students' understanding of course concepts as well as their opinions and perspectives.

Content for Course Management Systems

Instructors can access content specifically designed for *Media and Culture* like quizzing and activities for course management systems such as WebCT and Blackboard. Visit **bedfordstmartins.com/coursepacks** for more information.

The Bedford/St. Martin's Video Resource Library

Qualified instructors are eligible to receive videos from the resource library upon adoption of the text. The resource library includes full-length films; documentaries from Michael Moore, Bill Moyers, and Ken Burns; and news-show episodes from *Frontline* and *Now.* Please contact your local publisher's representative for more information.

Acknowledgments

We are very grateful to everyone at Bedford/St. Martin's who supported this project through its many stages. We wish that every textbook author could have the kind of experience we had with these people: Chuck Christensen, Joan Feinberg, Denise Wydra, Erika Gutierrez, Erica Appel, Stacey Propps, Simon Glick, and Noel Hohnstine. Over the years, we have also collaborated with superb and supportive developmental editors: on the ninth edition, Ada Fung Platt and Jesse Hassenger. We particularly appreciate the tireless work of Shuli Traub, managing editor, who oversaw the book's extremely tight schedule; William Imbornoni, senior project editor, who kept the book on schedule while making sure we got the details right; Dennis J. Conroy, senior production supervisor; and Alexis Smith, associate editor. Thanks also to Donna Dennison for a fantastic cover design and to Kim Cevoli for a striking brochure. We are especially grateful to our research assistant, Susan Coffin, who functioned as a one-person clipping service throughout the process. We are also grateful to Jimmie Reeves, our digital gaming expert, who contributed his great knowledge of this medium to the development of Chapter 3.

We also want to thank the many fine and thoughtful reviewers who contributed ideas to the ninth edition of *Media and Culture:* Glenda Alvarado, *University of South Carolina;* Lisa Burns, *Quinnipiac University;* Matthew Cecil, *South Dakota University;* John Dougan, *Middle Tennessee State University;* Lewis Freeman, *Fordham University;* Cindy Hing-Yuk Wong, *College of Staten Island;* K. Megan Hopper, *Illinois State University;* John Kerezy, *Cuyahoga Community College;* Marcia Ladendorff, *University of North Florida;* Julie Lellis, *Elon University;* Joy McDonald, *Hampton University;* Heather McIntosh, *Boston College;* Kenneth Nagelberg, *Delaware State University;* Eric Pierson, *University of San Diego;* Jennifer Tiernan, *South Dakota State University;* Erin Wilgenbusch, *Iowa State University.*

For the eighth edition: Frank A. Aycock, *Appalachian State University;* Carrie Buchanan, *John Carroll University;* Lisa M. Burns, *Quinnipiac University;* Rich Cameron, *Cerritos College;* Katherine Foss, *Middle Tennessee State University;* Myleea D. Hill, *Arkansas State University;* Sarah Alford Hock, *Santa Barbara City College;* Sharon R. Hollenback, *Syracuse University;* Drew

Jacobs, *Camden County College*; Susan Katz, *University of Bridgeport*; John Kerezy, *Cuyahoga Community College*; Les Kozaczek, *Franklin Pierce University*; Deborah L. Larson, *Missouri State University*; Susan Charles Lewis, *Minnesota State University–Mankato*; Rick B. Marks, *College of Southern Nevada*; Donna R. Munde, *Mercer County Community College*; Wendy Nelson, *Palomar College*; Charles B. Scholz, *New Mexico State University*; Don W. Stacks, *University of Miami*; Carl Sessions Stepp, *University of Maryland*; David Strukel, *University of Toledo*; Lisa Turowski, *Towson University*; Lisa M. Weidman, *Linfield College*.

For the seventh edition: Robert Blade, *Florida Community College*; Lisa Boragine, *Cape Cod Community College*; Joseph Clark, *University of Toledo*; Richard Craig, *San Jose State University*; Samuel Ebersole, *Colorado State University–Pueblo*; Brenda Edgerton-Webster, *Mississippi State University*; Tim Edwards, *University of Arkansas at Little Rock*; Mara Einstein, *Queens College*; Lillie M. Fears, *Arkansas State University*; Connie Fletcher, *Loyola University*; Monica Flippin-Wynn, *University of Oklahoma*; Gil Fowler, *Arkansas State University*; Donald G. Godfrey, *Arizona State University*; Patricia Homes, *University of Southwestern Louisiana*; Daniel McDonald, *Ohio State University*; Connie McMahon, *Barry University*; Steve Miller, *Rutgers University*; Siho Nam, *University of North Florida*; David Nelson, *University of Colorado–Colorado Springs*; Zengjun Peng, *St. Cloud State University*; Deidre Pike, *University of Nevada–Reno*; Neil Ralston, *Western Kentucky University*; Mike Reed, *Saddleback College*; David Roberts, *Missouri Valley College*; Donna Simmons, *California State University–Bakersfield*; Marc Skinner, *University of Idaho*; Michael Stamm, *University of Minnesota*; Bob Trumpbour, *Penn State University*; Kristin Watson, *Metro State University*; Jim Weaver, *Virginia Polytechnic and State University*; David Whitt, *Nebraska Wesleyan University*.

For the sixth edition: Boyd Dallos, *Lake Superior College*; Roger George, *Bellevue Community College*; Osvaldo Hirschmann, *Houston Community College*; Ed Kanis, *Butler University*; Dean A. Kruckeberg, *University of Northern Iowa*; Larry Leslie, *University of South Florida*; Lori Liggett, *Bowling Green State University*; Steve Miller, *Rutgers University*; Robert Pondillo, *Middle Tennessee State University*; David Silver, *University of San Francisco*; Chris White, *Sam Houston State University*; Marvin Williams, *Kingsborough Community College*.

For the fifth edition: Russell Barclay, *Quinnipiac University*; Kathy Battles, *University of Michigan*; Kenton Bird, *University of Idaho*; Ed Bonza, *Kennesaw State University*; Larry L. Burris, *Middle Tennessee State University*; Ceilidh Charleson-Jennings, *Collin County Community College*; Raymond Eugene Costain, *University of Central Florida*; Richard Craig, *San Jose State University*; Dave Deeley, *Truman State University*; Janine Gerzanics, *West Valley College*; Beth Haller, *Towson University*; Donna Hemmila, *Diablo Valley College*; Sharon Hollenback, *Syracuse University*; Marshall D. Katzman, *Bergen Community College*; Kimberly Lauffer, *Towson University*; Steve Miller, *Rutgers University*; Stu Minnis, *Virginia Wesleyan College*; Frank G. Perez, *University of Texas at El Paso*; Dave Perlmutter, *Louisiana State University–Baton Rouge*; Karen Pitcher, *University of Iowa*; Ronald C. Roat, *University of Southern Indiana*; Marshel Rossow, *Minnesota State University*; Roger Saathoff, *Texas Tech University*; Matthew Smith, *Wittenberg University*; Marlane C. Steinwart, *Valparaiso University*.

For the fourth edition: Fay Y. Akindes, *University of Wisconsin–Parkside*; Robert Arnett, *Mississippi State University*; Charles Aust, *Kennesaw State University*; Russell Barclay, *Quinnipiac University*; Bryan Brown, *Southwest Missouri State University*; Peter W. Croisant, *Geneva College*; Mark Goodman, *Mississippi State University*; Donna Halper, *Emerson College*; Rebecca Self Hill, *University of Colorado*; John G. Hodgson, *Oklahoma State University*; Cynthia P. King, *American University*; Deborah L. Larson, *Southwest Missouri State University*; Charles Lewis, *Minnesota State University–Mankato*; Lila Lieberman, *Rutgers University*; Abbus Malek, *Howard University*; Anthony A. Olorunnisola, *Pennsylvania State University*; Norma Pecora, *Ohio University–Athens*; Elizabeth M. Perse, *University of Delaware*; Hoyt Purvis, *University of Arkansas*; Alison Rostankowski, *University of Wisconsin–Milwaukee*; Roger A. Soenksen, *James Madison University*; Hazel Warlaumont, *California State University–Fullerton*.

For the third edition: Gerald J. Baldasty, *University of Washington*; Steve M. Barkin, *University of Maryland*; Ernest L. Bereman, *Truman State University*; Daniel Bernadi, *University of Arizona*; Kimberly L. Bissell, *Southern Illinois University*; Audrey Boxmann, *Merrimack College*; Todd Chatman, *University of Illinois*; Ray Chavez, *University of Colorado*; Vic Costello, *Gardner–Webb University*; Paul D'Angelo, *Villanova University*; James Shanahan, *Cornell University*; Scott A. Webber, *University of Colorado*.

For the second edition: Susan B. Barnes, *Fordham University*; Margaret Bates, *City College of New York*; Steven Alan Carr, *Indiana University/Purdue University–Fort Wayne*; William G. Covington Jr., *Bridgewater State College*; Roger Desmond, *University of Hartford*; Jules d'Hemecourt, *Louisiana State University*; Cheryl Evans, *Northwestern Oklahoma State University*; Douglas Gomery, *University of Maryland*; Colin Gromatzky, *New Mexico State University*; John L. Hochheimer, *Ithaca College*; Sheena Malhotra, *University of New Mexico*; Sharon R. Mazzarella, *Ithaca College*; David Marc McCoy, *Kent State University*; Beverly Merrick, *New Mexico State University*; John Pantalone, *University of Rhode Island*; John Durham Peters, *University of Iowa*; Lisa Pieraccini, *Oswego State College*; Susana Powell, *Borough of Manhattan Community College*; Felicia Jones Ross, *Ohio State University*; Enid Sefcovic, *Florida Atlantic University*; Keith Semmel, *Cumberland College*; Augusta Simon, *Embry–Riddle Aeronautical University*; Clifford E. Wexler, *Columbia–Greene Community College*.

For the first edition: Paul Ashdown, *University of Tennessee*; Terry Bales, *Rancho Santiago College*; Russell Barclay, *Quinnipiac University*; Thomas Beell, *Iowa State University*; Fred Blevens, *Southwest Texas State University*; Stuart Bullion, *University of Maine*; William G. Covington Jr., *Bridgewater State College*; Robert Daves, *Minneapolis Star Tribune*; Charles Davis, *Georgia Southern University*; Thomas Donahue, *Virginia Commonwealth University*; Ralph R. Donald, *University of Tennessee–Martin*; John P. Ferre, *University of Louisville*; Donald Fishman, *Boston College*; Elizabeth Atwood Gailey, *University of Tennessee*; Bob Gassaway, *University of New Mexico*; Anthony Giffard, *University of Washington*; Zhou He, *San Jose State University*; Barry Hollander, *University of Georgia*; Sharon Hollenbeck, *Syracuse University*; Anita Howard, *Austin Community College*; James Hoyt, *University of Wisconsin–Madison*; Joli Jensen, *University of Tulsa*; Frank Kaplan, *University of Colorado*; William Knowles, *University of Montana*; Michael Leslie, *University of Florida*; Janice Long, *University of Cincinnati*; Kathleen Maticheck, *Normandale Community College*; Maclyn McClary, *Humboldt State University*; Robert McGaughey, *Murray State University*; Joseph McKerns, *Ohio State University*; Debra Merskin, *University of Oregon*; David Morrissey, *Colorado State University*; Michael Murray, *University of Missouri at St. Louis*; Susan Dawson O'Brien, *Rose State College*; Patricia Bowie Orman, *University of Southern Colorado*; Jim Patton, *University of Arizona*; John Pauly, *St. Louis University*; Ted Pease, *Utah State University*; Janice Peck, *University of Colorado*; Tina Pieraccini, *University of New Mexico*; Peter Pringle, *University of Tennessee*; Sondra Rubenstein, *Hofstra University*; Jim St. Clair, *Indiana University Southeast*; Jim Seguin, *Robert Morris College*; Donald Shaw, *University of North Carolina*; Martin D. Sommernes, *Northern Arizona State University*; Linda Steiner, *Rutgers University*; Jill Diane Swensen, *Ithaca College*; Sharon Taylor, *Delaware State University*; Hazel Warlaumont, *California State University–Fullerton*; Richard Whitaker, *Buffalo State College*; Lynn Zoch, *University of South Carolina*.

Special thanks from Richard Campbell: I would also like to acknowledge the number of fine teachers at both the *University of Wisconsin–Milwaukee* and *Northwestern University* who helped shape the way I think about many of the issues raised in this book, and I am especially grateful to my former students at the *University of Wisconsin–Milwaukee, Mount Mary College,* the *University of Michigan, Middle Tennessee State University,* and my current students at *Miami University.* Some of my students have contributed directly to this text, and thousands have endured my courses over the years—and made them better. My all-time favorite former students, Chris Martin and Bettina Fabos, are now essential coauthors, as well as the creators of our book's Instructor's Resource Manual, Test Bank, and the *About the Media* DVD. I am grateful for Chris and Bettina's fine writing, research savvy, good stories, and tireless work amid their own teaching schedules and writing careers, all while raising two spirited daughters. I remain most grateful, though, to the people I most love: my son, Chris; my daughter, Caitlin; and, most of all, my wife, Dianna, whose line editing, content ideas, daily conversations, shared interests, and ongoing support are the resources that make this project go better with each edition.

Special thanks from Christopher Martin and Bettina Fabos: We would also like to thank Richard Campbell, with whom it is always a delight working on this project. We also appreciate the great energy, creativity, and talent that everyone at Bedford/St. Martin's brings to the book. From edition to edition, we also receive plenty of suggestions from *Media and Culture* users and reviewers and from our own journalism and media students. We would like to thank them for their input and for creating a community of sorts around the theme of critical perspectives on the media. Most of all, we'd like to thank our daughters, Olivia and Sabine, who bring us joy and laughter every day, and a sense of mission to better understand the world of media and culture in which they live.

Please feel free to email us at **mediaandculture@bedfordstmartins.com** with any comments, concerns, or suggestions!

Contents

PART 2: SOUNDS AND IMAGES   114

A BRAND NE...
Arianna: The Huffington Post & A...

Media ownership **affects the media you consume and how you receive that media.**

While the media used to be owned by numerous different companies, today six large conglomerates—**Sony, Disney, Comcast/NBC Universal, News Corp., Time Warner, and CBS**—dominate. However, in the wake of the digital turn, several more companies have emerged as leaders in digital media. These five digital companies—**Apple, Amazon, Google, Microsoft,** and **Facebook**—began in software or as Web sites, but their reach has expanded to compete with traditional media companies in many areas as they have begun producing, distributing, and consuming content. This visualization breaks down the media holdings of these digital companies to help you understand their growing influence.

As you examine this information, think about how much of your daily media consumption is owned by these top digital companies (as well as more traditional conglomerates like Sony or Disney). Which companies have the most influence on your entertainment and news consumption? What about on the technology you use every day? What does it mean that so few companies own so much of the media? Are there areas where the newer digital companies have a weaker hold?

Top Digital Companies and Their 2011 Revenue

Apple
$108 billion
The company Steve Jobs built sells computers, iPods, iPads, iPhones— and the music, movies, and e-books you consume on them.

Microsoft
$69.9 billion
Thanks to their widely used Windows operating system and their Xbox gaming console, Microsoft is still a major force in the digital world.

Amazon
$48.1 billion
What began as an online bookstore now commands a high share of printed and recorded media in traditional and digital forms—and dominates the e-reader market.

Google
$37.9 billion
Still the most-used search engine, Google has branched out into other media with its Google Play service and the Android phone.

Facebook
$3.7 billion
Facebook doesn't yet have as broad a multimedia reach as Amazon or Apple, but it is easily the biggest and most powerful social networking site, which provides a platform for games, music, news feeds, and plenty of crowd-sourced content.

How much do media companies make, really?

$613,900,000,000 — ◀ $613.9 billion Department of Defense proposed budget for 2013

$85,000,000,000 — ◀ $85 billion Amount of 2008 U.S. government loan to insurance giant AIG

$79,610,000,000 — ◀ $79.6 billion Libya's Gross Domestic Product (GDP) in 2012 (projected)

$79,000,000,000 — ◀ $79 billion Facebook's reported value in 2012

$78,600,000,000 — ◀ $78.6 billion Sony's 2012 revenue

$61,000,000,000 — ◀ $61 billion Net worth of Bill Gates in 2012

$50,175,000,000 — ◀ $50.18 billion Google's 2012 revenue

$42,300,000,000 — ◀ $42.3 billion Disney's 2012 revenue

$34,000,000,000 — ◀ $34 billion News Corp.'s 2012 revenue

$29,000,000,000 — ◀ $29 billion Time Warner's 2011 revenue

$28,200,000,000 — ◀ $28.2 billion President's fiscal year budget for the U.S. Department of Justice in 2011

$18,700,000,000 — ◀ $18.7 billion NASA proposed budget for 2011

$17,000,000,000 — ◀ $17 billion Total U.S. retail sales in the video game industry in 2011

$14,100,000,000 — ◀ $14.1 billion Net worth of Mark Zuckerberg (CEO of Facebook) in 2011

$13,900,000,000 — ◀ $13.9 billion Viacom's 2012 revenue

$10,800,000,000 — ◀ $10.8 billion Total U.S. movie box-office receipts in 2012

$8,340,000,000 — ◀ $8.34 billion Environmental Protection Agency proposed budget for 2013

$1,510,000,000 — ◀ $1.51 billion Worldwide gross for *The Avengers*

$315,000,000 — ◀ $315 million Amount AOL paid for the *Huffington Post* in 2011

$40,000,000 — ◀ $40 million Estimated cost of the 2012 London Olympics opening ceremony

$35,000,000 — ◀ $35 million Amount News Corp. sold MySpace for in 2011

$1,500,000 — ◀ $1.5 million Amount *People* magazine paid for the exclusive photos from Kim Kardashian's wedding

$142,544 — ◀ $142,544 Average four-year tuition and room and board at a private university

$50,054 — ◀ $50,054 Median U.S. household income in 2011

◢Media & Culture

Mass Communication

A Critical Approach

On November 6, 2012, shortly after 11 P.M., Fox News projected that Barack Obama had won Ohio, as he did in 2008, and would be reelected president of the United States. But Karl Rove, a Fox News analyst and the chief campaign fundraiser for the Republican Party, began questioning the news anchors, arguing it was too early to call the election for President Obama. Rove persuaded one anchor to walk down the hall, on live television, and confront the statisticians in the "decision room" about their projection. What followed was an uncomfortable yet dramatic period, with Fox News managers sticking by their projection while Rove and Republican candidate Mitt Romney's campaign protested. It turned out that the statisticians were right.

This news drama during the 2012 election highlighted a number of media issues that swirled around the campaign. Rove's prominence and influence at Fox News showcased the outsized role campaign contributors seemed to play in the election. While the campaigns raised more than $1 billion each, the parties themselves and outside partisan groups raised an additional

$4 billion, making it the most expensive federal election ever.[1] With unlimited funds raised by corporations, rich individuals, and unknown groups (thanks to the *Citizens United v. Federal Election Commission* ruling by the Supreme Court—see Chapter 16), partisan pundits and concerned citizens alike fretted about rich donors dictating election outcomes.

Much of this money was spent, of course, on political TV ads. By mid-October 2012, the Las Vegas TV market had already aired 73,000 political ads—10,000 per week—a new record with three weeks still to go.[2] The Richmond (VA) TV market stood to rake in as much as $18 million.[3] Many local retailers in swing states could not afford TV advertising during the political blitz—or got bumped off the air by political advertisers, as TV stations jacked up prices and even cut local news time to squeeze in more ads.[4] One often suggested solution: "Require . . . television to provide free air time to qualified candidates."[5]

But while Republicans outspent Democrats in nine of ten swing states where most of the TV ad money was concentrated, North Carolina was the only swing state that went to Romney.[6] Exit-poll data provides some reasons for President Obama's win: He won 55 percent of women voters, 93 percent of African American voters, 71 percent of Hispanic voters, 73 percent of Asian voters, and, perhaps most telling, 60 percent of eighteen- to twenty-nine-year olds—the social media generation.[7] In 2012 the president "had 32 million likes compared with 12 million for Romney" on Facebook; and on Twitter, he had 23 million followers "and out-tweeted Mitt Romney by a margin of eight to one."[8]

Given the rise of social media and the new clout of young voters, it's worth asking whether TV will continue to play such an outsized role in future federal elections—especially since much ad spending did not produce the desired results. With the ability to mute ads or bypass them with DVRs, and with young people less interested in television, will such outrageous spending continue?

In the end, how well did TV media—where most people get their political information—help us understand the complex issues of our time? In a democracy, we depend on news media to provide information about these issues. As citizens, therefore, we should expect that TV stations use a portion of their massive political advertising revenue to investigate the main issues of the day and serve as a counterpoint to the one-sided and mostly negative ads—and not lay off reporters or cut their news-block time to run more ads. Despite the limitations of our news media, their job of presenting the world to us and documenting what's going on is enormously important. But we also must point a critical lens back at the media and describe, analyze, and interpret the stories and ads to arrive at informed judgments. This textbook offers a map to help us become more *media literate*, critiquing the media—not as detached cynics, but as informed audiences with a stake in the outcome.

▲

"The two main principles of marketing—not spending more than the sale is worth; focusing the most resources on the most susceptible buyers—are thrown out in presidential elections."

MICHAEL WOLFF, *USA TODAY*, 2012

◢ SO WHAT EXACTLY ARE THE ROLES AND RESPONSIBILITIES OF THE MEDIA?

In the wake of the 2012 presidential election, the economic and unemployment crises, the Occupy Wall Street movement, the ongoing war in Afghanistan, and the political uprisings in several Arab nations, how do we demand the highest standards from our media to describe and analyze such complex events and issues? At their best, in all their various forms, from mainstream newspapers and radio talk shows to blogs, the media try to help us understand the events that affect us. But, at their worst, the media's appetite for telling and selling stories leads them not only to document tragedy but also to misrepresent or exploit it. Many viewers and social critics disapprove of how media, particularly TV and cable, seem to hurtle from one event to another, often dwelling on trivial, celebrity-driven content.

In this book, we examine the history and business of mass media, and discuss the media as a central force in shaping our culture and our democracy. We start by examining key concepts and introducing the critical process for investigating media industries and issues. In later chapters, we probe the history and structure of media's major institutions. In the process, we will develop an informed and critical view of the influence these institutions have had on national and global life. The goal is to become media literate—to become critical consumers of mass media institutions and engaged participants who accept part of the responsibility for the shape and direction of media culture. In this chapter, we will:

- Address key ideas including communication, culture, mass media, and mass communication
- Investigate important periods in communication history: the oral, written, print, electronic, and digital eras
- Examine the development of a mass medium from emergence to convergence
- Learn about how convergence has changed our relationship to media
- Look at the central role of storytelling in media and culture
- Discuss two models for organizing and categorizing culture: a skyscraper and a map
- Trace important cultural values in both the modern and postmodern societies
- Study media literacy and the five stages of the critical process: description, analysis, interpretation, evaluation, and engagement

As you read through this chapter, think about your early experiences with the media. Identify a favorite media product from your childhood—a song, book, TV show, or movie. Why was it so important to you? How much of an impact did your early taste in media have on your identity? How has your taste shifted over time to today? What does this change indicate about your identity now? For more questions to help you think about the role of media in your life, see "Questioning the Media" in the Chapter Review.

Past-Present-Future: The "Mass" Media Audience

In the sixties, seventies, and eighties—the height of the TV Network Era—people watched many of the same programs, like the *Beverly Hillbillies*, *All in the Family*, the *Cosby Show*, or the evening network news. But today, things have changed—especially for younger people. While almost all U.S. college students use Facebook every day, they are rarely posting or reading about the same experiences.

In a world where we can so easily customize our media use, the notion of truly "mass" media may no longer exist. Today's media marketplace is a fragmented world with more options than ever. Prime-time network TV has lost half its viewers in the last decade to the Internet and to hundreds of alternative channels. Traditional newspaper readership, too, continues to decline as young readers embrace social media, blogs, and their smartphones.

The former mass audience is morphing into individual users who engage with ever-narrowing politics, hobbies, and entertainment. As a result, media outlets that hope to survive must appeal not to mass audiences but to niche groups—whether these are conservatives, progressives, sports fans, history buffs, or reality TV addicts. But what does it mean for us as individuals with civic obligations to a larger society if we are tailoring media use and consumption so that we only engage with Facebook friends who share similar lifestyles, only visit media sites that affirm our personal interests, or only follow political blogs that echo our own views?

Culture and the Evolution of Mass Communication

One way to understand the impact of the media on our lives is to explore the cultural context in which the media operate. Often, culture is narrowly associated with art, the unique forms of creative expression that give pleasure and set standards about what is true, good, and beautiful. Culture, however, can be viewed more broadly as the ways in which people live and represent themselves at particular historical times. This idea of culture encompasses fashion, sports, literature, architecture, education, religion, and science, as well as mass media. Although we can study discrete cultural products, such as novels or songs from various historical periods, culture itself is always changing. It includes a society's art, beliefs, customs, games, technologies, traditions, and institutions. It also encompasses a society's modes of **communication**: the creation and use of symbol systems that convey information and meaning (e.g., languages, Morse code, motion pictures, and one-zero binary computer codes).

Culture is made up of both the products that a society fashions and, perhaps more important, the processes that forge those products and reflect a culture's diverse values. Thus **culture** may be defined as the symbols of expression that individuals, groups, and societies use to make sense of daily life and to articulate their values. According to this definition, when we listen to music, read a book, watch television, or scan the Internet, we usually are not asking "Is this art?" but are instead trying to identify or connect with something or someone. In other words, we are assigning meaning to the song, book, TV program, or Web site. Culture, therefore, is a process that delivers the values of a society through products or other meaning-making forms. The American ideal of "rugged individualism," for instance, has been depicted for decades through a tradition of westerns and detective stories on television, in movies and books, and even in political ads.

Culture links individuals to their society by providing both shared and contested values, and the mass media help circulate those values. The **mass media** are the cultural industries—the channels of communication—that produce and distribute songs, novels, TV shows, newspapers, movies, video games, Internet services, and other cultural products to large numbers of people. The historical development of media and communication can be traced through several overlapping phases or eras in which newer forms of technology disrupted and modified older forms—a process that many academics, critics, and media professionals began calling *convergence* with the arrival of the Internet.

These eras, which all still operate to some degree, are oral, written, print, electronic, and digital. The first two eras refer to the communication of tribal or feudal communities and agricultural economies. The last three phases feature the development of **mass communication**: the process of designing cultural messages and stories and delivering them to large and diverse audiences through media channels as old and distinctive as the printed book and as new and converged as the Internet. Hastened by the growth of industry and modern technology, mass communication accompanied the shift of rural populations to urban settings and the rise of a consumer culture.

CULTURAL VALUES AND IDEALS are transmitted through the media. Many cosmetics advertisements show beautiful people using a company's products; this implies that anyone who buys the products can obtain such ideal beauty. What other societal ideas are portrayed through the media?

Oral and Written Eras in Communication

In most early societies, information and knowledge first circulated slowly through oral traditions passed on by poets, teachers, and tribal storytellers. As alphabets and the written word emerged, however, a manuscript, or written, culture began to develop and eventually overshadowed oral communication. Documented and transcribed by philosophers, monks, and stenographers, the manuscript culture served the ruling classes. Working people were generally illiterate, and the economic and educational gap between rulers and the ruled was vast. These eras of oral and written communication developed slowly over many centuries. Although exact time frames are disputed, historians generally consider these eras as part of Western civilization's premodern period, spanning the epoch from roughly 1000 B.C.E. to the mid-fifteenth century.

Early tensions between oral and written communication played out among ancient Greek philosophers and writers. Socrates (470-399 B.C.E.), for instance, made his arguments through public conversations and debates. Known as the Socratic method, this dialogue style of communication and inquiry is still used in college classrooms and university law schools. Many philosophers who believed in the superiority of the oral tradition feared that the written word would threaten public discussion by offering fewer opportunities for the give-and-take of conversation. In fact, Socrates' most famous student, Plato (427-347 B.C.E.), sought to banish poets, whom he saw as purveyors of ideas less rigorous than those generated in oral, face-to-face, question-and-answer discussions. These debates foreshadowed similar discussions in our time regarding the dangers of television and the Internet. Do aspects of contemporary culture, such as reality TV shows, Twitter, and social networking sites, cheapen public discussion and discourage face-to-face communication?

The Print Revolution

While paper and block printing developed in China around 100 C.E. and 1045, respectively, what we recognize as modern printing did not emerge until the middle of the fifteenth century. At that time in Germany, Johannes Gutenberg's invention of movable metallic type and the printing press ushered in the modern print era. Printing presses and publications then spread rapidly across Europe in the late 1400s and early 1500s. Early on, many books were large, elaborate, and expensive. It took months to illustrate and publish these volumes, and they were usually purchased by wealthy aristocrats, royal families, church leaders, prominent merchants, and powerful politicians. Gradually, however, printers reduced the size and cost of books, making them available and affordable to more people. Books eventually became the first mass-marketed products in history.

The printing press combined three elements necessary for mass-market innovation. First, machine duplication replaced the tedious system in which scribes hand-copied texts. Second, duplication could occur rapidly, so large quantities of the same book could be reproduced easily. Third, the faster production of multiple copies brought down the cost of each unit, which made books more affordable to less affluent people.

Since mass-produced printed materials could spread information and ideas faster and farther than ever before, writers could use print to disseminate views counter to traditional civic doctrine and religious authority–views that paved the way for major social and cultural changes, such as the Protestant Reformation and the rise of modern nationalism. People started to resist traditional clerical authority and also to think of themselves not merely as members of families, isolated communities, or tribes, but as part of a country whose interests were broader than local or regional concerns. While oral

EARLY BOOKS
Before the invention of the printing press, books were copied by hand in a labor-intensive process. This beautifully illuminated page is from an Italian Bible made in the early 1300s.

and written societies had favored decentralized local governments, the print era supported the ascent of more centralized nation-states.

Eventually, the machine production of mass quantities that had resulted in a lowered cost per unit for books became an essential factor in the mass production of other goods, which led to the Industrial Revolution, modern capitalism, and the consumer culture in the twentieth century. With the revolution in industry came the rise of the middle class and an elite business class of owners and managers who acquired the kind of influence formerly held only by the nobility or the clergy. Print media became key tools that commercial and political leaders used to distribute information and maintain social order.

As with the Internet today, however, it was difficult for a single business or political leader, certainly in a democratic society, to gain exclusive control over printing technology (although the king or queen did control printing press licenses in England until the early nineteenth century, and even today governments in many countries control presses, access to paper, advertising, and distribution channels). Instead, the mass publication of pamphlets, magazines, and books in the United States helped democratize knowledge, and literacy rates rose among the working and middle classes. Industrialization required a more educated workforce, but printed literature and textbooks also encouraged compulsory education, thus promoting literacy and extending learning beyond the world of wealthy upper-class citizens.

Just as the printing press fostered nationalism, it also nourished the ideal of individualism. People came to rely less on their local community and their commercial, religious, and political leaders for guidance. By challenging tribal life, the printing press "fostered the modern idea of individuality," disrupting "the medieval sense of community and integration."[9] In urban and industrial environments, many individuals became cut off from the traditions of rural and small-town life, which had encouraged community cooperation in premodern times. By the mid-nineteenth century, the ideal of individualism affirmed the rise of commerce and increased resistance to government interference in the affairs of self-reliant entrepreneurs. The democratic impulse of individualism became a fundamental value in American society in the nineteenth and twentieth centuries.

The Electronic Era

In Europe and the United States, the impact of industry's rise was enormous: Factories replaced farms as the main centers of work and production. During the 1880s, roughly 80 percent of Americans lived on farms and in small towns; by the 1920s and 1930s, most had moved to urban areas, where new industries and economic opportunities beckoned. The city had overtaken the country as the focus of national life.

The gradual transformation from an industrial, print-based society to one grounded in the Information Age began with the development of the telegraph in the 1840s. Featuring dot-dash electronic signals, the telegraph made four key contributions to communication. First, it separated communication from transportation, making media messages instantaneous—unencumbered by stagecoaches, ships, or the pony express.[10] Second, the telegraph, in combination with the rise of mass-marketed newspapers, transformed "information into a commodity, a 'thing' that could be bought or sold irrespective of its uses or meaning."[11] By the time of the Civil War, news had become a valuable product. Third, the telegraph made it easier for military, business, and political leaders to coordinate commercial and military operations, especially after the installation of the transatlantic cable in the late 1860s. Fourth, the telegraph led to future technological developments, such as wireless telegraphy (later named radio), the fax machine, and the cell phone, which ironically resulted in the telegraph's demise: In 2006, Western Union telegraph offices sent their final messages.

The rise of film at the turn of the twentieth century and the development of radio in the 1920s were early signals, but the electronic phase of the Information Age really boomed in the 1950s and 1960s with the arrival of television and its dramatic impact on daily life. Then, with the coming of ever more communication gadgetry—personal computers, cable TV, DVDs, DVRs,

"We are in great haste to construct a magnetic telegraph from Maine to Texas; but Maine and Texas, it may be, have nothing important to communicate.... We are eager to tunnel under the Atlantic and bring the old world some weeks nearer to the new; but perchance the first news that will leak through into the broad flapping American ear will be that Princess Adelaide has the whooping cough."

HENRY DAVID THOREAU, *WALDEN*, 1854

direct broadcast satellites, cell phones, smartphones, PDAs, and e-mail–the Information Age passed into its digital phase where old and new media began to converge, thus dramatically changing our relationship to media and culture.

The Digital Era

In **digital communication**, images, texts, and sounds are converted (encoded) into electronic signals (represented as varied combinations of binary numbers–ones and zeros) that are then reassembled (decoded) as a precise reproduction of, say, a TV picture, a magazine article, a song, or a telephone voice. On the Internet, various images, texts, and sounds are all digitally reproduced and transmitted globally.

New technologies, particularly cable television and the Internet, developed so quickly that traditional leaders in communication lost some of their control over information. For example, starting with the 1992 presidential campaign, the network news shows (ABC, CBS, and NBC) began to lose their audiences, first to MTV and CNN, and later to MSNBC, Fox News, Comedy Central, and partisan radio talk shows. By the 2004 national elections, Internet **bloggers**– people who post commentary on cultural, personal, and political-opinion-based Web sites–had become key players in news.

Moreover, e-mail–a digital reinvention of oral culture–has assumed some of the functions of the postal service and is outpacing attempts to control communications beyond national borders. A professor sitting at her desk in Cedar Falls, Iowa, sends e-mail or Skype messages routinely to research scientists in Budapest. Yet as recently as 1990, letters–or "snail mail"– between the United States and former communist states might have been censored or taken months to reach their destinations. Moreover, many repressive and totalitarian regimes have had trouble controlling messages sent out over the borderless Internet.

Further reinventing oral culture has been the emergence of *social media*, such as Twitter and in particular Facebook, which now has nearly one billion users worldwide. Social media allow people from all over the world to have ongoing online conversations, share stories and interests, and generate their own media content. This turn to digital media forms has fundamentally overturned traditional media business models, the ways we engage with and consume media products, and the ways we organize our daily lives around various media choices.

The Linear Model of Mass Communication

The digital era also brought about a shift in the models that media researchers have used over the years to explain how media messages and meanings are constructed and communicated in everyday life. In one of the older and more enduring explanations about how media operate, mass communication has been conceptualized as a linear process of producing and delivering messages to large audiences. **Senders** (authors, producers, and organizations) transmit **messages** (programs, texts, images, sounds, and ads) through a **mass media channel** (newspapers, books, magazines, radio, television, or the Internet) to large groups of **receivers** (readers, viewers, and consumers). In the process, **gatekeepers** (news editors, executive producers, and other media managers) function as message filters. Media gatekeepers make decisions about what messages actually get produced for particular receivers. The process also allows for **feedback**, in which citizens and consumers, if they choose, return messages to senders or gatekeepers through letters-to-the-editor, phone calls, e-mail, Web postings, or talk shows.

But the problem with the linear model is that in reality media messages, especially in the digital era, do not usually move smoothly from a sender at point A to a receiver at point Z. Words and images are more likely to spill into one another, crisscrossing in the daily media deluge of ads, TV shows, news reports, social media, smartphone apps, and–of course–everyday conversation. Media messages and stories are encoded and sent in written and visual forms, but senders often have very little control over how their intended messages are decoded or whether the messages are ignored or misread by readers and viewers.

A Cultural Model for Understanding Mass Communication

A more contemporary approach to understanding media is through a cultural model. This concept recognizes that individuals bring diverse meanings to messages, given factors and differences such as gender, age, educational level, ethnicity, and occupation. In this model of mass communication, audiences actively affirm, interpret, refashion, or reject the messages and stories that flow through various media channels. For example, when controversial singer Lady Gaga released her nine-minute music video for the song "Telephone" in 2010, fans and critics had very different interpretations of the video. Some saw Lady Gaga as a cutting-edge artist pushing boundaries and celebrating alternative lifestyles—and the rightful heir to Madonna. Others, however, saw the video as tasteless and cruel, making fun of transsexuals and exploiting women—not to mention celebrating the poisoning of an old boyfriend.

While the linear model may demonstrate how a message gets from a sender to a receiver, the cultural model suggests the complexity of this process and the lack of control that "senders" (such as media executives, movie makers, writers, news editors, ad agencies, etc.) often have over how audiences receive messages and interpret their intended meanings. Sometimes, producers of media messages seem to be the active creators of communication while audiences are merely passive receptacles. But as the Lady Gaga example illustrates, consumers also shape media messages to fit or support their own values and viewpoints. This phenomenon is known as **selective exposure**: People typically seek messages and produce meanings that correspond to their own cultural beliefs, values, and interests. For example, studies have shown that people with political leanings toward the left or the right tend to seek out blogs or news outlets that reinforce their preexisting views.

The rise of the Internet and social media has also complicated the traditional roles in both the linear and cultural models of communication. While there are still senders and receivers, the borderless, decentralized, and democratic nature of the Internet means that anyone can become a sender of media messages—whether it's by uploading a video mash-up to YouTube or by writing a blog post. The Internet has also largely eliminated the gatekeeper role. Although some governments try to control Internet servers and some Web sites have restrictions on what can and cannot be posted, for the most part, the Internet allows senders to transmit content without first needing approval from, or editing by, a gatekeeper. For example, some authors who are unable to find a traditional book publisher for their work turn to self-publishing on the Internet. And musicians who don't have deals with major record labels can promote, circulate, and sell their music online.

The Development of Media and Their Role in Our Society

The mass media constitute a wide variety of industries and merchandise, from moving documentary news programs about famines in Africa to shady infomercials about how to retrieve millions of dollars in unclaimed money online. The word *media* is, after all, a Latin plural form of the singular noun *medium*, meaning an intervening substance through which something is conveyed or transmitted. Television, newspapers, music, movies, magazines, books, billboards, radio, broadcast satellites, and the Internet are all part of the media; and they are all quite capable of either producing worthy products or pandering to society's worst desires, prejudices, and stereotypes. Let's begin by looking at how mass media develop, and then at how they work and are interpreted in our society.

The Evolution of Media: From Emergence to Convergence

The development of most mass media is initiated not only by the diligence of inventors, such as Thomas Edison (see Chapters 4 and 7), but also by social, cultural, political, and economic circumstances. For instance, both telegraph and radio evolved as newly industrialized nations sought to expand their military and economic control and to transmit information more rapidly. The Internet is a contemporary response to new concerns: transporting messages and sharing information more rapidly for an increasingly mobile and interconnected global population.

Media innovations typically go through four stages. First is the *emergence*, or *novelty*, *stage*, in which inventors and technicians try to solve a particular problem, such as making pictures move, transmitting messages from ship to shore, or sending mail electronically. Second is the *entrepreneurial stage*, in which inventors and investors determine a practical and marketable use for the new device. For example, early radio relayed messages to and from places where telegraph wires could not go, such as military ships at sea. Part of the Internet also had its roots in the ideas of military leaders, who wanted a communication system that was decentralized and distributed widely enough to survive nuclear war or natural disasters.

The third phase in a medium's development involves a breakthrough to the *mass medium stage*. At this point, businesses figure out how to market the new device or medium as a consumer product. Although the government and the U.S. Navy played a central role in radio's early years, it was commercial entrepreneurs who pioneered radio broadcasting and figured out how to reach millions of people. In the same way, Pentagon and government researchers helped develop early prototypes for the Internet, but commercial interests extended the Internet's global reach and business potential.

Finally, the fourth and newest phase in a medium's evolution is the *convergence stage*. This is the stage in which older media are reconfigured in various forms on newer media. However, this does not mean that these older forms cease to exist. For example, you can still get the *New York Times* in print, but it's also now accessible on laptops and smartphones via the Internet. During this stage, we see the merging of many different media forms onto online platforms, but we also see the fragmenting of large audiences into smaller niche markets. With new technologies allowing access to more media options than ever, mass audiences are morphing into audience subsets that chase particular lifestyles, politics, hobbies, and forms of entertainment.

Media Convergence

Developments in the electronic and digital eras enabled and ushered in this latest stage in the development of media—**convergence**—a term that media critics and analysts use when describing all the changes that have occurred over the past decade, and are still occurring, in media content and within media companies. However, the term actually has two different meanings—one referring to technology and one to business—and has a great impact on how media companies are charting a course for the future.

The Dual Roles of Media Convergence

The first definition of media convergence involves the technological merging of content across different media channels—the magazine articles, radio programs, songs, TV shows, video games, and movies now available on the Internet through laptops, tablets, and smartphones.

MEDIA CONVERGENCE
In the 1950s, television sets—like radios in the 1930s and 1940s—were often encased in decorative wood and sold as stylish furniture that occupied a central place in many American homes. Today, using our computers, we can listen to a radio talk show, watch a movie, or download a favorite song—usually on the go—as older media forms now converge online.

Such technical convergence is not entirely new. For example, in the late 1920s, the Radio Corporation of America (RCA) purchased the Victor Talking Machine Company and introduced machines that could play both radio and recorded music. In the 1950s, this collaboration helped radio survive the emergence of television. Radio lost much of its content to TV and could not afford to hire live bands, so it became more dependent on deejays to play records produced by the music industry. However, contemporary media convergence is much broader than the simple merging of older and newer forms. In fact, the eras of communication are themselves reinvented in this "age of convergence." Oral communication, for example, finds itself reconfigured, in part, in e-mail and social media. And print communication is re-formed in the thousands of newspapers now available online. Also, keep in mind the wonderful ironies of media convergence: The first major digital retailer, Amazon.com, made its name by selling the world's oldest mass medium–the book–on the world's newest mass medium–the Internet.

A second definition of media convergence–sometimes called **cross platform** by media marketers–describes a business model that involves consolidating various media holdings, such as cable connections, phone services, television transmissions, and Internet access, under one corporate umbrella. The goal is not necessarily to offer consumers more choice in their media options, but to better manage resources and maximize profits. For example, a company that owns TV stations, radio outlets, and newspapers in multiple markets–as well as in the same cities–can deploy a reporter or producer to create three or four versions of the same story for various media outlets. So rather than having each radio station, TV station, newspaper, and online news site generate diverse and independent stories about an issue, a media corporation employing the convergence model can use fewer employees to generate multiple versions of the same story.

Media Businesses in a Converged World

The ramifications of media convergence are best revealed in the business strategies of digital age companies like Amazon, Facebook, Apple, and especially Google–the most successful company of the digital era so far (see Chapter 2). Google is the Internet's main organizer and aggregator because it finds both "new" and "old" media content–like blogs and newspapers– and delivers that content to vast numbers of online consumers. Google does not produce any of the content, and most consumers who find a news story or magazine article through a Google search pay nothing to the original media content provider nor to Google. Instead, as the "middleman" or distributor, Google makes most of its money by selling ads that accompany search results. But not all ads are created equal; as writer and journalism critic James Fallows points out, Google does not necessarily sell ads on the news sites it aggregates:

Virtually all of Google's (enormous) revenue comes from a tiny handful of its activities: mainly the searches people conduct when they're looking for something to buy. That money subsidizes all the other services the company offers—the classic "let me Google that" informational query (as opposed to the shopping query), Google Earth, driving directions, online storage for Gmail and Google Docs, the . . . YouTube video-hosting service. Structurally this is very much like the old newspaper bargain, in which the ad-crammed classified section, the weekly grocery-store pullout, and other commercial features underwrote state-house coverage and the bureau in Kabul.[12]

In fact, Fallows writes that Google, which has certainly done its part in contributing to the decline of newspapers, still has a large stake in seeing newspapers succeed online. Over the last few years, Google has undertaken a number of experiments to help older news media make the transition into the converged world. Google executives believe that since they aren't in the content business, they are dependent on news organizations to produce the quality information and journalism that healthy democracies need—and that Google can deliver.

Today's converged media world has broken down the old definitions of distinct media forms like newspapers and television—both now available online and across multiple platforms. And it favors players like Google, whose business model works in a world where customers expect to get their media in multiple places—and often for free. But the next challenge ahead in the new, converged world is to resolve who will pay for quality content and how that system will emerge. In the upcoming industry chapters, we take a closer look at how media convergence is affecting each industry in terms of both content production and business strategies.

Media Convergence and Cultural Change

The Internet and social media have led to significant changes in the ways we consume and engage with media culture. In pre-Internet days (say, back in the late 1980s), most people would watch popular TV shows like the *Cosby Show*, *A Different World*, *Cheers*, or *Roseanne* at the time they originally aired. Such scheduling provided common media experiences at specific times within our culture. While we still watch TV shows, we are increasingly likely to do so at our own convenience through Web sites like Hulu and Netflix or DVR/On-Demand options. We are also increasingly making our media choices on the basis of Facebook, YouTube, or Twitter recommendations from friends. Or we upload our own media—from photos of last night's party to homemade videos of our lives, pets, and hobbies—to share with friends instead of watching "mainstream" programming. While these options allow us to connect with friends or family and give us more choices, they also break down shared media experiences in favor of our individual interests and pursuits.

The ability to access many different forms of media in one place is also changing the ways we engage with and consume media. In the past, we read newspapers in print, watched TV on our televisions, and played video games on a console. Today, we are able to do all of those things on a computer, tablet, or smartphone, making it easy—and very tempting—to multitask. Media multitasking has led to growing media consumption, particularly for younger people. A recent Kaiser Family Foundation study found that today's youth—now doing two or more things at once—packed ten hours and forty-five minutes worth of media content into the seven and a half hours they spent daily consuming media.[13] But while we might be consuming more media, are we really engaging with it? And are we really engaging with our friends when we communicate with them by texting or posting on Facebook? Some critics and educators feel that media multitasking means that we are more distracted, that we engage less with each type of media we consume, and that we often pay closer attention to the media we are using than to people immediately in our presence.

However, media multitasking could have other effects. In the past, we would wait until the end of a TV program, if not until the next day, to discuss it with our friends. Now, with the proliferation of social media, and in particular Twitter, we can discuss that program with our friends—and with strangers—as we watch the show. Many TV shows now gauge their popularity with audiences by how many people are "live-tweeting" it, and by how many related trending topics they have on Twitter. In fact, commenting on a TV show on social media grew by 194 percent between April 2011 and April 2012.[14] This type of participation could indicate that audiences are in fact engaging more with the media they consume, even though they are multitasking. Some media critics even posit that having more choice actually makes us more engaged media consumers, because we have to actively choose the media we want to consume from the growing list of options.

Stories: The Foundation of Media

The stories that circulate in the media can shape a society's perceptions and attitudes. Throughout the twentieth century and during the recent wars in Afghanistan and Iraq, for instance, courageous professional journalists covered armed conflicts, telling stories that helped the public comprehend the magnitude and tragedy of such events. In the 1950s and 1960s, network television news stories on the Civil Rights movement led to crucial legislation that transformed the way many white people viewed the grievances and aspirations of African Americans. In the late 1960s to early 1970s, the persistent media coverage of the Vietnam War ultimately led to a loss of public support for the war. In the late 1990s, news and tabloid magazine stories about the President Clinton-Monica Lewinsky affair sparked heated debates over private codes of behavior and public abuses of authority. In each of these instances, the stories told through a variety of media outlets played a key role in changing individual awareness, cultural attitudes, and public perception.

While we continue to look to the media for narratives today, the kinds of stories we seek and tell are changing in the digital era. During Hollywood's Golden Age in the 1930s and 1940s, as many as ninety million people each week went to the movies on Saturday to take in a professionally produced double feature and a newsreel about the week's main events. In the 1980s, during TV's Network Era, most of us sat down at night to watch the polished evening news or the scripted sitcoms and dramas written by paid writers and performed by seasoned actors. But in the digital age, where reality TV and social media now seem to dominate storytelling, many of the performances are enacted by "ordinary" people. Audiences are fascinated by the stories of finding love, relationships gone bad, and backstabbing friends on such shows as *Jersey Shore*, *Keeping Up with the Kardashians*, and the *Real Housewives* series. Other reality shows like *Pawn Stars*, *The Deadliest Catch*, and *My Big Fat Gypsy Wedding* give us glimpses into the lives and careers of everyday people, while amateurs entertain us in singing, dancing, and cooking shows like *The Voice*, *Dancing with the Stars*, and *Top Chef*. While these shows are all professionally produced, the performers are almost all ordinary people (or celebrities and professionals performing alongside amateurs), which is part of the appeal of reality TV—we are better able to relate to the characters, or compare our lives against theirs, because they seem just like us.

Online, many of us are entertaining each other with videos of our pets, Facebook posts about our achievements or relationship issues, photos of a good meal, or tweets about a funny thing that happened at work. This cultural blending of old and new ways of telling stories—told both by professionals and amateurs—is just another form of convergence that has disrupted and altered the media landscape in the digital era. More than ever, ordinary citizens are able to participate in, and have an effect on, the stories being told in the media. For example, in 2011 and 2012, professional news reports and amateur tweets and blog posts about the Occupy Wall Street protests across the United States and the world led to important debates over income disparity, capitalism and power, government, and modern democracy. In fact, without the videos, tweets, and blog posts from ordinary people, the Occupy Wall Street movement might not have gotten the news media coverage that it did.

Our varied media institutions and outlets are basically in the **narrative**–or storytelling–business. Media stories put events in context, helping us to better understand both our daily lives and the larger world. As psychologist Jerome Bruner argues, we are storytelling creatures, and as children we acquire language to tell those stories that we have inside us. In his book *Making Stories*, he says, "Stories, finally, provide models of the world."[15] The common denominator, in fact, between our entertainment and information cultures is the narrative. It is the media's main cultural currency–whether it's Michael Jackson's "Thriller" video, a post on a gossip blog, a Fox News "exclusive," a *New York Times* article, a tweet about a bad breakfast, or a funny TV commercial. The point is that the popular narratives of our culture are complex and varied. Roger Rosenblatt, writing in *Time* magazine during the 2000 presidential election, made this observation about the importance of stories: "We are a narrative species. We exist by storytelling–by relating our situations–and the test of our evolution may lie in getting the story right."[16]

The Power of Media Stories in Everyday Life

The earliest debates, at least in Western society, about the impact of cultural narratives on daily life date back to the ancient Greeks. Socrates, himself accused of corrupting young minds, worried that children exposed to popular art forms and stories "without distinction" would "take into their souls teachings that are wholly opposite to those we wish them to be possessed of when they are grown up."[17] He believed art should uplift us from the ordinary routines of our lives. The playwright Euripides, however, believed that art should imitate life, that characters should be "real," and that artistic works should reflect the actual world–even when that reality is sordid.

In *The Republic*, Plato developed the classical view of art: It should aim to instruct and uplift. He worried that some staged performances glorified evil and that common folk watching might not be able to distinguish between art and reality. Aristotle, Plato's student, occupied a middle ground in these debates, arguing that art and stories should provide insight into the human condition but should entertain as well.

VideoCentral ◎
Mass Communication
bedfordstmartins.com
/mediaculture

Robin Sloan
Vice President of Strategy, Current TV
current

Agenda Setting and Gatekeeping
Experts discuss how the media exert influence over public discourse.
Discussion: How might the rise of the Internet cancel out or reduce the agenda-setting effect in media?

VIETNAM WAR PROTESTS
On October 21, 1967, a crowd of 100,000 protesters marched on the Pentagon demanding the end of the Vietnam War. Sadly, violence erupted when some protesters clashed with the U.S. Marshals protecting the Pentagon. However, this iconic image from the same protest appeared in the *Washington Post* the next day and went on to become a symbol for the peaceful ideals behind the protests. When has an image in the media made an event "real" to you?
◀

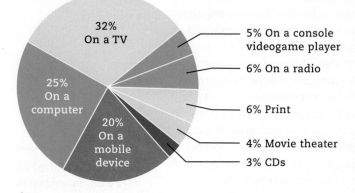

FIGURE 1.1

DAILY MEDIA CONSUMPTION BY PLATFORM, 2010 (8- TO 18-YEAR-OLDS)

Source: "Generation M²: Media in the Lives of 8- to 18-year-olds," a Kaiser Family Foundation Study, p. 10, accessed May 24, 2010, http://www.kff.org/entmedia/upload/8010.pdf.

The cultural concerns of classical philosophers are still with us. In the early 1900s, for example, newly arrived immigrants to the United States who spoke little English gravitated toward cultural events (such as boxing, vaudeville, and the emerging medium of silent film) whose enjoyment did not depend solely on understanding English. Consequently, these popular events occasionally became a flash point for some groups, including the Daughters of the American Revolution, local politicians, religious leaders, and police vice squads, who not only resented the commercial success of immigrant culture but also feared that these "low" cultural forms would undermine what they saw as traditional American values and interests.

In the United States in the 1950s, the emergence of television and rock and roll generated several points of contention. For instance, the phenomenal popularity of Elvis Presley set the stage for many of today's debates over hip-hop lyrics and television's influence, especially on young people. In 1956 and 1957, Presley made three appearances on the *Ed Sullivan Show*. The public outcry against Presley's "lascivious" hip movements was so great that by the third show the camera operators were instructed to shoot the singer only from the waist up. In some communities, objections to Presley were motivated by class bias and racism. Many white adults believed that this "poor white trash" singer from Mississippi was spreading rhythm and blues, a "dangerous" form of black popular culture.

Today, with the reach of print, electronic, and digital communications and the amount of time people spend consuming them (see Figure 1.1), mass media play an even more controversial role in society. Many people are critical of the quality of much contemporary culture and are concerned about the overwhelming amount of information now available. Many see popular media culture as unacceptably commercial and sensationalistic. Too many talk shows exploit personal problems for commercial gain, reality shows often glamorize outlandish behavior and sometimes dangerous stunts, and television research continues to document a connection between aggression in children and violent entertainment programs or video games. Children, who watch nearly forty thousand TV commercials each year, are particularly vulnerable to marketers selling junk food, toys, and "cool" clothing. Even the computer, once heralded as an educational salvation, has created confusion. Today, when kids announce that they are "on the computer," many parents wonder whether they are writing a term paper, playing a video game, chatting on Facebook, or peering at pornography.

Yet how much the media shape society—and how much they simply respond to existing cultural issues—is still unknown. Although some media depictions may worsen social problems, research has seldom demonstrated that the media directly cause our society's major afflictions. For instance, when a middle-school student shoots a fellow student over designer clothing, should society blame the ad that glamorized clothes and the network that carried the ad? Or are parents, teachers, and religious leaders failing to instill strong moral values? Or are economic and social issues involving gun legislation, consumerism, and income disparity at work as well? Even if the clothing manufacturer bears responsibility as a corporate citizen, did the ad alone bring about the tragedy, or is the ad symptomatic of a larger problem?

With American mass media industries earning more than $200 billion annually, the economic and societal stakes are high. Large portions of media resources now go toward studying audiences, capturing their attention through stories, and taking their consumer dollars. To increase their revenues, media outlets try to influence everything from how people shop to how they vote. Like the air we breathe, the commercially based culture that mass media help create surrounds us. Its impact, like the air, is often taken for granted. But to monitor that culture's "air quality"—to become media literate—we must attend more thoughtfully to diverse media stories that are too often taken for granted. (For further discussion, see "Examining Ethics: Covering War" on pages 18-19.)

Surveying the Cultural Landscape

Some cultural phenomena gain wide popular appeal, and others do not. Some appeal to certain age groups or social classes. Some, such as rock and roll, jazz, and classical music, are popular worldwide; other cultural forms, such as Tejano, salsa, and Cajun music, are popular primarily in certain regions or ethnic communities. Certain aspects of culture are considered elite in one place (e.g., opera in the United States) and popular in another (e.g., opera in Italy). Though categories may change over time and from one society to another, two metaphors offer contrasting views about the way culture operates in our daily lives: culture as a hierarchy, represented by a *skyscraper* model, and culture as a process, represented by a *map* model.

Culture as a Skyscraper

Throughout twentieth-century America, critics and audiences perceived culture as a hierarchy with supposedly superior products at the top and inferior ones at the bottom. This can be imagined, in some respects, as a modern skyscraper. In this model, the top floors of the building house **high culture**, such as ballet, the symphony, art museums, and classic literature. The bottom floors—and even the basement—house popular or **low culture**, including such icons as soap operas, rock music, radio shock jocks, and video games (see Figure 1.2). High culture, identified with "good taste," higher education, and supported by wealthy patrons and corporate donors, is associated with "fine art," which is available primarily in libraries, theaters, and museums. In contrast, low or popular culture is aligned with the "questionable" tastes of the masses, who enjoy the commercial "junk" circulated by the mass media, such as reality TV, celebrity gossip Web sites, and violent action films. Whether or not we agree with this cultural skyscraper model, the high-low hierarchy often determines or limits the ways in which we view and discuss culture today.[18] Using this model, critics have developed at least five areas of concern about so-called low culture.

An Inability to Appreciate Fine Art

Some critics claim that popular culture, in the form of contemporary movies, television, and music, distracts students from serious literature and philosophy, thus stunting their imagination and undermining their ability to recognize great art.[19] This critical view pits popular culture against high art, discounting a person's ability to value Bach and the Beatles or Shakespeare and *The Simpsons* concurrently. The assumption is that because popular forms of culture are made for profit, they cannot be experienced as valuable artistic experiences in the same way as more elite art forms such as classical ballet, Italian opera, modern sculpture, or Renaissance painting—even though many of what we regard as elite art forms today were once supported and even commissioned by wealthy patrons.

A Tendency to Exploit High Culture

Another concern is that popular culture exploits classic works of literature and art. A good example may be Mary Wollstonecraft Shelley's dark Gothic novel *Frankenstein*, written in 1818

EXAMINING ETHICS

Covering War

By early 2012, as the United States withdrew its military forces from Iraq and the Afghanistan war continued into its eleventh year, journalistic coverage of Middle East war efforts had declined dramatically. This was partly due to news organizations' losing interest in an event when it drags on for a long time and becomes "old news." The news media are often biased in favor of "current events." But war reporting also declined because of the financial crisis—twenty thousand reporters lost their jobs or took buyouts between 2009 and 2011 as papers cut staff to save money. In fact, many news organizations stopped sending reporters to cover the wars, depending instead on wire service reporters, foreign correspondents from other countries, or major news organizations

like the *New York Times* or CNN for their coverage. Despite the decreasing coverage, the news media confront ethical challenges about the best way to cover the wars, including reporting on the deaths of soldiers, documenting drug abuse or the high suicide rate among Iraq and Afghanistan war veterans, dealing with First Amendment issues, and knowing what is appropriate for their audiences to view, read, or hear.

When President Obama took office in 2009, he suspended the previous Bush administration ban on media coverage of soldiers' coffins returning to U.S. soil from the Iraq and Afghanistan wars. First Amendment advocates praised Obama's decision, although after a flurry of news coverage of these arrivals in April 2009, media outlets quickly grew less interested as the wars dragged on. Later, though, the Obama administration upset some of the same First Amendment supporters when it withheld more prisoner and detainee abuse photos from earlier in the wars, citing concerns for the safety of current U.S. troops and fears of further inflaming anti-American opinion. Both issues—one opening up news access and one

closing it down—suggest the difficult and often tense relationship between presidential administrations and the news media.

In May 2011, these issues surfaced again when U.S. Navy SEALs killed Osama bin Laden, long credited with perpetrating the 9/11 tragedy. As details of the SEAL operation began to emerge, the Obama administration weighed the appropriateness of releasing photos of bin Laden's body and video of his burial at sea. While some news organizations and First Amendment advocates demanded the release of the photos, the Obama administration ultimately decided against it, saying that they did not want to spur any further terrorist actions against the United States and its allies.

Back in 2006, then-President George W. Bush criticized the news media for not showing enough "good news" about U.S. efforts to bring democracy to Iraq. Bush's remarks raised ethical questions about the complex relationship between the government and the news media during times of war: How much freedom should the news media have to cover a war? How much control, if any, should the military have

---

IMAGES OF WAR

The photos and images that news outlets choose to show greatly influence their audience members' opinions. In each of the photos below, what message about war is being portrayed? How much freedom do you think news outlets should have in showing potentially controversial scenes from war?

How much freedom should the news media have to cover war?

over reporting a war? Are there topics that should not be covered?

These kinds of questions have also created ethical quagmires for local TV stations that cover war and its effects on communities where soldiers have been called to duty and then injured or killed. In one extreme case, the nation's largest TV station owner—Sinclair Broadcast Group—would not air the ABC News program *Nightline* in 2004 because it devoted an episode to reading the names of all U.S. soldiers killed in the Iraq war up to that time. Here is an excerpt from a *New York Times* account of that event:

> *Sinclair Broadcast Group, one of the largest owners of local television stations, will preempt tonight's edition of the ABC News program "Nightline," saying the program's plan to have Ted Koppel [who then anchored the program] read aloud the names of every member of the armed forces killed in action in Iraq was motivated by an antiwar agenda and threatened to undermine American efforts there.*

> *The decision means viewers in eight cities, including St. Louis and Columbus, Ohio, will not see "Nightline." ABC News disputed that the program carried a political message, calling it "an expression of respect which simply seeks to honor those who have laid down their lives for their country."*

> *But Mark Hyman, the vice president of corporate relations for Sinclair, who is also a conservative commentator on the company's newscasts, said tonight's edition of "Nightline" is biased journalism. "Mr. Koppel's reading of the fallen will have no proportionality," he said in a telephone interview, pointing out that the program will ignore other aspects of the war effort.*

> *Mr. Koppel and the producers of "Nightline" said earlier this week that they had no political motivation behind the decision to devote an entire show, expanded to 40 minutes, to reading the names and displaying the photos of those killed. They said they only intended to honor the dead and document what Mr. Koppel called "the human cost" of the war.*[1]

Given such a case, how might a local TV news director today—under pressure from the station's manager or owner—formulate guidelines to help negotiate such ethical territory? While most TV news divisions have ethical codes to guide journalists' behavior in certain situations, could ordinary citizens help shape ethical discussions and decisions? Following is a general plan for dealing with an array of ethical dilemmas that media practitioners face and for finding ways in which nonjournalists might participate in this decision-making process.

Arriving at ethical decisions is a particular kind of criticism involving several steps. These include (1) laying out the case; (2) pinpointing the key issues; (3) identifying the parties involved, their intents, and their potentially competing values; (4) studying ethical models and theories; (5) presenting strategies and options; and (6) formulating a decision or policy.[2]

As a test case, let's look at how local TV news directors might establish ethical guidelines for war-related events. By following the six steps above, our goal is to make some ethical decisions and to lay the groundwork for policies that address TV images or photographs—for example, those of protesters, supporters, memorials, or funerals—used in war coverage. (See Chapter 13 for details on confronting ethical problems.)

Examining Ethics Activity

As a class or in smaller groups, design policies that address one or more of the issues raised above. Start by researching the topic; find as much information as possible. For example, you can research guidelines that local stations already use by contacting local news directors and TV journalists.

Do they have guidelines? If so, are they adequate? Are there certain types of images they will not show? If the Obama administration had released photographic evidence of bin Laden's death, should a local station show it? Finally, if time allows, send the policies to various TV news directors and/or station managers; ask for their evaluations and whether they would consider implementing the policies. ◢

FIGURE 1.2

CULTURE AS A SKYSCRAPER

Culture is diverse and difficult to categorize. Yet throughout the twentieth century, we tended to think of culture not as a social process but as a set of products sorted into high, low, or middle positions on a cultural skyscraper. Look at this highly arbitrary arrangement and see if you agree or disagree. Write in some of your own examples.

Why do we categorize or classify culture in this way? Who controls this process? Is control of making cultural categories important? Why or why not?

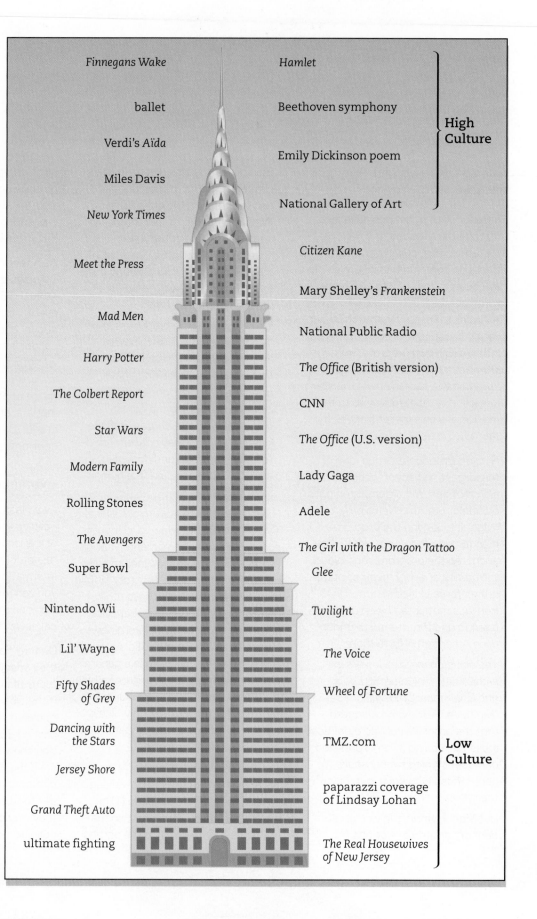

Finnegans Wake / Hamlet

ballet / Beethoven symphony

Verdi's Aïda / Emily Dickinson poem

Miles Davis / National Gallery of Art

High Culture

New York Times

Meet the Press / Citizen Kane

Mary Shelley's Frankenstein

Mad Men / National Public Radio

Harry Potter / The Office (British version)

The Colbert Report / CNN

Star Wars / The Office (U.S. version)

Modern Family / Lady Gaga

Rolling Stones / Adele

The Avengers / The Girl with the Dragon Tattoo

Super Bowl / Glee

Nintendo Wii / Twilight

Lil' Wayne / The Voice

Fifty Shades of Grey / Wheel of Fortune

Dancing with the Stars / TMZ.com

Jersey Shore / paparazzi coverage of Lindsay Lohan

Grand Theft Auto

ultimate fighting / The Real Housewives of New Jersey

Low Culture

EXPLOITING HIGH CULTURE

Mary Shelley, the author of *Frankenstein*, might not recognize our popular culture's mutations of her Gothic classic. First published in 1818, the novel has inspired numerous interpretations, everything from the scary—Boris Karloff in the classic 1931 movie—to the silly—the Munster family in the 1960s TV sitcom and the lovable creature in the 1974 movie *Young Frankenstein*. Can you think of another example of a story that has developed and changed over time and through various media transformations?

and ultimately transformed into multiple popular forms. Today, the tale is best remembered by virtue of two movies: a 1931 film version starring Boris Karloff as the towering and tragic monster, and the 1974 Mel Brooks comedy *Young Frankenstein*. In addition to the movies, television turned the tale into *The Munsters*, a mid-1960s situation comedy. The monster was even resurrected as sugar-coated Frankenberry cereal. In the recycled forms of the original story, Shelley's powerful themes about abusing science and judging people on the basis of appearances are often lost or trivialized in favor of a simplistic horror story, a comedy spoof, or a form of junk food.

A Throw-Away Ethic

Unlike an Italian opera or a Shakespearean tragedy, many elements of popular culture have a short life span. The average newspaper circulates for about twelve hours, then lands in a recycle bin or lines a litter box; a new Top 40 song on the radio lasts about one month; and most new Web sites or blogs are rarely visited and doomed to oblivion. Although endurance does not necessarily denote quality, many critics think that so-called better or "higher" forms of culture have more staying power. In this argument, lower or popular forms of culture are unstable and fleeting; they follow rather than lead public taste. In the TV industry in the 1960s and 1970s, for example, network executives employed the "least objectionable programming" (or LOP) strategy that critics said pandered to mediocrity with bland, disposable programs that a "regular" viewer would not find objectionable, challenging, or disturbing.

A Diminished Audience for High Culture

Some observers also warn that popular culture has inundated the cultural environment, driving out higher forms of culture and cheapening public life.[20] This concern is supported by data showing that TV sets are in use in the average American home for nearly eight hours a day, exposing adults and children each year to thousands of hours of trivial TV commercials, violent crime dramas, and superficial reality programs. According to one story critics tell, the prevalence of so many popular media products prevents the public from experiencing genuine art. Forty or more radio stations are available in large cities; cable and/or satellite systems with hundreds of channels are in place in 70 percent of all U.S. households; and Internet services and DVD players are in more than 90 percent of U.S. homes. In this scenario, the chances of audiences finding more refined forms of culture arguably become very small, although critics fail to note the choices that are also available on a variety of radio stations, cable channels, and Web sites. (For an alternate view, see "Case Study: The Sleeper Curve" on pages 22-23.)

The Sleeper Curve

In the 1973 science fiction comedy movie *Sleeper,* the film's director, Woody Allen, plays a character who reawakens two hundred years after being cryogenically frozen (after a routine ulcer operation had gone bad). The scientists who "unfreeze" Allen discuss how back in the 1970s people actually believed that "deep fat fried foods," "steaks," "cream pies," and "hot fudge" were unhealthy. But apparently in 2173 those food items will be good for us.

In his 2005 book, *Everything Bad Is Good for You,* Steven Johnson makes a controversial argument about TV and culture based on the movie. He calls his idea the "Sleeper Curve" and claims that "today's popular culture is actually making us smarter."[1] Johnson's ideas run counter to those of many critics who worry about popular culture and its potentially disastrous effects, particularly on young people. An influential argument in this strain of thinking appeared nearly thirty years ago in Neil Postman's 1985 book, *Amusing Ourselves to Death.* Postman

argued that we were moving from the "Age of Typology" to the "Age of Television," from the "Age of Exposition" to the "Age of Show Business."[2] Postman worried that an image-centered culture had overtaken words and a print-oriented culture, resulting in "all public discourse increasingly tak[ing] the form of entertainment." He pointed to the impact of advertising and how "American businessmen discovered, long before the rest of us, that the quality and usefulness of their goods are subordinate to the artifice of their display."[3] For Postman, image making has become central to choosing our government leaders, including the way politicians are branded and packaged as commodity goods in political ads. Postman argued that the TV ad has become the "chief instrument" for presenting political ideas, with these results: "that short simple messages are preferable to long and complex ones; that drama is to be preferred over exposition; that being sold solutions is better than being confronted with questions about problems."[4]

Across the converged cultural landscape, we are somewhere between the

Age of Television and the Age of the Internet. So Johnson's argument offers an opportunity to assess where our visual culture has taken us. According to Johnson, "For decades, we've worked under the assumption that mass culture follows a path declining steadily toward lowest-common-denominator standards, presumably because the 'masses' want dumb, simple pleasures and big media companies try to give the masses what they want. But, the exact opposite is happening: the culture is getting more cognitively demanding, not less."[5] While Johnson shares many of Postman's 1985 concerns, he disagrees with the point from *Amusing Ourselves to Death* that image-saturated media are only about "simple" messages and "trivial" culture. Instead, Johnson discusses the complexity of video and computer games and many of TV's dramatic prime-time series, especially when compared with less demanding TV programming from the 1970s and early 1980s.

As evidence, Johnson compares the plot complications of Fox's CIA/secret agent thriller *24* with *Dallas,* the prime-time soap opera that was America's most popular TV show in the early 1980s. "To make sense of an episode of *24*," Johnson maintains, "you have to integrate far more information than you would have a few decades ago watching a comparable show. Beneath the violence and the ethnic stereotypes, another trend appears: To keep up with entertainment like *24,* you have to pay attention, make inferences, track shifting social relationships." Johnson argues that today's

DALLAS (1978-1991)

BREAKING BAD (2008–)

audience would be "bored" watching a show like *Dallas*, in part "because the show contains far less information in each scene, despite the fact that its soap-opera structure made it one of the most complicated narratives on television in its prime. With *Dallas*, the modern viewer doesn't have to think to make sense of what's going on, and not having to think is boring."

In addition to *24*, a number of contemporary programs offer complex narratives, including *Mad Men*, *Breaking Bad*, *True Blood*, *Dexter*, *Game of Thrones*, *The Good Wife*, *Revolution*, *The Newsroom*, and *Girls*. Johnson says that in contrast to older popular programs like *Dallas* or *Dynasty*, the best TV storytelling today layers "each scene with a thick network of affiliations. You have to focus to follow the plot, and in focusing you're exercising the parts of your brain that map social networks, that fill in missing information, that connect multiple narrative threads." Johnson argues that younger audiences today—brought up in the Age of the Internet and in an era of complicated interactive visual games—bring high expectations to other kinds of popular culture as well, including television. "The mind," Johnson writes, "likes to be challenged; there's real pleasure to be found in solving puzzles, detecting patterns or unpacking a complex narrative system."

In countering the cultural fears expressed by critics like Postman and by many parents trying to make sense of the intricate media world that their children encounter each day, Johnson sees a hopeful sign: "I believe that the Sleeper Curve is the single most important new force altering the mental development of young people today, and I believe it is largely a force for good: enhancing our cognitive faculties, not dumbing them down. And yet you almost never hear this story in popular accounts of today's media."

Steven Johnson's theory is one of many about media impact on the way we live and learn. Do you accept Johnson's Sleeper Curve argument that certain TV programs—along with challenging interactive video and computer games—are intellectually demanding and are actually making us smarter? Why or why not?

Are you more persuaded by Postman's 1985 account—that the word has been displaced by an image-centered culture and, consequently, that popular culture has been dumbed down by its oversimplification and visual triviality? As you consider Postman, think about the Internet: Is it word based or image based? What kinds of opportunities for learning does it offer?

In thinking about both the 1985 and 2005 arguments by Postman and Johnson, consider as well generational differences. Do you enjoy TV shows and video games that your parents or grandparents don't understand? What types of stories and games do they enjoy? What did earlier generations value in storytelling, and what is similar and dissimilar about storytelling today? Interview someone who is close to you—but from an earlier generation—about media and story preferences. Then discuss or write about both the common ground and the cultural differences that you discovered.

"The Web has created a forum for annotation and commentary that allows more complicated shows to prosper, thanks to the fan sites where each episode of shows like *Lost* or *Alias* is dissected with an intensity usually reserved for Talmud scholars."

- Steven Johnson, 2005

THE POPULAR *HUNGER GAMES* book series, which has also become a blockbuster film franchise, mixes elements that have, in the past, been considered "low" culture (young-adult stories, science fiction) with the "high" culture of literature and satire. It also doubles as a cautionary story about media used to transform and suppress its audience: In the books and films, the media, controlled by a totalitarian government, broadcast a brutal fight to the death between child "tributes," fascinating the population while attempting to quash any hope of revolution.

Dulling Our Cultural Taste Buds

Another cautionary story, frequently recounted by academics, politicians, and TV pundits, tells how popular culture, especially its more visual forms (such as TV advertising and YouTube videos), undermines democratic ideals and reasoned argument. According to this view, popular media may inhibit not only rational thought but also social progress by transforming audiences into cultural dupes lured by the promise of products. A few multinational conglomerates that make large profits from media products may be distracting citizens from examining economic disparity and implementing change. Seductive advertising images showcasing the buffed and airbrushed bodies of professional models, for example, frequently contradict the actual lives of people who cannot hope to achieve a particular "look" or may not have the money to obtain the high-end cosmetic or clothing products offered. In this environment, art and commerce have become blurred, restricting the audience's ability to make cultural and economic distinctions. Sometimes called the "Big Mac" theory, this view suggests that people are so addicted to mass-produced media menus that they lose their discriminating taste for finer fare and, much worse, their ability to see and challenge social inequities.

Culture as a Map

The second way to view culture is as a map. Here, culture is an ongoing and complicated process—rather than a high/low vertical hierarchy—that allows us to better account for our diverse and individual tastes. In the map model, we judge forms of culture as good or bad based on a combination of personal taste and the aesthetic judgments a society makes at particular historical times. Because such tastes and evaluations are "all over the map," a cultural map suggests that we can pursue many connections from one cultural place to another and can appreciate a range of cultural experiences without simply ranking them from high to low.

Our attraction to and choice of cultural phenomena—such as the stories we read in books or watch at the movies—represent how we make our lives meaningful. Culture offers plenty of places to go that are conventional, familiar, and comforting. Yet at the same time, our culture's narrative storehouse contains other stories that tend toward the innovative, unfamiliar, and challenging. Most forms of culture, however, demonstrate multiple tendencies. We may use

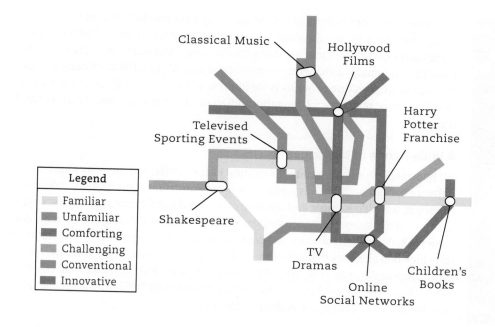

Classical Music
Hollywood Films
Harry Potter Franchise
Televised Sporting Events
Shakespeare
TV Dramas
Children's Books
Online Social Networks

Legend
- Familiar
- Unfamiliar
- Comforting
- Challenging
- Conventional
- Innovative

◀

FIGURE 1.3
CULTURE AS A MAP
In this map model, culture is not ranked as high or low. Instead, the model shows culture as spreading out in several directions across a variety of dimensions. For example, some cultural forms can be familiar, innovative, and challenging like the Harry Potter books and movies. This model accounts for the complexity of individual tastes and experiences. The map model also suggests that culture is a process by which we produce meaning—i.e., make our lives meaningful—as well as a complex collection of media products and texts. The map shown is just one interpretation of culture. What cultural products would you include in your own model? What dimensions would you link to and why?

online social networks because they are both comforting (an easy way to keep up with friends) and innovative (new tools or apps that engage us). We watch televised sporting events for their familiarity and conventional organization, and because the unknown outcome can be unpredictable or challenging. The map offered here (see Figure 1.3) is based on a familiar subway grid. Each station represents tendencies or elements related to why a person may be attracted to different cultural products. Also, more popular culture forms congregate in more congested areas of the map, while less popular cultural forms are outliers. Such a large, multidirectional map may be a more flexible, multidimensional, and inclusive way of imagining how culture works.

The Comfort of Familiar Stories

The appeal of culture is often its familiar stories, pulling audiences toward the security of repetition and common landmarks on the cultural map. Consider, for instance, early television's *Lassie* series, about the adventures of a collie named Lassie and her owner, young Timmy. Of the more than five hundred episodes, many have a familiar and repetitive plot line: Timmy, who arguably possessed the poorest sense of direction and suffered more concussions than any TV character in history, gets lost or knocked unconscious. After finding Timmy and licking his face, Lassie goes for help and saves the day. Adult critics might mock this melodramatic formula, but many children find comfort in the predictability of the story. This quality is also evident when night after night children ask their parents to read them the same book, such as Margaret Wise Brown's *Good Night, Moon* or Maurice Sendak's *Where the Wild Things Are*, or watch the same DVD, such as *Snow White* or *The Princess Bride*.

Innovation and the Attraction of "What's New"

Like children, adults also seek comfort, often returning to an old Beatles or Guns N' Roses song, a William Butler Yeats or Emily Dickinson poem, or a TV rerun of *Seinfeld* or *Andy Griffith*. But we also like cultural adventure. We may turn from a familiar film on cable's American Movie Classics to discover a new movie from Iran or India on the Independent Film Channel. We seek new stories and new places to go–those aspects of culture that demonstrate originality and complexity. For instance, James Joyce's *Finnegans Wake* (1939) created language anew and challenged readers, as the novel's poetic first sentence illustrates: "riverrun, past Eve and Adam's,

from swerve of shore to bend of bay, brings us by a commodius vicus of recirculation back to Howth Castle and Environs." A revolutionary work, crammed with historical names and topical references to events, myths, songs, jokes, and daily conversation, Joyce's novel remains a challenge to understand and decode. His work demonstrated that part of what culture provides is the impulse to explore new places, to strike out in new directions, searching for something different that may contribute to growth and change.

A Wide Range of Messages

We know that people have complex cultural tastes, needs, and interests based on different backgrounds and dispositions. It is not surprising, then, that our cultural treasures, from blues music and opera to comic books and classical literature, contain a variety of messages. Just as Shakespeare's plays—popular entertainments in his day—were packed with both obscure and popular references, TV episodes of *The Simpsons* have included allusions to the Beatles, Kafka, *Teletubbies*, Tennessee Williams, talk shows, Aerosmith, *Star Trek*, *The X-Files*, Freud, *Psycho*, and *Citizen Kane*. In other words, as part of an ongoing process, cultural products and their meanings are "all over the map," spreading out in diverse directions.

Challenging the Nostalgia for a Better Past

Some critics of popular culture assert—often without presenting supportive evidence—that society was better off before the latest developments in mass media. These critics resist the idea of re-imagining an established cultural hierarchy as a multidirectional map. The nostalgia for some imagined "better past" has often operated as a device for condemning new cultural phenomena. This impulse to criticize something that is new is often driven by fear of change or of cultural differences. Back in the nineteenth century, in fact, a number of intellectuals and politicians worried that rising literacy rates among the working class might create havoc: How would the aristocracy and intellectuals maintain their authority and status if everyone could read? A recent example includes the fear that some politicians, religious leaders, and citizens have expressed about the legalization of same-sex marriage, claiming that it would violate older religious tenets or the sanctity of past traditions.

Throughout history, a call to return to familiar terrain, to "the good old days," has been a frequent response to new, "threatening" forms of popular culture or to any ideas that are different from what we already believe. Yet over the years many of these forms, including the waltz, silent movies, ragtime, and jazz, have themselves become cultural "classics." How can we tell now what the future has in store for such cultural expressions as rock and roll, soap operas, fashion photography, dance music, hip-hop, tabloid newspapers, graphic novels, reality TV, and social media?

Cultural Values of the Modern Period

To understand how the mass media have come to occupy their current cultural position, we need to trace significant changes in cultural values from the modern period until today. In general, U.S. historians and literary scholars think of the **modern period** as beginning with the Industrial Revolution of the nineteenth century and extending until about the mid-twentieth century. Although there are many ways to define what it means to be "modern," we will focus on four major features or values that resonate best with changes across media and culture: efficiency, individualism, rationalism, and progress.

Modernization involved captains of industry using new technology to create efficient manufacturing centers, produce inexpensive products to make everyday life better, and make

PRIDE AND PREJUDICE AND ZOMBIES is a famous "mash-up"—a new creative work made by mixing together disparate cultural pieces. In this case, the classic novel by Jane Austen is re-imagined as taking place among zombies and ninjas, mixing elements of English literature and horror and action films. Usually intended as satire, such mash-ups allow us to enjoy an array of cultural elements in a single work and are a direct contradiction to the cultural hierarchy model.

commerce more profitable. Printing presses and assembly lines made major contributions in this transformation, and then modern advertising spread the word about new gadgets to American consumers. In terms of culture, the modern mantra has been "form follows function." For example, the growing populations of big cities placed a premium on space, creating a new form of building that fulfilled that functional demand by building upwards. Modern skyscrapers made of glass, steel, and concrete replaced the supposedly wasteful decorative and ornate styles of premodern Gothic cathedrals. This new value was echoed in journalism, where a front-page style rejected decorative and ornate adjectives and adverbs for "just the facts." To be lean and efficient, modern news de-emphasized complex analysis and historical context and elevated the new and the now.

Cultural responses to and critiques of modern efficiency often manifested themselves in the mass media. For example, Aldous Huxley, in *Brave New World* (1932), created a fictional world in which he cautioned readers that the efficiencies of modern science and technology posed a threat to individual dignity. Charlie Chaplin's film *Modern Times* (1936), set in a futuristic manufacturing plant, also told the story of the dehumanizing impact of modernization and machinery. Writers and artists, in their criticisms of the modern world, have often pointed to technology's ability to alienate people from one another, capitalism's tendency to foster greed, and government's inclination to create bureaucracies whose inefficiency oppresses rather than helps people.

While the values of the premodern period (before the Industrial Revolution) were guided by a strong belief in a natural or divine order, modernization elevated individual self-expression to a more central position. Modern print media allowed ordinary readers to engage with new ideas beyond what their religious leaders and local politicians communicated to them. Modern individualism and the Industrial Revolution also triggered new forms of hierarchy in which certain individuals and groups achieved higher standing in the social order. For example, those who managed commercial enterprises gained more control over the economic ladder, while an intellectual class of modern experts acquired increasing power over the nation's economic, political, and cultural agendas.

To be modern also meant valuing the ability of logical and scientific minds to solve problems by working in organized groups and expert teams. Progressive thinkers maintained that the printing press, the telegraph, and the railroad, in combination with a scientific attitude, would foster a new type of informed society. At the core of this society, the printed mass media—particularly newspapers—would educate the citizenry, helping to build and maintain an organized social framework.[21]

A leading champion for an informed rational society was Walter Lippmann, who wrote the influential book *Public Opinion* in 1922. He distrusted both the media and the public's ability to navigate a world that was "altogether too big, too complex, and too fleeting for direct acquaintance," and to reach the rational decisions needed in a democracy. Instead, he advocated a "machinery of knowledge" that might be established through "intelligence bureaus" staffed by experts. While such a concept might look like the modern "think tank," Lippmann saw these as independent of politics, unlike think tanks today, such as the Brookings Institution or Heritage Foundation, which have strong partisan ties.[22]

Walter Lippmann's ideas were influential throughout the twentieth century and were a product of the **Progressive Era**—a period of political and social reform that lasted roughly from the 1890s to the 1920s. On both local and national levels, Progressive Era reformers championed social movements that led to constitutional amendments for both women's suffrage and Prohibition, political reforms that led to the secret ballot during elections, and economic reforms that ushered in the federal income tax to try to foster a more equitable society. Muckrakers—journalists who exposed corruption, waste, and scandal in business and politics—represented media's significant contribution to this era (see Chapter 9).

Influenced by the Progressive movement, the notion of being modern in the twentieth century meant throwing off the chains of the past, breaking with tradition, and embracing progress. For example, twentieth-century journalists, in their quest for modern efficiency, focused on "the now" and the reporting of timely events. Newly standardized forms of front-page journalism that championed "just the facts" and events that "just happened yesterday" did help reporters efficiently meet tight deadlines. But realizing one of Walter Lippmann's fears, modern newspapers often failed to take a historical perspective or to analyze sufficiently the ideas and interests underlying these events.

Shifting Values in Postmodern Culture

For many people, the changes occurring in the **postmodern period**—from roughly the mid-twentieth century to today—are identified by a confusing array of examples: music videos, remote controls, Nike ads, shopping malls, fax machines, e-mail, video games, blogs, *USA Today*, YouTube, iPads, hip-hop, and reality TV (see Table 1.1). Some critics argue that postmodern culture represents a way of seeing—a new condition, or even a malady, of the human spirit. Although there are many ways to define the postmodern, this textbook focuses on four major features or values that resonate best with changes across media and culture: populism, diversity, nostalgia, and paradox.

As a political idea, *populism* tries to appeal to ordinary people by highlighting or even creating an argument or conflict between "the people" and "the elite." In virtually every campaign, populist politicians often tell stories and run ads that criticize big corporations and political favoritism. Meant to resonate with middle-class values and regional ties, such narratives generally pit Southern or Midwestern small-town "family values" against the supposedly coarser, even corrupt, urban lifestyles associated with big cities like Washington or Los Angeles.

In postmodern culture, populism has manifested itself in many ways. For example, artists and performers, like Chuck Berry in "Roll Over Beethoven" (1956) or Queen in "Bohemian Rhapsody" (1975), intentionally blurred the border between high and low culture. In the visual arts, following Andy Warhol's 1960s pop art style, advertisers have borrowed from both fine art and street art, while artists appropriated styles from commerce and popular art. Film stars, like

TABLE 1.1
TRENDS ACROSS HISTORICAL PERIODS

▼

Trend	Premodern (pre-1800s)	Modern Industrial Revolution (1800s–1950s)	Postmodern (1950s–present)
Work hierarchies	peasants/merchants/rulers	factory workers/managers/national CEOs	temp workers/global CEOs
Major work sites	field/farm	factory/office	office/home/"virtual" or mobile office
Communication reach	local	national	global
Communication transmission	oral/manuscript	print/electronic	electronic/digital
Communication channels	storytellers/elders/town criers	books/newspapers/magazines/radio	television/cable/Internet/multimedia
Communication at home	quill pen	typewriter/office computer	personal computer/laptop/smartphone/social networks
Key social values	belief in natural or divine order	individualism/rationalism/efficiency/antitradition	antihierarchy/skepticism (about science, business, government, etc.)/diversity/multiculturalism/irony & paradox
Journalism	oral & print-based/partisan/controlled by political parties	print-based/"objective"/efficient/timely/controlled by publishing families	TV & Internet-based/opinionated/conversational/controlled by global entertainment conglomerates

Angelina Jolie and Ben Affleck, often champion oppressed groups while appearing in movies that make the actors wealthy global icons of consumer culture.

Other forms of postmodern style blur modern distinctions not only between art and commerce but also between fact and fiction. For example, television vocabulary now includes infotainment (*Entertainment Tonight, Access Hollywood*) and infomercials (such as fading celebrities selling anti-wrinkle cream). On cable, MTV's reality programs—such as *Real World* and *Jersey Shore*—blur boundaries between the staged and the real, mixing serious themes with comedic interludes and romantic entanglements; Comedy Central's fake news programs, *The Daily Show with Jon Stewart* and *The Colbert Report*, combine real, insightful news stories with biting satires of traditional broadcast and cable news programs.

Closely associated with populism, another value (or vice) of the postmodern period emphasizes *diversity* and fragmentation, including the wild juxtaposition of old and new cultural styles. In a suburban shopping mall, for instance, Gap stores border a food court with Vietnamese, Italian, and Mexican options, while techno-digitized instrumental versions of 1960s protest music play in the background to accompany shoppers. Part of this stylistic diversity involves borrowing and transforming earlier ideas from the modern period. In music, hip-hop deejays and performers sample old R&B, soul, and rock classics, both reinventing old songs and creating something new. Critics of postmodern style contend that such borrowing devalues originality, emphasizing surface over depth and recycled ideas over new ones. Throughout the twentieth century, for example, films were adapted from books and short stories. More recently, films often derive from old popular TV series: *Mission Impossible*, *Charlie's Angels*, and *The A-Team*, to name just a few. Video games like the *Resident Evil* franchise and *Tomb Raider* have been made into Hollywood blockbusters. In fact, in 2012 more than twenty-five video games, including *BioShock* and the *Warcraft* series, were in various stages of film production.

Another tendency of postmodern culture involves rejecting rational thought as "the answer" to every social problem, reveling instead in *nostalgia* for the premodern values of small communities, traditional religion, and even mystical experience. Rather than seeing science purely as enlightened thinking or rational deduction that relies on evidence, some artists, critics, and politicians criticize modern values for laying the groundwork for dehumanizing technological advances and bureaucratic problems. For example, in the renewed debates over evolution, one cultural narrative that plays out often pits scientific evidence against religious belief and literal interpretations of the Bible. And in popular culture, many TV programs—such as *The X-Files*, *Buffy the Vampire Slayer*, *Charmed*, *Angel*, *Lost*, and *Fringe*—emerged to offer mystical and supernatural responses to the "evils" of our daily world and the limits of science and the purely rational.

In the 2012 presidential campaign, this nostalgia for the past was frequently deployed as a narrative device, with the Republican candidates depicting themselves as protectors of tradition and small-town values, and juxtaposing themselves against President Obama's messages of change and progressive reform. In fact, after winning the Nevada Republican primary in 2012, former Massachusetts governor Mitt Romney framed the story this way: "President Obama says he wants to fundamentally transform America. We [Romney and his supporters] want to restore to America the founding principles that made the country great." By portraying change—and present conditions—as sinister forces that could only be overcome by returning to some point in the past when we were somehow "better," Romney laid out what he saw as the central narrative conflicts of the 2012 presidential campaign: tradition versus change, and past versus present.

Lastly, the fourth aspect of our postmodern time is the willingness to accept *paradox*. While modern culture emphasized breaking with the past in the name of progress,

FILMS OFTEN REFLECT THE KEY SOCIAL VALUES of an era—as represented by the modern and postmodern movies pictured. Charlie Chaplin's *Modern Times* (1936, above left) satirized modern industry and the dehumanizing impact of a futuristic factory on its overwhelmed workers. Similarly, Ridley Scott's *Blade Runner* (1982, above right), set in futuristic Los Angeles in 2019, questioned the impact on humanity when technology overwhelms the natural world. As author William Romanowski said of *Blade Runner* in *Pop Culture Wars*, "It managed to quite vividly capture some postmodern themes that were not recognized at the time. . . . We are constantly trying to balance the promise of technology with the threats of technology."

"A cynic is a man who, when he smells flowers, looks around for a coffin."

H. L. MENCKEN, AMERICAN WRITER AND JOURNALIST

postmodern culture stresses integrating—or converging—retro beliefs and contemporary culture. So at the same time that we seem nostalgic for the past, we embrace new technologies with a vengeance. For example, fundamentalist religious movements that promote seemingly outdated traditions (e.g., rejecting women's rights to own property or seek higher education) still embrace the Internet and modern technology as recruiting tools or as channels for spreading messages. Culturally conservative politicians, who seem most comfortable with the values of the 1950s nuclear family, welcome talk shows, Twitter, Facebook, and Internet and social media ad campaigns as venues to advance their messages and causes.

Although new technologies can isolate people or encourage them to chase their personal agendas (e.g., a student perusing his individual interests online), as modernists warned, new technologies can also draw people together to advance causes or to solve community problems or to discuss politics on radio talk shows, on Facebook, or on smartphones. For example, in 2011 and 2012 Twitter made the world aware of protesters in many Arab nations, including Egypt and Libya, when governments there tried to suppress media access. Our lives today are full of such incongruities.

Critiquing Media and Culture

In contemporary life, cultural boundaries are being tested; the arbitrary lines between information and entertainment have become blurred. Consumers now read newspapers on their computers. Media corporations do business across vast geographic boundaries. We are witnessing media convergence, in which televisions, computers, and smartphones easily access new and old forms of mass communication. For a fee, everything from magazines to movies is channeled into homes through the Internet and cable or satellite TV.

Considering the diversity of mass media, to paint them all with the same broad brush would be inaccurate and unfair. Yet that is often what we seem to do, which may in fact reflect the distrust many of us have of prominent social institutions, from local governments to daily newspapers. Of course, when one recent president leads us into a long war based on faulty intelligence that mainstream news failed to uncover, or one of the world's leading media companies—with former editors in top government jobs—engages in phone hacking and privacy invasion, our distrust of both government and media may be understandable. It's ultimately more useful, however, to replace a cynical perception of the media with an attitude of genuine criticism. To deal with these shifts in how we experience media and culture and their impact, we need to develop a profound understanding of the media focused on what they offer or produce and what they downplay or ignore.

Media Literacy and the Critical Process

Developing **media literacy**—that is, attaining an understanding of mass media and how they construct meaning—requires following a **critical process** that takes us through the steps of description, analysis, interpretation, evaluation, and engagement (see "Media Literacy and the Critical Process" on pp. 32-33). We will be aided in our critical process by keeping an open mind, trying to understand the specific cultural forms we are critiquing, and acknowledging the complexity of contemporary culture.

Just as communication cannot always be reduced to the linear sender-message-receiver model, many forms of media and culture are not easily represented by the high-low model. We should, perhaps, strip culture of such adjectives as *high, low, popular,* and *mass.* These modifiers may artificially force media forms and products into predetermined categories. Rather than focusing on these worn-out labels, we might instead look at a wide range of issues generated by culture, from the role of storytelling in the mass media to the global influences of media industries on the consumer marketplace. We should also be moving toward a critical perspective that takes into account the intricacies of the cultural landscape. A fair critique of any cultural form, regardless of its social or artistic reputation, requires a working knowledge of the particular book, program, or music under scrutiny. For example, to understand W. E. B. Du Bois's essays, critics immerse themselves in his work and in the historical context in which he wrote. Similarly, if we want to develop a meaningful critique of TV's *Dexter* (where the protagonist is a serial killer) or Rush Limbaugh's radio program or a gossip magazine's obsession with Justin Bieber, it is essential to understand the contemporary context in which these cultural phenomena are produced.

To begin this process of critical assessment, we must imagine culture as more complicated and richer than the high-low model allows. We must also assume a critical stance that enables us to get outside our own preferences. We may like or dislike hip-hop, R&B, pop, or country, but if we want to criticize these musical genres intelligently, we should understand what the various types of music have to say and why their messages appeal to particular audiences that may be different from us. The same approach applies to other cultural forms. If we critique a newspaper article, we must account for the language that is chosen and what it means; if we analyze a film or TV program, we need to slow down the images in order to understand how they make sense and meaning.

Benefits of a Critical Perspective

Developing an informed critical perspective and becoming media literate allow us to participate in a debate about media culture as a force for both democracy and consumerism. On the one hand, the media can be a catalyst for democracy and social progress. Consider the role of television in spotlighting racism and injustice in the 1960s; the use of video

Media Literacy and the Critical Process

1 **DESCRIPTION.** If we decide to focus on how well the news media serve democracy, we might critique the fairness of several programs or individual stories from, say, *60 Minutes* or the *New York Times*. We start by describing the programs or articles, accounting for their reporting strategies, and noting those featured as interview subjects. We might further identify central characters, conflicts, topics, and themes. From the notes taken at this stage, we can begin comparing what we have found to other stories on similar topics. We can also document what we think is missing from these news narratives–the questions, viewpoints, and persons that were not included–and other ways to tell the story.

2 **ANALYSIS.** In the second stage of the critical process, we isolate patterns that call for closer attention. At this point, we decide how to focus the critique. Because *60 Minutes* has produced thousands of hours of programs in its nearly forty-five-year history, our critique might spotlight just a few key patterns. For example, many of the program's reports are organized like detective stories, reporters are almost always visually represented at a medium distance, and interview subjects are generally shot in tight close-ups. In studying the *New York Times*, in contrast, we might limit our analysis to social or political events in certain

It is easy to form a cynical view about the stream of TV advertising, reality programs, video games, celebrities, gossip blogs, tweets, and news tabloids that floods the cultural landscape. But cynicism is no substitute for criticism. To become literate about media involves striking a balance between taking a critical position (developing knowledgeable interpretations and judgments) and becoming tolerant of diverse forms of expression (appreciating the distinctive variety of cultural products and processes).

A cynical view usually involves some form of intolerance and either too little or too much information. For example, after enduring the glut of news coverage and political advertising devoted to the 2008 and 2012 presidential elections, we might easily become cynical about our political system. However, information in the form of "factual" news bits and knowledge about a complex social process such as a national election are not the same thing. The critical process stresses the subtle distinctions between amassing information and becoming media literate.

countries that get covered more often than events in other areas of the world. Or we could focus on recurring topics chosen for front-page treatment, or the number of quotes from male and female experts.

3 **INTERPRETATION.** In the interpretive stage, we try to determine the meanings of the patterns we have analyzed. The most difficult stage in criticism, interpretation demands an answer to the "So what?" question. For instance, the greater visual space granted to *60 Minutes*

reporters–compared with the close-up shots used for interview subjects–might mean that the reporters appear to be in control. They are given more visual space in which to operate, whereas interview subjects have little room to maneuver within the visual frame. As a result, the subjects often look guilty and the reporters look heroic–or, at least, in charge. Likewise, if we look again at the *New York Times*, its attention to particular countries could mean that the paper tends to cover

technology to reveal oppressive conditions in China and Eastern Europe or to document crimes by urban police departments; how the TV coverage of both business and government's slow response to the Gulf oil spill in 2010 impacted people's understanding of the event; and how blogs and Twitter can serve to debunk bogus claims or protest fraudulent elections. The media have also helped to renew interest in diverse cultures around the world and other emerging democracies (see "Global Village: Bedouins, Camels, Transistors, and Coke" on page 34).

Developing a media-literate critical perspective involves mastering five overlapping stages that build on one another:

- *Description:* paying close attention, taking notes, and researching the subject under study
- *Analysis:* discovering and focusing on significant patterns that emerge from the description stage
- *Interpretation:* asking and answering "What does that mean?" and "So what?" questions about one's findings
- *Evaluation:* arriving at a judgment about whether something is good, bad, or mediocre, which involves subordinating one's personal taste to the critical "bigger picture" resulting from the first three stages
- *Engagement:* taking some action that connects our critical perspective with our role as citizens to question our media institutions, adding our own voice to the process of shaping the cultural environment

Let's look at each of these stages in greater detail.

nations in which the United States has more vital political or economic interests, even though the *Times* might claim to be neutral and evenhanded in its reporting of news from around the world.

4 EVALUATION. The fourth stage of the critical process focuses on making an informed judgment. Building on description, analysis, and interpretation, we are better able to evaluate the fairness of a group of *60 Minutes* or *New York Times* reports. At this stage, we can grasp the strengths and weaknesses of the news media under study and make critical judgments measured against our own frames of reference—what we like and dislike, as well as what seems good or bad or missing, in the stories and coverage we analyzed.

This fourth stage differentiates the reviewer (or previewer) from the critic. Most newspaper reviews, for example, are limited by daily time or space constraints. Although these reviews may give us key information about particular programs, they often begin and end with personal judgments—"This is a quality show" or "That was a piece of trash"—that should be saved for the final stage in the critical process. Regrettably, many reviews do not reflect such a process; they do not move much beyond the writer's own frame of reference or personal taste.

5 ENGAGEMENT. To be fully media literate, we must actively work to create a media world that helps serve democracy. So we propose a fifth stage in the critical process—engagement. In our *60 Minutes* and *New York Times* examples, engagement might involve something as simple as writing a formal or e-mail letter to these media outlets to offer a critical take on the news narratives we are studying.

But engagement can also mean participating in Web discussions, contacting various media producers or governmental bodies like the Federal Communications Commission (FCC) with critiques and ideas, organizing or participating in public media literacy forums, or learning to construct different types of media narratives ourselves—whether print, audio, video, or online—to participate directly in the creation of mainstream or alternative media. Producing actual work for media outlets might involve doing news stories for a local newspaper (and its Web site), producing a radio program on a controversial or significant community issue, or constructing a Web site that critiques various news media. The key to this stage is to challenge our civic imaginations, to refuse to sit back and cynically complain about the media without taking some action that lends our own voices and critiques to the process.

On the other hand, competing against these democratic tendencies is a powerful commercial culture that reinforces a world economic order controlled by relatively few multinational corporations. For instance, when Poland threw off the shackles of the Soviet Union in the late 1980s, one of the first things its new leadership did was buy and dub the American soap operas *Santa Barbara* and *Dynasty*. For some, these shows were a relief from sober Soviet political propaganda, but others worried that Poles might inherit another kind of indoctrination—one starring American consumer culture and dominated by large international media companies.

Bedouins, Camels, Transistors, and Coke

Upon receiving the Philadelphia Liberty Medal in 1994, President Václav Havel of the Czech Republic described postmodernism as the fundamental condition of global culture, "when it seems that something is on the way out and something else is painfully being born." He described this "new world order" as a "multicultural era" or state in which consistent value systems break into mixed and blended cultures:

> For me, a symbol of that state is a Bedouin mounted on a camel and clad in traditional robes under which he is wearing jeans, with a transistor radio in his hands and an ad for Coca-Cola on the camel's back. . . . New meaning is gradually born from the . . . intersection of many different elements.[1]

Many critics, including Havel, think that there is a crucial tie between global politics and postmodern culture. They contend that the people who overthrew governments in the former Yugoslavia and the Soviet Union were the same people who valued American popular culture—especially movies, pop music, and television—for its free expression and democratic possibilities.

Back in the 1990s, as modern communist states were undermined by the growth and influence of transnational corporations, citizens in these nations capitalized on the developing global market, using portable video, digital cameras and phones, and audio technology to smuggle out recordings of repression perpetrated by totalitarian regimes. Thus it was difficult for political leaders to hide repressive acts from the rest of the world. In Newsweek, former CBS news anchor Dan Rather wrote about the role of television in the 1989 student uprising in China:

> Television brought Beijing's battle for democracy to Main Street. It made students who live on the other side of the planet just as human, just as vulnerable as the boy on the next block. The miracle of television is that the triumph and tragedy of Tiananmen Square would not have been any more vivid had it been Times Square.[2]

This trend continues today through the newer manifestations of our digital world like Facebook, Twitter, and YouTube. As protestors sent out messages and images on smartphones and laptops during the Arab Spring uprisings in 2011 and 2012, they spread stories that could not be contained by totalitarian governments.

At the same time, we need to examine the impact on other nations of the influx of U.S. popular culture (movies, TV shows, music, etc.), our second biggest export (after military and airplane equipment). Has access to an American consumer lifestyle fundamentally altered Havel's Bedouin on the camel? What happens when Westernized popular culture encroaches on the mores of Islamic countries, where the spread of American music, movies, and television is viewed as a danger to tradition? These questions still need answers. A global village, which through technology shares culture and communication, can also alter traditional customs forever.

To try to grasp this phenomenon, we might imagine how we would feel if the culture from a country far away gradually eroded our own established habits. This, in fact, is happening all over the world as U.S. culture has become the world's global currency. Although newer forms of communication such as tweeting and texting have in some ways increased citizen participation in global life, in what ways have they threatened the values of older cultures?

Our current postmodern period is double-coded: It is an agent both for the renewed possibilities of democracy and, even in tough economic times, for the worldwide spread of consumerism and American popular culture.

This example illustrates that contemporary culture cannot easily be characterized as one thing or another. Binary terms such as *liberal* and *conservative* or *high* and *low* have less meaning in an environment where so many boundaries have been blurred, so many media forms have converged, and so many diverse cultures coexist. Modern distinctions between print and electronic culture have begun to break down largely because of the increasing number of individuals who have come of age in what is *both* a print *and* an electronic culture.[23] Either/or models of culture, such as the high/low approach, are giving way to more inclusive ideas, like the map model for culture discussed earlier.

What are the social implications of the new, blended, and merging cultural phenomena? How do we deal with the fact that public debate and news about everyday life now seem as likely to come from *The View*, Jon Stewart, Stephen Colbert, or bloggers as from the *Wall Street Journal*, *NBC Nightly News*, or *Time*?[24] Clearly, such changes challenge us to reassess and rebuild the standards by which we judge our culture. The search for answers lies in recognizing the links between cultural expression and daily life. The search also involves monitoring how well the mass media serve democracy, not just by providing us with consumer culture but by encouraging us to help political, social, and economic practices work better. A healthy democracy requires the active involvement of everyone. Part of this involvement means watching over the role and impact of the mass media, a job that belongs to every one of us—not just the paid media critics and watchdog organizations. ▶

CHAPTER REVIEW

COMMON THREADS

In telling the story of mass media, several plotlines and major themes recur and help provide the "big picture"—the larger context for understanding the links between forms of mass media and popular culture. Under each thread that follows, we pose a set of questions that we will investigate together to help you explore media and culture:

- **Developmental stages of mass media.** How did the media evolve, from their origins in ancient oral traditions to their incarnation on the Internet today? What discoveries, inventions, and social circumstances drove the development of different media? What roles do new technologies play in changing contemporary media and culture?

- **The commercial nature of mass media.** What role do media ownership and government regulation play in the presentation of commercial media products and serious journalism? How do the desire for profit and other business demands affect and change the media landscape? What role should government oversight play? What role do we play as ordinary viewers, readers, students, critics, and citizens?

- **The converged nature of media.** How has convergence changed the experience of media from the print to the digital era? What are the significant differences between reading a printed newspaper and reading the news online? What changes have to be made in the media business to help older forms of media, like newspapers, in the transition to an online world?

- **The role that media play in a democracy.** How are policy decisions and government actions affected by the news media and other mass media? How do individuals find room in the media terrain to express alternative (nonmainstream) points of view? How do grassroots movements create media to influence and express political ideas?

- **Mass media, cultural expression, and storytelling.** What are the advantages and pitfalls of the media's appetite for telling and selling stories? As we reach the point where almost all media exist on the Internet in some form, how have our culture and our daily lives been affected?

- **Critical analysis of the mass media.** How can we use the critical process to understand, critique, and influence the media? How important is it to be media literate in today's world? At the end of each chapter, we will examine the historical contexts and current processes that shape media products. By becoming more critical consumers and engaged citizens, we will be in a better position to influence the relationships among mass media, democratic participation, and the complex cultural landscape that we all inhabit.

KEY TERMS

The definitions for the terms listed below can be found in the glossary at the end of the book. The page numbers listed with the terms indicate where the term is highlighted in the chapter.

communication, 6
culture, 6
mass media, 6
mass communication, 6
digital communication, 9
bloggers, 9
senders, 9
messages, 9
mass media channel, 9
receivers, 9

gatekeepers, 9
feedback, 9
selective exposure, 10
convergence, 11
cross platform, 12
narrative, 15
high culture, 17
low culture, 17
modern period, 26

Progressive Era, 27
postmodern period, 28
media literacy, 31
critical process, 31
description, 32
analysis, 32
interpretation, 32
evaluation, 33
engagement, 33

REVIEW QUESTIONS

Culture and the Evolution of Mass Communication

1. Define *culture, mass communication,* and *mass media,* and explain their interrelationships.

2. What are the key technological breakthroughs that accompanied the transition to the print and electronic eras? Why were these changes significant?

3. Explain the linear model of mass communication and its limitations.

The Development of Media and Their Role in Our Society

4. Describe the development of a mass medium from emergence to convergence.

5. In looking at the history of popular culture, explain why newer and emerging forms of media seem to threaten status quo values.

Surveying the Cultural Landscape

6. Describe the skyscraper model of culture. What are its strengths and limitations?

7. Describe the map model of culture. What are its strengths and limitations?

8. What are the chief differences between modern and postmodern values?

Critiquing Media and Culture

9. What are the five steps in the critical process? Which of these is the most difficult and why?

10. What is the difference between cynicism and criticism?

11. Why is the critical process important?

QUESTIONING THE MEDIA

1. Drawing on your experience, list the kinds of media stories you like and dislike. You might think mostly of movies and TV shows, but remember that news, sports, political ads, and product ads are also usually structured as stories. Conversations on Facebook can also be considered narratives. What kinds of stories do you like and dislike on Facebook, and why?

2. Cite some examples in which the media have been accused of unfairness. Draw on comments from parents, teachers, religious leaders, friends, news media, and so on. Discuss whether these criticisms have been justified.

3. Pick an example of a popular media product that you think is harmful to children. How would you make your concerns known? Should the product be removed from circulation? Why or why not? If you think the product should be banned, how would you do it?

4. Make a critical case either defending or condemning Comedy Central's *South Park,* a TV or radio talk show, a hip-hop group, a soap opera, or TV news coverage of the war in Afghanistan. Use the five-step critical process to develop your position.

5. Although in some ways postmodern forms of communication, such as e-mail, MTV, smartphones, and Twitter, have helped citizens participate in global life, in what ways might these forms harm more traditional or native cultures?

ADDITIONAL VIDEOS

Visit the ⊙ VideoCentral: Mass Communication *section at bedfordstmartins.com/mediaculture for additional exclusive videos related to Chapter 1, including:*

- THE MEDIA AND DEMOCRACY
  This video traces the history of the media's role in democracy from newspapers and television to the Internet.

PART 1
Digital Media and Convergence

Think about the main media technologies in your life ten or fifteen years ago. How did you watch TV shows, listen to music, or read books? How did you communicate with friends?

Now consider this: Apple began selling music through iTunes in 2003; Facebook was born in 2004, but was only opened to everyone in 2006; smartphones debuted in 2007; Hulu and Netflix launched their streaming video services in 2008; the iPad was introduced in 2010; and Apple's Siri first spoke to us in 2011. In just a little over ten years, we have moved from a world where each type of media was consumed separately and in its own distinct format to a world where we can experience every form of mass media content—books, music, newspapers, television, video games—on almost any Internet-connected device.

It used to be that things didn't move so quickly in the world of mass communication. After the world got wired with the invention of the telegraph in the 1840s and the telephone in the 1880s, the two next great electronic mass media were radio, popularized in the 1920s, and television, popularized in the 1950s. And until recently, print media like books, newspapers, and magazines remained much as they were when they were first invented.

The history of mass media has moved from the *emergence* of media to the *convergence* of media. While electronic media have been around for a long time, it is the development of the Web and the emergence of the Internet as a mass medium in the early 1990s that allowed an array of media—text, photos, audio, and video—to converge in one space and be easily shared. But while media have been converging since the early 1990s, in the past ten years we have experienced a great **digital turn**. Ever-growing download speeds and the development of more portable devices, from laptops to smartphones to tablets, have fundamentally changed the ways in which we access and consume media.

The digital turn has made us more fragmented than ever before, but ironically also more connected. We might not be able to count on our friends all having watched the same television show the night before, but Facebook and Twitter have made it easier for us to connect with friends—and strangers—and tell them what we watched, read, and listened to.

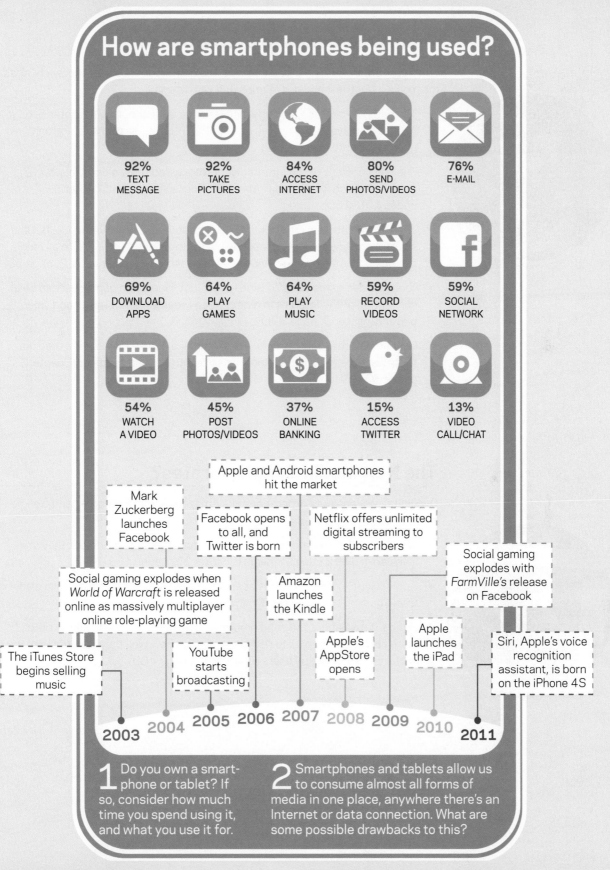

How are smartphones being used?

92% TEXT MESSAGE

92% TAKE PICTURES

84% ACCESS INTERNET

80% SEND PHOTOS/VIDEOS

76% E-MAIL

69% DOWNLOAD APPS

64% PLAY GAMES

64% PLAY MUSIC

59% RECORD VIDEOS

59% SOCIAL NETWORK

54% WATCH A VIDEO

45% POST PHOTOS/VIDEOS

37% ONLINE BANKING

15% ACCESS TWITTER

13% VIDEO CALL/CHAT

Apple and Android smartphones hit the market

Mark Zuckerberg launches Facebook

Facebook opens to all, and Twitter is born

Netflix offers unlimited digital streaming to subscribers

Social gaming explodes with *FarmVille's* release on Facebook

Social gaming explodes when *World of Warcraft* is released online as massively multiplayer online role-playing game

Amazon launches the Kindle

The iTunes Store begins selling music

YouTube starts broadcasting

Apple's AppStore opens

Apple launches the iPad

Siri, Apple's voice recognition assistant, is born on the iPhone 4S

2003 2004 **2005** **2006** **2007** 2008 **2009** 2010 **2011**

1 Do you own a smartphone or tablet? If so, consider how much time you spend using it, and what you use it for.

2 Smartphones and tablets allow us to consume almost all forms of media in one place, anywhere there's an Internet or data connection. What are some possible drawbacks to this?

See Notes for list of sources.

From Emergence to Convergence

While convergence is not a new concept, the digital turn has irrevocably changed the media industries, and our relationship with media.

- The cathode-ray tube, an early innovation in TV technology (Chapter 6, page 197), also played a part in the start of the Internet, as well as electronic gaming (Chapter 3, page 82).

- The development of the Internet went from wired to wireless (Chapter 2, page 58), much like the shift from the telegraph to radio (Chapter 5, pages 158–160).

- The PC and wireless Internet may have started media convergence, but the smartphone and tablet are responsible for the digital turn—where all media can be consumed on one device anywhere and anytime (Chapter 2, page 58).

- Today's video game console is no longer just for playing games—it can be a connection to the Internet, a digital video recorder, and a music and video player (Chapter 3, page 87).

- New times equal new formats. For example, a newspaper is still a medium for news, except it's increasingly less likely to be read on paper (Chapter 8, pages 304–305).

The New Media Conglomerates?

The digital turn has put corporations like Amazon, Apple, Facebook, and Google at the forefront of our media.

- These digital corporations might not produce media content, but they are involved in distributing *all* media (Chapter 13, pages 468–469).

- Apple, Google, Amazon, and Facebook are becoming major players in electronic gaming too (Chapter 3, page 110).

- But it's not all about the conglomerates. The digital turn also allows other, more nimble companies to rise depending on how well they connect with the social culture of digital users (Chapter 13, page 469).

Digital Media and Privacy Concerns

The massive amount of personal information flowing around the Internet puts our privacy at risk.

- Media companies have long used personal information in our Internet searches, e-mail, and social networking profiles to provide us with targeted ads (Chapter 2, page 66).

- But now with smartphones, it's easier than ever for media corporations to find out more about our private lives—even where we are at this precise moment (Chapter 2, pages 66–68).

- Who decides what information is legal for companies to use, and what isn't (Chapter 16, pages 570-573)?

The Digital Turn and Democracy

The old world of media was mostly a one-way street. As mass media users today, we have more power than ever.

- If we don't like what we see or read, we can easily provide immediate feedback—or better yet, create our own content (Chapter 2, page 52).

- But are Internet users, particularly in the closed world of apps, only seeking out those with similar interests and viewpoints (Chapter 2, pages 66–68)?

- Independent video game creators are now able to create games outside the über-popular first-person-shooter games (Chapter 3, page 110).

- And in journalism, blogging and citizen journalism are prime examples of how convergence and the Internet have allowed for more voices (Chapter 14, pages 507-510).

▶ **For more on Internet users creating their own content, watch the "User-Generated Content" video on** *VideoCentral: Mass Communication* **at bedfordstmartins.com/mediaculture.**

The Internet, Digital Media, and Media Convergence

In the mountains of North Carolina, four springtime hikers reported missing in the evening were back to safety by midnight. In a rugged park near the San Francisco Bay, two other hikers, lost after dark, were promptly found by a California Highway Patrol helicopter. In both cases, the hikers could have suffered from hypothermia, lack of food and water, and the scare of their lives. The key to their speedy rescue was a device from their more urban lives—their mobile phones, which had Global Positioning System (GPS) technology. The lost hikers simply had to call an emergency number, and rescuers found the lost callers using the latitude and longitude coordinates transmitted from the phone's built-in GPS signal.

Around the world, hikers with mobile phones are no longer lost—at least as long as their batteries last, and if they can find a signal. In the wilderness of Albuquerque, New Mexico, the rate of search and rescue missions in the area has dropped by more than half over the past decade as people use GPS to find their own way out. In Tasmania, Australia, local authorities retired their team of trained search and rescue dogs after mobile phones with GPS reduced the need for search missions for missing bushwalkers. "Everybody carries a mobile phone now, and the service is pretty good in most areas—if you are lost you can often climb to the top of a hill and get service," said the founder of Search and Rescue Dogs of Tasmania.[1]

Back in the cities and suburbs, mobile phones with GPS are less like survival tools and more like life trackers. On services like Facebook, Twitter, and Instagram, you can share, with precise coordinates, where you are, where you've been, and where your photos were taken. In fact, some of these services automatically geo-tag the location of photos and posts. As it turns out, sharing your every move on social media becomes much more valuable when you have GPS—to you, to your friends, and to advertisers. Several companies, such as Foursquare, Yelp, and Poynt, encourage users to check in at local business locations, earn points and savings, and share their reviews, recommendations, and locations with friends. Poynt combines GPS location data with users' search terms to more precisely target

consumers with location-based advertising. "We know where your customer is and what they are looking for so that you can tailor your advertising message accordingly," Poynt notes. But what is a boon for advertisers and customers— more specific, and therefore more useful, ads—needs to be balanced against concerns of too much consumer surveillance. Even though consumers are volunteering their location by allowing their social media posts to be geo-tagged or by using location-based services, some are balking at the idea of advertisers and their mobile phone companies collecting and even saving this information.

Wireless mobile technologies change our relationship with the Internet. It used to be that we would sit down, log on, and go "on" the Internet. Now, the Internet goes with us, and knows, at every moment, where we are.

▲

"We may be on the go, but now we aren't disconnected from the mass media—we take it with us."

▲ *THE INTERNET*, the vast network of telephone and cable lines, wireless connections, and satellite systems designed to link and carry digital information worldwide, was initially described as an *information superhighway*. This description implied that the goal of the Internet was to build a new media network, a new superhighway, to replace traditional media (e.g., books, newspapers, television, and radio), the old highway system. In many ways, the original description of the Internet has turned out to be true. The Internet has expanded dramatically from its initial establishment in the 1960s to an enormous media powerhouse that encompasses—but has not replaced—all other media today.

In this chapter, we examine the many dimensions of the Internet, digital media, and convergence. We will:

- Review the birth of the Internet and the development of the Web
- Provide an overview of the key features of the Internet, including instant messaging, search engines, and social media
- Discuss the convergence of the Internet with mobile media, such as smartphones and tablets, and how the Internet has changed our relationship with media
- Examine the economics of the Internet, including the structure of the "open web" vs. the "closed web," ownership issues, and the four leading Internet companies
- Investigate the critical issues of the Internet such as targeted advertising, free speech, security, net neutrality, and access

As you read through this chapter, think back to your first experiences with the Internet. What was your first encounter like? What were some of the things you remember using the Internet for then? How did it compare with your first encounters with other mass media? How has the Internet changed since your first experiences with it? For more questions to help you think through the role of the Internet in our lives, see "Questioning the Media" in the Chapter Review.

YOUTUBE is the most popular Web site for watching videos online. Full of amateur and home videos, the site now partners with mainstream television and movie companies to provide professional content as well (a change that occurred after Google bought the site in 2006).

Past-Present-Future: The Internet

From its inception, the Internet's main purpose has been for sharing information. In the 1960s, U.S. Defense Department researchers developed the forerunner of today's Internet as a way for military and academic researchers at various locations to share access to computers (which were bulky and expensive at the time). Soon, the researchers invented e-mail to share ideas and documents, and with the development of personal computers in the 1970s, the network grew to include more users at universities and research labs.

Today, sharing on the Internet is made easy with mobile devices and the ever-present social media "share" buttons. But perhaps we share a little *too* easily. The Internet economy is based on us sharing unprecedented amounts of information—our search interests, our e-mail content, our messages to friends, our photos, our birthdays, our musical tastes, our shopping habits—that companies like Google, Facebook, Apple, and Amazon track to better advertise and sell more products to us. Of course, Internet companies often give us free services—e-mail, social networks, search engines, apps—in exchange, but often we have no idea just how much of ourselves we are sharing. Conversely, when we share intellectual property, such as copyrighted music, movies, books, and images, we are monitored and tracked as well, and notified quickly of the inappropriate use.

The future debates about the Internet will continue to be about the nature of sharing on it. For example, should there be limits on the types and amount of personal data companies can compile on us through the Internet? In a digital world, should we be able to share small amounts of copyrighted music and images on the Internet as easily as we can currently quote and share text? Should all of us—individuals, small organizations, and large corporations—all be able to share equal access to the Internet at the same, reasonable cost? Should we be able to share anything on the Internet, even if it might offend some people? The answers to all of these questions about our rights to share (or not to share) on the Internet are essential to its function not only as an economic environment, but also as a democratic medium.

The Development of the Internet and the Web

> "The dream behind the Web is of a common information space in which we communicate by sharing information. Its universality is essential: the fact that a hyper-text link can point to anything, be it personal, local, or global, be it draft or highly polished."
>
> TIM BERNERS-LEE, INVENTOR OF THE WORLD WIDE WEB, 2000

From its humble origins as a military communications network in the 1960s, the **Internet** became increasingly interactive by the 1990s, allowing immediate two-way communication and one-to-many communication. By the 2000s, the Internet was a multimedia source for both information and entertainment as it quickly became an integral part of our daily lives. For example, in 2000, about 50 percent of American adults were connected to the Internet; by 2012 about 80 percent of American adults used the Internet.[2]

The Birth of the Internet

The Internet originated as a military-government project, with computer time-sharing as one of its goals. In the 1960s, computers were relatively new and there were only a few of the expensive, room-sized mainframe computers across the country for researchers to use. The Defense Department's Advanced Research Projects Agency (ARPA) developed a solution to enable researchers to share computer processing time starting in the late 1960s. This original Internet–called **ARPAnet** and nicknamed the Net–enabled military and academic researchers to communicate on a distributed network system (see Figure 2.1 on page 47). First, ARPA created a wired network system in which users from multiple locations could log into a computer whenever they needed it. Second, to prevent logjams in data communication, the network used a system called *packet switching*, which broke down messages into smaller pieces to more easily route them through the multiple paths on the network before reassembling them on the other end.

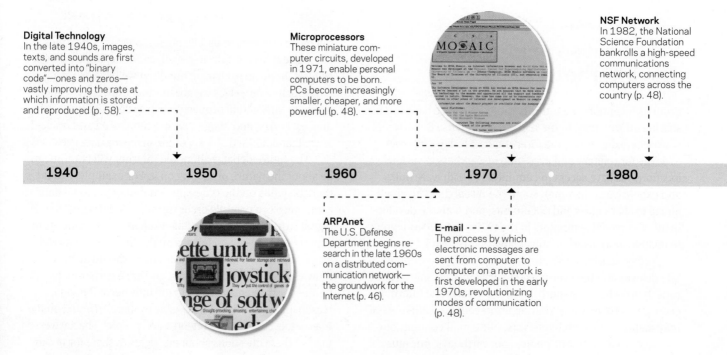

▼ The Internet, Digital Media, and Media Convergence

Digital Technology
In the late 1940s, images, texts, and sounds are first converted into "binary code"—ones and zeros—vastly improving the rate at which information is stored and reproduced (p. 58).

Microprocessors
These miniature computer circuits, developed in 1971, enable personal computers to be born. PCs become increasingly smaller, cheaper, and more powerful (p. 48).

NSF Network
In 1982, the National Science Foundation bankrolls a high-speed communications network, connecting computers across the country (p. 48).

| 1940 | 1950 | 1960 | 1970 | 1980 |

ARPAnet
The U.S. Defense Department begins research in the late 1960s on a distributed communication network—the groundwork for the Internet (p. 46).

E-mail
The process by which electronic messages are sent from computer to computer on a network is first developed in the early 1970s, revolutionizing modes of communication (p. 48).

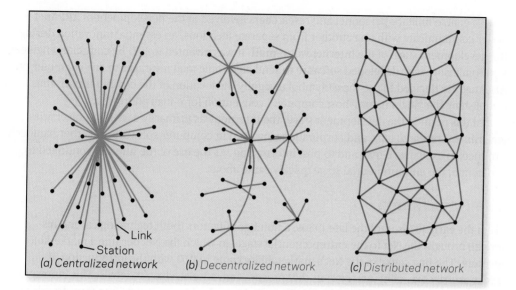

Link
Station
(a) Centralized network
(b) Decentralized network
(c) Distributed network

FIGURE 2.1

DISTRIBUTED NETWORKS

In a centralized network (*a*) all the paths lead to a single nerve center. Decentralized networks (*b*) contain several main nerve centers. In a distributed network (*c*), which resembles a net, there are no nerve centers; if any connection is severed, information can be immediately rerouted and delivered to its destination. But is there a downside to distributed networks when it comes to the circulation of network viruses?

Source: Katie Hafner and Matthew Lyon, Where Wizards Stay Up Late (New York: Simon & Schuster, 1996).

Ironically, one of the most hierarchically structured and centrally organized institutions in our culture–the national defense industry–created the Internet, possibly the least hierarchical and most decentralized social network ever conceived. Each computer hub in the Internet has similar status and power, so nobody can own the system outright and nobody has the power to kick others off the network. There isn't even a master power switch, so authority figures cannot shut off the Internet–although as we will discuss later, some nations and corporations have attempted to restrict access for political or commercial benefit.

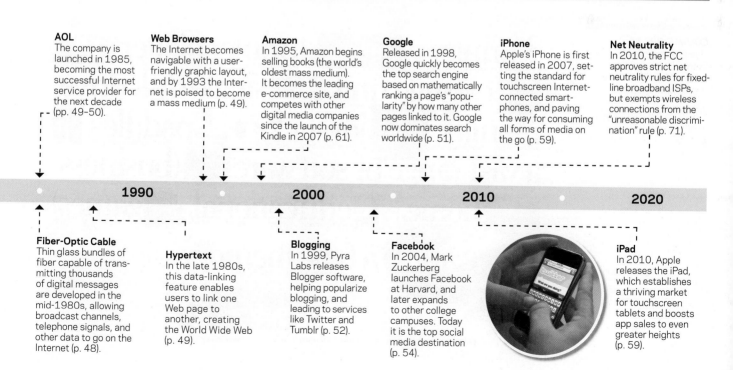

AOL
The company is launched in 1985, becoming the most successful Internet service provider for the next decade (pp. 49–50).

Web Browsers
The Internet becomes navigable with a user-friendly graphic layout, and by 1993 the Internet is poised to become a mass medium (p. 49).

Amazon
In 1995, Amazon begins selling books (the world's oldest mass medium). It becomes the leading e-commerce site, and competes with other digital media companies since the launch of the Kindle in 2007 (p. 61).

Google
Released in 1998, Google quickly becomes the top search engine based on mathematically ranking a page's "popularity" by how many other pages linked to it. Google now dominates search worldwide (p. 51).

iPhone
Apple's iPhone is first released in 2007, setting the standard for touchscreen Internet-connected smartphones, and paving the way for consuming all forms of media on the go (p. 59).

Net Neutrality
In 2010, the FCC approves strict net neutrality rules for fixed-line broadband ISPs, but exempts wireless connections from the "unreasonable discrimination" rule (p. 71).

1990   2000   2010   2020

Fiber-Optic Cable
Thin glass bundles of fiber capable of transmitting thousands of digital messages are developed in the mid-1980s, allowing broadcast channels, telephone signals, and other data to go on the Internet (p. 48).

Hypertext
In the late 1980s, this data-linking feature enables users to link one Web page to another, creating the World Wide Web (p. 49).

Blogging
In 1999, Pyra Labs releases Blogger software, helping popularize blogging, and leading to services like Twitter and Tumblr (p. 52).

Facebook
In 2004, Mark Zuckerberg launches Facebook at Harvard, and later expands to other college campuses. Today it is the top social media destination (p. 54).

iPad
In 2010, Apple releases the iPad, which establishes a thriving market for touchscreen tablets and boosts app sales to even greater heights (p. 59).

To enable military personnel and researchers involved in the development of ARPAnet to better communicate with one another from separate locations, an essential innovation during the development stage of the Internet was **e-mail**. It was invented in 1971 by computer engineer Ray Tomlinson, who developed software to send electronic mail messages to any computer on ARPAnet. He decided to use the @ symbol to signify the location of the computer user, thus establishing the "login name@host computer" convention for e-mail addresses.

At this point in the development stage, the Internet was primarily a tool for universities, government research labs, and corporations involved in computer software and other high-tech products to exchange e-mail and to post information. As the use of the Internet continued to proliferate, the entrepreneurial stage quickly came about.

The Net Widens

From the early 1970s until the late 1980s, a number of factors (both technological and historical) brought the Net to the entrepreneurial stage, in which the Net became a marketable medium. The first signal of the Net's marketability came in 1971 with the introduction of **microprocessors**, miniature circuits that process and store electronic signals. This innovation facilitated the integration of thousands of transistors and related circuitry into thin strands of silicon along which binary codes traveled. Using microprocessors, manufacturers were eventually able to introduce the first *personal computers* (*PCs*), which were smaller, cheaper, and more powerful than the bulky computer systems of the 1960s. With personal computers now readily available, a second opportunity for marketing the Net came in 1986, when the National Science Foundation developed a high-speed communications network (NSFNET) designed to link university research computer centers around the country and also encourage private investment in the Net. This innovation led to a dramatic increase in Internet use and further opened the door to the widespread commercial possibilities of the Internet.

In the mid-1980s, **fiber-optic cable** became the standard for transmitting communication data speedily. Featuring thin glass bundles of fiber capable of transmitting thousands of messages simultaneously (via laser light), fiber-optic cables began replacing the older, bulkier copper

"A fiber the size of a human hair can deliver every issue ever printed of the *Wall Street Journal* in less than a second."

NICHOLAS NEGROPONTE, *BEING DIGITAL*, 1995

COMMODORE 64
This advertisement for the Commodore 64, one of the first home PCs, touts the features of the computer. Although it was heralded in its time, today's PCs far exceed its abilities.

wire used to transmit computer information. This development made the commercial use of computers even more viable than before. With this increased speed, few limits exist with regard to the amount of information that digital technology can transport.

With the dissolution of the Soviet Union in the late 1980s, the ARPAnet military venture officially ended. By that time, a growing community of researchers, computer programmers, amateur hackers, and commercial interests had already tapped into the Net, creating tens of thousands of points on the network and the initial audience for its emergence as a mass medium.

The Commercialization of the Internet

The introduction of the World Wide Web and the first web browsers, Mosaic and Netscape, in the 1990s helped transform the Internet into a mass medium. Soon after these developments, the Internet quickly became commercialized, leading to battles between corporations vying to attract the most users, and others who wished to preserve the original public, nonprofit nature of the Net.

The World Begins to Browse

Prior to the 1990s, most of the Internet's traffic was for e-mail, file transfers, and remote access of computer databases. The **World Wide Web** (or the Web) changed all of that. Developed in the late 1980s by software engineer Tim Berners-Lee at the CERN particle physics lab in Switzerland to help scientists better collaborate, the Web was initially a text data-linking system that allowed computer-accessed information to associate with, or link to, other information no matter where it was on the Internet. Known as *hypertext*, this data-linking feature of the Web was a breakthrough for those attempting to use the Internet. **HTML (hypertext markup language)**, the written code that creates Web pages and links, is a language that all computers can read, so computers with different operating systems, such as Windows or Macintosh, can communicate easily. The Web and HTML allow information to be organized in an easy-to-use nonlinear manner, making way for the next step in using the Internet.

The release of Web **browsers**–the software packages that help users navigate the Web– brought the Web to mass audiences. In 1993, computer programmers led by Marc Andreessen at the National Center for Supercomputing Applications (NCSA) at the University of Illinois in Urbana-Champaign released Mosaic, the first window-based browser to load text and graphics together in a magazine-like layout, with attractive fonts and easy-to-use back, forward, home, and bookmark buttons at the top. In 1994, Andreessen joined investors in California's Silicon Valley to introduce a commercial browser, Netscape. As *USA Today* wrote that year, this "new way to travel the Internet, the World Wide Web," was "the latest rage among Net aficionados."[3] The Web soon became everyone else's rage, too, as universities and businesses, and later home users, got connected.

As the Web became the most popular part of the Internet, many thought that the key to commercial success on the Net would be through a Web browser. In 1995, Microsoft released its own Web browser, Internet Explorer; and within a few years, Internet Explorer–strategically bundled with Microsoft operating system software–overtook Netscape as the most popular Web browser. Today, Firefox and Google's Chrome are the top browsers, with Internet Explorer, Apple's Safari, and Opera as the leading alternatives.

Users Link In through Telephone and Cable Wires

In the first decades of the Internet, most people connected to "cyberspace" through telephone wires. AOL (formerly America Online) began connecting

WEB BROWSERS
The GUI (graphical user interface) of the World Wide Web changed overnight with the release of Mosaic in 1993 (above). As the first popular Web browser, Mosaic unleashed the multimedia potential of the Internet. Mosaic was the inspiration for the commercial browser Netscape, which was released in 1994.

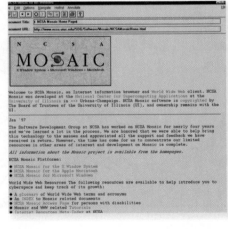

millions of home users in 1985 to its proprietary Web system through dial-up access, and quickly became the United States' top **Internet service provider (ISP)**. AOL's success was so great that by 2001, the Internet startup bought the world's largest media company, Time Warner–a deal that shocked the industry and signaled the Internet's economic significance as a vehicle for media content. As **broadband** connections, which can quickly download multimedia content, became more available (about 66 percent of all American households had such connections by 2012), users moved away from the slower telephone dial-up ISP service (AOL's main service) to high-speed service from cable, telephone, or satellite companies.[4] By 2007, both AT&T (offering DSL and cable broadband) and Comcast (cable broadband) surpassed AOL in numbers of customers. Today, other major ISPs include Verizon, Time Warner Cable, CenturyLink, Charter, and Cox. These are accompanied by hundreds of local services, many offered by regional telephone and cable companies that compete to provide consumers with access to the Internet.

People Embrace Digital Communication

In **digital communication**, an image, text, or sound is converted into electronic signals represented as a series of binary numbers–ones and zeros–which are then reassembled as a precise reproduction of an image, text, or sound. Digital signals operate as pieces, or bits (from *BI*nary dig*iTS*), of information representing two values, such as yes/no, on/off, or 0/1. For example, a typical compact disc track uses a binary code system in which zeros are microscopic pits in the surface of the disc and ones are represented on the unpitted surface. Used in various combinations, these digital codes can duplicate, store, and play back the most complex kinds of media content.

In the early days of e-mail, the news media constantly marveled at the immediacy of this new form of communication. Describing a man from Long Island e-mailing a colleague on the Galapagos Islands, the *New York Times* wrote in 1994 that his "magical new mailbox is inside his personal computer at his home, and his correspondence with the Galapagos now travels at the speed of electricity over the global computer network known as the Internet."[5] Other news media accounts worried about the brevity of e-mail interchanges, the loss of the art of letter writing, and the need for "netiquette," the manners of cyberspace. An e-mail sent by President Clinton in 1994 "COMPOSED ENTIRELY OF CAPITAL LETTERS" was reported as a "cardinal breach of netiquette."[6]

E-mail was one of the earliest services of the Internet, and people typically used the e-mail services connected to their ISPs before major Web corporations such as Google, Yahoo!, and Microsoft (Hotmail) began to offer free Web-based e-mail accounts to draw users to their sites; each now has millions of users. Today, all of the top e-mail services also include advertisements in their users' e-mail messages, one of the costs of the "free" e-mail accounts. Google's Gmail goes one step further by scanning messages to dynamically match a relevant ad to the text each time an e-mail message is opened. Such targeted advertising has become a hall-mark feature of the Internet.

As with e-mail, **instant messaging**, or IM, offered both a fascinating and troubling new part of media culture in the late 1990s. Teenagers were among the first to gravitate to IM and chat rooms, develop multitasking skills so they could IM multiple friends simultaneously, and discover that sometimes it was easier talking with friends online than face to face. In the early days of IM, there were concerns over the supposed lack of substance in IM conversations (was telephone dialogue any different?), and from teens talking to unseen strangers who might be asking them "What are you wearing?"[7] But as businesses found ways to integrate IM into the office culture, and as IM became as integrated as e-mail into our everyday lives, these worries subsided.

IM remains the easiest way to communicate over the Internet in real time and has become increasingly popular as a smartphone and tablet app, with free IM services supplanting costly text messages. Major IM services—many with voice and video chat capabilities—include AOL Instant Messenger (AIM), Microsoft's Messenger, Yahoo!'s Messenger, Apple's iChat, Skype (owned by eBay), Gmail's Chat, and Facebook Chat. IM users fill out detailed profiles when signing up for the service, providing advertisers with multiple ways to target them as they chat with their friends.

Search Engines Organize the Web

As the number of Web sites on the Internet quickly expanded, companies seized the opportunity to provide ways to navigate this vast amount of information by providing directories and search engines. One of the more popular search engines, Yahoo!, began as a directory. In 1994, Stanford University graduate students Jerry Yang and David Filo created a Web page—"Jerry and David's Guide to the World Wide Web"—to organize their favorite Web sites, first into categories, then into more and more subcategories as the Web grew. At that point, the entire World Wide Web was almost manageable, with only about twenty-two thousand Web sites. (By 2008, Google announced it had indexed more than one trillion Web pages, up from one billion in 2000.) The guide made a lot of sense to other people, and soon enough Yang and Filo renamed it the more memorable "Yahoo!"

Eventually, though, having employees catalog individual Web sites became impractical. **Search engines** offer a more automated route to finding content by allowing users to enter key words or queries to locate related Web pages. Search engines are built on mathematic algorithms, and the earliest ones directed them to search the entire Web and look for the number of times a key word showed up on a page. Soon search results were corrupted by Web sites that tried to trick search engines in order to get ranked higher on the results list. One common trick was to embed a popular search term in the page, often typed over and over again in the tiniest font possible and in the same color as the site's background. Although users didn't see the word, the search engines did, and they ranked the page higher.

Google, released in 1998, became a major success because it introduced a new algorithm that mathematically ranked a page's "popularity" on the basis of how many other pages linked to it. Users immediately recognized Google's algorithm as an improvement, and it became the favorite search engine almost overnight. Google also moved to maintain its search dominance with its Google Voice Search and Google Goggles apps, which allow smartphone users to conduct searches by voicing search terms or by taking a photo. By 2012, Google's market share accounted for 66.5 percent of searches in the United States, while Microsoft's Bing claimed about 15.4 percent and Yahoo!'s share was 13.5 percent.[8]

INSTANT MESSAGING
With early IM services like AOL Instant Messenger (http://en.wikipedia.org/wiki/AOL_Instant_Messenger [AIM]), users could bounce from chat room to chat room, sporting screen names that were often comical or ambiguous. Today, instant messaging is one of the principal modes of communication in professional settings.

"When search first started, if you searched for something and you found it, it was a miracle. Now, if you don't get exactly what you want in the first three results, something is wrong."

UDI MANBER, GOOGLE ENGINEER, 2007

The Web Goes Social

Aided by faster microprocessors, high-speed broadband networks, and a proliferation of digital content, the Internet has become more than just an information source in its second decade as a mass medium. The second generation of the Internet is a much more robust and social environment, having moved toward being a fully interactive medium with user-created content like blogs, Tumblrs, YouTube videos, Flickr photostreams, Photobucket albums, social networking, and other collaborative sites. In the words of law professor and media scholar Lawrence Lessig, we have moved from a "Read/Only" culture on the Internet, in which users can only read content, to a "Read/Write" culture, in which users have power not only to read content but also to develop their own.[9] It's the users who ultimately rule here, sharing the words, sounds, images, and creatively edited music remixes and mash-up videos that make these Web communities worth visiting.

What Are Social Media?

While it can be difficult to apply a singular definition to **social media**, given that they are a fairly new form of media that is still growing, practitioners and researchers have offered several ways of describing the world of social media, including:

- A venue for social interaction—a place where people can share creations, tell stories, and interact with others[10]
- Multiplatform, participatory, and digital . . . an essential feature of truly democratic public life[11]
- Platforms that enable the interactive Web by engaging users to participate in, comment on, and create content as a means of communicating with their social graph, other users, and the public[12]

Ironically, social media are a throwback to an older era of the Internet (the 1980s to the early 1990s) when bulletin boards and personal Web pages served as platforms for users to exchange information with other users.[13] Now, greater Internet bandwidth, inexpensive digital tools and mobile devices, and a generation willing to develop and share their own media content online have given rise to new kinds of social media. Social media have become a new distribution system for media as well, challenging the one-to-many model of traditional mass media with the many-to-many model of social media.

Types of Social Media

In less than a decade, a number of different types of social media have evolved, with multiple platforms for the creation of user-generated content. European researchers Andreas M. Kaplan and Michael Haenlein identify six categories of social media on the Internet: blogs, collaborative projects, content communities, social networking sites, virtual game worlds, and virtual social worlds.

Blogs

Years before there were status updates or Facebook, **blogs** enabled people to easily post their ideas to a Web site. Popularized with the release of Blogger (now owned by Google) in 1999, blogs contain articles or posts in chronological, journal-like form, often with reader comments

and links to other sites. Blogs can be personal or corporate multimedia sites, sometimes with photos, graphics, podcasts, and video. By 2012, there were at least 182 million blogs, the most common topics being personal accounts, movies/TV, sports, and politics.[14] Some blogs have developed into popular news and culture sites, such as the *Huffington Post*, *TechCrunch*, *Mashable!*, *Gawker*, *Engadget*, *HotAir*, *ThinkProgress*, and *TPM-Muckraker*.

Blogs have become part of the information and opinion culture of the Web, giving regular people and citizen reporters a forum for their ideas and views, and providing a place for even professional journalists to informally share ideas before a more formal news story gets published. Some of the leading platforms for blogging include Blogger, WordPress, Tumblr, Weebly, and Wix. But by 2012, the most popular form of blogging was microblogging, with about 140 million active users on Twitter, sending out 340 million tweets (a short message with a 140-character limit) per day.[15] Twitter users often follow the feeds of friends, businesses, politicians, or celebrities—like Lady Gaga, the most followed Twitterer in 2012.

THE HUFFINGTON POST, one of the top blogs today, aggregates the latest news in a wide variety of areas ranging from politics and the environment to style and entertainment. Recently, the site launched Twitter editions, gathering the most relevant and interesting Twitter feeds in one place for each of the site's nineteen sections.

Collaborative Projects

Another Internet development involves collaborative projects in which users build something together, often using *wiki* (which means "quick" in Hawaiian) technology. **Wiki Web sites** enable anyone to edit and contribute to them. There are several large wikis, such as Wikitravel (a global travel guide), WikiMapia (combining Google Maps with wiki comments), and WikiLeaks (an organization publishing sensitive documents leaked by anonymous whistleblowers). WikiLeaks gained notoriety for its release of thousands of United States diplomatic cables and other sensitive documents beginning in 2010 (see p. 514 in Chapter 14). But the most notable wiki is Wikipedia, an online encyclopedia launched in 2001 that is constantly updated and revised by interested volunteers. All previous page versions of Wikipedia are stored, allowing users to see how each individual topic develops. The English version of Wikipedia is the largest, containing about four million articles, but Wikipedias are also being developed in 284 other languages.

Businesses and other organizations have developed social media platforms for specific collaborative projects. Tools like Basecamp and Podio provide social media interfaces for organizing project and event-planning schedules, messages, to-do lists, and workflows. Kickstarter is a popular fund-raising tool for creative projects like books, recordings, and films. InnoCentive is a crowd-sourcing community that offers award payments for people who can solve business and scientific problems. And change.org has become an effective petition project to push for social change. For example, in 2012 a high school student from Michigan began a campaign that gained more than 500,000 signatures to persuade the MPAA to change the rating of the movie *Bully* from R to PG-13 so younger people could see it.

Content Communities

Content communities are the best examples of the many-to-many ethic of social media. **Content communities** exist for the sharing of all types of content from text (fanfiction.net) to photos (Flickr and Photobucket) and videos (YouTube, Vimeo). YouTube, created in 2005 and bought by Google in 2006, is the most well-known content community, with hundred of millions of users around the world uploading and watching amateur and professional videos. YouTube gave rise to the viral video—a video that becomes immediately popular by millions sharing it through social media platforms. The most popular video of all time—a fifty-six-second home

KICKSTARTER.COM has featured almost 64,000 creative projects since its launch in 2008. According to Kickstarter's raw data, 44 percent of these, or nearly 27,000 projects, were successfully funded. Some notable successes include an Oscar-nominated short documentary, a contemporary art exhibit featured in the Museum of Modern Art in 2011, and a highly anticipated smartwatch (http://en.wikipedia.org/wiki/Smartwatch) for iPhone and Android.

video titled "Charlie bit my finger—again!" has more than 457 million views. By 2012, YouTube reported that nearly sixty hours of video are uploaded to the site every minute, and its worldwide users generate four billion views per day.

Social Networking Sites

Perhaps the most visible examples of social media are **social networking sites** like MySpace, Facebook, LiveJournal, Hi5, Bebo, Orkut, LinkedIn, and Google+. On these sites, users can create content, share ideas, and interact with friends.

MySpace, founded in 2003, was the first big social media site. In addition to personal profiles, MySpace was known for its music listings, with millions of artists setting up profiles to promote their music, launch new albums, and allow users to buy songs. Its popularity with teens made it a major site for online advertising. That popularity attracted the attention of media conglomerate News Corp., which bought MySpace in 2005. But with competition from Facebook, by 2009 interest in MySpace was waning, and News Corp. sold it in 2011.

Facebook is now the most popular social media site on the Internet. Started at Harvard in 2004 as an online substitute to the printed facebooks the school created for incoming first-year students, Facebook was instantly a hit. The site enables users to construct personal profiles, upload photos, share music lists, play games, and post messages to connect with old friends and meet new ones. Originally, access was restricted to college students, but in 2006 the site expanded to include anyone. Soon after, Facebook grew at an astonishing rate, and by 2012 it had more than one billion active users and was available in more than seventy languages.

In 2011, Google introduced Google+, a social networking interface designed to compete with Facebook. Google+ enables users to develop distinct "circles," by dragging and dropping friends into separate groups, rather than having one long list of friends. In response, Facebook created new settings to enable users to control who sees their posts.

Virtual Game Worlds and Virtual Social Worlds

Virtual game worlds and virtual social worlds invite users to role-play in rich 3-D environments, in real-time, with players throughout the world. In virtual game worlds (also known as massively multiplayer online role-playing games, or MMORPGs) such as *World of Warcraft* and *Star Wars: The Old Republic*, players can customize their online identity, or avatar, and work with others through the game's challenges. Community forums for members extend discussion and shared play outside of the game. Virtual social worlds, like *Second Life*, enable players to take their avatars through simulated environments and even make transactions with virtual money. (See Chapter 3 for a closer look at virtual game worlds and virtual social worlds.)

Social Media and Democracy

In just a decade, social media have changed the way we consume and relate to media and the way we communicate with others. Social media tools have put unprecedented power in our hands to produce and distribute our own media. We can share our thoughts and opinions, write or update an encyclopedic entry, start a petition or fund-raising campaign, post a video, and create and explore virtual worlds. But social media have also proven to be an effective tool for democracy, and for undermining repressive regimes that thrive on serving up propaganda and hiding their atrocities from view.

The wave of protests in more than a dozen Arab nations in North Africa and the Middle East that began in late 2010 resulted in four rulers' being forced from power by mid-2012. The Arab Spring began in Tunisia, with a twenty-six-year-old street vendor named Mohamed Bouazizi, who had his vegetable cart confiscated by police. Humiliated when he tried to get it back, he set himself on fire. While there had been protests before in Tunisia, the stories were never communicated widely. This time, protesters posted videos on Facebook, and satellite news networks spread the story with reports based on those videos. The protests spread across Tunisia, and by January 2011, Tunisia's dictator of nearly twenty-four years fled the country.

In Egypt, a similar circumstance occurred when twenty-eight-year-old Khaled Said was pulled from a café and beaten to death by police. Said's fate might have made no impact but for the fact that his brother used his mobile phone to snap a photo of Said's dis-figured face and released it to the Internet. The success of protesters in Tunisia spurred Egyptians to organize their own protests, using the beating of Said as a rallying point. During the pro-democracy gatherings at Tahrir Square in Cairo, protesters used social media like Facebook, Twitter, and YouTube to stay in touch. Global news organizations tracked the protesters' feeds to stay abreast of what was happening, especially because the state news media ignored the protests and carried pro-Mubarak propaganda. Even though Egyptian leader Hosni Mubarak tried to shut down the Internet in Egypt, word of the protests spread quickly, and he was out within eighteen days after the demonstrations started. In Yemen and Libya, other dictators were ousted. And although Syria's repressive government was still in power after months of protests in 2012, citizens continued to use social media to provide the only evidence of the government's killing thousands of peaceful protestors.

Even in the United States, social media have helped call attention to issues that might not have received any media attention otherwise. In 2011 and 2012, protesters in the Occupy Wall Street movement in New York and at hundreds of sites across the country took to Twitter, Tumblr, YouTube, and Facebook to point out the inequalities of the economy and the income disparity between the wealthiest 1 percent and the rest of the population—the 99 percent.

The flexible and decentralized nature of the Internet and social media is in large part what makes them such powerful tools for subverting control. In China, the Communist Party has tightly controlled mass communication for decades. As more and more Chinese citizens take to the Internet, an estimated thirty thousand government censors monitor or even block Web pages, blogs, chat rooms, and e-mails. Social media sites like Twitter, YouTube, Bing, Flickr, WordPress, and Blogger have frequently been blocked, and Google moved its Chinese search engine (Google.cn) to Hong Kong after the Chinese government repeatedly censored it. And for those who persist in practicing "subversive" free speech, there can be severe penalties: Paris-based Reporters without Borders (www.rsf.org) reports that thirty Chinese journalists and sixty-eight netizens were in prison in 2012 for writing articles and blogs that criticized the government. Still, Chinese dissenters bravely play cat-and-mouse with Chinese censors, using free services like Hushmail, Tor, Freegate, and Ultrasurf (the latter two produced by Chinese immigrants in the United States) to break through the Chinese government's blockade. Today, for every social media site that gets blocked, a new one pops up, making it very difficult for the Chinese government to have the same kind of control over mass communication that they did just a decade ago. (For more on using the Internet for political and social statements, see "Examining Ethics: The 'Anonymous' Hackers of the Internet" on pages 56-57.)

NEW PROTEST LANGUAGE
It has become more and more commonplace to see protest signs with information about Facebook groups, Twitter hashtags, URLs, and other social media references.

EXAMINING ETHICS

The "Anonymous" Hackers of the Internet

Anonymous, the loosely organized hacktivist collective that would become known for its politically and socially motivated Internet vigilantism, first attracted major public attention in 2008.

If you haven't seen Anonymous, you have probably seen the chosen "face" of Anonymous—a Guy Fawkes mask, portraying the most renowned member of the 1605 anarchist plot to assassinate King James I of England. The mask has been a part of Guy Fawkes Day commemorations in England for centuries, but was made even more popular by the 2006 film *V for Vendetta*, based on the graphic novel series of the same name. Today, the mask has become a widespread international symbol for groups protesting financial institutions and politicians.

The issue was a video featuring a fervent Tom Cruise—meant for internal promotional use within the Church of Scientology—that had been leaked to the Web site *Gawker*. When the church tried to suppress the video footage on grounds of copyright, Anonymous went to work. They launched a DDoS, or Distributed Denial of Service, attack (flooding a server or network with external requests so that it becomes overloaded and slows down or crashes) on the church's Web sites, bombarded the church headquarters with prank phone calls and faxes, and "doxed" the church by publishing sensitive internal documents.

United by their libertarian distrust of government, their commitment to a free and open Internet, their opposition to child pornography, and their distaste for corporate conglomerates, Anonymous has targeted organizations as diverse as the Indian government (to protest the country's plan to block Web sites like The Pirate Bay and Vimeo) and the agricultural conglomerate Monsanto (to protest the company's malicious patent lawsuits and the company's dominant control of the food industry). As Anonymous wrote in a message to Monsanto:

You have continually introduced harmful, even deadly products into our food supply without warning, without care, all for your own profit. . . . Rest assured, we will continue to dox your employees and executives, continue to knock down your Web sites, continue to fry your mail servers, continue to be in your systems . . .[1]

While Anonymous agrees on an agenda and coordinates the campaign, the individual hackers all act independently of the group, without expecting recognition. A reporter from the *Baltimore Sun* aptly characterized Anonymous as "a group, in the sense that a flock of birds is a group. How do you know they're a group? Because they're traveling in the same direction. At any given moment, more birds could join,

leave, peel off in another direction entirely."[2]

In some cases, it's easy to find moral high ground in the activities of hacktivists. For example, Anonymous reportedly hacked the computer network of Tunisian tyrant Zine el-Abidine Ben Ali; his downfall in 2011 was the first victory of the Arab Spring movement. In 2011, Anonymous also hacked the Web site of the Westboro Baptist Church, known for spreading its extremist anti-gay rhetoric, picketing funerals of soldiers, and desecrating American flags. And in *The Girl with the Dragon Tattoo* book and film series, it is hard not to cheer on the master hacker character Lisbeth Salandar as she exacts justice on criminals and rapists. In a world of large, impersonal governments and organizations, hackers level the playing field for the ordinary people, responding quickly in ways much more powerful than traditional forms of protest, like writing a letter or publicly demonstrating in front of headquarters or embassies. In fact, hacktivism could be seen as an update on the long tradition of peaceful protests.

Yet, hackers can run afoul of ethics. Because the members of Anonymous are indeed anonymous, there aren't any checks or balances on those who "dox" a corporate site, revealing thousands of credit card or Social Security numbers and making regular citizens vulnerable to identity theft and fraud, as some hackers have done. Prosecutions in 2012 took down at least six international members of Anonymous when one hacker, known online as Sabu, turned out to be a government informant. One of the hackers arrested in Chicago was charged with stealing credit card data and using it to make more than $700,000 in charges.[3] Just a few "bad apples" can undermine the self-managed integrity of groups like Anonymous.

The very existence of Anonymous is a sign that many of our battles now are in the digital domain. We fight for equal access and free speech on the Internet. We are in a perpetual struggle with corporations and other institutions over the privacy of our digital information. And, although our government prosecutes hackers for computer crimes, governments themselves are increasingly using hacking to fight each other. For example, the United States has used computer viruses to attack the nuclear program of Iran. Yet this new kind of warfare carries risks for the United States as well. As the *New York Times*, which broke the story of cyberattacks against Iran, noted, "no country's infrastructure is more dependent on computer systems, and thus more vulnerable to attack, than that of the United States."[4] ◢

Convergence and Mobile Media

The innovation of digital communication—central to the development of the first computers in the 1940s—enables all media content to be created in the same basic way, which makes *media convergence*, the technological merging of content in different mass media, possible.

In recent years, the Internet has really become the hub for convergence, a place where music, television shows, radio stations, newspapers, magazines, books, games, and movies are created, distributed, and presented. Although convergence initially happened on desktop computers, it was the popularity of notebook computers, and then the introduction of smartphones and tablets, that have hastened the pace of media convergence and have made the idea of accessing any media content, anywhere, a reality.

Media Converges on Our PCs and TVs

First there was the telephone, invented in the 1870s. Then came radio in the 1920s, TV in the 1950s, and eventually the personal computer in the 1970s. Each device had its own unique and distinct function. Aside from a few exceptions, like the clock-radio (a popular hybrid device popular since the 1950s), that was how electronic devices worked.

The rise of the personal computer industry in the mid-1970s first opened the possibility for unprecedented technological convergence. A *New York Times* article on the new "home computers" in 1978 noted that "the long-predicted convergence of such consumer electronic products as television sets, videotape recorders, video games, stereo sound systems and the coming video-disk machines into a computer-based home information-entertainment center is getting closer."[16] However, PC-based convergence didn't really materialize until a few decades later when broadband Internet connections improved the multimedia capabilities of computers.

By the early 2000s, computers connected to the Internet allowed an array of digital media to converge in one space and be easily shared. A user can now access television shows (Hulu and Xfinity), movies (Netflix), music (iTunes and Spotify), books (Amazon, Google), games, newspapers, magazines, and lots of other Web content on a computer. And with Skype, iChat, and other live voice and video software, PCs can replace telephones. Other devices, like iPods, quickly capitalized on the Internet's ability to distribute such content, and adapted to play and exhibit multiple media content forms.

Media is also converging on our television sets, as the electronics industry manufactures Internet-ready TVs. Video game consoles like the Xbox, Wii, and PS3, and set-top boxes like Apple TV, Google TV, Roku, and Boxee also offer additional entertainment content access via their Internet connections. In the early years of the Web, it seemed that people would choose only one gateway to the Internet and media content, usually a computer or television. However, wireless networks and the recent technological developments in various media devices mean that consumers now regularly use more than one avenue to access all types of media content.

Mobile Devices Propel Convergence

Mobile telephones have been around for decades (like the giant "brick" mobile phones of the 1970s and 1980s), but the mobile phones of the twenty-first century are substantially different creatures—*smartphones* that go beyond voice calls. They can be used for texting, listening to music, watching movies, connecting to the Internet, playing games, and using hundreds of thousands of applications, or "apps" as they became quickly known.

The Blackberry was the first popular Internet-capable smartphone in the United States, introduced in 2002. Users' ability to check their e-mail messages at any time created addictive e-mail behavior and earned the phones their "Crackberry" nickname. Convergence on mobile phones took another big leap in 2007 with Apple's introduction of the iPhone, which combined qualities of its iPod digital music player and telephone and Internet service, all accessed through a sleek touchscreen. The next year, Apple opened its App Store, featuring free and low-cost software applications for the iPhone (and the iPod Touch and, later, the iPad) created by third-party developers, vastly increasing the utility of the iPhone. By 2012 there were more than 750,000 apps available to do thousands of things on Apple devices–from playing interactive games to finding locations with a GPS or using the iPhone like a carpenter's level.

In 2008, the first smartphone to run on Google's competing Android platform was released. By 2012, Android phones (sold by companies such as Samsung, HTC, LG, and Motorola, and supported by the Google Play app market and the Amazon Appstore) held more than 51 percent of the smartphone market share in the United States, while Apple's iPhone had a 31 percent share; Blackberry and Microsoft smartphones constituted the remainder of the market.[17] The precipitous drop of the Blackberry's market standing in just ten years (the company was late to add touchscreens and apps to its phones) illustrates the tumultuous competition in mobile devices. It also illustrates how apps and the ability to consume all types of media content on the go have surpassed voice call quality to become the most important feature to consumers purchasing a phone today.

In 2010, Apple introduced the iPad, a tablet computer that functions like a larger iPod Touch, making it more suitable for reading magazines, newspapers, and books; watching video; and using visual applications. The tablets became Apple's fastest-growing product line, selling at a rate of twenty-five million a year. Apple added cameras, faster graphics, and a thinner design to subsequent generations of the iPad, as other companies like Samsung rolled out competing tablets. Interestingly, two of the biggest rivals to the iPad are the Kindle Fire and the Nook Tablet, low-cost tablets developed by Amazon and Barnes & Noble, respectively. Both companies found success with their e-readers, but as more users expect their digital devices to perform multiple functions, they recognized that they would need to add a touchscreen, apps, and access to other content like music and movies to their devices in order to stay relevant in users' increasingly interconnected and converged lives.

The Impact of Media Convergence and Mobile Media

Convergence of media content and technology has forever changed our relationship with media. Today, media consumption is mobile and flexible; we don't have to miss out on media content just because we weren't home in time to catch a show, didn't find the book at the bookstore, or forgot to buy the newspaper yesterday. Increasingly, we demand access to our media when we want it, where we want it, and in multiple formats. In order to satisfy those demands and to stay relevant in today's converged world, traditional media companies have had to dramatically change their approach to media content and their business models.

Our Changing Relationship with the Media

The merging of all media onto one device such as a tablet or smartphone blurs the distinctions of what used to be separate media. For example, *USA Today* (a newspaper) and CBS News (network television news) used to deliver the news in completely different formats, but today look quite similar in their web forms, with listings of headlines, rankings of most popular stories, local weather forecasts, photo galleries, and video. On an Amazon Kindle, on which

GOOGLE'S ANDROID PHONES are proving to be stiff competition for Apple's ubiquitous iPhone. Americans are now buying more Android phones than iPhones, which could diminish the iPhone's dominance in the smartphone market.

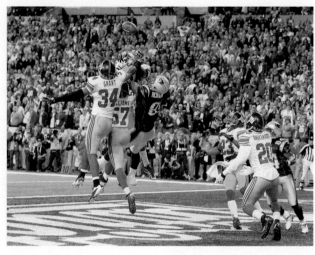

one can read books, newspapers, and magazines, new forms like the Kindle Single challenge old categories. Are the fictional Kindle Singles novellas, or more like the stories found in literary magazines? And what about the investigative reports released as Kindle Singles: Should they be considered long-form journalism, or are they closer to a nonfiction book? Is listening to an hourlong archived episode of Public Radio International's *This American Life* on an iPod more like experiencing a radio program, or an audio book? (It turns out you can listen to that show on the radio, as a downloadable podcast, as a Web stream, on mobile apps, or on a CD.)

Not only are the formats morphing, but we can now experience the media in more than one manner, simultaneously. Fans of television shows like *The Voice, Glee*, and *Top Chef* and viewers of live events like a presidential State of the Union address often multitask, reading live blogs during broadcasts or sharing their own commentary with friends on Facebook. Twitter encourages the same kind of multitasking with their search widget: "Displays search results in real time! Ideal for live events, broadcastings, conferences, TV shows, or even just keeping up with the news."[18] For those who miss the initial broadcasts, converged media offer a second life for media content through deep archive access and repurposed content on other platforms. For example, cable shows like *Game of Thrones* and *Mad Men* have found audiences beyond their initial broadcasts through their DVD collections and online video services like Amazon Instant Video and Apple's iTunes. In fact, some fans even prefer to watch these more complex shows this way, enjoying the ability to rewind an episode in order to catch a missed detail, as well as the ability to watch several episodes back-to-back. Similarly, *Arrested Development*, critically acclaimed but canceled by Fox in 2006, garnered new fans through the streaming episodes on Hulu and Netflix. As a result of this renewed interest, it was revived with new episodes produced for Netflix in 2013.

Our Changing Relationship with the Internet

Mobile devices and social media have altered our relationship with the Internet. Two trends are noteworthy: (1) Apple now makes more than five times as much money selling iPhones, iPads, and iPods and accessories as they do selling computers, and (2) the number of Facebook's users (one billion in 2012) keeps increasing. The significance of these two trends is that through our Apple devices and Facebook, we now inhabit a different kind of Internet—what some call a closed Internet, or a walled garden.[19]

In the world in which the small screens of smartphones are becoming the preferred medium for linking to the Internet, we typically don't get the full, open Internet, one represented by the vast searches brought to us by Google. Instead we get a more managed Internet, brought to us by apps or platforms that carry out specific functions via the Internet. Are you looking for a nearby restaurant? Don't search on the Internet—use this app especially designed for that purpose. And the distributors of these apps act as gatekeepers. Apple has more than 750,000 apps in its App Store, and Apple approves every one of them. The competing Android Appstores on Google Play and Amazon have a similar number of apps, but Google and Amazon exercise less control over approval of apps than Apple does.

Facebook offers a similar walled garden experience. Facebook began as a highly managed environment, only allowing those with .edu e-mail addresses. Although all are now invited to join Facebook, the interface and the user experience on the site is still highly managed by Facebook CEO Mark Zuckerberg and his staff. For example, if you click on a link to a news article that your friend has shared using a social reader app on Facebook, you will be prompted to add the same app–giving it permission to post your activity to your Wall–before you can access the article. In addition, Facebook has severely restricted what content can be accessed through the open Internet. Facebook has installed measures to stop search engines from indexing users' photos, Wall posts, videos, and other data. The effect of both Apple's devices and the Facebook interface is a clean, orderly, easy-to-use environment, but one in which we are "tethered" to the Apple App Store, or to Facebook.[20]

The open Internet–best represented by Google (but not its Google+ social networking service, which is more confining like Facebook) and a Web browser–promised to put the entire World Wide Web at your fingertips. On the one hand, the appeal of the Internet *is* its openness, its free-for-all nature. But of course, the trade-off is that the open Internet can be chaotic and unruly, and apps and other walled garden services have streamlined the cacophony of the Internet considerably for us.

The Changing Economics of Media and the Internet

The digital turn in the mass media has profoundly changed the economics of the Internet. Since the advent of Napster in 1999, which brought (illegal) file sharing to the music industry, each media industry has struggled to rethink how to distribute its content for the digital age. The content itself is still important–people still want quality news, television, movies, music, and games–but they want it in digital formats, and for mobile devices.

Apple's response to Napster established the new media economics. The late Apple CEO Steve Jobs struck a deal with the music industry. Apple would provide a new market for music on the iTunes store, selling digital music that customers could play on their iPods (and later on their iPhones and iPads). In return, Apple got a 30 percent cut of the revenue for all music sales on iTunes, simply for being the "pipes" that delivered the music. As music stores went out of business all across America, Apple sold billions of songs and hundreds of millions of iPods, all without requiring a large chain of retail stores.

Amazon.com started as a more traditional online retailer, taking orders online and delivering merchandise from its warehouses. As books took the turn into the digital era, Amazon created its own device, the Kindle, and followed Apple's model. Amazon started selling e-books, taking its cut for delivering the content. Along the way, Amazon and Apple (and Google through its Android apps) have become leading media companies. They don't make the content (although Amazon is now publishing books, too), but they are among the top digital distributors of books, newspapers, magazines, music, television, movies, and games.

The Next Era: The Semantic Web

Many Internet visionaries talk about the next generation of the Internet as the *Semantic Web*, a term that gained prominence after hypertext inventor Tim Berners-Lee and two coauthors published an influential article in a 2001 issue of *Scientific American*.[21] If "semantics" is the study of meanings, then the Semantic Web is about creating a more meaningful–or more organized–Web. To do that, the future promises a layered, connected database of information that software agents will sift through and process automatically for us. Whereas the search engines of today generate relevant Web pages for us to read, the software of the Semantic Web will make our lives even easier as it places the basic information of the Web into meaningful

Apple

Apple, Inc., was founded by Steven Jobs and Steve Wozniak in 1976 as a home computer company and is today the most valuable company in the world. Apple was only moderately successful until 2001, when Jobs, having been forced out of the company for a decade, returned. Apple introduced the iPod and iTunes in 2003, two innovations that led the company to become the No. 1 music retailer in the United States. Then in 2007, Jobs introduced the iPhone, the world's first smartphone that streamlined and redefined the way users access media content. Converging entertainment, computing, and communications, the iPhone transformed the mobile phone industry, and with Apple's release of the intensely anticipated iPad in 2010, the company further redefined portable computing.

With the iPhone and iPad now at the core of Apple's business, the company now expanded to include providing content—music, television shows, movies, games, newspapers, magazines—to sell its media devices. The next wave of Apple's innovations was the iCloud, a new storage and syncing service that enables users to access media content anywhere (with a wireless connection) on its mobile devices. The iCloud also helps to ensure that customers purchase their media content through Apple's iTunes store, further tethering users to its media systems. (For more on Apple devices and how they are made, see "Global Village: Designed in California, Assembled in China" on page 65.)

Amazon

Amazon started its business in 1995 in Seattle, selling the world's oldest mass medium (books) online. Since that time, Amazon has developed into the world's largest e-commerce store, selling books, but also electronics, garden tools, clothing, appliances, and toys. To keep its lead in e-commerce, Amazon also acquired Zappos, the popular online shoe seller. Yet, by 2007, with the introduction of its Kindle e-reader, Amazon followed Apple's model of using content to sell devices. The Kindle became the first widely successful e-reader, and by 2010 e-books were outselling hardcovers and paperbacks at Amazon. In 2011, in response to Apple's iPad, Amazon released its own color touchscreen tablet, the Kindle Fire, giving Amazon a device that can play all of the media—including music, TV, movies, and games—it sells online and in its Appstore. Like Apple, Amazon has a Cloud Player for making media content portable, and offers an additional five gigabytes of free Cloud Drive space to all users, to use however they like.

Facebook

Of all the leading Internet sites, Facebook is one of the "stickiest," with Americans staying on the social networking site, on average, about 20 percent of their overall time online.[25] Facebook's immense, socially dynamic audience (about two-thirds of the U.S. population, and one billion total users across the globe) is its biggest resource, and Facebook, like Google, has become a data processor as much as a social media service, collecting every tidbit of information about its users—what we "like," where we live, what we read, and what we want—and selling this information to advertisers. Because Facebook users reveal so much about themselves in their profiles and the messages they share with others, Facebook can offer advertisers exceptionally tailored ads: A user who recently got engaged gets ads like "Impress Your Valentine," "Vacation in Hawaii," and "Are You Pregnant?" while a teenage girl sees ads for prom dresses, sweet-sixteen party venues, and "Chat with Other Teens" Web sites.

As a young company, Facebook has suffered growing pains as it tried to balance its corporate interests (capitalizing on its millions of users) and its users' interest in controlling the privacy of their own information at the same time. In 2012, Facebook had the third-largest public offering in U.S. history, behind General Motors and Visa, with the company valued at $104 billion. Facebook's valuation is more of a statement of investors' hopes of what the company can do

Designed in California, Assembled in China

There is a now-famous story involving the release of the iPhone in 2007. The late Apple CEO Steve Jobs was carrying the prototype in his pocket about one month prior to its release, and discovered that his keys, also in his pocket, were scratching the plastic screen. Known as a stickler for design perfection, Jobs reportedly gathered his fellow executives in a room and told them (angrily), "I want a glass screen, and I want it perfect in six weeks."[1] This demand would have implications for a factory complex in China, called Foxconn, where iPhones are assembled. When the order trickled down to a Foxconn foreman, he woke up 8,000 workers in the middle of the night, gave them a biscuit and a cup of tea, and then started them on twelve-hour shifts fitting glass screens into the iPhone frames. Within four days, Foxconn workers were churning out ten thousand iPhones daily.

On its sleek packaging, Apple proudly proclaims that its products are "Designed by Apple in California," a slogan that evokes beaches, sunshine, and Silicon Valley—where the best and brightest in American engineering ingenuity reside. The products also say, usually in a less visible location, "Assembled in China," which suggests little, except that the components of the iPhone, iPad, iPod, or Apple computer were put together in a factory in the world's most populous country.

It wasn't until 2012 that most Apple customers learned that China's Foxconn was the company where their devices are assembled. Investigative reports by the New York Times revealed a company with ongoing problems with labor conditions and worker safety, including fatal explosions and a spate of worker suicides.[2] (Foxconn responded in part by erecting nets around its buildings to prevent fatal jumps.)

Foxconn (also known as Hon Hai Precision Industry Co., Ltd., with headquarters in Taiwan) is China's largest and most prominent private employer with 1.2 million employees—more than any American company except Walmart. Foxconn assembles an incredible 40 percent of the world's electronics, and earns more revenue than ten of its competitors combined.[3] And Foxconn is not just Apple's favorite place to outsource production; nearly every global electronics company is connected to the manufacturing giant: Amazon (Kindle), Microsoft (Xbox), Sony (PlayStation), Dell, Hewlett-Packard, IBM, Motorola, and Toshiba all feed their products to the vast Foxconn factory network.

Behind this manufacturing might is a network of factories now legendary for its enormity. Foxconn's largest factory compound is in Shenzhen. Dubbed "Factory City," it employs roughly 300,000 people—all squeezed into one square mile, many of whom live in the dormitories (dorms sleep seven to a room) on the Foxconn campus.[4] Workers, many of whom come from rural areas in China, often start a shift at 4 A.M. and work until late at night, performing monotonous, routinized work—for example, filing the aluminum shavings from iPad casings six thousand times a day. Thousands of these full-time workers are under the age of eighteen.

Conditions at Foxconn might, in some ways, be better than the conditions in the poverty-stricken small villages from which most of its workers come. But the low pay, long hours, dangerous work conditions, and suicide nets are likely not what the young workers had hoped for when they left their families behind.

In light of the news reports about the problems at Foxconn, Apple joined the Fair Labor Association (FLA), an international nonprofit that monitors labor conditions. The FLA inspected factories and surveyed more than 35,000 Foxconn workers. Their 2012 study verified a range of serious issues. Workers regularly labored more than sixty hours per week, with some employees working more than seven days in a row. Other workers weren't compensated for overtime. More than 43 percent of the workers reported they had witnessed or experienced an accident, and 64 percent of the employees surveyed said that the compensation does not meet their basic needs. In addition, the FLA found the labor union at Foxconn an unsatisfactory channel for addressing worker concerns, as representatives from the management dominated the union's membership.[5]

Apple now boasts on its Web site that it is the first technology company to be admitted to the Fair Labor Association. But Apple might not have taken that step had it not been for the New York Times investigative reports and the intense public scrutiny that followed. What is the role of consumers in ensuring that Apple and other companies are ethical and transparent in the treatment of the workers who make our electronic devices?

INSTAGRAM
Facebook's acquisition of Instagram will help secure the social networking site's future in the mobile interface. Yet questions remain as to the future of the Instagram brand and whether it will continue to grow independently of its parent company. Originally conceived as a user-generated content Web site, Instagram does not claim ownership for any material posted using its services, whereas Facebook owns all material posted to its site.

with one billion users rather than evidence of the company's financial successes so far. And as evidenced by its plummeting stock price during the first few weeks of trading, Facebook's next move and future area of growth is still somewhat uncertain. As Facebook moves forward, one of its shortcomings (and what Google and Apple control) is its mobile interface. In an attempt to build its mobile business, Facebook bought Instagram, a photo sharing mobile app for iPhone and Android, in 2012 for $1 billion.

Targeted Advertising and Data Mining

In the early years of the Web, advertising took the form of traditional display ads placed on pages. The display ads were no more effective than newspaper or magazine advertisements, and because they reached small, general audiences, they weren't very profitable. But in the late 1990s, Web advertising began to shift to search engines. Paid links appeared as "sponsored links" at the top, bottom, and side of a search engine result list and even, depending on the search engine, within the "objective" result list itself. Every time a user clicks on a sponsored link, the advertiser pays the search engine for the click-through. For online shopping, having paid placement in searches can be a good thing. But search engines doubling as ad brokers may undermine the utility of search engines as neutral locators of Web sites (see "Media Literacy and the Critical Process: Search Engines and Their Commercial Bias" on page 67).

Advertising has since spread to other parts of the Internet, including social networking sites, e-mail, and IM. For advertisers–who for years struggled with how to measure people's attention to ads–these activities make advertising easy to track, effective in reaching the desired niche audience, and relatively inexpensive because ads get wasted less often on the uninterested. For example, Yahoo! gleans information from search terms, Google scans the contents of Gmail messages, and Facebook uses profile information, status updates, and "likes" to deliver individualized, real-time ads to users' screens. Similarly, a mobile social networking application for smartphones, Foursquare, encourages users to earn points and "badges" by checking in at business locations, such as museums, restaurants, and airports (or other user-added locations), and to share that information via Twitter, Facebook, and text messages. Other companies, like Poynt and Yelp, are also part of the location-based ad market that is projected to account for one-third of all mobile advertising by 2015.[26] But by gathering users' location and purchasing habits, these data-collecting systems also function as consumer surveillance and **data mining** operations.

The practice of data mining also raises issues of Internet security and privacy. Millions of people, despite knowing that transmitting personal information online can make them vulnerable to online fraud, have embraced the ease of **e-commerce**: the buying and selling of products and services on the Internet, which took off in 1995 with the launch of Amazon.com. What many people don't know is that their personal information may be used without their knowledge for commercial purposes, such as targeted advertising. For example, in 2011, the Federal Trade Commission charged Facebook with a list of eight violations in which Facebook told consumers their information would be private, but made it public to advertisers and third-party applications. Facebook CEO Mark Zuckerberg admitted the company had made "a bunch of mistakes," and settled with the FTC by fixing the problems and agreeing to submit to privacy audits for twenty years.[27]

One common method that commercial interests use to track the browsing habits of computer users is **cookies**, or information profiles that are automatically collected and transferred between computer servers whenever users access Web sites. The legitimate purpose of a cookie

Media Literacy and the Critical Process

1 DESCRIPTION. Here's what we find in the first thirty results from Google: numerous sites for obesity research organizations (e.g., Obesity Society, MedicineNet, WebMD) and many government-funded sites like the CDC and NIH. Here's what we find in the top-rated results from Bing: numerous sponsored sites (e.g., the Scooter Store, Gastric Banding) and the same obesity research organizations.

2 ANALYSIS. A closer look at these results reveals a subtle but interesting pattern: All the sites listed in the top ten results (of both search engine result lists, and with the important exception of Wikipedia) offer loads of advice to help an individual lose weight (e.g., change eating habits, exercise, undergo surgery, take drugs). These "professional-looking" sites all frame obesity as a disease, a genetic disorder, or the result of personal inactivity. In other words, they put the blame squarely on the individual. But where is all the other research that links high obesity rates to social factors (e.g., constant streams of advertising for junk food, government subsidies of the giant corn syrup food sweetener industry, deceptive labeling practices)? These society-level views are not apparent in our Web searches.

Search Engines and Their Commercial Bias

How valuable are search engines for doing research? Are they the best resources for academic information? To test this premise, we're going to do a search for the topic "obesity," which is prevalent in the news and a highly controversial topic.

3 INTERPRETATION. What does it mean that our searches are so biased? Consider this series of connections: Obesity research organizations manufacture drugs and promote surgery treatments to "cure" obese individuals. They seem to offer legitimate information about the "obesity disease," but they are backed by big business, which is interested in selling more junk food (not taking social responsibility) and then promoting drugs to treat people's obesity problems. These wealthy sites can pay for placement through Search Engine Optimizer firms (which work relentlessly to outsmart Google's page rank algorithm) and by promoting themselves through various marketing channels to ensure their popularity (Google ranks pages by popularity). With the exception of Wikipedia, which is so interlinked it usually ranks high in search engines, search results today are skewed toward big business. Money speaks.

4 EVALUATION. Commercial search engines have evolved to be much like the commercial mass media: They tend to reflect the corporate perspective that finances them. This does not bode well for the researcher, who is interested in many angles of a single issue. Controversy is at the heart of every important research question.

5 ENGAGEMENT. What to do? Start by including the word *controversy* next to the search term, as in "obesity and controversy." Or learn about where alternative information sources exist on the Web. A search for "obesity" on the independent media publications AlterNet, MediaChannel, Common Dreams, and Salon, for example, and nonprofit digital archives like ibiblio and INFOMINE, will offer countless other perspectives to the obesity epidemic. Let's also not dismiss Wikipedia, a collaboratively built nonprofit encyclopedia that often lays out the controversies within a given research topic and can be a helpful launching pad for scholarly research. Good research does not mean clicking on the first link on a search engine list; it involves knowing that every topic has political, economic, and ideological biases, and looking for valuable and diverse perspectives.

---

is to verify that a user has been cleared for access to a particular Web site, such as a library database that is open only to university faculty and students. However, cookies can also be used to create marketing profiles of Web users to target them for advertising. Many Web sites require the user to accept cookies in order to gain access to the site.

Even more unethical and intrusive is **spyware**, information-gathering software that is often secretly bundled with free downloaded software. Spyware can be used to send pop-up ads to users' computer screens, to enable unauthorized parties to collect personal or account information of users, or even to plant a malicious click-fraud program on a computer, which generates phony clicks on Web ads that force an advertiser to pay for each click.

In 1998, the FTC developed fair information practice principles for online privacy to address the unauthorized collection of personal data. These principles require Web sites to

THE UNGOOGLABLE MAN

Even the most powerful search engines CANNOT DETECT HIM!

No Facebook page... no MySpace page... no NOTHING!

And yet HE WALKS AMONGST US.

**THIS *NEW YORKER*
CARTOON** illustrates
an increasingly rare
phenomenon.

(1) disclose their data-collection practices, (2) give consumers the option to choose whether their data may be collected and to provide information on how that data is collected, (3) permit individuals access to their records to ensure data accuracy, and (4) secure personal data from unauthorized use. Unfortunately, the FTC has no power to enforce these principles, and most Web sites either do not self-enforce them or deceptively appear to enforce them when they in fact don't.[28] As a result, consumer and privacy advocates are calling for stronger regulations, such as requiring Web sites to adopt **opt-in** or **opt-out policies**. Opt-in policies, favored by consumer and privacy advocates, require Web sites to obtain explicit permission from consumers before the sites can collect browsing history data. Opt-out policies, favored by data-mining corporations, allow for the automatic collection of browsing history data unless the consumer requests to "opt out" of the practice. In 2012, the Federal Trade Commission approved a report recommending that Congress adopt "Do Not Track" legislation to limit tracking of user information on Web sites and mobile devices, and enable users to easily opt out of data collection. Some Web browsers, such as Internet Explorer 9, are offering "Do Not Track" options, while other Web tools, like Ghostery.com, detect Web tags, bugs, and other trackers, generating a list of all of the sites following your moves.

Security: The Challenge to Keep Personal Information Private

When you watch television, listen to the radio, read a book, or go to a film, you do not need to provide personal information to others. However, when you use the Internet, whether you are signing up for an e-mail account, shopping online, or even just surfing the Web, you give away personal information—voluntarily or not. As a result, government surveillance, online fraud, and unethical data-gathering methods have become common, making the Internet a potentially treacherous place.

Government Surveillance

Since the inception of the Internet, government agencies worldwide have obtained communication logs, Web browser histories, and the online records of individual users who thought their online activities were private. In the United States, for example, the USA PATRIOT Act (which became law about a month after the September 11 attacks in 2001 and was renewed in 2006) grants sweeping powers to law-enforcement agencies to intercept individuals' online communications, including e-mail messages and browsing records. The act was intended to allow the government to more easily uncover and track potential terrorists and terrorist organizations, but many now argue that it is too vaguely worded, allowing the government to unconstitutionally probe the personal records of citizens without probable cause and for reasons other than preventing terrorism. Moreover, searches of the Internet permit law-enforcement agencies to gather huge amounts of data, including the communications of people who are not the targets of an investigation. For example, a traditional telephone wiretap would intercept only communication on a single telephone line. Internet surveillance involves tracking all of the communications over an ISP, which raises concerns about the privacy of thousands of other users.

Online Fraud

In addition to being an avenue for surveillance, the Internet is increasingly a conduit for online robbery and *identity theft*, the illegal obtaining of personal credit and identity information in order to fraudulently spend other people's money. Computer hackers have the ability to infiltrate Internet databases (from banks to hospitals to even the Pentagon) to obtain personal information and to steal credit card numbers from online retailers. Identity theft victimizes hundreds of thousands of people a year, and clearing one's name can take a very long time and cost a lot of money. About $3.4 billion in the United States is lost to online fraud artists every year. One particularly costly form of Internet identity theft is known as **phishing**. This scam involves phony e-mail messages that appear to be from official Web sites–such as eBay, PayPal, or the user's university or bank–asking customers to update their credit card numbers, account passwords, and other personal information.

Appropriateness: What Should Be Online?

The question of what constitutes appropriate content has been part of the story of most mass media, from debates over the morality of lurid pulp fiction books in the nineteenth century to arguments over the appropriateness of racist, sexist, and homophobic content in films and music. Although it is not the only material to come under intense scrutiny, most of the debate about appropriate media content, despite the medium, has centered on sexually explicit imagery.

As has always been the case, eliminating some forms of sexual content from books, films, television, and other media remains a top priority for many politicians and public interest groups. So it should not be surprising that public objection to indecent and obscene Internet content has led to various legislative efforts to tame the Web. Although the Communications Decency Act of 1996 and the Child Online Protection Act of 1998 were both judged unconstitutional, the Children's Internet Protection Act of 2000 was passed and upheld in 2003. This act requires schools and libraries that receive federal funding for Internet access to use software that filters out any visual content deemed obscene, pornographic, or harmful to minors, unless disabled at the request of adult users. Regardless of new laws, pornography continues to flourish on commercial sites, individuals' blogs, and social networking pages. As the American Library Association notes, there is "no filtering technology that will block out all illegal content, but allow access to constitutionally protected materials."[29]

Although the "back alleys of sex" on the Internet have caused considerable public concern, Internet sites that carry potentially dangerous information (e.g., bomb building instructions, hate speech) have also incited calls for Internet censorship, particularly after the terrorist attacks of September 11, 2001, and several tragic school shooting incidents. Nevertheless, many others–fearing that government regulation of speech would inhibit freedom of expression in a democratic society–want the Web to be completely unregulated.

Access: The Fight to Prevent a Digital Divide

A key economic issue related to the Internet is whether the cost of purchasing a personal computer and paying for Internet services will undermine equal access. Coined to echo the term *economic divide* (the disparity of wealth between the rich and poor), the term **digital divide** refers to the growing contrast between the "information haves," those who can afford to purchase computers and pay for Internet services, and the "information have-nots," those who may not be able to afford a computer or pay for Internet services.

Although about 80 percent of U.S. households are connected to the Internet, there are big gaps in access, particularly in terms of age and education. For example, a 2012 study found that only 41 percent of Americans over the age of sixty-five go online, compared with 74 percent of Americans ages fifty to sixty-four, 87 percent of Americans ages thirty to forty-nine, and 94 percent of Americans ages eighteen to twenty-nine. Education has an even more pronounced effect: Only 43 percent of those who did not graduate from high school have Internet access, compared with 71 percent of high school graduates and 94 percent of college graduates.[30]

"Given that the Internet has become an indispensable tool for realizing a range of human rights, combating inequality, and accelerating development and human progress, ensuring universal access to the Internet should be a priority."

UNITED NATIONS REPORT, 2011

Another digital divide has developed in the United States as Americans have switched over from slow dial-up connections to high-speed broadband service. By 2012, 68 percent of all Internet users in the United States had broadband connections, but given that prices are tiered so that the higher the speed of service the more it costs, those in lower-income households were much less likely to have high-speed service. A Pew Internet & American Life Project study found that one in five American adults does not use the Internet. Non-users were predominantly senior citizens, Spanish-language speakers, those with less than a high school education, and those living in households earning less than $30,000 per year. The primary reason given by non-users for why they don't go online is they don't think the Internet is relevant to them.[31]

The rising use of smartphones is helping to narrow the digital divide, particularly along racial lines. In the United States, African American families generally have lagged behind whites in home access to the Internet, which requires a computer and broadband access. However, the Pew Internet & American Life Project reported that African Americans are the most active users of mobile Internet devices. Thus, the report concluded, "the digital divide between African Americans and white Americans diminishes when mobile use is taken into account."[32]

Globally, though, the have-nots face an even greater obstacle crossing the digital divide. Although the Web claims to be worldwide, the most economically powerful countries like the United States, Sweden, Japan, South Korea, Australia, and the United Kingdom account for most of its international flavor. In nations such as Jordan, Saudi Arabia, Syria, and Myanmar (Burma), the governments permit limited or no access to the Web. In other countries, an inadequate telecommunications infrastructure hampers access to the Internet. And in underdeveloped countries, phone lines and computers are almost nonexistent. For example, in Sierra Leone, a nation of about six million in West Africa with poor public utilities and intermittent electrical service, only about ten thousand people—about 0.16 percent of the population—are Internet users.[33] However, as mobile phones become more popular in the developing world, they could provide one remedy to the global digital divide.

NICHOLAS NEGROPONTE, founder of the Media Lab at MIT, began a project to provide $100 laptops to children in developing countries (shown). These laptops, the first supply of which was funded by Negroponte, need to survive in rural environments where challenges include battling adverse weather conditions (dust and high heat) and providing reliable power, Internet access, and maintenance.

Even as the Internet matures and becomes more accessible, wealthy users are still more able to buy higher levels of privacy and faster speeds of Internet access than other users. Whereas traditional media made the same information available to everyone who owned a radio or a TV set, the Internet creates economic tiers and classes of service. Policy groups, media critics, and concerned citizens continue to debate the implications of the digital divide, valuing the equal opportunity to acquire knowledge.

Net Neutrality: Maintaining an Open Internet

For more than a decade, the debate over net neutrality has framed the shape of the Internet's future. **Net neutrality** refers to the principle that every Web site and every user–whether a multinational corporation or you–has the right to the same Internet network speed and access. The idea of an open and neutral network has existed since the origins of the Internet, but there had never been a formal policy until 2010, when the Federal Communications Commission approved a limited set of net neutrality rules. Still, the debate forges on.

The dispute over net neutrality and the future of the Internet is dominated by some of the biggest communications corporations. These major telephone and cable companies–Verizon, Comcast, AT&T, Time Warner Cable, and CenturyLink–control 98 percent of broadband access in the United States through DSL and cable modem service. They want to offer faster connections and priority to clients willing to pay higher rates, and provide preferential service for their own content or for content providers who make special deals with them–effectively eliminating net neutrality. For example, tiered Internet access might mean that these companies would charge customers more for data-heavy services like Netflix, YouTube, Hulu, or iTunes. These companies argue that the profits they could make with tiered Internet access will allow them to build expensive new networks, benefiting everyone.

But supporters of net neutrality–mostly bloggers, video gamers, educators, religious groups, unions, and small businesses–argue that the cable and telephone giants actually have incentive to rig their services and cause net congestion in order to force customers to pay a premium for higher speed connections. They claim that an Internet without net neutrality would hurt small businesses, nonprofits, and Internet innovators, who might be stuck in the "slow lane" and not be able to afford the fastest connections that large corporations can afford. Large Internet corporations like Google, Yahoo!, Amazon, eBay, Microsoft, Skype, and Facebook also support net neutrality because their businesses depend on their millions of customers having equal access to the Web.

In late 2010, the FCC adopted rules on net neutrality, noting "the Internet's openness promotes innovation, investment, competition, free expression, and other national broadband goals."[34] On a split vote, the FCC approved firm net neutrality guidelines for fixed-line broadband ISPs (like cable and DSL connections), but required less strict net neutrality rules for wireless broadband connections (mobile phone companies). Both fixed-line and mobile providers must disclose their network management practices and are prohibited from blocking sites or applications. However, while the FCC prohibited fixed-line providers from unreasonable discrimination, mobile phone companies are exempt from this rule, and they are also allowed to offer tiered service prices for data packages. The FCC explained that these differences in rules were in part due to the fact that the mobile industry is more competitive. But neither side of the net neutrality debate is 100 percent happy with the FCC's ruling: Net neutrality proponents have argued that these rules don't go far enough, while opponents have tried to get the courts and Congress to overturn the FCC's policy.

Alternative Voices

Independent programmers continue to invent new ways to use the Internet and communicate over it. While some of their innovations have remained free of corporate control, others have

VideoCentral ⊚
Mass Communication
bedfordstmartins.com
/mediaculture

Net Neutrality
Experts discuss net neutrality and privatization of the Internet
Discussion: Do you support net neutrality? Why or why not?

"The choice for American consumers is between the open broadband they have come to expect—in which they can view any content from sources big and small—and a walled garden somewhat like cable TV, where providers can decide what we can see, and at what price."

NEW YORK TIMES, 2011

been taken over by commercial interests. Despite commercial buyouts, however, the pioneering spirit of the Internet's independent early days endures; the Internet continues to be a participatory medium where anyone can be involved. Two of the most prominent areas in which alternative voices continue to flourish relate to open-source software and digital archiving.

Open-Source Software

Microsoft has long been the dominant software corporation of the digital age, but independent software creators persist in developing alternatives. One of the best examples of this is the continued development of **open-source software**. In the early days of computer code writing, amateur programmers developed software on the principle that it was a collective effort. Programmers openly shared program source codes and their ideas to upgrade and improve programs. Beginning in the 1970s, Microsoft put an end to much of this activity by transforming software development into a business in which programs were developed privately and users were required to pay for both the software and its periodic upgrades.

However, programmers are still developing noncommercial, open-source software, if on a more limited scale. One open-source operating system, Linux, was established in 1991 by Linus Torvalds, a twenty-one-year-old student at the University of Helsinki in Finland. Since the establishment of Linux, professional computer programmers and hobbyists alike around the world have participated in improving it, creating a sophisticated software system that even Microsoft has acknowledged is a credible alternative to expensive commercial programs. Linux can operate across disparate platforms, and companies such as IBM, Dell, and Sun Microsystems, as well as other corporations and governmental organizations, have developed applications and systems that run on it. Still, the greatest impact of Linux is not evident on the desktop screens of everyday computer users but in the operation of behind-the-scenes computer servers.

Digital Archiving

Librarians have worked tirelessly to build nonprofit digital archives that exist outside of any commercial system in order to preserve libraries' tradition of open access to information. One of the biggest and most impressive digital preservation initiatives is the Internet Archive, established in 1996. The Internet Archive aims to ensure that researchers, historians, scholars, and all citizens have universal access to human knowledge–that is, everything that's digital: text, moving images, audio, software, and more than eighty-five billion archived Web pages reaching back to the earliest days of the Internet. The archive is growing at staggering rates as the general public and partners such as the Smithsonian and the Library of Congress upload cultural artifacts. For example, the Internet Archive stores sixty-five thousand live music concerts, including performances by Jack Johnson, the Grateful Dead, and the Smashing Pumpkins.

The archive has also partnered with the Open Content Alliance to digitize every book in the public domain (generally, those published before 1922). This book-scanning effort is the nonprofit alternative to Google's "Google Book Search" program, which, beginning in 2004, has scanned books from the New York Public Library as well as the libraries of Harvard, Stanford, and the University of Michigan despite many books' copyright status. Google pays to scan each book (which can cost up to $30 in labor) and then includes book contents in its search results, significantly adding to the usefulness and value of its search engine. Since Google forbids other commercial search engines from accessing the scanned material, the deal has the library community concerned. "Scanning the great libraries is a wonderful idea," says Brewster Kahle, head of the Internet Archive, "but if only one corporation controls access to this digital collection, we'll have handed too much control to a private entity."[35] Under the terms of the Open Content Alliance, all search engines, including Google, will have access to the Alliance's ever-growing repository of scanned books. Media activist David Bollier has likened open access initiatives to an information "commons," underscoring the idea that the public collectively owns (or should own) certain public resources, like airwaves, the Internet, and public spaces (such as parks). "Libraries are one of the few, if not the key, public institutions defending popular access and sharing of information as a right of all citizens, not just those who can afford access," Bollier says.[36]

The Internet and Democracy

Throughout the twentieth century, Americans closely examined emerging mass media for their potential contributions to democracy. As radio became more affordable in the 1920s and 1930s, we hailed the medium for its ability to reach and entertain even the poorest Americans caught in the Great Depression. When television developed in the 1950s and 1960s, it also held promise as a medium that could reach everyone, including those who were illiterate or cut off from printed information. Despite continuing concerns over the digital divide, many have praised the Internet for its democratic possibilities. Some advocates even tout the Internet as the most democratic social network ever conceived.

The biggest threat to the Internet's democratic potential may well be its increasing commercialization. Similar to what happened with radio and television, the growth of commercial "channels" on the Internet has far outpaced the emergence of viable nonprofit channels, as fewer and fewer corporations have gained more and more control. The passage of the 1996 Telecommunications Act cleared the way for cable TV systems, computer firms, and telephone companies to merge their interests and become even larger commercial powers. Although there was a great deal of buzz about lucrative Internet startups in the 1990s and 2000s, it has been large corporations such as Microsoft, Apple, Amazon, and Google that have weathered the low points of the dot-com economy and maintained a controlling hand.

About three-quarters of households in the United States are now linked to the Internet, thus greatly increasing its democratic possibilities but also tempting commercial interests to gain even greater control over it and intensifying problems for agencies trying to regulate it. If the histories of other media are any predictor, it seems realistic to expect that the Internet's potential for widespread use by all could be partially preempted by narrower commercial interests. As media economist Douglas Gomery warns, "Technology alone does not a communication revolution make. Economics trumps technology every time."[37]

However, defenders of the Digital Age argue that inexpensive digital production and social media distribution allow greater participation than any other traditional medium. In response to these new media forms, older media are using Internet technology to increase their access to and feedback from varied audiences. Skeptics raise doubts about the participatory nature of discussions on the Internet. For instance, they warn that Internet users may be communicating with those people whose beliefs and values are similar to their own—in other words, just their Facebook friends and Google+ circles. Although it is important to be able to communicate across vast distances with people who have similar viewpoints, these kinds of discussions may not serve to extend the diversity and tolerance that are central to democratic ideals. There is also the threat that we may not be interacting with anyone at all. In the wide world of the Web, we are in a shared environment of billions of people. In the emerging ecosystem of apps, we live in an efficient but gated community, walled off from the rest of the Internet. However, we are still in the early years of the Internet. The democratic possibilities of the Internet's future are still endless. ▶

CHAPTER REVIEW

COMMON THREADS

One of the Common Threads discussed in Chapter 1 is about the commercial nature of the mass media. The Internet is no exception, as advertisers have capitalized on its ability to be customized. How might this affect other media industries?

Most people love the simplicity of the classic Google search page. The iGoogle home page builds on that by offering the ability to "Create your own homepage in under 30 seconds." Enter your city, and the page's design theme will dynamically change images to reflect day and night. Enter your zip code, and you get your hometown weather information or local movie schedules. Tailor the page to bring up your favorite RSS feeds, and stay on top of the information that interests you the most.

This is just one form of mass customization—something no other mass medium has been able to provide. (When is the last time a television, radio, newspaper, or movie spoke directly to you?) This is one of the Web's greatest strengths—it can connect us to the world in a personally meaningful way. But a casualty of the Internet may be our shared common culture. A generation ago, students and coworkers across the country gathered on Friday mornings to discuss what happened on NBC's "must-see" TV shows like *Cosby*, *Seinfeld*, *Friends*, and *Will & Grace*. Today it's

more likely that they watched vastly different media the night before. And if they did share something—say, a funny YouTube video—it's likely they all laughed alone, as they watched it individually, although they may have later shared it with their friends on a social media site.

We have become a society divided by the media, often split into our basic entity, the individual. One would think that advertisers dislike this, since it is easier to reach a mass audience by showing commercials during *The Voice*. But mass customization gives advertisers the kind of personal information they once only dreamed about: your e-mail address, hometown, zip code, birthday, and a record of your interests—what Web pages you visit and what you buy online. If you have a Facebook profile or a Gmail account, they may know even more about you—what you did last night or what you are doing right now. What will advertisers want to sell to you with all this information? With the mass-customized Internet, you may have already told them.

KEY TERMS

The definitions for the terms listed below can be found in the glossary at the end of the book. The page numbers listed with the terms indicate where the term is highlighted in the chapter.

Internet, 46
ARPAnet, 46
e-mail, 48
microprocessors, 48
fiber-optic cable, 48
World Wide Web, 49
HTML (hypertext markup language), 49
browsers, 49
Internet service provider (ISP), 50

broadband, 50
digital communication, 50
instant messaging, 51
search engines, 51
social media, 52
blogs, 52
wiki Web sites, 53
content communities, 53
social networking sites, 54
Telecommunications Act of 1996, 62

portal, 63
data mining, 66
e-commerce, 66
cookies, 66
spyware, 67
opt-in or opt-out policies, 68
phishing, 69
digital divide, 69
net neutrality, 71
open-source software, 72

REVIEW QUESTIONS

The Development of the Internet and the Web

1. When did the Internet reach the novelty (development), entrepreneurial, and mass medium stages?

2. How did the Internet originate? What role did the government play?

3. How does the World Wide Web work? What is the significance of it in the development of the Internet?

4. Why did Google become such a force in Web searching?

The Web Goes Social

5. What is the difference between a "Read/Only" culture and a "Read/Write" culture of the Internet?

6. What are the six main types of social media?

7. What are the democratic possibilities of social media? How can social media aid political repression?

Convergence and Mobile Media

8. What were the conditions that enabled media convergence?

9. What are the significant milestones for mobile devices as playing a part in media convergence?

10. How has convergence changed our relationship with media, and with the Internet?

11. What elements of today's digital world are part of the Semantic Web?

The Economics and Issues of the Internet

12. Which of the four major digital companies are most aligned with the "open Internet," and which are most aligned with the "closed Internet"?

13. What is the role of data mining in the digital economy? What are the ethical concerns?

14. What is the digital divide, and what is being done to close the gap?

15. Why is net neutrality such an important debate?

16. What are the major alternative voices on the Internet?

The Internet and Democracy

17. How can the Internet make democracy work better?

18. What are the key challenges to making the Internet itself more democratic?

QUESTIONING THE MEDIA

1. What possibilities for the Internet's future are you most excited about? Why? What possibilities are most troubling? Why?

2. What are the advantages of media convergence that enable all types of media content to be accessed on a single device?

3. Google's corporate motto is "Don't be evil." Which of the four major digital corporations (Google, Apple, Amazon, and Facebook) seems to have the greatest tendency for evil? Which seems to do the most good? Why?

4. As we move from a print-oriented Industrial Age to a digitally based Information Age, how do you think individuals, communities, and nations have been affected positively? How have they been affected negatively?

ADDITIONAL VIDEOS

Visit the Ⓥ VideoCentral: Mass Communication *section at bedfordstmartins.com/mediaculture for additional exclusive videos related to Chapter 2, including:*

- USER-GENERATED CONTENT
  Editors, producers, and advertisers discuss the varieties of user-generated content and how it can contribute to the democratization of media.

- INTERNET MEDIA ENTREPRENEURS: NEWSY
  Jim Spencer, the founder of Newsy.com, describes his news service that delivers multiple sources on individual stories straight to laptops and other mobile devices.

3

Digital Gaming and the Media Playground

In October 2011, producers released the trailer film for the latest blockbuster sequel coming to screens around the world. As the trailer revealed, the next installation of the series featured new special effects and more pitched battles between the Alliance and the Horde on the planet Azeroth. Critics wrote positive advance reviews, and with young target audiences and a big distribution push planned for Asia, it had the makings of another Hollywood blockbuster.

Except that the sequel wasn't a film—it was an expansion of *World of Warcraft* (*WoW*), the most successful massively multiplayer online role-playing game (MMORPG), with more than ten million players worldwide. The fantastical setting of Azeroth was first introduced in the strategy game *Warcraft: Orcs and Humans*, released on CD-ROM in 1994 by Blizzard Entertainment. But it wasn't until 2004 with the release of *World of Warcraft* that the playing environment became completely immersive and online, enabling millions of players from around the world to participate.

Since then, *World of Warcraft* and its culture have spread beyond the gaming community to become a part of the mainstream. Not only did *WoW* spawn a parody episode of *South Park* ("Make Love, Not Warcraft"), there is a Sam Raimi–directed film in the works. And the famous "Leeroy Jenkins" video that captures the breakdown in communication among a group of *WoW* players on a dangerous dungeon raid has garnered more than thirty-one million views on YouTube.

The beginner's guide for *World of Warcraft* reads something like the narrative of an epic novel, describing the "two large, opposing factions. On one side is the noble Alliance, which comprises the valiant humans, the stalwart dwarves, the ingenious gnomes, the spiritual night elves, the mystical draenei, and the bestial worgen[;] . . . on the other side is the mighty Horde, made up of the battle-hardened orcs, the cunning trolls, the hulking tauren, the cursed Forsaken, the extravagant blood elves, and the devious goblins. Your character's race will determine whose side you are on, so choose carefully." [1]

Since the original game, there have been four expansions: *The Burning Crusade* (2007), the *Wrath of the Lich King* (2008), *Cataclysm* (2010), and *Mists of Pandaria* (2012). Each expansion opens up new continents on Azeroth for exploration, introduces new characters, and adds new play features. For example, the *Cataclysm* expansion brought more than thirty-five hundred new quests, enabling players to have an enormous range of playing possibilities and ways to unfold the experience of the narrative.

Mists of Pandaria, the latest expansion, is set in "lush forests and cloud-ringed mountains" and is "home to a complex ecosystem of indigenous races and exotic creatures." [2] The Pandarians (who look like pandas and live in a land that appears to be a fantasy version of ancient China) have been at peace for ten thousand years, now disrupted by the arrival of the Alliance and the Horde. Pandarians are a "playable" race, and gamers can ally their Pandarian avatar with either the Alliance or the Horde. *Mists of Pandaria* feels like a movie in many ways, with its cinematic music, sound effects, expansive vistas, and grand stories. But there are also ninety levels of play in which players use the unique powers of their characters to complete quests, creating their own "narratives." Playing *World of Warcraft* is a social experience as well, as players chat and form "guilds" with others for the more difficult quests. *World of Warcraft* costs $14.99 per month to play. What players get is not only the experience of the game's rich narratives—just like watching a movie—but also the ability to create their own narratives by themselves and with fellow players.

▲

"In the outside world, I am a simple geologist. But in here, I am Falcorn, defender of the Alliance. I've braved the Fargodeep Mine, and defeated the Blood Fish at Jerod's Landing."

RANDY MARSH, *SOUTH PARK,* "MAKE LOVE, NOT WARCRAFT," 2006

◢ **ELECTRONIC GAMES OFFER PLAY, ENTERTAINMENT, AND SOCIAL INTERAC-TION**. Like the Internet, they combine text, audio, and moving images. But they go even further than the Internet by enabling players to interact with aspects of the medium in the context of the game–from deciding when an onscreen character jumps or punches to controlling the direction of the "story" in *World of Warcraft*. This interactive quality creates an experience so compelling that vibrant communities of fans have cropped up around the globe. And the games have powerfully shaped the everyday lives of millions of people. Indeed, for players around the world, digital gaming has become a social medium as compelling and distracting as other social media. The U.S. Supreme Court has even granted digital gaming First Amendment freedom of speech rights, ensuring its place as a mass medium.

In this chapter, we take a look at the evolving mass medium of digital gaming and:

- Examine the early history of electronic gaming, including its roots in penny arcades
- Trace the evolution of electronic gaming from arcades and bars into living rooms and our hands
- Discuss gaming as a social medium that forms communities of play
- Analyze the economics of gaming, including the industry's major players and various revenue streams
- Raise questions about the role of digital gaming in our democratic society

"Print has been around for 570 years, cinema for 120, television for 80. Yet in just four decades, the video-game industry has beaten them all, becoming the most profitable—and, arguably, the most dynamic and innovative— entertainment medium on the planet."

JAMIE RUSSELL, *SUNDAY TIMES* (LONDON), 2012

DISNEY EPIC MICKEY 2: THE POWER OF TWO, the sequel to 2010's platform video game *Epic Mickey*, debuted at the Electronic Entertainment Expo (E3) in June 2012. Recent video game sequels, such as Disney's *Epic Mickey 2*, *Mass Effect 3*, and *Halo 4* in 2012, highlight the ways in which game developers have adopted the storytelling approach of traditional media like television, comic books, and film, where a narrative can develop over the course of several installments. Meanwhile, gamers now anticipate the next installment of their favorite video game as passionately as filmgoers anticipate the sequels to their favorite movies.

Past-Present-Future: Digital Gaming

Playing games is part of being human. As we discuss later in this chapter, the business of playing games is a more modern pursuit, designed to take advantage of our leisure time. The rise of amusement parks in the late 1800s, with rides and carnival games, brought people together to enjoy created experiences. Later, mechanical and electronic games brought those experiences into year-round use at bars, arcades, and homes.

Today's gaming environment has gone digital–on a console, on a computer, on a mobile device–and as a result become more popular than ever. Mirroring our lives in which work can be done everywhere (at home or out, on our computers, or on our mobile devices), games are everywhere, too, offering a few minutes of downtime with a casual game like *Fruit Ninja* or complete release with an immersive experience like *Dark Souls*. The ubiquity and wide price range of digital games mean that the "gamer" demographic has also broadened to include males and females, of every age and race, in every location.

Our current experience with video games hints at their future. On one hand, games will become more and more realistic and immersive, reading our body movement (as the Wii or the Kinect do now), our facial expressions, and our thoughts, and inserting us into even more highly developed fantasy worlds. (Think of the movie *Avatar*.) On the other hand, games will become even more enmeshed with everyday life, as motivating forces in our workplaces, schools, media, and social lives.

The Development of Digital Gaming

When the Industrial Revolution swept Western civilization two centuries ago, the technological advances involved weren't simply about mass production. They also promoted mass consumption and the emergence of *leisure time*–both of which created money-making opportunities for media makers. By the late nineteenth century, the availability of leisure time sparked the creation of mechanical games like pinball. Technology continued to grow, and by the 1950s computer science students in the United States had developed early versions of the video games we know today.

In their most basic form, digital games involve users in an interactive computerized environment where they strive to achieve a desired outcome. These days, most digital games go beyond a simple competition like the 1975 tennis-style game of *Pong*: They often entail sweeping narratives and offer imaginative and exciting adventures, sophisticated problem-solving opportunities, and multiple possible outcomes.

But the boundaries were not always so varied. Digital games evolved from their simplest forms in the arcade into four major formats: television, handheld devices, computers, and the Internet. As these formats evolved and graphics advanced, distinctive types of games emerged and became popular. These included action games, sports games, shooter games, family entertainment games, role-playing games, adventure games, racing games, strategy games, fighting games, simulation games, computerized versions of card games, fantasy sports leagues, and virtual social environments. Together, these varied formats constitute an industry that analysts predict will reach $91 billion in annual revenues worldwide by 2015–and one that has become a socially driven mass medium.[3]

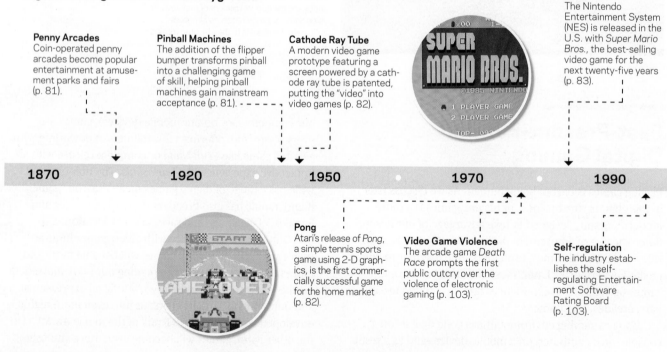

▼ **Digital Gaming and the Media Playground**

Penny Arcades
Coin-operated penny arcades become popular entertainment at amusement parks and fairs (p. 81).

Pinball Machines
The addition of the flipper bumper transforms pinball into a challenging game of skill, helping pinball machines gain mainstream acceptance (p. 81).

Cathode Ray Tube
A modern video game prototype featuring a screen powered by a cathode ray tube is patented, putting the "video" into video games (p. 82).

NES
The Nintendo Entertainment System (NES) is released in the U.S. with *Super Mario Bros.*, the best-selling video game for the next twenty-five years (p. 83).

1870　　1920　　1950　　1970　　1990

Pong
Atari's release of *Pong*, a simple tennis sports game using 2-D graphics, is the first commercially successful game for the home market (p. 82).

Video Game Violence
The arcade game *Death Race* prompts the first public outcry over the violence of electronic gaming (p. 103).

Self-regulation
The industry establishes the self-regulating Entertainment Software Rating Board (p. 103).

Mechanical Gaming

In the 1880s, the seeds of the modern entertainment industry were planted by a series of coin-operated contraptions devoted to cashing in on idleness. First appearing in train depots, hotel lobbies, bars, and restaurants, these leisure machines (also called "counter machines") would find a permanent home in the first thoroughly modern indoor playground: the **penny arcade**.[4]

Arcades were like nurseries for fledgling forms of amusement that would mature into mass entertainment industries during the twentieth century. They offered fun even as they began shaping future media technology. For example, automated phonographs used in arcade machines evolved into the jukebox, while the kinetoscope (see Chapter 7) set the stage for the coming wonders of the movies. But the machines most relevant to today's electronic gaming were more interactive and primitive than the phonograph and kinetoscope. Some were strength testers that dared young men to show off their muscles by punching a boxing bag or arm wrestling a robotlike Uncle Sam. Others required more refined skills and sustained play, such as those that simulated bowling, horse racing, and football.[5]

Another arcade game, the bagatelle, spawned the **pinball machine**, the most prominent of the mechanical games. In pinball, players score points by manipulating the path of a metal ball on a playfield in a glass-covered case. In the 1930s and 1940s, players could control only the launch of the ball. For this reason, pinball was considered a sinister game of chance that, like

MODERN, BIG-BUDGET GAMING EVENTS like the launch of *Mass Effects 3* can be traced back to the emergence of penny arcades in the late nineteenth century.

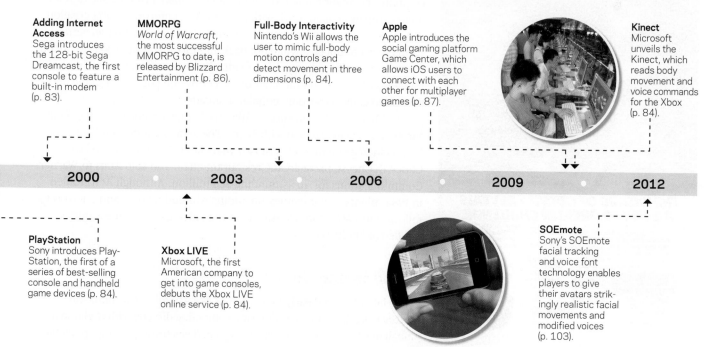

Adding Internet Access
Sega introduces the 128-bit Sega Dreamcast, the first console to feature a built-in modem (p. 83).

MMORPG
World of Warcraft, the most successful MMORPG to date, is released by Blizzard Entertainment (p. 86).

Full-Body Interactivity
Nintendo's Wii allows the user to mimic full-body motion controls and detect movement in three dimensions (p. 84).

Apple
Apple introduces the social gaming platform Game Center, which allows iOS users to connect with each other for multiplayer games (p. 87).

Kinect
Microsoft unveils the Kinect, which reads body movement and voice commands for the Xbox (p. 84).

| 2000 | | 2003 | | 2006 | | 2009 | | 2012 |

PlayStation
Sony introduces PlayStation, the first of a series of best-selling console and handheld game devices (p. 84).

Xbox LIVE
Microsoft, the first American company to get into game consoles, debuts the Xbox LIVE online service (p. 84).

SOEmote
Sony's SOEmote facial tracking and voice font technology enables players to give their avatars strikingly realistic facial movements and modified voices (p. 103).

THE ODYSSEY², a later model of the Odyssey console, was released in 1978 and featured a full keyboard that could be used for educational games.

the slot machine, fed the coffers of the gambling underworld. As a result, pinball was banned in most American cities, including New York, Chicago, and Los Angeles.[6] However, pinball gained mainstream acceptance and popularity after World War II with the addition of the flipper bumper, which enables players to careen the ball back up the play table. This innovation transformed pinball into a challenging game of skill, touch, and timing—all of which would become vital abilities for video game players years later.

The First Video Games

Not long after the growth of pinball, the first video game patent was issued on December 14, 1948, to Thomas T. Goldsmith and Estle Ray Mann for what they described as a "Cathode Ray Tube Amusement Device." The invention would not make much of a splash in the history of digital gaming, but it did feature the key component of the first video games: the cathode ray tube (CRT).

CRT-powered screens provided the images for analog television and for early computers' displays, where the first video games appeared a few years later. Computer science students developed these games as novelties in the 1950s and 1960s. But because computers consisted of massive mainframes at the time, the games couldn't be easily distributed.

However, more and more people owned televisions, and this development provided a platform for video games. The first home television game, called *Odyssey*, was developed by German immigrant and television engineer Ralph Baer. Released by Magnavox in 1972 and sold for a whopping $100, *Odyssey* used player controllers that moved dots of light around the screen in a twelve-game inventory of simple aiming and sports games. From 1972 until *Odyssey*'s replacement by a simpler model (the *Odyssey 100*) in 1975, Magnavox sold roughly 330,000 consoles.[7]

In the next decade, a ripped-off version of one of the *Odyssey* games brought the delights of video gaming into modern **arcades**. These establishments gather multiple coin-operated games together and can be thought of as a later version of the penny arcade. The same year that Magnavox released *Odyssey*, a young American computer engineer named Nolan Bushnell formed a video game development company, called Atari, with a friend. The enterprise's first creation was *Pong*, a simple two-dimensional tennis-style game with two vertical paddles that bounced a white dot back and forth. The game kept score on the screen. Unlike *Odyssey*, *Pong* made blip noises when the ball hit the paddles or bounced off the sides of the court. Pong quickly became the first video game to become popular in arcades.

In 1975, Atari began successfully marketing a home version of *Pong* through an exclusive deal with Sears. The arrangement established the home video game market. Just two years later, Bushnell started the Chuck E. Cheese pizza-arcade restaurant chain and sold Atari to Warner Communications for an astounding $28 million. Although Atari folded in 1984, plenty of companies—including Nintendo, Sony, and Microsoft—followed its early lead, transforming the video game business into a full-fledged industry.

Arcades and Classic Games

By the late 1970s and early 1980s, games like *Asteroids*, *Pac-Man*, and *Donkey Kong* filled arcades and bars, competing directly with traditional pinball machines. In a way, arcades signaled electronic gaming's potential as a social medium, because many games allowed players to compete with or against each other, standing side by side. To be sure, arcade gaming has been superseded by the console and computer. But the industry still attracts fun-seekers to businesses like Dave and Buster's, a gaming/restaurant chain operating in more than fifty locations, as well as to amusement parks, malls, and casinos.

To play the classic arcade games, and many of today's popular console games, players use controllers like joysticks and buttons to interact with graphical elements on a video screen. With a few notable exceptions (puzzle games like *Tetris*, for instance), these types of video games require players to identify with a position on the screen. In *Pong*, this position is represented by an electronic paddle; in *Space Invaders*, it's an earthbound shooting position. After *Pac-Man*, the **avatar** (a graphic interactive "character" situated within the world of the game) became the most common figure of player control and position identification. In the United States, the most popular video games today assume a "first-person" perspective in which the player "sees" the virtual environment through the eyes of an avatar. In South Korea and other Asian countries, many real-time strategy games take an elevated "three-quarters" perspective, which affords a grander and more strategic vantage point on the field of play.

POPULAR ARCADE GAMES in the 1970s and 1980s were simple two-dimensional games with straightforward goals like driving a racecar, destroying asteroids, or gobbling up little dots. Today, most video games have more complex storylines based in fully fleshed-out worlds.

Consoles and Advancing Graphics

Today, many electronic games are played on home **consoles**, devices specifically used to play video games. These systems have become increasingly more powerful since the appearance of the early Atari consoles in the 1970s. One way of charting the evolution of consoles is to track the number of bits (binary digits) that they can process at one time. The bit rating of a console is a measure of its power at rendering computer graphics. The higher the bit rating, the more detailed and sophisticated the graphics. The Atari 2600, released in 1977, used an 8-bit processor, as did the wildly popular Nintendo Entertainment System, first released in Japan in 1983. Sega Genesis, the first 16-bit console, appeared in 1989. In 1992, 32-bit computers appeared on the market; the following year, 64 bits became the new standard. The 128-bit era dawned with the marketing of Sega Dreamcast in 1999. With the current generation of consoles, 256-bit processors are the standard.

THE ATARI 2600 was followed by the Atari 400, Atari 800, and Atari 5200, but none matched the earlier success of the 2600 model.

But more detailed graphics have not always replaced simpler games. Nintendo, for example, offers many of its older, classic games for download onto its newest consoles even as updated versions are released, for the nostalgic gamers as well as new fans. Perhaps the best example of enduring games is the *Super Mario Bros.* series. Created by Nintendo mainstay Shigeru Miyamoto in 1983, the original *Mario Bros.* game began in arcades. The 1985 sequel *Super Mario Bros.*, developed for the 8-bit Nintendo Entertainment System, became the best-selling video game of all time. It held this title until as recently as 2009, when it was unseated by Nintendo's *Wii Sports*. Graphical elements

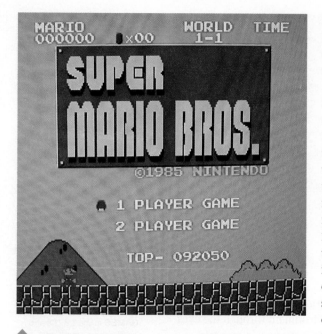

THE ORIGINAL *MARIO BROS.* GAME made its arcade debut in 1983, but it was the 1985 home console sequel *Super Mario Bros.* that made the series a household name. *Super Mario* titles have been developed for the original Nintendo, Super Nintendo, Nintendo 64, Game Cube, Game Boy, Wii, and 3Ds, for which *New Super Mario Bros. 2* was released in 2012.

"In Mario, the squat Italian plumber who bops around the Mushroom Kingdom in a quest to rescue Princess Toadstool, [Shigeru] Miyamoto created a folk hero—gaming's first—with as great a reach as Mickey Mouse's."

NICK PAUMGARTEN, *NEW YORKER*, DECEMBER 2010

from the *Mario Bros.* games, like the "1UP" mushroom that gives players an extra life, remain instantly recognizable to gamers of many ages. Some even appear on nostalgic T-shirts, as toys and cartoons, and in updated versions of newer games.

Through decades of ups and downs in the electronic gaming industry (Atari folded in 1984, and Sega no longer makes video consoles), three major home console makers emerged: Nintendo, Microsoft, and Sony. Nintendo has been making consoles since the 1980s; Microsoft and Sony came later, but both companies were already major media conglomerates and thus well positioned to support and promote their interests in the video game market. Veteran electronics manufacturer Sony has the third most popular console, with its PlayStation series, introduced in 1994. Its current console, the PlayStation 3 (PS3), boasts more than ninety million users on its online PlayStation Network. Sony introduced PlayStation Move, its handheld remote motion sensing controller, in 2010. Microsoft's first foray into video game consoles was the Xbox, released in 2001 and linked to the Xbox LIVE online service in 2002. Xbox LIVE lets its forty million subscribers play online and enables users to download new content directly to the Xbox 360. In 2011, this was the world's second most popular console, and its sales grew faster than any competitor with the introduction of the Kinect motion sensing controller in 2010.[8] The Kinect reads the body motion of users without requiring them to hold a controller, and has voice recognition as well.

Nintendo released its most recent console, the Wii, in 2006. The device supports traditional video games like *New Super Mario Bros.* However, it was the first of the three major consoles to add a wireless motion-sensing controller, which took the often-sedentary nature out of gameplay. Games like Wii Sports require the user to mimic the full-body motion of bowling or playing tennis, while Wii Fit uses a wireless balance board for interactive yoga, strength, aerobic, and balance games. Although the Wii has lagged behind Xbox and PlayStation in establishing an online community, its controller enabled a host of games that appealed to broader audiences, and it became the best-selling of the three major console systems. In 2012, Nintendo introduced the Wii U, which features the GamePad, a controller with an embedded touchscreen, on which games can be played without a television set (making it like a handheld video player).

The three major consoles share some game content, but not every popular game works on all three platforms, a selling point which might cause users to prefer one system over another. For example, *Call of Duty: Black Ops 2* (by Activision Blizzard), *Epic Mickey 2* (by Disney Interactive Studios), and *Just Dance 4* (by Ubisoft) come in versions for all three consoles (and personal computers running Microsoft Windows, too). But the console makers also create games just for their own platform: *Halo 4* for the Xbox 360, *Tokyo Jungle* for the PlayStation 3, and *The Last Story* for the Wii.

Gaming on Home Computers

Very early home computer games, like the early console games, often mimicked (and sometimes ripped off) popular arcade games like *Frogger, Centipede, Pac-Man*, and *Space Invaders*. Computer-based gaming also featured certain genres not often seen on consoles, like the digitization of card and board games. The early days of the personal computer saw the creation of electronic versions of games like Solitaire, Hearts, Spades, and Chess, all simple games still popular today. But for a time in the late 1980s and much of the 1990s, personal computers held some clear advantages over console gaming. The versatility of keyboards, compared with the relatively simple early console controllers, allowed for ambitious puzzle-solving games like *Myst*. Moreover, faster processing speeds gave some computer games richer, more detailed three-dimensional (3-D) graphics. Many of the most popular early first-person shooter games like *Doom* and *Quake* were developed for home computers rather than consoles.

As consoles caught up with greater processing speeds and disc-based games in the late 1990s, elaborate personal computer games attracted less attention. But more recently, PC gaming has experienced a resurgence, due to the advent of free-to-play games (like *Spelunky* and *Neptune's Pride*), subscription games (such as *World of Warcraft* and *Diablo 3*), and social media games (such as *FarmVille*)—all trends aided by the Internet. With powerful processors for handling rich graphics, and more stable Internet connectivity for downloading games or playing games via social media sites and other gaming sites, personal computers can adeptly handle a wide range of activities.

DOOM, an early first-person shooter that influenced later hits like *Halo*, was first developed for home computers. The first game was released in 1993. It has spawned several sequels and a 2005 feature film.

The Internet Transforms Gaming

With the introduction of the Sega Dreamcast in 1999, the first console to feature a built-in modem, gaming emerged as an online, multiplayer social activity. The Dreamcast didn't last, but online connections are now a normal part of console video games, with Internet-connected players opposing one another in combat, working together against a common enemy, or teaming up to achieve a common goal (like sustain a medieval community). Some of the biggest titles have been first-person shooter games like *Counter-Strike*, an online spin-off of the popular *Half-Life* console game. Each player views the game from the first-person perspective but also plays in a team as terrorists or counterterrorists.

The ability to play online has added a new dimension to other, less combat-oriented games, too. For example, football and music enthusiasts playing already-popular console games like *Madden NFL* and *Rock Band* can now engage with others in live online multiplayer play. And young and old alike can compete against teams in other locations in Internet-based bowling tournaments using the Wii.

The Internet enabled the spread of video games to converged devices, like tablets and mobile phones, making games more portable, and creating whole new segments in the gaming industry. The connectivity of the Internet also opened the door to social gaming, virtual worlds, and massively multiplayer online games.

"Wii sounds like 'we,' which emphasizes that the console is for everyone. Wii can easily be remembered by people around the world, no matter what language they speak. No confusion."

NINTENDO WII WEB SITE, 2006

MMORPGs, Virtual Worlds, and Social Gaming

It is one of the longest acronyms in the world of gaming: **massively multiplayer online role-playing games (MMORPGs)**. These games are set in virtual worlds that require users to play through an avatar of their own design. The "massively multiplayer" aspect of MMORPGs indicates that electronic games—once designed for solo or small-group play—have expanded to reach large groups, similar to traditional mass media.

The fantasy adventure game *World of Warcraft* is the most popular MMORPG, boasting more than ten million players around the globe. Users can select from twelve different "races" of avatars, including dwarves, gnomes, night elves, orcs, trolls, goblins, and humans. To succeed in the game, many players join with other players to form guilds or tribes, working together toward in-game goals that can be achieved only by teams. *Second Life*, a 3-D social simulation set in real time, also features social interaction. Players build human avatars, selecting from an array of physical characteristics and clothing. Then they use real money to buy virtual land and to trade in virtual goods and services.

Simulations like *Second Life* and MMORPGs like *World of Warcraft* are aimed at teenagers and adults. One of the most overlooked areas (at least by adults) in online gaming is the children's market. *Club Penguin*, a moderated virtual world purchased by Disney, enables kids to play games and chat as colorful penguins. Disney later developed additional *Club Penguin* games for handheld players. Toy maker Ganz developed the online *Webkinz* game to revive its stuffed animal sales. Each Webkinz stuffed animal comes with a code that lets players access the online game and care for the virtual version of their plush pets. In 2009, as Webkinz sales declined, Ganz started *Webkinz Jr.* to market bigger, more expensive plush animals to preschoolers. *Woozworld* offers a virtual shopping world and chat for the tween market, ages nine to fourteen. All of these virtual worlds offer younger players their own age-appropriate environment to experiment with virtual socializing, but they have also attracted criticism for their messages of consumerism. In many of these games, children can buy items with virtual currency, or acquire "bling" more quickly through a premium membership. The games also market merchandise to their young players, such as stuffed animals, movies, and clothing.

Online fantasy sports games also reach a mass audience with a major social component. Players—real-life friends, virtual acquaintances, or a mix of both—assemble teams and use actual sports results to determine scores in their online games. But rather than experiencing the visceral thrills of, say, *Madden NFL 13*, fantasy football participants take a more detached, managerial perspective on the game—a departure from the classic video game experience. Fantasy sports' managerial angle makes it even more fun to watch almost any televised game because players focus more on making strategic investments in individual performances scattered across the various professional teams than they do in rooting for local teams. In the process, players become statistically savvy aficionados of the game overall, rather than rabid fans of a particular team. In 2012, about thirty-four million people played fantasy sports in the United States and Canada; the Fantasy Sports Trade Association currently estimates a market size in the neighborhood of $2 billion.[9]

The increasingly social nature of video games has made them a natural fit for social networking sites. Game apps for Facebook have drawn millions of fans. Zynga is the maker of several of the

THE COMPANY ZYNGA has made massive social gaming hits out of *CityVille*, *FarmVille*, and *Words with Friends*, but has still struggled with how to increase profits from its popular lineup. The company may expand its casino-style games if real-money online betting is legalized in the United States.

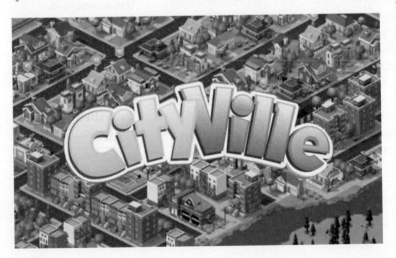

most popular games on Facebook, including *CityVille, FarmVille,* and *Words with Friends. Zynga Poker,* a top social media game in 2012, has more than thirty-four million monthly users, making it what Zynga claims is the world's largest poker game.

Convergence: From Consoles to Mobile Gaming

Digital games made their initial appearances on computers and consoles, and were very much wedded to those platforms. Today, though, games can be consumed the same way so much music, books, television shows, and films are consumed: just about anywhere, and in a number of different ways. And video game consoles are increasingly part of the same technological convergence that gives devices like smartphones and tablets multiple functions.

Consoles Become Entertainment Centers

Video game consoles, once used exclusively for games, now work as part computer, part cable box. They've become powerful entertainment centers, with multiple forms of media converging in a single device. For example, the Xbox 360 and PS3 can function as DVD players and digital video recorders (with hard drives of up to 250 gigabytes) and offer access to Twitter, Facebook, blogs, and video chat. The PS3 can also play Blu-ray discs, and all three console systems offer connections to stream programming from sources like Netflix and Hulu Plus. Microsoft's Xbox, which offers the greatest selection of video channels (including ESPN, HBO Go, YouTube, SyFy, and Amazon Instant Video) and has Kinect's voice recognition system for viewers to communicate with the box, has been the most successful in becoming a converged device for home entertainment. In 2012, for the first time, "subscribers to Xbox's LIVE online service in the U.S. spent more time consuming video and music than multiplayer games," *Forbes* magazine reported, declaring that "Microsoft Xbox is winning the living room war."[10]

Portable Players and Mobile Gaming

Simple handheld players made games portable long before the advent of Internet-connected touchscreen mobile devices. Nintendo's Game Boy, a two-color handheld console introduced in 1989, was one early success and popularized the game *Tetris,* which came preloaded on it. The early handhelds gave way to later generations of devices offering more advanced graphics and wireless capabilities. These include the top-selling Nintendo DS, released in 2004, and PlayStation Portable (PSP), released in 2005 and succeeded by the PlayStation Vita in 2012. Both brands are Wi-Fi capable, so players can interface with other users to play games or browse the Internet.

While portable players remain immensely popular (the Nintendo DS sold more than 151 million units through 2012), they face competition from the widespread use of smartphones and touchscreen tablets like iPads. These devices are not designed principally for gaming, but their capabilities have given casual gamers who may not have been interested in owning a handheld console another option. Manufacturers of these converged devices are catching on to their gaming potential: After years of relatively little interest in video games, Apple introduced Game Center in 2010. This social gaming network enabled users to invite friends or find others for multiplayer gaming, track their scores, and view high scores on a leader board–which the DS and PSP do as well. With more than 108 million iPhones and 67 million iPads sold worldwide by 2012 (and millions more iPod Touch devices in circulation), plus more than 103,000 games (like *Cut the Rope* and *Asphalt 7: Heat*) available in its App Store, Apple's devices, games, and distribution system are transforming the portable video game business.[11] Handheld video games have made the medium more accessible and widespread. Even people who wouldn't identify themselves

"The Xbox has never been a game system. The Xbox is Microsoft's idea lab. It's the one market where Microsoft is indisputably considered both serious and cool."

TIM CARMODY, *WIRED,* MARCH 2012

HANDHELD GAMING
used to require a specific piece of hardware, like the classic Game Boy. But as technology has grown more sophisticated, handheld games can be played on smaller, more versatile devices like smartphones and PDAs, and some handheld gaming systems can do more than just games.

"Now, smartphones and tablets are quickly approaching the resolution and computing power of today's consoles, and that's opened up a whole new market for games. There are about 223 million game-console owners in the world right now—but there are 500 million smartphone owners walking around, and that's expected to reach 1.5 billion by 2015."

JEFF BEER, *CANADIAN BUSINESS*, APRIL 2012

as gamers may kill time between classes or waiting in line by playing *Angry Birds* on their phones.

Google Play (formerly the Android Market) rivals Apple's App Store in its number of apps and provides a substantial platform for gaming on Android mobile phones and tablet devices like the Kindle, Nook, and Galaxy. Microsoft is also looking to improve its new generations of Windows Phones to better interface with its Xbox 360 entertainment system.

This convergence is changing the way people look at video games and their systems. The games themselves are no longer confined to arcades or home television sets, while the latter have gained power as entertainment tools, reaching a wider and more diverse audience. Many phones and PDAs operate as de facto handheld consoles, and many home consoles serve as comprehensive entertainment centers. Thus, gaming has become an everyday form of entertainment, rather than the niche pursuit of hard-core enthusiasts.

With its increased profile and flexibility across platforms, the gaming industry has achieved a mass medium status on a par with film or television. This rise in status has come with stiffer and more complex competition, not just within the gaming industry but across media. Rather than Sony competing with Nintendo, or TV networks competing among themselves for viewers, or new movies facing off at the box office, media must now compete against other media for an audience's attention.

The Media Playground

To fully explore the larger media playground, we need to look beyond electronic gaming's technical aspects and consider the human faces of gaming. The attractions of this interactive playground validate electronic gaming's status as one of today's most powerful social media. Electronic games occupy an enormous range of styles, from casual games like *Tetris, Angry Birds, Bejeweled*, and *Fruit Ninja*, etc.–what one writer called "stupid games"–that are typically "a repetitive, storyless puzzle that could be picked up, with no loss of potency, at any moment, in any situation," to the full-blown, Hollywood-like immersive adventures and stories of games like *The Elder Scrolls V: Skyrim*.[12] No matter what the style, digital games are compelling entertainment and mass media because they pose challenges (mental and physical), allow us to engage in situations both realistic and fantastical, and allow us to socialize with others as we play with friends and form communities inside and outside of games. (See "Case Study: Thoughts on Video Game Narrative" on page 89 for more on the narrative power of video games.)

Video Game Genres

Electronic games inhabit so many playing platforms and devices, and cover so many genres, it is not easy to categorize them. The game industry, as represented by the Electronic Software Association, organizes games by **gameplay**–the way in which the rules structure how players

CASE STUDY

Thoughts on Video Game Narrative

by Isaac Butler

In the beginning, things were simple. Bowser has kidnapped the Princess. You go to a variety of castles until you find the one she's in, jumping on, over or under things all the way. In the beginning, narrative existed to justify the mashing of B and A, the cursing and gnashing of teeth, the subscribing to magazines filled with tricks and tips.

Googling around one day, I found a web site dedicated to writing a novelization of the video game *Heavy Rain*. It's a crowdsourced project in which various denizens of the website try to write the prose narrative equivalent of what happens as you play through Quantic Dream's neo-Gothic serial killer thriller.

This novelization quest is loveably quixotic and difficult not to condescend to. *Heavy Rain* is a work of interactive fiction that is unadaptable. It is one of the few video games to fully take advantage of its medium as a vehicle for telling stories. We can see its roots in everything from old Sierra games and *Space Ace* to recent titles like *Bioshock* and *Fallout 3* and (especially) *Uncharted*. But the particular ways that it creates story are worth exploring.

In *Heavy Rain*, you play a chorus of characters all affected by The Origami Killer, a murderer who kidnaps young boys and allows them to drown in rainwater before lovingly burying them. As a PI investigating the crimes, an FBI profiler brought in to solve the latest disappearance, a (sexy female) reporter working on the story and a father trying to save his son, you gradually put the pieces together and use your characters (who are often unaware of each other's existence) to solve the killings.

Or not. Throughout each chapter, the various characters are presented with a number of options for dialogue, interior thoughts and actions and none of them are guaranteed success. I am unsure how many endings *Heavy Rain* has, as all four of your characters can die over the course of the game. You can solve the murders or not. You can rescue your son, or not. You can start a love affair between two of your characters or not. You can turn one of your characters into a drug addict or not. You can even solve the murders and rescue your son and the killer can still get away with it.

Here's the kicker: These are simply endings to the story. They aren't "Game Over," they're just options. You're always free to reboot a chapter and try a different path.

If you read *Heavy Rain* or saw it as a film, you'd probably laugh at it. Yet playing it is a profound emotional experience. You may even find yourself worried about the child you are trying to save, or upset about what happens to the characters. When you are given the choice to kill an innocent man to get a clue to save your son, you may hesitate wondering what it says about you, not the character Ethan Marks but you sitting there in the chair and whether you're okay living as the person who choice [sic] to make one character kill another.

The insertion of choice is the insertion of you the player into the world of the game. That is *Heavy Rain*'s real genius. *Heavy Rain* is not the only game to do this. The games from Bethesda Softworks (*Fallout 3, Fallout: New Vegas, Elder Scrolls*, etc.) and BioWare (*Mass Effect, Dragon Age*, etc.) create games based on choice as well. But in those games, choice and narrative are serving the game. This is why the choices are frequently binary. Paragon or Renegade. Blow up Megaton or don't. In *Heavy Rain*, the choices serve a narrative experience. ◢

Source: Excerpted from Isaac Butler, "Thoughts on Narrative II: Video Games in the Sweet Spot," Parabasis, March 30, 2011, http://parabasis .typepad.com/blog/2011/03/thoughts-on-narrative-ii-video-games-in-the-sweet-spot.html.

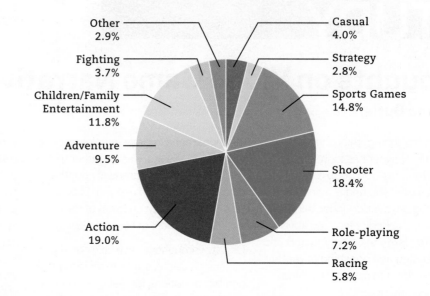

FIGURE 3.1

TOP VIDEO GAME GENRES BY UNITS SOLD, 2011

Source: Entertainment Software Association, "Essential Facts about the Computer and Video Game Industry," 2012

Note: Percentages were rounded up to the next decimal point.

Other 2.9%
Casual 4.0%
Fighting 3.7%
Strategy 2.8%
Children/Family Entertainment 11.8%
Sports Games 14.8%
Adventure 9.5%
Shooter 18.4%
Action 19.0%
Role-playing 7.2%
Racing 5.8%

interact with the game, rather than by any sort of visual or narrative style. There are many hybrid forms, but the major gameplay genres are discussed in the following sections. (See Figure 3.1 for a breakdown of top video game genres.)

Action and Shooter Games

Usually emphasizing combat-type situations, **action games** ask players to test their reflexes, and to punch, slash, shoot, or throw as strategically and accurately as possible so as to strategically make their way through a series of levels. Some action games feature hand-to-hand combat (e.g., *Street Fighter, Marvel vs. Capcom*); others feature more sophisticated weaponry and obstacles, such as bladed spears against groups of enemy combatants (e.g., *Hidden Blade; Bushido Blade*). Shooter games offer a selection of guns and missiles for obliterating opponents.

Most *shooter games* have a **first-person shooter (FPS)** perspective, which allows players to feel like they are actually holding the weapon and to feel physically immersed in the drama. (See Table 3.1 for more on major video game conventions.) *Doom*, for example, released in 1993, was one of the first major FPS breakthroughs, requiring players to shoot their way through a military base on Mars' moon, killing the demons from Hell using a pistol, and moving up to a chainsaw, shotgun, chaingun, rocket launcher, plasma rifle, and finally the coveted "BFG 9000," all the while negotiating pits of toxic slime and locating the "exit door" that leads to the next level. *Halo*, Microsoft's impressive launch title for the Xbox 360 in 2001, has become the top FSP game of all time. In the *Halo* series (the fourth sequel was released in 2012), players assume the identity of "Master Chief," a super soldier living in the twenty-sixth century and fighting aliens, with the ultimate goal of uncovering secrets about the secret ring-shaped world, Halo. The weapons allotted to "Master Chief" all require the player to think strategically about how and when to launch them. Plasma weapons need time to cool if fired too quickly; guns need both ammunition and time to reload; fragmentation grenades bounce and detonate immediately; plasma grenades attach to the target before exploding. Players have to negotiate all of these (and many more) variables as they move through various futuristic landscapes in order to unlock the secrets of *Halo*.

Maze games like *Pac-Man* also fit into the "action" genre, involving maze navigation to avoid or chase adversaries. Finally, *platform games* gained notoriety through the very successful *Super Mario Bros.* series. Using quick reflexes and strategic time management, players move Mario and

Convention	Description	Examples	Visual Representation
Avatars	Onscreen figures of player identification	Pac-Man, Mario from the *Mario Bros.* series, *Sonic the Hedgehog*, Link from *Legend of Zelda*	
Bosses	Powerful enemy characters that represent the final challenge in a stage or the entire game	Ganon from the *Zelda* series, Hitler in *Castle Wolfenstein*, Dr. Eggman from *Sonic the Hedgehog*, Mother Brain from *Metroid*	
Vertical and Side Scrolling	As opposed to a fixed screen, scrolling that follows the action as it moves up, down, or sideways in what is called a "tracking shot" in the cinema	Platform games like *Jump Bug*, *Donkey Kong*, and *Super Mario Bros.*; also integrated into the design of *Angry Birds*	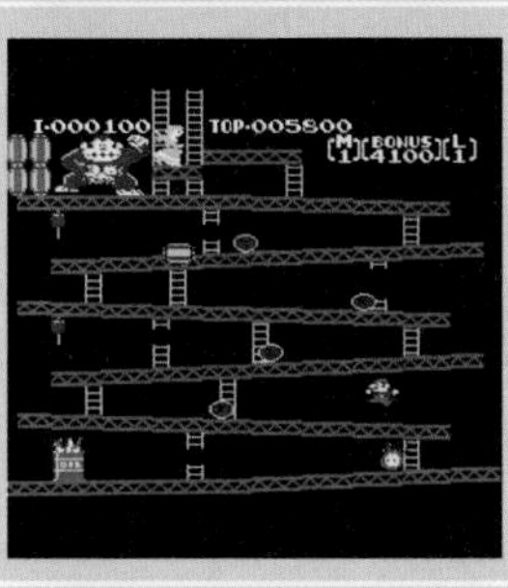
Isometric Perspective (also called *Three-Quarters Perspective*)	An elevated and angled perspective that enhances the sense of three-dimensionality by allowing players to see the tops and sides of objects	*Zaxxon*, *StarCraft*, *Civilization*, and *Populous*	
First-Person Perspective	Presents the gameplay through the eyes of your avatar	First-person shooter (FPS) games like *Quake*, *Doom*, *Halo*, and *Call of Duty*	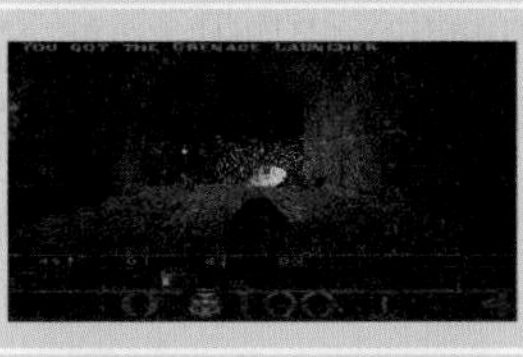
Third-Person Perspective (or *Over-the-Shoulders Perspective*)	Enables you to view your heroic avatar in action from an external viewpoint	*Tomb Raider*, *Assassin's Creed*, and the default viewpoint in *World of Warcraft*	

TABLE 3.1

MAJOR VIDEO GAME CONVENTIONS

This table breaks down six common elements of video game layout. Many of these elements have been in place since the earliest games and continue to be used today.

◀

Luigi between various platform levels of the Mushroom Kingdom in order to rescue Princess Toadstool (later called Princess Peach) from Bowser.

Adventure Games

"Any game that does move at your own pace, like adventure games do, you don't have to worry about dying or dealing with enemies and bosses and monsters; you have a more ponderous, thoughtful experience."

TIM SCHAFER, FOUNDER OF DOUBLE FINE PRODUCTIONS, APRIL 2012

Developed in the 1970s, **adventure games** involve a type of gameplay that is in many ways the opposite of action games. Typically nonconfrontational in nature, adventure games such as *Myst* require players to interact with individual characters and the sometimes hostile environment in order to solve puzzles. In the case of *Myst* (released in 1991), the player is "the Stranger" who travels to different worlds and finds clues to solve various puzzles, that, if solved correctly, lead to the "deserted" island of Myst. The genre peaked in popularity in 1993 and has spawned derivative genres such as *action-adventure* (e.g., *Zelda*, *Metroid*) and *survival horror* games (e.g., *Resident Evil*), which are inspired by horror fiction.

Role-playing Games

Role-playing games (RPGs) are typically set in a fantasy or sci-fi world in which each player (there can be multiple players in a game) chooses to play as a character that specializes in a particular skill set (such as magic spells or "finesse"). Players embark on a predetermined adventure and interact with the game's other inhabitants and each other, making choices throughout the game that bring about various diverse outcomes. *Neverwinter Nights* (2002), for example, challenges its players to collaboratively collect four "Waterdhavian creatures" needed to stop the "Wailing Death plague," defeat the cult that is spreading the plague, and finally thwart an attack on the city of Neverwinter. The game is derived from *Dungeons & Dragons*, one of the most popular face-to-face, paper-and-pencil role-playing games. More complex role-playing games, like the *Final Fantasy* series, involve branching plots and changing character destinies. MMORPGs are obviously a subgenre of this game category. Other subgenres, such as the action-role player games, are some of the most successful video games on the market. A good example is the *Diablo* series, which combines combat and role-playing in a horror and dark fantasy setting. When Blizzard released the third installment, *Diablo III*, in May 2012, it sold 3.5 million copies in twenty-four hours, becoming the fastest-selling PC game of all time.[13]

Strategy and Simulation Games

Strategy video games often involve military battles (real or imaginary), and focus on gameplay that requires careful thinking and skillful planning in order to achieve victory. Unlike FPS games, the perspective in **strategy games** is omniscient, with the player surveying the entire "world" or playing field and making strategic decisions–such as building bases, researching technologies, managing resources, and waging battles–that will make or break this world. No doubt the most popular *real-time strategy game* (*RTS*) is Blizzard's *StarCraft*, which is played competitively throughout South Korea and televised to large audiences. Taking place during the twenty-sixth century in a distant part of the Milky Way galaxy, *StarCraft* involves three races (one human) that are at war with each other. To develop better strategic advantages, players download and memorize maps, study up on minute game details (such as race characteristics), and participate in *StarCraft*-centered advice boards.

Like strategy games, **simulation games** involve managing resources and planning worlds, but these worlds are typically based in reality. A good example is *Sim City*, which asks players to build a city given real-world constraints, such as land-use zoning (commercial, industrial, residential); tax rates (to tax or not to tax); and transportation (buses, cars, trams). A player may also face unanticipated natural disasters such as floods or tornadoes. Another example is *The Oregon Trail*, an educational simulation game that aims at reproducing the circumstances and drastic choices faced by white settlers traveling the 2,000-mile journey from Independence,

Kansas, to the Willamette Valley in Oregon. Throughout the game, players make choices to help their ox-driven wagon parties survive numerous potential horrors, including measles, dysentery, typhoid, cholera, snake bites, drowning, physical injuries, floods, mountains, heat, and cold, all the while maintaining provisions and predicting weather conditions. First developed by educators in 1971, *The Oregon Trail* has been played by millions of students.

Casual Games

This category of gaming, which encompasses everything from *Minesweeper* to *Angry Birds* to *Words with Friends*, includes games that have very simple rules and are usually quick to play. **Casual games** have a historical starting point–1989–when the game *Tetris* came bundled with every new Game Boy (Nintendo). *Tetris* requires players to continuously (frantically, for some) rotate colored blocks and fit them into snug spaces before the screen fills up with badly stacked blocks. There is no story to *Tetris*, and no real challenge other than mastering the rather numbing pattern of rotating and stacking, a process that keeps getting faster the higher the level achieved. For many people, the ceaseless puzzle became like a drug: millions of people have purchased and played *Tetris* since its release. Today, *Tetris* has given way to *Angry Birds* and other such games that have exploded in popularity due in large part to the rise in mobile devices.

Sports, Music, and Dance Games

"There is apparently a video game for every sport except for competitive mushroom picking," commented a *Milwaukee Journal* editorial in 1981.[14] Today, there really does seem to be a 3-D game for every sport. Gaming consoles first featured 3-D graphics in the early to mid-1990s with the arrival of Sega Saturn and Sony's PlayStation in 1994. Today's game technology, with infrared motion detectors, accelerometers (a device that measures proper acceleration), and tuning fork gyroscopes (a device that determines rotational motion), allows players to control their avatar through physical movements, making the 3-D sports games experience even more realistic. Players in a soccer game, for example, might feel as though they are in the thick of things, kicking, dribbling, shooting, and even getting away with a foul if referees aren't watching. In sports games, players either engage in competitive gameplay (player vs. player) or cooperative gameplay (two or more teammates work together against the artificial intelligence, or A.I., opponents within the game).

One of the most consistently best-selling sports games is *Madden NFL*, which is based on famed NFL football player and then coach John Madden. Among the game's realistic features are character collisions with varying speeds and trajectories that differ based on player control, sophisticated playbooks and player statistics, and voice commentary that allows players to hear the game as if it were a real TV broadcast. With XBox Kinect functionality, players can even select and alter screen actions with the power of their own voice (*they* are Madden, screaming from the sidelines).

Other experiential games tie into music and dance categories. *Rock Band*, developed by Harmonix Systems and published by MTV Games and Electronic Arts, allows up to four players to simulate the popular rock band performances of fifty-eight songs–from the Pixies and OK Go to Black Sabbath and the Rolling Stones–as well as more than fourteen hundred additional downloadable songs for $1.99 apiece. Each instrument part (lead guitar, bass, drums, and vocal) can be played at one of four difficulty levels (Easy, Medium, Hard, and Expert), and if a player doesn't keep up, they "fail" out of the song and their instrument is muted. The gameplay is derivative of *Guitar Hero* (vertical scrolling, colored music notes, and karaoke-like vocals), but the experience of *Rock Band*–with four players, a variety of venues from clubs to concert halls, and screaming fans (who are also prone to boo)–is far

"I remember carefully managing my bank roll, stocking up with supplies, spare wagon parts, clothes, victuals. I charted my course, past Fort Kearney, on towards Laramie, then making the choice at South Pass: the long route to Fort Bridger, or brave the ford and head right to Soda Springs? I recall well the warning the game gave as winter approached; I felt myself shivering in my chair, checking my stock of food and ammunition nervously."

PHILIP A. LOBO, *OPEN LETTERS MONTHLY*, FEBRUARY 2010

"These games are not for everyone, it's true, but it's for more of everyone than anything else I know."

JOHN DOERR, ON CASUAL GAMES, 2011

ROCKBAND became a popular experiential game; it has also provided a new revenue stream for the music industry, which can offer licensed downloads of current and classic songs for use with the game.

"The real world just doesn't offer up as easily the carefully designed pleasures, the thrilling challenges, and the powerful social bonding afforded by virtual environments."

JANE MCGONIGAL,
REALITY IS BROKEN,
2011

more "real." Dance-oriented video games such as *Dance Dance Revolution* and *Just Dance* use motion-detecting technology and challenge players to match their rhythm and dance moves to figures on the screen.

Communities of Play: Inside the Game

Virtual communities often crop up around online video games and fantasy sports leagues. Indeed, players may get to know each other through games without ever meeting in person. They can interact in two basic types of groups. **PUGs** (short for "Pick-Up Groups") are temporary teams usually assembled by match-making programs integrated into the game. The members of a PUG may range from elite players to **noobs** (clueless beginners) and may be geographically and generationally diverse. PUGs are notorious for harboring ninjas and trolls–two universally despised player types (not to be confused with ninja or troll avatars). **Ninjas** are players who snatch loot out of turn and then leave the group; **trolls** are players who delight in intentionally spoiling the gaming experience for others.

Because of the frustration of dealing with noobs, ninjas, and trolls, most experienced players join organized groups called **guilds** or **clans**. These groups can be small and easy-going or large and demanding. Guild members can usually avoid PUGs and team up with guildmates to complete difficult challenges requiring coordinated group activity. As the terms *ninja, troll,* and *noob* suggest, online communication is often encoded in gamespeak, a language filled with jargon, abbreviations, and acronyms relevant to gameplay. The typical codes of text messaging (OMG, LOL, ROFL, and so forth) form the bedrock of this language system.

Players communicate in two forms of in-game chat–voice and text. Xbox LIVE, for example, uses three types of voice chat that allow players to socialize and strategize, in groups or one-on-one, even as they are playing the game. Other in-game chat systems are text-based, with chat channels for trading in-game goods or coordinating missions within a guild. These methods of communicating with fellow players who may or may not know each other outside the game create a sense of community around gameplay. Some players have formed lasting friendships or romantic relationships through their video game habit. Avid gamers have even held in-game ceremonies, like weddings or funerals–sometimes for game-only characters, sometimes for real-life events.

Communities of Play: Outside the Game

Communities also form outside games, through Web sites and even face-to-face gatherings dedicated to electronic gaming in its many forms. This is similar to when online and in-person groups form to discuss other mass media like movies, TV shows, and books. These communities extend beyond gameplay, enhancing the social experience gained through the games.

Collective Intelligence

Mass media productions are almost always collaborative efforts, as is evident in the credits for movies, television shows, and music recordings. The same goes for digital games. But what is unusual about game developers and the game industry is their interest in listening to gamers and their communities to gather new ideas and constructive criticism, and to gauge popularity. Gamers, too, collaborate with each other to share shortcuts and "cheats" to solving tasks and quests, and to create their own modifications to games. This sharing of knowledge and ideas is an excellent example of **collective intelligence**. French professor Pierre Lévy coined the term *collective intelligence* in 1997 to describe the Internet, "this new dimension of communication," and its ability to "enable us to share our knowledge and acknowledge it to others."[15] In the world of gaming, where users are active participants (more than in any other medium), the collective intelligence of players informs the entire game environment.

For example, collective intelligence (and action) is necessary to work through levels of many games. In *World of Warcraft*, collective intelligence is highly recommended. According to the beginner's guide, "if you want to take on the greatest challenges *World of Warcraft* has to offer, you will need allies to fight by your side against the tides of darkness."[16] Players form guilds and use their play experience and characters' skills to complete quests and move to higher levels. Gamers also share ideas through chats and wikis, and those looking for tips and cheats provided by fellow players need only Google what they want. The largest of the sites devoted to sharing collective intelligence is the *World of Warcraft* wiki (http://wowwiki .com). Similar user-generated sites are dedicated to a range of digital games including *Age of Conan, Assassin's Creed, Grand Theft Auto, Halo, Mario, Metal Gear, Pokémon, Sonic the Hedgehog,* and *Spore.*

The most advanced form of collective intelligence in gaming is **modding**, slang for "modifying game software or hardware." In many mass communication industries, modifying hardware or content would land someone in a copyright lawsuit. In gaming, modding is often encouraged, as it is yet another way players become more deeply invested in a game, and can improve the game for others. For example, *Counter-Strike*, a popular first-person shooter game, is a mod of the game *Half-Life. Half-Life* is a critically acclaimed science-fiction first-person shooter game (a physicist fighting aliens) released by Valve Corporation in 1998 for PCs, and later PlayStation. The developers of *Half-Life* encouraged mods by including software development tools with it. By 1999, *Counter-Strike*, in which counterterrorists fight terrorists, emerged as the most popular of many mods, and Valve formed a partnership with the game's developers. *Counter-Strike* was released to retailers as a PC game in 2000 and an Xbox game in 2004, eventually selling more copies than *Half-Life.* Today, many other games, such as *The Elder Scrolls*, have active modding communities.

Game Sites

Game sites and blogs are among the most popular external communities for gamers. IGN.com (owned by News Corp.), GameSpot.com (owned by CBS), GameTrailers.com (MTV Networks/Viacom), and Kotaku (Gawker Media) are four of the leading Web sites for gaming. Gamespot.com and IGN.com are apt examples of giant industry sites, each with sixteen to nineteen million unique visitors per month. The ownership of these sites is a sign of the desirability of this audience—mostly male, ages eighteen to thirty-four—to major media corporations. IGN.com covers all the major gaming platforms and provides reviews, news, videos, cheats, and forums, as well as the regular Webcast of a news show about games called *The Daily Fix.* GameSpot has similar elements, and a culture section that features interviews with game designers and other creative artists. In 2011, GameSpot launched Fuse, a social networking service for gamers that is designed to be "your personal gaming dashboard."[17]

Penny-arcade.com is perhaps the best-known of the independent community-building sites. Founded by Jerry Holkins and Mike Krahulik, the site started out as a Webcomic focused on video game culture. It has since expanded to include forums and a Webcast called PATV that documents behind-the-scenes work at Penny Arcade. Penny Arcade organizes a live festival for gamers called the Penny Arcade Expo (PAX), a celebration of gamer culture, and a children's charity called Child's Play.

USHER performs at the Electronic Entertainment Expo in 2012. Other musicians who have played E3 in recent years include David Guetta, deadmau5, and Eminem, showing increased convergence of the video game and music industries.

Conventions

In addition to online gaming communities, there are conventions and expos where video game enthusiasts can come together in person to test out new games and other new products, play old games in competition, and meet video game developers. One of the most significant is the Electronic Entertainment Expo (E3), which draws more than 45,000 industry professionals, investors, developers, and retailers to its annual meeting. E3 is the place where the biggest new game titles and products are unveiled, and is covered by hundreds of journalists, televised on Spike TV, and streamed to mobile devices and Xbox consoles. At the 2012 E3, Nintendo introduced its Wii U controller, Microsoft sponsored a performance by Usher to promote *Dance Central 3* for the Xbox, and game publisher Ubisoft brought Flo Rida to perform at its presentation for *Just Dance 4*.

The Penny Arcade Expo (PAX) convention is a convention created by gamers for gamers, held each year in Seattle. One of its main attractions is the Omegathon, a three-day elimination game tournament, in which twenty randomly selected attendees compete in games across several genres, culminating in the championship match at the convention's closing. In 2010, a PAX East convention debuted in Boston, and the original event in Seattle was renamed PAX Prime. Both events draw in excess of 70,000 attendees.

Other conventions include Blizzcon (operated by Blizzard Entertainment to feature developments to their games, including their top franchises—*World of Warcraft, Diablo,* and *StarCraft*) and the Tokyo Game Show, the world's largest gaming convention with more than 200,000 attendees annually.

Trends and Issues in Digital Gaming

The ever-growing relationship between video games and other media like books, movies, and television leaves no doubt that digital gaming has a permanent place in our culture. Like other media, games are also a venue for advertising. A virtual billboard in a video game is likely more than just a digital prop; as in television and the movies, it's a paid placement. And like other media, games are a subject of social concern, too. Violent and misogynistic content has from time to time spurred calls for more regulation of electronic games. But, as games permeate more of culture and increasingly come in nonstandard formats and genres, they may also become harder to define, and therefore, regulate.

Electronic Gaming and Media Culture

Beyond the immediate industry, electronic games have had a pronounced effect on media culture. For example, fantasy league sports have spawned a number of draft specials on ESPN as well as a regular podcast, Fantasy Focus, on ESPN Radio. On FX, fantasy football has even inspired an adult comedy called *The League*.

Like television shows, books, and comics before them, electronic games have also inspired movies, such as *Super Mario Bros.* (1993), *Lara Croft: Tomb Raider* (2001), and the *Resident Evil* series (2001–present, including a fifth installment in 2012). A movie inspired by video games, *Tron* (1982), spurred an entire franchise of books, comic books, and arcade and console video games in the 1980s; and it was revived a generation later with an Xbox LIVE game in 2008, a movie sequel (*Tron: Legacy*) in 2010, and a Disney television series. For many Hollywood blockbusters today, a video game spin-off is a must-have item. Box office hits like *Avatar* (2009), *Up* (2009), *Shrek: Forever After* (2010), *Transformers: Dark of the Moon* (2011), and *Brave* (2012) all have companion video games for consoles and portable players.

Books and electronic games have also had a long history of influencing each other. Japanese manga and animé (comic books and animation) have also inspired video games, such as *Akira*, *Astro Boy*, and *Naruto*. *Batman: Arkham Asylum*, a top video game title introduced in 2009, is based closely on the *Batman* comic book stories, while *The Witcher*, an action role-playing game for PCs, is based on Polish fantasy writer Andrzej Sapkowski's *The Witcher* saga. Perhaps the most unusual link between books and electronic games is the *Marvel vs. Capcom* series. In this series, characters from Marvel comic books (e.g., Captain America, Hulk, Spider-Man, Wolverine) battle characters from Capcom games like *Street Fighter* and *Resident Evil* (e.g., Akuma, Chun-Li, Ryu, Albert Wesker).

Electronic Gaming and Advertising

Commercialism is as prevalent in video games as it is in most entertainment media. **Advergames**, like television's infomercials or newspaper and magazines' advertorials, are video games created for purely promotional purposes. The first notable advergame debuted in 1992, when Chester Cheetah, the official mascot for Cheetos snacks, starred in two video games for the Sega Genesis and Super Nintendo systems—*Chester Cheetah: Too Cool to Fool* and *Chester Cheetah: Wild Wild Quest*. In late 2006, Burger King sold three advergame titles for Xbox and Xbox 360 consoles for $3.99 each with value-meal purchases. One title, *Sneak King*, required the player to have the Burger King mascot deliver food to other characters before they faint from hunger. More recent is the innovative interactive Web commercial, "Magnum Pleasure Hunt," for gourmet Magnum chocolate ice cream bars. In this platform game, the user manipulates the constantly jogging, barefoot "Magnum Girl" up and over the game's Internet-based environments (such as Bing travel pages, YouTube videos, and luxury hotel Web sites). A player earns points by strategically timing her jumps so that she connects with—or consumes—the game's many chocolate bon bons, and the Magnum's specialty chocolate bar is the final reward for Magnum Girl's (and the player's) hard work. **In-game advertisements** are more subtle, and integrate advertisements as billboards, logos, or storefronts in the game (e.g., a Farmers Insurance airship floating by in *FarmVille* or Dove soap spas appearing in *The Sims Social*), or making the product a component of the game (e.g., in the game *Splinter Cell: Chaos Theory*, a large glowing billboard for AXE deodorant becomes an obstacle for the player to overcome).[18]

Some in-game advertisements are static, which means the ads are permanently placed in the game. Others in-game ads are dynamic, which means the game ads are digitally networked and can be altered remotely, so agencies can tailor them according to release time,

"Prose is an art form, movies and acting in general are art forms, so is music, painting, graphics, sculpture, and so on. Some might even consider classic games like chess to be an art form. Video games use elements of all of these to create something new. Why wouldn't video games be an art form?"

SAM LAKE, WRITER OF THE *MAX PAYNE* SERIES, 2004

"Video games can never be art."

ROGER EBERT, FILM CRITIC, 2010

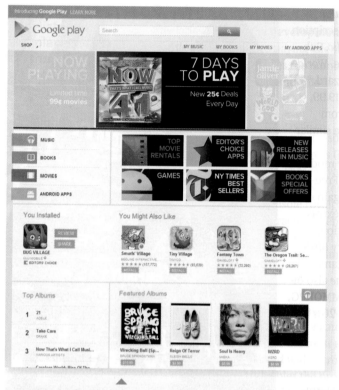

GOOGLE PLAY, formerly known as the Android market, allows Android users to browse and download their favorite video games directly to their mobiles. And while it has been shown that Apple customers are more likely to purchase apps, Google highlighted its digital distribution strategy when it announced that as of October 2012, Google Play had 700,000 apps available for download, the same number of apps found in Apple's App Store.

Wi-Fi capable and each has its own digital store–Xbox LIVE Marketplace, Wii Shop Channel, and PlayStation Store. Customers can purchase and download games, get extra downloadable content, and buy other media like television shows and movies as the consoles compete to be the sole entertainment center of people's living rooms. These console-connected digital stores present the biggest threat to brick-and-mortar game stores.

Although the three major console companies control digital downloads to their devices, several companies compete for the download market in PC games. The largest is Steam, with more than forty million subscribers and about 50 percent of the PC game distribution market.[44] Steam is owned by Valve Corporation, which used the digital store to help distribute its *Counter-Strike* game online starting in 2003. Steam also carries more than eighteen hundred games from a wide range of game publishers. Other companies that sell digital game downloads for PCs include Amazon's AppStore, GameStop, Microsoft's Games Marketplace, Origin (owned by EA), and GameFly.

Of course, the most ubiquitous digital game distributors are Apple's App Store and Google Play, where users can purchase games on mobile devices. Although Google's Android system has surpassed the iPhone in market penetration, Apple customers are more likely to purchase apps, including games. That has drawn more independent developers to work in the Apple operating system. As one technology writer summarized, "Quite simply, developers have long known that Apple device owners are closely locked into the Apple ecosystem, with credit cards on file."[45]

Alternative Voices

The advent of mobile gaming has provided a new entry point for independent game developers. As *Canadian Business* magazine noted, the cost of entry has decreased substantially. "The average cost of making a major console game for Xbox 360 and Playstation3 is about $20 million, but almost anyone can churn out a new game app for the iPhone. And independent developers need only pay Apple's $99 fee for a developer's account to get their creations to the market–no Best Buy or Walmart shelf space required."[46]

But even so, time and money are still required to develop quality games. Many independent game developers and smaller game companies, shunned by big game publishers who are focused on the next big blockbuster games, are finding funding through Kickstarter, the crowd-source fund-raising social media Web site for creative projects. Video game developers make a brief pitch on Kickstarter and then request a modest amount–sometimes just a few thousand dollars–from supporters to get started. "Rather than seeking help from publishers who demand a high rate of return and, thus, a product that appeals to a broad group of gamers, developers can turn directly to their most devoted fans," the *Washington Post* explained. "And if enough of those fans are willing to pony up cash for the promise of a game that suits their tastes, it gets made, regardless of how quirky or niche-oriented it is."[47]

Another social network, GAMEiFESTO, links together game developers for collaboration on projects. Participants select their role–including artist, coder, game designer, musician, producer, animator, writer, actor, sound engineer, quality assurance tester, and project manager–and request invitations to work with others. A number of top games at Apple's App Store—including *Temple Run*, *Tiny Wings*, and *Jetpack Joyride*—are great success stories, started by small independent developers. But the cautionary tale is that it takes incredible persistence against great odds to make a successful game. Rovio made fifty-one failed app games in six years and nearly folded before *Angry Birds* became a worldwide success in 2009.

Digital Gaming, Free Speech, and Democracy

Though 80 percent of retail outlets voluntarily chose to observe the ESRB guidelines and not sell M- and AO-rated games to minors, the ratings did not have force of law. That changed in 2005, when California enacted a law to make renting or selling an M-rated game to a minor an offense enforced by fines. The law was immediately challenged by the industry and struck down by a lower court as unconstitutional. California petitioned the Supreme Court to hear the case. In a landmark decision handed down in 2011, the Supreme Court granted electronic games speech protections afforded by the First Amendment. According to the opinion written by Justice Antonin Scalia, video games communicate ideas worthy of such protection:

Like the protected books, plays, and movies that preceded them, video games communicate ideas—and even social messages—through many familiar literary devices (such as characters, dialogue, plot, and music) and through features distinctive to the medium (such as the player's interaction with the virtual world).[48]

Scalia even mentions *Mortal Kombat* in Footnote 4 of the decision:

Reading Dante is unquestionably more cultured and intellectually edifying than playing Mortal Kombat. *But these cultural and intellectual differences are not constitutional ones. Crudely violent video games, tawdry TV shows, and cheap novels and magazines are no less forms of speech than* The Divine Comedy. *. . . Even if we can see in them "nothing of any possible value to society . . . they are as much entitled to the protection of free speech as the best of literature."*

With the Supreme Court decision, electronic games achieved the same First Amendment protection afforded to other mass media. However, as in the music, television, and film industries, First Amendment protections will not make the rating system for the gaming industry go away. Parents continue to have legitimate concerns about the games their children play. Game publishers and retailers understand it is still in their best interest to respect those concerns even though the ratings cannot be enforced by law. ▶

"It's not unheard of for an unknown, upstart game creator to find a successful round of funding through [Kickstarter], but it is monumentally easier if you're a developer that has either nostalgia, name recognition, or a solid reputation that gamers (and potential backers) can bank on. It's just like in stand-up comedy or music—it's easy to be successful at crowd-funding if you're Louis C.K., Radiohead, Tim Schafer, or Paul Trowe. It's going to be much more difficult if you're the local garage band."

SCOTT NEUMYER, *POPULAR MECHANICS*, MAY 2012

CHAPTER REVIEW

COMMON THREADS

Chapter 1 of this book contains one of our favorite quotes. It's from writer Joan Didion, in her book The White Album. *She wrote: "We tell ourselves stories in order to live." Telling stories is one of the constants of cultural expression across the mass media. But, with digital games, is it still a story—or, better yet, what is it that is being communicated— if we are crafting our own individual narrative as we play through a game?*

Books, television, movies, newspapers, magazines, and even musical recordings tell us stories about the human experience. Digital games, especially ones where we play as a character or an avatar, offer perhaps the most immersive storytelling experiences of any medium.

Gamers have already shifted away from traditional media stories to those of video games. The Entertainment Software Association reported in 2012 that gamers who played more video games than they had three years earlier were spending less time going to the movies (50 percent of respondents), watching TV (47 percent), and watching movies at home (47 percent).[49] Clearly, video games are in competition with movies and television for consumers' attention. But, as we move from the kind of storytelling as audience members of TV and movies to the storytelling as players of games, what happens to the story? Is it still a mass mediated story, or something else?

Jon Spaihts, screenwriter of the science fiction film *Prometheus* (2012), identified an essential difference between the stories and storytelling in games and films. "The central character of a game is most often a cipher—an avatar into which the player projects himself or herself. The story has to have a looseness to accommodate the player's choices," Spaihts said. Conversely, "A filmmaker is trying to make you look at something a certain way—almost to force an experience on you," he added.[50] Thus, the question

of who is doing the storytelling—a producer/director or the game player—is a significant one.

Such was the case in the furor over *Mass Effect* 3 in 2012. After players spent from 120 to 150 hours advancing through the trilogy in which they could make hundreds of choices in the sequence of events, the final act took that power away from them with a tightly scripted finish. The players complained loudly, and the cofounder of BioWare, the game's developer, issued an apology: "*Mass Effect* 3 concludes a trilogy with so much player control and ownership of the story that it was hard for us to predict the range of emotions players would feel when they finished playing through it. The journey you undertake in *Mass Effect* provokes an intense range of highly personal emotions in the player; even so, the passionate reaction of some of our most loyal players to the current endings in *Mass Effect* 3 is something that has genuinely surprised us." BioWare said that they would create a new ending with "a number of game content initiatives that will help answer the questions, providing more clarity for those seeking further closure to their journey."[51]

Certainly the audience of a movie will have a range of interpretations of the movie's story. But what of the stories we are telling ourselves as players of games like *Mass Effect*? Is such personally immersive storytelling better, worse, or just different? And who is doing the storytelling?

KEY TERMS

The definitions for the terms listed below can be found in the glossary at the end of the book. The page numbers listed with the terms indicate where the term is highlighted in the chapter.

REVIEW QUESTIONS

The Development of Digital Gaming

1. What sparked the creation of mechanical games in the nineteenth and then the twentieth centuries?
2. What technology enabled the evolution of the first video games?
3. How are classic arcade games and the culture of the arcade similar to today's popular console games and gaming culture?
4. What are the three major consoles, and what distinguishes them from each other?
5. What advantages did personal computers have over video game consoles in the late 1980s and much of the 1990s?

The Internet Transforms Gaming

6. How are MMORPGs, virtual worlds, and online fantasy sports built around online social interaction?
7. How has digital convergence changed the function of gaming consoles?

The Media Playground

8. What are the main genres within digital gaming?
9. What are the two basic kinds of virtual communities?
10. How do collective intelligence, gaming Web sites, and game conventions enhance the social experience of gaming, and make games different from other mass media?

Trends and Issues in Digital Gaming

11. How have digital games influenced media culture, and vice versa?
12. In what ways has advertising become incorporated into electronic games?
13. To what extent are video game addiction, and violent and misogynistic representations, a problem for the gaming industry?
14. How are digital games regulated?
15. What will video games be like in the future?

The Business of Digital Gaming

16. What are the roles of two major components of the gaming industry—console makers and game publishers?
17. How do game publishers develop, license, and market new titles?
18. What are the three major pay models for selling video games today?
19. How can small, independent game developers get their start in the industry?

Digital Gaming, Free Speech, and Democracy

20. Why did the U.S. Supreme Court rule that games count as speech?
21. Why does the game industry still rate digital games, even if they aren't required by law to do so?

QUESTIONING THE MEDIA

1. Do you have any strong memories from playing early video games? To what extent did these games define your childhood?
2. What role does digital gaming play in your life today? Are you more inclined to play casual games or more involved games, and why?
3. Do you have a story about game addiction, either from yourself or someone you know? Explain.
4. Have you ever been appalled at the level of violence, misogyny, or racism in a video game you played (or watched being played)? Discuss the game narrative and what made it problematic.
5. Most electronic games produced have a white, male, heterosexual point of view. Why is that? If you were a game developer, what kinds of game narratives would you like to see developed?

ADDITIONAL VIDEOS

Visit the ⊚ VideoCentral: Mass Communication *section at* bedfordstmartins.com/mediaculture *for additional exclusive videos related to Chapter 3.*

PART 2

Sounds and Images

The dominant media of the twentieth century were all about sounds and images: music, radio, television, and film. Each of these media industries was built around a handful of powerful groups—record labels, radio networks, television networks, and film studios—that set the terms for creating and distributing this popular media content. The main story of these media industries was one of ever-improving technology. For example, television moved from black and white to color, from analog broadcast transmissions to digital cable.

Music, radio, TV, and movies are still significant media in our lives. But convergence and the digital turn have changed the story of our sound and image media. Starting with the music industry and the introduction of Napster in 1999, one by one these media industries have had to cope with revolutionary changes. More than a decade later, the traditional media corporations have much less power in dictating what we listen to and watch. The narrative of ever-improving technology has been upended and replaced with wholly different technology.

We now live in a world in which any and all media can be consumed via the Internet on laptops, tablets, smartphones, and video game consoles. As a result, we have seen the demise of record stores and video stores, local radio deejays, and the big network TV hit. Traditional media corporations are playing catch-up, devising new online services to bring their offerings to us and still make money. (Hulu, NBC.com, and iHeartRadio are good examples.) Meanwhile, start-up technology and content companies and anyone with a video camera and a YouTube account are competing with the major media corporations on the same Internet playing field. Pandora, iTunes, Vevo, YouTube, Amazon.com, and Netflix have all become significant distributors of sounds and images.

Moreover, as we consume all types of media content on a single device or through a single service, the traditionally separate "identities" of music, radio, television, and film have become blurred. For example, people might download a radio podcast and the latest pop single onto their iPods, or stream an album on a subscription service like Spotify and then switch to listening to its radio function. Similarly, more and more people are choosing to watch their video content on Netflix or Hulu—where TV programs and movies exist side by side.

The major media of the twentieth century are mostly still with us, but the twenty-first century story of what form that content will take, how we will experience it, and even what we might call the activity (we may need new words for watching a bunch of TV episodes in a row online, or creating a customized Internet radio channel) are still up for grabs.

How We Watch TV, Movies, and Video Today

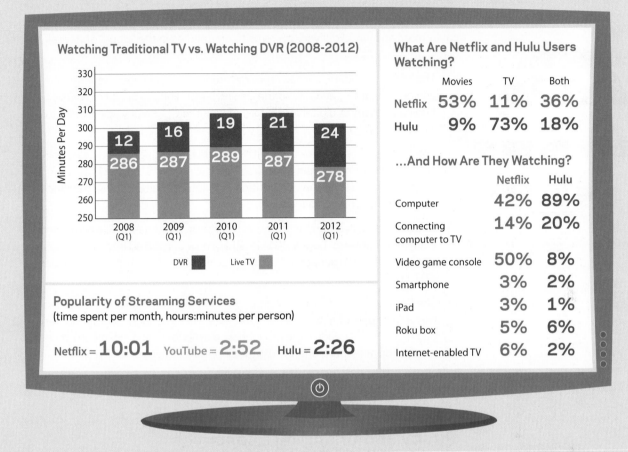

Watching Traditional TV vs. Watching DVR (2008-2012)

Minutes Per Day

Year	DVR	Live TV
2008 (Q1)	12	286
2009 (Q1)	16	287
2010 (Q1)	19	289
2011 (Q1)	21	287
2012 (Q1)	24	278

DVR ■   Live TV ■

Popularity of Streaming Services
(time spent per month, hours:minutes per person)

Netflix = **10:01**   YouTube = **2:52**   Hulu = **2:26**

What Are Netflix and Hulu Users Watching?

	Movies	TV	Both
Netflix	53%	11%	36%
Hulu	9%	73%	18%

...And How Are They Watching?

	Netflix	Hulu
Computer	42%	89%
Connecting computer to TV	14%	20%
Video game console	50%	8%
Smartphone	3%	2%
iPad	3%	1%
Roku box	5%	6%
Internet-enabled TV	6%	2%

How We Listen to Music and Radio Today

Digital listening is on the rise. Digital channels now account for an estimated 32% of record company revenues globally. This compares with 5% for newspapers, 4% for books and 1% for films.

WHERE ARE MUSIC LISTENERS LISTENING?

79% living room (HiFi, DVD players, games console, TV)

76% in car

20% on mobile devices

39% on PCs

...AND HOW ARE THEY LISTENING?

Music videos on computer
Downloaded song without paying
Streamed music on computer
Music videos on smartphone
Streamed on mobile phone
Downloaded on mobile phone
Paid downloaded on computer

INTERNET RADIO–PANDORA'S SUCCESS STORY ▼

Number of unique monthly visitors:
16,763,000

Number of registered users:
80 million

Number of hours streamed in 2011:
3.9 billion

Pandora's Active Users from 2009 to 2012

MILLION

Year	Users
2009	7
2010	16
2011	29
2012	47

1 Do you regularly stream music, movie, or TV content through Netflix, Hulu, Pandora, or some other service? If so, consider how much time you spend streaming, and compare it to how much time you spend consuming the same media in their "traditional" settings (e.g., at a movie theater, using a music player).

2 Streaming means we never really "own" the digital files we listen to and watch, but rather lease or rent them from one service or another. What are some possible drawbacks to this?

See Notes for list of sources.

Changing Formats

Thanks to the digital turn, our sound and image media have moved from physical formats and wired delivery systems to digital files in the "cloud" and wireless distribution.

- The tin foil cylinders, shellac and vinyl records, and cassette tapes—all analog formats—gave way to the 0s and 1s of digitally produced music. Ironically, the first digital music format was the CD—a physical product (Chapter 4, pages 122-125).

- The sounds of radio were transmitted wirelessly through analog electromagnetic waves for more than a hundred years (Chapter 5, pages 159-162). But terrestrial radio is now in competition with Internet alternatives transmitted wirelessly (Chapter 5, page 183).

- Television shows broadcast through terrestrial antennas, cable wires, and satellite (Chapter 6, pages 201-202) are now converted into digital files and streamed through services like YouTube, Hulu, and Netflix (Chapter 6, pages 207-209).

- The flexible celluloid film that looped through film cameras and then projectors was a fixed part of film production for more than a hundred years (Chapter 7, pages 242-244). Today, the production, distribution, and exhibition processes are, for the most part, entirely digital (Chapter 7, pages 266-267).

Piracy and Changing Economics

As digital technology made audio and video production affordable to amateurs, it broke the hold media corporations had over producing and distributing media content, changing media economics and creating opportunities for media pirates to exploit.

- The recording industry threw its weight against Internet piracy but was slow to shift distribution to for-profit digital distribution (Chapter 4, page 127).

- Digital music in the recording industry creates several new opportunities for revenue but unclear systems for sharing royalties with artists (Chapter 4, pages 145-149).

- Government regulators and the recording industry responded to digital streaming radio music services with oppressively high performance royalty rates (Chapter 4, page 147).

- Meanwhile, the broadcast radio industry has long paid no performance royalties to artists, which streaming services called unfair (Chapter 5, page 183).

- The movie industry, concerned that downloading and streaming will cannibalize box-office and DVD sales and undermine movie theaters, has been slow to embrace Internet distribution for newer releases (Chapter 7, pages 266-267).

Fragmenting Audiences

Producing mass media used to mean producing for a single mass audience, but today convergence has led to smaller "niche" audiences: We have more choice, but we also don't listen or watch content in the same way as previous generations.

- The radio show *Amos 'n' Andy* was so popular in the 1930s that restaurants and movie theaters would need to broadcast it to their customers or else lose their business (Chapter 5, page 171). With Internet radio sites, users can tailor their experience by creating stations based off a single artist or even song (Chapter 5, page 183).

- Prior to the 1980s, discussion at school or work used to revolve around what was on the three main television networks the night before. Now, only Super Bowl audiences and crisis news coverage bring people together around television the same way (Chapter 6, pages 226–227).

- The development of cable introduced the idea of narrowcasting (Chapter 6, page 202). In 2011 and 2012, YouTube launched more than a hundred channels of original programming, each devoted to a niche topic, ensuring even more choice and further fragmenting audiences (Chapter 6, pages 226–227).

- The peak movie audience was in 1946, at 90 million a week (at a time when the entire national population was 141 million). With multiple avenues for watching movies, today's box-office revenue is sustained by a much smaller audience (Chapter 7, pages 265–266).

- With such fragmented media, is the era of a "mass" audience over (Chapter 1, page 5)?

Convergence Benefits Independent Media Makers

While digital convergence has upset the economics of the traditional media industries, it has created opportunities for alternative voices of independent media makers.

- Some sound recording artists are distributing their work directly to their audience, and even engaging their audience as investors in music projects (Chapter 4, pages 119–120).

- Web shows offer outlets for producers who want to do shows that might be too experimental or niche for broadcast or cable networks (Chapter 6, pages 228–229).

- Digital technology makes filmmaking within reach; young filmmakers created the hit *Paranormal Activity* (2007) for the cost of an inexpensive car (Chapter 7, page 267).

▶ **For more on Internet users creating their own content, watch the "User-Generated Content" video on *VideoCentral: Mass Communication* at bedfordstmartins.com/mediaculture.**

4

Sound Recording and Popular Music

◀

AMANDA PALMER
funded her bold album online via Kickstarter.

For years, the recording industry has been panicking about file swappers who illegally download songs and thereby decrease recorded music sales. So it struck many in the industry as unusual when the Grammy Award–winning British alternative rock group Radiohead decided to sell its 2007 album *In Rainbows* online for whatever price fans wished to pay, including nothing at all.

Radiohead was able to try this business model because its contract with the record corporation EMI had expired after its previous album, 2003's *Hail to the Thief*. Knowing it had millions of fans around the world, the group turned down multi-million-dollar offers to sign a new contract with major labels, and instead decided to experiment by offering its seventh studio album online with a "pay what you wish" approach. "It's not supposed to be a model for anything else. It was simply a response to a situation," Thom Yorke, the lead singer of Radiohead, said. "We're out of contract. We have our own studio. We have this new server. What the hell else would we do?"[1]

Radiohead didn't disclose the sales revenue or numbers of the downloads, but one source claimed at least 1.2 million copies of the album were downloaded in the first two days.[2] In an interview with an Australian newspaper, Yorke mentioned that about 50 percent of the downloaders took the album for free.[3] But a study conservatively estimated that Radiohead made an average of $2.26 on each album download. If that's the case, Radiohead may have made more money per recording than the traditional royalties the group might have earned with a release by a major label.[4] Radiohead continued to sell its recordings independently through its own Web site, but without a "name-your-price" option.

Although Radiohead's Thom Yorke said the online album release experiment was not supposed to be a model for anyone else, it ended up being just that. Hip-hop artist Saul Williams released digital downloads of *The Inevitable Rise and Liberation of Niggy Tardust* (saulwilliams.com) for $5, with a "free" option to the first hundred thousand customers. In March 2008, Nine Inch Nails released *Ghosts I–IV*, a four-album recording with thirty-six songs, at ghosts.nin.com. *Ghost I*, the package of the first nine songs, was available as a free download, with the rest available for purchase.

An alternate avenue for music artists to promote their music is posting their music videos to sites like YouTube, Dailymotion, and Vevo, which are a way to get less expensive (free) and much wider music video distribution. In 2006, the band OK Go gained enormous attention by posting its treadmill dancing video for its song "Here It Goes Again" on YouTube. The video went viral and made OK Go a profitable act for EMI. Yet EMI later prohibited OK Go's videos from being embedded on any site but YouTube, since only YouTube paid royalties to

EMI for views on its site. Immediately, views of the group's videos dropped by 90 percent, and OK Go lost one of its best methods of promotion. In March 2010, OK Go parted ways with EMI and released an imaginative Rube Goldberg machine video for "This Too Shall Pass" that, absent EMI's constraints on distribution, became another viral music video. Without a major label, the band creatively financed the video with support from State Farm Insurance, whose logo appears a few times in the video.

Recently, some musical artists have chosen to go straight to their fans to "crowdsource" financial support for their next project. Boston singer Amanda Palmer, who left Roadrunner Records (a Warner Music Group label) a few years earlier, appealed to her fans on a Kickstarter page in 2012 to get funding for her new studio album. Contributions of $1 or more would get a digital download of the album. For a pledge of $25 or more, individuals would receive a limited edition CD, a twenty-four-page art booklet, a digital download, and a thank-you card. In two days she raised $379,000.[5] In a month, she raised almost $1.2 million from nearly twenty-five thousand backers. "Since I'm now without a giant label to front the gazillions of dollars that it always takes to manufacture and promote a record this big, I'm coming to you to gather funds," Palmer wrote on her Kickstarter page.[6]

▲
___

"I think Kickstarter and other crowdfunding platforms like this are the BEST way to put out music right now—no label, no rules, no fuss, no muss."

AMANDA PALMER

▲ *THE MEDIUM OF SOUND RECORDING* has had an immense impact on our culture. The music that helps shape our identities and comforts us during the transition from childhood to adulthood resonates throughout our lives, and it often stirs debate among parents and teenagers, teachers and students, and politicians and performers, many times leading to social change. Throughout its history, popular music has been banned by parents, school officials, and even governments under the guise of protecting young people from corrupting influences. As far back as the late 1700s, authorities in Europe, thinking that it was immoral for young people to dance close together, outlawed waltz music as "savagery." Between the 1920s and the 1940s, jazz music was criticized for its unbridled and sometimes free-form sound and the unrestrained dance crazes (such as the Charleston and the jitterbug) it inspired. Rock and roll from the 1950s onward and hip-hop from the 1980s to today have also added their own chapters to the age-old musical battle between generations.

In this chapter, we will place the impact of popular music in context and:

- Investigate the origins of recording's technological "hardware," from Thomas Edison's early phonograph to Emile Berliner's invention of the flat disk record and the development of audiotape, compact discs, and MP3s
- Study radio's early threat to sound recording and the subsequent alliance between the two media when television arrived in the 1950s
- Explore the impact of the Internet on music, including the effects of online piracy and how the industry is adapting to the new era of convergence with new models for distributing and promoting music
- Examine the content and culture of the music industry, focusing on the predominant role of rock music and its extraordinary impact on mass media forms and a diverse array of cultures, both American and international
- Explore the economic and democratic issues facing the recording industry

As you consider these topics, think about your own relationship with popular music and sound recordings. Who was your first favorite group or singer? How old were you, and what was important to you about this music? How has the way you listen to music changed in the past five years? For more questions to help you think through the role of music in our lives, see "Questioning the Media" in the Chapter Review.

> **"If people knew what this stuff was about, we'd probably all get arrested."**
>
> BOB DYLAN, 1966, TALKING ABOUT ROCK AND ROLL

Past-Present-Future: Sound Recording

For about half a century starting in the 1950s, the economics of the sound recording industry were pretty simple. Retailers, the record label, the artists, and the songwriters would each get their share of revenue (and radio stations got free content).

Then, in 1999, the music industry was completely caught off guard by the introduction of Napster, the music file-sharing service. After years of panicked lawsuits over file sharing, Apple convinced the industry to go where the customers had already moved in 2003, and iTunes was born. Today, fans listen to music in any number of ways—downloads, music videos, and online streaming services.

The sound recording industry was the first of the mass media industries to see its business upended by digital culture. Now it is slowly figuring out how to monetize and make its business profitable again. Digital downloads have surpassed CDs as the main source of income, and the proliferation of other distribution models—ringtones, subscription services, video sites, and even radio (the recording industry would now like to charge radio for playing songs)—means that the music industry will never be as uncomplicated again. Music fans will largely decide how they like to consume music, and the industry will have to follow and figure out how to set pricing for new avenues like streaming services.

The Development of Sound Recording

New mass media have often been defined in terms of the communication technologies that preceded them. For example, movies were initially called *motion pictures*, a term that derived from photography; radio was referred to as *wireless telegraphy*, referring back to telegraphs; and television was often called *picture radio*. Likewise, sound recording instruments were initially described as talking machines and later as phonographs, indicating the existing innovations, the tele*phone* and the tele*graph*. This early blending of technology foreshadowed our contemporary era, in which media as diverse as newspapers and movies converge on the Internet. Long before the Internet, however, the first major media convergence involved the relationship between the sound recording and radio industries.

From Cylinders to Disks: Sound Recording Becomes a Mass Medium

In the 1850s, the French printer Édouard-Léon Scott de Martinville conducted the first experiments with sound recording. Using a hog's hair bristle as a needle, he tied one end to a thin membrane stretched over the narrow part of a funnel. When the inventor spoke into the funnel, the membrane vibrated and the free end of the bristle made grooves on a revolving cylinder coated with a thick liquid called *lamp black*. De Martinville noticed that different sounds made different trails in the lamp black, but he could not figure out how to play back the sound. However, his experiments did usher in the *development stage* of sound recording as a mass medium. In 2008, audio researchers using high-resolution scans of the recordings and a digital stylus were able to finally play back some of de Martinville's recordings for the first time.[7]

THOMAS EDISON
In addition to the phonograph, Edison (1847–1931) ran an industrial research lab that is credited with inventing the motion picture camera and the first commercially successful light bulb, and a system for distributing electricity.

Sound Recording and Popular Music

de Martinville
The first experiments with sound are conducted in the 1850s using a hog's hair bristle as a needle; de Martinville can record sound, but he can't play it back (p. 122).

Flat Disk
Berliner invents the flat disk in 1887 and develops the gramophone to play it. The disks are easily mass-produced, a labeling system is introduced, and sound recording becomes a mass medium (p. 123).

MAPLE LEAF RAG.
Scott Joplin.

Radio Threatens the Sound Recording Industry
By 1925, "free" music can be heard over the airwaves (p. 124).

Audiotape
Developed in Germany in the early 1940s, audiotape enables multitrack recording. Taping technology comes to the United States after WWII (p. 124).

| 1850 | 1880 | 1890 | 1900 | 1910 | 1920 | 1930 | 1940 |

Phonograph
In 1877, Edison figures out how to play back sound, thinking this invention would make a good answering machine (p. 123).

Victrolas
Around 1910, music players enter living rooms as elaborate furniture centerpieces, replacing pianos as musical entertainment (p. 124).

In 1877, Thomas Edison had success playing back sound. He recorded his own voice by using a needle to press his voice's sound waves onto tinfoil wrapped around a metal cylinder about the size of a cardboard toilet-paper roll. After recording his voice, Edison played it back by repositioning the needle to retrace the grooves in the foil. The machine that played these cylinders became known as the *phonograph*, derived from the Greek terms for "sound" and "writing."

Thomas Edison was more than an inventor—he was also able to envision the practical uses of his inventions and ways to market them. Moving sound recording into its *entrepreneurial stage*, Edison patented his phonograph in 1878 as a kind of answering machine. He thought the phonograph would be used as a "telephone repeater" that would "provide invaluable records, instead of being the recipient of momentary and fleeting communication."[8] Edison's phonograph patent was specifically for a device that recorded and played back foil cylinders. Because of this limitation, in 1886 Chichester Bell (cousin of telephone inventor Alexander Graham Bell) and Charles Sumner Tainter were able to further sound recording by patenting an improvement on the phonograph. Their sound recording device, known as the *graphophone,* played back more durable wax cylinders.[9] Both Edison's phonograph and Bell and Tainter's graphophone had only marginal success as voice-recording office machines. Eventually, both sets of inventors began to produce cylinders with prerecorded music, which proved to be more popular but difficult to mass-produce and not very durable for repeated plays.

Using ideas from Edison, Bell, and Tainter, Emile Berliner, a German engineer who had immigrated to America, developed a better machine that played round, flat disks, or records. Made of zinc and coated with beeswax, these records played on a turntable, which Berliner called a *gramophone* and patented in 1887. Berliner also developed a technique that enabled him to mass-produce his round records, bringing sound recording into its *mass medium stage*. Previously, using Edison's cylinder, performers had to play or sing into the speaker for each separate recording. Berliner's technique featured a master recording from which copies could be easily duplicated in mass quantities. In addition, Berliner's records could be stamped with labels, allowing the music to be differentiated by title, performer, and songwriter. This led to the development of a "star system," because fans could identify and choose their favorite sounds and artists.

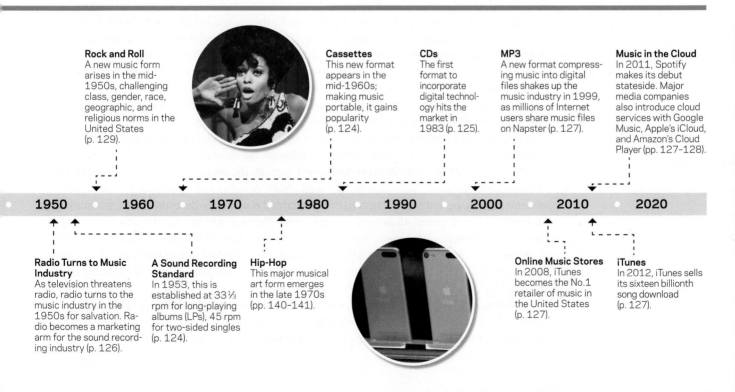

Rock and Roll
A new music form arises in the mid-1950s, challenging class, gender, race, geographic, and religious norms in the United States (p. 129).

Cassettes
This new format appears in the mid-1960s; making music portable, it gains popularity (p. 124).

CDs
The first format to incorporate digital technology hits the market in 1983 (p. 125).

MP3
A new format compressing music into digital files shakes up the music industry in 1999, as millions of Internet users share music files on Napster (p. 127).

Music in the Cloud
In 2011, Spotify makes its debut stateside. Major media companies also introduce cloud services with Google Music, Apple's iCloud, and Amazon's Cloud Player (pp. 127–128).

1950   1960   1970   1980   1990   2000   2010   2020

Radio Turns to Music Industry
As television threatens radio, radio turns to the music industry in the 1950s for salvation. Radio becomes a marketing arm for the sound recording industry (p. 126).

A Sound Recording Standard
In 1953, this is established at 33⅓ rpm for long-playing albums (LPs), 45 rpm for two-sided singles (p. 124).

Hip-Hop
This major musical art form emerges in the late 1970s (pp. 140–141).

Online Music Stores
In 2008, iTunes becomes the No.1 retailer of music in the United States (p. 127).

iTunes
In 2012, iTunes sells its sixteen billionth song download (p. 127).

By the early 1900s, record-playing phonographs were widely available for home use. In 1906, the Victor Talking Machine Company placed the hardware, or "guts," of the record player inside a piece of furniture. These early record players, known as Victrolas, were mechanical and had to be primed with a crank handle. The introduction of electric record players, first available in 1925, gradually replaced Victrolas as more homes were wired for electricity; this led to the gramophone becoming an essential appliance in most American homes.

The appeal of recorded music was limited at first because of sound quality. While the original wax records were replaced by shellac discs, shellac records were also very fragile and didn't improve the sound quality much. By the 1930s, in part because of the advent of radio and in part because of the Great Depression, record and phonograph sales declined dramatically. However, in the early 1940s shellac was needed for World War II munitions production, so the record industry turned to manufacturing polyvinyl plastic records instead. The vinyl recordings turned out to be more durable than shellac records and less noisy, paving the way for a renewed consumer desire to buy recorded music.

In 1948, CBS Records introduced the 33⅓-rpm (revolutions-per-minute) *long-playing record* (LP), with about twenty minutes of music on each side of the record, creating a market for multisong albums and classical music. This was an improvement over the three to four minutes of music contained on the existing 78-rpm records. The next year, RCA developed a competing 45-rpm record that featured a quarter-size hole (best for jukeboxes) and invigorated the sales of songs heard on jukeboxes throughout the country. Unfortunately, the two new record standards were not technically compatible, meaning they could not be played on each other's machines. A five-year marketing battle ensued, similar to the Macintosh vs. Windows battle over computer-operating-system standards in the 1980s and 1990s or the mid-2000s battle between Blu-ray and HD DVD. In 1953, CBS and RCA compromised. The LP became the standard for long-playing albums, the 45 became the standard for singles, and record players were designed to accommodate 45s, LPs, and, for a while, 78s.

From Phonographs to CDs: Analog Goes Digital

The invention of the phonograph and the record were the key sound recording advancements until the advent of magnetic **audiotape** and tape players in the 1940s. Magnetic tape sound recording was first developed as early as 1929 and further refined in the 1930s, but it didn't catch on initially because the first machines were bulky reel-to-reel devices, the amount of tape required to make a recording was unwieldy, and the tape itself broke or damaged easily. However, owing largely to improvements by German engineers who developed plastic magnetic tape during World War II, audiotape eventually found its place.

Audiotape's lightweight magnetized strands finally made possible sound editing and multiple-track mixing, in which instrumentals or vocals could be recorded at one location and later mixed onto a master recording in another studio. This led to a vast improvement of studio recordings and subsequent increases in sales, although the recordings continued to be sold primarily in vinyl format rather than on reel-to-reel tape. By the mid-1960s, engineers had placed miniaturized reel-to-reel audiotape inside small plastic *cassettes* and had developed portable cassette players, permitting listeners to bring recorded music anywhere and creating a market for prerecorded cassettes. Audiotape also permitted "home dubbing": Consumers could copy their favorite records onto tape or record songs from the radio. This practice denied sales to the recording industry, resulting in a drop in record sales, the doubling of blank audiotape sales during a period in the 1970s, and the later rise of the Sony Walkman, a portable cassette player that foreshadowed the release of the iPod two decades later.

Some thought the portability, superior sound, and recording capabilities of audiotape would mean the demise of records. Although records had retained essentially the same format since the advent of vinyl, the popularity of records continued, in part due to the improved sound fidelity that came with stereophonic sound. Invented in 1931 by engineer Alan Blumlein, but not put to commercial use until 1958, **stereo** permitted the recording of two separate channels, or tracks, of sound. Recording-studio engineers, using audiotape, could now record many instrumental or vocal tracks, which they "mixed down" to two stereo tracks. When played back through two loudspeakers, stereo creates a more natural sound distribution. By 1971, stereo sound had been advanced into *quadrophonic*, or four-track, sound, but that never caught on commercially.

The biggest recording advancement came in the 1970s, when electrical engineer Thomas Stockham made the first digital audio recordings on standard computer equipment. Although the digital recorder was invented in 1967, Stockham was the first to put it to practical use. In contrast to **analog recording**, which captures the fluctuations of sound waves and stores those signals in a record's grooves or a tape's continuous stream of magnetized particles, **digital recording** translates sound waves into binary on-off pulses and stores that information as numerical code. When a digital recording is played back, a microprocessor translates these numerical codes back into sounds and sends them to loudspeakers. By the late 1970s, Sony and Philips were jointly working on a way to design a digitally recorded disc and player to take advantage of this new technology, which could be produced at a lower cost than either vinyl records or audiocassettes. As a result of their efforts, digitally recorded **compact discs (CDs)** hit the market in 1983.

By 1987, CD sales were double the amount of LP record album sales (see Figure 4.1). By 2000, CDs rendered records and audiocassettes nearly obsolete, except for DJs and record enthusiasts who continued to play and collect vinyl LPs. In an effort to create new product lines and maintain consumer sales, the music industry promoted two advanced digital disc formats in the late 1990s, which it hoped would eventually replace standard CDs. However, the introduction of these formats was ill-timed for the industry, because the biggest development in music formatting was already on the horizon–the MP3.

The Rocky Relationship between Records and Radio

The recording industry and radio have always been closely linked. Although they work almost in unison now, in the beginning they had a tumultuous relationship. Radio's very existence sparked the first battle. By 1915, the phonograph had become a popular form of

FIGURE 4.1

ANNUAL VINYL, TAPE, CD, MOBILE, AND DIGITAL SALES

Source: Recording Industry Association of America, 2011 year-end statistics.

Note: "Digital" includes singles, albums, music videos, and kiosk sales. Cassette tapes fell under $1 million in sales in 2008.

▼

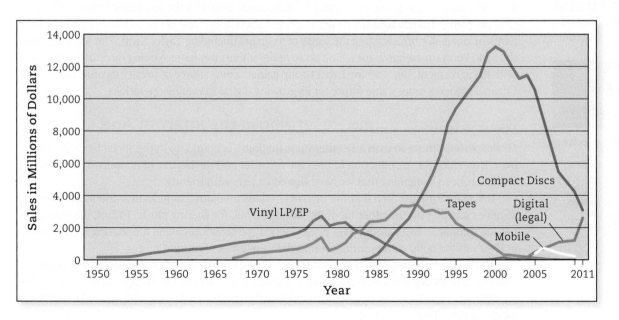

entertainment. The recording industry sold thirty million records that year, and by the end of the decade sales more than tripled each year. In 1924, though, record sales dropped to only half of what they had been the previous year. Why? Because radio had arrived as a competing mass medium, providing free entertainment over the airwaves, independent of the recording industry.

The battle heated up when, to the alarm of the recording industry, radio stations began broadcasting recorded music without compensating the music industry. The American Society of Composers, Authors, and Publishers (ASCAP), founded in 1914 to collect copyright fees for music publishers and writers, charged that radio was contributing to plummeting sales of records and sheet music. By 1925, ASCAP established music rights fees for radio, charging stations between $250 and $2,500 a week to play recorded music—and causing many stations to leave the air.

But other stations countered by establishing their own live, in-house orchestras, disseminating "free" music to listeners. This time, the recording industry could do nothing, as original radio music did not infringe on any copyrights. Throughout the late 1920s and 1930s, record and phonograph sales continued to fall, although the recording industry got a small boost when Prohibition ended in 1933 and record-playing jukeboxes became the standard musical entertainment in neighborhood taverns.

The recording and radio industries only began to cooperate with each other after television became popular in the early 1950s. Television pilfered radio's variety shows, crime dramas, and comedy programs and, along with those formats, much of its advertising revenue and audience. Seeking to reinvent itself, radio turned to the record industry, and this time both industries greatly benefited from radio's new "hit songs" format. The alliance between the recording industry and radio was aided enormously by rock and roll music, which was just emerging in the 1950s. Rock created an enduring consumer youth market for sound recordings and provided much-needed new content for radio precisely when television made it seem like an obsolete medium.

After the digital turn, that mutually beneficial arrangement between the recording and radio industries began to fray. While Internet streaming radio stations were being required to pay royalties to music companies when they played their songs, radio stations still got to play music royalty-free over the air. In 2012, Clear Channel, the largest radio station chain in the United States and one of the largest music streaming companies, with more than a thousand live stations on iHeartRadio.com, was the first company to strike a new deal with the recording industry. Clear Channel pledged to pay royalties to Big Machine Label Group—one of the country's largest independent labels—for broadcasting the songs of its artists (including Taylor Swift, Tim McGraw, and the Band Perry) in exchange for a limit on royalties it must pay for streaming those artists' music. With the agreement, Big Machine Label Group gained a new source of royalty income, and Clear Channel crafted a more stable future for its growing digital streaming operations.

Convergence: Sound Recording in the Internet Age

Music, perhaps more so than any other mass medium, is bound up in the social fabric of our lives. Ever since the introduction of the tape recorder and the heyday of homemade mixtapes, music has been something that we have shared eagerly with friends.

It is not surprising then that the Internet, a mass medium that links individuals and communities together like no other medium, became a hub for sharing music. In fact, the reason college student Shawn Fanning said he developed the groundbreaking file-sharing site Napster in 1999 was "to build communities around different types of music."[10]

Music's convergence with radio saved the radio industry in the 1950s. But music's convergence with the Internet began to unravel the music industry in the 2000s. The changes in the music industry were set in motion about two decades ago with the proliferation of Internet use and the development of a new digital file format.

MP3s and File Sharing

The **MP3** file format, developed in 1992, enables digital recordings to be compressed into smaller, more manageable files. With the increasing popularity of the Internet in the mid-1990s, computer users began swapping MP3 music files online because they could be uploaded or downloaded in a fraction of the time it took to exchange noncompressed music and because they use up less memory.

By 1999, the year Napster's infamous free file-sharing service brought the MP3 format to popular attention, music files were widely available on the Internet—some for sale, some legally available for free downloading, and many traded in violation of copyright laws. Despite the higher quality of industry-manufactured CDs, music fans enjoyed the convenience of downloading and burning MP3 files to CD. Some listeners skipped CDs altogether, storing their music on hard drives and essentially using their computers as stereo systems. Losing countless music sales to illegal downloading, the music industry fought the proliferation of the MP3 format with an array of lawsuits (aimed at file-sharing companies and at individual downloaders), but the popularity of MP3s continued to increase.

In 2001, the U.S. Supreme Court ruled in favor of the music industry and against Napster, declaring free music file-swapping illegal and in violation of music copyrights held by recording labels and artists. It was relatively easy for the music industry to shut down Napster (which later relaunched as a legal service), because it required users to log into a centralized system. However, the music industry's elimination of illegal file-sharing was not complete, as decentralized *peer-to-peer* (P2P) systems, such as Grokster, LimeWire, Morpheus, Kazaa, eDonkey, eMule, and BitTorrent, once again enabled online free music file-sharing.

The recording industry fought back with thousands of lawsuits, many of them successful. In 2005, P2P service Grokster shut down after it was fined $50 million by U.S. federal courts and, in upholding the lower court rulings, the Supreme Court reaffirmed that the music industry could pursue legal action against any P2P service that encouraged its users to illegally share music or other media. By 2010, eDonkey, Morpheus, and LimeWire had been shut down, while Kazaa settled a lawsuit with the music industry and became a legal service. By 2011, several major Internet service providers, including AT&T, Cablevision, Comcast, Time Warner Cable, and Verizon, agreed to help the music industry identify customers who may be illegally downloading music and try to prevent them from doing so by sending them "copyright alert" warning letters, redirecting them to Web pages about digital piracy, and ultimately slowing download speeds, or closing their broadband accounts.

As it cracked down on digital theft, the music industry also realized that it would have to somehow adapt its business to the digital format and embraced services like iTunes (launched by Apple in 2003, to accompany the iPod), which has become the model for legal online distribution. In 2008, iTunes became the top music retailer in the United States, surpassing Walmart, and by 2012 iTunes had sold more than sixteen billion songs. Even with the success of Apple's iTunes and other online music stores, illegal music file-sharing still accounts for four out of five music downloads in the United States.[11]

Music in the Stream, Music in the Cloud

If the history of recorded music tells us anything, it's that over time tastes change and formats change. While artists take care of the musical possibilities, technology companies are developing formats for the future. One such format is "music in the cloud," which eliminates the physical ownership of music entirely. This format first became

APPLE'S iPOD, the leading portable music and video player, began a revolution in digital music.

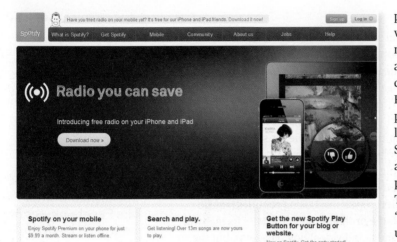

popular with streaming radio services like Pandora, where users can create personalized Internet music radio channels for free (Pandora is financed by ads), although they can't select individual songs. Then came subscription music services, including MOG, Rhapsody, Rdio, Audiogalaxy, AudioBox, and the popular European service co-owned by major music labels, Spotify, which made its debut in the United States in 2011. With these services, listeners can pay a monthly subscription of $5 to $10 and instantly play millions of songs on demand via the Internet. Three major media companies also jumped on the "cloud-based music" bandwagon in 2011. Although users still need to purchase copies of individual songs, Amazon's Cloud Player, Google Music, and Apple's iCloud provide users with a "storage locker" on the Web for their music, so they can access it almost anywhere, on almost any Internet-connected device.

U.S. Popular Music and the Formation of Rock

Popular or **pop music** is music that appeals either to a wide cross section of the public or to sizable subdivisions within the larger public based on age, region, or ethnic background (e.g., teenagers, southerners, Mexican Americans). U.S. pop music today encompasses styles as diverse as blues, country, Tejano, salsa, jazz, rock, reggae, punk, hip-hop, and dance. The word *pop* has also been used to distinguish popular music from classical music, which is written primarily for ballet, opera, ensemble, or symphony. As various subcultures have intersected, U.S. popular music has developed organically, constantly creating new forms and reinvigorating older musical styles.

The Rise of Pop Music

SCOTT JOPLIN (1868–1917) published more than fifty compositions during his life, including "Maple Leaf Rag"—arguably his most famous piece.

Although it is commonly assumed that pop music developed simultaneously with the phonograph and radio, it actually existed prior to these media. In the late nineteenth century, the sale of sheet music for piano and other instruments sprang from a section of Broadway in Manhattan known as Tin Pan Alley, a derisive term used to describe the way that these quickly produced tunes supposedly sounded like cheap pans clanging together. Tin Pan Alley's tradition of song publishing began in the late 1880s with music like the marches of John Philip Sousa and the ragtime piano pieces of Scott Joplin. It continued through the first half of the twentieth century with the show tunes and vocal ballads of Irving Berlin, George Gershwin, and Cole Porter, and into the 1950s and 1960s with such rock-and-roll writing teams as Jerry Leiber–Mike Stoller and Carole King–Gerry Goffin.

At the turn of the twentieth century, with the newfound ability of song publishers to mass-produce sheet music for a growing middle class, popular songs moved from being a novelty to being a major business enterprise. With the emergence of the phonograph, song publishers also discovered that recorded tunes boosted interest in and sales of sheet music. Songwriting and Tin Pan Alley played a key role in transforming popular music into a mass medium.

As sheet music grew in popularity, **jazz** developed in New Orleans. An improvisational and mostly instrumental musical form, jazz absorbed and integrated a diverse body of musical styles, including African rhythms, blues, and gospel. Jazz influenced many bandleaders throughout the 1930s and 1940s. Groups led by Louis Armstrong, Count Basie, Tommy Dorsey, Duke Ellington, Benny Goodman, and Glenn Miller were among the most popular of the "swing" jazz bands, whose rhythmic music also dominated radio, recording, and dance halls in their day.

The first pop vocalists of the twentieth century were products of the vaudeville circuit, which radio, movies, and the Depression would bring to an end in the 1930s. In the 1920s, Eddie Cantor, Belle Baker, Sophie Tucker, and Al Jolson were all extremely popular. By the 1930s, Rudy Vallée and Bing Crosby had established themselves as the first "crooners," or singers of pop standards. Bing Crosby also popularized Irving Berlin's "White Christmas," one of the most covered songs in recording history. (A song recorded or performed by another artist is known as **cover music**.) Meanwhile, the Andrews Sisters' boogie-woogie style helped them sell more than sixty million records in the late 1930s and 1940s. In one of the first mutually beneficial alliances between sound recording and radio, many early pop vocalists had their own network of regional radio programs, which vastly increased their exposure.

Frank Sinatra arrived in the 1940s, and his romantic ballads foreshadowed the teen love songs of rock and roll's early years. Nicknamed "The Voice" early in his career, Sinatra, like Crosby, parlayed his music and radio exposure into movie stardom. (Both singers made more than fifty films apiece.) Helped by radio, pop vocalists like Sinatra were among the first vocalists to become popular with a large national teen audience. Their record sales helped stabilize the industry, and in the early 1940s Sinatra's concerts caused the kind of audience riots that would later characterize rock-and-roll performances.

Rock and Roll Is Here to Stay

The cultural storm called **rock and roll** hit in the mid-1950s. As with the term *jazz*, *rock and roll* was a blues slang term for "sex," lending it instant controversy. Early rock and roll was considered the first "integrationist music," merging the black sounds of rhythm and blues, gospel, and Robert Johnson's screeching blues guitar with the white influences of country, folk, and pop vocals.[12] From a cultural perspective, only a few musical forms have ever sprung from such a diverse set of influences, and no new style of music has ever had such a widespread impact on so many different cultures as rock and roll. From an economic perspective, rock and roll was the first musical form to simultaneously transform the structure of sound recording and radio. Rock's development set the stage for how music is produced, distributed, and performed today. Many social, cultural, economic, and political factors leading up to the 1950s contributed to the growth of rock and roll, including black migration, the growth of youth culture, and the beginnings of racial integration.

The migration of southern blacks to northern cities in search of better jobs during the first half of the twentieth century had helped spread different popular music styles. In particular, **blues** music, the foundation of rock and roll, came to the North. Influenced by African American spirituals, ballads, and work songs from the rural South, blues music was exemplified in the work of Robert Johnson, Ma Rainey, Son House, Bessie Smith, Charley Patton, and others. The introduction in the 1930s of the electric guitar—a major contribution to rock music—gave southern blues its urban style, popularized in the work of Muddy Waters, Howlin' Wolf, Sonny Boy Williamson, B.B. King, and Buddy Guy.[13]

> "Frank Sinatra was categorized in 1943 as 'the glorification of ignorance and musical illiteracy.'"
>
> DICK CLARK, *THE FIRST 25 YEARS OF ROCK & ROLL*

ROBERT JOHNSON (1911–1938), who ranks among the most influential and innovative American guitarists, played the Mississippi delta blues and was a major influence on early rock and rollers, especially the Rolling Stones and Eric Clapton. His intense slide-guitar and finger-style playing also inspired generations of blues artists, including Muddy Waters, Howlin' Wolf, Bonnie Raitt, and Stevie Ray Vaughan. To get a sense of his style, visit The Robert Johnson Notebooks, http://xroads .virginia.edu/~MUSIC/ rjhome.html.

The North and the South

Not only did rock and roll muddy the urban and rural terrain, it also combined northern and southern influences. In fact, with so much blues, R&B, and rock and roll rising from the South in the 1950s, this region regained some of its cultural flavor, which (along with a sizable portion of the population) had migrated to the North after the Civil War and during the early twentieth century. Meanwhile, musicians and audiences in the North had absorbed blues music as their own, eliminating the understanding of blues as specifically a southern style. Like the many white teens today who are fascinated by hip-hop, Carl Perkins, Elvis Presley, and Buddy Holly—all from the rural South—were fascinated with and influenced by the black urban styles they had heard on the radio or seen in nightclubs. These artists in turn brought southern culture to northern listeners.

But the key to record sales and the spread of rock and roll, according to famed record producer Sam Phillips of Sun Records, was to find a white man who sounded black. Phillips found that man in Elvis Presley. Commenting on Presley's cultural importance, one critic wrote: "White rockabillies like Elvis took poor white southern mannerisms of speech and behavior deeper into mainstream culture than they had ever been taken."[18]

The Sacred and the Secular

Although many mainstream adults in the 1950s complained that rock and roll's sexuality and questioning of moral norms constituted an offense against God, in fact many early rock figures had close ties to religion. Jerry Lee Lewis attended a Bible institute in Texas (although he was eventually thrown out); Ray Charles converted an old gospel tune he had first heard in church as a youth into "I Got a Woman," one of his signature songs; and many other artists transformed gospel songs into rock and roll.

Still, many people did not appreciate the blurring of boundaries between the sacred and the secular. In the late 1950s, public outrage over rock and roll was so great that even Little Richard and Jerry Lee Lewis, both sons of southern preachers, became convinced that they were playing the "devil's music." By 1959, Little Richard had left rock and roll to become a minister. Lewis had to be coerced into recording "Great Balls of Fire," a song by Otis Blackwell that turned an apocalyptic biblical phrase into a highly charged sexual teen love song that was banned by many radio stations, but nevertheless climbed to No. 2 on the pop charts in 1957. Throughout the rock-and-roll era to today, the boundaries between sacred and secular music and religious and secular concerns continue to blur, with some churches using rock and roll to appeal to youth, and some Christian-themed rock groups recording music as seemingly incongruous as heavy metal.

Battles in Rock and Roll

The blurring of racial lines and the breakdown of other conventional boundaries meant that performers and producers were forced to play a tricky game to get rock and roll accepted by the masses. Two prominent white disc jockeys used different methods. Cleveland deejay Alan Freed, credited with popularizing the term *rock and roll*, played original R&B recordings from the race charts and black versions of early rock and roll on his program. In contrast, Philadelphia deejay Dick Clark believed that making black music acceptable to white audiences required cover versions by white artists. By the mid-1950s, rock and roll was gaining acceptance with the masses, but rock-and-roll artists and promoters still faced further obstacles: Black artists found that their music was often undermined by white cover versions; the payola scandals portrayed rock and roll as a corrupt industry; and fears of rock and roll as a contributing factor in juvenile delinquency resulted in censorship.

KATY PERRY
Many of today's biggest pop music stars show off not just catchy radio-ready singles, but eye-grabbing fashion, memorable music videos, and multimillion-dollar live shows. Perry's 3-D concert movie, *Part of Me,* was released in theaters in 2012.

"[Elvis Presley's] kind of music is deplorable, a rancid smelling aphrodisiac."

FRANK SINATRA, 1956

"There have been many accolades uttered about [Presley's] talent and performances through the years, all of which I agree with wholeheartedly."

FRANK SINATRA, 1977

ELVIS PRESLEY AND HIS LEGACY
Elvis Presley remains the most popular solo artist of all time. From 1956 to 1962, he recorded seventeen No. 1 hits, from "Heartbreak Hotel" to "Good Luck Charm." According to Little Richard, Presley's main legacy was that he opened doors for many young performers and made black music popular in mainstream America. Presley's influence continues to be felt today in the music of artists like Bruno Mars.

White Cover Music Undermines Black Artists

By the mid-1960s, black and white artists routinely recorded and performed one another's original tunes. For example, established black R&B artist Otis Redding covered the Rolling Stones' "Satisfaction" and Jimi Hendrix covered Bob Dylan's "All along the Watchtower," while just about every white rock-and-roll band established its career by covering R&B classics. Most notably, the Beatles covered "Twist and Shout" and "Money" and the Rolling Stones—whose name came from a Muddy Waters song—covered numerous Robert Johnson songs and other blues staples.

Although today we take such rerecordings for granted, in the 1950s the covering of black artists' songs by white musicians was almost always an attempt to capitalize on popular songs from the R&B "race" charts and transform them into hits on the white pop charts. Often, white producers would not only give co-writing credit to white performers for the tunes they only covered, but they would also buy the rights to potential hits from black songwriters who seldom saw a penny in royalties or received songwriting credit.

During this period, black R&B artists, working for small record labels, saw many of their popular songs covered by white artists working for major labels. These cover records, boosted by better marketing and ties to white deejays, usually outsold the original black versions. For instance, the 1954 R&B song "Sh-Boom," by the Chords on Atlantic's Cat label, was immediately covered by a white group, the Crew Cuts, for the major Mercury label. Record sales declined for the Chords, although jukebox and R&B radio play remained strong for their original version. By 1955, R&B hits regularly crossed over to the pop charts, but inevitably the cover music versions were more successful. Pat Boone's cover of Fats Domino's "Ain't That a Shame" went to No. 1 and stayed on the Top 40's pop chart for twenty weeks, whereas Domino's original made it only to No. 10. During this time, Pat Boone ranked as the king of cover music, with thirty-eight Top 40 songs between 1955 and 1962. His records were second in sales only to Elvis Presley's. Slowly, however, the cover situation changed. After watching Boone outsell his song "Tutti-Frutti" in 1956, Little Richard wrote "Long Tall Sally," which included lyrics written and delivered in such a way that he believed Boone would not be able to adequately replicate them. "Long Tall Sally" went to No. 6 for Little Richard and charted for twelve weeks; Boone's version got to No. 8 and stayed there for nine weeks.

Overt racism lingered in the music business well into the 1960s. A turning point, however, came in 1962, the last year that Pat Boone, then age twenty-eight, ever had a Top 40 rock-and-roll hit. That year, Ray Charles covered "I Can't Stop Loving You," a 1958 country song by the Grand Ole Opry's Don Gibson. This marked the first time that a black artist, covering a white artist's song, had notched a No. 1 pop hit. With Charles's cover, the rock-and-roll merger between gospel and R&B, on one hand, and white country and pop, on the other, was complete. In fact, the relative acceptance of black crossover music provided a more favorable cultural context for the political activism that spurred important Civil Rights legislation in the mid-1960s.

Payola Scandals Tarnish Rock and Roll

The payola scandals of the 1950s were another cloud over rock-and-roll music and its artists. In the music industry, *payola* is the practice of record promoters paying deejays or radio programmers to play particular songs. As recorded rock and roll became central to commercial radio's success in the 1950s and the demand for airplay grew enormous, independent promoters hired by record labels used payola to pressure deejays into playing songs by the artists they represented.

Although payola was considered a form of bribery, no laws prohibited its practice. However, following closely on the heels of television's quiz-show scandals (see Chapter 6), congressional hearings on radio payola began in December 1959. The hearings were partly a response to generally fraudulent business practices, but they were also an opportunity to blame deejays and radio for rock and roll's negative impact on teens by portraying it as a corrupt industry.

The payola scandals threatened, ended, or damaged the careers of a number of rock-and-roll deejays and undermined rock and roll's credibility for a number of years. In 1959, shortly before the hearings, Chicago deejay Phil Lind decided to clear the air. He broadcast secretly taped discussions in which a representative of a small independent record label acknowledged that it had paid $22,000 to ensure that a record would get airplay. Lind received calls threatening his life and had to have police protection. At the hearings in 1960, Alan Freed admitted to participating in payola, although he said he did not believe there was anything illegal about such deals, and his career soon ended. Dick Clark, then an influential deejay and the host of TV's *American Bandstand*, would not admit to participating in payola. But the hearings committee chastised Clark and alleged that some of his complicated business deals were ethically questionable, a censure that hung over him for years. Congress eventually added a law concerning payola to the Federal Communications Act, prescribing a $10,000 fine and/or a year in jail for each violation (see Chapter 5).

Fears of Corruption Lead to Censorship

Since rock and roll's inception, one of the uphill battles it faced was the perception that it was a cause of juvenile delinquency, which was statistically on the rise in the 1950s. Looking for an easy culprit rather than considering contributing factors such as neglect, the rising consumer culture, or the growing youth population, many assigned blame to rock and roll. The view that rock and roll corrupted youth was widely accepted by social authorities, and rock-and-roll music was often censored, eventually even by the industry itself.

By late 1959, many key figures in rock and roll had been tamed. Jerry Lee Lewis was exiled from the industry, labeled southern "white trash" for marrying his thirteen-year-old third cousin; Elvis Presley, having already been censored on television, was drafted into the army; Chuck Berry was run out of Mississippi and eventually jailed for gun possession and transporting a minor across state lines; and Little Richard felt forced to tone down his image and left rock and roll to sing gospel music. A tragic accident led to the final taming of rock and roll's first frontline. In February 1959, Buddy Holly ("Peggy Sue"), Ritchie Valens ("La Bamba"), and the Big Bopper ("Chantilly Lace") all died in an Iowa plane crash—a tragedy mourned in Don McLean's 1971 hit "American Pie" as "the day the music died."

Although rock and roll did not die in the late 1950s, the U.S. recording industry decided that it needed a makeover. To protect the enormous profits the new music had been generating, record companies began to discipline some of rock and roll's rebellious impulses. In the early 1960s, the industry introduced a new generation of clean-cut white singers, like Frankie Avalon, Connie Francis, Ricky Nelson, Lesley Gore, and Fabian. Rock and roll's explosive violations of racial, class, and other boundaries were transformed into simpler generation gap problems, and the music developed a milder reputation.

A Changing Industry: Reformations in Popular Music

> "Hard rock was rock's blues base electrified and upped in volume . . . heavy metal wanted to be the rock music equivalent of a horror movie—loud, exaggerated, rude, out for thrills only."
>
> KEN TUCKER, *ROCK OF AGES*, 1986

As the 1960s began, rock and roll was tamer and "safer," as reflected in the surf and road music of the Beach Boys and Jan & Dean, but it was also beginning to branch out. For instance, the success of all-female groups, such as the Shangri-Las ("Leader of the Pack") and the Angels ("My Boyfriend's Back"), challenged the male-dominated world of early rock and roll. In addition, rock-and-roll music and other popular styles went through cultural reformations that significantly changed the industry, including the international appeal of the "British invasion"; the development of soul and Motown; the political impact of folk-rock; the experimentalism of psychedelic music; the rejection of music's mainstream by punk, grunge, and alternative rock movements; and the reassertion of black urban style in hip-hop.

The British Are Coming!

Rock recordings today remain among America's largest economic exports, bringing in billions of dollars a year from abroad. In cultural terms, the global trade of rock and roll is even more evident in the exchanges and melding of rhythms, beats, vocal styles, and musical instruments. The origin of rock's global impact can be traced to England in the late 1950s, when the young Rolling Stones listened to the blues of Robert Johnson and Muddy Waters, and the young Beatles tried to imitate Chuck Berry and Little Richard.

Until 1964, rock-and-roll recordings had traveled on a one-way ticket to Europe. Even though American artists regularly reached the top of the charts overseas, no British performers had yet appeared on any Top 10 pop lists in the States. This changed almost overnight. In 1964, the Beatles invaded America with their mop haircuts and pop reinterpretations of American blues and rock and roll. Within the next few years, more British bands as diverse as the Kinks, the Rolling Stones, the Zombies, the Animals, Herman's Hermits, the Who, the Yardbirds, Them, and the Troggs had hit the American Top 40 charts.

With the British invasion, "rock and roll" unofficially became "rock," sending popular music and the industry in two directions. On the one hand, the Rolling Stones would influence generations of musicians emphasizing gritty, chord-driven, high-volume rock, including bands in the glam rock, hard rock, punk, heavy metal, and grunge genres. On the other hand, the Beatles would influence countless artists interested in a more accessible, melodic, and softer sound, in genres such as pop-rock, power-pop, new wave, and alternative rock. In the end, the British invasion verified what Chuck Berry and Little Richard had already demonstrated–that rock-and-roll performers could write and produce popular songs as well as Tin Pan Alley had. The success of British groups helped change an industry arrangement in which most pop music was produced by songwriting teams hired by major labels and matched with selected performers. Even more

BRITISH ROCK GROUPS
Ed Sullivan, who booked the Beatles several times on his TV variety show in 1964, helped promote their early success. Sullivan, though, reacted differently to the Rolling Stones, who were perceived as the "bad boys" of rock and roll in contrast to the "good" Beatles. The Stones performed black-influenced music without "whitening" the sound and exuded a palpable aura of sexuality, particularly frontman Mick Jagger. Although the Stones appeared on his program as early as 1964 and returned on several occasions, Sullivan remained wary and forced them to change the lyrics of "Let's Spend the Night Together" to "Let's Spend Some Time Together" for a 1967 broadcast.

important, the British invasion showed the recording industry how older American musical forms, especially blues and R&B, could be repackaged as rock and exported around the world.

Motor City Music: Detroit Gives America Soul

Ironically, the British invasion, which drew much of its inspiration from black influences, drew many white listeners away from a new generation of black performers. Gradually, however, throughout the 1960s, black singers like James Brown, Aretha Franklin, Otis Redding, Ike and Tina Turner, and Wilson Pickett found large and diverse audiences. Transforming the rhythms and melodies of older R&B, pop, and early rock and roll into what became labeled as **soul**, they countered the British invaders with powerful vocal performances. Mixing gospel and blues with emotion and lyrics drawn from the American black experience, soul contrasted sharply with the emphasis on loud, fast instrumentals and lighter lyrical concerns that characterized much of rock music.[19]

The most prominent independent label that nourished soul and black popular music was Motown, started in 1959 by former Detroit autoworker and songwriter Berry Gordy with a $700 investment and named after Detroit's "Motor City" nickname. Beginning with Smokey Robinson and the Miracles' "Shop Around," which hit No. 2 in 1960, Motown enjoyed a long string of hit records that rivaled the pop success of British bands throughout the decade. Motown's many successful artists included the Temptations ("My Girl"), Mary Wells ("My Guy"), the Four Tops ("I Can't Help Myself"), Martha and the Vandellas ("Heat Wave"), Marvin Gaye ("I Heard It through the Grapevine"), and, in the early 1970s, the Jackson 5 ("ABC"). But the label's most successful group was the Supremes, featuring Diana Ross, who scored twelve No. 1 singles between 1964 and 1969 ("Where Did Our Love Go," "Stop! In the Name of Love"). The Motown groups had a more stylized, softer sound than the grittier southern soul (later known as funk) of Brown and Pickett.

Folk and Psychedelic Music Reflect the Times

Popular music has always been a product of its time, so the social upheavals of the Civil Rights movement, the women's movement, the environmental movement, and the Vietnam War naturally brought social concerns into the music of the 1960s and early 1970s. Even Motown

acts sounded edgy, with hits like Edwin Starr's "War" (1970) and Marvin Gaye's "What's Goin' On" (1971). By the late 1960s, the Beatles had transformed themselves from a relatively lightweight pop band to one that spoke for the social and political concerns of their generation, and many other groups followed the same trajectory. (To explore how the times and personal taste influence music choices, see "Media Literacy and the Critical Process: Music Preferences across Generations" on page 138.)

Folk Inspires Protest

The musical genre that most clearly responded to the political happenings of the time was folk music, which had long been the sound of social activism. In its broadest sense, **folk music** in any culture refers to songs performed by untrained musicians and passed down mainly through oral traditions, from the banjo and fiddle tunes of Appalachia to the accordion-led zydeco of Louisiana and the folk-blues of the legendary Lead Belly (Huddie Ledbetter). During the 1930s, folk was defined by the music of Woody Guthrie ("This Land Is Your Land"), who not only brought folk to the city but also was extremely active in social reforms. Groups such as the Weavers, featuring labor activist and songwriter Pete Seeger, carried on Guthrie's legacy and inspired a new generation of singer-songwriters, including Joan Baez; Arlo Guthrie; Peter, Paul, and Mary; Phil Ochs; and–perhaps the most influential–Bob Dylan. Dylan's career as a folk artist began with acoustic performances in New York's Greenwich Village in 1961, and his notoriety was spurred by his measured nonchalance and unique nasal voice. Significantly influenced by the blues, Dylan identified folk as "finger pointin'" music that addressed current social circumstances. At a key moment in popular music's history, Dylan walked onstage at the 1965 Newport Folk Festival fronting a full, electric rock band. He was booed and cursed by traditional "folkies," who saw amplified music as a sellout to the commercial recording industry. However, Dylan's move to rock was aimed at reaching a broader and younger constituency, and in doing so he inspired the formation of **folk-rock** artists like the Byrds, who had a No. 1 hit with a cover of Dylan's "Mr. Tambourine Man," and led millions to protest during the turbulent 1960s.

Media Literacy and the Critical Process

Music Preferences across Generations

We make judgments about music all the time. Older generations don't like some of the music younger people prefer, and young people often dismiss some of the music of previous generations. Even among our peers, we have different tastes in music and often reject certain kinds of music that have become too popular or that don't conform to our own preferences. The following exercise aims to understand musical tastes beyond our own individual choices. Always include yourself in this project.

1 DESCRIPTION. Arrange to interview four to eight friends or relatives of different ages about their musical tastes and influences. Devise questions about what music they listen to and have listened to at different stages of their lives. What music do they buy or collect? What's the first album (or single) they acquired? What's the latest album? What stories or vivid memories do they relate to particular songs or artists? Collect demographic and consumer information: age, gender, occupation, educational background, place of birth, and current place of residence.

2 ANALYSIS. Chart and organize your results. Do you recognize any patterns emerging from the data or stories? What kinds of music did your interview subjects listen to when they were younger? What kinds of music do they listen to now? What formed/influenced their musical interests? If their musical interests changed, what happened? (If they stopped listening to music, note that and find out why.) Do they have any associations between music and their everyday lives? Are these music associations and lifetime interactions with songs and artists important to them?

3 INTERPRETATION. Based on what you have discovered and the patterns you have charted, determine what the patterns mean. Does age, gender, geographic location, or education matter in musical tastes? Over time, are the changes in musical tastes and buying habits significant? Why or why not? What kind of music is most important to your subjects? Finally, and most important, why do you think their music preferences developed as they did?

4 EVALUATION. Determine how your interview subjects came to like particular kinds of music. What constitutes "good" and "bad" music for them? Did their ideas change over time? How? Are they open- or closed-minded about music? How do they form judgments about music? What criteria did your interview subjects offer for making judgments about music? Do you think their criteria are a valid way to judge music?

5 ENGAGEMENT. To expand on your findings and see how they match up with industry practices, contact music professionals. Track down record label representatives from a small indie label and a large mainstream label, and ask them whom they are trying to target with their music. How do they find out about the musical tastes of their consumers? Share your findings with them, and discuss whether these match their practices. Speculate whether the music industry is serving the needs and tastes of you and your interview subjects. If not, what might be done to change the current system?

> "Through their raw, nihilistic singles and violent performances, the [Sex Pistols] revolutionized the idea of what rock and roll could be."
>
> STEPHEN THOMAS ERLEWINE, *ALL-MUSIC GUIDE*, 1996

Rock Turns Psychedelic

Alcohol and drugs have long been associated with the private lives of blues, jazz, country, and rock musicians. These links, however, became much more public in the late 1960s and early 1970s, when authorities busted members of the Rolling Stones and the Beatles. With the increasing role of drugs in youth culture and the availability of LSD (not illegal until the mid-1960s), more and more rock musicians experimented with and sang about drugs in what were frequently labeled rock's psychedelic years. Many groups and performers of the *psychedelic* era (named for the mind-altering effects of LSD and other drugs) like the Jefferson Airplane, Big Brother and the Holding Company (featuring Janis Joplin), the Jimi Hendrix Experience, the Doors, and the Grateful Dead (as well as established artists like the Beatles and the Stones) believed that artistic expression could be enhanced by mind-altering drugs. The 1960s drug explorations coincided with the free-speech movement, in which many artists and followers saw experimenting with drugs as a form of personal expression and a response to the failure of traditional institutions to deal with social and political problems such as racism and America's involvement in the Vietnam War. But after a surge of optimism that culminated in the historic Woodstock concert in August 1969, the psychedelic movement was quickly overshadowed. In 1969, a similar concert at the Altamont racetrack in California started in chaos and ended in tragedy when one of the Hell's Angels hired as a bodyguard for the show murdered a concertgoer. Around the same time, the shocking multiple murders committed by the Charles Manson "family" cast a negative light on hippies, drug use, and psychedelic culture. Then, in quick succession, a number of the psychedelic movement's greatest stars died from drug overdoses, including Janis Joplin, Jimi Hendrix, and Jim Morrison of the Doors.

Punk, Grunge, and Alternative Respond to Mainstream Rock

By the 1970s, rock music was increasingly viewed as just another part of mainstream consumer culture. With major music acts earning huge profits, rock soon became another product line for manufacturers and retailers to promote, package, and sell—primarily to middle-class white male teens. According to critic Ken Tucker, this situation gave rise to "faceless rock—crisply recorded, eminently catchy," featuring anonymous hits by bands with "no established individual personalities outside their own large but essentially discrete audiences" of young white males.[20] Some rock musicians like Bruce Springsteen and Elton John; glam artists like David Bowie, Lou Reed, and Iggy Pop; and soul artists like Curtis Mayfield and Marvin Gaye continued to explore the social possibilities of rock or at least keep its legacy of outrageousness alive. But they had, for the most part, been replaced by "faceless" supergroups like REO Speedwagon, Styx, Boston, and Kansas. By the late 1970s, rock could only seem to define itself by saying what it wasn't; "Disco Sucks" became a standard rock slogan against the popular dance music of the era.

BOB DYLAN
Born Robert Allen Zimmerman in Minnesota, Bob Dylan took his stage name from Welsh poet Dylan Thomas. He led a folk music movement in the early 1960s with engaging, socially provocative lyrics. He also was an astute media critic, as is evident in the seminal documentary *Dont Look Back* (1967).

Punk Revives Rock's Rebelliousness

After a few years, **punk rock** rose in the late 1970s to challenge the orthodoxy and commercialism of the record business. By this time, the glory days of rock's competitive independent labels had ended, and rock music was controlled by just a half-dozen major companies. By avoiding rock's consumer popularity, punk attempted to return to the basics of rock and roll: simple chord structures, catchy melodies, and politically or socially challenging lyrics. The premise was "do it yourself": Any teenager with a few weeks of guitar practice could learn the sound and make music that was both more democratic and more provocative than commercial rock.

The punk movement took root in the small dive bar CBGB in New York City around bands such as the Ramones, Blondie, and the Talking Heads. (The roots of punk essentially lay in four pre-punk groups from the late 1960s and early 1970s—the Velvet Underground, the Stooges, the New York Dolls, and the MC5—none of whom experienced commercial success in their day.) Punk quickly spread to England, where a soaring unemployment rate and growing class inequality ensured the success of socially critical rock. Groups like the Sex Pistols, the Clash, the Buzzcocks, and Siouxsie and the Banshees sprang up and even scored Top 40 hits on the U.K. charts.

Punk was not a commercial success in the United States, where (not surprisingly) it was shunned by radio. However, punk's contributions continue to be felt. Punk broke down the "boy's club" mentality of rock, launching unapologetic and unadorned frontwomen like Patti

WILD FLAG
All-female bands like Wild Flag continue to take on the boy's-club mentality of rock and roll. The band formed in 2010, featuring members of the 1990s alternative/punk trio Sleater-Kinney and developing a style that combines the energy of punk with some elements of classic rock.

"We're like reporters. We give them [our listeners] the truth. People where we come from hear so many lies the truth stands out like a sore thumb."

EAZY-E, N.W.A, 1989

Smith, Joan Jett, Debbie Harry, and Chrissie Hynde; and it introduced all-women bands (writing and performing their own music) like the Go-Go's into the mainstream. It also reopened the door to rock experimentation at a time when the industry had turned music into a purely commercial enterprise. The influence of experimental, or post-punk, music is still felt today in alternative bands such as the Yeah Yeah Yeahs, Wild Flag, and Dirty Projectors.

Grunge and Alternative Reinterpret Rock

Taking the spirit of punk and updating it, the **grunge** scene represented a significant development in rock in the 1990s. Getting its name from its often messy guitar sound and the anti-fashion torn jeans and flannel shirt appearance of its musicians and fans, grunge's lineage can be traced back to 1980s bands like Sonic Youth, the Minutemen, and Hüsker Dü. In 1992, after years of limited commercial success, the younger cousin of punk finally broke into the American mainstream with the success of Nirvana's "Smells Like Teen Spirit" on the album *Nevermind*. Led by enigmatic singer Kurt Cobain—who committed suicide in 1994—Nirvana produced songs that one critic described as "stunning, concise bursts of melody and rage that occasionally spilled over into haunting, folk-styled acoustic ballad."[21] Nirvana opened up the floodgates to bands such as Green Day, Pearl Jam, Soundgarden, the Breeders, Hole, Nine Inch Nails, and many others.

In some critical circles, both punk and grunge are considered subcategories or fringe movements of **alternative rock**. This vague label describes many types of experimental rock music that offered a departure from the theatrics and staged extravaganzas of 1970s glam rock, which showcased such performers as David Bowie and Kiss. Appealing chiefly to college students and twentysomethings, alternative rock has traditionally opposed the sounds of Top 40 and commercial FM radio. In the 1980s and 1990s, U2 and R.E.M. emerged as successful groups often associated with alternative rock. A key dilemma for successful alternative performers, however, is that their popularity results in commercial success, ironically a situation that their music often criticizes. While alternative rock music has more variety than ever, it is also not producing new mega-groups like Nirvana, Pearl Jam, and Green Day. Still, alternative groups like Arctic Monkeys, Vampire Weekend, and MGMT have launched successful recording careers the old-school way, but with a twist: starting out on independent labels, playing small concerts, and growing popular quickly with alternative music audiences through the immediate buzz of the Internet.

Hip-Hop Redraws Musical Lines

With the growing segregation of radio formats and the dominance of mainstream rock by white male performers, the place of black artists in the rock world diminished from the late 1970s onward. By the 1980s, few popular black successors to Chuck Berry or Jimi Hendrix had emerged in rock, though Michael Jackson and Prince were extremely popular exceptions. These trends, combined with the rise of "safe" dance disco by white bands (the Bee Gees), black artists (Donna Summer), and integrated groups (the Village People), created a space for a new sound to emerge: **hip-hop**, a term for the urban culture that includes *rapping*, *cutting* (or *sampling*) by deejays, breakdancing, street clothing, poetry slams, and graffiti art.

Similar to punk's opposition to commercial rock, hip-hop music stood in direct opposition to the polished, professional, and often less political world of soul. Its combination of

social politics, swagger, and confrontational lyrics carried forward long-standing traditions in blues, R&B, soul, and rock and roll. Like punk and early rock and roll, hip-hop was driven by a democratic, nonprofessional spirit and was cheap to produce, requiring only a few mikes, speakers, amps, turntables, and vinyl records. Deejays, like the pioneering Jamaica émigré Clive Campbell (a.k.a. DJ Kool Herc), emerged first in New York, scratching and re-cueing old reggae, disco, soul, and rock albums. These deejays, or MCs (masters of ceremony), used humor, boasts, and "trash talking" to entertain and keep the peace at parties.

The music industry initially saw hip-hop as a novelty, despite the enormous success of the Sugarhill Gang's "Rapper's Delight" in 1979 (which sampled the bass beat of a disco hit from the same year, Chic's "Good Times"). Then, in 1982, Grandmaster Flash and the Furious Five released "The Message" and forever infused hip-hop with a political take on ghetto life, a tradition continued by artists like Public Enemy and Ice-T. By 1985, hip-hop exploded as a popular genre with the commercial successes of groups like Run-DMC, the Fat Boys, and LL Cool J. That year, Run-DMC's album *Raising Hell* became a major crossover hit, the first No. 1 hip-hop album on the popular charts (thanks in part to a collaboration with Aerosmith on a rap version of the group's 1976 hit "Walk This Way"). But because most major labels and many black radio stations rejected the rawness of hip-hop, the music spawned hundreds of new independent labels. Although initially dominated by male performers, hip-hop was open to women, and some–Salt-N-Pepa and Queen Latifah among them–quickly became major players. Soon, white groups like the Beastie Boys, Limp Bizkit, and Kid Rock were combining hip-hop and punk rock in a commercially successful way, while Eminem found enormous success emulating black rap artists.

On the one hand, the conversational style of rap makes it a forum in which performers can debate issues of gender, class, sexuality, violence, and drugs. On the other hand, hip-hop, like punk, has often drawn criticism for lyrics that degrade women, espouse homophobia, and applaud violence. Although hip-hop encompasses many different styles, including various Latin and Asian offshoots, its most controversial subgenre is probably **gangster rap**, which, in seeking to tell the truth about gang violence in American culture, has been accused of creating violence. Gangster rap drew national attention in 1996 with the shooting death of Tupac Shakur, who lived the violent life he rapped about on albums like *Thug Life*. Then, in 1997, Notorious B.I.G. (Christopher Wallace, a.k.a. Biggie Smalls), whose followers were prominent suspects in Shakur's death, was shot to death in Hollywood. The result was a change in the hip-hop industry. Most prominently, Sean "Diddy" Combs led Bad Boy Entertainment (former home of Notorious B.I.G.) away from gangster rap to a more danceable hip-hop that combined singing and rapping with musical elements of rock and soul. Today, hip-hop's stars include artists such as 50 Cent, who emulates the gangster genre, and artists like will.i.am, Lupe Fiasco, Talib Kweli, and M.I.A. who bring an old-school social consciousness to their performances.

The Reemergence of Pop

After waves of punk, grunge, alternative, and hip-hop, the decline of Top 40 radio, and the demise of MTV's *Total Request Live* countdown show, it seemed like pop music and the era of big pop

NIRVANA'S lead singer, Kurt Cobain, during his brief career in the early 1990s. The release of Nirvana's *Nevermind* in September 1991 bumped Michael Jackson's *Dangerous* from the top of the charts and signaled a new direction in popular music. Other grunge bands soon followed Nirvana onto the charts, including Pearl Jam, Alice in Chains, Stone Temple Pilots, and Soundgarden.

KANYE WEST AND JAY-Z, two of the biggest names in the music industry, released a collaborative album, *Watch The Throne*, in 2011.

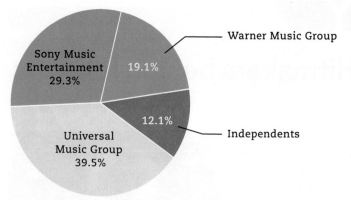

▲

FIGURE 4.2

**U.S. MARKET SHARE
OF THE MAJOR LABELS
IN THE RECORDING
INDUSTRY, 2011**

*Source: Nielsen
SoundScan, 2012*

Note: Figure combines UMG's and
EMI's pre-merger market shares.

INDIE LABELS are able
to take chances on artists
like Bon Iver, who became
a break-out success on the
Jagjaguwar label in 2008.
Bon Iver has remained on an
indie even after the band's
founder, Justin Verbon, has
worked with major-label
stars like Kanye West.

▼

Fewer Major Labels Control More Music

From the 1950s through the 1980s, the music industry, though powerful, consisted of a large number of competing major labels, along with numerous independent labels. Over time, the major labels began swallowing up the independents and then buying one another. By 1998, only six major labels remained–Universal, Warner, Sony, BMG, EMI, and Polygram. That year, Universal acquired Polygram, and in 2003 BMG and Sony merged. (BMG left the partnership in 2008.) In 2012, Universal gained regulatory approval to purchase EMI's recorded music division. Now, only three major music corporations will remain: Universal Music Group, Sony Music Entertainment, and Warner Music Group. Together, these companies control nearly 90 percent of the recording industry market in the United States (see Figure 4.2). Although their revenue has eroded over the past decade, the major music corporations still wield great power, as they can control when and how their artists' music will be licensed to play on new distribution services.

The Indies Spot the Trends

The rise of rock and roll in the 1950s and early 1960s showcased a rich diversity of independent labels–including Sun, Stax, Chess, and Motown–all vying for a share of the new music. That tradition lives on today. In contrast to the three global players, some five thousand large and small independent production houses–or **indies**–record less commercially viable music, or music they hope will become commercially viable. Often struggling enterprises, indies require only a handful of people to operate them. Producing between 11 and 15 percent of America's music, indies often depend on wholesale distributors to promote and sell their music, or enter into deals with majors to gain wider distribution for their artists. The Internet has also become a low-cost distribution outlet for independent labels, which sell recordings and merchandise and list tour schedules online. (See "Alternative Voices" on page 149.)

Indies play a major role as the music industry's risk-takers, since major labels are reluctant to invest in commercially unproven artists. The majors frequently rely on indies to discover and initiate distinctive musical trends that first appear on a local level. For instance, indies such as Sugarhill, Tommy Boy, and Uptown emerged in the 1980s to produce regional hip-hop. In the early 2000s, bands of the "indie-rock" movement, such as Yo La Tengo and Arcade Fire, found their home on indie labels Matador and Merge. Once indies become successful, the financial inducement to sell out to a major label is enormous. Seattle indie Sub Pop (Nirvana's initial recording label) sold 49 percent of its stock to Time Warner for $20 million in 1994. However, the punk label Epitaph rejected takeover offers as high as $50 million in the 1990s and remains independent. All the major labels look for and swallow up independent labels that have successfully developed artists with national or global appeal.

Making, Selling, and Profiting from Music

Like most mass media, the music business is divided into several areas, each working in a different capacity. In the music industry, those areas are making the music (signing, developing, and recording the artist), selling the music (selling, distributing, advertising, and promoting the music), and sharing the profits. All of these areas are essential to the industry but have always shared in the conflict between business concerns and artistic concerns.

Making the Music

Labels are driven by **A&R (artist & repertoire) agents**, the talent scouts of the music business, who discover, develop, and sometimes manage artists. A&R executives scan online music sites and listen to demonstration tapes, or *demos*, from new artists and decide whom to sign and which songs to record. A&R executives naturally look for artists who they think will sell, and they are often forced to avoid artists with limited commercial possibilities or to tailor artists to make them viable for the recording studio.

A typical recording session is a complex process that involves the artist, the producer, the session engineer, and audio technicians. In charge of the overall recording process, the producer handles most nontechnical elements of the session, including reserving studio space, hiring session musicians (if necessary), and making final decisions about the sound of the recording. The session engineer oversees the technical aspects of the recording session, everything from choosing recording equipment to managing the audio technicians. Most popular records are recorded part by part. Using separate microphones, the vocalists, guitarists, drummers, and other musical sections are digitally recorded onto separate audio tracks, which are edited and remixed during postproduction and ultimately mixed down to a two-track stereo master copy for reproduction to CD or online digital distribution.

Selling the Music

Selling and distributing music is a tricky part of the business. For years, the primary sales outlets for music were direct-retail record stores (independents or chains such as Sam Goody) and general retail outlets like Walmart, Best Buy, and Target. Such direct retailers could specialize in music, carefully monitoring new releases and keeping large, varied inventories. But as digital sales climbed, CD sales fell, hurting direct retail sales considerably. In 2006, Tower Records declared bankruptcy, closed its retail locations, and became an online-only retailer. Sam Goody stores were shuttered in 2008, and Virgin closed its last U.S. megastore in 2009. Meanwhile, other independent record stores either went out of business or experienced great losses, and general retail outlets began to offer considerably less variety, stocking only top-selling CDs.

At the same time, digital sales have grown to capture 50 percent of the U.S. market and 32 percent of the global market.[22] Apple's iTunes now sells songs at prices ranging from $0.69 to $1.49. It has become the leading music retailer, selling 38.2 percent of all music purchased in the United States. (See "What Apple Owns" at right.) Anderson Merchandisers, the behind-the-scenes wholesaler that stocks and manages music inventories at Walmart and Best Buy, is the second biggest music seller, at about 18 percent of the market, followed by Amazon (which also sells digital downloads) in third place, with 8 percent of the market. Alliance Entertainment, a wholesaler that manages and ships recorded music for several hundred online stores, is fourth, with a 6 percent market share.[23]

In addition to the top music retailers who sell digital downloads and physical CDs, subscription music streaming services like Rhapsody, Spotify, MOG, and Rdio are a small but growing market that can also generate revenue for music labels and their artists. But some leading

▶

WHAT APPLE OWNS

Consider how Apple connects to your life; turn the page for the bigger picture.

ELECTRONICS
- iPod
- iPod Classic
- iPod Nano
- iPod Shuffle
- iPod Touch
- iPhone
- iPad
- Apple TV
- iMac
- MacBook Air
- MacBook Pro
- Mac Mini
- Mac Pro
- Magic Mouse
- Time Capsule
- Magic Track Pad
- Airport Express
- Airport Extreme

RETAIL SERVICES
- iTunes
- App Store
- iBooks
- iMusic
- Apple Retail Stores

OPERATING SYSTEMS
- iOS
- OS X

SOFTWARE
- Aperture (photograph manipulation software)
- Apple Remote (desktop management software)
- FaceTime for Mac (video calling interface)
- Final Cut Pro X (digital video editing software)
- iMovie
- iPhoto
- iWork
- iWeb
- iDVD
- Keynote
- Pages
- Numbers
- GarageBand
- Logic Studio
- Safari

CLOUD SERVICES
- iCloud

Turn page for more ▶

artists—including Adele, the Black Keys, and Coldplay—have held back their new releases from such services due to concerns that streaming eats into their digital download and CD sales. "Part of the reason is that a song has to be played between 100 and 150 times on a streaming service in order to generate the same licensing revenue as a single download sale," the *Los Angeles Times* reported.[24] Yet, a later analysis by the same newspaper suggested there isn't a clear relationship between streaming activity and digital download sales.[25]

As noted earlier, some established rock acts like Nine Inch Nails and Amanda Palmer are taking the "alternative" approach to their business model, shunning major labels and using the Internet to directly reach their fans. By selling music online at their own Web sites or CDs at live concerts, music acts generally do better, cutting out the retailer and keeping more of the revenue themselves.

Legitimate online music sales are now a growing success, and in 2011 the music industry recorded its first year of growth since 2004. Although **online piracy**—unauthorized online file sharing—is still a problem, with about one-quarter of Internet users worldwide accessing unauthorized music content each month, the international recording industry group IPFI reported in 2012 that "we are undoubtedly making important progress" toward "developing a sustainable legitimate digital music sector." There are now about five hundred legal online music services worldwide.[26]

Dividing the Profits

The upheaval in the music industry in recent years has shaken up the once predictable sale of music through CDs. Now there are multiple digital venues for selling music.[27] But for the sake of example, we will first look at the various costs and profits from a typical CD that retails at $17.98. The wholesale price for that CD is about $12.50, leaving the remainder as retail profit. Discount retailers like Walmart and Best Buy sell closer to the wholesale price to lure customers to buy other things (even if they make less profit on the CD itself). The wholesale price represents the actual cost of producing and promoting the recording, plus the recording label's profits. The record company reaps the highest revenue (close to $9.74 on a typical CD) but, along with the artist, bears the bulk of the expenses: manufacturing costs, packaging and CD design, advertising and promotion, and artists' royalties (see Figure 4.3 on page 147). The physical product of the CD itself costs less than a quarter to manufacture.

New artists usually negotiate a royalty rate of between 8 and 12 percent on the retail price of a CD, while more established performers might negotiate for 15 percent or higher. An artist who has negotiated a typical 11 percent royalty rate would earn about $1.93 per CD whose suggested retail price is $17.98. So a CD that "goes gold"—that is, sells 500,000 units—would net the artist around $965,000. But out of this amount, artists must repay the record company the money they have been advanced (from $100,000 to $500,000). And after band members, managers, and attorneys are paid with the remaining money, it's quite possible that an artist will end up with almost nothing—even after a certified gold CD. (See "Case Study: In the Jungle, the Unjust Jungle, a Small Victory" on page 148.) The financial risk is much lower for the songwriter/publisher, who makes a standard mechanical royalty rate of about 9.1 cents per song, or $0.91 for a ten-song CD, without having to bear any production or promotional costs.

The profits are divided somewhat differently in digital download sales. A $1.29 iTunes download generates about $0.40 for iTunes (iTunes gets 30 percent of every song sale) and a standard $0.09 mechanical royalty for the song publisher and writer, leaving about $0.60 for the record company. Artists at a typical royalty rate of about 15 percent would get $0.20 from the song download. With no CD printing and packaging costs, record companies can retain more of the revenue on download sales.

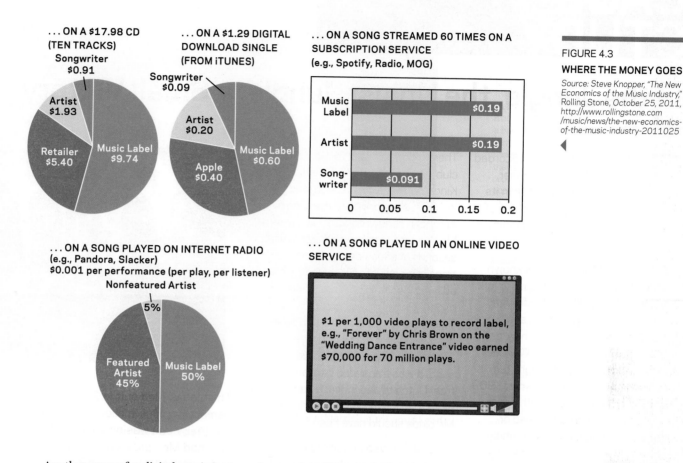

... ON A $17.98 CD (TEN TRACKS)

Songwriter $0.91
Artist $1.93
Retailer $5.40
Music Label $9.74

... ON A $1.29 DIGITAL DOWNLOAD SINGLE (FROM iTUNES)

Songwriter $0.09
Artist $0.20
Apple $0.40
Music Label $0.60

... ON A SONG STREAMED 60 TIMES ON A SUBSCRIPTION SERVICE (e.g., Spotify, Radio, MOG)

Music Label	$0.19
Artist	$0.19
Songwriter	$0.091

0   0.05   0.1   0.15   0.2

... ON A SONG PLAYED ON INTERNET RADIO (e.g., Pandora, Slacker)
$0.001 per performance (per play, per listener)

Nonfeatured Artist 5%
Featured Artist 45%
Music Label 50%

... ON A SONG PLAYED IN AN ONLINE VIDEO SERVICE

$1 per 1,000 video plays to record label, e.g., "Forever" by Chris Brown on the "Wedding Dance Entrance" video earned $70,000 for 70 million plays.

FIGURE 4.3
WHERE THE MONEY GOES
Source: Steve Knopper, "The New Economics of the Music Industry," Rolling Stone, *October 25, 2011,* http://www.rollingstone.com /music/news/the-new-economics- of-the-music-industry-2011025

Another venue for digital music is streaming services like Spotify, MOG, and Rdio. A single stream isn't worth much, but collectively, they generate more substantial revenue. A song streamed sixty times is about the equivalent of one download and generates about $0.38 for the label and the artist, who—depending on the contract—typically split this 50-50.

Songs played on Internet radio, like Pandora, Slacker, or iHeartRadio, have yet another formula for determining royalties. In 2000, the nonprofit group SoundExchange was established to collect royalties for Internet radio. (The significant difference between Internet radio and subscription streaming services is that on Internet radio, listeners can't select specific songs to play. Instead, Internet stations have "theme" stations.) SoundExchange charges fees of $0.002 per play, per listener. Large Internet radio stations can pay up to 25 percent of their gross revenue (less for smaller Internet radio stations, and a small flat fee for streaming nonprofit stations). About 50 percent of the fees go to the music label, 45 percent goes to the featured artists, and 5 percent goes to nonfeatured artists.

Finally, video services like YouTube and Vevo have become sites to generate advertising revenue through music videos, which can attract tens of millions of views. For example, OK Go's video for "Needing/Getting" in 2012 drew more than twenty-one million views in just a few months. Even popular amateur videos that use copyrighted music can create substantial revenue for music labels and artists. The 2009 amateur video JK "Wedding Entrance Dance" (reprised in a wedding scene in TV's *The Office*) has more than seventy-six million views. Instead of asking YouTube to remove the wedding video for its unauthorized use of Chris Brown's song "Forever," Sony licensed the video to stay on YouTube. At the rate of $1 per thousand video plays, it ultimately generated over $70,000 in ad revenue.

There aren't standard formulas for sharing ad revenue from music videos, but there is movement in that direction. In 2012, Universal Music Group and the National Music Publishers

VideoCentral ⊚
Mass Communication
bedfordstmartins.com /mediaculture

Alternative Strategies for Music Marketing
This video explores the strategies independent artists and marketers now employ to reach audiences.
Discussion: Even with the ability to bypass major record companies, many of the most popular artists still sign with those companies. Why do you think that is?

CHAPTER REVIEW

COMMON THREADS

One of the Common Threads discussed in Chapter 1 is about the developmental stages of the mass media. But as new audio and sound recording technologies evolve, do they drive the kind of music we hear?

In the recent history of the music industry, it would seem as if technology has been the driving force behind the kind of music we hear. Case in point: The advent of the MP3 file as a new format in 1999 has led to a new emphasis on single songs as the primary unit of music sales. The Recording Industry Association of America reports that there were more than 1.3 billion downloads of digital singles in 2011. In that year, digital singles outsold physical CD albums more than 5 to 1, digital albums 12 to 1, and vinyl LP/EPs 237 to 1. In the past decade, we have come to live in a music business dominated by digital singles.

What have we gained by this transition? Thankfully, there are fewer CD jewel boxes (which always shattered with the greatest of ease). And there is no requirement to buy the lackluster "filler" songs that often come with the price of an album, when all we want are the two or three hit songs. But what have we lost culturally in the transition away from albums?

First, there is no album art for digital singles (although department stores now sell frames to turn vintage 12-inch album covers into art). And second, we have lost the concept of an album as a thematic collection of music, and a medium that provides a much broader canvas to a talented musical artist. Consider this: How would the Beatles' *The White Album* have been created in a business dominated by singles? A look at *Rolling Stone* magazine's 500 Greatest Albums and *Time* magazine's All-Time 100 Albums indicates the apex of album creativity in earlier decades, with selections such as Jimi Hendrix's *Are You Experienced*

(1967), the Beatles' *Sgt. Pepper's Lonely Hearts Club Band* (1967), David Bowie's *The Rise and Fall of Ziggy Stardust* (1972), Public Enemy's *It Takes a Nation of Millions to Hold Us Back* (1988), and Radiohead's *OK Computer* (1997). Has the movement away from albums changed possibilities for musical artists? That is, if an artist is to be commercially successful, is there more pressure just to generate hit singles instead of larger bodies of work that constitute the album? Have the styles of artists like Ke$ha, Nicki Minaj, One Republic, and Lil Wayne been shaped by the predominance of the single?

Still, there is a clear case against technological determinism—the idea that technological innovations determine the direction of the culture. Back in the 1950s, the vinyl album caught on despite there having been no album format prior to it and despite the popularity of the 45-rpm single format, which competed with it at the same time. When the MP3 single format emerged in the late 1990s, the music industry had just rolled out two formats of advanced album discs that were technological improvements on the CD. Neither caught on. Of course, music fans may have been lured by the ease of acquiring music digitally via the Internet, and by the price—usually free (but illegal).

So, if it isn't technological determinism, why doesn't a strong digital album market coexist with the digital singles today? Can you think of any albums of the past few years that merit being listed with the greatest albums of all time?

KEY TERMS

The definitions for the terms listed below can be found in the glossary at the end of the book. The page numbers listed with the terms indicate where the term is highlighted in the chapter.

audiotape, 124
stereo, 125
analog recording, 125
digital recording, 125
compact discs (CDs), 125
MP3, 127
pop music, 128
jazz, 129
cover music, 129

rock and roll, 129
blues, 129
rhythm and blues (R&B), 130
rockabilly, 131
soul, 136
folk music, 137
folk-rock, 137
punk rock, 139
grunge, 140

alternative rock, 140
hip-hop, 140
gangster rap, 141
oligopoly, 142
indies, 144
A&R (artist & repertoire) agents, 145
online piracy, 146

REVIEW QUESTIONS

The Development of Sound Recording

1. The technological configuration of a particular medium sometimes elevates it to mass market status. Why did Emile Berliner's flat disk replace the wax cylinder, and why did this reconfiguration of records matter in the history of the mass media? Can you think of other mass media examples in which the size and shape of the technology have made a difference?

2. How did sound recording survive the advent of radio?

3. How did the music industry attempt to curb illegal downloading and file-sharing?

U.S. Popular Music and the Formation of Rock

4. How did rock and roll significantly influence two mass media industries?

5. Although many rock-and-roll lyrics from the 1950s are tame by today's standards, this new musical development represented a threat to many parents and adults at that time. Why?

6. What moral and cultural boundaries were blurred by rock and roll in the 1950s?

7. Why did cover music figure so prominently in the development of rock and roll and the record industry in the 1950s?

A Changing Industry: Reformations in Popular Music

8. Explain the British invasion. What was its impact on the recording industry?

9. What were the major influences of folk music on the recording industry?

10. Why did hip-hop and punk rock emerge as significant musical forms in the late 1970s and 1980s? What do their developments have in common, and how are they different?

11. Why does pop music continue to remain powerful today?

The Business of Sound Recording

12. What companies control the bulk of worldwide music production and distribution?

13. Why are independent labels so important to the music industry?

14. Who are the major parties who receive profits when a digital download, music stream, or physical CD is sold?

15. How is a mechanical royalty different from a performance royalty?

Sound Recording, Free Expression, and Democracy

16. Why is it ironic that so many forms of alternative music become commercially successful?

QUESTIONING THE MEDIA

1. If you ran a noncommercial campus radio station, what kind of music would you play and why?

2. Think about the role of the 1960s drug culture in rock's history. How are drugs and alcohol treated in contemporary and alternative forms of rock and hip-hop today?

3. Is it healthy for, or detrimental to, the music business that so much of the recording industry is controlled by just a few large international companies? Explain.

4. Do you think the Internet as a technology helps or hurts musical artists? Why do so many contemporary musical performers differ in their opinions about the Internet?

5. How has the Internet changed your musical tastes? Has it exposed you to more global music? Do you listen to a wider range of music because of the Internet?

ADDITIONAL VIDEOS

Visit the Ⓥ VideoCentral: Mass Communication *section at* bedfordstmartins.com/mediaculture *for additional exclusive videos related to Chapter 4.*

5

Popular Radio and the Origins of Broadcasting

A few years ago, a young woman named Kristin* took an entry-level position running the audio board for the on-air radio personalities at an AM radio station. She loved radio, and hoped that this job would jump-start her career in the industry. "When I went to college to get my bachelor's degree, that's what I wanted to do," she said. Kristin got her break when she was asked to fill in at the microphone while one of the radio personalities went on maternity leave. Soon, she won a regular shift while just a college student. And because the station was owned by Atlanta-based Cumulus Media, one of the largest radio groups in the country with 350 stations in 68 markets, there were opportunities for Kristin to grow within the company. She was transferred to host a show on a popular contemporary hits FM station in a larger market, playing the latest songs. "I was so excited to be living my dream," Kristin said, so much so that she didn't mind that she was earning only minimum wage.

Name has been changed for confidentiality reasons.

That dream soon revealed its darker side—the realities of today's homogenized radio industry. Kristin's station was one of three FM stations owned by Cumulus in that market. Kristin was asked to do voice-tracking, a cost-saving measure in which a radio deejay prerecords voice breaks that are then inserted into an automated shift. To the listeners, it may have seemed like they were getting three different deejays on Cumulus's contemporary hits station, rock station, and country station. After all, they were hearing three different names, with three slightly different personalities. In reality, Kristin was the midday deejay on the contemporary hits radio station; she was the evening deejay on the rock format station; and she was also the weekend voice of the company's country format station. Some days, due to scheduling, Kristin's three on-air personalities could be heard at the exact same time. But she would only be paid for the one hour it took her to lay down a voice track for each four-to-five hour shift.

Kristin and her fellow voice-tracked deejays felt disconnected from their listeners. "You can see that the phones ring all day long," as listeners call in requests, she said. "Even if you voice track, you say, 'Call in with your request, or leave a message.'" But because the songs are scheduled days in advance in the automated system, if a request happens to be played, it's only by coincidence.

After four years, Kristin finished her B.A. in communication, left the radio station, and went to grad school. "I wouldn't be able to pay my college loans with the money I was making," she said.

But even with the low wages, for Kristin, the biggest disappointment was that the kind of commercial radio she grew up listening to was being phased out by the time she went to work in the business.

The consolidation of stations into massive radio groups like Cumulus and Clear Channel in the 1990s and 2000s resulted in budget-cutting demands from the corporate offices and, ultimately, stations with less connection to their local audience. And even with growing complaints from listeners and community groups about the decline in minority ownership, the lack of musical diversity on the airwaves, and the near-disappearance of local radio news, little has changed. It is simply more profitable for radio conglomerates to use prerecorded or syndicated programming, even if it means losing sight of their duty to serve the public's interests and stifling their deejays' individuality and passion for the medium. Kristin's contemporary hits station had five full-time on-air deejays when she started. Today, it has just one.

▲

"When you take away the interaction with people and the live aspect, you lose the magic."

KRISTIN, FORMER RADIO DEEJAY

◢ *EVEN WITH THE ARRIVAL OF TV IN THE 1950s* and the "corporatization" of broadcasting in the 1990s, the historical and contemporary roles played by radio have been immense. From the early days of network radio, which gave us "a national identity" and "a chance to share in a common experience,"[1] to the more customized, demographically segmented medium today, radio's influence continues to reverberate throughout our society. Though television displaced radio as our most common media experience, radio specialized and adapted. The daily music and persistent talk that resonate from radios all over the world continue to play a key role in contemporary culture.

In this chapter, we examine the scientific, cultural, political, and economic factors surrounding radio's development and perseverance. We will:

- Explore the origins of broadcasting, from the early theories about radio waves to the critical formation of RCA as a national radio monopoly
- Probe the evolution of commercial radio, including the rise of NBC as the first network, the development of CBS, and the establishment of the first federal radio legislation
- Review the fascinating ways in which radio reinvented itself in the 1950s
- Examine television's impact on radio programming, the invention of FM radio, radio's convergence with sound recording, and the influence of various formats
- Investigate newer developments like satellite and HD radio, their impact on the radio industry, and the convergence of radio with the Internet
- Survey the economic health, increasing conglomeration, and cultural impact of commercial and noncommercial radio today, including the emergence of noncommercial low-power FM service

As you read through this chapter, think about your own relationship with radio. What are your earliest memories of listening to radio? Do you remember a favorite song or station? How old were you when you started listening? Why did you listen? What types of radio stations are in your area today? If you could own and manage a commercial radio station, what format would you choose, and why? For more questions to help you think through the role of radio in our lives, see "Questioning the Media" in the Chapter Review.

Past-Present-Future: Radio

As radio undergoes a transformation in the face of the digital turn, it's worth remembering how radio was first imagined in its development. The earliest radio technology was developed to improve on a task previously done by lighthouses and flags: ship-to-shore communication. Thus, the first concept of radio was point-to-point—no one had yet thought of *broadcasting*.

By the 1920s, the idea of casting the radio signal broadly caught on, and it was the first time the nation was brought together with shared electronic media programming. But when television became the new electronic hearth in the 1950s, radio turned to more segmented programming: news, sports, and lots of music formats. Today, there are about fifteen thousand radio stations, but ironically many of them sound alike, in part because many of them are owned by the same companies and carry the same syndicated national programming. If you listen to

a contemporary hits radio station throughout the country, you'll likely hear the same syndicated Ryan Seacrest program in the mornings or midday, and the Billy Bush program in the evening.

The future is already here in radio, as Internet radio has been pulling listeners away from AM and FM stations. Online, listeners can make even more customized channels based on artists or songs they like. Internet radio sites like Pandora are clearly popular, but what does it mean when a news headline says (as it did in 2012) that "Pandora Is Number One Radio Station in L.A."?[1] If Pandora has a seemingly infinite number of "stations" that one can choose and create, does the term "station" even apply? Are Los Angeles radio listeners having a shared experience on Pandora, compared to the shared experience they might have listening to 102.7 KISS-FM in Los Angeles, the station it displaced from number one? Is having a more customized radio station better than having a radio station that originates in the local culture of a city? Or is the question moot, since many local stations have already lost their distinct local voice?

Early Technology and the Development of Radio

Radio did not emerge as a full-blown mass medium until the 1920s, though the technology that made radio possible had been evolving for years. The **telegraph**–the precursor of radio technology–was invented in the 1840s. American inventor Samuel Morse developed the first practical system, sending electrical impulses from a transmitter through a cable to a reception point. Using what became known as **Morse code**–a series of dots and dashes that stood for letters in the alphabet–telegraph operators transmitted news and messages simply by interrupting the electrical current along a wire cable. By 1844, Morse had set up the first telegraph line between Washington, D.C., and Baltimore. By 1861, telegraph lines ran coast to coast. By 1866, the first transatlantic cable, capable of transmitting about six words a minute, ran between Newfoundland and Ireland along the ocean floor.

Although it was a revolutionary technology, the telegraph had its limitations. For instance, while it dispatched complicated language codes, it was unable to transmit the human voice. Moreover, ships at sea still had no contact with the rest of the world. As a result, navies could not find out that wars had ceased on land and often continued fighting for months. Commercial shipping interests also lacked an efficient way to coordinate and relay information from land and between ships. What was needed was a telegraph without the wires.

▼ **Popular Radio and the Origins of Broadcasting**

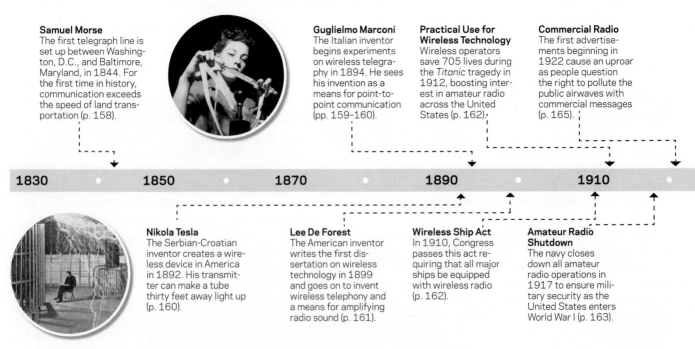

Samuel Morse
The first telegraph line is set up between Washington, D.C., and Baltimore, Maryland, in 1844. For the first time in history, communication exceeds the speed of land transportation (p. 158).

Guglielmo Marconi
The Italian inventor begins experiments on wireless telegraphy in 1894. He sees his invention as a means for point-to-point communication (pp. 159–160).

Practical Use for Wireless Technology
Wireless operators save 705 lives during the *Titanic* tragedy in 1912, boosting interest in amateur radio across the United States (p. 162).

Commercial Radio
The first advertisements beginning in 1922 cause an uproar as people question the right to pollute the public airwaves with commercial messages (p. 165).

| 1830 | 1850 | 1870 | 1890 | 1910 |

Nikola Tesla
The Serbian-Croatian inventor creates a wireless device in America in 1892. His transmitter can make a tube thirty feet away light up (p. 160).

Lee De Forest
The American inventor writes the first dissertation on wireless technology in 1899 and goes on to invent wireless telephony and a means for amplifying radio sound (p. 161).

Wireless Ship Act
In 1910, Congress passes this act requiring that all major ships be equipped with wireless radio (p. 162).

Amateur Radio Shutdown
The navy closes down all amateur radio operations in 1917 to ensure military security as the United States enters World War I (p. 163).

Maxwell and Hertz Discover Radio Waves

The key development in wireless transmissions came from James Maxwell, a Scottish physicist who in the mid-1860s theorized the existence of **electromagnetic waves**: invisible electronic impulses similar to visible light. Maxwell's equations showed that electricity, magnetism, light, and heat are part of the same electromagnetic spectrum and that they radiate in space at the speed of light, about 186,000 miles per second (see Figure 5.1). Maxwell further theorized that a portion of these phenomena, later known as **radio waves**, could be harnessed so that signals could be sent from a transmission point to a reception point.

It was German physicist Heinrich Hertz, however, who in the 1880s proved Maxwell's theories. Hertz created a crude device that permitted an electrical spark to leap across a small gap between two steel balls. As the electricity jumped the gap, it emitted waves; this was the first recorded transmission and reception of an electromagnetic wave. Hertz's experiments significantly advanced the development of wireless communication.

Marconi and the Inventors of Wireless Telegraphy

In 1894, Guglielmo Marconi, a twenty-year-old, self-educated Italian engineer, read Hertz's work and understood that developing a way to send high-speed messages over great distances would transform communication, the military, and commercial shipping. Although revolutionary, the

A TELEGRAPH OPERATOR reads the perforated tape. Sending messages using Morse code across telegraph wires was the precursor to radio, which did not fully become a mass medium until the 1920s.

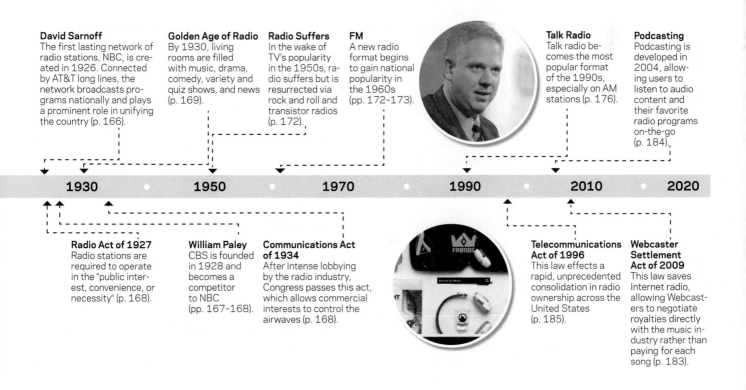

David Sarnoff
The first lasting network of radio stations, NBC, is created in 1926. Connected by AT&T long lines, the network broadcasts programs nationally and plays a prominent role in unifying the country (p. 166).

Golden Age of Radio
By 1930, living rooms are filled with music, drama, comedy, variety and quiz shows, and news (p. 169).

Radio Suffers
In the wake of TV's popularity in the 1950s, radio suffers but is resurrected via rock and roll and transistor radios (p. 172).

FM
A new radio format begins to gain national popularity in the 1960s (pp. 172-173).

Talk Radio
Talk radio becomes the most popular format of the 1990s, especially on AM stations (p. 176).

Podcasting
Podcasting is developed in 2004, allowing users to listen to audio content and their favorite radio programs on-the-go (p. 184).

1930 • **1950** • **1970** • **1990** • **2010** • **2020**

Radio Act of 1927
Radio stations are required to operate in the "public interest, convenience, or necessity" (p. 168).

William Paley
CBS is founded in 1928 and becomes a competitor to NBC (pp. 167-168).

Communications Act of 1934
After intense lobbying by the radio industry, Congress passes this act, which allows commercial interests to control the airwaves (p. 168).

Telecommunications Act of 1996
This law effects a rapid, unprecedented consolidation in radio ownership across the United States (p. 185).

Webcaster Settlement Act of 2009
This law saves Internet radio, allowing Webcasters to negotiate royalties directly with the music industry rather than paying for each song (p. 183).

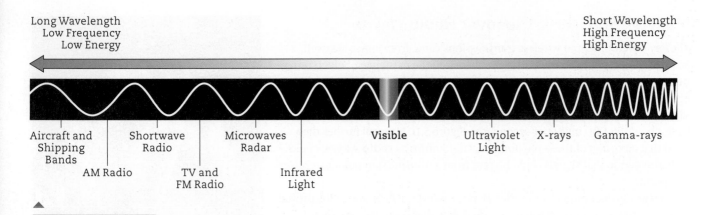

Long Wavelength
Low Frequency
Low Energy

Short Wavelength
High Frequency
High Energy

Aircraft and
Shipping
Bands

Shortwave
Radio

Microwaves
Radar

Visible

Ultraviolet
Light

X-rays

Gamma-rays

AM Radio

TV and
FM Radio

Infrared
Light

FIGURE 5.1

**THE ELECTROMAGNETIC
SPECTRUM**

*Source: NASA, http://imagine.gsfc
.nasa.gov/docs/science/know_l1/
emspectrum.html.*

telephone and the telegraph were limited by their wires, so Marconi set about trying to make wireless technology practical. First, he attached Hertz's spark-gap transmitter to a Morse telegraph key, which could send out dot-dash signals. The electrical impulses traveled into a Morse inker, the machine that telegraph operators used to record the dots and dashes onto narrow strips of paper. Second, Marconi discovered that grounding–connecting the transmitter and receiver to the earth–greatly increased the distance over which he could send signals.

In 1896, Marconi traveled to England, where he received a patent on **wireless telegraphy**, a form of voiceless point-to-point communication. In London, in 1897, he formed the Marconi Wireless Telegraph Company, later known as British Marconi, and began installing wireless technology on British naval and private commercial ships. In 1899, he opened a branch in the United States, establishing a company nicknamed American Marconi. That same year, he sent the first wireless Morse code signal across the English Channel to France, and in 1901 he relayed the first wireless signal across the Atlantic Ocean. Although Marconi was a successful innovator and entrepreneur, he saw wireless telegraphy only as point-to-point communication, much like the telegraph and the telephone, not as a one-to-many mass medium. He also confined his applications to Morse code messages for military and commercial ships, leaving others to explore the wireless transmission of voice and music.

History often cites Marconi as the "father of radio," but another inventor unknown to him was making parallel discoveries about wireless telegraphy in Russia. Alexander Popov, a professor of physics in St. Petersburg, was also experimenting with sending wireless messages over distances. Popov announced to the Russian Physicist Society of St. Petersburg on May 7, 1895, that he had transmitted and received signals over a distance of six hundred yards.[2] Yet Popov was an academic, not an entrepreneur, and after Marconi accomplished a similar feat that same summer, Marconi was the first to apply for and receive a patent. However, May 7 is celebrated as "Radio Day" in Russia.

It is important to note that the work of Popov and Marconi was preceded by that of Nikola Tesla, a Serbian-Croatian inventor who immigrated to New York in 1884. Tesla, who also conceived the high-capacity alternating current systems that made worldwide electrification possible, invented a wireless system in 1892. A year later, Tesla successfully demonstrated his device in St. Louis, with his transmitter lighting up a receiver tube thirty feet away.[3] However, Tesla's work was overshadowed by Marconi's; Marconi used much of Tesla's work in his own developments, and for years Tesla was not associated with the invention of radio. Tesla never received great financial benefits from his breakthroughs, but in 1943 (a few months after he died penniless in New York) the U.S. Supreme Court overturned Marconi's wireless patent and deemed Tesla the inventor of radio.[4]

NIKOLA TESLA
A double-exposed photograph combines the image of inventor Nikola Tesla reading a book in his Colorado Springs, Colorado, laboratory in 1899 with the image of his Tesla coil discharging several million volts.

Wireless Telephony: De Forest and Fessenden

In 1899, inventor Lee De Forest (who, in defiance of other inventors, liked to call himself the "father of radio") wrote the first Ph.D. dissertation on wireless technology, building on others' innovations. In 1901, De Forest challenged Marconi, who was covering New York's International Yacht Races for the Associated Press, by signing up to report the races for a rival news service. The competing transmitters jammed each other's signals so badly, however, that officials ended up relaying information on the races in the traditional way—with flags and hand signals. The event exemplified a problem that would persist throughout radio's early development: noise and interference from competition for the finite supply of radio frequencies.

In 1902, De Forest set up the Wireless Telephone Company to compete head-on with American Marconi, by then the leader in wireless communication. A major difference between Marconi and De Forest was the latter's interest in wireless voice and music transmissions, later known as **wireless telephony** and, eventually, radio. Although sometimes an unscrupulous competitor (inventor Reginald Fessenden won a lawsuit against De Forest for using one of his patents without permission), De Forest went on to patent more than three hundred inventions.

De Forest's biggest breakthrough was the development of the Audion, or triode, vacuum tube, which detected radio signals and then amplified them. De Forest's improvements greatly increased listeners' ability to hear dots and dashes and, later, speech and music on a receiver set. His modifications were essential to the development of voice transmission, long-distance radio, and television. In fact, the Audion vacuum tube, which powered radios until the arrival of transistors and solid-state circuits in the 1950s, is considered by many historians to be the beginning of modern electronics. But again, bitter competition taints De Forest's legacy; although De Forest won a twenty-year court battle for the rights to the Audion patent, most engineers at the time agreed that Edwin Armstrong (who later developed FM radio) was the true inventor and disagreed with the U.S. Supreme Court's 1934 decision on the case that favored De Forest.[5]

> "I discovered an Invisible Empire of the Air, intangible, yet solid as granite."
>
> LEE DE FOREST, INVENTOR

The credit for the first voice broadcast belongs to Canadian engineer Reginald Fessenden, formerly a chief chemist for Thomas Edison. Fessenden went to work for the U.S. Navy and eventually for General Electric (GE), where he played a central role in improving wireless signals. Both the navy and GE were interested in the potential for voice transmissions. On Christmas Eve in 1906, after GE built Fessenden a powerful transmitter, he gave his first public demonstration, sending a voice through the airwaves from his station at Brant Rock, Massachusetts. A radio historian describes what happened:

That night, ship operators and amateurs around Brant Rock heard the results: "someone speaking! . . . a woman's voice rose in song. . . . Next someone was heard reading a poem." Fessenden himself played "O Holy Night" on his violin. Though the fidelity was not all that it might be, listeners were captivated by the voices and notes they heard. No more would sounds be restricted to mere dots and dashes of the Morse code.[6]

Ship operators were astonished to hear voices rather than the familiar Morse code. (Some operators actually thought they were having a supernatural encounter.) This event showed that the wireless medium was moving from a point-to-point communication tool (wireless operator to wireless operator) toward a one-to-many communication tool. **Broadcasting**, once an agricultural term that referred to the process of casting seeds over a large area, would come to mean the transmission of radio waves (and, later, TV signals) to a broad public audience. Prior to radio broadcasting, wireless was considered a form of **narrowcasting**, or person-to-person communication, like the telegraph and telephone.

In 1910, De Forest transmitted a performance of *Tosca* by the Metropolitan Opera to friends in the New York area with wireless receivers. At this point in time, radio passed from the novelty stage to the entrepreneurial stage, where various practical uses would be tested before radio would launch as a mass medium.

Regulating a New Medium

The two most important international issues affecting radio in the 1900s were ship radio requirements and signal interference. Congress passed the Wireless Ship Act in 1910, which required that all major U.S. seagoing ships carrying more than fifty passengers and traveling more than two hundred miles off the coast be equipped with wireless equipment with a one-hundred-mile range. The importance of this act was underscored by the *Titanic* disaster two years later. A brand-new British luxury steamer, the *Titanic* sank in 1912. Although more than fifteen hundred people died in the tragedy, wireless reports played a critical role in pinpointing the *Titanic*'s location, enabling rescue ships to save over seven hundred lives.

Radio Waves as a Natural Resource

In the wake of the *Titanic* tragedy, Congress passed the **Radio Act of 1912**, which addressed the problem of amateur radio operators increasingly cramming the airwaves. Because radio waves crossed state and national borders, legislators determined that broadcasting constituted a "natural resource"–a kind of interstate commerce. This meant that radio waves could not be owned; they were the collective property of all Americans, just like national parks. Therefore, transmitting on radio waves would require licensing in the same way that driving a car requires a license.

A short policy guide, the first Radio Act required all wireless stations to obtain radio licenses from the Commerce Department.

NEWS OF THE *TITANIC*
Despite the headline in the *St. Louis Post-Dispatch*, actually 1,523 people died and only 705 were rescued when the *Titanic* hit an iceberg on April 14, 1912 (the ship technically sank at 2:20 A.M. on April 15). The crew of the *Titanic* used the Marconi wireless equipment on board to send distress signals to other ships. Of the eight ships nearby, the *Carpathia* was the first to respond with lifeboats.

This act, which governed radio until 1927, also formally adopted the SOS Morse-code distress signal that other countries had been using for several years. Further, the "natural resource" mandate led to the idea that radio, and eventually television, should provide a benefit to society–in the form of education and public service. The eventual establishment of public radio stations was one consequence of this idea, and the Fairness Doctrine was another.

The Impact of World War I

By 1915, more than twenty American companies sold wireless point-to-point communication systems, primarily for use in ship-to-shore communication. Having established a reputation for efficiency and honesty, American Marconi (a subsidiary of British Marconi) was the biggest and best of these companies. But in 1914, with World War I beginning in Europe and with America warily watching the conflict, the U.S. Navy questioned the wisdom of allowing a foreign-controlled company to wield so much power. American corporations, especially GE and AT&T, capitalized on the navy's xenophobia and succeeded in undercutting Marconi's influence.

As wireless telegraphy played an increasingly large role in military operations, the navy sought tight controls on information. When the United States entered the war in 1917, the navy closed down all amateur radio operations and took control of key radio transmitters to ensure military security. As the war was nearing its end in 1919, British Marconi placed an order with GE for twenty-four potent new alternators, which were strong enough to power a transoceanic system of radio stations that could connect the world. But the U.S. Navy–influenced by Franklin Roosevelt, at that time the navy's assistant secretary–grew concerned and moved to ensure that such powerful new radio technology would not fall under foreign control.

Roosevelt was guided in turn by President Woodrow Wilson's goal of developing the United States as an international power, a position greatly enhanced by American military successes during the war. Wilson and the navy saw an opportunity to slow Britain's influence over communication and to promote a U.S. plan for the control of the emerging wireless operations. Thus corporate heads and government leaders conspired to make sure radio communication would serve American interests.

The Formation of RCA

Some members of Congress and the corporate community opposed federal legislation that would grant the government or the navy a radio monopoly. Consequently, GE developed a compromise plan that would create a *private sector monopoly*–that is, a private company that would have the government's approval to dominate the radio industry. First, GE broke off negotiations to sell key radio technologies to European-owned companies like British Marconi, thereby limiting those companies' global reach. Second, GE took the lead in founding a new company, **Radio Corporation of America (RCA)**, which soon acquired American Marconi and radio patents of other U.S. companies. Upon its founding in 1919, RCA had pooled the necessary technology and patents to monopolize the wireless industry and expand American communication technology throughout the world.[7]

Under RCA's patents pool arrangement, wireless patents from the navy, AT&T, GE, the former American Marconi, and other companies were combined to ensure U.S. control over the manufacture of radio transmitters and receivers. Initially, AT&T, then the government-sanctioned monopoly provider of telephone services, manufactured most transmitters, while GE (and later Westinghouse) made radio receivers. RCA administered the pool, collecting patent royalties and distributing them to pool members. To protect these profits, the government did not permit RCA to manufacture equipment or to operate radio stations under its own name for several years. Instead, RCA's initial function was to ensure that radio parts were standardized by manufacturers and to control frequency interference by amateur radio operators, which increasingly became a problem after the war.

A government restriction at the time mandated that no more than 20 percent of RCA–and eventually any U.S. broadcasting facility–could be owned by foreigners. This restriction, later raised to 25 percent, became law in 1927 and applied to all U.S. broadcasting stocks and facilities. It is because of this rule that in 1985 Rupert Murdoch, the head of Australia's giant News Corp., became a U.S. citizen so he could buy a number of TV stations and form the Fox television network.

RCA's most significant impact was that it gave the United States almost total control over the emerging mass medium of broadcasting. At the time, the United States was the only country that placed broadcasting under the care of commercial, rather than military or government, interests. By pooling more than two thousand patents and sharing research developments, RCA ensured the global dominance of the United States in mass communication, a position it maintained in electronic hardware into the 1960s and maintains in program content today.

The Evolution of Radio

> "I believe the quickest way to kill broadcasting would be to use it for direct advertising."
>
> HERBERT HOOVER, SECRETARY OF COMMERCE, 1924

When Westinghouse engineer Frank Conrad set up a crude radio studio above his Pittsburgh garage in 1916, placing a microphone in front of a phonograph to broadcast music and news to his friends (whom Conrad supplied with receivers) two evenings a week on experimental station 8XK, he unofficially became one of the medium's first disc jockeys. In 1920, a Westinghouse executive, intrigued by Conrad's curious hobby, realized the potential of radio as a mass medium. Westinghouse then established station KDKA, which is generally regarded as the first commercial broadcast station. KDKA is most noted for airing national returns from the Cox-Harding presidential election on November 2, 1920, an event most historians consider the first professional broadcast.

Other amateur broadcasters could also lay claim to being first. One of the earliest stations, operated by Charles "Doc" Herrold in San Jose, California, began in 1909 and later became KCBS. Additional experimental stations–in places like New York; Detroit; Medford, Massachusetts; and Pierre, South Dakota–broadcast voice and music prior to the establishment of KDKA. But KDKA's success, with the financial backing of Westinghouse, signaled the start of broadcast radio.

In 1921, the U.S. Commerce Department officially licensed five radio stations for operation; by early 1923, more than six hundred commercial and noncommercial stations were operating. Some stations were owned by AT&T, GE, and Westinghouse, but many were run by amateurs or were independently owned by universities or businesses. By the end of 1923, as many as 550,000 radio receivers, most manufactured by GE and Westinghouse, had been sold for about $55 each (about $701 in today's dollars). Just as the "guts" of the phonograph had been put inside a piece of furniture to create a consumer product, the vacuum tubes, electrical posts, and bulky batteries that made up the radio receiver were placed inside stylish furniture and marketed to households. By 1925, 5.5 million radio sets were in use across America, and radio was officially a mass medium.

The RCA Partnership Unravels

In 1922, in a major power grab, AT&T, which already had a government-sanctioned monopoly in the telephone business, decided to break its RCA agreements in an attempt to monopolize radio as well. Identifying the new medium as the "wireless telephone," AT&T argued that broadcasting was merely an extension of its control over the telephone. Ultimately, the corporate giant complained that RCA had gained too much monopoly power. In violation of its early agreements with RCA, AT&T began making and selling its own radio receivers.

In the same year, AT&T started WEAF (now WNBC) in New York, the first radio station to regularly sell commercial time to advertisers. AT&T claimed that under the RCA agreements it had the exclusive right to sell ads, which AT&T called *toll broadcasting*. Most people in radio at the time recoiled at the idea of using the medium for crass advertising, viewing it instead as a public information service. In fact, stations that had earlier tried to sell ads received "cease and desist" letters from the Department of Commerce. But by August 1922, AT&T had nonetheless sold its first ad to a New York real estate developer for $50. The idea of promoting the new medium as a public service, along the lines of today's noncommercial National Public Radio (NPR), ended when executives realized that radio ads offered another opportunity for profits long after radio-set sales had saturated the consumer market.

The initial strategy behind AT&T's toll broadcasting idea was an effort to conquer radio. By its agreements with RCA, AT&T retained the rights to interconnect the signals between two or more radio stations via telephone wires. In 1923, when AT&T aired a program simultaneously on its flagship WEAF station and on WNAC in Boston, the phone company created the first **network**: a cost-saving operation that links (at that time, through special phone lines; today, through satellite relays) a group of broadcast stations that share programming produced at a central location. By the end of 1924, AT&T had interconnected twenty-two stations to air a talk by President Calvin Coolidge. Some of these stations were owned by AT&T, but most simply consented to become AT&T "affiliates," agreeing to air the phone company's programs. These network stations informally became known as the *telephone group* and later as the Broadcasting Corporation of America (BCA).

In response, GE, Westinghouse, and RCA interconnected a smaller set of competing stations, known as the *radio group*. Initially, their network linked WGY in Schenectady, New York (then GE's national headquarters), and WJZ in Manhattan. The radio group had to use inferior Western Union telegraph lines when AT&T denied them access to telephone wires. By this time, AT&T had sold its stock in RCA and refused to lease its lines to competing radio networks. The telephone monopoly was now enmeshed in a battle to defeat RCA for control of radio.

This clash, among other problems, eventually led to a government investigation and an arbitration settlement in 1925. In the agreement, the Justice Department, irritated by AT&T's power grab, redefined patent agreements. AT&T received a monopoly on providing the wires, known as *long lines*, to interconnect stations nationwide. In exchange, AT&T sold its BCA network to RCA for $1 million and agreed not to reenter broadcasting for eight years (a banishment that actually extended into the 1990s).

Sarnoff and NBC: Building the "Blue" and "Red" Networks

After Lee De Forest, David Sarnoff was among the first to envision wireless telegraphy as a modern mass medium. From the time he served as Marconi's personal messenger (at age fifteen), Sarnoff rose rapidly at American Marconi. He became a wireless operator, helping to relay information about the *Titanic* survivors in 1912. Promoted to a series of management positions, Sarnoff was closely involved in RCA's creation in 1919, when most radio executives saw wireless merely as point-to-point communication. But with Sarnoff as RCA's first commercial manager,

WESTINGHOUSE ENGINEER FRANK CONRAD
Broadcasting from his garage, Conrad turned his hobby into Pittsburgh's KDKA, one of the first radio stations. Although this early station is widely celebrated in history books as the first broadcasting outlet, one can't underestimate the influence Westinghouse had in promoting this "historical first." Westinghouse clearly saw the celebration of Conrad's garage studio as a way to market the company and its radio equipment. The resulting legacy of Conrad's garage studio has thus overshadowed other individuals who also experimented with radio broadcasting.

radio's potential as a mass medium was quickly realized. In 1921, at age thirty, Sarnoff became RCA's general manager.

After RCA bought AT&T's telephone group network (BCA), Sarnoff created a new subsidiary in September 1926 called the National Broadcasting Company (NBC). Its ownership was shared by RCA (50 percent), General Electric (30 percent), and Westinghouse (20 percent). This loose network of stations would be hooked together by AT&T long lines. Shortly thereafter, the original telephone group became known as the NBC-Red network, and the radio group (the network previously established by RCA, GE, and Westinghouse) became the NBC-Blue network.

Although NBC owned a number of stations by the late 1920s, many independent stations also began affiliating with the NBC networks to receive programming. NBC affiliates, though independently owned, signed contracts to be part of the network and paid NBC to carry its programs. In exchange, NBC reserved time slots, which it sold to national advertisers. NBC centralized costs and programming by bringing the best musical, dramatic, and comedic talent to one place, where programs could be produced and then distributed all over the country. By 1933, NBC-Red had twenty-eight affiliates and NBC-Blue had twenty-four.

Network radio may actually have helped modernize America by de-emphasizing the local and the regional in favor of national programs broadcast to nearly everyone. For example, when Charles Lindbergh returned from the first solo transatlantic flight in 1927, an estimated twenty-five to thirty million people listened to his welcome-home party on the six million radio sets then in use. At the time, it was the largest shared audience experience in the history of any mass medium.

David Sarnoff's leadership at RCA was capped by two other negotiations that solidified his stature as the driving force behind radio's development as a modern medium: cutting a deal with General Motors for the manufacture of car radios (under the brand name Motorola) in 1929, and merging RCA with the Victor Talking Machine Company. Afterward, until the mid-1960s, the company was known as RCA Victor, adopting as its corporate symbol the famous terrier sitting alertly next to a Victrola radio-phonograph. The merger gave RCA control over Victor's records and recording equipment, making the radio company a major player in the sound recording industry. In 1930, David Sarnoff became president of RCA, and he ran it for the next forty years.

Government Scrutiny Ends RCA-NBC Monopoly

As early as 1923, the Federal Trade Commission had charged RCA with violations of antitrust laws but allowed the monopoly to continue. By the late 1920s, the government, concerned about NBC's growing control over radio content, intensified its scrutiny. Then, in 1930, federal marshals charged RCA/NBC with a number of violations, including exercising too much control over manufacturing and programming. Although the government had originally sanctioned a closely supervised monopoly for wireless communication, after the collapse of the stock market in 1929, the public became increasingly distrustful of big business.

RCA acted quickly. To eliminate its monopolizing partnerships, Sarnoff's company proposed buying out GE's and Westinghouse's remaining shares in RCA's manufacturing business. Now RCA would compete directly against GE, Westinghouse, and other radio manufacturers, encouraging more competition in the radio manufacturing industry. In 1932, days before the antitrust case against RCA was to go to trial, the government accepted RCA's proposal for breaking up its monopoly. Ironically, in the mid-1980s, GE bought RCA, a shell of its former self and no longer competitive with foreign electronics firms.[8] GE was chiefly interested in RCA's brand-name status and its still-lucrative subsidiary, NBC.

CBS and Paley: Challenging NBC

Even with RCA's head start and its favored status, the two NBC networks faced competitors in the late 1920s. The competitors, however, all found it tough going. One group, United Independent Broadcasters (UIB), even lined up twelve prospective affiliates and offered them $500 a week for access to ten hours of station time in exchange for quality programs. UIB was cash-poor, however, and AT&T would not rent the new company its lines to link the affiliates.

Enter the Columbia Phonograph Company, which was looking for a way to preempt RCA's merger with the Victor Company, then the record company's major competitor. With backing from Columbia, UIB launched the new Columbia Phonograph Broadcasting System (CPBS), a wobbly sixteen-affiliate network, in 1927. But after losing $100,000 in the first month, the record company pulled out. Later, CPBS dropped the word *Phonograph* from its title, creating the Columbia Broadcasting System (CBS).

In 1928, William Paley, the twenty-seven-year-old son of Sam Paley, owner of a Philadelphia cigar company, bought a controlling interest in CBS to sponsor their cigar brand, La Palina. One of Paley's first moves was to hire the public relations pioneer Edward Bernays to polish the new network's image. (Bernays played a significant role in the development of the public relations industry; see Chapter 12.) Paley and Bernays modified a concept called **option time**, in which CBS paid affiliate stations $50 per hour for an option on a portion of their time. The network provided programs to the affiliates and sold ad space or sponsorships to various product companies. In theory, CBS could now control up to twenty-four hours a day of its affiliates' radio time. Some affiliates received thousands of dollars per week merely to serve

CBS HELPED ESTABLISH ITSELF as a premier radio network by attracting top talent like comedic duo George Burns and Gracie Allen from NBC. They first brought their "Dumb Dora" and straight man act from stage to radio in 1929, and then continued on various radio programs in the 1930s and 1940s, with the most well known being *The Burns and Allen Show*. CBS also reaped the benefits when Burns and Allen moved their eponymous show to television in 1950.

as conduits for CBS programs and ads. Because NBC was still charging some of its affiliates as much as $96 a week to carry its network programs, the CBS offer was extremely appealing.

By 1933, Paley's efforts had netted CBS more than ninety affiliates, many of them defecting from NBC. Paley also concentrated on developing news programs and entertainment shows, particularly soap operas and comedy-variety series. In the process, CBS successfully raided NBC, not just for affiliates but for top talent as well. Throughout the 1930s and 1940s, Paley lured a number of radio stars from NBC, including Jack Benny, Frank Sinatra, George Burns, Gracie Allen, and Groucho Marx. During World War II, Edward R. Murrow's powerful firsthand news reports from bomb-riddled London established CBS as the premier radio news network, a reputation it carried forward to television. In 1949, near the end of big-time network radio, CBS finally surpassed NBC as the highest-rated network. Although William Paley had intended to run CBS only for six months to help get it off the ground, he ultimately ran it for more than fifty years.

Bringing Order to Chaos with the Radio Act of 1927

In the 1920s, as radio moved from narrowcasting to broadcasting, the battle for more frequency space and less channel interference intensified. Manufacturers, engineers, station operators, network executives, and the listening public demanded action. Many wanted more sweeping regulation than the simple licensing function granted under the Radio Act of 1912, which gave the Commerce Department little power to deny a license or to unclog the airwaves.

Beginning in 1924, Commerce Secretary Herbert Hoover ordered radio stations to share time by setting aside certain frequencies for entertainment and news and others for farm and weather reports. To challenge Hoover, a station in Chicago jammed the airwaves, intentionally moving its signal onto an unauthorized frequency. In 1926, the courts decided that based on the existing Radio Act, Hoover had the power only to grant licenses, not to restrict stations from operating. Within the year, two hundred new stations clogged the airwaves, creating a chaotic period in which nearly all radios had poor reception. By early 1927, sales of radio sets had declined sharply.

To restore order to the airwaves, Congress passed the **Radio Act of 1927**, which stated an extremely important principle–licensees did not *own* their channels but could only license them as long as they operated to serve the "public interest, convenience, or necessity." To oversee licenses and negotiate channel problems, the 1927 act created the **Federal Radio Commission (FRC)**, whose members were appointed by the president. Although the FRC was intended as a temporary committee, it grew into a powerful regulatory agency. With passage of the **Communications Act of 1934**, the FRC became the **Federal Communications Commission (FCC)**. Its jurisdiction covered not only radio but also the telephone and the telegraph (and later television, cable, and the Internet). More significantly, by this time Congress and the president had sided with the already-powerful radio networks and acceded to a system of advertising-supported commercial broadcasting as best serving "public interest, convenience, or necessity," overriding the concerns of educational, labor, and citizen broadcasting advocates.[9] (See Table 5.1.)

In 1941, an activist FCC went after the networks. Declaring that NBC and CBS could no longer force affiliates to carry programs they did not want, the government outlawed the practice of option time that Paley had used to build CBS into a major network. The FCC also demanded that RCA sell one of its two NBC networks. RCA and NBC claimed that the rulings would bankrupt them. The Supreme Court sided with the FCC, however, and RCA eventually sold NBC-Blue to a group of businessmen for $8 million in the mid-1940s. It became the American Broadcasting Company (ABC). These government crackdowns brought long-overdue reform to the radio industry, but they had not come soon enough to prevent considerable damage to noncommercial radio.

> "Overnight, it seemed, everyone had gone into broadcasting: newspapers, banks, public utilities, department stores, universities and colleges, cities and towns, pharmacies, creameries, and hospitals."
>
> TOM LEWIS,
> RADIO HISTORIAN

Act	Provisions	Effects
Wireless Ship Act of 1910	Required U.S. seagoing ships carrying more than fifty passengers and traveling more than two hundred miles off the coast to be equipped with wireless equipment with a one-hundred-mile range.	Saved lives at sea, including more than seven hundred rescued by ships responding to the *Titanic*'s distress signals two years later.
Radio Act of 1912	Required radio operators to obtain a license, gave the Commerce Department the power to deny a license, and began a uniform system of assigning call letters to identify stations.	The federal government began to assert control over radio. Penalties were established for stations that interfere with other stations' signals.
Radio Act of 1927	Established the Federal Radio Commission (FRC) as a temporary agency to oversee licenses and negotiate channel assignments.	First expressed the now-fundamental principle that licensees did not *own* their channels but could only license them as long as they operated to serve the "public interest, convenience, or necessity."
Communications Act of 1934	Established the Federal Communications Commission (FCC) to replace the FRC. The FCC regulated radio, the telephone, the telegraph, and later television, cable, and the Internet.	Congress tacitly agreed to a system of advertising-supported commercial broadcasting despite concerns of the public.
Telecommunications Act of 1996	Eliminated most radio and television station ownership rules, some dating back more than fifty years.	Enormous national and regional station groups formed, dramatically changing the sound and localism of radio in the United States.

▲

TABLE 5.1

MAJOR ACTS IN THE HISTORY OF U.S. RADIO

The Golden Age of Radio

Many programs on television today were initially formulated for radio. The first weather forecasts and farm reports on radio began in the 1920s. Regularly scheduled radio news analysis started in 1927, with H. V. Kaltenborn, a reporter for the *Brooklyn Eagle*, providing commentary on AT&T's WEAF. The first regular network news analysis began on CBS in 1930, featuring Lowell Thomas, who would remain on radio for forty-four years.

Early Radio Programming

Early on, only a handful of stations operated in most large radio markets, and popular stations were affiliated with CBS, NBC-Red, or NBC-Blue. Many large stations employed their own in-house orchestras and aired live music daily. Listeners had favorite evening programs, usually fifteen minutes long, to which they would tune in each night. Families gathered around the radio to hear such shows as *Amos 'n' Andy*, *The Shadow*, *The Lone Ranger*, *The Green Hornet*, and *Fibber McGee and Molly*, or one of President Franklin Roosevelt's fireside chats.

Among the most popular early programs on radio, the variety show was the forerunner to popular TV shows like the *Ed Sullivan Show*. The variety show, developed from stage acts and vaudeville, began with the *Eveready Hour* in 1923 on WEAF. Considered experimental, the program presented classical music, minstrel shows, comedy sketches, and dramatic readings. Stars from vaudeville, musical comedy, and New York theater and opera would occasionally make guest appearances.

By the 1930s, studio-audience quiz shows—*Professor Quiz* and the *Old Time Spelling Bee*—had emerged. Other quiz formats, used on *Information Please* and *Quiz Kids*, featured guest panelists. The quiz formats were later copied by television, particularly in the 1950s. *Truth or Consequences*, based on a nineteenth-century parlor game, first aired on radio in 1940 and featured guests performing goofy stunts. It ran for seventeen years on radio and another twenty-seven on television, influencing TV stunt shows like CBS's *Beat the Clock* in the 1950s and NBC's *Fear Factor* in the early 2000s.

Dramatic programs, mostly radio plays that were broadcast live from theaters, developed as early as 1922. Historians mark the appearance of *Clara, Lu, and Em* on WGN in 1931 as the first

"There are three things which I shall never forget about America—the Rocky Mountains, Niagara Falls, and *Amos 'n' Andy*."

GEORGE BERNARD SHAW, IRISH PLAYWRIGHT

FIRESIDE CHATS
This giant bank of radio network microphones makes us wonder today how President Franklin D. Roosevelt managed to project such an intimate and reassuring tone in his famous fireside chats. Conceived originally to promote FDR's New Deal policies amid the Great Depression, these chats were delivered between 1933 and 1944 and touched on topics of national interest. Roosevelt was the first president to effectively use broadcasting to communicate with citizens; he also gave nearly a thousand press conferences during his twelve-plus years as president, revealing a strong commitment to use media and news to speak early and often with the American people.

soap opera. One year later, Colgate-Palmolive bought the program, put it on NBC, and began selling the soap products that gave this dramatic genre its distinctive nickname. Early "soaps" were fifteen minutes in length and ran five or six days a week. By 1940, sixty different soap operas occupied nearly eighty hours of network radio time each week.

Most radio programs had a single sponsor that created and produced each show. The networks distributed these programs live around the country, charging the sponsors advertising fees. Many shows—the *Palmolive Hour*, *General Motors Family Party*, the *Lucky Strike Orchestra*, and the *Eveready Hour* among them—were named after the sole sponsor's product.

Radio Programming as a Cultural Mirror

The situation comedy, a major staple of TV programming today, began on radio in the mid-1920s. By the early 1930s, the most popular comedy was *Amos 'n' Andy*, which started on Chicago radio in 1925 before moving to NBC-Blue in 1929. *Amos 'n' Andy* was based on the conventions of the nineteenth-century minstrel show and featured black characters stereotyped as shiftless and stupid. Created as a blackface stage act by two white comedians, Charles Correll and Freeman Gosden, the program was criticized as racist. But NBC and the program's producers claimed that *Amos 'n' Andy* was as popular among black audiences as among white listeners.[10]

Amos 'n' Andy also launched the idea of the serial show: a program that featured continuing story lines from one day to the next. The format was soon copied by soap operas and other radio dramas. The show aired six nights a week from 7:00 to 7:15 P.M. During the show's first year on the network, radio-set sales rose nearly 25 percent nationally. To keep people coming to restaurants and movie theaters, owners broadcast *Amos 'n' Andy* in lobbies, rest rooms, and entryways. Early radio research estimated that the program aired in more than half of all radio homes in the nation during the 1930-31 season, making it the most popular radio series in history. In 1951, it made a brief transition to television (Correll and Gosden sold the rights to CBS for $1 million), becoming the first TV series to have an entirely black cast. But amid a strengthening Civil Rights movement and a formal protest by the NAACP (which argued that "every character is either a clown or a crook"), CBS canceled the program in 1953.[11]

The Authority of Radio

The most famous single radio broadcast of all time was an adaptation of H. G. Wells's *War of the Worlds* on the radio series *Mercury Theater of the Air*. Orson Welles produced, hosted, and acted in this popular series, which adapted science fiction, mystery, and historical adventure dramas for radio. On Halloween eve in 1938, the twenty-three-year-old Welles aired the 1898 Martian invasion novel in the style of a radio news program. For people who missed the opening disclaimer, the program sounded like a real news report, with eyewitness accounts of battles between Martian invaders and the U.S. Army.

The program created a panic that lasted several hours. In New Jersey, some people walked through the streets with wet towels around their heads for protection from deadly Martian heat rays. In New York, young men reported to their National Guard headquarters to prepare for battle. Across the nation, calls jammed police switchboards. Afterward, Orson Welles, once the radio voice of *The Shadow*, used the notoriety of this broadcast to launch a film career. Meanwhile, the FCC called for stricter warnings both before and during programs that imitated the style of radio news.

Radio Reinvents Itself

New from Motorola
ALL-TRANSISTOR
Shirt-pocket radio
with powerful built-in speaker

Slips into your pocket...plays with the sound of a set twice its size.
New miniaturized transistor radio lets you enjoy favorite programs wherever you go. Powerful chassis pulls in stations loud and clean . . . plays them clear and mellow through a newly designed built-in speaker. A *single* low-cost battery gives many hours of listening pleasure. Motorola extras include magnifying lens for easy-to-read dial . . . durable case in black, blue, red, or green. 90-day warranty on all parts and labor at no additional cost.

Perfect gift for you or someone extra special

ONLY $29.95

Built-In Easel Stand in back for stable "stand-up" position.   Power-Packed Chassis with 6 transistors provides plenty of volume.   Built-In Antenna pulls in stations like a magnet for finest reception.   Perfect Companion for sports events. Earphone jack for private listening.

More to enjoy **MOTOROLA**

ADVERTISEMENTS for pocket transistor radios, which became popular in the 1950s, emphasized their portability.

"Armstrong was a lone experimenter, Sarnoff a company man."

ERIK BARNOUW, MEDIA HISTORIAN

Older media forms do not generally disappear when confronted by newer forms. Instead, they adapt. Although radio threatened sound recording in the 1920s, the recording industry adjusted to the economic and social challenges posed by radio's arrival. Remarkably, the arrival of television in the 1950s marked the only time in media history in which a new medium stole virtually every national programming and advertising strategy from an older medium. Television snatched radio's advertisers, program genres, major celebrities, and large evening audiences. The TV set even physically displaced the radio as the living room centerpiece across America. Nevertheless, radio adapted and continued to reach an audience.

The story of radio's evolution and survival is especially important today, as newspapers and magazines appear online and as publishers produce e-books for new generations of readers. In contemporary culture, we have grown accustomed to such media convergence, but to best understand this blurring of the boundaries between media forms, it is useful to look at the 1950s and the ways in which radio responded to the advent of television.

Transistors Make Radio Portable

A key development in radio's adaptation to television occurred with the invention of the transistor by Bell Laboratories in 1947. **Transistors** were small electrical devices that, like vacuum tubes, could receive and amplify radio signals. However, they used less power and produced less heat than vacuum tubes, and they were more durable and less expensive. Best of all, they were tiny. Transistors, which also revolutionized hearing aids, constituted the first step in replacing bulky and delicate tubes, leading eventually to today's integrated circuits.

Texas Instruments marketed the first transistor radio in 1953 for about $40. Using even smaller transistors, Sony introduced the pocket radio in 1957. But it wasn't until the 1960s that transistor radios became cheaper than conventional tube and battery radios. For a while, the term *transistor* became a synonym for a small, portable radio.

The development of transistors let radio go where television could not—to the beach, to the office, into bedrooms and bathrooms, and into nearly all new cars. (Before the transistor, car radios were a luxury item.) By the 1960s, most radio listening took place outside the home.

The FM Revolution and Edwin Armstrong

By the time the broadcast industry launched commercial television in the 1950s, many people, including David Sarnoff of RCA, were predicting radio's demise. To fund television's development and to protect his radio holdings, Sarnoff had even delayed a dramatic breakthrough in broadcast sound, what he himself called a "revolution"—FM radio.

Edwin Armstrong, who first discovered and developed FM radio in the 1920s and early 1930s, is often considered the most prolific and influential inventor in radio history. He used De Forest's vacuum tube to invent an amplifying system that enabled radio receivers to pick up distant signals, rendering the enormous alternators used for generating power in early radio transmitters obsolete. In 1922, he sold a "super" version of his circuit to RCA for $200,000 and sixty thousand shares of RCA stock, which made him a millionaire as well as RCA's largest private stockholder.

Armstrong also worked on the major problem of radio reception–electrical interference. Between 1930 and 1933, the inventor filed five patents on **FM**, or frequency modulation. Offering static-free radio reception, FM supplied greater fidelity and clarity than AM, making FM ideal for music. **AM**, or amplitude modulation (*modulation* refers to the variation in waveforms), stressed the volume, or height, of radio waves; FM accentuated the pitch, or distance, between radio waves (see Figure 5.2).

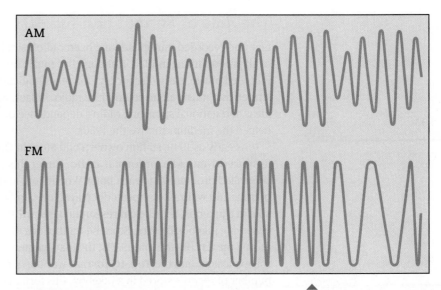

FIGURE 5.2
AM AND FM WAVES
Source: Adapted from David Cheshire, The Video Manual, 1982.

Although David Sarnoff, the president of RCA, thought that television would replace radio, he helped Armstrong set up the first experimental FM station atop the Empire State Building in New York City. Eventually, though, Sarnoff thwarted FM's development (which he was able to do because RCA had an option on Armstrong's new patents). Instead, in 1935 Sarnoff threw RCA's considerable weight behind the development of television. With the FCC allocating and reassigning scarce frequency spaces, RCA wanted to ensure that channels went to television before they went to FM. But most of all, Sarnoff wanted to protect RCA's existing AM empire. Given the high costs of converting to FM and the revenue needed for TV experiments, Sarnoff decided to close down Armstrong's station.

Armstrong forged ahead without RCA. He founded a new FM station and advised other engineers, who started more than twenty experimental stations between 1935 and the early 1940s. In 1941, the FCC approved limited space allocations for commercial FM licenses. During the next few years, FM grew in fits and starts. Between 1946 and early 1949, the number of commercial FM stations expanded from 48 to 700. But then the FCC moved FM's frequency space to a new band on the electromagnetic spectrum, rendering some 400,000 prewar FM receiver sets useless. FM's future became uncertain, and by 1954 the number of FM stations had fallen to 560.

On January 31, 1954, Edwin Armstrong, weary from years of legal skirmishes over patents with RCA, Lee De Forest, and others, wrote a note apologizing to his wife, removed the air conditioner from his thirteenth-story New York apartment window, and jumped to his death. A month later, David Sarnoff announced record profits of $850 million for RCA, with TV sales accounting for 54 percent of the company's earnings. In the early 1960s, the FCC opened up more spectrum space for the superior sound of FM, infusing new life into radio.

Although AM stations had greater reach, they could not match the crisp fidelity of FM, which made FM preferable for music. In the early 1970s, about 70 percent of listeners tuned almost exclusively to AM radio. By the 1980s, however, FM had surpassed AM in profitability. By the 2000s, more than 75 percent of all listeners preferred FM, and about 6,500 commercial and more than 3,400 educational FM stations were in operation. The expansion of FM represented one of the chief ways radio survived television and Sarnoff's gloomy predictions.

The Rise of Format and Top 40 Radio

Live and recorded music had long been radio's single biggest staple, accounting for 48 percent of all programming in 1938. Although live music on radio was generally considered superior to recorded music, early disc jockeys made a significant contribution to the latter. They demonstrated that music alone could drive radio. In fact, when television snatched radio's program ideas and national sponsors, radio's dependence on recorded music became a necessity and helped the medium survive the 1950s.

As early as 1949, station owner Todd Storz in Omaha, Nebraska, experimented with formula-driven radio, or **format radio**. Under this system, management rather than deejays controlled programming each hour. When Storz and his program manager noticed that bar patrons and waitresses repeatedly played certain favorite songs from the forty records available in a jukebox, they began researching record sales to identify the most popular tunes. From observing jukebox culture, Storz hit on the idea of **rotation**: playing the top songs many times during the day. By the mid-1950s, the management-control idea combined with the rock-and-roll explosion, and the **Top 40 format** was born. Although the term *Top 40* derived from the number of records stored in a jukebox, this format came to refer to the forty most popular hits in a given week as measured by record sales.

As format radio grew, program managers combined rapid deejay chatter with the best-selling songs of the day and occasional oldies–popular songs from a few months earlier. By the early 1960s, to avoid "dead air," managers asked deejays to talk over the beginning and the end of a song so that listeners would feel less compelled to switch stations. Ads, news, weather forecasts, and station identifications were all designed to fit a consistent station environment. Listeners, tuning in at any moment, would recognize the station by its distinctive sound.

In format radio, management carefully coordinates, or programs, each hour, dictating what the deejay will do at various intervals throughout each hour of the day (see Figure 5.3). Management creates a program log–once called a *hot clock* in radio jargon–that deejays must follow. By the mid-1960s, one study had determined that in a typical hour on Top 40, listeners could expect to hear about twenty ads; numerous weather, time, and contest announcements; multiple recitations of the station's call letters; about three minutes of news; and approximately twelve songs.

Radio managers further sectioned off programming into *day parts*, which typically consisted of time blocks covering 6 to 10 A.M., 10 A.M. to 3 P.M., 3 to 7 P.M., and 7 P.M. to midnight. Each day part, or block, was programmed through ratings research according to who was listening. For instance, a Top 40 station would feature its top deejays in the morning and afternoon periods when audiences, many riding in cars, were largest. From 10 A.M. to 3 P.M., research determined that women at home and secretaries at work usually controlled the dial, so program managers, capitalizing on the gender stereotypes of the day, played more romantic ballads and less hard rock. Teenagers tended to be heavy evening listeners, so program managers often discarded news breaks at this time, since research showed that teens turned the dial when news came on.

Critics of format radio argued that only the top songs received play and that lesser-known songs deserving air time received meager attention. Although a few popular star deejays

```
******************************* MusicMaster *******************************

93.5 The Mix                                                      12N-1PM
Lunch Time    Rewind    LIVE

  0:00        01890     DON HENLEY                    :26/5:59/FADE
                        SUNSET GRILL

  5:59        00617     ROBERT PALMER                 :24/3:45/FADE
                        ADDICTED TO LOVE

  9:44        00852     JOHN LENNON                   :14/2:49/FADE
                        IMAGINE

 12:33        00405     MADONNA                 :17/:32/4:00/FADE
                        PAPA DON'T PREACH

 16:33        02252     EDDIE MONEY                   15/3:28/COLD
                        BABY HOLD ON

----------------------------------------------------------------------
 20:01                  STOP SET
----------------------------------------------------------------------

 22:01        02225     DOOBIE BROTHERS               11/3:24/FADE
                        TAKE ME IN YOUR ARMS

 25:25        02396     STEVIE WONDER                 07/3:18/FADE
                        ISN'T SHE LOVELY

 28:43        01679     A-HA                          08/3:42/FADE
                        TAKE ON ME

 32:25        00110     THE GUESS WHO                 :21/3:39/FADE
                        THESE EYES
```

▲

FIGURE 5.3

RADIO PROGRAM LOG FOR AN ADULT CONTEMPORARY (AC) STATION

Source: KCVM, Cedar Falls, IA, 2010.

continued to play a role in programming, many others quit when managers introduced formats. Owners approached programming as a science, but deejays considered it an art form. Program managers argued that deejays had different tastes from those of the average listener and therefore could not be fully trusted to know popular audience tastes. The owners' position, which generated more revenue, triumphed.

Resisting the Top 40

The expansion of FM in the mid-1960s created room for experimenting, particularly with classical music, jazz, blues, and non-Top 40 rock songs. **Progressive rock** emerged as an alternative to conventional formats. Many noncommercial stations broadcast from college campuses, where student deejays and managers rejected the commercialism associated with Top 40 tunes and began playing lesser-known alternative music and longer album cuts (such as Bob Dylan's "Desolation Row" and the Doors' "The End"). Until that time, most rock on radio had been consigned almost exclusively to Top 40 AM formats, with song length averaging about three minutes.

Experimental FM stations, both commercial and noncommercial, offered a cultural space for hard-edged political folk music and for rock music that commented on the Civil Rights movement and protested America's involvement in the Vietnam War. By the 1970s, however, progressive rock had been copied, tamed, and absorbed by mainstream radio under the format labeled **album-oriented rock (AOR)**. By 1972, AOR-driven album sales accounted for more than 85 percent of the retail record business. By the 1980s, as first-generation rock and rollers aged and became more affluent, AOR stations became less political and played mostly white, post-Beatles music featuring such groups as Pink Floyd, Led Zeppelin, Cream, and Queen. Today, AOR has been subsumed under the more general classic rock format.

The Sounds of Commercial Radio

Contemporary radio sounds very different from its predecessor. In contrast to the few stations per market in the 1930s, most large markets today include more than forty stations that vie for listener loyalty. With the exception of national network-sponsored news segments and nationally syndicated programs, most programming is locally produced and heavily dependent on the music industry for content. Although a few radio personalities, such as Glenn Beck, Ryan Seacrest, Rush Limbaugh, Tom Joyner, Tavis Smiley, and Jim Rome, are nationally prominent, local deejays and their music are the stars at most radio stations.

However, listeners today are unlike radio's first audiences in several ways. First, listeners in the 1930s tuned in to their favorite shows at set times. Listeners today do not say, "Gee, my favorite song is coming on at 8 P.M., so I'd better be home to listen." Instead, radio has become a secondary, or background, medium that follows the rhythms of daily life. Radio programmers today worry about channel cruising–listeners' tendency to search the dial until they find a song they like.

Second, in the 1930s, peak listening time occurred during the evening hours–dubbed *prime time* in the TV era–when people were home from work and school. Now, the heaviest radio listening occurs during **drive time**, between 6 and 9 A.M. and 4 and 7 P.M., when people are commuting to and from work or school.

Third, stations today are more specialized. Listeners are loyal to favorite stations, music formats, and even radio personalities, rather than to specific shows. People

RYAN SEACREST may be best known for his job hosting TV's *American Idol*, but he began his career in radio when he hosted a local radio show while attending the University of Georgia. In the style of his own idols—Dick Clark and Casey Kasem—Seacrest now hosts two nationally syndicated radio shows, *On Air with Ryan Seacrest* and *American Top 40*, in addition to his television projects.

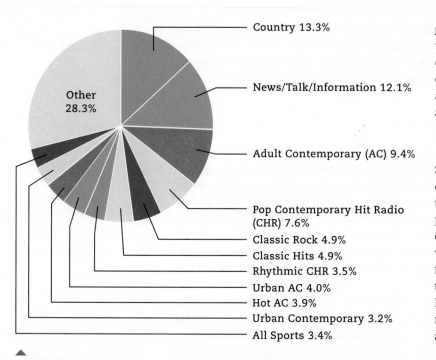

Country 13.3%

News/Talk/Information 12.1%

Adult Contemporary (AC) 9.4%

Pop Contemporary Hit Radio (CHR) 7.6%

Classic Rock 4.9%

Classic Hits 4.9%

Rhythmic CHR 3.5%

Urban AC 4.0%

Hot AC 3.9%

Urban Contemporary 3.2%

All Sports 3.4%

Other 28.3%

FIGURE 5.4

THE MOST POPULAR RADIO FORMATS IN THE UNITED STATES AMONG PERSONS AGE TWELVE AND OLDER

Source: Arbitron, Radio Today, 2011 Edition.

Note: Based on listener shares for primary AM and FM stations, plus HD stations and Internet streams of radio stations.

generally listen to only four or five stations that target them. Almost fifteen thousand radio stations now operate in the United States, customizing their sounds to reach niche audiences through format specialization and alternative programming.

Format Specialization

Stations today use a variety of formats based on managed program logs and day parts. All told, more than forty different radio formats, plus variations, serve diverse groups of listeners (see Figure 5.4). To please advertisers, who want to know exactly who is listening, formats usually target audiences according to their age, income, gender, or race/ethnicity. Radio's specialization enables advertisers to reach smaller target audiences at costs that are much lower than those for television.

Targeting listeners has become extremely competitive, however, because forty or fifty stations may be available in a large radio market. About 10 percent of all stations across the country switch formats each year in an effort to find a formula that generates more advertising money. Some stations, particularly those in large cities, even rent blocks of time to various local ethnic or civic groups; this enables the groups to dictate their own formats and sell ads.

News, Talk, and Information Radio

The nation's fastest-growing format throughout much of the 1990s was the **news/talk/information** format (see "Case Study: Host: The Origins of Talk Radio" on page 177). In 1987, only 170 radio stations operated formats dominated by either news programs or talk shows, which tend to appeal to adults over age thirty-five (except for sports talk programs, which draw mostly male sports fans of all ages). By 2012, more than 1,920 stations carried the format—the most stations of any format. It is the most dominant format on AM radio and the second most popular format (by number of listeners) in the nation (see Figure 5.4 and Table 5.2). A news/talk/information format, though more expensive to produce than a music format, appeals to advertisers looking to target working- and middle-class adult consumers. Nevertheless, most radio stations continue to be driven by a variety of less expensive music formats.

TABLE 5.2

TALK RADIO WEEKLY AUDIENCE (IN MILLIONS)

Source: Talkers magazine, "The Top Talk Radio Audiences," Winter, 2012.

Note: * = Information unavailable; N/A = Talk host not nationally broadcast.

Talk Show Host	2003	2006	2012
Rush Limbaugh (Conservative)	14.5	13.5	15
Sean Hannity (Conservative)	11.75	12.5	14
Michael Savage (Conservative)	7	8.25	9
Glenn Beck (Conservative)	*	3	8.5
Mark Levin (Conservative)	N/A	1	8.5
Dave Ramsey (Financial Advice)	*	2.75	8.5
Laura Ingraham (Conservative)	1.25	5	6
Neal Boortz (Conservative)	*	*	6

Host: The Origins of Talk Radio

by David Foster Wallace

The origins of contemporary political talk radio can be traced to three phenomena of the 1980s. The first of these involved AM music stations getting absolutely murdered by FM, which could broadcast music in stereo and allowed for much better fidelity on high and low notes. The human voice, on the other hand, is midrange and doesn't require high fidelity. The eighties' proliferation of talk formats on the AM band also provided new careers for some music deejays—e.g., Don Imus, Morton Downey Jr.—whose chatty personas didn't fit well with FM's all-about-the-music ethos.

The second big factor was the repeal, late in Ronald Reagan's second term, of what was known as the Fairness Doctrine. This was a 1949 FCC rule designed to minimize any possible restrictions on free speech caused by limited access to broadcasting outlets. The idea was that, as one of the conditions for receiving an FCC broadcast license, a station had to "devote

GLENN BECK, the conservative host of *The Glenn Beck Program*, a nationally syndicated talk radio show that also promulgates the MMLB idea.

reasonable attention to the coverage of controversial issues of public importance," and consequently had to provide "reasonable, although not necessarily equal" opportunities for opposing sides to express their views. Because of the Fairness Doctrine, talk stations had to hire and program symmetrically: if you had a three-hour program whose host's politics were on one side of the ideological spectrum, you had to have another long-form program whose host more or less spoke for the other side. Weirdly enough, up through the mid-eighties it was usually the U.S. right that benefited most from the Doctrine. Pioneer talk syndicator Ed McLaughlin, who managed San Francisco's KGO in the 1960s, recalls that "I had more liberals on the air than I had conservatives or even moderates for that matter, and I had a hell of a time finding the other voice."

The Fairness Doctrine's repeal was part of the sweeping deregulations of the Reagan era, which aimed to liberate all sorts of industries from government interference and allow them to compete freely in the marketplace. The old, Rooseveltian logic of the Doctrine had been that since the airwaves belonged to everyone, a license to profit from those airwaves conferred on the broadcast industry some special obligation to serve the public interest. Commercial radio broadcasting was not, in other words, originally conceived as just another for-profit industry; it was supposed to meet a higher standard of social responsibility. After 1987, though, just another industry is pretty much what radio became, and its only real responsibility now is to attract and retain

listeners in order to generate revenue. In other words, the sort of distinction explicitly drawn by FCC Chairman Newton Minow in the 1960s—namely, that between "the public interest" and "merely what interests the public"—no longer exists.

More or less on the heels of the Fairness Doctrine's repeal came the West Coast and then national syndication of *The Rush Limbaugh Show* through Mr. McLaughlin's EFM Media. Limbaugh is the third great progenitor of today's political talk radio partly because he's a host of extraordinary, once-in-a-generation talent and charisma—bright, loquacious, witty, complexly authoritative—whose show's blend of news, entertainment, and partisan analysis became the model for legions of imitators. But he was also the first great promulgator of the Mainstream Media's Liberal Bias (MMLB) idea. This turned out to be a brilliantly effective rhetorical move, since the MMLB concept functioned simultaneously as a standard around which Rush's audience could rally, as an articulation of the need for right-wing (i.e., unbiased) media, and as a mechanism by which any criticism or refutation of conservative ideas could be dismissed (either as biased or as the product of indoctrination by biased media). Boiled way down, the MMLB thesis is able both to exploit and to perpetuate many conservatives' dissatisfaction with extant media sources—and it's this dissatisfaction that cements political talk radio's large and loyal audience.

Source: Excerpted from David Foster Wallace, "Host: The Origins of Talk Radio," Atlantic, April 2005, 66–68.

Music Formats

The **adult contemporary (AC)** format, also known as middle-of-the-road or MOR, is among radio's oldest and most popular formats, reaching about 9.4 percent of all listeners, most of them over age forty, with an eclectic mix of news, talk, oldies, and soft rock music—what *Broadcasting* magazine describes as "not too soft, not too loud, not too fast, not too slow, not too hard, not too lush, not too old, not too new." Variations on the AC format include urban AC, hot AC, rhythmic AC, modern AC, and smooth AC. Now encompassing everything from rap to pop punk songs, Top 40 radio—also called **contemporary hit radio (CHR)**—still appeals to many teens and young adults. A renewed focus on producing pop singles in the sound recording industry has boosted listenership of this format lately.

Country is the most popular format in the nation (except during morning drive time, when news/talk/information is number one). Many stations are in tiny markets where country is traditionally the default format for communities with only one radio station. Country music has old roots in radio, starting in 1925 with the influential *Grand Ole Opry* program on WSM in Nashville. Although Top 40 drove country music out of many radio markets in the 1950s, the growth of FM in the 1960s brought it back, as station managers looked for market niches not served by rock music.

Many formats appeal to particular ethnic or racial groups. In 1947, WDIA in Memphis was the first station to program exclusively for black listeners. Now called **urban contemporary**, this format targets a wide variety of African American listeners, primarily in large cities. Urban contemporary, which typically plays popular dance, rap, R&B, and hip-hop music (featuring performers like Rihanna and Ludacris), also subdivides by age, featuring an Urban AC category with performers like Maxwell, Alicia Keys, and Mary J. Blige.

Spanish-language radio, one of radio's fastest-growing formats, is concentrated mostly in large Hispanic markets such as Miami, New York, Chicago, Las Vegas, California, Arizona,

WENDY WILLIAMS
refers to herself as the "Queen of All Media," but before her daytime TV talk show, she got her start with a nearly two-decade career in radio. She began as a substitute deejay on an urban contemporary station in New York before gaining notoriety with her celebrity interviews and gossip.

EDDIE "PIOLÍN" SOTELO
is a popular Los Angeles radio personality on Univision-owned KSCA (101.9 FM), which has a regional Mexican format and is the highest-rated station in the market. Sotelo is a major supporter of immigrant rights and helped to organize a huge rally in 2006. His nickname, "Piolín," means "Tweety Bird" in Spanish.

New Mexico, and Texas (where KCOR, the first all-Spanish-language station, originated in San Antonio in 1947). Besides talk shows and news segments in Spanish, this format features a variety of Spanish, Caribbean, and Latin American musical styles, including calypso, flamenco, mariachi, merengue, reggae, samba, salsa, and Tejano.

In addition, today there are other formats that are spin-offs from AOR. Classic rock serves up rock favorites from the mid-1960s through the 1980s to the baby-boom generation and other listeners who have outgrown Top 40. The oldies format originally served adults who grew up on 1950s and early 1960s rock and roll. As that audience has aged, oldies formats now target younger audiences with the classic hits format featuring songs from the 1970s, 1980s, and 1990s. The alternative music format recaptures some of the experimental approach of the FM stations of the 1960s, although with much more controlled playlists, and has helped to introduce artists such as the Dead Weather and Cage the Elephant.

Research indicates that most people identify closely with the music they listened to as adolescents and young adults. This tendency partially explains why classic hits and classic rock stations combined have surpassed CHR stations today. It also helps to explain the recent nostalgia for music from the 1980s and early 1990s.

Nonprofit Radio and NPR

Although commercial radio (particularly those stations owned by huge radio conglomerates) dominates the radio spectrum, nonprofit radio maintains a voice. But the road to viability for nonprofit radio in the United States has not been easy. In the 1930s, the Wagner-Hatfield Amendment to the 1934 Communications Act intended to set aside 25 percent of radio for a wide variety of nonprofit stations. When the amendment was defeated in 1935, the future of educational and noncommercial radio looked bleak. Many nonprofits had sold out to for-profit owners during the Great Depression of the 1930s. The stations that remained were often banished from the air during the evening hours or assigned weak signals by federal regulators who favored commercial owners and their lobbying agents. Still, nonprofit public radio survived. Today, more than three thousand nonprofit stations operate, most of them on the FM band.

The Early Years of Nonprofit Radio

Two government rulings, both in 1948, aided nonprofit radio. First, the government began authorizing noncommercial licenses to stations not affiliated with a labor, religious, education, or civic group. The first license went to Lewis Kimball Hill, a radio reporter and pacifist during World War II who started the **Pacifica Foundation** to run experimental public stations. Pacifica stations, like Hill, have often challenged the status quo in radio as well as in government. Most notably, in the 1950s they aired the poetry, prose, and music of performers considered radical, left-wing, or communist who were blacklisted by television and seldom acknowledged by AM stations. Over the years, Pacifica has also been fined and reprimanded by the FCC and Congress for airing programs that critics considered inappropriate for public airwaves. Today, Pacifica has more than ninety affiliate stations.

Second, the FCC approved 10-watt FM stations. Prior to this time, radio stations had to have at least 250 watts to get licensed. A 10-watt station with a broadcast range of only about seven miles took very little capital to operate, so more people could participate, and they became training sites for students interested in broadcasting. Although the FCC stopped licensing new 10-watt stations in 1978, about one hundred longtime 10-watters are still in operation.

> "We have a huge responsibility to keep the airwaves open for what I think is the majority—representing the voices that are locked out of the mainstream media."
>
> AMY GOODMAN, CO-HOST OF RADIO'S *DEMOCRACY NOW!* 2001

PUBLIC RADIO STATIONS in rural areas, like WMMT, which services eastern Kentucky, southwestern Virginia, and southern West Virginia, connect people in far-flung and remote areas by broadcasting local programming that speaks to their listeners' needs and tastes. Rural stations like this one rely heavily on federal funding and thus are more likely to go under if budgets are cut.

▼

Media Literacy and the Critical Process

1 DESCRIPTION. Listen to a typical morning or late afternoon hour of a popular local commercial talk-news radio station and a typical hour of your local NPR station from the same time period over a two- to three-day period. Keep a log of what topics are covered and what news stories are reported. For the commercial station, log what commercials are carried and how much time in an hour is devoted to ads. For the noncommercial station, note how much time is devoted to recognizing the station's sources of funding support and who the supporters are.

2 ANALYSIS. Look for patterns. What kinds of stories are covered? What kinds of topics are discussed? Create a chart to categorize the stories. To cover events and issues, do the stations use actual reporters at the scene? How much time is given to reporting compared to time devoted to opinion? How many sources are cited in each story? What kinds of interview sources are used? Are they expert sources or regular person-on-the-street interviews? How many sources are men and how many are women?

Comparing Commercial and Noncommercial Radio

After the arrival and growth of commercial TV, the Corporation for Public Broadcasting (CPB) was created in 1967 as the funding agent for public broadcasting—an alternative to commercial TV and radio for educational and cultural programming that could not be easily sustained by commercial broadcasters in search of large general audiences. As a result, NPR (National Public Radio) developed to provide national programming to public stations to supplement local programming efforts. Today, NPR affiliates get just 2 percent of their funding from the federal government. Most money for public radio comes instead from corporate sponsorships, individual grants, and private donations.

3 INTERPRETATION. What do these patterns mean? Is there a balance between reporting and opinion? Do you detect any bias, and if so, how did you determine this? Are the stations serving as watchdogs to ensure that democracy's best interests are being served? What effect, if any, do you think the advertisers/supporters have on the programming? What arguments might you make about commercial and noncommercial radio based on your findings?

4 EVALUATION. Which station seems to be doing a better job serving its local audience? Why? Do you buy the 1930s argument that noncommercial stations serve narrow, special interests while commercial stations serve capitalism and the public interest? Why or why not? From which station did you learn the most, and which station did you find most entertaining? Explain. What did you like and dislike about each station?

5 ENGAGEMENT. Join your college radio station. Talk to the station manager about the goals for a typical hour of programming and what audience they are trying to reach. Finally, pitch program or topic ideas that would improve your college station's programming.

Creation of the First Noncommercial Networks

During the 1960s, nonprofit broadcasting found a Congress sympathetic to an old idea: using radio and television as educational tools. As a result, **National Public Radio (NPR)** and the **Public Broadcasting Service (PBS)** were created as the first noncommercial networks. Under the provisions of the **Public Broadcasting Act of 1967** and the **Corporation for Public Broadcasting (CPB)**, NPR and PBS were mandated to provide alternatives to commercial broadcasting. Now, NPR's popular news and interview programs, *Morning Edition* and *All Things Considered*, are thriving, and they contribute to the network's audience of thirty-two million listeners per week.

Over the years, however, public radio has faced waning government support and the threat of losing its federal funding. In 1994, a conservative majority in Congress cut financial support and threatened to scrap the CPB, the funding authority for public broadcasting. And again in 2011, the House voted to end financing for the CPB, but the Senate voted against the measure. Consequently, stations have become more reliant on private donations and corporate sponsorship, which could cause some public broadcasters to steer clear of controversial subjects, especially those that critically examine corporations. (See "Media Literacy and the Critical Process: Comparing Commercial and Noncommercial Radio" on page 180.)

Like commercial stations, nonprofit radio has adopted the format style. However, the dominant style in public radio is a loose variety format whereby a station may actually switch from jazz, classical music, and alternative rock to news and talk during different parts of the day. Noncommercial radio remains the place for both tradition and experimentation, as well as for programs that do not draw enough listeners for commercial success. (See "Global Village: Radio Mogadishu" on page 182 for more on public radio internationally.)

New Radio Technologies Offer More Stations

Over the past decade or so, two alternative radio technologies have helped expand radio beyond its traditional AM and FM bands and bring more diverse sounds to listeners: satellite and HD (digital) radio.

Satellite Radio

A series of satellites launched to cover the continental United States created a subscription national **satellite radio** service. Two companies, XM and Sirius, completed their national introduction by 2002 and merged into a single provider in 2008. The merger was precipitated by their struggles to make a profit after building competing satellite systems and battling for listeners. SiriusXM offers about 160 digital music, news, and talk channels to the continental United States (and about 130 online-only channels), with monthly prices starting at $14.49 and satellite radio receivers costing from $50 to $300. SiriusXM access is also available to mobile devices via an app.

Programming includes a range of music channels, from rock to reggae, to Spanish Top 40 and opera, as well as channels dedicated to NASCAR, NPR, cooking, and comedy. Another feature of satellite radio's programming is popular personalities who host their own shows or have their own channels, including Howard Stern, Martha Stewart, Oprah Winfrey, and Bruce Springsteen. U.S. automakers (investors in the satellite radio companies) now equip most new cars with a satellite band, in addition to AM and FM, in order to promote further adoption of satellite radio. SiriusXM had nearly twenty-three million subscribers by 2012.

HD Radio

Available to the public since 2004, **HD radio** is a digital technology that enables AM and FM radio broadcasters to multicast two to three additional compressed digital signals within their traditional analog frequency. For example, KNOW, a public radio station at 91.1 FM in Minneapolis-St. Paul, runs its National Public Radio news/talk/information format on 91.1 HD1, Radio Heartland (acoustic and Americana music) on 91.1 HD2, and the BBC News service on 91.1 HD3. About 2,100 radio stations now broadcast in HD. To tune in, listeners need a radio with the HD band, which brings in CD-quality digital signals. Digital HD radio also provides program data, like artist name and song title, and enables listeners to tag songs for playlists that can later be downloaded to an iPod and purchased on iTunes. The roll-out of HD has been slow, but by 2012, major auto manufacturers were putting HD-equipped radios in most of their new models.

Radio and Convergence

Like every other mass medium, radio is moving into the future by converging with the Internet. Interestingly, this convergence is taking radio back to its roots in some aspects. Internet radio allows for much more variety in radio, which is reminiscent of radio's earliest years when nearly any individual or group with some technical skill could start a radio station. Moreover, *podcasts* bring back content like storytelling, instructional programs, and local topics of interest that

"[Pandora's iPhone app has] changed the perception people have of what Internet radio is, from computer-radio to radio, because you can take the iPhone and just plug it into your car, or take it to the gym."

TIM WESTERGREN, PANDORA FOUNDER, WIRED.COM, 2010

Radio Mogadishu

For two decades, Somalia has been without a properly functioning government. The nation of about nine million people on the eastern coast of Africa has been embroiled in a civil war since 1991 in which competing clans and militias have fought in see-saw battles for control of the country. During this time, more than a half-million Somalis have died from famine and war. Once a great economic and cultural center, Somalia's biggest contribution to global culture in recent years has been modern-day seagoing pirates.

A more moderate transitional government has tried to take leadership of the war-weary nation, but radical Islamist militias, including one with ties to Al Qaeda called Al-Shabaab, have been its biggest adversaries. Al-Shabaab has terrorized African Union peacekeepers and humanitarian aid workers with assassinations and suicide bombings, and it has used amputations, stonings, and beatings to enforce its harsh rules against civilians.

Journalists in Somalia have not been immune from the terror. More than twenty-five journalists have been killed there since 2005, earning Somalia the title "Africa's deadliest country for the media" from the international organization Reporters Without Borders.[1] The media workers under attack include radio workers, who were threatened by militias in April 2010 to stop playing foreign programs from the BBC and Voice of America, and then to stop playing all music (which was deemed un-Islamic) or face "serious consequences."[2] Although most radio stations in Somalia's capital, Mogadishu, have succumbed to the threats, they have found creative (and ironic) ways to jab back at the militants, like playing sound effects instead of music to introduce programs. A newscast, for example, might be introduced by recorded gunshots, animal noises, or car sounds.

One station, Radio Mogadishu, is still bravely broadcasting music and independent newscasts. The station is supported by the transitional government as a critical tool in bringing democracy back to the country, but radio work in the name of democracy has never been more dangerous than it is in Somalia today. "Radio Mogadishu's 100 or so employees are marked men and women, because the insurgents associate them with the government," the *New York Times* reported.[3] Many of the journalists, sound engineers, and deejays eat and sleep at the station for fear of being killed; some have not left the radio station compound to visit their families for months, even though they live in the same city. Their fears are well-founded: One veteran reporter who still lived at home was gunned down by hooded assassins as he returned to his house one night in May 2010.

Radio Mogadishu (in English, Somali, and Arabic on the Web at http://radio muqdisho.net/) speaks to the enduring power of independent radio around the globe and its particular connection to Somali citizens, for whom it is a cultural lifeline. The BBC reports that Somali citizens love pop music (like that of popular Somali artists Abdi Shire Jama [Joogle] and K'Naan, who record abroad), and they resent being told that they cannot listen to it on the radio. Somali bus drivers reportedly sneak music radio for their passengers, turning the music on and off depending on whether they are in a safe, government-controlled district or a dangerous, militia-controlled area. The news portion of radio broadcasts is also important, especially in a country where only about 1 percent of the population has Internet access. "In a fractured state like Somalia, radio remains the most influential medium," the BBC noted.[4]

For radio stations in the United States, the most momentous decision is deciding what kind of music to play—maybe CHR, country, or hot AC. For Radio Mogadishu, simply deciding to play music and broadcast independent news is a far more serious, and life-threatening, matter. ◢

have largely been missing in corporate radio. And portable listening devices like the iPod and radio apps for the iPad and smartphones harken back to the compact portability that first came with the popularization of transistor radios in the 1950s.

Internet Radio

Internet radio emerged in the 1990s with the popularity of the Web. Internet radio stations come in two types. The first involves an existing AM, FM, satellite, or HD station "streaming" a simulcast version of its on-air signal over the Web. According to the Arbitron radio rating service, more than 8,200 radio stations stream their programming over the Web today.[12] Clear Channel's iHeartRadio is one of the major streaming sites for broadcast and custom digital stations. The second kind of online radio station is one that has been created exclusively for the Internet. Pandora, Grooveshark, Yahoo! Music, AOL Radio, and Last.fm are some of the leading Internet radio station services. In fact, services like Pandora allow users to have more control over their listening experience and the selections that are played. Listeners can create individualized stations based on a specific artist or song that they request. Pandora also enables users to share their musical choices on Facebook. Internet radio is clearly in sync with younger radio listeners: A majority of younger consumers, ages twelve to thirty-four, select the Internet (52 percent) over radio (32 percent) as the medium to which they turn first to learn about music.[13]

Beginning in 2002, a Copyright Royalty Board established by the Library of Congress began to assess royalty fees for streaming copyrighted songs over the Internet based on a percentage of each station's revenue. Webcasters have complained that royalty rates set by the board are too high and threaten their financial viability, particularly compared to satellite radio, which pays a lower royalty rate, and broadcasters, who pay no royalty rates at all. For decades, radio broadcasters have paid mechanical royalties to songwriters and music publishers, but no royalties to the performing artists or record companies. Broadcasters have argued that the promotional value of getting songs played is sufficient compensation.

In 2009, Congress passed the Webcaster Settlement Act, which was considered a lifeline for Internet radio. The act enabled Internet stations to negotiate royalty fees directly with the music industry, at rates presumably more reasonable than what the Copyright Royalty Board had proposed. In 2012, Clear Channel became the first company to strike a deal directly with the recording industry. Clear Channel pledged to pay royalties to Big Machine Label Group—one of the country's largest independent labels—for broadcasting the songs of Taylor Swift and its other artists, in exchange for a limit on royalties it must pay for streaming those artists' music on its iHeartRadio.com site. The chairman and CEO of the Recording Industry Association of America said he was pleased to hear "Clear Channel is stating that artists and record companies deserve to be paid and that promotion isn't enough."[14]

Clear Channel's deal with the music industry opened up new dialogue about equalizing the royalty rates paid by broadcast radio, satellite radio, and Internet radio. Tim Westergren, founder of Pandora, argued before Congress in 2012 that the rates were most unfair to companies like his. In the previous year, Westergren said, Pandora paid 50 percent of its revenue to performance royalties, whereas satellite radio service SiriusXM paid 7.5 percent of its revenues to performance royalties, and broadcast radio paid nothing. He noted that a car equipped with an AM/FM radio, satellite radio, and streaming Internet radio could deliver the same song to a listener through all three technologies, but the various radio services would pay markedly different levels of performance royalties to the artist and recording company.[15]

ONE OF THE MOST POPULAR Internet radio sites, Grooveshark allows you to search for streaming songs, browse other users' playlists, or view friends' recent listening. Users can also listen to genre customized radio stations or create their own.

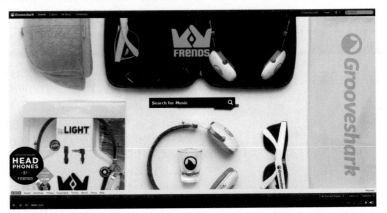

Podcasting and Portable Listening

Developed in 2004, **podcasting** (the term marries *iPod* and *broadcasting*) refers to the practice of making audio files available on the Internet so listeners can download them onto their computers and transfer them to portable MP3 players or listen to the files on the computer. This popular distribution method quickly became mainstream, as mass media companies created commercial podcasts to promote and extend existing content, such as news and reality TV, while independent producers kept pace with their own podcasts on niche topics like knitting, fly fishing, and learning Russian.

Podcasts have led the way for people to listen to radio on mobile devices like the iPod and smartphones. Satellite radio, Internet-only stations like Pandora and Grooveshark, sites that stream traditional broadcast radio like iHeartRadio, and public radio like NPR all offer apps for smartphones and touchscreen devices like the iPad, which has also led to a resurgence in portable listening. Traditional broadcast radio stations are becoming increasingly mindful that they need to reach younger listeners on the Internet, and that Internet radio is no longer tethered to a computer.

For the broadcast radio industry, portability used to mean listening on a transistor or car radio. But with the digital turn to iPods and mobile phones, broadcasters haven't been as easily available on today's primary portable audio devices. Hoping to change that, the National Association of Broadcasters (NAB) has been lobbying the FCC and mobile phone industry to include FM radio capability in all mobile phones. According to the NAB, adding an FM radio chip in the manufacturing of mobile phones would cost less than a dollar, and add little bulk, with the chip just the size of a nail head. In a survey, about two-thirds of mobile phone users reported they would use a built-in radio.[16] The NAB argues that the radio chip would be most important for enabling listeners to access broadcast radio in times of emergencies and disasters. But the chip would also be commercially beneficial for radio broadcasters, putting them on the same digital devices as their non-broadcast radio competitors like Pandora.

The Economics of Broadcast Radio

Radio continues to be one of the most-used mass media, reaching 93 percent of American teenagers and adults every week.[17] Because of radio's broad reach, the airwaves are very desirable real estate for advertisers, who want to reach people in and out of their homes; for record labels, who want their songs played; and for radio station owners, who want to create large radio groups to dominate multiple markets.

Local and National Advertising

About 8 percent of all U.S. spending on media advertising goes to radio stations. Like newspapers, radio generates its largest profits by selling local and regional ads. Thirty-second radio spot ads range from $1,500 in large markets to just a few dollars in the smallest markets. Today, gross advertising receipts for radio are more than $17.4 billion (about 80 percent of the revenues from local ad sales, with the remainder in national spot, network, and digital radio sales), up from about $16 billion in 2009.[18] Although industry revenue has dropped from a peak of $21.7 billion in 2006, the number of stations keeps growing, now totaling about 15,000 stations (almost 4,800 AM stations, about 6,500 FM commercial stations, and about 3,700 FM educational stations).[19] Unlike television, where nearly 40 percent of a station's expenses goes to buy syndicated programs, local radio stations get much of their content free from the recording industry. Therefore, only about 20 percent of a typical radio station's budget goes to cover programming costs. But, as noted earlier, that free music content is in doubt as the music industry–which already charges performance royalties for Internet radio stations–moves toward charging radio broadcast performance royalty fees for playing music on the air.

When radio stations want to purchase programming, they often turn to national network radio, which generates more than $1 billion in ad sales annually by offering dozens of specialized services. For example, Dial Global (formerly Westwood One), the nation's largest radio network service, managed by CBS Radio, syndicates more than 200 programs, including regular news features (e.g., CBS Radio News, NBC Radio News), entertainment programs (e.g., *Country Countdown USA*, the *Billy Bush Show*), talk shows (e.g., the *Dennis Miller Show*, *Ed Schultz*), and complete twenty-four-hour formats (e.g., hot AC, hot country, mainstream country, and classic rock). More than sixty companies offer national program and format services, typically providing local stations with programming in exchange for time slots for national ads. The most successful radio network programs are the shows broadcast by affiliates in the Top 20 markets, which offer advertisers half of the country's radio audience.

Manipulating Playlists with Payola

Radio's impact on music industry profits–radio airplay can help to popularize recordings–has required ongoing government oversight to expose illegal playlist manipulation. **Payola**, the practice by which record promoters pay deejays to play particular records, was rampant during the 1950s as record companies sought to guarantee record sales (see Chapter 4). In response, management took control of programming, arguing that if individual deejays had less impact on which records would be played, the deejays would be less susceptible to bribery.

Despite congressional hearings and new regulations, payola persisted. Record promoters showered their favors on a few influential, high-profile deejays, whose backing could make or break a record nationally, or on key program managers in charge of Top 40 formats in large urban markets. Although a 1984 congressional hearing determined that there was "no credible evidence" of payola, NBC News broke a story in 1986 about independent promoters who had alleged ties to organized crime. A subsequent investigation led major recording companies to break most of their ties with independent promoters. Prominent record labels had been paying such promoters up to $80 million per year to help records become hits.

Recently, there has been increased enforcement of payola laws. In 2005, two major labels–Sony-BMG and Warner Music–paid $10 million and $5 million, respectively, to settle payola cases in New York State, where label executives were discovered bribing radio station programmers to play particular songs. A year later in New York State, Universal Music Group paid $12 million to settle payola charges, which included allegations of bribing radio program directors with baseball tickets, hotel rooms, and laptop computers. And in 2007, four of the largest broadcasting companies–CBS Radio, Clear Channel, Citadel, and Entercom–agreed to pay $12.5 million to settle an FCC payola investigation. The companies also agreed to an unprecedented "independent music content commitment," which required them to provide 8,400 half-hour blocks of airtime to play music from independent record labels over three years.

Radio Ownership: From Diversity to Consolidation

The **Telecommunications Act of 1996** substantially changed the rules concerning ownership of the public airwaves because the FCC eliminated most ownership restrictions on radio. As a result, 2,100 stations and $15 billion changed hands that year alone. From 1995 to 2005, the number of radio station owners declined by one-third, from 6,600 to about 4,400.[20]

LOW-POWER FM RADIO
To help communities or organizations set up LPFM stations, some nonprofit groups like the Prometheus Radio Project provide support in obtaining government licenses as well as actually constructing stations. For construction endeavors known as "barn raisings," the Prometheus project will send volunteers "to raise the antenna mast, build the studio, and flip on the station switch." Shown above is the barn raising for station WRFU 104.5 FM in Urbana, Illinois.

low-power FM signals of 1 to 10 watts. The NAB and other industry groups pressed to have the pirate broadcasters closed down, citing their illegality and their potential to create interference with existing stations. Between 1995 and 2000, more than five hundred illegal micropower radio stations were shut down. Still, an estimated one hundred to one thousand pirate stations are in operation in the United States, in both large urban areas and small rural towns.

The major complaint of pirate radio station operators was that the FCC had long ago ceased licensing low-power community radio stations. In 2000, the FCC, responding to tens of thousands of inquiries about the development of a new local radio broadcasting service, approved a new noncommercial **low-power FM (LPFM)** class of 10- and 100-watt stations in order to give voice to local groups lacking access to the public airwaves. LPFM station licensees included mostly religious groups but also high schools, colleges and universities, Native American tribes, labor groups, and museums.

The technical plans for LPFM located the stations in unused frequencies on the FM dial. Still, the NAB and National Public Radio fought to delay and limit the number of LPFM stations, arguing that such stations would cause interference with existing full-power FM stations. Then-FCC chairman William E. Kennard, who fostered the LPFM initiative, responded: "This is about the haves–the broadcast industry–trying to prevent many have-nots–small community and educational organizations–from having just a little piece of the pie. Just a little piece of the airwaves which belong to all of the people."[21] By 2012, about 833 LPFM stations were broadcasting. The passage of the Local Community Radio Act in 2011 will create opportunities for more LPFM stations. A major advocate of LPFM stations is the Prometheus Radio Project, a nonprofit formed by radio activists in 1998. Prometheus has helped to educate community organizations about low-power radio and has sponsored at least a dozen "barn raisings" to build community stations in places like Hudson, New York; Opelousas, Louisiana; and Woodburn, Oregon.

Radio and the Democracy of the Airwaves

As radio was the first national electronic mass medium, its influence in the formation of American culture cannot be overestimated. Radio has given us soap operas, situation comedies, and broadcast news; it helped popularize rock and roll, car culture, and the politics of talk radio. Yet, for all of its national influence, broadcast radio is still a supremely local medium. For decades, listeners have tuned in to hear the familiar voices of their community's deejays and talk-show hosts and hear the regional flavor of popular music over airwaves that the public owns.

The early debates over radio gave us one of the most important and enduring ideas in communication policy: a requirement to operate in the "public interest, convenience, or necessity." But the broadcasting industry has long been at odds with this policy, arguing that radio corporations invest heavily in technology and should be able to have more control over the radio frequencies on which they operate, and moreover own as many stations as they want. Deregulation in the past few decades has moved closer to that corporate vision, as nearly every radio market in the nation is dominated by a few owners, and those owners are required to renew their broadcasting licenses only every eight years.

This trend in ownership has moved radio away from its localism, as radio groups often manage hundreds of stations from afar. Given broadcasters' reluctance to publicly raise questions about their own economic arrangements, public debate regarding radio as a natural resource has remained minuscule. As citizens look to the future, a big question remains to be answered: With a few large broadcast companies now permitted to dominate radio ownership nationwide, how much is consolidation of power restricting the number and kinds of voices permitted to speak over public airwaves? To ensure that mass media industries continue to serve democracy and local communities, the public needs to play a role in developing the answer to this question. ▶

CHAPTER REVIEW

COMMON THREADS

One of the Common Threads discussed in Chapter 1 is about the development of the mass media. Like other mass media, radio evolved in three stages. But it also influenced an important dichotomy in mass media technology: wired versus wireless.

In radio's novelty stage, several inventors transcended the wires of the telegraph and telephone to solve the problem of wireless communication. In the entrepreneurial stage, inventors tested ship-to-shore radio, while others developed person-to-person toll radio transmissions and other schemes to make money from wireless communication. Finally, when radio stations began broadcasting to the general public (who bought radio receivers for their homes), radio became a mass medium.

As the first electronic mass medium, radio set the pattern for an ongoing battle between wired and wireless technologies. For example, television brought images to wireless broadcasting. Then, cable television's wires brought television signals to places where receiving antennas didn't work. Satellite television (wireless from outer space) followed as an innovation to bring TV where cable didn't exist.

Now, broadcast, cable, and satellite all compete against one another.

Similarly, think of how cell phones have eliminated millions of traditional phone, or land, lines. The Internet, like the telephone, also began with wires, but Wi-Fi and home wireless systems are eliminating those wires, too. And radio? Most listeners get traditional local (wireless) radio broadcast signals, but now listeners may use a wired Internet connection to stream Internet radio or download Webcasts and podcasts.

Both wired and wireless technology have advantages and disadvantages. Do we want the stability but the tethers of a wired connection? Or do we want the freedom and occasional instability ("Can you hear me now?") of wireless media? Can radio's development help us understand wired versus wireless battles in other media?

KEY TERMS

The definitions for the terms listed below can be found in the glossary at the end of the book. The page numbers listed with the terms indicate where the term is highlighted in the chapter.

telegraph, 158
Morse code, 158
electromagnetic waves, 159
radio waves, 159
wireless telegraphy, 160
wireless telephony, 161
broadcasting, 162
narrowcasting, 162
Radio Act of 1912, 162
Radio Corporation of
  America (RCA), 163
network, 165
option time, 167
Radio Act of 1927, 168
Federal Radio Commission (FRC), 168

Communications Act of 1934, 168
Federal Communications Commission
  (FCC), 168
transistors, 172
FM, 173
AM, 173
format radio, 174
rotation, 174
Top 40 format, 174
progressive rock, 175
album-oriented rock (AOR), 175
drive time, 175
news/talk/information, 176
adult contemporary (AC), 178
contemporary hit radio (CHR), 178

country, 178
urban contemporary, 178
Pacifica Foundation, 179
National Public Radio (NPR), 180
Public Broadcasting Service (PBS), 180
Public Broadcasting Act of 1967, 180
Corporation for Public
  Broadcasting (CPB), 180
satellite radio, 181
HD radio, 181
Internet radio, 183
podcasting, 184
payola, 185
Telecommunications Act of 1996, 185
low-power FM (LPFM), 188

REVIEW QUESTIONS

Early Technology and the Development of Radio

1. Why was the development of the telegraph important in media history? What were some of the disadvantages of telegraph technology?

2. How is the concept of wireless different from that of radio?

3. What was Guglielmo Marconi's role in the development of the wireless?

4. What were Lee De Forest's contributions to radio?

5. Why were there so many patent disputes in the development of radio?

6. Why was the RCA monopoly formed?

7. How did broadcasting, unlike print media, come to be federally regulated?

The Evolution of Radio

8. What was AT&T's role in the early days of radio?

9. How did the radio networks develop? What were the contributions of David Sarnoff and William Paley to network radio?

10. Why did the government-sanctioned RCA monopoly end?

11. What is the significance of the Radio Act of 1927 and the Federal Communications Act of 1934?

Radio Reinvents Itself

12. How did radio adapt to the arrival of television?

13. What was Edwin Armstrong's role in the advancement of radio technology? Why did RCA hamper Armstrong's work?

14. How did music on radio change in the 1950s?

15. What is format radio, and why was it important to the survival of radio?

The Sounds of Commercial Radio

16. Why are there so many radio formats today?

17. Why did Top 40 radio diminish as a format in the 1980s and 1990s?

18. What is the state of nonprofit radio today?

19. Why are performance royalties a topic of debate between broadcast radio, satellite radio, Internet radio, and the recording industry?

20. Why do radio broadcasters want FM radio chips required in mobile phones?

The Economics of Broadcast Radio

21. What are the current ownership rules governing American radio?

22. What has been the main effect of the Telecommunications Act of 1996 on radio station ownership?

23. Why did the FCC create a new class of low-power FM stations?

Radio and the Democracy of the Airwaves

24. Throughout the history of radio, why did the government encourage monopoly or oligopoly ownership of radio broadcasting?

25. What is the relevance of localism to debates about ownership in radio?

QUESTIONING THE MEDIA

1. Count the number and types of radio stations in your area today. What formats do they use? Do a little research, and find out who are the owners of the stations in your market. How much diversity is there among the highest-rated stations?

2. If you could own and manage a commercial radio station, what format would you choose, and why?

3. If you ran a noncommercial radio station in your area, what services would you provide that are not being met by commercial format radio?

4. How might radio be used to improve social and political discussions in the United States?

5. If you were a broadcast radio executive, what arguments would you make in favor of broadcast radio over Internet radio?

ADDITIONAL VIDEOS

Visit the Ⓥ VideoCentral: Mass Communication *section at* bedfordstmartins.com/mediaculture *for additional exclusive videos related to Chapter 5.*

6

Television and Cable

The Power of Visual Culture

Television may be our final link to true "mass" communication—a medium that in the 1960s through the 1980s could attract nearly 30 to 40 million viewers to a single episode of a popular prime-time drama like *Bonanza* (1959–73) or a "must-see" comedy like the *Cosby Show* (1984–92). Today, the only program that attracts that kind of audience happens once a year—the Super Bowl. Back in its full-blown mass media stage, television was available only on traditional TV sets, and we mostly watched only the original broadcast networks—ABC, CBS, and NBC.

Things are different today as television has entered the fourth stage in the life cycle of a mass medium—convergence. Today, audiences watch TV on everything from big flat-screen digital sets to tiny smartphones and tablet screens. Back in the day, the networks either made or bought almost all TV shows, usually bankrolled by Hollywood film studios. Now everyone from broadcast networks to cable channels to Internet services like Netflix and Hulu are producing original shows.

The first major crack in the networks' mass audience dominance came when cable TV developed in the 1970s. At first, cable channels like HBO and TNT survived by redistributing old movies and network TV programs. But then when HBO (and its parent company, Time Warner, a major owner of cable companies) began producing popular award-winning original series like *The Sopranos*, the networks' hold on viewers started to erode. Originally, premium cable services like HBO (*True Blood*) and Showtime (*Weeds*) led the way, but now basic cable channels like USA Network (*Burn Notice*), TNT (*The Closer*), Syfy (*Battlestar Galactica*), and FX (*Justified*) all have produced popular original programming. Cable shows routinely win more Emmys each year than broadcast networks (AMC's *Mad Men* won the Emmy for Best Drama from 2008 to 2011).

What cable really did was introduce a better business model—earning money from monthly subscription fees *and* advertising. The old network model relied solely on advertising revenue. The networks, worried about both the loss of viewers and of ad dollars to its upstart competitor, decided they wanted a piece of that action. Some networks started buying cable channels (NBC, for example, has purchased stakes in Bravo, E!, SyFy, USA Network, and the Weather Channel). The networks and local TV stations also championed something called *retransmission consent*—fees that cable providers like Comcast and Time Warner pay to local TV stations and the major networks each month for the right to carry their channels. Typically, cable companies in large-market cities pay their local broadcasters and the national networks about fifty to seventy-five cents per month for each cable subscriber. Those fees are then passed along to cable subscribers.

In recent years, retransmission fees have caused some friction between broadcasters and cable companies. For example, in 2010, when negotiations for higher fees between WABC (the New York City ABC affiliate) and Cablevision broke down, the station was dropped from Cablevision's lineup for twenty hours. In the same year, the evolving relationship between broadcasters and cable TV took a dramatic turn when General Electric, which started and owned NBC (and Universal Studios), sold majority control of its flagship network (and the film company) to Comcast, the nation's largest cable provider. Comcast now produces or owns a significant amount of programming for use on both its broadcast and cable channels, and exercises better control over retransmission fees.

While the major tensions between cable and broadcasters appear to have quieted down, a new battle is brewing as the Internet and smaller screens are quickly becoming the future of television. On the surface, there seems to be a mutually beneficial relationship among streaming online services and broadcasters and cable providers—Hulu, after all, is jointly owned by Disney (ABC), News Corp. (Fox), and Comcast (NBC). Internet streaming services help cable and broadcast networks increase their audiences through time-shifting, as viewers watch favorite TV shows days, even weeks, after they originally aired. But these services are no longer content to distribute network reruns and older cable shows—Hulu (*Battleground*), Netflix (*Lilyhammer*), and YouTube (*Black Box TV*) have begun developing original programming.

As the newest TV battle shakes up the television landscape, one thing remains unchanged: high-quality stories that resonate with viewers. But in the fragmented marketplace, in which the "mass" audience has shrunk and morphed into niche viewers, there may be plenty of room for small, quirky shows that attract younger fans who grew up on the Internet.

◢ *BROADCAST NETWORKS TODAY* may resent cable developing original programming, but in the beginning network television actually stole most of its programming and business ideas from radio. Old radio scripts began reappearing in TV form, snatching radio's sponsors, program ideas, and even its prime-time evening audience. In 1949, for instance, *The Lone Ranger* rode over to television from radio, where the program had originated in 1933. *Amos 'n' Andy*, a fixture on network radio since 1928, became the first TV series to have an entirely black cast in 1951. Since replacing radio in the 1950s as our most popular mass medium, television has sparked repeated arguments about its social and cultural impact. Television has been accused of having a negative impact on children and young people, and has also faced criticism for enabling and sustaining a sharply partisan political system. But there is another side to this story. In times of crisis, our fragmented and pluralistic society has embraced television as common ground. It was TV that exposed us to Civil Rights violations in the South, and to the shared pain and healing rituals after the Kennedy and King assassinations in the 1960s. On September 11, 2001–in shock and horror–we turned on television sets to learn that nearly three thousand people had been killed in that day's terrorist attacks. And in 2011, we viewed the Arab Spring and Occupy Wall Street protests–on our TVs and online. For better or worse, television has become a central touchstone in our daily lives.

In this chapter, we examine television and cable's cultural, social, and economic impact. We will:

- Review television's early technological development
- Discuss TV's boom in the 1950s and the impact of the quiz-show scandals
- Examine cable's technological development and basic services
- Explore new viewing technologies such as computers, smartphones, and tablets
- Learn about major programming genres: comedy, drama, news, and reality TV
- Trace the key rules and regulations of television and cable
- Inspect the costs related to the production, distribution, and syndication of programs
- Investigate television and cable's impact on democracy and culture

As you read through this chapter, think about your own experiences with television programs and the impact they have on you. What was your favorite show as a child? Were there shows you weren't allowed to watch when you were young? If so, why? What attracts you to your favorite programs now? For more questions to help you think through the role of television and cable in our lives, see "Questioning the Media" in the Chapter Review.

Past-Present-Future: Television

During the network era, the "Big Three" (ABC, CBS, and NBC) often put on bland, noncontroversial programming, known as LOP (or "least objectionable programming"), which meant westerns in the 1950s and 1960s, and sitcoms in the 1970s and 1980s. The idea was to avoid offending people in order to attract big prime-time audiences, and therefore advertisers.

However, mass audiences began to shrink as cable and then the Internet siphoned off viewers. Cable began "narrowcasting" to smaller but loyal audiences, with edgier programs like *The Sopranos* on HBO, *South Park* on Comedy Central, and *It's Always Sunny in Philadelphia* on FX, whose depictions of violence, use of coarse language, and choice of subject matter would have offended many in the old prime-time TV audiences. Shorter seasons on cable–ten to thirteen episodes versus twenty-two to twenty-four on the broadcast networks–often meant an improvement in quality of the stories as well as lower costs. Today, a typical network drama costs about $4 million per episode to produce while a cable drama averages about $3 million per episode.[1]

TV's future will be about serving smaller rather than larger audiences. As sites like YouTube develop original programming and as niche cable services like the Weather Channel produce reality TV series about storms, no audience seems too small and no subject matter too narrow for today's TV world. For example, in 2012, Spike TV promoted *Rat Bastards*, a program that follows a pack of industrious men in Louisiana who hunt nutria, an invasive and elusive species of swamp rat. An overwhelming number of programming choices like this now exist for big and small TV screens alike. How might this converged TV landscape change how we watch, and pay, for TV? With hundreds of shows available, will we adopt "à la carte" viewing habits, where we download or stream only the shows that interest us, rather than pay for cable (or DBS) packages with hundreds of channels we don't watch?

The Origins and Development of Television

CIVIL RIGHTS
In the 1950s and 1960s, television images of Civil Rights struggles visually documented the inequalities faced by black citizens. Seeing these images made the events and struggles more "real" to a nation of viewers and helped garner support for the movement.

In 1948, only 1 percent of America's households had a TV set; by 1953, more than 50 percent had one; and since the early 1960s, more than 90 percent of all homes have TV. Television's rise throughout the 1950s created fears that radio—as well as books, magazines, and movies—would become irrelevant and unnecessary; but both radio and print media adapted. In fact, today more radio stations are operating and more books and magazines are being published than ever before; only ticket sales for movies have declined slightly since the 1960s.

Three major historical developments in television's early years helped shape it: (1) technological innovations and patent wars, (2) wresting control of content away from advertisers, and (3) the sociocultural impact of the infamous quiz-show scandals.

Early Innovations in TV Technology

In its novelty stage, television's earliest pioneers were trying to isolate TV waves from the electromagnetic spectrum (as radio's pioneers had done with radio waves). The big question was: If a person could transmit audio signals from one place to another, why not visual images as well? Inventors from a number of nations toyed with the idea of sending "tele-visual" images for nearly a hundred years before what we know as TV developed.

▼ **Television and Cable: The Power of Visual Culture**

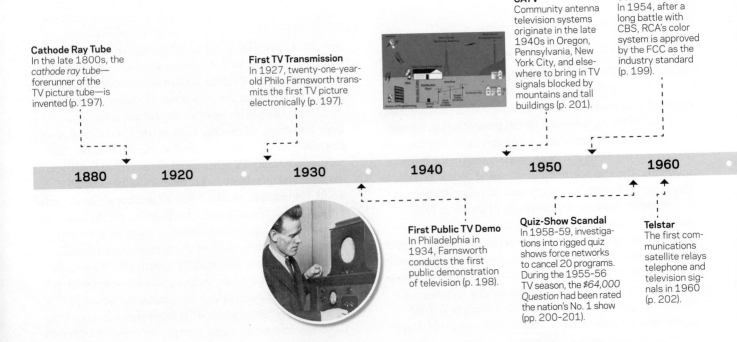

Cathode Ray Tube
In the late 1800s, the *cathode ray tube*—forerunner of the TV picture tube—is invented (p. 197).

First TV Transmission
In 1927, twenty-one-year-old Philo Farnsworth transmits the first TV picture electronically (p. 197).

CATV
Community antenna television systems originate in the late 1940s in Oregon, Pennsylvania, New York City, and elsewhere to bring in TV signals blocked by mountains and tall buildings (p. 201).

Color TV Standard
In 1954, after a long battle with CBS, RCA's color system is approved by the FCC as the industry standard (p. 199).

1880	1920	1930	1940	1950	1960

First Public TV Demo
In Philadelphia in 1934, Farnsworth conducts the first public demonstration of television (p. 198).

Quiz-Show Scandal
In 1958–59, investigations into rigged quiz shows force networks to cancel 20 programs. During the 1955–56 TV season, the *$64,000 Question* had been rated the nation's No. 1 show (pp. 200–201).

Telstar
The first communications satellite relays telephone and television signals in 1960 (p. 202).

In the late 1800s, the invention of the *cathode ray tube*, the forerunner of the TV picture tube, combined principles of the camera and electricity. Because television images could not physically float through the air, technicians and inventors developed a method of encoding them at a transmission point (TV station) and decoding them at a reception point (TV set). In the 1880s, German inventor Paul Nipkow developed the *scanning disk*, a large flat metal disk with a series of small perforations organized in a spiral pattern. As the disk rotated, it separated pictures into pinpoints of light that could be transmitted as a series of electronic lines. As the disk spun, each small hole scanned one line of a scene to be televised. For years, Nipkow's mechanical disk served as the foundation for experiments on the transmission of visual images.

Electronic Technology: Zworykin and Farnsworth

The story of television's invention included a complex patents battle between two independent inventors: Vladimir Zworykin and Philo Farnsworth. It began in Russia in 1907, when physicist Boris Rosing improved Nipkow's mechanical scanning device. Rosing's lab assistant, Vladimir Zworykin, left Russia for America in 1919 and went to work for Westinghouse and then RCA. In 1923, Zworykin invented the *iconoscope*, the first TV camera tube to convert light rays into electrical signals, and he received a patent for it in 1928.

Around the same time, Idaho teenager Philo Farnsworth also figured out that a mechanical scanning system would not send pictures through the air over long distances. On September 7, 1927, the twenty-one-year-old Farnsworth transmitted the first electronic TV picture: He rotated a straight line scratched on a square of painted glass by 90 degrees. RCA, then the world leader in broadcasting technology, challenged Farnsworth in a major patents battle, in part over Zworykin's innovations for Westinghouse and RCA. Farnsworth had to rely on his high-school science teacher to retrieve his original drawings from 1922. Finally, in 1930, Farnsworth received a patent for the first electronic television.

After the company's court defeat, RCA's president, David Sarnoff, had to negotiate to use Farnsworth's patents. Farnsworth later licensed these patents to RCA and AT&T for use in

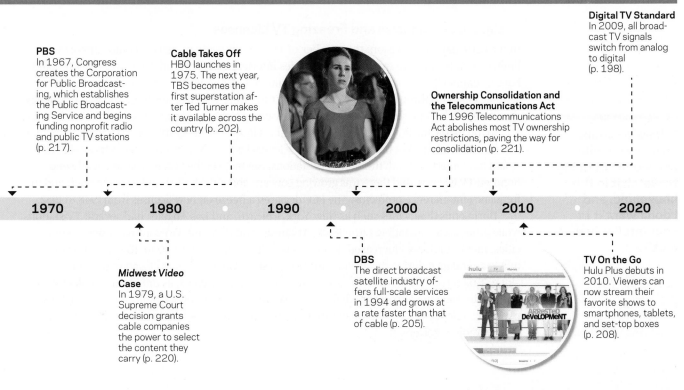

PBS
In 1967, Congress creates the Corporation for Public Broadcasting, which establishes the Public Broadcasting Service and begins funding nonprofit radio and public TV stations (p. 217).

Cable Takes Off
HBO launches in 1975. The next year, TBS becomes the first superstation after Ted Turner makes it available across the country (p. 202).

Ownership Consolidation and the Telecommunications Act
The 1996 Telecommunications Act abolishes most TV ownership restrictions, paving the way for consolidation (p. 221).

Digital TV Standard
In 2009, all broadcast TV signals switch from analog to digital (p. 198).

| 1970 | 1980 | 1990 | 2000 | 2010 | 2020 |

Midwest Video Case
In 1979, a U.S. Supreme Court decision grants cable companies the power to select the content they carry (p. 220).

DBS
The direct broadcast satellite industry offers full-scale services in 1994 and grows at a rate faster than that of cable (p. 205).

TV On the Go
Hulu Plus debuts in 2010. Viewers can now stream their favorite shows to smartphones, tablets, and set-top boxes (p. 208).

PHILO FARNSWORTH, one of the inventors of television, experiments with an early version of an electronic TV set.

"There's nothing on it worthwhile, and we're not going to watch it in this household, and I don't want it in your intellectual diet."

KENT FARNSWORTH, RECALLING THE ATTITUDE OF HIS FATHER (PHILO) TOWARD TV WHEN KENT WAS GROWING UP

the commercial development of television. At the end of television's development stage, Farnsworth conducted the first public demonstration of television at the Franklin Institute in Philadelphia in 1934–five years *before* RCA's famous public demonstration at the 1939 World's Fair.

Setting Technical Standards

Figuring out how to push TV as a business and elevate it to a mass medium meant creating a coherent set of technical standards for product manufacturers. In the late 1930s, the National Television Systems Committee (NTSC), a group representing major electronics firms, began outlining industry-wide manufacturing practices and compromising on technical standards. As a result, in 1941 the Federal Communications Commission (FCC) adopted an **analog** standard (based on radio waves) for all U.S. TV sets. About thirty countries, including Japan, Canada, Mexico, Saudi Arabia, and most Latin American nations, also adopted this system. (Most of Europe and Asia, however, adopted a slightly superior technical system shortly thereafter.)

The United States continued to use analog signals until 2009, when they were replaced by **digital** signals. These translate TV images and sounds into binary codes (ones and zeros like computers use) and allow for increased channel capacity and improved image quality and sound. HDTV, or *high-definition television*, digital signals offer the highest resolution and sharpest image. Receiving a "hi-def" picture depends on two things: the programmer must use a high-definition signal, and consumers must have HDTV equipment to receive and view it. The switch to digital signals has also opened up new avenues for receiving and viewing television on laptops, smartphones, and tablets.

Assigning Frequencies and Freezing TV Licenses

In the early days of television, the number of TV stations a city or market could support was limited because airwave spectrum frequencies interfered with one another. So a market could have a channel 2 and a channel 4 but not a channel 3. Cable systems "fixed" this problem by sending channels through cable wires that don't interfere with one another. Today, a frequency that once carried one analog TV signal can now carry eight or nine compressed digital channels.

In the 1940s, the FCC began assigning channels in specific geographic areas to make sure there was no interference. As a result, for years New Jersey had no TV stations because those signals would have interfered with the New York stations. But by 1948 the FCC had issued nearly one hundred TV licenses, and there was growing concern about the finite number of channels and the frequency-interference problems. The FCC declared a freeze on new licenses from 1948 to 1952.

During this time, cities such as New York, Chicago, and Los Angeles had several TV stations, while other areas–including Little Rock, Arkansas, and Portland, Oregon–had none. In non-TV cities, movie audiences increased. But cities with TV stations saw a 20 to 40 percent drop in movie attendance during this period; more than sixty movie theaters closed in the Chicago area alone. Taxi receipts and nightclub attendance also fell in TV cities, as did library book circulation. Radio listening also declined; for example, Bob Hope's network radio show lost half its national audience between 1949 and 1951. By 1951, the sales of television sets had surpassed the sales of radio receivers.

After a second NTSC conference in 1952 sorted out the technical problems, the FCC ended the licensing freeze, and almost thirteen hundred communities received TV channel allocations. By the mid-1950s, there were more than four hundred television stations in operation—a 400 percent surge since the prefreeze era—and television became a mass medium. Today, about seventeen hundred TV stations are in operation.

The Introduction of Color Television

In 1952, the FCC tentatively approved an experimental CBS color system. However, because black-and-white TV sets could not receive its signal, the system was incompatible with the sets most Americans owned. In 1954, RCA's color system, which sent TV images in color but allowed older sets to receive the color images as black-and-white, usurped CBS's system to become the color standard. Although NBC began broadcasting a few shows in color in the mid-1950s, it wasn't until 1966, when the consumer market for color sets had taken off, that the Big Three networks (CBS, NBC, and ABC) broadcast their entire evening lineups in color.

Controlling Content—TV Grows Up

By the early 1960s, television had become a dominant mass medium and cultural force, with more than 90 percent of U.S. households owning at least one set. Television's new standing came as its programs moved away from the influence of radio and established a separate identity. Two important contributors to this identity were a major change in the sponsorship structure of television programming and, more significant, a major scandal.

Program Format Changes Inhibit Sponsorship

Like radio in the 1930s and 1940s, early TV programs were often developed, produced, and supported by a single sponsor. Many of the top-rated programs in the 1950s even included the sponsor's name in the title: *Buick Circus Hour*, *Camel News Caravan*, and *Colgate Comedy Hour*. Having a single sponsor for a show meant that the advertiser could easily influence the program's content. In the early 1950s, the broadcast networks became increasingly unhappy with the lack of creative control in this arrangement. Luckily, the growing popularity, and growing cost, of television offered opportunities to alter this financial setup. In 1952, for example, a single one-hour TV show cost a sponsor about $35,000, a figure that rose to $90,000 by the end of the decade.

David Sarnoff, then head of RCA/NBC, and William Paley, head of CBS, saw an opportunity to diminish the sponsors' role. In 1953, Sarnoff appointed Sylvester "Pat" Weaver (father of actress Sigourney Weaver) as the president of NBC. Previously an advertising executive, Weaver undermined his former profession by increasing program length from fifteen minutes (then the standard for radio programs) to thirty minutes or longer, substantially raising program costs for advertisers and discouraging some from sponsoring programs.

In addition, the introduction of two new types of programs—the magazine format and the TV spectacular—greatly helped the networks gain control over content. The *magazine program* featured multiple segments—news, talk, comedy, and music—similar to the content variety found in a general

THE TODAY SHOW, the first magazine-style show, has been on the air since 1952. A groundbreaking concept that forever changed television, morning news shows are now common. They include *Good Morning America* (ABC), *The Early Show* (CBS), *Fox & Friends* (Fox), and *American Morning* (CNN).

interest or news magazine of the day, such as *Life* or *Time*. In January 1952, NBC introduced the *Today* show as a three-hour morning talk-news program. Then, in September 1954, NBC premiered the ninety-minute *Tonight Show*. Because both shows ran daily rather than weekly, studio production costs were prohibitive for a single sponsor. Consequently, NBC offered spot ads within the shows: Advertisers paid the network for thirty- or sixty-second time slots. The network, not the sponsor, now produced and owned the programs or bought them from independent producers.

The television spectacular is today recognized by a more modest term, the *television special*. At NBC, Weaver bought the rights to special programs, like the Broadway production of *Peter Pan*, and sold spot ads to multiple sponsors. The 1955 TV version of *Peter Pan* was a particular success, with sixty-five million viewers. More typical specials featured music-variety shows hosted by famous singers such as Judy Garland, Frank Sinatra, and Nat King Cole.

The Rise and Fall of Quiz Shows

In 1955, CBS aired the *$64,000 Question*, reviving radio's quiz-show genre (radio's version was the more modest *$64 Question*). Sponsored by Revlon, the program ran in **prime time** (the hours between 8 and 11 P.M., when networks traditionally draw their largest audiences and charge their highest advertising rates) and became the most popular TV show in America during its first year. Revlon followed the show's success with the *$64,000 Challenge* in 1956; by the end of 1958, twenty-two quiz shows aired on network television. Revlon's cosmetic sales skyrocketed from $1.2 million before its sponsorship of the quiz shows to nearly $10 million by 1959.

Compared with dramas and sitcoms, quiz shows were (and are) cheap to produce, with inexpensive sets and mostly nonactors as guests. The problem was that most of these shows were rigged. To heighten the drama, key contestants were rehearsed and given the answers.

The most notorious rigging occurred on *Twenty-One*, a quiz show owned by Geritol (whose profits climbed by $4 million one year after it began to sponsor the program in 1956). A young Columbia University English professor from a famous literary family, Charles Van Doren won $129,000 in 1957 during his fifteen-week run on the program; his fame even landed him a job on

TWENTY-ONE
In 1957, the most popular contestant on the quiz show *Twenty-One* was college professor Charles Van Doren (left). Congressional hearings on rigged quiz shows revealed that Van Doren had been given some answers. Host Jack Barry, pictured here above the sponsor's logo, nearly had his career ruined, but made a comeback in the late 1960s with the syndicated game show *The Joker's Wild*.

NBC's *Today* show. But in 1958, after a series of contestants accused the quiz show *Dotto* of being fixed, the networks quickly dropped twenty quiz shows. Following further rumors, a *TV Guide* story, a New York grand jury probe, and a 1959 congressional investigation during which Van Doren admitted to cheating, big-money prime-time quiz shows ended.

Quiz-Show Scandal Hurts the Promise of TV

The impact of the quiz-show scandals was enormous. First, the sponsors' pressure on TV executives to rig the programs and the subsequent fraud put an end to any role that major sponsors had in creating TV content. Second, and more important, the fraud undermined Americans' expectation of the democratic promise of television–to bring inexpensive information and entertainment into every household. Many people had trusted their own eyes–what they saw on TV–more than the *words* they heard on radio or read in print. But the scandals provided the first dramatic indication that TV images could be manipulated. In fact, our contemporary love-hate relationship with electronic culture and new gadgets began during this time.

The third, and most important, impact of the quiz-show scandals was that they magnified the division between "high" and "low" culture attitudes toward television. The fact that Charles Van Doren had come from a family of Ivy League intellectuals and cheated for fame and money drove a wedge between intellectuals–who were already skeptical of television–and the popular new medium. This was best expressed in 1961 by FCC commissioner Newton Minow, who labeled game shows, westerns, cartoons, and other popular genres as part of television's "vast wasteland." Critics have used the wasteland metaphor ever since to admonish the TV industry for failing to live up to its potential.

After the scandal, quiz shows were kept out of network prime time for forty years. Finally, in 1999, ABC gambled that the nation was ready once again for a quiz show in prime time. The network, at least for a couple of years, had great success with *Who Wants to Be a Millionaire*, the No. 1 program in 1999-2000.

> "I was fascinated by the seduction of [Charles] Van Doren, by the Faustian bargain that lured entirely good and honest people into careers of deception."
>
> ROBERT REDFORD, DIRECTOR, *QUIZ SHOW*, 1995

The Development of Cable

Most historians mark the period from the late 1950s, when the networks gained control over TV's content, to the end of the 1970s as the **network era**. Except for British and American anthology dramas on PBS, this was a time when the Big Three broadcast networks–CBS, NBC, and ABC–dictated virtually every trend in programming and collectively accounted for more than 95 percent of all prime-time TV viewing. In 2012, however, this figure was less than 40 percent. Why the drastic drop? Because cable television systems–along with VCRs and DVD players–had cut into the broadcast networks' audience.

CATV—Community Antenna Television

The first small cable systems–called **CATV**, or community antenna television–originated in Oregon, Pennsylvania, and New York City, where mountains or tall buildings blocked TV signals. These systems served roughly 10 percent of the country and, because of early technical and regulatory limits, contained only twelve channels. Even at this early stage, though, TV sales personnel, broadcasters, and electronics firms recognized two big advantages of cable. First, by routing and reamplifying each channel in a separate wire, cable eliminated over-the-air interference. Second, running signals through coaxial cable increased channel capacity.

In the beginning, small communities with CATV often received twice as many channels as were available over the air in much larger cities. That technological advantage, combined with cable's ability to deliver clear reception, would soon propel the new cable industry into competition with conventional broadcast television. But unlike radio, which freed mass communication from unwieldy wires, early cable technology relied on wires.

The Wires and Satellites behind Cable Television

The idea of using space satellites to receive and transmit communication signals is right out of science fiction: In 1945, Arthur C. Clarke (who studied physics and mathematics and would later write dozens of sci-fi books, including *2001: A Space Odyssey*) published the original theories for a global communications system based on three satellites equally spaced from one another, rotating with the earth's orbit. In the mid-1950s, these theories became reality, as the Soviet Union and then the United States successfully sent satellites into orbit around the earth.

In 1960, AT&T launched Telstar, the first communication satellite capable of receiving, amplifying, and returning signals. Telstar was able to process and relay telephone and occasional television signals between the United States and Europe. By the mid-1960s, scientists figured out how to lock communication satellites into *geosynchronous orbit*. Hovering 22,300 miles above the earth, satellites travel at nearly 7,000 mph and circle the earth at the same speed at which the earth revolves on its axis. For cable television, the breakthrough was the launch of domestic communications satellites: Canada's *Anik* in 1972 and the United States' *Westar* in 1974.

Cable TV signals are processed at a computerized nerve center, or *headend*, which operates various large satellite dishes that receive and distribute long-distance signals from, say, CNN in Atlanta or ESPN in Connecticut. In addition, the headend's receiving equipment can pick up an area's local signals or a nearby city's PBS station. The headend relays each channel, local network affiliate, or public TV signal along its own separate line. Headend computers relay the channels in the same way that telephone calls and electric power reach individual households: through *trunk* and *feeder cables* attached to existing utility poles. Cable companies rent space on these poles from phone and electric companies. Signals are then transmitted to *drop* or *tap lines* that run from the utility poles into subscribers' homes (see Figure 6.1).

Advances in satellite technology in the 1970s dramatically changed the fortunes of cable by creating a reliable system for the distribution of programming to cable companies across the nation. The first cable network to use satellites for regular transmission of TV programming was Home Box Office (HBO), which began delivering programming such as uncut, commercial-free movies and exclusive live coverage of major boxing matches for a monthly fee in 1975. The second cable network began in 1976, when media owner Ted Turner distributed his small Atlanta broadcast TV station, WTBS, to cable systems across the country.

FIGURE 6.1

A BASIC CABLE TELEVISION SYSTEM

Source: Clear Creek Telephone & TeleVision, www.ccmtc.com.

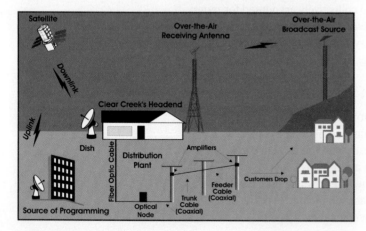

Cable Threatens Broadcasting

While only 14 percent of all U.S. homes received cable in 1977, by 1985 that percentage had climbed to 46. By the summer of 1997, basic cable channels had captured a larger prime-time audience than the broadcast networks had. The cable industry's rapid rise to prominence was partly due to the shortcomings of broadcast television. Beyond improving signal reception in most communities, the cable era introduced **narrowcasting**–the providing of specialized programming for diverse and fragmented groups. Attracting both advertisers and audiences, cable programs provide access to certain target audiences that cannot be guaranteed in broadcasting. For example, a golf-equipment manufacturer can buy ads on the Golf Channel and reach only golf enthusiasts. (See "Case Study: ESPN: Sports and Stories" on page 204 for more on narrowcasting.)

As cable channels have become more and more like specialized magazines or radio formats, they have siphoned off network viewers, and the networks' role as the chief programmer of our shared culture has eroded. For example, back in 1980 the Big Three evening news programs had a combined audience of more than fifty million on a typical weekday evening. In 2012, though, that audience had shrunk to about twenty million.[1] In addition, through its greater channel capacity, cable has provided more access. In many communities, various public, government, and educational channels have made it possible for anyone to air a point of view or produce a TV program. When it has lived up to its potential, cable has offered the public greater opportunities to participate more fully in the democratic promise of television.

Cable Services

Cable consumers usually choose programming from a two-tiered structure: basic cable services like CNN and premium cable services like HBO. These services are the production arm of the cable industry, supplying programming to the nation's six-thousand-plus cable operations, which function as program distributors to cable households.

Basic Cable Services

A typical **basic cable** system today includes a hundred-plus channel lineup composed of local broadcast signals, access channels (for local government, education, and general public use), regional PBS stations, and a variety of cable channels, such as ESPN, CNN, MTV, USA, Bravo, Nickelodeon, Disney, Comedy Central, BET, Telemundo, the Weather Channel, **superstations**

"FAKE NEWS" SHOWS like *The Daily Show* and *The Colbert Report* are available on the basic cable channel Comedy Central. While their nightly audiences are not as large as those of other basic cable news shows like *The O'Reilly Factor*, critics argue that the satiric shows have become a major source for news for the eighteen- to thirty-four-year-old age group because of their satire and sharp-witted lampoon of politics and news media.

ESPN: Sports and Stories

A common way many of us satisfy our cultural and personal need for storytelling is through sports: We form loyalties to local and national teams. We follow the exploits of favorite players. We boo our team's rivals. We suffer with our team when the players have a bad game or an awful season. We celebrate the victories.

The appeal of following sports is similar to the appeal of our favorite books, TV shows, and movies—we are interested in characters, in plot development, in conflict and drama. Sporting events have all of this. It's no coincidence, then, that the Super Bowl is annually the most watched single TV show around the world.

One of the best sports stories on television over the past thirty years, though, may not be a single sporting event but the tale of an upstart cable network based in Bristol, Connecticut. ESPN (Entertainment Sports Programming Network) began in 1979 and has now surpassed all the major broadcast networks as the "brand" that frames and presents sports on TV. In fact, cable operators around the country regard ESPN as the top service when it comes to helping them "gain and retain customers."[1] One of ESPN's main attractions is its "live" aspect and its ability to draw large TV and cable audiences—many of them young men—to events in real time. In a third-screen world full of mobile devices, this is a big plus for ESPN and something that advertisers especially like.

Today, the ESPN flagship channel reaches more than 100 million U.S. homes. And ESPN, Inc., now provides a sports smorgasbord—a menu of media offerings that includes ESPN2 (sporting events, news, and original programs), ESPN Classic (historic sporting events), ESPN Deportes (Spanish-language sports network), ESPN HD (a high-definition channel), ESPN Radio, *ESPN The Magazine,* ESPNEWS (twenty-four-hour sports news channel), ESPN Outdoors, and ESPNU (college games). ESPN also creates original programming for TV and radio and operates ESPN.com, which is among the most popular sites on the Internet. Like CNN and MTV, ESPN makes its various channels available in more than two hundred countries.

Each year, ESPN's channels air more than five thousand live and original hours of sports programming, covering more than sixty-five different sports. In 2002, ESPN even outbid NBC for six years of NBA games—offering $2.4 billion, which at the time was just over a year's worth of ESPN revenues. But the major triumph of ESPN over the broadcast networks was probably wrestling the *Monday Night Football* contract from its sports partner, ABC (both ESPN and ABC are owned by Disney). For eight years, starting in 2006, ESPN agreed to pay the NFL $1.1 billion a year for the broadcasting rights to *MNF*, the most highly rated sports series in prime-time TV history. In 2006, ABC turned over control of its sports programming division, ABC Sports, to ESPN, which now carries games on ABC under the ESPN logo.

The story of ESPN's "birth" also has its share of drama.

The creator of ESPN was Bill Rasmussen, an out-of-work sports announcer who had been fired in 1978 by the New England Whalers (now the Carolina Hurricanes), a professional hockey team. Rasmussen wanted to bring sports programs to cable TV, which was just emerging from the shadow of broadcast television. But few backers thought this would be a good idea. Eventually, Rasmussen managed to land a contract with the NCAA to cover college games. He also lured Anheuser-Busch to become cable's first million-dollar advertiser. Getty Oil then agreed to put up $10 million to finance this sports adventure, and ESPN took off.

Today, ESPN is 80 percent owned by the Disney Company, while the Hearst Corporation holds the other 20 percent interest. The sports giant earned around $7 billion in worldwide revenue in 2010 and ESPN's cable ad sales and higher subscription fees were major reasons why Disney's net income rose 21 percent to more than $40 billion in 2011. ◢

(independent TV stations uplinked to a satellite such as WGN in Chicago), and others, depending on the cable system's capacity and regional interests. Typically, local cable companies pay each of these satellite-delivered services between a few cents per month per subscriber (for low-cost, low-demand channels like C-Span) and as much as $3.50 per month per subscriber (for high-cost, high-demand channels like ESPN). That fee is passed along to consumers as part of their basic monthly cable rate, which averaged more than $70 per month in 2011. In addition, cable system capacities continue to increase as a result of high-bandwidth fiber-optic cable and *digital cable*, allowing for expanded offerings such as additional premium, pay-per-view, video-on-demand, and audio music channels.

Premium Cable Services

Besides basic programming, cable offers a wide range of special channels, known as **premium channels**, which lure customers with the promise of no advertising, recent and classic Hollywood movies, and original movies or series like HBO's *True Blood* or *Boardwalk Empire* and Showtime's *Dexter* or *Homeland*. These channels are a major source of revenue for cable companies: The cost to them is $4 to $6 per month per subscriber to carry a premium channel, but the cable company can charge customers $10 or more per month and reap a nice profit. Premium services also include pay-per-view (PPV) programs; video-on-demand (VOD); and interactive services that enable consumers to use their televisions to bank, shop, play games, and access the Internet.

Beginning in 1985, cable companies began introducing new viewing options for their customers. **Pay-per-view (PPV)** channels came first, offering recently released movies or special one-time sporting events to subscribers who paid a designated charge to their cable company, allowing them to view the program. In the early 2000s, cable companies introduced **video-on-demand (VOD)**. This service enables customers to choose among hundreds of titles and watch their selection whenever they want in the same way as a video, pausing and fast-forwarding when desired. Along with online downloading and streaming services, and digital video recorders (DVRs), VOD services today are ending the era of the local video store.

DBS: Cable without Wires

By 1999, cable penetration had hit 70 percent. But **direct broadcast satellite (DBS)** services presented a big challenge to cable—especially in regions with rugged terrain and isolated homes, where the installation of cable wiring hasn't always been possible or profitable. Instead of using wires, DBS transmits its signal directly to small satellite dishes near or on customers' homes. As a result, cable penetration dropped to 44 percent by 2012. In addition, new over-the-air digital signals and better online options meant that many customers began moving away from subscribing to either cable or DBS services (see Figure 6.2).

Satellite service began in the mid-1970s when satellite dishes were set up to receive cable programming. Small-town and rural residents bypassed FCC restrictions by buying receiving dishes and downlinking, for free, the same channels that cable companies were supplying to wired communities. Not surprisingly, satellite programmers filed a flurry of legal challenges against those who were receiving their signals for free. Rural communities countered that they had the rights to

HBO series don't always attract massive audiences by broadcast standards: *Girls*, for example, a comedy about twentysomething women in New York city, averages about a million views per episode. But they attract positive buzz, Emmy nominations, and pay-channel subscribers.

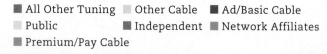

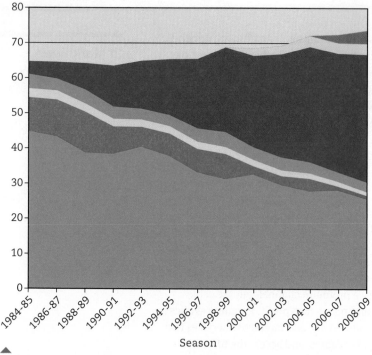

the airspace above their own property; the satellite firms contended that their signals were being stolen. Because the law was unclear, a number of cable channels began scrambling their signals and most satellite users had to buy or rent descramblers and subscribe to services, just as cable customers did.

Signal scrambling spawned companies that provided both receiving dishes and satellite program services for a monthly fee. In 1978, Japanese companies, which had been experimenting with "wireless cable" alternatives for years, started the first DBS system in Florida. By 1994, full-scale DBS service was available. Today, DBS companies like DirecTV and the DISH Network offer consumers most of the channels and tiers of service that cable companies carry (including Internet, television, and phone services), at a comparable and often cheaper monthly cost.

FIGURE 6.2
PRIME-TIME TV AUDIENCE, 1984–2009

Source: Nielsen TV Ratings Data: © 2010 The Nielsen Company. Note: All years prior to 2006–09 are Live Data; 2006–09 are Live+7 data.

Technology and Convergence Change Viewing Habits

Among the biggest technical innovations in TV are nontelevision delivery systems. We can skip a network broadcast and still watch our favorite shows on DVRs, on laptops, or on mobile devices for free or for a nominal cost. Not only is TV being reinvented, but its audiences–although fragmented–are also growing. A few years ago, televisions glimmered in the average U.S. household just over seven hours a day; but by 2012, when you add in downloading, streaming, and smartphone/tablet viewing, that figure has expanded to more than eight hours a day. And with DVR systems like TiVo, television viewing was up 5 percent in DVR-equipped homes. All these options mean that we are still watching TV, but at different times, places, and on different kinds of screens.

Home Video

In 1975-76, the consumer introduction of videocassettes and *videocassette recorders (VCRs)* enabled viewers to tape-record TV programs and play them back later. Sony introduced the Betamax ("Beta") in 1975, and in 1976 JVC in Japan introduced a slightly larger format, VHS (Video Home System), which was incompatible with Beta. This triggered a marketing war, which helped drive costs down and put VCRs in more homes. Beta ultimately lost the consumer marketplace battle to VHS, whose larger tapes held more programming space.

VCRs also got a boost from a failed suit brought against Sony by Disney and MCA (now NBC Universal) in 1976: The two film studios alleged that home taping violated their movie copyrights. In 1979, a federal court ruled in favor of Sony and permitted home taping for personal use. In response, the movie studios quickly set up videotaping facilities so that they could rent and sell movies in video stores, which became popular in the early 1980s.

VideoCentral ◉
Mass Communication
bedfordstmartins.com
/mediaculture

David Gale
VP of New Media, MTV

Television Networks Evolve
Insiders discuss how cable and satellite have changed the television market.
Discussion: How might definitions of a TV network change in the realm of new digital media?

Over time, the VHS format gave way to DVDs. But today the standard DVD is threatened by both the Internet and a consumer market move toward *high-definition* DVDs. In fact, in 2007 another format war pitted high-definition Blu-ray DVDs (developed by Sony and used in the PlayStation 3) against the HD DVD format (developed by Toshiba and backed by Microsoft). Blu-ray was declared the victor when, in February 2008, Best Buy and Walmart, the nation's leading sellers of DVDs, decided to stop carrying HD DVD players and disks.

By 2012, more than 50 percent of U.S. homes had *DVRs (digital video recorders)*, which enable users to download specific programs onto the DVR's computer memory and watch at a later time. While offering greater flexibility for viewers, DVRs also provide a means to "watch" the watchers. DVRs give advertisers information about what each household views, allowing them to target viewers with specific ads when they play back their programs. This kind of technology has raised concerns among some lawmakers and consumer groups over having our personal viewing and buying habits tracked by marketers.

The impact of home video has been enormous. More than 95 percent of American homes today are equipped with either DVD or DVR players, which serve two major purposes: video rentals and time shifting. Video rental, formerly the province of walk-in video stores like Blockbuster, have given way to mail services like Netflix or online services like iTunes. **Time shifting**, which began during the VCR era, occurs when viewers record shows and watch them at a later, more convenient time. Time shifting and video rentals, however, have threatened the TV industry's advertising-driven business model; when viewers watch DVDs and DVRs, they often aren't watching the ads that normally accompany network or cable shows.

The Third Screen: TV Converges with the Internet

The Internet has transformed the way many of us, especially younger generations, watch movies, TV, and cable programming. These new online viewing experiences are often labeled **third screens**, usually meaning that computer screens are the third major way we view content (movie screens and traditional TV sets are the first and second screens, respectively). By far the most popular site for viewing video online is YouTube. Containing some original shows, classic TV episodes, full-length films, and of course the homemade user-uploaded clips that first made the site famous, YouTube remains at the center of video consumption online. Owned by Google, YouTube by early 2012 was drawing more than 800 million unique visitors per month and uploading forty-eight hours of new video per minute.[2]

But YouTube has competition from sites that offer full-length episodes of current and recent programming. While viewers might be able to watch snippets of a show on YouTube, it's rare that they will find a full episode of popular, professionally produced TV shows like *Mad Men*, *30 Rock*, and *Homeland*. Services like iTunes or Amazon Instant Video offer the ability to download full seasons of these shows, charging just $0.99 to $2.99 per episode. And streaming site Hulu (a partnership among NBC, Fox, and Disney) allows viewers to watch a certain number of episodes of a show for free—but with ads.

WATCHING TV ONLINE
Hulu.com is the second-most popular site for watching videos online—after Google's YouTube. Launched in 2008, the site offers content from NBC, ABC/Disney, Fox, PBS, Bravo, Current TV, FX, USA, E!, movie studios, and others. Many viewers use Hulu for catch-up viewing, or watching episodes of current shows after they first air.

LILYHAMMER, starring Steven Van Zandt as a New York mobster relocated to Norway after joining the witness protection program, is the first original television series from online provider Netflix. All 8 episodes of the series were available for instant streaming the day it premiered, a decision that merged Netflix's online streaming model with network-quality television.

In late 2010, Hulu started Hulu Plus, a paid subscription service. For $8 a month, viewers can stream full seasons of current and older programs and some movies and documentaries on their computer, TV, or mobile device. Hulu Plus had more than 2 million subscribers by early 2012. Netflix, which started streaming videos back in 2008, has moved further away from a DVD-through-mail model and become more focused on a less expensive (no postal costs) online streaming model. More than 66 percent of Netflix's subscribers are now streaming movies and TV shows online.[3] With 26 million subscribers by 2012, it's become bigger than Comcast, the largest cable company, with its 23 million subscribers.[4] Netflix is also negotiating with major film and TV studios for the rights to stream current episodes of prime-time television shows—and seemed willing to pay between $70,000 and $100,000 per episode.[5]

In addition, cable TV giants like Comcast, Time Warner, and HBO are making programs available to download or stream through sites like TV Everywhere, Xfinity TV, and HBO GO. These programs are only open to subscribers who can download cable TV shows using a password and username. In 2012, Netflix, looking to increase its subscriber base, started talks with some of the largest U.S. cable operators about adding Netflix as part of their cable packages. However, cable and DBS companies are, thus far, resisting Netflix's proposition, and are rolling out their own video-streaming services instead. Comcast introduced Xfinity Streampix in February 2012, expanding the Xfinity offerings to include even more movies from top Hollywood studios and past seasons of TV shows. The goal, according to Comcast executive Marcien Jenckes, is "to be the single stop for video needs for consumers."[6] In addition, DirecTV and Blockbuster have partnered—as have Verizon and Redbox—to create streaming services of their own.

In most cases, these third-screen sites operate as *catch-up services* rather than as replacements for broadcast or cable TV, allowing viewers and fans to "catch-up" on movies and programs that played earlier in theaters or on television (see Figure 6.3). Now with devices like the Roku box and gaming consoles that can stream programming directly to our television sets, and newer television sets that are Internet ready, the TV has become one of the latest converged devices.

FIGURE 6.3

CROSS-PLATFORM VIEWING

Source: Nielsen, The Cross Platform Report Q3 2011, http://www.nielsen.com/content /dam/corporate/us/en/reports -downloads/2012-Reports /Nielsen-Cross-Platform-Report -Q3-2011.pdf.

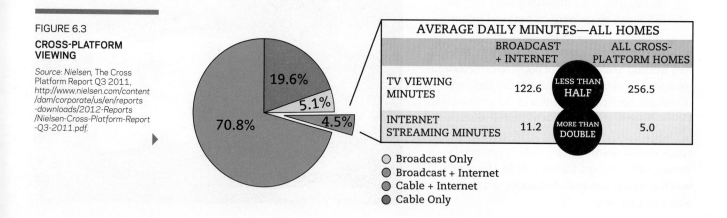

Fourth Screens: Smartphones and Mobile Video

A 2010 Nielsen survey found that in a one-month period, an average viewer spent three and a half hours using a computer and television at the same time. Nielsen also estimated that 60 percent of viewers are online at least once a month while they are watching television.[7] Such multitasking has further accelerated with new **fourth-screen** technologies like smartphones, iPods, iPads, and mobile TV devices. These devices are forcing major changes in consumer viewing habits and media content creation. For example, between January 2010 and January 2011, online viewers "streamed 28 percent more video, and spent 45 percent more time watching."[8] Cable and DBS operators are capitalizing on this trend: Cablevision, Time Warner, and DISH Network released iPad apps in 2011, allowing their subscribers to watch live TV on their iPads at no additional charge, in the hopes of deterring their customers from cutting their subscriptions. However, some cable programmers like Discovery and Viacom are pushing back, arguing that their existing contracts with cable and DBS operators don't cover third or fourth screens.

The multifunctionality and portability of third- and fourth-screen devices means that consumers may no longer need television sets—just as landline telephones have fallen out of favor as more people rely solely on their mobile phones. If *where* we watch TV programming changes, does TV programming also need to change to keep up? Reality shows like *Jersey Shore* and dramas like *Game of Thrones*—with extended casts and multiple plot lines—are considered best suited for the digital age, enabling viewers to talk to one another on various social networks about favorite characters and plots at the same time as they watch these programs on traditional—or nontraditional—TV.

MEDIA ON THE GO
Downloading or streaming TV episodes to smartphones and other mobile devices lets us take our favorite shows with us wherever we go. By expanding where and when we consume such programming, these devices will encourage new ways to view and engage with the media. How have your own viewing habits changed over the last few years?

"Teenagers today barely understand the idea of watching TV on someone else's schedule. When you tell them we didn't leave home because our show was coming on at 9 P.M., to them it sounds like our great-grandparents talking to us about horses and buggies."

JEFFREY COLE, DIRECTOR, CENTER FOR THE DIGITAL FUTURE, 2009

Major Programming Trends

Television programming began by borrowing genres from radio such as variety shows, sitcoms, soap operas, and newscasts. Starting in 1955, the Big Three networks gradually moved their entertainment divisions to Los Angeles because of its proximity to Hollywood production studios. Network news operations, however, remained in New York. Ever since, Los Angeles and New York came to represent the two major branches of TV programming: *entertainment* and *information*. Although there is considerable blurring between these categories today, the two were once more distinct. In the sections that follow, we focus on these long-standing program developments and explore newer trends (see Figure 6.4).

TV Entertainment: Our Comic Culture

The networks began to move their entertainment divisions to Los Angeles partly because of the success of the pioneering comedy series *I Love Lucy* (1951-57). *Lucy*'s owners and costars,

Anthology Drama and the Miniseries

In the early 1950s, television–like cable in the early 1980s–served a more elite and wealthier audience. **Anthology dramas** brought live dramatic theater to that television audience. Influenced by stage plays, anthologies offered new, artistically significant *teleplays* (scripts written for television), casts, directors, writers, and sets from one week to the next. In the 1952-53 season alone, there were eighteen anthology dramas, including *Studio One* (1948-58), *Alfred Hitchcock Presents* (1955-65), the *Twilight Zone* (1959-64), and *Kraft Television Theater* (1947-58), which was created to introduce Kraft's Cheez Whiz.

The anthology's brief run as a dramatic staple on television ended for both economic and political reasons. First, advertisers disliked anthologies because they often presented stories containing complex human problems that were not easily resolved. The commercials that interrupted the drama, however, told upbeat stories in which problems were easily solved by purchasing a product; by contrast, anthologies made the simplicity of the commercial pitch ring false. A second reason for the demise of anthology dramas was a change in audience. The people who could afford TV sets in the early 1950s could also afford tickets to a play. For these viewers, the anthology drama was a welcome addition given their cultural tastes. By 1956, however, working- and middle-class families were increasingly able to afford television, and the prices of sets dropped. Anthology dramas were not as popular in this newly expanded market.

Third, anthology dramas were expensive to produce–double the cost of most other TV genres in the 1950s. Each week meant a completely new story line, as well as new writers, casts, and expensive sets. (Many anthology dramas also took more than a week to produce and had to alternate biweekly with other programs.) Sponsors and networks came to realize that it would be less expensive and easier to build audience allegiance with an ongoing program featuring the same cast and set.

Finally, anthologies that dealt seriously with the changing social landscape were sometimes labeled "politically controversial." This was especially true during the attempts by Senator Joseph McCarthy and his followers to rid media industries and government agencies of left-leaning political influences (see Chapter 16 on blacklisting). By the early 1960s, this dramatic form had virtually disappeared from network television, although its legacy continues on public television with the imported British program *Masterpiece Theatre* (1971-), now known as either *Masterpiece Classic* or *Masterpiece Mystery!*–the longest-running prime-time drama series on U.S. television.

In fact, these British shows carry on the legacy of the U.S. TV *miniseries*–a serialized TV show that ran over a two-day to two-week period, usually on consecutive evenings. A cross between an extended anthology drama and a network serial, the most famous U.S. miniseries were probably the twelve-hour *Rich Man, Poor Man* (1976), based on the 1970 Irwin Shaw novel, and *Roots* (1977), based on Alex Haley's novelized version of his family's slave history. The final episode of *Roots,* which ran on eight consecutive nights, drew an audience of more than 100 million viewers. Contemporary British series like *Downton Abbey* (2010-), *Inspector Lewis* (2005-), and *Sherlock* (2011-) last three to eight episodes over a few weeks, making it more like a miniseries than a traditional network drama, even though they have multiple seasons. The miniseries has also experienced a recent resurgence in the United States with quality and popular miniseries on cable like *John Adams* (HBO), *American Horror Story* (FX), and *Hatfields and McCoys* (History Channel).

Episodic Series

Abandoning anthologies, producers and writers increasingly developed **episodic series**, first used on radio in 1929. In this format, main characters continue from week to week, sets and locales remain the same, and technical crews stay with the program. The episodic series comes in two general types: chapter shows and serial programs.

> "Aristotle once said that a play should have a beginning, a middle, and an end. But what did he know? Today, a play must have a first half, a second half, and a station break."
>
> ALFRED HITCHCOCK, DIRECTOR

Chapter shows are self-contained stories with a recurring set of main characters who confront a problem, face a series of conflicts, and find a resolution. This structure can be used in a wide range of sitcoms like *The Big Bang Theory* (2007-) and dramatic genres, including adult westerns like *Gunsmoke* (1955-75); police/detective shows like *CSI: Crime Scene Investigation* (2000-); and fantasy/science fiction like *Star Trek* (1966-69). Culturally, television dramas often function as a window into the hopes and fears of the American psyche. For example, in the 1970s police/detective dramas became a staple, mirroring anxieties about the urban unrest of the time, precipitated by the decline of manufacturing and the loss of factory jobs. Americans' popular entertainment reflected the idea of heroic police and tenacious detectives protecting a nation from menacing forces that were undermining the economy and the cities. Such shows as *Ironside* (1967-75), *Hawaii Five-O* (1968-80), *The Mod Squad* (1968-73), and *The Rockford Files* (1974-80) all ranked among the nation's top-rated programs during that time.

DOWNTON ABBEY, a British period drama series, has amassed a large international fan base since premiering in the United Kingdom in 2010. Part of PBS' *Masterpiece Classic* anthology, each *Downton Abbey* season depicts a distinct period in English history and in the personal lives of the aristocratic Crawley family and their live-in servants. In the second season, the Earl of Grantham, and head of the Crawley family estate, creates a makeshift hospital in his home to treat soldiers wounded in World War I, an act of charity that initially disrupts day-to-day life at the family's sprawling country house.

In contrast to chapter shows, **serial programs** are open-ended episodic shows; that is, most story lines continue from episode to episode. Cheaper to produce than chapter shows, employing just a few indoor sets, and running five days a week, daytime *soap operas* are among the longest-running serial programs in the history of television. Acquiring their name from soap product ads that sponsored these programs in the days of fifteen-minute radio dramas, soaps feature cliff-hanging story lines and intimate close-up shots that tend to create strong audience allegiance. Soaps also probably do the best job of any genre at imitating the actual open-ended rhythms of daily life. Popular daytime network soaps include *As the World Turns* (1956-2010) and *General Hospital* (1963-).

Another type of drama is the *hybrid,* which developed in the early 1980s with the appearance of *Hill Street Blues* (1981-87). Often mixing comic situations and grim plots, this multiple-cast show looked like an open-ended soap opera. On occasion, as in real life, crimes were not solved and recurring characters died. As a hybrid form, *Hill Street Blues* combined elements of both chapter and serial television by featuring some self-contained plots that were resolved in a single episode as well as other plot lines that continued from week to week. This blend has been used by many successful dramatic hybrids, including *The X-Files* (1993-2002), *Buffy the Vampire Slayer* (1997-2003), *Lost* (2004-2010), TNT's *The Closer* (2005-2012), USA's *Burn Notice* (2007-), and AMC's *Mad Men* (2007-).

TV Information: Our Daily News Culture

Since the 1960s, broadcast news, especially on local TV stations, has consistently topped print journalism in national research polls that ask which news medium is most trustworthy. Most studies suggest this has to do with television's intimacy as a medium–its ability to create loyalty with viewers who connect personally with the news anchors we "invite" into our living rooms each evening. Print reporters and editors, by comparison, seem anonymous and detached. In this section, we focus on the traditional network evening news, its history, and the changes in TV news ushered in by twenty-four-hour cable news channels.

Media Literacy and the Critical Process

1 DESCRIPTION. Pick a current reality program and a current sitcom or drama. Choose programs that either started in the last year or two or that have been on television for roughly the same period of time. Now develop a "viewing sheet" that allows you to take notes as you watch the two programs over a three- to four-week period. Keep track of main characters, plot lines, settings, conflicts, and resolutions. Also track the main problems that are posed in the programs and how they are worked out in each episode. Find out and compare the basic production costs of each program.

2 ANALYSIS. Look for patterns and differences in the ways stories are told in the two programs. At a general level, what are the conflicts about (e.g., men versus women, managers versus employees, tradition versus change, individuals versus institutions, honesty versus dishonesty, authenticity versus artificiality)? How complicated or simple are the tensions in the two programs, and how are problems resolved? Are there some conflicts that should not be permitted–like pitting white against black contestants? Are there noticeable differences between "the look" of each program?

TV and the State of Storytelling

The rise of the reality program over the past decade has more to do with the cheaper costs of this genre than with the wild popularity of these programs. In fact, in the history of television and viewer numbers, traditional sitcoms and dramas—and even prime-time news programs like *60 Minutes* and *20/20*—have been far more popular than successful reality programs like *American Idol*. But when national broadcast TV executives cut costs by reducing writing and production staffs and hiring "regular people" instead of trained actors, does the craft of storytelling suffer at the expense of commercial savings? Can good stories be told in a reality program? In this exercise, let's compare the storytelling competence of a reality program with that of a more traditional comedy or dramatic genre.

3 INTERPRETATION. What do some of the patterns mean? What seems to be the point of each program? What do they say about relationships, values, masculinity or femininity, power, social class, and so on?

4 EVALUATION. What are the strengths and weaknesses of each program? Which program would you judge as better at telling a compelling story that you want to watch each week? How could each program improve its storytelling?

5 ENGAGEMENT. Either through online forums or via personal contacts, find other viewers of these programs. Ask them follow-up questions about what they like or don't like about such shows, about what they might change, about what the programs' creators might do differently. Then report your findings to the programs' producers through a letter, a phone call, or an e-mail. Try to elicit responses from the producers about the status of their programs. How did they respond to your findings?

> "I may have destroyed world culture, but MTV wouldn't exist today if it wasn't for me."
>
> ADVERTISING ART DIRECTOR GEORGE LOIS, WHO COINED THE PHRASE "I WANT MY MTV," 2003

people who seem more like us and less like celebrities. Additionally, these programs have helped the networks and cable providers deal with the high cost of programming. Featuring nonactors, cheap sets, and no extensive scripts, reality shows are much less expensive to produce than sitcoms and dramas. While reality-based programs have played a major role in network prime time since the late 1990s, the genre was actually inspired by cable's *The Real World* (1992–), the longest-running program on MTV. Changing locations and casts from season to season, *The Real World* follows a group of strangers who live and work together for a few months and records their interpersonal entanglements and up-and-down relationships. *The Real World* has significantly influenced the structure of today's reality TV programs, including *Survivor*, *Project Runway*, *Jersey Shore*, and *Dancing with the Stars*. (See "Media Literacy and the Critical Process: TV and the State of Storytelling" on this page.)

Another growing trend is Spanish-language television like Univision and Telemundo. For the 2011-12 TV season, the popular network Univision reached about 3.6 million viewers in prime time each day (compared with 1.7 million for the CW or 11.6 million for CBS, the top-rated network). The first foreign-language U.S. network began in 1961 when the owners of the nation's first Spanish-language TV station in San Antonio acquired a TV station in Los Angeles, setting up what was then called the Spanish International Network. It officially became Univision in 1986 and has built audiences in major urban areas with large Hispanic populations through its popular talk-variety programs and *telenovelas* (Spanish-language soap operas, mostly produced in Mexico), which air each weekday evening. Today, Univision Communications owns and operates more than sixty TV stations in the United States. Its Univision Network, carried by seventeen hundred cable affiliates, reaches almost all U.S. Hispanic households.

Public Television Struggles to Find Its Place

Another key programmer in TV history has been public television. Under President Lyndon Johnson, and in response to a report from the Carnegie Commission on Educational Television, Congress passed the Public Broadcasting Act of 1967, establishing the Corporation for Public Broadcasting (CPB) and later, in 1969, the Public Broadcasting Service (PBS). In part, Congress intended public television to target viewers who were "less attractive" to commercial networks and advertisers. Besides providing programs for viewers over age fifty, public television has figured prominently in programming for audiences under age twelve with children's series like *Mister Rogers' Neighborhood* (1968-2001), *Sesame Street* (1969-), and *Barney & Friends* (1991-). With the exception of CBS's long-running *Captain Kangaroo* (1955-84), the major networks have largely abdicated the responsibility of developing educational series aimed at children under age twelve. When Congress passed a law in 1996 ordering the networks to offer three hours of children's educational programming per week, the networks sidestepped this mandate by taking advantage of the law's vagueness on what constituted "educational" to claim that many of their routine sitcoms, cartoons, and dramatic shows satisfied the legislation's requirements.

The original Carnegie Commission report also recommended that Congress create a financial plan to provide long-term support for public television, in part to protect it from political interference. However, Congress did not do this, nor did it require wealthy commercial broadcasters to subsidize public television (as many other countries do). As federal funding levels dropped in the 1980s, PBS depended more and more on corporate underwriting. By the early 2000s, corporate sponsors funded more than 25 percent of all public television, although corporate sponsorship declined in 2009 as the economy suffered. In 2010, Congress gave an extra $25 million to PBS to help during the economic downturn.[13] However, only about 15 percent of funding for public broadcasting has come from the federal government, with the bulk of support being provided by viewers, listeners, and corporations.

Despite support from the Obama administration, in 2011 the Republican-controlled House voted to ax all funding of the CPB in 2013. The Senate killed this effort, and eventually the CPB did receive $430 million in federal funding for 2012. Anticipating decreased government support, public broadcasting hoped to increase its corporate contributions by inserting promotional messages every fifteen minutes in its programs, starting in fall 2011.[14] Some critics and public TV executives worried that such corporate messages would offend loyal viewers accustomed to uninterrupted programming, and compromise public television's mission to air programs that might be considered controversial or commercially less viable.

PUBLIC TELEVISION
The most influential children's show in TV history, *Sesame Street* (below, 1969-) has been teaching children their letters and numbers for more than forty years. The program has also helped break down ethnic, racial, and class barriers by introducing TV audiences to a rich and diverse cast of puppets and people.

Cable's Role: Electronic Publisher or Common Carrier?

Because the Communications Act of 1934 had not anticipated cable, the industry's regulatory status was unclear at first. In the 1970s, cable operators argued that they should be considered **electronic publishers** and be able to choose which channels and content to carry. Cable companies wanted the same "publishing" freedoms and legal protections that broadcast and print media enjoyed in selecting content. Just as local broadcasters could choose to carry local news or *Jeopardy!* at 6 P.M., cable companies wanted to choose what channels to carry.

At the time, the FCC argued the opposite: Cable systems were **common carriers**–services that do not get involved in content. Like telephone operators, who do not question the topics of personal conversations ("Hi, I'm the phone company, and what are you going to be talking about today?"), cable companies, the FCC argued, should offer at least part of their services on a first-come, first-served basis to whoever could pay the rate.

In 1979, the debate over this issue ended in the landmark *Midwest Video* case, when the U.S. Supreme Court upheld the rights of cable companies to determine channel content and defined the industry as a form of "electronic publishing."[18] Although the FCC could no longer mandate channels' content, the Court said that communities could "request" access channels as part of contract negotiations in the franchising process. Access channels are no longer a requirement, but most cable companies continue to offer them in some form to remain on good terms with their communities.

Intriguingly, must-carry rules seem to contradict the *Midwest Video* ruling since they require cable operators to carry certain local content. But this is a quirky exception to the *Midwest Video* ruling–mostly due to politics and economics. Must-carry rules have endured because of the lobbying power of the National Association of Broadcasters (NAB) and the major TV networks. Over the years, these groups have successfully argued that cable companies should carry most local over-the-air broadcast stations on their systems so local broadcasters can stay financially viable as cable systems expand their menus of channels and services.

Franchising Frenzy

After the *Midwest Video* decision, the future of cable programming was secure and competition to obtain franchises to supply local cable service became intense. Essentially, a cable franchise is a mini-monopoly awarded by a local community to the most attractive bidder, usually for a fifteen-year period. Although a few large cities permitted two companies to build different parts of their cable systems, most communities granted franchises to only one company so that there wouldn't be more than one operator trampling over private property to string wire from utility poles or to bury cables underground. Most of the nation's cable systems were built between the late 1970s and the early 1990s.

During the franchising process, a city (or state) would outline its cable system needs and request bids from various cable companies. (Potential cable companies were prohibited from also owning broadcast stations or newspapers in the community.) In its bid, a company would make a list of promises to the city about construction schedules, system design, subscription rates, channel capacity, types of programming, financial backing, deadlines, and a *franchise fee*: the money the cable company would pay the city annually for the right to operate the local cable system. Lots of wheeling and dealing transpired in these negotiations, along with occasional corruption, as few laws existed to regulate franchise negotiations (e.g., paying off local city officials who voted on which company got the franchise). Often, battles over broken promises, unreasonable contracts, or escalating rates ended up in court.

Today, a federal cable policy act from 1984 dictates the franchise fees for most U.S. municipalities. This act helps cities and municipalities use such fees to establish and fund access

"Cable companies have monopoly power, and this shows in the prices they charge."

CONSUMERS UNION, 2003

channels for local government, educational, and community programming as part of their license agreement. For example, Groton, Massachusetts (population around ten thousand), has a cable contract with Charter Communications. According to the terms of the contract with Groton, Charter returned 4.25 percent of its revenue to the town (5 percent is the maximum a city can charge a cable operator). This money, which has amounted to about $100,000 a year, helped underwrite the city's cable access programs and other community services.

The Telecommunications Act of 1996

Between 1984 and 1996, lawmakers went back and forth on cable rates and rules, creating a number of cable acts. One Congress would try to end *must-carry rules* or abandon rate regulation, and then a later one would restore the rules. Congress finally rewrote the nation's communications laws in the **Telecommunications Act of 1996**, bringing cable fully under the federal rules that had long governed the telephone, radio, and TV industries. In its most significant move, Congress used the Telecommunications Act to knock down regulatory barriers, allowing regional phone companies, long-distance carriers, and cable companies to enter one another's markets. The act allows cable companies to offer telephone services, and it permits phone companies to offer Internet services and buy or construct cable systems in communities with fewer than fifty thousand residents. For the first time, owners could operate TV or radio stations in the same market where they owned a cable system. Congress hoped that the new rules would spur competition and lower both phone and cable rates, but this has not usually happened. Instead, cable and phone companies have merged operations in many markets, keeping prices at a premium and competition to a minimum.

The 1996 act has had a mixed impact on cable customers. Cable companies argued that it would lead to more competition and innovations in programming, services, and technology. But in fact, there is not extensive competition in cable. About 90 percent of communities in the United States still have only one local cable company. In these areas, cable rates have risen faster, and in communities with multiple cable providers the competition makes a difference—monthly rates are an average of 10 percent lower, according to one FCC study.[19] The rise of DBS companies like DISH in the last few years has also made cable prices more competitive.

Still, the cable industry has delivered on some of its technology promises, investing nearly $150 billion in technological infrastructure between 1996 and 2009—mostly installing high-speed fiber-optic wires to carry TV and phone services. This has enabled cable companies to offer what they call the "triple play"—or *bundling* digital cable television, broadband Internet, and telephone service. By early 2012, U.S. cable companies had signed more than forty-six million households to digital programming packages, while another forty-seven million households had high speed cable Internet service and twenty-five million households received their telephone service from cable companies.[20]

"If this [telecommunications] bill is a blueprint, it's written in washable ink. Congress is putting out a picture of how things will evolve. But technology is transforming the industry in ways that we don't yet understand."

MARK ROTENBERG, ELECTRONIC PRIVACY INFORMATION CENTER, 1996

The Economics and Ownership of Television and Cable

It is not much of a stretch to define TV programming as a system that mostly delivers viewers to merchandise displayed in blocks of ads. And with more than $60 billion at stake in advertising revenues each year, networks and cable services work hard to attract the audiences and subscribers that bring in the advertising dollars. But although broadcast

FIGURE 6.5

PRIME-TIME NETWORK TV PRICING, 2011

The average costs for a thirty-second commercial during prime-time programs on Monday and Thursday nights in 2011 is shown.

Source: Brian Steinberg, "American Idol, NFL Duke It out for Priciest TV Spot," AdAge, October 24, 2011, http://adage.com/article/media/chart-american-idol-nfl-duke-priciest-tv-spot/230547/.

* = Canceled shows

Monday

	8:00pm	8:30pm	9:00pm	9:30pm	10:00pm
ABC	*Dancing with the Stars* ($233,482)				*Castle* ($121,914)
CBS	*How I Met Your Mother* ($168,829)	*Two Broke Girls* ($166,678)	*Two and a Half Men* ($252,418)	*Mike and Molly* ($196,497)	*Hawaii Five-0* ($130,514)
NBC	*The Voice* ($206,500)		*Awake* ($117,550)*		*Smash* ($154,000)
FOX	*House* ($236,500)		*Alcatraz** ($160,000)		no programming

Thursday

	8:00pm	8:30pm	9:00pm	9:30pm	10:00pm
ABC	*Charlie's Angels** ($69,640)		*Grey's Anatomy* ($203,078)		*Scandal* ($92,800)
CBS	*Big Bang Theory* ($198,348)	*How to Be a Gentleman** ($128,147)	*Person of Interest* ($174,574)		*The Mentalist* ($154,718)
NBC	*Community* ($93,533)	*Parks and Recreation* ($116,883)	*The Office** ($178,840)	*30 Rock** ($133,000)	*Prime Suspect* ($93,092)
FOX	*American Idol Results* ($468,100)		*The Finder** ($152,100)		no programming

and cable advertising declined slightly during the 2008-09 financial crisis, one recent study reported that more than 80 percent of consumers say that TV advertising—of all ad formats—has the most impact or influence on their buying decisions. A distant second, third, and fourth in the study were magazines (50 percent), online (47 percent), and newspapers (44 percent).[21] (See Figure 6.5 for costs for a thirty-second commercial during prime-time programs.) To understand the TV economy today, we need to examine the production, distribution, and syndication of programming; the rating systems that set advertising rates; and the ownership structure that controls programming and delivers content to our homes.

Production

The key to the TV industry's success is offering programs that viewers will habitually watch each week—whether at scheduled times or via catch-up viewing. The networks, producers, and film studios spend fortunes creating programs that they hope will keep us coming back.

Production costs generally fall into two categories: below-the-line and above-the-line. *Below-the-line* costs, which account for roughly 40 percent of a new program's production budget, include the technical, or "hardware," side of production: equipment, special effects, cameras and crews, sets and designers, carpenters, electricians, art directors, wardrobe, lighting, and transportation. *Above-the-line*, or "software," costs include the creative talent: actors, writers, producers, editors, and directors. These costs account for about 60 percent of a program's budget, except in the case of successful long-running series (like *Friends* or *CSI*), in which salary demands by actors can drive up above-the-line costs to more than 90 percent.

Most prime-time programs today are developed by independent production companies that are owned or backed by a major film studio such as Sony or Disney. In addition to providing and renting production facilities, these film studios serve as a bank, offering enough capital to carry producers through one or more seasons. In television, programs are funded through **deficit financing**. This means that the production company leases the show to a network or cable channel for a license fee that is actually lower than the cost of production. (The company hopes to recoup this loss later in lucrative rerun syndication.) Typically, a network leases an episode of a one-hour drama for about $1.5 million for two airings. Each episode, however, might cost the program's producers about $2.5 million to make, meaning they lose about $1 million per episode. After two years of production (usually forty-four episodes), an average network show builds up a large deficit.

Because of smaller audiences and fewer episodes per season, costs for original programs on cable channels are lower than those for network broadcasts.[22] On average, in 2012-13 cable channels pay about $1 million per episode in licensing fees to production companies. Some cable shows, like AMC's *Breaking Bad*, cost about $3 million per episode; but since cable seasons are shorter (usually eight to twelve episodes per season, compared to twenty-two or so for broadcast networks), cable channels build up smaller deficits. And unlike networks, cable channels have two revenue streams to pay for original programs—monthly subscription fees and advertising. (However, because network audiences are usually much larger, ad revenue is higher for networks.) Cable channels also keep costs down by airing three to four new programs a year at most, compared to the ten to twenty that the broadcast networks air.

Still, both networks and cable channels build up deficits. This is where film studios like Disney, Sony, and Twentieth Century Fox have been playing a crucial role: They finance the deficit and hope to profit on lucrative deals when the show—like *CSI*, *Friends*, *Bones*, or *The Office*—goes into domestic and international syndication.

To save money and control content, many networks and cable stations create programs that are less expensive than sitcoms and dramas. These include TV newsmagazines and reality programs. For example, NBC's *Dateline* requires only about half the outlay (between $700,000 and $900,000 per episode) demanded by a new hour-long drama. In addition, by producing projects in-house, networks and cable channels avoid paying license fees to independent producers and movie studio production companies.

OFF-NETWORK SYNDICATION programs often include reruns of popular network sitcoms like *How I Met Your Mother*, which airs on local stations as well as two different major cable channels, FX and Lifetime.

Distribution

Programs are paid for in a variety of ways. Cable service providers (e.g., Time Warner Cable or Cablevision) rely mostly on customer subscriptions to pay for distributing their channels, but they also have to pay the broadcast networks **retransmission fees** to carry network channels and programming. While broadcast networks do earn carriage fees from cable and DBS providers, they pay *affiliate stations* license fees to carry their programs. In return, the networks sell the bulk of advertising time to recoup their fees and their investments in these programs. In this arrangement, local stations receive national programs that attract large local audiences and are allotted some local ad time to sell during the programs to generate their own revenue.

A common misconception is that TV networks own their affiliated stations. This is not usually true. Although networks own stations in major markets like New York, Los Angeles, and Chicago, throughout most of the country networks sign short-term contracts to rent time on local stations. Years ago, the FCC placed restrictions on network-owned-and-operated stations (called **O & Os**). But the sweeping Telecommunications Act of 1996 abolished most ownership restrictions. Today, one owner is permitted to reach up to 39 percent of the nation's 120 million-plus TV households.

Although a local affiliate typically carries a network's entire line-up, a station may substitute a network's program. According to *clearance rules*, established in the 1940s by the Justice Department and the FCC, all local affiliates are ultimately responsible for the content of their channels and must clear, or approve, all network programming. Over the years, some of the circumstances in which local affiliates have rejected the network's programming have been controversial. For example, in 1956 Nat King Cole (singer Natalie Cole's father) was one of the first African American performers to host a network variety program. As a result of pressure applied by several white southern organizations, though, the program had trouble attracting a national sponsor. When some affiliates, both southern and northern, refused to carry the program, NBC canceled it in 1957. More recently, affiliates may occasionally substitute other programming for network programs they think may offend their local audiences, especially if the programs contain excessive violence or explicit sexual content.

Syndication Keeps Shows Going and Going . . .

Syndication–leasing TV stations or cable networks the exclusive right to air TV shows–is a critical component of the distribution process. Each year, executives from thousands of local TV stations and cable firms gather at the National Association of Television Program Executives (NATPE) convention to buy or barter for programs that are up for syndication. In so doing, they acquire the exclusive local market rights, usually for two- or three-year periods, to game shows, talk shows, and **evergreens**–popular old network reruns such as *I Love Lucy*.

Syndication plays a large role in programming for both broadcast and cable networks. For local network-affiliated stations, syndicated programs are often used during **fringe time**– programming immediately before the evening's prime-time schedule (*early fringe*) and following the local evening news or a network late-night talk show (*late fringe*). Cable channels also syndicate network shows but are more flexible with time slots; for example, TNT may run older network syndicated episodes of *Law & Order* or *Bones* during its prime-time schedule, along with original cable programs like *The Closer* or *Burn Notice*.

Types of Syndication

In **off-network syndication** (commonly called reruns), older programs that no longer run during network prime time are made available for reruns to local stations, cable operators, online services, and foreign markets. This type of syndication occurs when a program builds up a supply of episodes (usually four seasons' worth) that are then leased to hundreds of TV stations and cable or DBS providers in the United States and overseas. A show can be put into rerun syndication even if new episodes are airing on network television. Rerun, or off-network, syndication is the key to erasing the losses generated by deficit financing. With a successful program, the profits can be enormous. For instance, the early rerun cycle of *Friends* earned nearly $4 million an episode from syndication in 250-plus markets, plus cable, totaling over $1 billion. Because the show's success meant the original production costs were already covered, the syndication market became almost pure profit for the producers and their backers. This is why deficit financing endures: Although investors rarely hit the jackpot, when they do, the revenues more than cover a lot of losses and failed programs.

First-run syndication is any program specifically produced for sale into syndication markets. Quiz programs such as *Wheel of Fortune* and daytime talk or advice shows like the *Ellen DeGeneres Show* or *Dr. Phil* are made for first-run syndication. The producers of these programs usually sell them directly to local markets around the country and the world.

FIRST-RUN SYNDICATION programs often include talk shows like the *Ellen DeGeneres Show,* which debuted in 2003 and is now one of the highest-rated daytime series.

Barter vs. Cash Deals

Most financing of television syndication is either a cash deal or a barter deal. In a *cash deal,* the distributor offers a series for syndication to the highest bidder. Because of exclusive contractual arrangements, programs air on only one broadcast outlet per city in a major TV market or, in the case of cable, on one cable channel's service across the country. Whoever bids the most gets to syndicate the program (which can range from a few thousand dollars for a week's worth of episodes in a small market to $250,000 a week in a large market). In a variation of a cash deal called *cash-plus,* distributors retain some time to sell national commercial spots in successful syndicated shows (when the show is distributed, it already contains the national ads). While this means the local station has less ad time to sell, it also usually pays less for the syndicated show.

Although syndicators prefer cash deals, *barter deals* are usually arranged for new, untested, or older but less popular programs. In a straight barter deal, no money changes hands. Instead, a syndicator offers a program to a local TV station in exchange for a split of the advertising revenue. For example, in a 7/5 barter deal, during each airing the show's producers and syndicator retain seven minutes of ad time for national spots and leave stations with five minutes of ad time for local spots. As programs become more profitable, syndicators repackage and lease the shows as cash-plus deals.

Measuring Television Viewing

Primarily, TV shows live or die based on how satisfied advertisers are with the quantity and quality of the viewing audience. Since 1950, the major organization that tracks and rates prime-time viewing has been the A.C. Nielsen Market Research Company, which estimates what viewers are watching in the nation's major markets. Ratings services like Nielsen provide advertisers, broadcast networks, local stations, and cable channels with considerable detail about viewers—from race and gender to age, occupation, and educational background.

The Impact of Ratings and Shares on Programming

In TV measurement, a **rating** is a statistical estimate expressed as the percentage of households that are tuned to a program in the market being sampled. Another audience measure is the **share**, a statistical estimate of the percentage of homes that are tuned to a specific program compared with those using their sets at the time of the sample. For instance, let's say on a typical night that 5,000 metered homes are sampled by Nielsen in 210 large U.S. cities, and 4,000 of those households have their TV sets turned on. Of those 4,000, about 1,000 are tuned to *The Voice on* NBC. The rating for that show is 20 percent—that is, 1,000 households watching *The Voice* out of 5,000 TV sets monitored. The share is 25 percent—1,000 homes watching *The Voice* out of a total of 4,000 sets turned on.

The importance of ratings and shares to the survival of TV programs cannot be overestimated. In practice, television is an industry in which networks, producers, and distributors target, guarantee, and "sell" viewers in blocks to advertisers. Audience measurement tells advertisers not only how many people are watching but, more important, what kinds of people are watching. Prime-time advertisers on the broadcast networks have mainly been interested in reaching relatively affluent eighteen- to forty-nine-year-old viewers, who account for most consumer spending. If a show is attracting those viewers, advertisers will compete to buy time during that program. Typically, as many as nine out of ten new shows introduced each fall on the networks either do not attain the required ratings or fail to reach the "right" viewers. The result is cancellation. Cable, in contrast, targets smaller audiences, so programs that would not attract a large audience might survive on cable because most of cable's revenues come from subscription fees and not advertising. For example, on cable, AMC's *Breaking Bad* and FX's *It's Always Sunny in Philadelphia* are considered reasonably successful. However, neither show attracts an audience of over two million; in comparison, Fox network's *American Idol* draws an audience of between fifteen and twenty-five million.

Assessing Today's Converged and Multi-Screen Markets

During the height of the network era, a prime-time series with a rating of 17 or 18 and a share of between 28 and 30 was generally a success. By the late 2000s, though, with increasing competition from cable, DVDs, and the Internet, the threshold for success had dropped to a rating of 3 or 4 and a share of under 10. In fact, with all the screen options and targeted audiences, it is almost impossible for a TV program today to crack the highest-rated series list (see Table 6.1 on page 227). Unfortunately, many popular programs have been canceled over the years because advertisers considered their audiences too young, too old, or too poor. To account for the rise of DVRs, Nielsen now offers three versions of its ratings: "live . . . ; live plus 24 hours, counting how many people who own

NICHE MARKETS
As TV's audience gets fragmented among broadcast, cable, DVRs, and the Internet, some shows have focused on targeting smaller niche audiences instead of the broad public. IFC's *Portlandia*, for example, has a relatively small but devoted fan base that supports the show's culturally specific satire.

Program	Network	Date	Rating
1 M*A*S*H (final episode)	CBS	2/28/83	60.2
2 Dallas ("Who Shot J.R.?" episode)	CBS	11/21/80	53.3
3 The Fugitive (final episode)	ABC	8/29/67	45.9
4 Cheers (final episode)	NBC	5/20/93	45.5
5 Ed Sullivan Show (Beatles' first U.S. TV appearance)	CBS	2/9/64	45.3
6 Beverly Hillbillies	CBS	1/8/64	44.0
7 Ed Sullivan Show (Beatles' second U.S. TV appearance)	CBS	2/16/64	43.8
8 Beverly Hillbillies	CBS	1/15/64	42.8
9 Beverly Hillbillies	CBS	2/26/64	42.4
10 Beverly Hillbillies	CBS	3/25/64	42.2

TABLE 6.1

THE TOP 10 HIGHEST-RATED TV SERIES; INDIVIDUAL PROGRAMS (SINCE 1960)

Note: The Seinfeld finale, which aired in May 1998, drew a rating of 41-plus and a total viewership of 76 million; in contrast, the final episode of Friends in May 2004 had a 25 rating and drew about 52 million viewers. (The M*A*S*H finale in 1983 had more than 100 million viewers.)

Source: The World Almanac and Book of Facts 1997 (Mahwah, N.J.: World Almanac Books, 1996), 296; Corbett Steinberg, TV Facts (New York: Facts on File Publications, 1985); A.C. Nielsen Media Research.

DVRs played back shows within a day of recording them; and live plus seven days."[23] During the 2011-12 TV season, many shows—including ABC's Fringe and CW's Vampire Diaries—actually drew larger audiences just from DVR playback than through their original first-time showing on the networks.[24]

In its efforts to keep up with the TV's move to smaller screens, Nielsen is also using special software to track TV viewing on computers and mobile devices. Today, with the fragmentation of media audiences, the increase in third- and fourth-screen technologies, and the decline in traditional TV set viewing, targeting smaller niche markets and consumers has become advertisers' main game.

The biggest revenue game changer in the small-screen world will probably be Google's YouTube, which in 2011 and 2012 entered into a joint venture with nearly a hundred content producers to create niche online channels. YouTube advances up to $5 million to each content producer, and it keeps the ad money it collects until the advance is paid off; revenue after that is split between YouTube and the content producer. Some familiar names have signed on including Madonna, Shaquille O'Neal, and Amy Poehler (from NBC's Parks & Recreation). Among the popular channels already launched are the music video site, Noisey, which had twenty-seven million visits in its first two months, and Drive, a channel for auto fans, which had seven million views in its first four months. (See "Tracking Technology: Streaming Dreams: YouTube Turns Pro" on page 228 for more on YouTube's foray into original programming.)

The way advertising works online differs substantially from network TV, where advertisers pay as much as $400,000 to buy one thirty-second ad during NBC's The Voice or ABC's Modern Family. Online advertisers pay a rate called a CPM ("cost per mille"; mille is Latin for "one thousand"), meaning the rate per one thousand impressions—which is a single ad shown to a person visiting an online site. So if a product company or ad agency purchases one thousand online impressions at a $1 CPM rate, that means the company or agency would spend $10 to have its advertisement displayed ten thousand times. Popular online sites where advertisers are reaching targeted audiences could set a CPM rate between $10 and $100, while less popular sites might command only a 10- to 20-cent CPM rate from ad agencies and product companies. For some of its new YouTube TV channels, analysts predicted that Google might be able to charge as much as $20 CPM for a relatively popular site.

TRACKING TECHNOLOGY

Streaming Dreams: YouTube Turns Pro

by John Seabrook

For the past sixty years, TV executives have been making the decisions about what we watch in our living rooms. Robert Kyncl, a senior executive at Google's YouTube, would like to change that. Therefore YouTube, the home of

Though Hulu remains a go-to destination for network and cable shows streaming online, some shows both new and archival are available on YouTube—usually through a paid subscription. But despite these moves toward more polished content, many users still visit YouTube for shorter, more eclectic fare.

grainy cell-phone videos and skate-boarding dogs, is going pro. Streaming video, delivered over the Internet, is about to engage traditional TV in a skirmish in the looming war for screen time.

YouTube was created by three former employees of PayPal, in a Silicon Valley garage, in early 2005. The founders envisioned a video version of Flickr, a popular photo-sharing site. On the evening of April 23, 2005, one of the founders, Jawed Karim, uploaded the first video to YouTube—an eighteen-

second clip of him, standing in front of the elephant enclosure at the San Diego Zoo, wearing an ill-fitting hiking jacket. Civilization would never be the same.

In October 2006, Google bought YouTube, for $1.65 billion. Within a year, Google had tamed the Wild West of copyright infringement that characterized YouTube's pioneer days, both through licensing deals with major content providers and through a content-management program, called Content ID, that alerted copyright

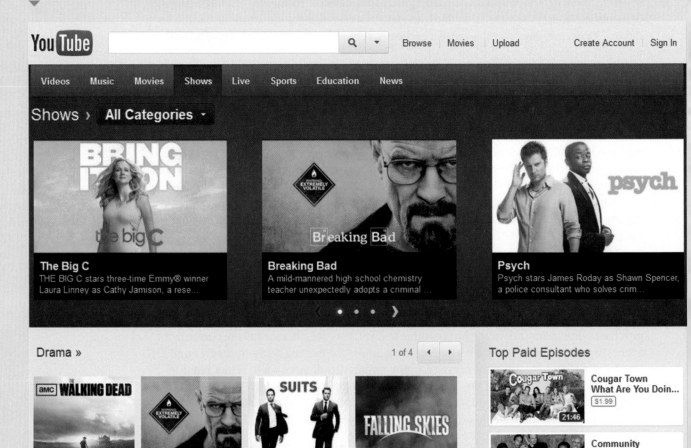

holders automatically whenever any part of their content went up on YouTube. Today, YouTube has eight hundred million unique users a month, and generates more than three billion views a day. Forty-eight hours of new video are uploaded to the site every minute.

But the average 'Tuber spends only fifteen minutes a day on the site—a paltry showing when compared with the four or five hours the average American spends in front of the TV each day. The standard block of programming on TV lasts twenty-two minutes; on YouTube, it's three minutes. If YouTube could get people to stay on the site longer, it could sell more advertising, and raise the rates it charges advertisers for each thousand views. Advertisers spend some $60 billion a year on television; they spend only about $3 billion on online video. Clearly, YouTube would benefit from premium content, the kind of stuff you could watch on Netflix and Hulu.

The senior vice-president of YouTube, Salar Kamangar, hired Robert Kyncl to help chart YouTube's future. In his first months on the job, Kyncl concentrated on beefing up YouTube's streaming-movie-rental business—the company's first foray into paid content—which, at that point, had mostly indie titles. But while Kamangar and Kyncl were expanding YouTube's movie titles, they were also exploring a more radical idea. What if YouTube could get professional writers, directors, and producers to create original content for the site?

Early in 2011, Kyncl began meeting content creators in a variety of media—film, TV, music, print—and inviting them to participate in it by creating new YouTube channels. He offered several million dollars in funding, in the form of advances against future ad revenues, to be used as development money. Once the advances are earned back, YouTube will share ad revenues with the creators. YouTube will have an exclusive right to the content for a year, but the creators will retain ownership. YouTube will be responsible for selling ads but will not invest in promoting or marketing the channels in the way that traditional television channels do.

In all, Kyncl received more than a thousand proposals for new YouTube channels. Madonna and her longtime manager, Guy Oseary, are developing a dance channel called Dance On. Amy Poehler is creating a channel called Smart Girls at the Party. Shaquille O'Neal is behind the Comedy Shaq Network, and there is a skateboard channel, RIDE, from Tony Hawk. The *Onion*, *Slate*, and the *Wall Street Journal* are also creating channels, as are Hearst and Meredith. Even Disney, which had not made its films available to YouTube until November, agreed to partner with the company.

Anthony Zuiker, who created the crime show *C.S.I.* for CBS, got a deal, along with his colleagues, to develop a channel called BlackBoxTV, a "Night Gallery"-like chiller theatre. When asked what attracted him to the opportunity, Zuiker said, "This world of online video is the future, and for an artist you want to be first in, to be a pioneer. And that time is now. We've had amateur content on the Web, and we've had network shows rebroadcast on the Web, but now we are combining those two into a bigger game."

But is there any danger to the brand, in moving so decisively from the user-generated anarchy of the old YouTube to YouTV? In its attempt to increase watch time and attract more viewers, YouTube risks alienating its core constituency—everyday people. ◢

Source: http://www.newyorker.com/reporting /2012/01/16/120116fa_fact_seabrook.

The Major Programming Corporations

After deregulation began in the 1980s, many players in TV and cable consolidated to broaden their offerings, expand their market share, and lower expenses. For example, Disney now owns both ABC and ESPN and can spread the costs of sports programming over their networks and their various ESPN cable channels. This business strategy has produced an *oligopoly* in which just a handful of media corporations now controls programming.

The Major Broadcast Networks

Despite their declining reach and the rise of cable, the traditional networks have remained attractive business investments. In 1985, General Electric, which once helped start RCA/NBC, bought back NBC. In 1995, Disney bought ABC for $19 billion; in 1999, Viacom acquired CBS for $37 billion (Viacom and CBS split in 2005, but Viacom's CEO remains CBS's main stockholder). And in January 2011, the FCC and the Department of Justice approved Comcast's purchase of NBC Universal from GE—a deal valued at $30 billion.

To combat audience erosion in the 1990s, the major networks began acquiring or developing cable channels to recapture viewers. Thus, what appears to be competition between TV and cable is sometimes an illusion. NBC, for example, operates MSNBC, CNBC, and Bravo. ABC owns ESPN along with portions of Lifetime, A&E, History, and the E! channel. However, the networks continue to attract larger audiences than their cable or online competitors. For the 2011-2012 season, CBS led the broadcast networks in ratings, followed by Fox, ABC, NBC, Univision, and the CW. CBS averaged 11.6 million viewers while CW drew about 1.7 million viewers each evening, although Fox reached more of the viewers most cherished by advertisers—eighteen- to forty-nine-year-olds. (For more on Fox, see "What News Corp. Owns" on page 231.)

Major Cable and DBS Companies

In the late 1990s, cable became a coveted investment, not so much for its ability to carry television programming as for its access to households connected with high-bandwidth wires. Today, there are about 7,100 U.S. cable systems, down from 11,200 in 1994. Since the 1990s, thousands of cable systems have been bought by large **multiple-system operators (MSOs)**, corporations like Comcast and Time Warner Cable that own many cable systems. The industry now calls its major players **multichannel video programming distributors (MVPDs)**; this includes DBS

TABLE 6.2

Top 10 Multichannel Video Programming Distributors (MVPD), 2012

Source: National Cable & Telecommunications Association, "Top 25 Multichannel Video Programming Distributors as of March 2012," http://www.ncta.com/Stats /TopMSOs.aspx.

Rank	MVPD	Subscribers
1	Comcast Corporation	22,294,000
2	DirecTV	19,966,000
3	DISH Network Corporation	14,071,000
4	Time Warner Cable, Inc.	12,653,000
5	Cox Communications, Inc.	4,756,000
6	Verizon Communications, Inc.	4,473,000
7	Charter Communications, Inc.	4,269,000
8	AT&T, Inc.	3,991,000
9	Cablevision Systems Corporation	3,257,000
10	Bright House Networks LLC	2,079,000

providers like DirecTV and DISH Network. By 2012, the Top 10 companies controlled about 70 percent of cable and DBS households (see Table 6.2 on page 230).

In cable, the industry behemoth is Comcast, especially after its takeover of NBC and move into network broadcasting. Back in 2001, AT&T had merged its cable and broadband industry in a $72 billion deal with Comcast, then the third-largest MSO. The new Comcast instantly became the cable industry leader, and it now serves more than twenty-five million households. Comcast's cable properties also include interests in Versus, E!, and the Golf Channel. Other major cable MSOs include Time Warner Cable (formerly part of Time Warner), Cox Communications, Charter Communications, and Cablevision Systems.

In the DBS market, DirecTV and DISH Network control virtually all of the DBS service in the continental United States. In 2008, News Corp. sold DirecTV to cable service provider Liberty Media, which also owns the Encore and Starz movie channels. The independently owned DISH Network was founded as EchoStar Communications in 1980. DBS's market share has grown from 14 percent in 2000 to nearly 40 percent in 2011. Television services (combined with existing voice and Internet services) offered by telephone giants Verizon (FiOS) and AT&T (U-verse) are also developing into viable competition for cable and DBS companies.

The Effects of Consolidation

There are some concerns that the trend toward cable, broadcasting, and telephone companies merging will limit expression of political viewpoints, programming options, and technical innovation, and lead to price-fixing. These concerns raise an important question: *In an economic climate in which fewer owners control the circulation of communication, what happens to new ideas or controversial views that may not always be profitable to circulate?*

The response from the industries is that, given the tremendous capital investment it takes to run television, cable, and other media enterprises, it is necessary to form business conglomerates in order to buy up struggling companies and keep them afloat. This argument suggests that without today's MVPD-type services, many smaller ventures in programming would not be possible. However, there is evidence that large MVPDs can wield their monopoly power unfairly. Business disputes have caused disruptions as networks and cable providers have dropped one another from their services, leaving customers in the dark. For example, in October 2010 News Corp. pulled six channels including the Fox network from over three million Cablevision customers for two weeks. This unusually long and bitter standoff meant Cablevision subscribers missed two World Series games, various professional football matches, and popular programs like *Family Guy*. This shows what can happen when a few large corporations engage in relatively minor arguments over prices and programs: Consumers are often left with little recourse or choice in markets with minimal or no competition and programming from just a handful of large media companies.

Alternative Voices

After suffering through years of rising rates and limited expansion of services, some small U.S. cities have decided to challenge the private monopolies of cable giants by building competing, publicly owned cable systems. So far, the municipally owned cable systems number in the hundreds and can be found in places like Glasgow, Kentucky; Kutztown, Pennsylvania; Cedar Falls, Iowa; and Provo, Utah. In most cases, they're operated by the community-owned, nonprofit electric utilities. There are more than two thousand such municipal utilities across the United States, serving about 14 percent of the population and creating the potential for more municipal utilities to expand into communications services. As nonprofit entities, the municipal operations are less expensive for cable subscribers, too.

Turn page for more ▶

The first town to take on a national commercial cable provider (Comcast now runs the cable service there) was Glasgow, Kentucky, which built a competing municipal cable system in 1989. The town of fourteen thousand now has seven thousand municipal cable customers. William J. Ray, the town's Electric Plant Board superintendent and the visionary behind the municipal communications service, argues that this is not a new idea:

Cities have long been turning a limited number of formerly private businesses into public-works projects. This happens only when the people making up a local government believe that the service has become so essential to the citizens that it is better if it is operated by the government. In colonial America, it was all about drinking water. . . . In the twentieth century, the issue was electric power and natural gas service. Now, we are facing the same transformation in broadband networks.[25]

More than a quarter of the country's two thousand municipal utilities offer broadband services, including cable, high-speed Internet, and telephone. How will commercial cable operators fend off this unprecedented competition? According to Ray: "If cable operators are afraid of cities competing with them, there is a defense that is impregnable–they can charge reasonable rates, offer consummate customer service, improve their product, and conduct their business as if they were a guest that owes their existence to the benevolence of the city that has invited them in."[26]

Television, Cable, and Democracy

In the 1950s, television's appearance significantly changed the media landscape–particularly the radio and magazine industries, both of which had to cultivate specialized audiences and markets to survive. In its heyday, television carried the egalitarian promise that it could bypass traditional print literacy and reach all segments of society. This promise was reenergized in the 1970s when cable-access channels gave local communities the chance to create their own TV programming. In such a heterogeneous and diverse nation, the concept of a visual, affordable mass medium, giving citizens entertainment and information that they could all talk about the next day, held great appeal. However, since its creation, commercial television has tended to serve the interests of profit more often than those of democracy. Despite this, television remains the main storytelling medium of our time.

The development of cable, VCRs and DVD players, DVRs, the Internet, and smartphone services has fragmented television's audience by appealing to viewers' individual and special needs. These changes and services, by providing more specialized and individual choices, also alter television's former role as a national unifying cultural force, potentially de-emphasizing the idea that we are all citizens who are part of a larger nation and world. Moreover, many cable channels survive mostly by recycling old television shows and movies. Although cable is creating more and more original quality programming, it hasn't fully become an alternative to traditional broadcasting. In fact, given that the television networks and many leading cable channels are now owned by the same media conglomerates, cable has evolved into something of an extension of the networks. And even though cable audiences are growing and network viewership is contracting, the division between the two is blurring. For years now, new generations that grow up on cable and the Internet rarely make a distinction between a broadcast network and a cable service. In addition, iPods, iPads, smartphones, and Internet services that

now offer or create our favorite "TV" programs are breaking down the distinctions between mobile devices and TV screens. Today, the promise that cable once offered as a place for alternative programming and noncommercial voices is now usurped by the Internet, where all kinds of TV experiments are under way.

The bottom line is that television, despite the audience fragmentation, still provides a gathering place for friends and family at the same time that it provides access anywhere to a favorite show. Like all media forms before it, television is adapting to changing technology and shifting economics. As the technology becomes more portable and personal, TV-related industries continue to search for less expensive ways to produce stories and more channels on which to deliver them. But what will remain common ground on this shifting terrain is that television continues as our nation's chief storyteller, whether those stories come in the form of news bulletins, sporting events, cable dramas, or network sitcoms. ▶

"Those who complain about a lack of community among television viewers might pay attention to the vitality and interaction of TV sports watchers wherever they assemble."

BARBRA MORRIS, UNIVERSITY OF MICHIGAN, 1997

CHAPTER REVIEW

COMMON THREADS

One of the Common Threads discussed in Chapter 1 is about mass media, cultural expression, and storytelling. As television and cable change their shape and size, do they remain the dominant way our culture tells stories?

By the end of the 1950s, television had become an "electronic hearth" where families gathered in living rooms to share cultural experiences. By 2012, though, the television experience had splintered. Now we watch programming on our laptops, smartphones, and iPads, making it increasingly an individual rather than a communal experience. Still, television remains the mass medium that can reach most of us at a single moment in time, whether it's during a popular sitcom or a presidential debate.

In this shift, what has been lost and what has been gained? As an electronic hearth, television has offered coverage of special moments—inaugurations, assassinations, moonwalks, space disasters, Super Bowls, *Roots*, the Olympics, 9/11, hurricanes, presidential campaigns, Arab uprisings—that brought large heterogeneous groups together for the common experience of sharing information, celebrating triumphs, mourning loss, and electing presidents. Accessible now in multiple digitized versions, the TV image has become portable—just as radio became portable in the 1950s. Today, we can watch TV in cars, in the park, even in class (often when we're not supposed to).

The bottom line is that today television in all its configurations is both electronic hearth and digital encounter. It still provides a gathering place for friends and family, but now we can also watch a favorite show almost whenever or wherever we want. Like all media forms before it, television is adapting to changing technology and shifting economics. As technology becomes more portable and personal, the TV, cable, and DBS industries search for less expensive ways to produce and deliver television. Still, television remains the main place—whether it's the big LED screen or the handheld smartphone—where we go for stories. In what ways do you think this will change or remain the case in the future? Where do you prefer to get your stories?

KEY TERMS

The definitions for the terms listed below can be found in the glossary at the end of the book. The page numbers listed with the terms indicate where the term is highlighted in the chapter.

analog, 198
digital, 198
prime time, 200
network era, 201
CATV, 201
narrowcasting, 202
basic cable, 203
superstations, 203
premium channels, 205
pay-per-view (PPV), 205
video-on-demand (VOD), 205
direct broadcast satellite (DBS), 205
time shifting, 207
third screens, 207
fourth screens, 209

kinescope, 210
sketch comedy, 210
situation comedy, 211
domestic comedy, 211
anthology dramas, 212
episodic series, 212
chapter shows, 213
serial programs, 213
affiliate stations, 214
Prime Time Access Rule (PTAR), 218
fin-syn, 218
must-carry rules, 219
access channels, 219
leased channels, 219
electronic publishers, 220
common carriers, 220

Telecommunications Act of 1996, 221
deficit financing, 223
retransmission fees, 224
O & Os, 224
syndication, 224
evergreens, 224
fringe time, 224
off-network syndication, 224
first-run syndication, 225
rating, 226
share, 226
multiple-system operators (MSOs), 230
multichannel video programming distributors (MVPDs), 230

REVIEW QUESTIONS

The Origins and Development of Television

1. What were the major technical standards established for television in the 1940s? What happened to analog television?

2. Why did the FCC freeze the allocation of TV licenses between 1948 and 1952?

3. How did the sponsorship of network programs change during the 1950s?

The Development of Cable

4. What is CATV, and what were its advantages over broadcast television?

5. How did satellite distribution change the cable industry?

6. What is DBS? How well does it compete with the cable industry?

Technology and Convergence Change Viewing Habits

7. How have computers and mobile devices challenged the TV and cable industries?

8. What has happened to the audience in the digital era of third and fourth screens?

Major Programming Trends

9. What are the differences among sketch, situation, and domestic comedies on television?

10. Why did the anthology drama fade as a network programming staple?

11. How did news develop at the networks in the late 1940s and 1950s?

12. What are the challenges faced by public broadcasting today?

Regulatory Challenges to Television and Cable

13. What rules and regulations did the government impose to restrict the networks' power?

14. How did cable pose a challenge to broadcasting, and how did the FCC respond to cable's early development?

15. Why are cable companies treated more like electronic publishers than common carriers?

16. How did the Telecommunications Act of 1996 change the economic shape and future of the television and cable industries?

The Economics and Ownership of Television and Cable

17. Why has it become more difficult for independent producers to create programs for television?

18. What are the differences between off-network and first-run syndication?

19. What are ratings and shares in TV audience measurement?

20. What are the main reasons some municipalities are building their own cable systems?

Television, Cable, and Democracy

21. Why has television's role as a national cultural center changed over the years? What are programmers doing to retain some of their influence?

QUESTIONING THE MEDIA

1. How much television do you watch today? How has technology influenced your current viewing habits?

2. If you were a television or cable executive, what changes would you try to make in today's programs? How would you try to adapt to third- and fourth-screen technologies?

3. Do you think the must-carry rules violate a cable company's First Amendment rights? Why or why not?

4. If you ran a public television station, what programming would you provide that isn't currently being supplied by commercial television? How would you finance such programming?

5. How do you think new technologies will further change TV viewing habits?

6. How could television be used to improve our social and political life?

ADDITIONAL VIDEOS

Visit the © VideoCentral: Mass Communication **section at bedfordstmartins.com/mediaculture for additional exclusive videos related to Chapter 6, including:**

- CHANGES IN PRIME TIME
  Television industry experts discuss shifts in programming, including the fading influence of the prime-time block.

- WIRED OR WIRELESS: TELEVISION DELIVERY TODAY
  This video explores the switch to digital TV signals in 2009 and how it is changing television delivery.

A generation later, the space epic *Star Wars* (1977) changed the culture of the movie industry. *Star Wars*, produced, written, and directed by George Lucas, departed from the personal filmmaking of the early 1970s and spawned a blockbuster mentality that formed a new primary audience for Hollywood—teenagers. It had all of the now-typical blockbuster characteristics like massive promotion and lucrative merchandising tie-ins. Repeat attendance and positive buzz among young people made the first *Star Wars* the most successful movie of its generation.

Star Wars has impacted not only the cultural side of moviemaking but also the technical form. In the first *Star Wars* trilogy, produced in the 1970s and 1980s, Lucas developed technologies that are now commonplace in moviemaking—digital animation, special effects, and computer-based film editing. With the second trilogy, Lucas again broke new ground in the film industry. Several scenes of *Star Wars: Episode I—The Phantom Menace* (1999) were shot on digital video, easing integration with digital special effects. *The Phantom Menace* also used digital exhibition, becoming the first full-length motion picture from a major studio to use digital projectors, which have steadily been replacing standard film projectors.

For the current generation, no film has shaken up the film industry like *Avatar* (2009). Like *Star Wars* before it, *Avatar* was a groundbreaking blockbuster. Made for an estimated $250–$300 million, it became the all-time domestic box office champion, pulling in about $760 million, and more than $2.7 billion worldwide. *Avatar* integrated 3-D movie technology seamlessly, allowing viewers to immerse themselves in the computer-generated world of the ethereal planet Pandora, home of the eleven-foot-tall blue beings called the Na'vi. Director James Cameron worked with Sony to develop new 3-D cameras (a major technical innovation), which were an essential element of the filmmaking process and story, rather than a gimmicky add-on. Esteemed film critic Roger Ebert likened the movie to a blockbuster he saw a generation earlier: "Watching *Avatar*, I felt sort of the same as when I saw *Star Wars* in 1977. That was another movie I walked into with uncertain expectations. . . . *Avatar* is not simply a sensational entertainment, although it is that. It's a technical breakthrough."[2]

Though *Avatar* was released in both conventional 2-D and 3-D versions, it was the 3-D version that not only most impressed viewers but also changed the business of Hollywood. Theaters discovered they could charge a premium for the 3-D screenings and still draw record crowds. The success of *Avatar* paved the way for more 3-D movies like *Transformers: Dark of the Moon, Harry Potter and the Deathly Hallows: Part 2*, and *The Hobbit*. But 3-D, which can add 20 to 30 percent to the budget of a film, isn't a guarantee of success. In fact, savvy filmgoers are rejecting 3-D films where the format seems like an unnecessary gimmick.

▲

"In one way or another all the big studios have been trying to make another *Star Wars* ever since."

ROGER EBERT

▲ *DATING BACK TO THE LATE 1800s,* films have had a substantial social and cultural impact on society. Blockbuster movies such as *Star Wars, E.T., Titanic, Lord of the Rings, Shrek, Avatar,* and *The Avengers* represent what Hollywood has become–America's storyteller. Movies tell communal stories that evoke and symbolize our most enduring values and our secret desires (from *The Wizard of Oz* to *The Godfather* and the Batman series).

Films have also helped moviegoers sort through experiences that either affirmed or deviated from their own values. Some movies–for instance, *Last Tango in Paris* (1972), *Scarface* (1983), *Brokeback Mountain* (2005), *Fahrenheit 9/11* (2004), and *The Dictator* (2012)–have allowed audiences to survey "the boundary between the permitted and the forbidden" and to experience, in a controlled way, "the possibility of stepping across this boundary."[3] Such films–criticized by some for appearing to glorify crime and violence, verge on pornography, trample on sacred beliefs, or promote unpatriotic viewpoints– have even, on occasion, been banned from public viewing.

Finally, movies have acted to bring people together. Movies distract us from our daily struggles: They evoke and symbolize universal themes of human experience (the experience of childhood, coming of age, family relations, growing older, and coping with death); they can help us understand and respond to major historical events and tragedies (for instance, the Holocaust and 9/11); and they encourage us to rethink contemporary ideas as the world evolves, particularly in terms of how we think about race, class, spirituality, gender, and sexuality.

In this chapter, we examine the rich legacy and current standing of movies. We will:

- Consider film's early technology and the evolution of film as a mass medium
- Look at the arrival of silent feature films, the emergence of Hollywood, and the development of the studio system with regard to production, distribution, and exhibition
- Explore the coming of sound and the power of movie storytelling
- Analyze major film genres, directors, and alternatives to Hollywood's style, including independent films, foreign films, and documentaries
- Survey the movie business today–its major players, economic clout, technological advances, and implications for democracy
- Examine how convergence has changed the way the industry distributes movies and the ways we experience them

As you consider these topics, think about your own relationship with movies. What is the first movie you remember watching? What are your movie-watching experiences like today? How have certain movies made you think differently about an issue, yourself, or others? For more questions to help you think through the role of movies in our lives, see "Questioning the Media" in the Chapter Review.

> **"The movie is not only a supreme expression of mechanism, but paradoxically it offers as product the most magical of consumer commodities, namely dreams."**
>
> MARSHALL MCLUHAN, *UNDERSTANDING MEDIA,* 1964

Past-Present-Future: Movies

In film technology's nascent years, just seeing a few minutes of film screened on a white wall was an event, the fascination of moving images being sufficiently entertaining. Soon, nickelodeons brought movies to the masses, and they have remained shared cultural experiences ever since, continuing on to today's digital screens and giant IMAX theaters.

There have been points in the history of film in which Hollywood was concerned that television, then videotapes and DVDs, would end the movie industry. For example, the video industry took off in the 1970s only after the motion picture industry lost a court battle. But people still flocked to theaters. Similar concerns about the movie industry's demise are popping up today. Movie theater owners fear that the ease of watching movies at home and on mobile devices will mean fewer people going to the theaters. Because of this fear, they have insisted on maintaining a longer "window" between a theatrical release and video on demand release. Are these concerns valid? Would a shorter waiting period between theatrical releases and streaming undermine the theater box office? Should movies open in all venues–streaming, downloads, and theaters–at the same time? If they did, would theaters still survive? As the film industry confronts its future, it might take solace in the fact that throughout its history, disruptions in media technology never stopped people from desiring the shared cultural experience that movies offer.

Early Technology and the Evolution of Movies

History often credits a handful of enterprising individuals with developing the new technologies that lead to new categories of mass media. Such innovations, however, are usually the result of simultaneous investigations by numerous people. In addition, the innovations of both known and unknown inventors are propelled by economic and social forces as well as by individual abilities.[4]

The Development of Film

The concept of film goes back as early as Leonardo DaVinci, who theorized in the late 1400s about creating a device that would reproduce reality. Other early precursors to film included the Magic Lantern in the seventeenth century, which projected images painted on glass plates using an oil lamp as a light source; the invention of the *thaumatrope* in 1824, a two-sided card with different images on each side that appeared to combine the images when twirled; and finally, the introduction in 1834 of the *zoetrope*, a cylindrical device that rapidly twirled images inside a cylinder, which appeared to make the images move.

Muybridge and Goodwin Make Pictures Move

The development stage of movies began when inventors started manipulating photographs to make them appear to move while simultaneously projecting them on a screen. Eadweard Muybridge, an English photographer living in America, is credited with being the first to do both. He studied motion by using multiple cameras to take successive photographs of humans and animals in motion. One of Muybridge's first projects involved using photography to determine if

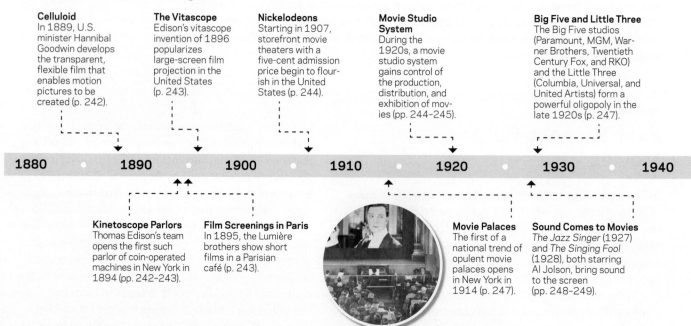

Movies and the Impact of Images

Celluloid
In 1889, U.S. minister Hannibal Goodwin develops the transparent, flexible film that enables motion pictures to be created (p. 242).

The Vitascope
Edison's vitascope invention of 1896 popularizes large-screen film projection in the United States (p. 243).

Nickelodeons
Starting in 1907, storefront movie theaters with a five-cent admission price begin to flourish in the United States (p. 244).

Movie Studio System
During the 1920s, a movie studio system gains control of the production, distribution, and exhibition of movies (pp. 244–245).

Big Five and Little Three
The Big Five studios (Paramount, MGM, Warner Brothers, Twentieth Century Fox, and RKO) and the Little Three (Columbia, Universal, and United Artists) form a powerful oligopoly in the late 1920s (p. 247).

1880   1890   1900   1910   1920   1930   1940

Kinetoscope Parlors
Thomas Edison's team opens the first such parlor of coin-operated machines in New York in 1894 (pp. 242–243).

Film Screenings in Paris
In 1895, the Lumière brothers show short films in a Parisian café (p. 243).

Movie Palaces
The first of a national trend of opulent movie palaces opens in New York in 1914 (p. 247).

Sound Comes to Movies
The Jazz Singer (1927) and *The Singing Fool* (1928), both starring Al Jolson, bring sound to the screen (pp. 248–249).

EADWEARD MUYBRIDGE'S study of horses in motion, like the one shown, proved that a racehorse gets all four feet off the ground during a gallop. In his various studies of motion, Muybridge would use up to twelve cameras at a time.

◀

a racehorse actually lifts all four feet from the ground at full gallop (it does). By 1880, Muybridge had developed a method for projecting the photographic images on a wall for public viewing. These early image sequences were extremely brief, showing only a horse jumping over a fence or a man running a few feet, because only so many photographs could be mounted inside the spinning cylinder that projected the images.

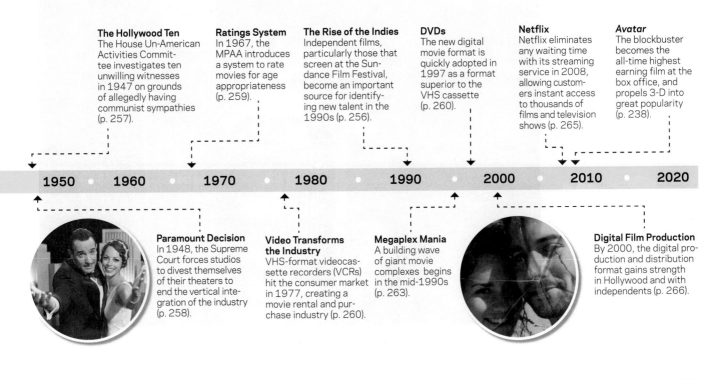

The Hollywood Ten
The House Un-American Activities Committee investigates ten unwilling witnesses in 1947 on grounds of allegedly having communist sympathies (p. 257).

Ratings System
In 1967, the MPAA introduces a system to rate movies for age appropriateness (p. 259).

The Rise of the Indies
Independent films, particularly those that screen at the Sundance Film Festival, become an important source for identifying new talent in the 1990s (p. 256).

DVDs
The new digital movie format is quickly adopted in 1997 as a format superior to the VHS cassette (p. 260).

Netflix
Netflix eliminates any waiting time with its streaming service in 2008, allowing customers instant access to thousands of films and television shows (p. 265).

Avatar
The blockbuster becomes the all-time highest earning film at the box office, and propels 3-D into great popularity (p. 238).

| 1950 | 1960 | 1970 | 1980 | 1990 | 2000 | 2010 | 2020 |

Paramount Decision
In 1948, the Supreme Court forces studios to divest themselves of their theaters to end the vertical integration of the industry (p. 258).

Video Transforms the Industry
VHS-format videocassette recorders (VCRs) hit the consumer market in 1977, creating a movie rental and purchase industry (p. 260).

Megaplex Mania
A building wave of giant movie complexes begins in the mid-1990s (p. 263).

Digital Film Production
By 2000, the digital production and distribution format gains strength in Hollywood and with independents (p. 266).

Hollywood Narrative and the Silent Era

D. W. Griffith, among the first "star" directors, was the single most important director in Hollywood's early days. Griffith paved the way for all future narrative filmmakers by refining many of the narrative techniques introduced by Méliès and Porter and using nearly all of them in one film for the first time, including varied camera distances, close-up shots, multiple story lines, fast-paced editing, and symbolic imagery. Despite the cringe-inducing racism of this pioneering and controversial film, *The Birth of a Nation* (1915) was the first *feature-length film* (more than an hour long) produced in America. The three-hour epic was also the first **blockbuster** and cost moviegoers a record $2 admission. Although considered a technical masterpiece, the film glorified the Ku Klux Klan and stereotyped southern blacks, leading to a campaign against the film by the NAACP and protests and riots at many screenings. Nevertheless, the movie triggered Hollywood's fascination with narrative films.

Feature films became the standard throughout the 1920s and introduced many of the film genres we continue to see produced today. The most popular films during the silent era were historical and religious epics, including *Napoleon* (1927), *Ben-Hur* (1925), and *The Ten Commandments* (1923); but the silent era also produced pioneering social dramas, mysteries, comedies, horror films, science fiction films, war films, crime dramas, westerns, and even spy films. The silent era also introduced numerous technical innovations, established the Hollywood star system, and cemented the reputation of movies as a viable art form, when previously they had been seen as novelty entertainment.

The Introduction of Sound

With the studio system and Hollywood's worldwide dominance firmly in place, the next big challenge was to bring sound to moving pictures. Various attempts at **talkies** had failed since Edison first tried to link phonograph and moving picture technologies in the 1890s. During the 1910s, however, technical breakthroughs at AT&T's research arm, Bell Labs, produced prototypes of loudspeakers and sound amplifiers. Experiments with sound continued during the 1920s, particularly at Warner Brothers studios, which released numerous short sound films of vaudeville acts, featuring singers and comedians. The studio packaged them as a novelty along with silent feature films.

In 1927, Warner Brothers produced a feature-length film, *The Jazz Singer*, starring Al Jolson, a charismatic and popular vaudeville singer who wore blackface makeup as part of his act. This further demonstrated, as did *The Birth of a Nation*, that racism in America carried into the film industry. An experiment, *The Jazz Singer* was basically a silent film interspersed with musical numbers and brief dialogue. At first, there was only modest interest in the movie, which featured just 354 spoken words. But the film grew in popularity as it toured the Midwest, where audiences stood and cheered the short bursts of dialogue. The breakthrough film, however, was Warner Brothers' 1928 release *The Singing Fool*, which also starred Jolson. Costing $200,000 to make, the film took in $5 million and "proved to all doubters that talkies were here to stay."[6]

A SILENT COMEBACK
The Artist, a tribute to silent movies set around the dawn of the talkies, won the Academy Award for Best Picture of 2011. It was the first (mostly) silent movie to win since the first Academy Awards in 1927.

Warner Brothers, however, was not the only studio exploring sound technology. Five months before *The Jazz Singer* opened, Fox studio premiered sound-film **newsreels**. Fox's newsreel company, Movietone, captured the first film footage with sound of the takeoff and return of Charles Lindbergh, who piloted the first solo, nonstop flight across the Atlantic Ocean in May 1927. Fox's Movietone system recorded sound directly onto the film, running it on a narrow filmstrip that ran alongside the larger, image portion of the film. Superior to the sound-on-record system, the Movietone method eventually became film's standard sound system.

Boosted by the innovation of sound, annual movie attendance in the United States rose from sixty million a week in 1927 to ninety million a week in 1929. By 1931, nearly 85 percent of America's twenty thousand theaters accommodated sound pictures, and by 1935 the world had adopted talking films as the commercial standard.

The Development of the Hollywood Style

By the time sound came to movies, Hollywood dictated not only the business but also the style of most moviemaking worldwide. That style, or model, for storytelling developed with the rise of the studio system in the 1920s, solidified during the first two decades of the sound era, and continues to dominate American filmmaking today. The model serves up three ingredients that give Hollywood movies their distinctive flavor: the narrative, the genre, and the author (or director). The right blend of these ingredients—combined with timing, marketing, and luck—has led to many movie hits, from 1930s and 1940s classics like *It Happened One Night*, *Gone with the Wind*, *The Philadelphia Story*, and *Casablanca* to recent successes like *Inception* (2010) and *The Hunger Games* (2012).

Hollywood Narratives

American filmmakers from D. W. Griffith to Steven Spielberg have understood the allure of *narrative*, which always includes two basic components: the story (what happens to whom) and the discourse (how the story is told). Further, Hollywood codified a familiar narrative structure across all genres. Most movies, like most TV shows and novels, feature recognizable character types (protagonist, antagonist, romantic interest, sidekick); a clear beginning, middle, and end (even with flashbacks and flash-forwards, the sequence of events is usually clear to the viewer); and a plot propelled by the main character experiencing and resolving a conflict by the end of the movie.

Within Hollywood's classic narratives, filmgoers find an amazing array of intriguing cultural variations. For example, familiar narrative conventions of heroes, villains, conflicts, and resolutions may be made more unique with inventions like computer-generated imagery (CGI) or digital remastering for an IMAX 3-D Experience release. This combination of convention and invention—standardized Hollywood stories and differentiated special effects—provides a powerful economic package that satisfies most audiences' appetites for both the familiar and the distinctive.

Hollywood Genres

In general, Hollywood narratives fit a **genre**, or category, in which conventions regarding similar characters, scenes, structures, and themes recur in combination. Grouping films by category is another way for the industry to achieve the two related economic goals of *product standardization* and *product differentiation*. By making films that fall into popular genres, the movie industry provides familiar models that can be imitated. It is much easier for a studio to promote a film that already fits into a preexisting category with which viewers are familiar. Among the most familiar genres are comedy, drama, romance, action/adventure, mystery/suspense,

"I think that American movies, to be honest, are just simple. You blow things up, you shoot people, you have sex and you have a movie. And I think it appeals to just the more base emotions of people anywhere."

ANTHONY KAUFMANN, FILM JOURNALIST, 2004

"The thing of a musical is that you take a simple story, and tell it in a complicated way."

BAZ LUHRMANN, AT THE 2002 ACADEMY AWARDS, ON *MOULIN ROUGE!*

> "My stuff always starts with interviews. I start interviewing people, and then slowly but surely, a movie insinuates itself."
>
> ERROL MORRIS, DOCUMENTARY FILMMAKER, 2008

INDEPENDENT FILM FESTIVALS, like the Sundance Film Festival, are widely recognized in the film industry as a major place to discover new talent and acquire independently made films on topics that might otherwise be too controversial, too niche, or too original for a major studio-backed picture. One of the breakout hits of Sundance 2012, *Beasts of the Southern Wild*, is a magical realist drama about a little girl (played by newcomer Quvenzhané Wallis) who lives in a bayou outside New Orleans and faces a hurricane, as well as mythical creatures. Fox Searchlight acquired distribution rights, releasing it to great acclaim and strong limited-release box office grosses that summer.

Perhaps the major contribution of documentaries has been their willingness to tackle controversial or unpopular subject matter. For example, American documentary filmmaker Michael Moore often addresses complex topics that target corporations or the government. His films include *Roger and Me* (1989), a comic and controversial look at the relationship between the city of Flint, Michigan, and General Motors; the Oscar-winning *Bowling for Columbine* (2002), which explored gun violence; *Fahrenheit 9/11* (2004), a critique of the Bush administration's Middle East policies; *Sicko* (2007), an investigation of the U.S. health-care system; and *Capitalism: A Love Story* (2009), about corporate culture in the United States. Moore's recent films were part of a resurgence in high-profile documentary filmmaking in the United States, which included *The Fog of War* (2003), *Super Size Me* (2004), *An Inconvenient Truth* (2006), *The Cove* (2009), *Waiting for Superman* (2010), and *Bully* (2012).

The Rise of Independent Films

The success of documentary films like *Super Size Me* and *Fahrenheit 9/11* dovetails with the rise of **indies**, or independently produced films. As opposed to directors working in the Hollywood system, independent filmmakers typically operate on a shoestring budget and show their movies in thousands of campus auditoriums and at hundreds of small film festivals. The decreasing costs of portable technology, including smaller digital cameras and computer editing, have kept many documentary and independent filmmakers in business. They make movies inexpensively, relying on real-life situations, stage actors and nonactors, crews made up of friends and students, and local nonstudio settings. Successful independents like Kevin Smith (*Clerks*, 1994; *Cop Out*, 2010), Darren Aronofsky (*The Fountain*, 2006; *The Wrestler*, 2008; *Black Swan*, 2010), and Sofia Coppola (*Lost in Translation*, 2003; *The Bling Ring*, 2013) continue to find substantial audiences in college and art-house theaters and through online DVD services like Netflix, which promote work produced outside the studio system.

The rise of independent film festivals in the 1990s—especially the Sundance Film Festival held every January in Park City, Utah—helped Hollywood rediscover low-cost independent films as an alternative to traditional movies with *Titanic*-size budgets. Films such as *Little Miss Sunshine* (2006), *500 Days of Summer* (2009), *Our Idiot Brother* (2011), and *Beasts of the Southern Wild* (2012) were able to generate industry buzz and garner major studio distribution deals through Sundance screenings, becoming star vehicles for several directors and actors. As with the recording industry, the major studios see these festivals—which also include New York's Tribeca Film Festival, the South by Southwest festival in Austin, and international film festivals in Toronto and Cannes—as important venues for discovering new talent. Some major studios even purchased successful independent film companies (Disney's purchase of Miramax) or have developed in-house indie divisions (Sony's Sony Pictures Classics) to specifically handle the development and distribution of indies.

But by 2010, the independent film business as a feeder system for major studios was declining due to the poor economy and studios' waning interest in smaller, specialty films. Disney sold Miramax for $660 million to an investor group comprised of Hollywood outsiders. Viacom folded its independent unit, Paramount Vantage, into its main studio; and Time Warner closed its Warner Independent and Picturehouse in-house indie divisions. Meanwhile, producers of low-budget independent films increasingly looked to alternative digital distribution models, such as Internet downloads, direct DVD sales, and on-demand screenings via cable and services like Netflix.

The Transformation of the Studio System

After years of thriving, the Hollywood movie industry began to falter after 1946. Weekly movie attendance in the United States peaked at ninety million in 1946, then fell to under twenty-five million by 1963. Critics and observers began talking about the death of Hollywood, claiming that the Golden Age was over. However, the movie industry adapted and survived, just as it continues to do today. Among the changing conditions facing the film industry were the communist witch-hunts in Hollywood, the end of the industry's vertical integration, suburbanization, the arrival of television, and the appearance of home entertainment.

The Hollywood Ten

In 1947, in the wake of the unfolding Cold War with the Soviet Union, conservative members of Congress began investigating Hollywood for alleged subversive and communist ties. That year, aggressive witch-hunts for political radicals in the film industry by the House Un-American Activities Committee (HUAC) led to the famous **Hollywood Ten** hearings and subsequent trial. (HUAC included future president Richard M. Nixon, then a congressman from California.)

During the investigations, HUAC coerced prominent people from the film industry to declare their patriotism and to give up the names of colleagues suspected of having politically unfriendly tendencies. Upset over labor union strikes and outspoken writers, many film executives were eager to testify and provide names. For instance, Jack L. Warner of Warner Brothers suggested that whenever film writers made fun of the wealthy or America's political system in their work, or if their movies were sympathetic to "Indians and the colored folks,"[11] they were engaging in communist propaganda. In addition, film producer Sam Wood, who had directed Marx Brothers comedies in the mid-1930s, testified that communist writers could be spotted because they portrayed bankers and senators as villainous characters. Other "friendly" HUAC witnesses included actors Gary Cooper and Ronald Reagan, director Elia Kazan, and producer Walt Disney. Whether they believed it was their patriotic duty or they feared losing their jobs, many prominent actors, directors, and other film executives also "named names."

Eventually, HUAC subpoenaed ten unwilling witnesses who were questioned about their memberships in various organizations. The so-called Hollywood Ten—nine screenwriters and one director—refused to discuss their memberships or to identify communist sympathizers. Charged with contempt of Congress in November 1947, they were eventually sent to prison. Although jailing the Hollywood Ten clearly violated their free-speech rights, in the atmosphere of the Cold War many people worried that "the American way" could be sabotaged via unpatriotic messages planted in films. Upon release from jail, the Hollywood Ten found themselves

"After the success of *The Blair Witch Project* . . . it seemed that anyone with a dream, a camera and an Internet account could get a film made—or, at least, market it cheaply once it was made."

ABBY ELLIN,
NEW YORK TIMES,
2000

THE HOLLYWOOD TEN
While many studio heads, producers, and actors "named names" to HUAC, others, such as the group shown below, held protests to demand the release of the Hollywood Ten.

Hollywood Adapts to Home Entertainment

Just as nickelodeons, movie palaces, and drive-ins transformed movie exhibition in earlier times, the introduction of cable television and the videocassette in the 1970s transformed contemporary movie exhibition. Despite advances in movie exhibition, most people prefer the convenience of watching movies at home. In fact, about 30 percent of domestic revenue for Hollywood studios comes from DVD/Blu-ray rentals and sales as well as Internet downloads and streaming, leaving domestic box-office receipts accounting for just 20 percent of total film revenue.

Although the video market became a financial bonanza for the movie industry, Hollywood ironically tried to stall the arrival of the VCR in the 1970s—even filing lawsuits to prohibit customers from copying movies from television. The 1997 introduction of the DVD helped reinvigorate the flat sales of the home video market as people began to acquire new movie collections on DVD. Today, home movie exhibition is again in transition, this time from DVD to Internet video. As DVD sales began to decline, Hollywood endorsed the high-definition format Blu-ray in 2008 to revive sales, but the format hasn't grown quickly enough to help the video store business.

The biggest chain, Blockbuster, filed for bankruptcy in 2010, closed hundreds of stores, and was auctioned to the DISH Network in 2011, while the Movie Gallery/Hollywood Video chain shuttered all of its stores. The only bright spot in DVD rentals has been at the low end of the market—automated kiosks like Redbox and Blockbuster Express that rent movies for $1.20 to $2.00 a day. Online rental company Netflix became a success by delivering DVDs by mail to its subscribers. But the future of the video rental business is in Internet distribution. Movie fans can also download or stream movies and television shows from services like Netflix, Amazon, Hulu, Google, and the iTunes store to their television sets through devices like Roku, AppleTV, TiVo Premiere, videogame consoles, and Internet-ready TVs. As people invest in wide-screen TVs (including 3-D televisions) and sophisticated sound systems, home entertainment is getting bigger and keeping pace with the movie theater experience. Interestingly, home entertainment is also getting smaller—movies are increasingly available to stream and download on portable devices like tablets, laptop computers, and smartphones.

> "(Blu-ray is) the last hardware.... There won't be any other hardware now. It's gonna be on a digital phone, it's gonna be on a computer or TV screen."
>
> OLIVER STONE, DIRECTOR, 2011

The Economics of the Movie Business

Despite the development of network and cable television, video-on-demand, DVDs, and Internet downloads and streaming, the movie business has continued to thrive. In fact, since 1963 Americans have purchased roughly 1 billion movie tickets each year; in 2011, 1.28 billion tickets were sold.[13] With first-run movie tickets in some areas rising to more than $13 (and 3-D movies costing even more), gross revenues from domestic box-office sales have climbed to $10.2 billion, up from $3.8 billion annually in the mid-1980s (see Figure 7.1). In addition, home video, which includes domestic DVD and Blu-ray disc rentals and sales and digital streaming and downloads, produced another $18 billion a year, substantially more than box-office receipts. (Digital sales accounted for $3.4 billion of the home video total in 2011.[14]) In order to continually flourish, the movie industry revamped its production, distribution, and exhibition system and consolidated its ownership.

Production, Distribution, and Exhibition Today

In the 1970s, attendance by young moviegoers at new suburban multiplex theaters made megahits of *The Godfather* (1972), *The Exorcist* (1973), *Jaws* (1975), *Rocky* (1976), and *Star Wars* (1977). During this period, *Jaws* and *Star Wars* became the first movies to gross more than $100 million

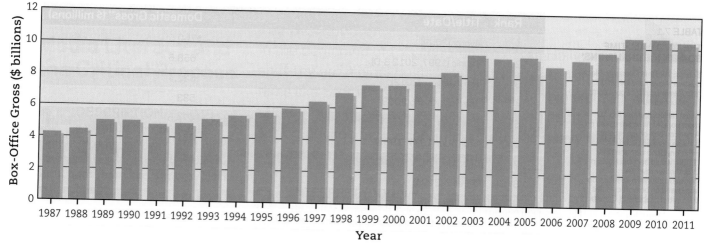

at the U.S. box office in a single year. In trying to copy the success of these blockbuster hits, the major studios set in place economic strategies for future decades. (See "Media Literacy and the Critical Process: The Blockbuster Mentality" on page 263.)

Making Money on Movies Today

With 80 to 90 percent of newly released movies failing to make money at the domestic box office, studios need a couple of major hits each year to offset losses on other films. (See Table 7.1 on page 262 for a list of the highest-grossing films of all time.) The potential losses are great: Over the past decade, a major studio film, on average, cost about $66 million to produce and about $37 million for domestic marketing, advertising, and print costs.[15]

With climbing film costs, creating revenue from a movie is a formidable task. Studios make money on movies from six major sources: First, the studios get a portion of the theater box-office revenue—about 40 percent of the box-office take (the theaters get the rest). Overall, box-office receipts provide studios with approximately 20 percent of a movie's domestic revenue. More recently, studios have found that they often can reel in bigger box-office receipts for 3-D films and their higher ticket prices. For example, admission to the 2-D version of a film costs $14 at a New York City multiplex, while the 3-D version costs $18 at the same theater. In 2011, 25 percent of major studio releases were 3-D films, and they generated 18 percent of Hollywood's box-office revenue that year. As Hollywood makes more 3-D films (the latest form of product differentiation), the challenge for major studios has been to increase the number of digital 3-D screens across the country. By 2012, about 32 percent of theater screens were digital 3-D.

Second, about four months after the theatrical release come the DVD sales and rentals, and digital downloads and streaming. This "window" accounts for about 30 percent of all domestic-film income for major studios, and has been declining since 2004 as DVD sales falter. Discount rental kiosk companies like Redbox must wait twenty-eight days after DVDs go on sale before they can rent them, and Netflix has entered into a similar agreement with movie studios in exchange for more video streaming content—a concession to Hollywood's preference for the greater profits in selling DVDs rather than renting them. A small percentage of this market includes "direct-to-DVD" films, which don't have a theatrical release.

Third are the next "windows" of release for a film: pay-per-view, premium cable (such as HBO), then network and basic cable, and, finally, the syndicated TV market. The price these cable and television outlets pay to the studios is negotiated on a film-by-film basis, although digital services like Netflix and premium channels also negotiate agreements with studios to gain access to a library of films. The cable window has traditionally begun with the DVD release window, but DirecTV threatened that system in 2011 by offering Hollywood films on demand

FIGURE 7.1

GROSS REVENUES FROM BOX-OFFICE SALES, 1987–2011

Source: Motion Picture Association of America, "Theatrical Market Statistics, 2011, U.S./ Canada," http://www.mpaa.org.

"The skill that movie executives have honed over the years is audience-creation. Even if it takes $30 to $50 million to herd teens to the multiplexes, and the movie fails to earn back that outlay, they hope it will lead to a future franchise. To abandon that hope means the end of Hollywood, as they know it."

EDWARD JAY EPSTEIN, *THE HOLLYWOOD ECONOMIST: THE HIDDEN FINANCIAL REALITY BEHIND THE MOVIES*, 2010

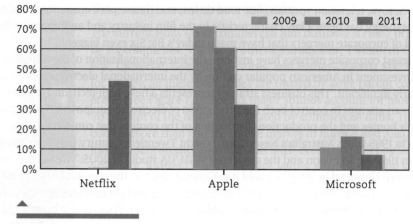

FIGURE 7.3

ONLINE MOVIE MARKET SHARE RANKING IN 2011

Source: IHS Screen Digest June 2012.

service that enables buyers of movies on DVD/Blu-ray to enter a code and stream or download those same movies to multiple devices.

The digital turn creates two long-term paths for Hollywood. One path is that studios and theaters will lean even more heavily toward making and showing big-budget blockbuster film franchises with a lot of special effects, since people will want to watch those on the big screen (especially IMAX and 3-D) for the full effect—and they are easy to export for international audiences. The other path features inexpensive digital distribution for lower-budget documentaries and independent films, which likely wouldn't get wide theatrical distribution anyway but could find an audience in those who watch from home.

The Internet has also become an essential tool for movie marketing, and one that studios are finding less expensive than traditional methods like television ads or billboards. Films regularly have Web pages, but many studios also now use a full menu of social media to promote films in advance of their release. For example, Lionsgate's 2012 movie *The Hunger Games* employed "near-constant use of Facebook and Twitter, a YouTube channel, a Tumblr blog, iPhone games and live Yahoo streaming from the premiere" to build interest that made it a hit film.[19]

Alternative Voices

With the major studios exerting such a profound influence on the worldwide production, distribution, and exhibition of movies, new alternatives have helped open and redefine the movie industry. The digital revolution in movie production is the most recent opportunity to wrest some power away from the Hollywood studios. Substantially cheaper and more accessible than standard film equipment, **digital video** is a shift from celluloid film; it allows filmmakers to replace expensive and bulky 16-mm and 35-mm film cameras with less expensive, lightweight digital video cameras. For moviemakers, digital video also means seeing camera work instantly instead of waiting for film to be developed and being able to capture additional footage without concern for the high cost of film stock and processing.

By 2002, a number of major directors—including Steven Soderbergh, Spike Lee, Francis Ford Coppola, George Lucas, and Gus Van Sant—began testing the digital video format. British director Mike Figgis achieved the milestone of producing the first fully digital release from a major studio with his film *Time Code* (2000). But the greatest impact of digital technology is on independent filmmakers. Low-cost digital video opens up the creative process to countless new artists. With digital video camera equipment and computer-based desktop editors, movies can now be made for just a few thousand dollars, a fraction of what the cost would be on film. For example, *Paranormal Activity* (2007) was made for about $15,000 with digital equipment and went on to be a top box-office feature. Digital cameras are now the norm for independent filmmakers, and many directors at venues like the Sundance Film Festival have upgraded to high-definition digital cameras, which rival film's visual quality. Ironically, both independent and Hollywood filmmakers have to contend with issues of preserving digital content: Celluloid film stock can last a hundred years, whereas digital formats can be lost as storage formats fail and devices become obsolete.[20]

Because digital production puts movies in the same format as DVDs and the Internet, independent filmmakers have new distribution venues beyond film festivals or the major studios. For example, Vimeo, YouTube, and Netflix have grown into leading Internet sites for the screening and distribution of short films and film festivals, providing filmmakers with their most valuable asset—an audience. Others have used the Web to sell DVDs directly, sell merchandise, or accept contributions for free movie downloads.

PARANORMAL ACTIVITY (2007), the horror film made by first-time director Oren Peli for a mere $15,000 with digital equipment, proves that you don't always need a big budget to make a successful film. Peli asked fans to "demand" the film be shown in their area via the Web site www.eventful.com, and Paramount agreed to a nationwide release if the film received 1 million "demands." *Paranormal Activity* was released nationwide on October 16, 2009, and went on to gross close to $200 million worldwide, spawning several sequels.

Popular Movies and Democracy

At the cultural level, movies function as **consensus narratives**, a term that describes cultural products that become popular and provide shared cultural experiences. These consensus narratives operate across different times and cultures. In this sense, movies are part of a long narrative tradition, encompassing "the oral formulaic of Homer's day, the theater of Sophocles, the Elizabethan theater, the English novel from Defoe to Dickens, . . . the silent film, the sound film, and television during the Network Era."[21] Consensus narratives—whether they are dramas, romances, westerns, or mysteries—speak to central myths and values in an accessible language that often bridges global boundaries.

At the international level, countries continue to struggle with questions about the influence of American films on local customs and culture. Like other American mass media industries, the long reach of Hollywood movies is one of the key contradictions of contemporary life: Do such films contribute to a global village in which people throughout the world share a universal culture that breaks down barriers? Or does an American-based common culture stifle the development of local cultures worldwide and diversity in moviemaking? Clearly, the steady production of profitable action/adventure movies—whether they originate in the United States, Africa, France, or China—continues, not only because these movies appeal to mass audiences, but also because they translate easily into other languages.

With the rise of international media conglomerates, it has become more difficult to awaken public debate over issues of movie diversity and America's domination of the film business. Consequently, issues concerning greater competition and a better variety of movies sometimes fall by the wayside. As critical consumers, those of us who enjoy movies and recognize their cultural significance must raise these broader issues in public forums as well as in our personal conversations. ▶

CHAPTER REVIEW

COMMON THREADS

One of the Common Threads discussed in Chapter 1 is about mass media, cultural expression, and storytelling. The movie industry is a particularly potent example of this, as Hollywood movies dominate international screens. But Hollywood dominates our domestic screens as well. Does this limit our exposure to other kinds of stories?

Since the 1920s, after the burgeoning film industries in Europe lay in ruins from World War I, Hollywood gained an international dominance it has never relinquished. Critics have long cited America's *cultural imperialism*, flooding the world with our movies, music, television shows, fashion, and products. The strength of American cultural and economic power is evident when you witness a Thai man in a Tommy Hilfiger shirt watching *Transformers* at a Bangkok bar while eating a hamburger and drinking a Coke. Critics feel that American-produced culture overwhelms indigenous cultural industries, which will never be able to compete at the same level.

But other cultures are good at bending and blending our content. Hip-hop has been remade into regional music in places like Senegal, Portugal, Taiwan, and the Philippines. McDonald's is global, but in India you can get a McAlooTikki sandwich—a spicy fried potato and pea vegetarian patty. In Turkey, you can get a McTurco, a kebab with lamb or chicken. Or in France you can order a beer with your meal.

While some may be proud of the success of America's cultural exports, we might also ask ourselves this: What is the impact of our cultural dominance on our own media environment? Foreign films, for example, account for less than 2 percent of all releases in the United States. Is this because we find subtitles or other languages too challenging? At points in the twentieth century, American movie-goers were much more likely to see foreign films. Did our taste in movies change on our own accord, or did we simply forget how to appreciate different narratives and styles?

Of course, international content does make it to our shores. We exported rock and roll, and the British sent it back to us, with long hair. They also gave us *American Idol* and *The Office*. Japan gave us anime, Pokémon, *Iron Chef*, and Hello Kitty.

But in a world where globalization is a key phenomenon, Hollywood rarely shows us the world through another's eyes. The burden falls to us to search out and watch those movies until Hollywood finally gets the message.

KEY TERMS

The definitions for the terms listed below can be found in the glossary at the end of the book. The page numbers listed with the terms indicate where the term is highlighted in the chapter.

celluloid, 242
kinetograph, 242
kinetoscope, 242
vitascope, 243
narrative films, 243
nickelodeons, 244
vertical integration, 245
oligopoly, 245
studio system, 245
block booking, 246

movie palaces, 247
multiplexes, 247
Big Five, 247
Little Three, 247
blockbuster, 248
talkies, 248
newsreels, 249
genre, 249
documentary, 254
cinema verité, 254

indies, 256
Hollywood Ten, 257
Paramount decision, 258
megaplexes, 263
Big Six, 264
synergy, 264
digital video, 266
consensus narratives, 267

For review quizzes, chapter summaries, links to media-related Web sites, and more, go to bedfordstmartins.com/mediaculture.

REVIEW QUESTIONS

Early Technology and the Evolution of Movies

1. How did film go from the novelty stage to the mass medium stage?
2. Why were early silent films popular?
3. What contribution did nickelodeons make to film history?

The Rise of the Hollywood Studio System

4. Why did Hollywood end up as the center of film production?
5. Why did Thomas Edison and the patents Trust fail to shape and control the film industry, and why did Adolph Zukor of Paramount succeed?
6. How does vertical integration work in the film business?

The Studio System's Golden Age

7. Why did a certain structure of film—called classic Hollywood narrative—become so dominant in moviemaking?
8. Why are genres and directors important to the film industry?
9. Why are documentaries an important alternative to traditional Hollywood filmmaking? What contributions have they made to the film industry?

The Transformation of the Studio System

10. What political and cultural forces changed the Hollywood system in the 1950s?
11. How did the movie industry respond to the advent of television?
12. How has the home entertainment industry developed and changed since the 1970s?

The Economics of the Movie Business

13. What are the various ways in which major movie studios make money from the film business?
14. How do a few large film studios manage to control more than 90 percent of the commercial industry?
15. How is the movie industry adapting to the Internet?
16. What is the impact of inexpensive digital technology on filmmaking?

Popular Movies and Democracy

17. Do films contribute to a global village in which people throughout the world share a universal culture? Or do U.S.-based films overwhelm the development of other cultures worldwide? Discuss.

QUESTIONING THE MEDIA

1. Do some research, and compare your earliest memory of going to a movie with a parent's or grandparent's earliest memory. Compare the different experiences.
2. Do you remember seeing a movie you were not allowed to see? Discuss the experience.
3. Do you prefer viewing films at a movie theater or at home, either by playing a DVD or streaming/downloading from the Internet? How might your viewing preferences connect to the way in which the film industry is evolving?
4. If you were a Hollywood film producer or executive, what kinds of films would you like to see made? What changes would you make in what we see at the movies?
5. Look at the international film box-office statistics in the latest issue of *Variety* magazine or online at www.boxofficemojo.com. Note which films are the most popular worldwide. What do you think about the significant role U.S. movies play in global culture? Should their role be less significant? Explain your answer.

ADDITIONAL VIDEOS

Visit the Ⓥ *VideoCentral: Mass Communication section at bedfordstmartins.com/mediaculture for additional exclusive videos related to the issues discussed in Chapter 7.*

The Roots and Roles of Print Media

One reason that print media will endure in some form is its rich and varied role in shaping our society and in serving as the repository of knowledge and stories over centuries.

- The invention of the printing press in the 1450s may seem far removed from our current media landscape, but the social and cultural transformations this invention allowed cannot be overestimated (Chapter 10, pages 350–351).

- The rise of yellow journalism in the late 1800s influenced both today's tabloids and, more important, investigative journalism that still crusades on behalf of society, rather than simply reporting news items (Chapter 8, pages 282–284).

- Similarly, longer-form investigative journalism found a home in magazines, thanks to the muckrakers of the early 1900s (Chapter 9, pages 320–321). Investigative news pieces that may now run on news sites or blogs are the current descendants of these practices.

- By blazing the trail for media, print forms have also advanced social equality, as with the pioneering journalism of Nellie Bly (Chapter 14, pages 485–486) and the women's magazines of the late 1960s and 1970s that gave voice to the feminist movement (Chapter 9, page 331).

- Just as the Internet has provided a platform for people, interests, and causes that may not have otherwise had a voice among the media, minority writers and audiences not always recognized by mainstream sources have been given platforms by specialized newspapers (Chapter 8, pages 293–296) and magazines (Chapter 9, pages 329–336).

The Struggles of Print Media in the Digital Turn

The digital turn has led to a unique set of challenges for print media, both structurally and economically.

- The emergence of blogs has challenged more traditional methods of news delivery (Chapter 8, page 302).

- Online journalism has vastly expanded over the past two decades, but it comes with its own set of pressures and pitfalls (Chapter 14, pages 503–505).

- Free online content, like blogs, Twitter feeds, and news aggregators, has led to drops in newspaper staffs and profits, which in turn has led to some newspapers' attempts to devise new business models, like paywalls or the expansion of successful online companies into journalism (Chapter 8, pages 306–307).

- Brick-and-mortar bookstores have also faced economic challenges in the face of online booksellers and e-books (Chapter 9, pages 368–370), while sellers of e-books as well as the Big Six publishers grapple with pricing strategies (Chapter 10, pages 362, 364).

Reimagining Print Media in the Digital Age

The digital turn has also created a wealth of opportunities for print media, which are often more adaptable than new media forms. For example, unlike a Hollywood movie, a network TV program, or a music industry CD, it is still inexpensive by comparison to publish a book. Even if physical print media forms disappear in the distant future, we will continue to identify these media as newspapers, magazines, and books even in their tablet or smartphone configurations.

- The popularity of tablets and e-readers means that the basic concept of books can be rethought—e-books can include content that was unthinkable on the printed page (Chapter 10, pages 361–362). Magazines, too, have potential for interactivity in these new platforms (Chapter 9, pages 327–328).

- Online news speeds up the news cycle; stories can now "break" on Twitter before moving on to blogs, Web sites, and eventually television and print media (Chapter 8, pages 304–305).

- Convergence allows even more specialization across media—print and otherwise. Self-publishing books is easier than ever (Chapter 10, pages 371–372); anyone with a video camera can produce a show for YouTube (Chapter 6, page 228); and the variety of news sources eliminates some of the pressure for those sources to stay nonpartisan (Chapter 14, pages 507–508).

▶ **For more on Internet users creating their own content, watch the "User-Generated Content" video on *VideoCentral: Mass Communication* at bedfordstmartins.com/mediaculture.**

Table of Contents

WEDNESDAY **2nd** FEBRUARY

TAP FOR TOP STORIES

Tap to
how to
The D

Quick tip
The Dai

Carousel

Control panel

Visual browser

Sharing &
commenting

Saving articles
for later

NEWS

Mubarak: I'll step down — eventually

The Egyptian president won't run for re-election – but a million marchers tell him to quit now.

NEWS

Here we snow again, America

A monster storm sweeps from the Southwest to New England and could affect as many as 100 million people.

NEWS

Creating joy from maximum security

A video look inside the prison where convicted murderers find redemption in making kids' toys.

NEWS

Arf, arf, arf, arf, stayin' alive ...

Manhattan's doggie disco is a late-night haven for hard-partying pooches and their owners.

Newspapers

The Rise and Decline of Modern Journalism

In his provocatively titled book, *The Deal from Hell: How Moguls and Wall Street Plundered Great American Newspapers* (2011), James O'Shea, former top editor at the *Chicago Tribune* and the *Los Angeles Times*, tells the sad story of the once-mighty Tribune Company (owner of both newspapers). The Tribune Company, which declared bankruptcy in 2008, had become *overleveraged*. That is, like other troubled media companies, it borrowed lots of money in the 1990s to buy more media companies and extend its media empire. The company used some of the borrowed money to fund new purchases, and some it invested. Then executives used the interest from investments, plus profits from ad revenue, to pay bankers and loan debt. But when advertising tanked and their investments began losing money in fall 2008 (as the stock market crashed), the Tribune Company, along with other big media firms in the same dire straits, could not pay all the bills. To raise capital, reorganize their debt, and avoid bankruptcy, media companies laid off hundreds of reporters and sold valuable assets.

So against the backdrop of this grim tale, what will happen to newspapers? Just as the music and radio industries adapted and survived, newspapers will survive, too—probably by delivering a print version two or three days a week—like AnnArbor.com in Michigan. In fact, the new owners of the New Orleans *Times Picayune*, among the nation's oldest newspapers, announced just such a switch, reducing the paper's print editions to Wednesday, Friday, and Sunday. Other newspapers have decided to go online only (like the *Christian Science Monitor*), or develop "papers" for new digital platforms—like the touchscreen tablet. That's the route Rupert Murdoch's News Corp. bet on in February 2011 with its launch of *The Daily*—the first "newspaper" designed especially for an iPad.

For News Corp., *The Daily* represented a way to cater to readers' increasingly digital lifestyles, and "an opportunity to try to reinvent the business model for news publishing."[1] After all, consider this big benefit touted by Murdoch at *The Daily*'s launch: "There is no paper, no multimillion-dollar presses, no trucks. We are passing the savings on to the readers."[2]

The Daily offers two weeks of free content to readers who download the app, and then asks them to subscribe for 99 cents a week or $40 a year. News Corp. invested $30 million in the project, started with a staff of a hundred, and featured six sections, including news, gossip, opinion, arts & life, apps & games, and sports. Operating costs were estimated at around $500,000 per week, which meant the paper needed to attract about 650,000 subscribers to break even.[3] Although

the new venture lost about $10 million in its first few months, it did boast one million downloads of its app in those early months.

But by late 2012 *The Daily* had only about 120,000 subscribers and was reportedly losing $30 million a year. With News Corp. splitting its newspaper and entertainment divisions into separate companies in 2012, the company closed the groundbreaking tablet newspaper in December 2012.[4]

Whether *The Daily* and similar tablet apps are the future of newspapers is still to be determined. As Joshua Benton of Harvard's Nieman Journalism Lab noted at the time of the launch, "I'm not sold that there's a vision for who, exactly, *The Daily* was trying to reach and what problem, exactly, it's trying to solve."[5] In other words, by 2012 the online-only *Daily* had not distinguished itself through its reporting or storytelling from better-staffed, conventional papers like the *New York Times*, which has its own very popular iPad app. But we *do* know that, just like movies shifted from film to digital and music moved from shellac disks to MP3s, newspapers will change in the near future, too—and it's a good bet that several incarnations of the interactive digital tablet will be involved.

▲

"We will stop printing the *New York Times* sometime in the future, date TBD."

ARTHUR SULZBERGER, *NEW YORK TIMES* PUBLISHER, 2010

◢ *DESPITE THEIR CURRENT PREDICAMENTS,* newspapers and their online offspring play many roles in contemporary culture. As chroniclers of daily life, newspapers both inform and entertain. By reporting on scientific, technological, and medical issues, newspapers disseminate specialized knowledge to the public. In reviews of films, concerts, and plays, they shape cultural trends. Opinion pages trigger public debates and offer differing points of view. Columnists provide everything from advice on raising children to opinions on the U.S. role as an economic and military superpower. Newspapers help readers make choices about everything from what kind of food to eat to what kind of leaders to elect.

Despite the importance of newspapers in daily life, in today's digital age the industry is losing both papers and readers. Newspapers have lost their near monopoly on classified advertising, much of which has shifted to free Web sites like eBay, monster.com, and craigslist. According to the Newspaper Association of America (NAA), in 2011 total newspaper ad revenues fell 9.2 percent (compared to a 28 percent decline in 2009 and 8.2 percent fall in 2010). Online ad sales increased only 6 percent in 2011 after an 11 percent decline in 2009 during the recession. In 2011, online ads accounted for about $3.2 billion in total revenue, while print advertising brought in more than $20 billion in ad revenue for the nation's papers—still less than half of the ad money generated as recently as 2006. The NAA reported that in 2011 digital ad revenue was up over $200 million compared to 2010; however, print ads were down more than $2 billion. The loss of papers, readers, advertising, and investor confidence raises significant concerns in a nation where daily news has historically functioned to "speak truth to power" by holding elected officials responsible and acting as a watchdog for democratic life.[6]

In this chapter, we examine the cultural, social, and economic impact of newspapers. We will:

- Trace the history of newspapers through a number of influential periods and styles
- Explore the early political-commercial press, the penny press, and yellow journalism
- Examine the modern era through the influence of the *New York Times* and journalism's embrace of objectivity
- Look at interpretive journalism in the 1920s and 1930s and the revival of literary journalism in the 1960s
- Review issues of newspaper ownership, new technologies, citizen journalism, declining revenue, and the crucial role of newspapers in our democracy

As you read this chapter, think about your own early experiences with newspapers and the impact they have had on you and your family. Did you read certain sections of the paper, like sports or comics? What do you remember from your childhood about your parents' reading habits? What are your own newspaper reading habits today? How often do you actually hold a newspaper? How often do you get your news online? For more questions to help you think through the role of newspapers in our lives, see "Questioning the Media" in the Chapter Review.

> "There's almost no media experience sweeter . . . than poring over a good newspaper. In the quiet morning, with a cup of coffee—so long as you haven't turned on the TV, listened to the radio, or checked in online—it's as comfortable and personal as information gets."
>
> JON KATZ, *WIRED,* 1994

Past-Present-Future: Newspapers

As late as the 1980s, many adults started their day reading a newspaper that was delivered to their front door. For most of the nation's first two hundred years, these home-delivered newspapers played a key role in informing people and helping them make sense of events and issues that affected their communities and country.

Today this job has been usurped, first by radio and TV and, most recently, by online news sites, blogs, and social media. Traditional printed newspapers are struggling as the page turns from a print world to a digital one, and they have lost both young readers and ad revenue to Internet news sources. Nonetheless, newspapers still play a central role in informing and educating people. After all, aggregators like Yahoo! and Google most often send their search-engine users looking for the best information and daily reports to newspaper sites. In fact, newspapers are still considered the most dependable and trustworthy source for news.

Think about your own use of actual printed newspaper. Track how often you look at one during a typical week. Compare this to how often you look for news online in that same week. Where do you tend to go for your news? Finally, how do you think the newspaper industry can keep publishing good journalism and train new journalists in the digital age . . . and still make money?

> "Oral news systems must have arrived early in the development of language, some tens or even hundreds of thousands of years ago.... And the dissemination of news accomplishes some of the basic purposes of language: informing others, entertaining others, protecting the tribe."
>
> MITCHELL STEPHENS,
> *A HISTORY OF NEWS*,
> 1988

The Evolution of American Newspapers

The idea of news is as old as language itself. The earliest news was passed along orally from family to family, from tribe to tribe, by community leaders and oral historians. The earliest known written news account, or news sheet, *Acta Diurna* (Latin for "daily events"), was developed by Julius Caesar and posted in public spaces and on buildings in Rome in 59 B.C.E. Even in its oral and early written stages, news informed people on the state of their relations with neighboring tribes and towns. The development of the printing press in the fifteenth century greatly accelerated a society's ability to send and receive information. Throughout history, news has satisfied our need to know things we cannot experience personally. Newspapers today continue to document daily life and bear witness to both ordinary and extraordinary events.

Colonial Newspapers and the Partisan Press

The novelty and entrepreneurial stages of print media development first happened in Europe with the rise of the printing press. In North America, the first newspaper, *Publick Occurrences, Both Foreign and Domestick*, was published on September 25, 1690, by Boston printer Benjamin Harris. The colonial government objected to Harris's negative tone regarding British rule, and local ministers were offended by his published report that the king of France had an affair with his son's wife. The newspaper was banned after one issue.

▼ **Newspapers: The Rise and Decline of Modern Journalism**

First Colonial Newspaper
In 1690, Boston printer Benjamin Harris publishes the first North American newspaper—*Publick Occurrences, Both Foreign and Domestick* (p. 278).

First Precedent for Libel and Press Freedom
In 1734, printer John Peter Zenger is arrested for seditious libel; jury rules in Zenger's favor in 1735—establishing freedom of the press and newspapers' right to criticize government (p. 279).

First Native American Newspaper
The *Cherokee Phoenix* appears in Georgia in 1828, giving a voice to tribal concerns as settlers encroach and move west (p. 295).

Yellow Journalism
Joseph Pulitzer buys the *New York World* in 1883; William Randolph Hearst buys the *New York Journal* in 1895 and battles Pulitzer during the heyday of the yellow journalism era (pp. 282-284).

1650	1800	1850

First U.S.-Based Spanish Paper
New Orleans' *El Misisipi* is founded in 1808 to serve Spanish-language readers (p. 294).

First African American Newspaper
Freedom's Journal begins short-lived operation in 1827, establishing a tradition of newspapers speaking out against racism (p. 293).

Penny Press
Printer Benjamin Day founds the *New York Sun* in 1833 and sets the price at one cent, helping usher in the penny press era and news for the working and emerging middle classes (p. 280).

In 1704, the first regularly published newspaper appeared in the American colonies–the *Boston News-Letter*, published by John Campbell. Because European news took weeks to travel by ship, these early colonial papers were not very timely. In their more spirited sections, however, the papers did report local illnesses, public floggings, and even suicides. In 1721, also in Boston, James Franklin, the older brother of Benjamin Franklin, started the *New England Courant*. The *Courant* established a tradition of running stories that interested ordinary readers rather than printing articles that appealed primarily to business and colonial leaders. In 1729, Benjamin Franklin, at age twenty-four, took over the *Pennsylvania Gazette* and created, according to historians, the best of the colonial papers. Although a number of colonial papers operated solely on subsidies from political parties, the *Gazette* also made money by advertising products.

Another important colonial paper, the *New-York Weekly Journal*, appeared in 1733. John Peter Zenger had been installed as the printer of the *Journal* by the Popular Party, a political group that opposed British rule and ran articles that criticized the royal governor of New York. After a Popular Party judge was dismissed from office, the *Journal* escalated its attack on the governor. When Zenger shielded the writers of the critical articles, he was arrested in 1734 for *seditious libel*–defaming a public official's character in print. Championed by famed Philadelphia lawyer Andrew Hamilton, Zenger ultimately won his case in 1735. A sympathetic jury, in revolt against the colonial government, decided that newspapers had the right to criticize government leaders as long as the reports were true. After the Zenger case, the British never prosecuted another colonial printer. The Zenger decision would later provide a key foundation– the right of a democratic press to criticize public officials–for the First Amendment to the Constitution, adopted as part of the Bill of Rights in 1791. (See Chapter 16 for more on the First Amendment.)

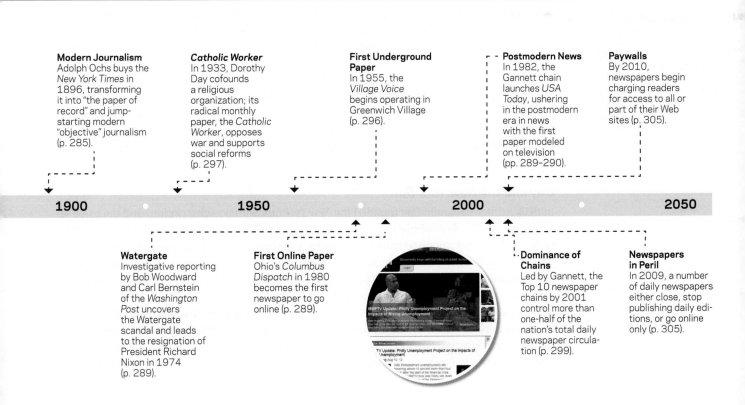

Modern Journalism
Adolph Ochs buys the *New York Times* in 1896, transforming it into "the paper of record" and jump-starting modern "objective" journalism (p. 285).

Catholic Worker
In 1933, Dorothy Day cofounds a religious organization; its radical monthly paper, the *Catholic Worker*, opposes war and supports social reforms (p. 297).

First Underground Paper
In 1955, the *Village Voice* begins operating in Greenwich Village (p. 296).

Postmodern News
In 1982, the Gannett chain launches *USA Today*, ushering in the postmodern era in news with the first paper modeled on television (pp. 289–290).

Paywalls
By 2010, newspapers begin charging readers for access to all or part of their Web sites (p. 305).

1900   **1950**   **2000**   **2050**

Watergate
Investigative reporting by Bob Woodward and Carl Bernstein of the *Washington Post* uncovers the Watergate scandal and leads to the resignation of President Richard Nixon in 1974 (p. 289).

First Online Paper
Ohio's *Columbus Dispatch* in 1980 becomes the first newspaper to go online (p. 289).

Dominance of Chains
Led by Gannett, the Top 10 newspaper chains by 2001 control more than one-half of the nation's total daily newspaper circulation (p. 299).

Newspapers in Peril
In 2009, a number of daily newspapers either close, stop publishing daily editions, or go online only (p. 305).

THE
New-York Weekly JOURNAL.

Containing the freſheſt Advices, Foreign, and Domeſtick.

MUNDAT December 2d, 1734.

By 1765, about thirty newspapers operated in the American colonies, with the first daily paper beginning in 1784. Newspapers were of two general types: political or commercial. Their development was shaped in large part by social, cultural, and political responses to British rule and by its eventual overthrow. The gradual rise of political parties and the spread of commerce also influenced the development of early papers. Although the political and commercial papers carried both party news and business news, they had different agendas. Political papers, known as the **partisan press**, generally pushed the plan of the particular political group that subsidized the paper. The *commercial press*, by contrast, served business leaders, who were interested in economic issues. Both types of journalism left a legacy. The partisan press gave us the editorial pages, while the early commercial press was the forerunner of the business section.

From the early 1700s to the early 1800s, even the largest of these papers rarely reached a circulation of fifteen hundred. Readership was primarily confined to educated or wealthy men who controlled local politics and commerce. During this time, though, a few pioneering women operated newspapers, including Elizabeth Timothy, the first American woman newspaper publisher (and mother of eight children). After her husband died of smallpox in 1738, Timothy took over the *South Carolina Gazette*, established in 1734 by Benjamin Franklin and the Timothy family. Also during this period, Anna Maul Zenger ran the *New-York Weekly Journal* throughout her husband's trial and after his death in 1746.[7]

The Penny Press Era: Newspapers Become Mass Media

By the late 1820s, the average newspaper cost six cents a copy and was sold through yearly subscriptions priced at ten to twelve dollars. Because that price was more than a week's salary for most skilled workers, newspaper readers were mostly affluent. By the 1830s, however, the Industrial Revolution made possible the replacement of expensive handmade paper with cheaper machine-made paper. During this time, the rise of the middle class spurred the growth of literacy, setting the stage for a more popular and inclusive press. In addition, breakthroughs in technology, particularly steam-powered presses replacing mechanical presses, permitted publishers to produce as many as four thousand newspapers an hour, which lowered the cost of newspapers. **Penny papers** soon began competing with six-cent papers. Though subscriptions remained the preferred sales tool of many penny papers, they began relying increasingly on daily street sales of individual copies.

Day and the *New York Sun*

In 1833, printer Benjamin Day founded the *New York Sun* with no subscriptions and the price set at one penny. The *Sun*—whose slogan was "It shines for all"—highlighted local events, scandals, police reports, and serialized stories. Like today's supermarket tabloids, the *Sun* fabricated stories, including the infamous moon hoax, which reported "scientific" evidence of life on the moon. Within six months, the *Sun*'s lower price had generated a circulation of eight thousand, twice that of its nearest New York competitor.

The *Sun*'s success initiated a wave of penny papers that favored **human-interest stories**: news accounts that focus on the daily trials and triumphs of the human condition, often featuring ordinary individuals facing extraordinary challenges. These kinds of stories reveal journalism's ties to literary traditions, such as the archetypal conflicts between good and evil, normal and deviant, or between individuals and institutions. Today, this can be found in everyday feature stories that chronicle the lives of remarkable people or in crime news that details the daily work of police and the misadventures of criminals. As in the nineteenth century, crime stories remain popular and widely read.

Bennett and the *New York Morning Herald*

The penny press era also featured James Gordon Bennett's *New York Morning Herald*, founded in 1835. Bennett, considered the first U.S. press baron, freed his newspaper from political influence. He established an independent paper serving middle- and working-class readers as well as his own business ambitions. The *Herald* carried political essays and news about scandals, business stories, a letters section, fashion notes, moral reflections, religious news, society gossip, colloquial tales and jokes, sports stories, and, later, reports from the Civil War. In addition, Bennett's paper sponsored balloon races, financed safaris, and overplayed crime stories. Charles Dickens, after returning to Britain from his first visit to America in the early 1840s, used the *Herald* as a model for the sleazy *Rowdy Journal*, the fictional newspaper in his novel *Martin Chuzzlewit*. By 1860, the *Herald* reached nearly eighty thousand readers, making it the world's largest daily paper at the time.

Changing Economics and the Founding of the Associated Press

The penny papers were innovative. For example, they were the first to assign reporters to cover crime, and readers enthusiastically embraced the reporting of local news and crime. By gradually separating daily front-page reporting from overt political viewpoints on an editorial page, penny papers shifted their economic base from political parties to the market—to advertising revenue, classified ads, and street sales. Although many partisan papers had taken a moral stand against advertising some controversial products and "services"—such as medical "miracle" cures, abortionists, and especially the slave trade—the penny press became more neutral toward advertisers and printed virtually any ad. In fact, many penny papers regarded advertising as consumer news. The rise in ad revenues and circulation accelerated the growth of the newspaper industry. In 1830, 650 weekly and 65 daily papers operated in the United States, reaching a circulation of 80,000. By 1840, a total of 1,140 weeklies and 140 dailies attracted more than 300,000 readers.

In 1848, six New York newspapers formed a cooperative arrangement and founded the Associated Press (AP), the first major news wire service. **Wire services** began as commercial organizations that relayed news stories and information around the country and the world using telegraph lines and, later, radio waves and digital transmissions. In the case of the AP, the New York papers provided access to both their own stories and those from other newspapers. In the 1850s, papers started sending reporters to cover Washington, D.C.; and in the early 1860s more than a hundred reporters from northern papers went south to cover the Civil War, relaying their reports back to their home papers via telegraph and wire services. The news wire companies enabled news to travel rapidly from coast to coast and set the stage for modern journalism.

The marketing of news as a product and the use of modern technology to dramatically cut costs gradually elevated newspapers from an entrepreneurial stage to the status of a mass medium. By adapting news content, penny papers captured the middle- and working-class readers who could now afford the paper and also had more leisure time to read it. As newspapers sought to sustain their mass appeal, news and "factual" reports about crimes and other items of human interest eventually superseded the importance of partisan articles about politics and commerce.

The Age of Yellow Journalism: Sensationalism and Investigation

The rise of competitive dailies and the penny press triggered the next significant period in American journalism. In the late 1800s, **yellow journalism** emphasized profitable papers that carried exciting human-interest stories, crime news, large headlines, and more readable copy. Generally regarded as sensationalistic and the direct forerunner of today's tabloid papers, reality TV, and celebrity-centered shows like *Access Hollywood*, yellow journalism featured two

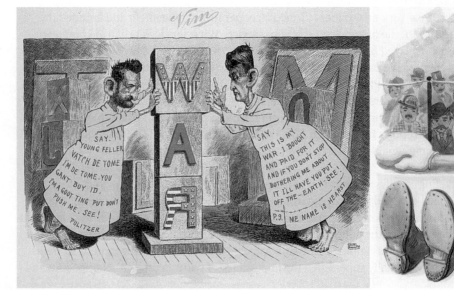

major characteristics. First were the overly dramatic—or sensational—stories about crimes, celebrities, disasters, scandals, and intrigue. Second, and sometimes forgotten, are the legacy and roots that the yellow press provided for **investigative journalism**: news reports that hunt out and expose corruption, particularly in business and government. Reporting increasingly became a crusading force for common people, with the press assuming a watchdog role on their behalf.

During this period, a newspaper circulation war pitted Joseph Pulitzer's *New York World* against William Randolph Hearst's *New York Journal*. A key player in the war was the first popular cartoon strip, *The Yellow Kid*, created in 1895 by artist R. F. Outcault, who once worked for Thomas Edison. The phrase *yellow journalism* has since become associated with the cartoon strip, which was shuttled back and forth between the Hearst and Pulitzer papers during their furious battle for readers in the mid- to late 1890s.

Pulitzer and the *New York World*

Joseph Pulitzer, a Jewish-Hungarian immigrant, began his career in newspaper publishing in the early 1870s as part owner of the *St. Louis Post*. He then bought the bankrupt *St. Louis Dispatch* for $2,500 at an auction in 1878 and merged it with the *Post*. The *Post-Dispatch* became known for stories that highlighted "sex and sin" ("A Denver Maiden Taken from Disreputable House") and satires of the upper class ("St. Louis Swells"). Pulitzer also viewed the *Post-Dispatch* as a "national conscience" that promoted the public good. He carried on the legacies of James Gordon Bennett: making money and developing a "free and impartial" paper that would "serve no party but the people." Within five years, the *Post-Dispatch* became one of the most influential newspapers in the Midwest.

In 1883, Pulitzer bought the *New York World* for $346,000. He encouraged plain writing and the inclusion of maps and illustrations to help immigrant and working-class readers understand the written text. In addition to running sensational stories on crime and sex, Pulitzer instituted advice columns and women's pages. Like Bennett, Pulitzer treated advertising as a kind of news that displayed consumer products for readers. In fact, department stores became major advertisers during this period. This development contributed directly to the expansion of consumer culture and indirectly to the acknowledgment of women as newspaper readers. Eventually (because of pioneers like Nellie Bly—see Chapter 14), newspapers began employing women as reporters.

The *World* reflected the contradictory spirit of the yellow press. It crusaded for improved urban housing, better conditions for women, and equitable labor laws. It campaigned against monopoly practices by AT&T, Standard Oil, and Equitable Insurance. Such popular crusades helped lay the groundwork for tightening federal antitrust laws in the early 1910s. At the same time, Pulitzer's paper manufactured news events and staged stunts, such as sending star reporter Nellie Bly around the world in seventy-two days to beat the fictional "record" in the popular 1873 Jules Verne novel *Around the World in Eighty Days*. By 1887, the *World*'s Sunday circulation had soared to more than 250,000, the largest anywhere.

Pulitzer created a lasting legacy by leaving $2 million to start the graduate school of journalism at Columbia University in 1912. In 1917, part of Pulitzer's Columbia endowment established the Pulitzer Prizes, the prestigious awards given each year for achievements in journalism, literature, drama, and music.

Hearst and the *New York Journal*

The *World* faced its fiercest competition when William Randolph Hearst bought the *New York Journal* (a penny paper founded by Pulitzer's brother Albert). Before moving to New York, the

> "There is room in this great and growing city for a journal that is not only cheap but bright, not only bright but large . . . that will expose all fraud and sham, fight all public evils and abuses—that will serve and battle for the people."
>
> JOSEPH PULITZER, PUBLISHER, *NEW YORK WORLD*, 1883

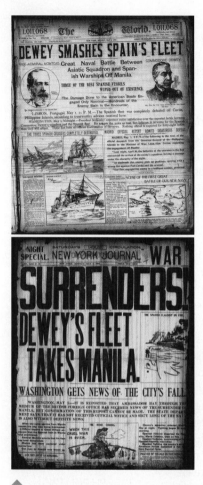

twenty-four-year-old Hearst took control of the *San Francisco Examiner* when his father, George Hearst, was elected to the U.S. Senate in 1887 (the younger Hearst had recently been expelled from Harvard for playing a practical joke on his professors). In 1895, with an inheritance from his father, Hearst bought the ailing *Journal* and then raided Joseph Pulitzer's paper for editors, writers, and cartoonists.

Taking his cue from Bennett and Pulitzer, Hearst focused on lurid, sensational stories and appealed to immigrant readers by using large headlines and bold layout designs. To boost circulation, the *Journal* invented interviews, faked pictures, and encouraged conflicts that might result in a story. One tabloid account describes "tales about two-headed virgins" and "prehistoric creatures roaming the plains of Wyoming."[8] In promoting journalism as mere dramatic storytelling, Hearst reportedly said, "The modern editor of the popular journal does not care for facts. The editor wants novelty. The editor has no objection to facts if they are also novel. But he would prefer a novelty that is not a fact to a fact that is not a novelty."[9]

Hearst is remembered as an unscrupulous publisher who once hired gangsters to distribute his newspapers. He was also, however, considered a champion of the underdog, and his paper's readership soared among the working and middle classes. In 1896, the *Journal*'s daily circulation reached 450,000, and by 1897 the Sunday edition of the paper rivaled the 600,000 circulation of the *World*. By the 1930s, Hearst's holdings included more than forty daily and Sunday papers, thirteen magazines (including *Good Housekeeping* and *Cosmopolitan*), eight radio stations, and two film companies. In addition, he controlled King Features Syndicate, which sold and distributed articles, comics, and features to many of the nation's dailies. Hearst, the model for Charles Foster Kane, the ruthless publisher in Orson Welles's classic 1940 film *Citizen Kane*, operated the largest media business in the world–the News Corp. of its day.

Competing Models of Modern Print Journalism

The early commercial and partisan presses were, to some extent, covering important events impartially. These papers often carried verbatim reports of presidential addresses and murder trials, or the annual statements of the U.S. Treasury. In the late 1800s, as newspapers pushed for greater circulation, newspaper reporting changed. Two distinct types of journalism emerged: the *story-driven model*, dramatizing important events and used by the penny papers and the yellow press; and the *"just the facts" model*, an approach that appeared to package information more impartially and that the six-cent papers favored.[10] Implicit in these efforts was the question (still debated today): Is there, in journalism, an ideal, attainable, objective model, or does the quest for objectivity actually conflict with journalists' traditional role of raising important issues about potential abuses of power in a democratic society?

"Objectivity" in Modern Journalism

As the consumer marketplace expanded during the Industrial Revolution, facts and news became marketable products. Throughout the mid-1800s, the more a newspaper appeared not to take sides on its front pages, the more its readership base grew (although, as they are today, editorial pages were still often partisan). In addition, wire service organizations were serving a variety of newspaper clients in different regions of the country. To satisfy all their clients and the wide range of political views, newspapers tried to appear more impartial.

Ochs and the *New York Times*

The ideal of an impartial, or purely informational, news model was championed by Adolph Ochs, who bought the *New York Times* in 1896. The son of immigrant German Jews, Ochs grew up in Ohio and Tennessee, where at age twenty-one he took over the *Chattanooga Times* in 1878. Known more for his business and organizational ability than for his writing and editing skills, he transformed the Tennessee paper. Seeking a national stage and business expansion, Ochs moved to New York and invested $75,000 in the struggling *Times*. Through strategic hiring, Ochs and his editors rebuilt the paper around substantial news coverage and provocative editorial pages. To distance his New York paper from the yellow press, the editors also downplayed sensational stories, favoring the documentation of major events or issues.

Partly as a marketing strategy, Ochs offered a distinct contrast to the more sensational Hearst and Pulitzer newspapers: an informational paper that provided stock and real estate reports to businesses, court reports to legal professionals, treaty summaries to political leaders, and theater and book reviews to educated general readers and intellectuals. Ochs's promotional gimmicks took direct aim at yellow journalism, advertising the *Times* under the motto "It does not soil the breakfast cloth." Ochs's strategy is similar to today's advertising tactic of targeting upscale viewers and readers who control a disproportionate share of consumer dollars.

With the Hearst and Pulitzer papers capturing the bulk of working- and middle-class readers, managers at the *Times* first tried to use their straightforward, "no frills" reporting to appeal to more affluent and educated readers. In 1898, however, Ochs lowered the paper's price to a penny. He believed that people bought the *World* and the *Journal* primarily because they were cheap, not because of their stories. The *Times* began attracting middle-class readers who gravitated to the now affordable paper as a status marker for the educated and well informed. Between 1898 and 1899, its circulation rose from 25,000 to 75,000. By 1921, the *Times* had a daily circulation of 330,000, and 500,000 on Sunday. (For contemporary print and digital circulation figures, see Table 8.1 on the next page.)

"Just the Facts, Please"

Early in the twentieth century, with reporters adopting a more "scientific" attitude to news- and fact-gathering, the ideal of objectivity began to anchor journalism. In **objective journalism**, which distinguishes factual reports from opinion columns, modern reporters strive to maintain a neutral attitude toward the issue or event they cover; they also search out competing points of view among the sources for a story.

The story form for packaging and presenting this kind of reporting has been traditionally labeled the **inverted-pyramid style**. Civil War correspondents developed this style by imitating the terse, compact press releases (summarizing or imitating telegrams to generals) that came from President Abraham Lincoln and his secretary of war, Edwin M. Stanton.[11] Often stripped of adverbs and adjectives, inverted-pyramid reports began—as they do today—with the most dramatic or newsworthy information. They answered who, what, where, when (and, less frequently, why or how) questions at the top of the story and then narrowed down the story to presumably

THE *NEW YORK TIMES* established itself as the official paper of record by the 1920s. The *Times* was the first modern newspaper, gathering information and presenting news in a straightforward way—without the opinion of the reporter. Today, the *Times* is known for its opinion columns and editorial pages as much as for its original reporting. In 2011, Jill Abramson (pictured) became its first woman executive editor.

JOAN DIDION'S two essay collections—*Slouching Towards Bethlehem* (1968) and *The White Album* (1979)—are considered iconic pieces from the new journalism movement. Both books detail and analyze Didion's life in California, where she experienced everything from the counterculture movement in San Francisco to meeting members of the Black Panther Party, the Doors, and even followers of Charles Manson.

movement were not easily explained. Faced with so much change and turmoil, many individuals began to lose faith in the ability of institutions to oversee and ensure the social order. Members of protest movements as well as many middle- and working-class Americans began to suspect the privileges and power of traditional authority. As a result, key institutions—including journalism—lost some of their credibility.

Journalism as an Art Form

Throughout the first part of the twentieth century—journalism's modern era—journalistic storytelling was downplayed in favor of the inverted-pyramid style and the separation of fact from opinion. Dissatisfied with these limitations, some reporters began exploring a new model of reporting. **Literary journalism**, sometimes dubbed "new journalism," adapted fictional techniques, such as descriptive details and settings and extensive character dialogue, to nonfiction material and in-depth reporting. In the United States, literary journalism's roots are evident in the work of nineteenth-century novelists like Mark Twain, Stephen Crane, and Theodore Dreiser, all of whom started out as reporters. In the late 1930s and 1940s, literary journalism surfaced: Journalists, such as James Agee and John Hersey, began to demonstrate how writing about real events could achieve an artistry often associated only with fiction.

In the 1960s, Tom Wolfe, a leading practitioner of new journalism, argued for mixing the *content* of reporting with the *form* of fiction to create "both the kind of objective reality of journalism" and "the subjective reality" of the novel.[17] Writers such as Wolfe (*The Electric Kool-Aid Acid Test*), Truman Capote (*In Cold Blood*), Joan Didion (*The White Album*), Norman Mailer (*Armies of the Night*), and Hunter S. Thompson (*Hell's Angels*) turned to new journalism to overcome flaws they perceived in routine reporting. Their often self-conscious treatment of social problems gave their writing a perspective that conventional journalism did not offer. After the 1960s' tide of intense social upheaval ebbed, new journalism subsided as well. However, literary journalism not only influenced magazines like *Mother Jones* and *Rolling Stone*, but it also affected daily newspapers by emphasizing longer feature stories on cultural trends and social issues with detailed description or dialogue. Today, writers such as Adrian Nicole LeBlanc (*Random Family*), Dexter Filkins (*The Forever War*), and Asne Seierstad (*The Bookseller of Kabul*) keep this tradition alive.

The Attack on Journalistic Objectivity

Former *New York Times* columnist Tom Wicker argued that in the early 1960s an objective approach to news remained the dominant model. According to Wicker, the "press had so wrapped itself in the paper chains of 'objective journalism' that it had little ability to report anything beyond the bare and undeniable facts."[18] Through the 1960s, attacks on the detachment of reporters escalated. News critic Jack Newfield rejected the possibility of genuine journalistic

	Journalists	Title or Subject	Publisher	Year
1	John Hersey	"Hiroshima"	*New Yorker*	1946
2	Rachel Carson	*Silent Spring*	Houghton Mifflin	1962
3	Bob Woodward/ Carl Bernstein	Watergate investigation	*Washington Post*	1972-73
4	Edward R. Murrow	Battle of Britain	CBS Radio	1940
5	Ida Tarbell	"The History of the Standard Oil Company"	*McClure's Magazine*	1902-04
6	Lincoln Steffens	"The Shame of the Cities"	*McClure's Magazine*	1902-04
7	John Reed	*Ten Days That Shook the World*	Random House	1919
8	H. L. Mencken	Coverage of the Scopes "monkey" trial	*Baltimore Sun*	1925
9	Ernie Pyle	Reports from Europe and the Pacific during World War II	Scripps-Howard newspapers	1940-45
10	Edward R. Murrow/ Fred Friendly	Investigation of Senator Joseph McCarthy	CBS Television	1954

TABLE 8.2

EXCEPTIONAL WORKS OF AMERICAN JOURNALISM

Working under the aegis of New York University's journalism department, thirty-six judges compiled a list of the Top 100 works of American journalism in the twentieth century. The list takes into account not just the newsworthiness of the event but the craft of the writing and reporting. What do you think of the Top 10 works listed here? What are some problems associated with a list like this? Do you think newswriting should be judged in the same way we judge novels or movies?

Source: New York University, Department of Journalism, New York, N.Y., 1999.

impartiality and argued that many reporters had become too trusting and uncritical of the powerful: "Objectivity is believing people with power and printing their press releases."[19] Eventually, the ideal of objectivity became suspect along with the authority of experts and professionals in various fields.

A number of reporters responded to the criticism by rethinking the framework of conventional journalism and adopting a variety of alternative techniques. One of these was *advocacy journalism*, in which the reporter actively promotes a particular cause or viewpoint. *Precision journalism*, another technique, attempts to make the news more scientifically accurate by using poll surveys and questionnaires. Throughout the 1990s, precision journalism became increasingly important. However, critics have charged that in every modern presidential campaign—including that of 2012—too many newspapers and TV stations became overly reliant on political polls, thus reducing campaign coverage to "racehorse" journalism, telling only "who's ahead" and "who's behind" stories rather than promoting substantial debates on serious issues. (See Table 8.2 for top works in American journalism.)

Contemporary Journalism in the TV and Internet Age

In the early 1980s, a postmodern brand of journalism arose from two important developments. In 1980 the *Columbus Dispatch* became the first paper to go online; today, nearly all U.S. papers offer some Web services. Then the colorful *USA Today* arrived in 1982, radically changing the look of most major U.S. dailies.

USA Today Colors the Print Landscape

USA Today made its mark by incorporating features closely associated with postmodern forms, including an emphasis on visual style over substantive news or analysis and the use of brief news items that appealed to readers' busy schedules and shortened attention spans.

Now the second most widely circulated paper in the nation, *USA Today* represents the only successful launch of a new major U.S. daily newspaper in the last several decades. Showing its marketing savvy, *USA Today* was the first paper to openly acknowledge television's central role

"Critics [in the 1960s] claimed that urban planning created slums, that school made people stupid, that medicine caused disease, that psychiatry invented mental illness, and that the courts promoted injustice.... And objectivity in journalism, regarded as an antidote to bias, came to be looked upon as the most insidious bias of all. For 'objective' reporting reproduced a vision of social reality which refused to examine the basic structures of power and privilege."

MICHAEL SCHUDSON, *DISCOVERING THE NEWS*, 1978

in mass culture: The paper used TV-inspired color and designed its first vending boxes to look like color TVs. Even the writing style of *USA Today* mimics TV news by casting many reports in present tense rather than the past tense (which was the print-news norm throughout the twentieth century).

Writing for *Rolling Stone* in March 1992, media critic Jon Katz argued that the authority of modern newspapers suffered in the wake of a variety of "new news" forms that combined immediacy, information, entertainment, persuasion, and analysis. Katz claimed that the news supremacy of most prominent daily papers, such as the *New York Times* and the *Washington Post*, was being challenged by "news" coming from talk shows, television sitcoms, popular films, and even rap music. In other words, we were changing from a society in which the transmission of knowledge depended mainly on books, newspapers, and magazines to a society dominated by a mix of print, visual, and digital information.

Online Journalism Redefines News

What started out in the 1980s as simple, text-only experiments for newspapers developed into more robust Web sites in the 1990s, allowing newspapers to develop an online presence. Today, online journalism is completely changing the industry. First, rather than subscribing to a traditional paper, many readers now begin their day on their iPads, smartphones, or computers scanning a wide variety of news Web sites, including those of print papers, cable news channels, newsmagazines, bloggers, and online-only news organizations. Such sources are increasingly taking over the roles of more traditional forms of news, helping to set the nation's cultural, social, and political agendas. One of the biggest changes is that online news has sped up the news cycle to a constant stream of information and has challenged traditional news services to keep up. For instance, Matt Drudge, the conservative Internet gossip and news source behind the *Drudge Report*, hijacked the national agenda in January 1998 and launched a scandal when he posted a report that *Newsweek* had delayed the story about President Clinton's having an affair with White House intern Monica Lewinsky.

Another change is the way nontraditional sources and even newer digital technology help drive news stories. For example, the Occupy Wall Street (OWS) movement, inspired by the Arab Spring uprisings, began in September 2011 when a group of protestors gathered in Zuccotti Park in New York's financial district to express discontentment with overpaid CEOs, big banks, and Wall Street, all of whom helped cause the 2008-09 financial collapse but still enjoyed a government bailout.

Mainstream media was slow to cover OWS, with early coverage simply pitting angry protesters against dismissive Wall Street executives and politicians, many of whom questioned the movement's longevity as well as its vague agenda. But as retirees, teachers, labor unions, off-duty police officers, firefighters, and other government workers joined the college students, the jobless, and the homeless in OWS protests across the country, the coverage and narratives in the media became more complicated and nuanced. As in the Arab uprisings, sites like Tumblr, Facebook, and Twitter became key organizational tools. But more than that, they became alternative media sources, documenting incidents of police brutality and arrests, and covering the issues protestors championed. In both the Arab Spring and OWS stories, the Internet and social media gave ordinary people more agency than ever before. Still, it's important to remember that while successful movements need good communication and media coverage, they also require enough people willing to challenge power, just as they did in the days of the American Revolution and the Civil Rights movement.

In the digital age, newsrooms are integrating their digital and print operations, and asking their journalists to tweet breaking news that links back to newspapers' Web sites. However,

editors are still facing a challenge to get reporters and editors to fully embrace what news executives regard as a reporter's online responsibilities. In 2011, for example, executive editor of the *New York Times* Jill Abramson noted that although the *Times* had fully integrated its online and print operations, some editors still tried to hold back on publishing a timely story online, hoping that it would make the front page of the print paper instead. "That's a culture I'd like to break down, without diminishing the [reporters'] thrill of having their story on the front page of the paper," said Abramson.[20] For more about how online news ventures are changing the newspaper industry, see pages 304-306.

The Business and Ownership of Newspapers

In the news industry today, there are several kinds of papers. *National newspapers* (such as the *Wall Street Journal*, the *New York Times*, and *USA Today*) serve a broad readership across the country. Other papers primarily serve specific geographic regions. Roughly 100 *metropolitan dailies* have a circulation of 100,000 or more. About 30 of these papers have a circulation of more than 200,000. In addition, about 100 daily newspapers are classified as medium dailies, with circulations between 50,000 and 100,000. By far the largest number of U.S. dailies—about 1,200 papers—fall into the small daily category, with circulations under 50,000. While dailies serve urban and suburban centers, about 7,500 nondaily and *weekly newspapers* (down from 14,000 back in 1910) serve smaller communities and average just over 5,000 copies per issue.[21] No matter the size of the paper, each must determine its approach, target readers, and deal with ownership issues in a time of technological transition and declining revenue.

Consensus vs. Conflict: Newspapers Play Different Roles

Smaller nondaily papers tend to promote social and economic harmony in their communities. Besides providing community calendars and meeting notices, nondaily papers focus on **consensus-oriented journalism**, carrying articles on local schools, social events, town government, property crimes, and zoning issues. Recalling the partisan spirit of an earlier era, small newspapers are often owned by business leaders who may also serve in local politics. Because consensus-oriented papers have a small advertising base, they are generally careful not to offend local advertisers, who provide the financial underpinnings for many of these papers. At their best, these small-town papers foster a sense of community; at their worst, they overlook or downplay discord and problems.

In contrast, national and metro dailies practice **conflict-oriented journalism**, in which front-page news is often

THE *WALL STREET JOURNAL* not only has the largest circulation of any newspaper in the United States, it also has the most online subscriptions—over 400,000 members pay for access to the paper's Web site. Its online success has been attributed to two facts: It instituted a paywall as soon as the paper went online in 1995, and it provides specialized business and financial information that its readers can't get elsewhere. (Pictured is News Corp. CEO Rupert Murdoch reading the *Wall Street Journal*.)

Media Literacy and the Critical Process

1 DESCRIPTION. Check a week's worth of business news in your local paper. Examine both the business pages and the front and local sections for these stories. Devise a chart and create categories for sorting stories (e.g., promotion news, scandal stories, earnings reports, home foreclosures, auto news, and media-related news), and gauge whether these stories are positive or negative. If possible, compare this coverage to a week's worth of news from the economic crisis in late 2008. Or compare your local paper's coverage of home foreclosures or company bankruptcies to the coverage in one of the nation's dailies like the *New York Times*.

2 ANALYSIS. Look for patterns in the coverage. How many stories are positive? How many are negative? Do the stories show any kind of gender favoritism (such as more men covered than women) or class bias (management favored over workers)? Compared to the local paper, are there differences in the frequency and kinds of coverage offered in the national newspaper? Does your paper routinely cover the business of the parent company that owns the local paper? Does it cover national business stories? How many stories are there on the business of newspapers and media in general?

3 INTERPRETATION. What do some of the patterns mean? Did

Covering Business and Economic News

The financial crisis and subsequent recession spotlighted newspapers' coverage of issues such as corporate corruption. For example, since 2008 articles have detailed the collapse of major investment firms like Lehman Brothers, the GM and Chrysler bailouts, fraud charges against Goldman Sachs, and of course the scandals surrounding the subprime mortgage/home foreclosure crisis. Over the years, critics have claimed that business news pages tend to favor issues related to management and downplay the role of everyday employees. Critics have also charged that business pages favor positive business stories—such as managers' promotions—and minimizes negative news (unlike regional newspaper front pages, which often emphasize crime stories). In an era of Wall Street scandals and major bankruptcies, check the business coverage in your local daily paper to see if these charges are accurate or if this pattern has changed since 2008.

you find examples where the coverage of business seems comprehensive and fair? If business news gets more positive coverage than political news, what might this mean? If managers get more coverage than employees, what does this mean, given that there are many more regular employees than managers at most businesses? What might it mean if men are more prominently featured than women in business stories? What does it mean if certain businesses are not being covered adequately by local and national news operations? How do business stories cover the recession now in comparison to late 2008?

4 EVALUATION. Determine which papers and stories you would judge as stronger models and which ones you would judge as weaker models for how business should be covered. Are some elements that should be included missing from coverage? If so, make suggestions.

5 ENGAGEMENT. Either write or e-mail the editor to report your findings, or make an appointment with the editor to discuss what you discovered. Note what the newspaper is doing well and make a recommendation on how to improve coverage.

defined primarily as events, issues, or experiences that deviate from social norms. Under this news orientation, journalists see their role not merely as neutral fact-gatherers but also as observers who monitor their city's institutions and problems. They often maintain an adversarial relationship with local politicians and public officials. These papers offer competing perspectives on such issues as education, government, poverty, crime, and the economy; and their publishers, editors, or reporters avoid playing major, overt roles in community politics. In theory, modern newspapers believe their role in large cities is to keep a wary eye fixed on recent local and state intrigue and events.

In telling stories about complex and controversial topics, conflict-oriented journalists often turn such topics into two-dimensional stories, pitting one idea or person against another. This convention, or "telling both sides of a story," allows a reporter to take the position of a detached observer. Although this practice offers the appearance of balance, it usually functions to generate conflict and sustain a lively news story; sometimes, reporters ignore the idea that there may be more than two sides to a story. But faced with deadline pressures, reporters often do not have the time—or the space—to develop a multifaceted and complex report or series of reports. (See "Media Literacy and the Critical Process: Covering Business and Economic News" on page 292.)

Newspapers Target Specific Readers

Historically, small-town weeklies and daily newspapers have served predominantly white, mainstream readers. However, ever since Benjamin Franklin launched the short-lived German-language *Philadelphische Zeitung* in 1732, newspapers aimed at ethnic groups have played a major role in initiating immigrants into American society. During the nineteenth century, Swedish- and Norwegian-language papers informed various immigrant communities in the Midwest. The early twentieth century gave rise to papers written in German, Yiddish, Russian, and Polish, assisting the massive influx of European immigrants.

Throughout the 1990s and into the twenty-first century, several hundred foreign-language daily and nondaily presses published papers in at least forty different languages in the United States. Many are financially healthy today, supported by classified ads, local businesses, and increased ad revenue from long-distance phone companies and Internet services, which see the ethnic press as an ideal place to reach those customers most likely to need international communication services.[22] While the financial crisis took its toll and some ethnic newspapers failed, overall, loyal readers allowed such papers to fare better than the mainstream press.[23]

Most of these weekly and monthly newspapers serve some of the same functions for their constituencies—minorities and immigrants, as well as disabled veterans, retired workers, gay and lesbian communities, and the homeless—that the "majority" papers do. These papers, however, are often published outside the social mainstream. Consequently, they provide viewpoints that are different from the mostly middle- and upper-class establishment attitudes that have shaped the media throughout much of America's history. As noted by the Pew Research Center's Project for Excellence in Journalism, ethnic newspapers and media "cover stories about the activities of those ethnic groups in the United States that are largely ignored by the mainstream press, they provide ethnic angles to news that actually is covered more widely, and they report on events and issues taking place back in the home countries from which those populations or their family members emigrated. These outlets have also traditionally been leaders in their communities."[24]

African American Newspapers

Between 1827 and the end of the Civil War in 1865, forty newspapers directed at black readers and opposed to slavery struggled for survival. These papers faced not only higher rates of illiteracy among potential readers but also hostility from white society and the majority press of the day. The first black newspaper, *Freedom's Journal*, operated from 1827 to 1829 and opposed the racism of many New York newspapers. In addition, it offered a public voice for antislavery societies. Other notable papers included the *Alienated American* (1852-56) and the *New Orleans Daily Creole*, which began its short life in 1856 as the first black-owned daily in the South. The most influential oppositional

FREDERICK DOUGLASS helped found the *North Star* in 1847. It was printed in the basement of the Memorial African Methodist Episcopal Zion Church, a gathering spot for abolitionists and "underground" activities in Rochester, New York. At the time, the white-owned *New York Herald* urged Rochester's citizens to throw the *North Star*'s printing press into Lake Ontario. Under Douglass's leadership, the paper came out weekly until 1860, addressing problems facing blacks around the country and offering a forum for Douglass to debate his fellow black activists.

"We wish to plead our own cause. Too long have others spoken for us."

FREEDOM'S JOURNAL, 1827

AFRICAN AMERICAN NEWSPAPERS
This 1936 scene reveals the newsroom of Harlem's *Amsterdam News,* one of the nation's leading African American newspapers. Ironically, the Civil Rights movement and affirmative action policies since the 1960s served to drain talented reporters from the black press by encouraging them to work for larger, mainstream newspapers.

newspaper was Frederick Douglass's *North Star*, a weekly antislavery newspaper in Rochester, New York, which was published from 1847 to 1860 and reached a circulation of three thousand. Douglass, a former slave, wrote essays on slavery and on a variety of national and international topics.

Since 1827, 5,500 newspapers have been edited or started by African Americans.[25] These papers, with an average life span of nine years, have taken stands against race baiting, lynching, and the Ku Klux Klan. They also promoted racial pride long before the Civil Rights movement. The most widely circulated black-owned paper was Robert C. Vann's weekly *Pittsburgh Courier*, founded in 1910. Its circulation peaked at 350,000 in 1947–the year professional baseball was integrated by Jackie Robinson, thanks in part to relentless editorials in the *Courier* that denounced the color barrier in pro sports. As they have throughout their history, these papers offer oppositional viewpoints to the mainstream press and record the daily activities of black communities by listing weddings, births, deaths, graduations, meetings, and church functions. Today, the National Association of Black Journalists (NABJ) reports that there are roughly two hundred African American newspapers, including Baltimore's *Afro-American*, New York's *Amsterdam News*, and the *Chicago Defender*, which celebrated its one hundredth anniversary in 2005.[26] None of these publish daily editions any longer, and most are weeklies.

The circulation rates of most black papers dropped sharply after the 1960s. The combined circulation of the local and national editions of the *Pittsburgh Courier*, for instance, dropped from 202,080 in 1944 to 20,000 in 1970. Several factors contributed to these declines. First, television and black radio stations tapped into the limited pool of money that businesses allocated for advertising. Second, some advertisers, to avoid controversy, withdrew their support when the black press started giving favorable coverage to the Civil Rights movement in the 1960s. Third, the loss of industrial urban jobs in the 1970s and 1980s not only diminished readership but also hurt small neighborhood businesses, which could no longer afford to advertise in both the mainstream and the black press. Finally, after the enactment of Civil Rights and affirmative action laws, mainstream papers raided black papers, seeking to integrate their newsrooms with African American journalists. Black papers could seldom match the offers from large white-owned dailies.

While a more integrated mainstream press hurt black papers then–an ironic effect of the Civil Rights laws–today that trend is reversing a bit as some black reporters and editors return to black newsrooms.[27] Overall, however, the number of African Americans in newsrooms is declining–between 2006 and 2012, African American representation fell from 5.5 to 4.65 percent. The NABJ reports that there are a thousand fewer African American journalists now than a decade ago.[28]

Spanish-Language Newspapers

Bilingual and Spanish-language newspapers have served a variety of Mexican, Puerto Rican, Cuban, and other Hispanic readerships since 1808, when *El Misisipi* was founded in New Orleans. In the 1800s alone, Texas had more than 150 Spanish-language papers.[29] Los Angeles' *La Opinión,* founded in 1926, is now the nation's largest Spanish-language daily. Other prominent publications are in Miami (*La Voz* and *Diario Las Americas*), Houston (*La Información*), Chicago (*El Mañana Daily News* and *La Raza*), and New York

(*El Diario-La Prensa*). In 2011, no more than eight hundred Spanish-language papers operated in the United States, most of them weekly and nondaily papers.[30]

Until the late 1960s, mainstream newspapers virtually ignored Hispanic issues and culture. But with the influx of Mexican, Puerto Rican, and Cuban immigrants throughout the 1980s and 1990s, many mainstream papers began to feature weekly Spanish-language supplements. The first was the *Miami Herald*'s "El Nuevo Herald," introduced in 1976. Other mainstream papers also joined in, but many folded their Spanish-language supplements by the mid-1990s. In 1995, the *Los Angeles Times* discontinued its supplement, "Nuestro Tiempo," and the *Miami Herald* trimmed budgets and staff for "El Nuevo Herald." Spanish-language radio and television had beaten newspapers to these potential customers and advertisers. As the U.S. Hispanic population reached 16 percent by 2011, Hispanic journalists accounted for only about 4.5 percent of the newsroom workforce at U.S. daily newspapers.[31]

Asian American Newspapers

In the 1980s, hundreds of small papers emerged to serve immigrants from Pakistan, Laos, Cambodia, and China. While people of Asian descent made up only about 4.8 percent of the U.S. population in 2010, this percentage is expected to rise to 9 percent by 2050.[32] Today, fifty small U.S. papers are printed in Vietnamese. Ethnic papers like these help readers both adjust to foreign surroundings and retain ties to their traditional heritage. In addition, these papers often cover major stories downplayed in the mainstream press. For example, in the aftermath of 9/11, airport security teams detained thousands of Middle Eastern–looking men. The *Weekly Bangla Patrika*, a Long Island, New York, paper, reported on the one hundred people the Bangladeshi community lost in the 9/11 attacks and on how it feels to be innocent yet targeted by ethnic profiling.[33]

A growth area in newspapers is Chinese publications. Even amid a poor economy, a new Chinese newspaper, *News for Chinese*, started in 2008. The Chinese-language paper began as a free monthly distributed in the San Francisco area. By early 2009, it began publishing twice a week. The *World Journal*, the largest U.S.-based Chinese-language paper, publishes six editions on the East Coast; on the West Coast, the paper is known as the *Chinese Daily News*.[34] In 2011, Asian American journalists accounted for 2.9 percent of newsroom jobs in the United States.[35]

Native American Newspapers

An activist Native American press has provided oppositional voices to mainstream American media since 1828, when the *Cherokee Phoenix* appeared in Georgia. Another prominent early paper was the *Cherokee Rose Bud*, founded in 1848 by tribal women in the Oklahoma territory. The Native American Press Association has documented more than 350 different Native American papers, most of them printed in English but a few in tribal languages. Currently, two national papers are the *Native American Times*, which offers perspectives on "sovereign rights, civil rights, and government-to-government relationships with the federal government," and *Indian Country Today*, owned by the Oneida Nation in New York. In 2012, Native American journalists accounted for 0.33 percent of newsroom jobs in the United States (down from 0.5 in 2011).

To counter the neglect of their culture's viewpoints by the mainstream press, Native American newspapers have helped educate various tribes about their heritage and build

THE *WORLD JOURNAL* is a national daily paper that targets Chinese immigrants by focusing on news from China, Hong Kong, Taiwan, and other Southeast Asian communities.

On a more promising note, in 2012 billionaire philanthropist Warren Buffett, CEO of the investment firm Berkshire Hathaway, spent $142 million and bought sixty-three newspapers (the company plans to retain about thirty). A newspaper junkie and former paperboy, Buffet has owned the *Buffalo News* in New York since 1977 and run it profitably. In 2011, he also bought his hometown paper, the *Omaha World-Herald,* for $200 million. Buffett has argued that many newspapers will thrive if they have "a strong sense of community" and do a good job of mixing their print and digital products. Buffet says he plans to buy more papers—"three years after telling shareholders that he would not buy a newspaper at any price."[40]

While Warren Buffett has concentrated on purchasing smaller regional papers, ownership of one of the nation's three national newspapers also changed hands. Back in 2007, the *Wall Street Journal*, held by the Bancroft family for more than one hundred years, accepted a bid of nearly $5.8 billion from News Corp. head Rupert Murdoch (News Corp. also owns the *New York Post* and many papers in the United Kingdom and Australia). At the time, critics also raised serious concerns about takeovers of newspapers by large entertainment conglomerates (Murdoch's company also owns TV stations, a network, cable channels, and a movie studio). As small subsidiaries in large media empires, newspapers are increasingly treated as just another product line that is expected to perform in the same way that a movie or TV program does. But in 2012, News Corp. decided to split its news and entertainment divisions, leading some critics to hope that Murdoch's news operations would no longer be subject to the same high profit expectations of Hollywood movies and sitcoms.

As chains lose their grip, there are concerns about who will own papers in the future and the effect this will have on content and press freedoms. Recent purchases by private equity groups are alarming since these companies are usually more interested in turning a profit than supporting journalism. However, ideas exist for how to avoid this fate. For example, more support could be rallied for small, independent owners who could then make decisions based on what's best for the paper and not just the quarterly report. For more on how newspapers and owners are trying new business models, see "New Models for Journalism" on page 306.

Joint Operating Agreements Combat Declining Competition

Although the amount of regulation preventing newspaper monopolies has lessened, the government continues to monitor the declining number of newspapers in various American cities as well as mergers in cities where competition among papers might be endangered. In the mid-1920s, about five hundred American cities had two or more newspapers with separate owners. However, by 2010 fewer than fifteen cities had independent, competing papers.

In 1970, Congress passed the Newspaper Preservation Act, which enabled failing papers to continue operating through a **joint operating agreement (JOA)**. Under a JOA, two competing papers keep separate news divisions while merging business and production operations for a period of years. Since the act's passage, twenty-eight cities have adopted JOAs. In 2012, just six JOAs remained in place—in Charleston, West Virginia; Detroit; Fort Wayne, Indiana; Las Vegas; Salt Lake City; and York, Pennsylvania. Although JOAs and mergers have monopolistic tendencies, they sometimes have been the only way to maintain competition between newspapers.

For example, Detroit was one of the most competitive newspaper cities in the nation until 1989. The *Detroit News* and the *Detroit Free Press*, then owned by Gannett and Knight Ridder, respectively, both ranked among the ten most widely circulated papers in the country and sold their weekday editions for just fifteen cents a copy. Faced with declining revenue and increased costs, the papers' managers asked for and received a JOA in 1989. But problems continued. Then, in 1995, a prolonged and bitter strike by several unions sharply reduced circulation, as the strikers formed a union-backed paper to compete against the existing newspapers. Many readers dropped their subscriptions to the *Free Press* and the *News* to support the strikers. Before the strike (and the rise of the Internet), Gannett and Knight Ridder had both reported profit margins of well over 15 percent on all their newspaper holdings.[41] By 2010, Knight Ridder was out of the newspaper chain business, and neither Detroit paper ranked in the Top 20. In addition, the *News* and *Free Press* became the first major papers to stop daily home delivery for part of the week, instead directing readers to the Web or brief newsstand editions.

Challenges Facing Newspapers Today

Publishers and journalists today face worrisome issues, such as the decline in newspaper readership and the failure of many papers to attract younger readers. However, other problems persist as newspapers continue to converge with the Internet and grapple with the future of digital news.

Readership Declines in the United States

The decline in daily newspaper readership actually began during the Great Depression, with the rise of radio. Between 1931 and 1939, six hundred newspapers ceased operation. Another circulation crisis occurred from the late 1960s through the 1970s with the rise in network television viewing and greater competition from suburban weeklies. In addition, with an increasing number of women working full-time outside the home, newspapers could no longer consistently count on one of their core readership groups.

Throughout the first decade of the 2000s, U.S. newspaper circulation dropped again, this time by more than 25 percent.[42] In the face of such steep circulation and readership declines, however, overall audiences did start growing again thanks to online readers, but some digital audience numbers seemed unclear. According to Pew's *State of the News Media 2012* report:

The newspaper industry enters 2012 neither dying nor assured of a stable future. The industry has rallied around a story about itself–that year-by-year it is developing new digital products and new revenue streams to transition from dependence on print advertising. . . .

By the available measures, the industry's 2011 digital audience performance was mixed. For December 2011, the most recent month measured by the Newspaper Association of America, unique visitors were up by about 7.4% year-to-year, but time per visit was down 5.4% and page views were down about 2%.[43]

Remarkably, while the United States continues to experience declines in newspaper readership and advertising dollars, many other nations–where Internet news is still emerging–have experienced increases. For example, the World Association of Newspapers (WAN) reported that between 2003 and 2009, there was an 8.8 percent growth in newspaper readership worldwide, mostly in regions where the Internet had not become ubiquitous.[44] These increases are concentrated in Asia, Africa, and South America, while sales are declining in North America and Europe. In 2010, WAN's Web site also boasted that newspapers are still the world's "second largest advertising medium" (after television) and that worldwide newspapers have "more than 1.6 billion readers a day."[45] (See "Global Village: For U.S. Newspaper Industry, an Example in Germany?" on page 303.)

▶

WHAT GANNETT OWNS

Consider how Gannett connects to your life; then turn the page for the bigger picture.

NEWSPAPERS

- 80 daily papers and 600 nondaily publications, including
  - *USA Today*
  - *Asbury Park Press* (N.J.)
  - *Detroit Free Press*
  - *Rochester Democrat and Chronicle* (N.Y.)
  - *Arizona Republic* (Phoenix)
  - *Cincinnati Enquirer*
  - *Courier-Journal* (Louisville, Ky.)
  - *Des Moines Register* (Iowa)
  - *Indianapolis Star*
  - *News Journal* (Wilmington, Del.)
  - *Tennessean* (Nashville)
  - Army Times Publishing Company (newspapers)
  - Newsquest plc (newspaper publishing, United Kingdom)

TELEVISION

- Captivate Network (advertising-based television in elevators)
- 23 TV stations, including
  - KARE-TV (Minneapolis)
  - KNAZ-TV (Flagstaff, Ariz.)
  - KSDK-TV (St. Louis)
  - KTHV-TV (Little Rock, Ark.)
  - KUSA-TV (Denver)
  - KXTV-TV (Sacramento, Calif.)
  - WATL-TV (Atlanta)
  - WBIR-TV (Knoxville, Tenn.)
  - WCSH-TV (Portland, Me.)
  - WGRZ-TV (Buffalo, N.Y.)
  - WJXX-TV (Jacksonville)
  - WKYC-TV (Cleveland)
  - WTLV-TV (Jacksonville)
  - WTSP-TV (Tampa)
  - WZZM-TV (Grand Rapids, Mich.)

INTERNET

- CareerBuilder (50 percent)
- Metromix.com (51 percent)
- ShopLocal.com
- Topix (34 percent)

MAGAZINES AND PRINTING

- Clipper Magazine (direct mail advertising)
- Gannett Healthcare Group (periodical publishing)
- Gannett Offset (commercial printing)
- USA Weekend

Turn page for more ▶

Web and tablet access, or $35 per month for an "all-you-can-eat" plan that would allow access to all the *Times* platforms. In its first few weeks of operation, the paper gained more than 100,000 new subscribers and lost only about 15 percent of traffic from the days of free Web access–a more positive scenario than the 50 percent loss in online traffic some observers had predicted. And by early 2013 the *Times* reported 668,000 paid subscribers to all its various digital options.[53]

By 2012, more than 150 newspapers had launched various paywalls, many of them based on the *New York Times* metered models, trying to reverse years of giving away their print content online for free. One smaller daily, the *Augusta Chronicle* in Georgia, is being studied closely by other newspapers. According the Pew *State of the News Media 2012* report:

Morris Communications' Augusta Chronicle *began a metered-model pay wall four months before the* Times *in December 2010. Page views actually went up 5% in the next three months. The* Augusta *offer began by allowing up to 100 page views per month free, gradually reducing that threshold to 15. It charges digital-only subscribers $6.95 per month and print subscribers an additional $2.95 for digital access.*

Larger metro dailies, including the *Boston Globe, Dallas Morning News, Milwaukee Journal Sentinel,* and *Los Angeles Times* have also started their own paywalls and metered models. Pew's annual report on the news media explains "why now," especially since many newspaper executives for years believed that free digital news would attract readers to their print editions or that charging readers for online content would irritate them and drive them away.

The pay systems re-establish the principle that users should pay for valued content, expensive to produce, whatever the platform. It gives flexibility to raise the subscription price in later years or charge more for a particularly convenient medium like tablets. The change is unlikely to have a big financial impact, positive or negative, right away, but it better positions newspaper organizations eventually to wean themselves away from print.[54]

Still, only time will tell if the new paywalls will bring in badly needed revenue from newspaper readers . . . or drive them to find "free" news elsewhere.

New Models for Journalism

In response to the challenges newspapers face, a number of journalists, economists, and citizens are calling for new business models for combatting newspapers' decline. One avenue is developing new business ventures such as the online papers begun by former print reporters. Another idea is for wealthy universities like Harvard and Yale to buy and support papers, thereby better insulating their public service and watchdog operations from the high profit expectations of the marketplace. Another possibility might be to get Internet companies involved. Google, worried that a decline in quality journalism means fewer sites on which to post ads and earn online revenue, pledged $5 million to news foundations and companies to encourage innovation in digital journalism. Wealthy Internet companies like Microsoft and Google could expand into the news business and start producing content for both online and print papers. In fact, in March 2010 Yahoo! began hiring reporters to increase the presence of its online news site. The company hired reporters from Politico.com, *BusinessWeek*, the *New York Observer*, the *Washington Post*, and *Talking Points Memo*, among others.

Additional ideas are coming from universities (where journalism school enrollments are actually increasing). For example, the dean of Columbia University's Journalism School (started once upon a time with money bequeathed by nineteenth-century newspaper mogul Joseph Pulitzer) commissioned a study from Leonard Downie, former executive editor of the *Washington Post*, and Michael Schudson, Columbia journalism professor and media scholar. Their report,

"Now, like hundreds of other mid-career journalists who are walking away from media institutions across the country, I'm looking for other ways to tell the stories I care about. At the same time, the world of online news is maturing, looking for depth and context. I think the timing couldn't be better."

NANCY CLEELAND, ON WHY SHE WAS LEAVING THE *LOS ANGELES TIMES*, POSTED ON THE *HUFFINGTON POST*, 2007

"The Reconstruction of American Journalism," focused on the lost circulation, advertising revenue, and news jobs and aimed to create a strategy for reporting that would hold public and government officials accountable.[55] After all, citizens in democracies require basic access to reports, data, and documentation in order to be well informed. Here is an overview of their recommendations, some of which have already been implemented:

- News organizations "substantially devoted to reporting on public affairs" should be allowed to operate as nonprofit entities in order to take in tax-deductible contributions while still collecting ad and subscription revenues. For example, the Poynter Institute owns and operates the *St. Petersburg Times*, Florida's largest newspaper. As a nonprofit, the *St. Petersburg Times* is protected from the unrealistic 16 to 20 percent profit margins that publicly held newspapers had been expected to earn in the 1980s and 1990s.
- Public radio and TV, through federal reforms in the Corporation for Public Broadcasting (CPB), should reorient their focus to "significant local news reporting in every community served by public stations and their Web sites."
- Operating their own news services or supporting regional news organizations, public and private universities "should become ongoing sources of local, state, specialized subject and accountability news reporting as part of their educational mission."
- A national Fund for Local News should be created with money the Federal Communications Commission (FCC) collects from "telecom users, television and radio broadcast licensees, or Internet service providers."
- Via use of the Internet, news services, nonprofit organizations, and government agencies should "increase the accessibility and usefulness of public information collected by federal, state, and local governments."

As the journalism industry continues to reinvent itself and tries new avenues to ensure its future, not every "great" idea will work out. Some of the immediate backlash to this report raised questions about the government becoming involved with traditionally independent news media. What is important, however, is that newspapers continue to experiment with new ideas and business models so they can adapt and even thrive in the Internet age. (For more on the challenges facing journalism, see Chapter 14.)

Alternative Voices

The combination of the online news surge and traditional newsroom cutbacks has led to a new phenomenon known as **citizen journalism**, or *citizen media*, or *community journalism* (in those projects where the participants might not be citizens). As a grassroots movement, citizen journalism refers to people–activist amateurs and concerned citizens, not professional journalists–who use the Internet and blogs to disseminate news and information. In fact, with steep declines in newsroom staffs, many professional news media organizations–like CNN's iReport and many regional newspapers–are increasingly trying to corral citizen journalists as an inexpensive way to make up for journalists lost to newsroom "downsizing."

A 2008 study by J-Lab: The Institute for Interactive Journalism reported that more than one thousand community-based Web sites were in operation, posting citizen stories about local government, police, and city development. This represented twice the number of community

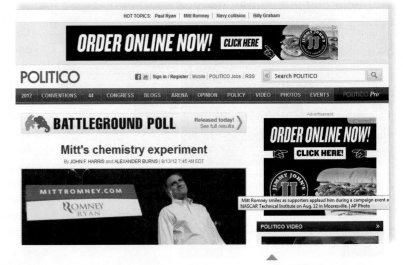

POLITICO quickly became a reputable place for Washington insiders as well as the general population to go for political news and reporting, allowing the organization to thrive at a time when other papers were struggling. As editor in chief John Harris states on the site, Politico aims to be more than just a place for politics; it also "hope[s] to add to the conversation about what's next for journalism." What do you think its success means for the future of the news media?

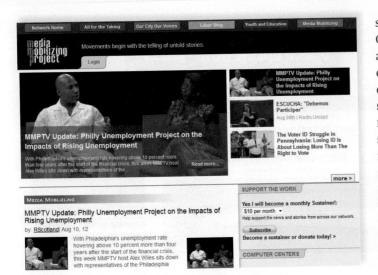

sites from a year earlier. J-Lab also operates the Knight Citizen News Network, "a Web site that advises citizens and traditional journalists on how to launch and operate community news and information sites."[56] In 2009, academics examined "60 of the most highly regarded citizen sites identified by nationally known experts in new media." While the study found that "a number of these sites individually revealed some impressive work," the funding and "resources to provide these services at the same level of full news operations, day-in and day-out, do not exist, at least as of now." The report also found "fairly limited levels of new content," many sites that were not very transparent about funding and daily operations, and policies "no more likely to encourage citizen postings" than traditional commercial news media sites.[57] While many of these sites do not yet have the resources to provide the kind of regional news coverage that local newspapers once provided, there is still a lot of hope for community journalism moving forward. These sites provide an outlet for people to voice their stories and opinions, and new sites are emerging daily.

MEDIA MOBILIZING PROJECT (mediamobilizing .org) is a community-based organization in Philadelphia that helps nonprofit and grassroots organizations create and distribute news pieces about their causes and stories. Such organizations are key to getting out messages that matter deeply to communities but that the mainstream media often ignore, such as documentation about wealth disparity at the heart of the Occupy Wall Street movement in 2011 and 2012.

"It may not be essential to save or promote any particular news medium, including printed newspapers. What is paramount is preserving independent, original, credible reporting, whether or not it is popular or profitable, and regardless of the medium in which it appears."

LEONARD DOWNIE AND MICHAEL SCHUDSON

Newspapers and Democracy

Of all mass media, newspapers have played the leading role in sustaining democracy and championing freedom. Over the years, newspapers have fought heroic battles in places that had little tolerance for differing points of view. According to the Committee to Protect Journalists (CPJ), from 1992 through August 2012, 962 reporters from around the world were killed while doing their jobs. Of those, more than 600 were murdered, more than 150 were killed in combat assignments and war reporting, and another 100 were killed while performing "dangerous assignments."[58] In the first half of 2012, 32 reporters had died, including 13 in Syria and 5 in Somalia. Many deaths in the 2000s reported by the CPJ came from the war in Iraq. From 2003 to 2011, 225 reporters, media workers, and support staff died in Iraq. For comparison, 63 reporters were killed while covering the Vietnam War; 17 died covering the Korean War; and 69 were killed during World War II.[59] Our nation is dependent on journalists who are willing to do this very dangerous reporting in order to keep us informed about what is going on around the world.

In addition to the physical danger, newsroom cutbacks, and the closing of foreign bureaus, a number of smaller concerns remain as we consider the future of newspapers. For instance, some charge that newspapers have become so formulaic in their design and reporting styles that they may actually discourage new approaches to telling stories and reporting news. Another criticism is that in many one-newspaper cities, only issues and events of interest to middle- and upper-middle-class readers are covered, resulting in the underreporting of the experiences and events that affect poorer and working-class citizens. In addition, given the rise of newspaper chains, the likelihood of including new opinions, ideas, and information in mainstream daily papers may be diminishing. Moreover, chain ownership tends to discourage watchdog journalism and the crusading traditions of newspapers. Like other business managers, many news executives have preferred not to offend investors or outrage potential advertisers by running too many investigative reports—especially business probes. This may be most evident in the fact that reporters have generally not reported adequately on the business and ownership arrangements in their own industry.

Finally, as print journalism shifts to digital culture, the greatest challenge is the upheaval of print journalism's business model. Most economists say that newspapers need new business models, but some observers think that local papers, ones that are not part of big overleveraged chains, will survive on the basis of local ads and coupons or "big sale" inserts. Increasingly, independent online firms will help bolster national reporting through special projects. In 2009, the Associated Press wire service initiated an experiment to distribute investigative reports from several nonprofit groups—including the Center for Public Integrity, the Center for Investigative Reporting, and ProPublica—to its fifteen hundred members as a news source for struggling papers that have cut back on staff. Also in 2009, the news aggregator *Huffington Post* hired a team of reporters to cover the economic crisis. And by 2011, AOL (which purchased the *Huffington Post* for $315 million) had more than thirteen hundred reporters—most of them for Patch.com, its hyperlocal news initiative with over eight hundred separate editorial units serving small to midsize towns and cities across the United States. This initiative hopes to restore local news coverage to areas that have been neglected due to newsroom cutbacks.[60]

ProPublica, for example, has published more than a hundred investigative stories a year, often teaming up with traditional newspapers or public radio stations from around the country. They then offer these reports to traditional news outlets for free. In 2010, one story won a Pulitzer Prize for investigative reporting. Regional examples of this kind of public service news include the *Voice of San Diego* and *MinnPost*, both nonprofit online news ventures that feature news about the San Diego and the Twin Cities areas, respectively. Many of these news services have tried to provide reports for news outlets that have downsized and no longer have the reporting resources to do some kinds of major investigations.

As print journalism loses readers and advertisers to digital culture, what will become of newspapers, which do most of the nation's primary journalistic work? John Carroll presided over thirteen Pulitzer Prize-winning reports at the *Los Angeles Times* as editor from 2000 to 2005, but he left the paper to protest deep corporate cuts to the newsroom. He has lamented the future of newspapers and their unique role: "Newspapers are doing the reporting in this country. Google and Yahoo! and those people aren't putting reporters on the street in any numbers at all. Blogs can't afford it. Network television is taking reporters off the street. Commercial radio is almost nonexistent. And newspapers are the last ones standing, and newspapers are threatened. And reporting is absolutely an essential thing for democratic self-government. Who's going to do it? Who's going to pay for the news? If newspapers fall by the wayside, what will we know?"[61] In the end, there will be no returning to any golden age of newspapers; the Internet is transforming journalism and relocating where we get our news. ▶

"The primary purpose of journalism is to provide citizens with the information they need to be free and self-governing."

BILL KOVACH AND TOM ROSENSTIEL, *THE ELEMENTS OF JOURNALISM*, 2007

CHAPTER REVIEW

COMMON THREADS

One of the Common Threads discussed in Chapter 1 is about the role that media play in a democracy. The newspaper industry has always played a strong role in our democracy by reporting news and investigating stories. Even in the Internet age, newspapers remain our primary source for content. How will the industry's current financial struggles affect our ability to demand and access reliable news?

With the coming of radio and television, newspapers in the twentieth century surrendered their title as the mass medium shared by the largest audience. However, to this day newspapers remain the single most important source of news for the nation, even in the age of the Internet. Although many readers today cite Yahoo! and Google as the primary places they search for news, Yahoo! and Google are directories and aggregators that guide readers to other news stories—most often to online newspaper sites. This means that newspaper organizations are still the primary institutions doing the work of gathering and reporting the news. Even with all the newsroom cutbacks across the United States, newspapers remain the only journalistic organization in most towns and cities that still employs a significant staff to report news and tell the community's stories.

Newspapers link people to what matters in their communities, their nation, and their world. Few other journalistic institutions serve society as well. But with smaller news resources and the industry no longer able to sustain high profit margins, what will become of newspapers? Are digital news sites serving readers in their communities as well as newspapers once did? Who will gather the information needed to sustain a democracy, to serve as the watchdog over our key institutions, to document the comings and goings of everyday life? And perhaps more important, who will act on behalf of the people who don't have the news media's access to authorities or the ability to influence them?

KEY TERMS

The definitions for the terms listed below can be found in the glossary at the end of the book. The page numbers listed with the terms indicate where the term is highlighted in the chapter.

partisan press, 280
penny papers, 280
human-interest stories, 280
wire services, 281
yellow journalism, 282
investigative journalism, 283
objective journalism, 285

inverted-pyramid style, 285
interpretive journalism, 286
literary journalism, 288
consensus-oriented journalism, 291
conflict-oriented journalism, 291
underground press, 296
newshole, 298

feature syndicates, 299
newspaper chain, 299
joint operating agreement
  (JOA), 300
paywall, 305
citizen journalism, 307

REVIEW QUESTIONS

The Evolution of American Newspapers

1. What are the limitations of a press that serves only partisan interests? Why did the earliest papers appeal mainly to more privileged readers?

2. How did newspapers emerge as a mass medium during the penny press era? How did content changes make this happen?

3. What are the two main features of yellow journalism? How have Joseph Pulitzer and William Randolph Hearst contributed to newspaper history?

Competing Models of Modern Print Journalism

4. Why did objective journalism develop? What are its characteristics? What are its strengths and limitations?

5. Why did interpretive forms of journalism develop in the modern era? What are the limits of objectivity?

6. How would you define *literary journalism*? Why did it emerge in such an intense way in the 1960s? How did literary journalism provide a critique of so-called objective news?

The Business and Ownership of Newspapers

7. What is the difference between consensus- and conflict-oriented newspapers?

8. What role have ethnic, minority, and oppositional newspapers played in the United States?

9. Define *wire service* and *syndication*.

10. Why did newspaper chains become an economic trend in the twentieth century?

11. What is the impact of a joint operating agreement (JOA) on the business and editorial divisions of competing newspapers?

Challenges Facing Newspapers Today

12. What are the major reasons for the decline in U.S. newspaper circulation figures? How do these figures compare with circulations in other nations?

13. What major challenges does new technology pose to the newspaper industry?

14. With traditional ownership in jeopardy today, what are some other possible business models for running a newspaper?

15. What is the current state of citizen journalism?

16. What are the challenges that new online news sites face?

Newspapers and Democracy

17. What is a newspaper's role in a democracy?

18. What makes newspaper journalism different from the journalism of other mass media?

QUESTIONING THE MEDIA

1. What kinds of stories, topics, or issues are not being covered well by mainstream papers?

2. Why do you think people aren't reading U.S. daily newspapers as frequently as they once did? Why is newspaper readership going up in other countries?

3. Discuss whether newspaper chains are ultimately good or bad for the future of journalism.

4. Do newspapers today play a vigorous role as watchdogs of our powerful institutions? Why or why not? What impact will the "downsizing" and closing of newspapers have on this watchdog role?

5. Will tablets, or some other format, eventually replace the printed newspaper? Explain your response.

ADDITIONAL VIDEOS

Visit the ◉ VideoCentral: Mass Communication *section at* bedfordstmartins.com/mediaculture *for additional exclusive videos related to Chapter 8, including:*

- THE MEDIA AND DEMOCRACY
  This video traces the history of media's role in democracy from newspapers and television to the Internet.

- NEWSPAPERS NOW: BALANCING CITIZEN JOURNALISM AND INVESTIGATIVE REPORTING
  Reporters explain the value of investigative journalism and debate how citizen journalism fits within the spectrum of traditional reporting.

The magazine featured writers like Edith Wharton, Rudyard Kipling, and Theodore Dreiser and serialized entire books, including H. G. Wells's *The War of the Worlds*. Walker, seeing the success of contemporary newspapers in New York, was not above stunt reporting either. When Joseph Pulitzer's *New York World* sent off reporter Nellie Bly to travel the world in less than eighty days in 1889 (challenging the premise of Jules Verne's 1873 novel, *Around the World in Eighty Days*), Walker sent reporter Elizabeth Bisland around the world in the opposite direction for a more literary travel account.[3] Walker's leadership turned *Cosmopolitan* into a respected magazine with increased circulation and a strong advertising base.

Walker sold *Cosmopolitan* at a profit to William Randolph Hearst (Pulitzer's main competitor) in 1905. Under Hearst, *Cosmopolitan* had its third rebirth—this time as a muckraking magazine. As magazine historians explain, Hearst was a U.S. representative who "had his eye on the presidency and planned to use his newspapers and the recently bought *Cosmopolitan* to stir up further discontent over the trusts and big business."[4] *Cosmopolitan*'s first big muckraking series, David Graham Phillips's "The Treason of the Senate" in 1906, didn't help Hearst's political career, but it did boost the circulation of the magazine

by 50 percent, and was reprinted in Hearst newspapers for even more exposure.

But by 1912, the progressive political movement that had given impetus to muckraking journalism was waning. *Cosmopolitan*, in its fourth incarnation, became like a version of its former self, an illustrated literary monthly targeted to women, with short stories and serialized novels by popular writers like Damon Runyon, Sinclair Lewis, and Faith Baldwin.

Cosmopolitan had great success as an upscale literary magazine, but by the early 1960s the format had become outdated and readership and advertising had declined. At this point, the magazine had its most radical makeover. In 1962, Helen Gurley Brown, one of the country's top advertising copywriters, was recently married (at age forty) and wrote the best-selling book *Sex and the Single Girl*. When she proposed a magazine modeled on the book's vision of strong, sexually liberated women, the Hearst Corporation hired her in 1965 as editor in chief to reinvent *Cosmopolitan*. The new *Cosmopolitan* helped spark a sexual revolution and was marketed to the "Cosmo Girl": women age eighteen to thirty-four with an interest in love, sex, fashion, and their careers.

Brown maintained a pink corner office in the Hearst Tower in New York until her death in 2012, but her vision of *Cosmo* continues today. It's the top women's fashion magazine—surpassing competitors like *Glamour*, *Marie Claire*, and *Vogue*—and has wide global influence with 63 international editions. Although its present format is far from its origins, *Cosmopolitan* endures based on its successful reinventions for over 126 years.

▲ *Since the 1740s,* magazines have played a key role in our social and cultural lives, becoming America's earliest national mass medium. They created some of the first spaces for discussing the broad issues of the age, including public education, the abolition of slavery, women's suffrage, literacy, and the Civil War.

In the nineteenth century, magazines became an educational forum for women, who were barred from higher education and from the nation's political life. At the turn of the twentieth century, magazines' probing reports would influence investigative journalism, while their use of engraving and photography provided a hint of the visual culture to come. Economically, magazines brought advertised products into households, hastening the rise of a consumer society.

Today, more than twenty thousand commercial, alternative, and noncommercial magazines are published in the United States annually. Like newspapers, radio, movies, and television, magazines reflect and construct portraits of American life. They are catalogues for daily events and experiences, but they also show us the latest products, fostering our consumer culture. We read magazines to learn something about our community, our nation, our world, and ourselves.

In this chapter, we will:

- Investigate the history of the magazine industry, highlighting the colonial and early American eras, the arrival of national magazines, and the development of photojournalism
- Focus on the age of muckraking and the rise of general-interest and consumer magazines in the modern American era
- Look at the decline of mass market magazines, TV's impact, and how magazines have specialized in order to survive in a fragmented and converged market
- Investigate the organization and economics of magazines and their function in a democracy

As you think about the evolution of magazine culture, consider your own experiences. When did you first start reading magazines, and what magazines were they? What sort of magazines do you read today—popular mainstream magazines like *Cosmo* or *Sports Illustrated*, or niche publications that target very specific subcultures? How do you think printed magazines can best adapt to the age of the Internet? For more questions to help you think through the role of magazines in our lives, see "Questioning the Media" in the Chapter Review.

> "For generations, *Time* and *Newsweek* fought to define the national news agenda. . . . That era seems to be ending. . . . The circulations of *Time* and *Newsweek* now stand about where they were in 1966."
>
> NEW YORK TIMES, 2010

Past-Present-Future: Magazines

Long before the arrival of motion pictures or cable television, magazines were the first medium to bring visuals to the masses, and the first to segment the masses into groups of various interests or demographics. Early magazines used engravings and illustrations to visualize life; later, magazines of the twentieth century used photographs to disseminate some of the most iconic images of modern times. Although some of the largest magazines once targeted a general-interest audience, most magazines succeeded by creating content for a specific audience—e.g., *Latina*, for Hispanic women, or *Golf Digest*, for fans of the sport.

Today, the magazine industry is in the midst of a digital transition that is eviscerating its print business. Newsstand sales continue to fall, as readers sometimes find print magazine content less timely. Industry consultant John Harrington noted that timeliness poses a particular problem in celebrity magazines, where celebrity gossip can be found online. "By the time the magazine comes out, it's old news," he said.[1]

Yet, for all of the laments of the magazine industry in the present, magazines might be particularly well suited to adapt their content to the digital turn in a creative and compelling way. The relatively bite-sized content of magazines—articles, essays, photos, glorified ads—is compatible with online reading habits, and the visual nature of magazines translates well to tablet and online environments. And while most magazines have always focused on driving sales for their advertisers, tablet editions go one step better, and offer immediate links to e-commerce. One success story is the *Atlantic* (founded in 1857), which still distributes a print edition, but also has a network of Web sites with multimedia and timely blog posts. The *Atlantic* offers hope to others: in 2011, it became the first major magazine in which digital advertising revenue exceeded print ad revenue.[2]

The Early History of Magazines

The first magazines appeared in seventeenth-century France in the form of bookseller catalogues and notices that book publishers inserted in newspapers. In fact, the word *magazine* derives from the French term *magasin*, meaning "storehouse." The earliest magazines were "storehouses" of writing and reports taken mostly from newspapers. Today, the word **magazine** broadly refers to collections of articles, stories, and advertisements appearing in nondaily (such as weekly or monthly) periodicals that are published in the smaller tabloid style rather than the larger broadsheet newspaper style.

The First Magazines

The first political magazine, called the *Review*, appeared in London in 1704. Edited by political activist and novelist Daniel Defoe (author of *Robinson Crusoe*), the *Review* was printed sporadically until 1713. Like the *Nation*, the *National Review*, and the *Progressive* in the United States today, early European magazines were channels for political commentary and argument. These periodicals looked like newspapers of the time, but they appeared less frequently and were oriented toward broad domestic and political commentary rather than recent news.

Regularly published magazines or pamphlets, such as the *Tatler* and the *Spectator*, also appeared in England around this time. They offered poetry, politics, and philosophy for London's elite, and they served readerships of a few thousand. The first publication to use the term *magazine* was *Gentleman's Magazine*, which appeared in London in 1731 and consisted of

COLONIAL MAGAZINES
The first issue of Benjamin Franklin's *General Magazine and Historical Chronicle* appeared in January 1741. While it lasted only six months, Franklin found success in other publications, like his annual *Poor Richard's Almanac*, starting in 1732 and lasting twenty-five years.

▼ **Magazines in the Age of Specialization**

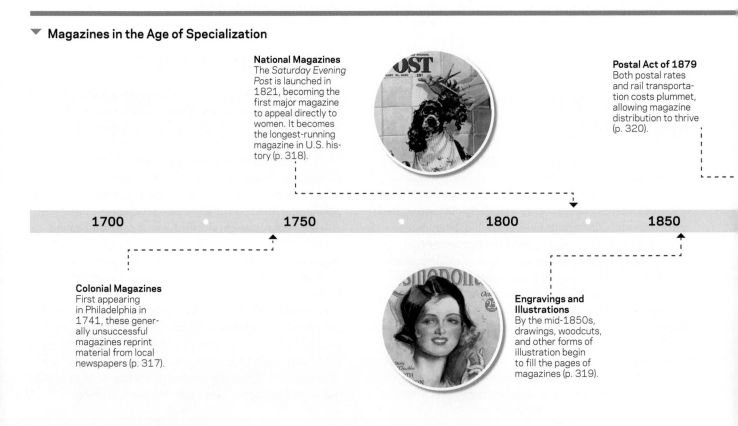

National Magazines
The *Saturday Evening Post* is launched in 1821, becoming the first major magazine to appeal directly to women. It becomes the longest-running magazine in U.S. history (p. 318).

Postal Act of 1879
Both postal rates and rail transportation costs plummet, allowing magazine distribution to thrive (p. 320).

1700	1750	1800	1850

Colonial Magazines
First appearing in Philadelphia in 1741, these generally unsuccessful magazines reprint material from local newspapers (p. 317).

Engravings and Illustrations
By the mid-1850s, drawings, woodcuts, and other forms of illustration begin to fill the pages of magazines (p. 319).

reprinted articles from newspapers, books, and political pamphlets. Later, the magazine began publishing original work by such writers as Defoe, Samuel Johnson, and Alexander Pope.

Magazines in Colonial America

Without a substantial middle class, widespread literacy, or advanced printing technology, magazines developed slowly in colonial America. Like the partisan newspapers of the time, these magazines served politicians, the educated, and the merchant classes. Paid circulations were slight–between one hundred and fifteen hundred copies. However, early magazines did serve the more widespread purpose of documenting a new nation coming to terms with issues of taxation, state versus federal power, Indian treaties, public education, and the end of colonialism. George Washington, Alexander Hamilton, and John Hancock all wrote for early magazines, and Paul Revere worked as a magazine illustrator for a time.

The first colonial magazines appeared in Philadelphia in 1741, about fifty years after the first newspapers. Andrew Bradford started it all with *American Magazine, or A Monthly View of the Political State of the British Colonies*. Three days later, Benjamin Franklin's *General Magazine and Historical Chronicle* appeared. Bradford's magazine lasted only three monthly issues, due to circulation and postal obstacles that Franklin, who had replaced Bradford as Philadelphia's postmaster, put in its way. For instance, Franklin mailed his magazine without paying the high postal rates that he subsequently charged others. Franklin's magazine primarily duplicated what was already available in local papers. After six months it, too, stopped publication.

Nonetheless, following the Philadelphia experiments, magazines began to emerge in the other colonies, beginning in Boston in the 1740s. The most successful magazines simply reprinted articles from leading London periodicals, keeping readers abreast of European events. These magazines included New York's *Independent Reflector* and the *Pennsylvania Magazine*, edited by activist Thomas Paine, which helped rally the colonies against British rule. By 1776, about

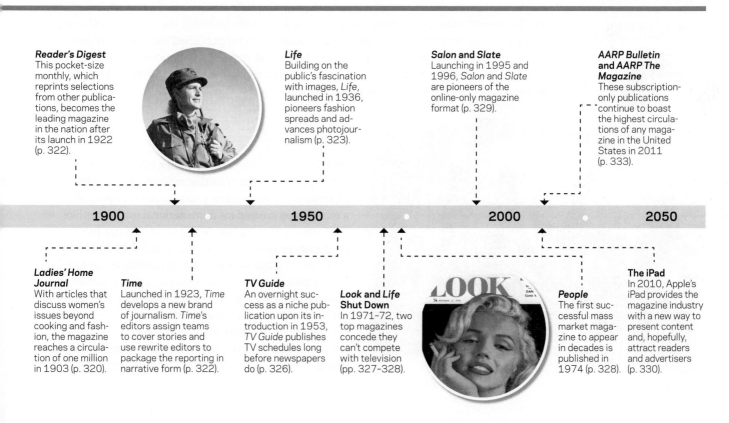

Reader's Digest
This pocket-size monthly, which reprints selections from other publications, becomes the leading magazine in the nation after its launch in 1922 (p. 322).

Life
Building on the public's fascination with images, *Life*, launched in 1936, pioneers fashion spreads and advances photojournalism (p. 323).

Salon and Slate
Launching in 1995 and 1996, *Salon* and *Slate* are pioneers of the online-only magazine format (p. 329).

AARP Bulletin and AARP The Magazine
These subscription-only publications continue to boast the highest circulations of any magazine in the United States in 2011 (p. 333).

1900   1950   2000   2050

Ladies' Home Journal
With articles that discuss women's issues beyond cooking and fashion, the magazine reaches a circulation of one million in 1903 (p. 320).

Time
Launched in 1923, *Time* develops a new brand of journalism. *Time*'s editors assign teams to cover stories and use rewrite editors to package the reporting in narrative form (p. 322).

TV Guide
An overnight success as a niche publication upon its introduction in 1953, *TV Guide* publishes TV schedules long before newspapers do (p. 326).

Look and Life Shut Down
In 1971–72, two top magazines concede they can't compete with television (pp. 327–328).

People
The first successful mass market magazine to appear in decades is published in 1974 (p. 328).

The iPad
In 2010, Apple's iPad provides the magazine industry with a new way to present content and, hopefully, attract readers and advertisers (p. 330).

a hundred colonial magazines had appeared and disappeared. Although historians consider them dull and uninspired for the most part, these magazines helped launch a new medium that caught on after the American Revolution.

U.S. Magazines in the Nineteenth Century

After the revolution, the growth of the magazine industry in the newly independent United States remained slow. Delivery costs remained high, and some postal carriers refused to carry magazines because of their weight. Only twelve magazines operated in 1800. By 1825, about a hundred magazines existed, although about another five hundred had failed between 1800 and 1825. Nevertheless, during the first quarter of the nineteenth century, most communities had their own weekly magazines. These magazines featured essays on local issues, government activities, and political intrigue, as well as material reprinted from other sources. They sold some advertising but were usually in precarious financial straits because of their small circulations.

As the nineteenth century progressed, the idea of specialized magazines devoted to certain categories of readers developed. Many early magazines were overtly religious and boasted the largest readerships of the day. The Methodist *Christian Journal and Advocate*, for example, claimed twenty-five thousand subscribers by 1826. Literary magazines also emerged at this time. The *North American Review*, for instance, established the work of important writers such as Ralph Waldo Emerson, Henry David Thoreau, and Mark Twain. In addition to religious and literary magazines, specialty magazines that addressed various professions, lifestyles, and topics also appeared. Some of these magazines included the *American Farmer*, the *American Journal of Education*, the *American Law Journal*, *Medical Repository*, and the *American Journal of Science*. Such specialization spawned the modern trend of reaching readers who share a profession, a set of beliefs, cultural tastes, or a social identity.

The nineteenth century also saw the birth of the first general-interest magazine aimed at a national audience. In 1821, two young Philadelphia printers, Charles Alexander and Samuel Coate Atkinson, launched the *Saturday Evening Post*, which became the longest-running magazine in U.S. history. Like most magazines of the day, the early *Post* included a few original essays but "borrowed" many pieces from other sources. Eventually, however, the *Post* grew to incorporate news, poetry, essays, play reviews, and more. The *Post* published the writings of such prominent popular authors as Nathaniel Hawthorne and Harriet Beecher Stowe. Although the *Post* was a general-interest magazine, it also was the first major magazine to appeal directly to women, via its "Lady's Friend" column, which addressed women's issues.

National, Women's, and Illustrated Magazines

With increases in literacy and public education, the development of faster printing technologies, and improvements in mail delivery (due to rail transportation), a market was created for more national magazines like the *Saturday Evening Post*. Whereas in 1825 one hundred magazines struggled for survival, by 1850 nearly six hundred magazines were being published regularly. (Thousands of others lasted less than a year.) Significant national magazines of the era included *Graham's Magazine* (1840-58), one of the most influential and entertaining magazines in the country; *Knickerbocker* (1833-64), which published essays and literary works by Washington Irving, James Fenimore Cooper, and Nathaniel

> "They spring up as fast as mushrooms, in every corner, and like all rapid vegetation, bear the seeds of early decay within them. . . . And then comes a 'frost, a killing frost,' in the form of bills due and debts unpaid. . . . The average age of periodicals in this country is found to be six months."
>
> *NEW-YORK MIRROR, 1828*

COLOR ILLUSTRATIONS first became popular in the fashion sections of women's magazines in the mid-1800s. The color for this fashion image from *Godey's Lady's Book* was added to the illustration by hand.

Hawthorne (preceding such national cultural magazines as the *New Yorker* and *Harper's*); the *Nation* (1865–present), which pioneered the national political magazine format; and *Youth's Companion* (1826-1929), one of the first successful national magazines for younger readers.

Besides the move to national circulation, other important developments in the magazine industry were under way. In 1828, Sarah Josepha Hale started the first magazine directed exclusively to a female audience: the *Ladies' Magazine*. In addition to general-interest articles, the magazine advocated for women's education, work, and property rights. After nine years and marginal success, Hale merged her magazine with its main rival, *Godey's Lady's Book* (1830-98), which she edited for the next forty years. By 1850, *Godey's*, known for its colorful fashion illustrations in addition to its advocacy, achieved a circulation of 40,000 copies—at the time, the biggest distribution ever for a U.S. magazine. By 1860, circulation swelled to 150,000. Hale's magazine played a central role in educating working- and middle-class women, who were denied access to higher education throughout the nineteenth century.

The other major development in magazine publishing during the mid-nineteenth century was the arrival of illustration. Like the first newspapers, early magazines were totally dependent on the printed word. By the mid-1850s, drawings, engravings, woodcuts, and other forms of illustration had become a major feature of magazines. During this time, *Godey's Lady's Book* employed up to 150 women to color-tint its magazine illustrations and stencil drawings by hand. Meanwhile, *Harper's New Monthly Magazine*, founded in 1850, offered extensive woodcut illustrations with each issue. During the Civil War, many readers relied on *Harper's* for its elaborate battlefield sketches. Publications like *Harper's* married visual language to the printed word, helping to transform magazines into a mass medium. Bringing photographs into magazines took a bit longer. Mathew Brady and his colleagues, whose thirty-five hundred photos documented the Civil War, helped to popularize photography by the 1860s. But it was not until the 1890s that magazines and newspapers possessed the technology to reproduce photos in print media.

CIVIL WAR PHOTOGRAPHY
Famed portrait photographer Mathew Brady coordinated many photographers to document the Civil War (although all the resulting photos were credited "Photograph by Brady," he did not take them all). This effort allowed people at home to see and understand the true carnage of the war. Photo critics now acknowledge that some of Brady's photos were posed or reenactments.

The Development of Modern American Magazines

In 1870, about twelve hundred magazines were produced in the United States; by 1890, that number reached forty-five hundred; and by 1905, more than six thousand magazines existed. Part of this surge in titles and readership was facilitated by the Postal Act of 1879, which assigned magazines lower postage rates and put them on an equal footing with newspapers delivered by mail, reducing distribution costs. Meanwhile, advances in mass-production printing, conveyor systems, assembly lines, and faster presses reduced production costs and made large-circulation national magazines possible.[5]

The combination of reduced distribution and production costs enabled publishers to slash magazine prices. As prices dropped from thirty-five cents to fifteen and then to ten cents, the working class was gradually able to purchase national publications. By 1905, there were about twenty-five national magazines, available from coast to coast and serving millions of readers.[6] As jobs and the population began shifting from farms and small towns to urban areas, magazines helped readers imagine themselves as part of a nation rather than as individuals with only local or regional identities. In addition, the dramatic growth of drugstores and dime stores, supermarkets, and department stores offered new venues and shelf space for selling consumer goods, including magazines.

As magazine circulation started to skyrocket, advertising revenue soared. The economics behind the rise of advertising was simple: A magazine publisher could dramatically expand circulation by dropping the price of an issue below the actual production cost for a single copy. The publisher recouped the loss through ad revenue, guaranteeing large readerships to advertisers who were willing to pay to reach more readers. The number of ad pages in national magazines proliferated. *Harper's*, for instance, devoted only seven pages to ads in the mid-1880s, nearly fifty pages in 1890, and more than ninety pages in 1900.[7]

By the turn of the century, advertisers increasingly used national magazines to capture consumers' attention and build a national marketplace. One magazine that took advantage of these changes was *Ladies' Home Journal*, begun in 1883 by Cyrus Curtis. The women's magazine began publishing more than the usual homemaking tips, including also popular fiction, sheet music, and—most important, perhaps—the latest consumer ads. The magazine's broadened scope was a reflection of the editors' and advertisers' realization that women consumers constituted a growing and lucrative market. *Ladies' Home Journal* reached a circulation of over 500,000 by the early 1890s—the highest circulation of any magazine in the country. In 1903, it became the first magazine to reach a circulation of one million.

Social Reform and the Muckrakers

Better distribution and lower costs had attracted readers, but to maintain sales, magazines had to change content as well. While printing the fiction and essays of the best writers of the day was one way to maintain circulation, many magazines also engaged in one aspect of *yellow journalism*—crusading for social reform on behalf of the public good. In the 1890s, for example, *Ladies' Home Journal* (*LHJ*) and its editor, Edward Bok, led the fight against unregulated patent medicines (which often contained nearly 50 percent alcohol), while other magazines joined the fight against phony medicines, poor living and working conditions, and unsanitary practices in various food industries.

The rise in magazine circulation coincided with rapid social changes in America. While hundreds of thousands of Americans moved from the country to the city in search of industrial

A NAUSEATING JOB, BUT IT MUST BE DONE

(President Roosevelt takes hold of the investigating muck-rake himself in the packing-house scandal.)

From the *Saturday Globe* (Utica)

jobs, millions of new immigrants also poured in. Thus, the nation that journalists had long written about had grown increasingly complex by the turn of the century. Many newspaper reporters became dissatisfied with the simplistic and conventional style of newspaper journalism and turned to magazines, where they were able to write at greater length and in greater depth about broader issues. They wrote about such topics as corruption in big business and government, urban problems faced by immigrants, labor conflicts, and race relations.

In 1902, *McClure's* magazine (1893-1933) touched off an investigative era in magazine reporting with a series of probing stories, including Ida Tarbell's "The History of the Standard Oil Company," which took on John D. Rockefeller's oil monopoly, and Lincoln Steffens's "Shame of the Cities," which tackled urban problems. In 1906, *Cosmopolitan* magazine joined the fray with a series called "The Treason of the Senate," and *Collier's* magazine (1888-1957) developed "The Great American Fraud" series, focusing on patent medicines (whose ads accounted for 30 percent of the profits made by the American press by the 1890s). Much of this new reporting style was critical of American institutions. Angry with so much negative reporting, in 1906 President Theodore Roosevelt dubbed these investigative reporters **muckrakers**, because they were willing to crawl through society's muck to uncover a story. Muckraking was a label that Roosevelt used with disdain, but it was worn with pride by reporters such as Ray Stannard Baker, Frank Norris, and Lincoln Steffens.

Influenced by Upton Sinclair's novel *The Jungle*–a fictional account of Chicago's meatpacking industry–and

SATURDAY EVENING POST artist Albert Staehle's first cover featuring Butch, a mischievous black-and-white cocker spaniel, was so popular that Staehle was asked to do a series of them. Readers couldn't wait to see what scrape Butch would get himself into next. Butch's many adventures included playing baseball, knocking over a lamp, chewing up war rations, and getting a haircut.

by the muckraking reports of *Collier's* and *LHJ*, in 1906 Congress passed the Pure Food and Drug Act and the Meat Inspection Act. Other reforms stemming from muckraking journalism and the politics of the era include antitrust laws for increased government oversight of business, a fair and progressive income tax, and the direct election of U.S. senators.

The Rise of General-Interest Magazines

The heyday of the muckraking era lasted into the mid-1910s, when America was drawn into World War I. After the war and through the 1950s, **general-interest magazines** were the most prominent publications, offering occasional investigative articles but also covering a wide variety of topics aimed at a broad national audience. A key aspect of these magazines was **photojournalism**—the use of photos to document the rhythms of daily life (see "Case Study: The Evolution of Photojournalism" on pages 324-325). High-quality photos gave general-interest magazines a visual advantage over radio, which was the most popular medium of the day. In 1920, about fifty-five magazines fit the general-interest category; by 1946, more than one hundred such magazines competed with radio networks for the national audience.

Saturday Evening Post

Although it had been around since 1821, the *Saturday Evening Post* concluded the nineteenth century as only a modest success, with a circulation of about ten thousand. In 1897, Cyrus Curtis, who had already made *Ladies' Home Journal* the nation's top magazine, bought the *Post* and remade it into the first widely popular general-interest magazine. Curtis's strategy for reinvigorating the magazine included printing popular fiction and romanticizing American virtues through words and pictures (a *Post* tradition best depicted in the three-hundred-plus cover illustrations by Norman Rockwell). Curtis also featured articles that celebrated the business boom of the 1920s. This reversed the journalistic direction of the muckraking era, in which business corruption was often the focus. By the 1920s, the *Post* had reached two million in circulation, the first magazine to hit that mark.

Reader's Digest

The most widely circulated general-interest magazine during this period was *Reader's Digest*. Started in a Greenwich Village basement in 1922 by Dewitt Wallace and Lila Acheson Wallace, *Reader's Digest* championed one of the earliest functions of magazines: printing condensed versions of selected articles from other magazines. In the magazine's early years, the Wallaces refused to accept ads and sold the *Digest* only through subscriptions. With its inexpensive production costs, low price, and popular pocket-size format, the magazine's circulation climbed to over a million during the Great Depression, and by 1946 it was the nation's most popular magazine. By the mid-1980s, it was the most popular magazine in the world with a circulation of twenty million in America and ten to twelve million abroad. However, by 2012 it was recovering from bankruptcy, and working to cut costs and adjusting its circulation base to about 5.5 million.

Time

During the general-interest era, national newsmagazines such as *Time* were also major commercial successes. Begun in 1923 by Henry Luce and Briton Hadden, *Time* developed a magazine brand of interpretive journalism, assigning reporter-researcher teams to cover stories while a

rewrite editor would put the article in narrative form with an interpretive point of view. *Time* had a circulation of 200,000 by 1930, increasing to more than 3 million by the mid-1960s. *Time*'s success encouraged prominent imitators, including *Newsweek* (1933-), *U.S. News & World Report* (1948-), and more recently the *Week* (2001-). By 2012, economic decline, competition from the Web, and a shrinking number of readers and advertisers took their toll on the three top news-weeklies. *Time*'s circulation stagnated at 3.3 million while *U.S. News* became a monthly magazine in 2008 with less than 1.3 million in circulation. After losing $30 million in 2009, *Newsweek* was sold for $1 and its debts. In an attempt to attract new readers and better compete online, *Newsweek* merged with the *Daily Beast*, a Web site run by former magazine editor Tina Brown, but its profitability continued to be an issue.

Life

Despite the commercial success of *Reader's Digest* and *Time* in the twentieth century, the magazines that really symbolized the general-interest genre during this era were the oversized pictorial weeklies *Look* and *Life*. More than any other magazine of its day, *Life* developed an effective strategy for competing with popular radio by advancing photojournalism. Launched as a weekly by Henry Luce in 1936, *Life* combined the public's fascination with images (invigorated by the movie industry), radio journalism, and the popularity of advertising and fashion photography. By the end of the 1930s, *Life* had a **pass-along readership**—the total number of people who come into contact with a single copy of a magazine—of more than seventeen million, rivaling the ratings of popular national radio programs.

Life's first editor, Wilson Hicks—formerly a picture editor for the Associated Press—built a staff of renowned photographer-reporters who chronicled the world's ordinary and extraordinary events from the late 1930s through the 1960s. Among *Life*'s most famous photojournalists were Margaret Bourke-White, the first woman war correspondent to fly combat missions during World War II, and Gordon Parks, who later became Hollywood's first African American director of major feature films. Today, *Life*'s photographic archive is hosted online by Google (images.google.com/hosted/life).

The Fall of General-Interest Magazines

The decline of the weekly general-interest magazines, which had dominated the industry for thirty years, began in the 1950s. By 1957, both *Collier's* (founded in 1888) and *Woman's Home Companion* (founded in 1873) had folded. Each magazine had a national circulation of more than

The Evolution of Photojournalism

by Christopher R. Harris

What we now recognize as photojournalism started with the assignment of photographer Roger Fenton, of the *Sunday Times of London*, to document the Crimean War in 1856. Technical limitations did not allow direct reproduction of photodocumentary images in the publications of the day, however. Woodcut artists had to interpret the photographic images as black-and-white-toned woodblocks that could be reproduced by the presses of the period. Images interpreted by artists therefore lost the inherent qualities of photographic visual documentation: an on-site visual representation of facts for those who weren't present.

Woodcuts remained the basic method of press reproduction until 1880, when *New York Daily Graphic* photographer Stephen Horgan invented half-tone reproduction using a dot-pattern screen. This screen enabled metallic plates to directly represent photographic images in the printing process; now periodicals could bring exciting visual reportage to their pages.

In the mid-1890s, Jimmy Hare became the first photographer recognized as a photojournalist in the United States. Taken for *Collier's Weekly*, Hare's photoreportage on the sinking of the battleship *Maine* in 1898 near Havana, Cuba, established his reputation as a newsman traveling the world to bring back images of news events. Hare's images fed into growing popular support for Cuban independence from Spain and eventual U.S. involvement in the Spanish-American War.

In 1888, George Eastman opened photography to the working and middle classes when he introduced the first flexible-film camera from Kodak, his company in Rochester, New York. Gone were the bulky equipment and fragile photographic plates of the past. Now families and journalists could more easily and affordably document gatherings and events.

As photography became easier and more widespread, photojournalism began to take on an increasingly important social role. At the turn of the century, the documentary photography of Jacob Riis and Lewis Hine captured the harsh working and living conditions of the nation's many child laborers, including crowded ghettos and unsafe mills and factories. Reaction to these shockingly honest photographs resulted in public outcry and new laws against the exploitation of children. Photographs also brought the horrors of World War I to people far from the battlefields.

In 1923, visionaries Henry Luce and Briton Hadden published *Time*, the first modern photographic newsweekly; *Life* and *Fortune* soon followed. From coverage of the Roaring Twenties to the Great Depression, these magazines used images that changed the way people viewed the world.

Life, with its spacious 10-by-13-inch format and large photographs, became one of the most influential magazines in America, printing what are now classic images from World War II and the Korean War. Often, *Life* offered images that were unavailable anywhere else: Margaret Bourke-White's photographic proof of the unspeakably horrific concentration camps; W. Eugene Smith's gentle portraits of the humanitarian Albert Schweitzer in Africa; David Duncan's gritty images of the faces of U.S. troops fighting in Korea.

Television photojournalism made its quantum leap into the public mind as it documented the assassination of President Kennedy in 1963. In televised images that were broadcast and rebroadcast, the public witnessed the actual assassination and the

◀

JACOB RIIS
The Tramp, c. 1890. Riis, who emigrated from Denmark in 1870, lived in poverty in New York for several years before becoming a photojournalist. He spent much of his later life chronicling the lives of the poor in New York City. *Courtesy: The Jacob A. Riis Collection, Museum of the City of New York.*

confusing aftermath, including live coverage of the murder of alleged assassin Lee Harvey Oswald and of President Kennedy's funeral procession. Photojournalism also provided visual documentation of the turbulent 1960s, including aggressive photographic coverage of the Vietnam War—its protesters and supporters. Pulitzer Prize–winning photographer Eddie Adams shook the emotions of the American public with his photographs of a South Vietnamese general's summary execution of a suspected Vietcong terrorist. Closer to home, shocking images of the Civil Rights movement culminated in pictures of Birmingham police and police dogs attacking Civil Rights protesters.

In the 1970s, new computer technologies emerged that were embraced by print and television media worldwide. By the late 1980s, computers could transform images into digital form and easily manipulate them with sophisticated software programs. Today, a reporter can take a picture and within minutes send it to news offices in Tokyo, Berlin, and New York; moments later, the image can be used in a late-breaking TV story or sent directly to that organization's Twitter followers. Such digital technology has revolutionized photojournalism, perhaps even more than the advent of roll film did in the late nineteenth century. Today's photojournalists post entire interactive photo slideshows alongside stories, sometimes adding audio explaining their artistic and journalistic process. Their photographs live on through online news archives and through photojournalism blogs such as the Lens of the *New York Times*, where photojournalists are able to gain recognition for their work and find new audiences.

However, there is a dark side to all this digital technology. Because of the absence of physical film, there is a loss of proof, or veracity, of the authenticity of images. Original film has qualities that make it easy to determine whether it has been tampered with. Digital images, by contrast, can be easily altered, and such alteration can be very difficult to detect.

TIM HETHERINGTON, a British-American photographer, was killed on April 20, 2011, along with American photographer Chris Hondros while they were covering the conflict in Libya. Hetherington was forty. He had previously photographed the human side of conflicts in Liberia, Sierra Leone, Nigeria, Afghanistan, and Libya. Regarding his war photographs, Hetherington told the *New York Times* in 2007, "I wanted to be part of the solution, not part of the problem." His work is collected in several books and in *Restrepo*, the acclaimed 2010 documentary he codirected about an American platoon fighting in Afghanistan. (Above photo is from Hetherington's collection on the civil war in Liberia.)

A recent example of image-tampering involved the Ralph Lauren fashion model Filippa Hamilton. She appeared in a drastically Photoshopped advertisement that showed her hips as being thinner than her head—like a Bratz doll. The ad, published only in Japan, received intense criticism when the picture went viral. The 5'10", 120-pound model was subsequently dropped by the fashion label, because, as Hamilton explained, "they said I was overweight and I couldn't fit in their clothes anymore."[1] In today's age of Photoshop, it is common practice to make thin female models look even thinner and make male models look unnaturally muscled. "Every picture has been worked on, some twenty, thirty rounds," Ken Harris, a fashion magazine photo-retoucher said; "going between the retoucher, the client, and the agency . . . [photos] are retouched to death."[2] And since there is no disclaimer saying these images have been retouched, it can be hard for viewers to know the truth.

Photojournalists and news sources are confronted today with unprecedented concerns over truth-telling. In the past, trust in documentary photojournalism rested solely on the verifiability of images ("what you see is what you get"). This is no longer the case. Just as we must evaluate the words we read, now we must also take a more critical eye to the images we view.

Christopher R. Harris is a professor in the Department of Electronic Media Communication at Middle Tennessee State University.

four million the year it died. No magazine with this kind of circulation had ever shut down before. Together, the two publications brought in advertising revenues of more than $26 million in 1956. Although some critics blamed poor management, both magazines were victims of changing consumer tastes, rising postal costs, falling ad revenues, and, perhaps most important, television, which began usurping the role of magazines as the preferred family medium.

TV Guide Is Born

While other magazines were just beginning to make sense of the impact of television on their readers, *TV Guide* appeared in 1953. Taking its cue from the pocket-size format of *Reader's Digest* and the supermarket sales strategy used by women's magazines, *TV Guide*, started by Walter Annenberg's Triangle Publications, soon rivaled the success of *Reader's Digest* by addressing the nation's growing fascination with television by publishing TV listings. The first issue sold a record 1.5 million copies in ten urban markets. Because many newspapers were not yet listing TV programs, by 1962 the magazine became the first weekly to reach a circulation of 8 million with its seventy regional editions tailoring its listings to TV channels in specific areas of the country. (See Table 9.1 for the circulation figures of the Top 10 U.S. magazines.)

TV Guide's story illustrates a number of key trends that impacted magazines beginning in the 1950s. First, *TV Guide* highlighted America's new interest in specialized magazines. Second, it demonstrated the growing sales power of the nation's checkout lines, which also sustained the high circulation rates of women's magazines and supermarket tabloids. Third, *TV Guide* underscored the fact that magazines were facing the same challenge as other mass media in the 1950s: the growing power of television. *TV Guide* would rank among the nation's most popular magazines in the twentieth century.

In 1988, media baron Rupert Murdoch acquired Triangle Publications for $3 billion. Murdoch's News Corp. owned the new Fox network, and buying the then-influential *TV Guide* ensured that the fledgling network would have its programs listed. By the mid-1990s, Fox was using *TV Guide* to promote the network's programming in the magazine's hundred-plus regional editions. In 2005, after years of declining circulation (TV schedules in local newspapers undermined its regional editions), *TV Guide* became a full-size entertainment magazine, dropping its smaller digest format and its 140 regional editions. In 2008, *TV Guide*, once the most widely distributed magazine, was sold to a private venture capital firm for $1–less than the cost of a single issue. The TV Guide Network and TVGuide.com–both deemed more valuable assets–were sold

"Starting a magazine is an intensely complicated business, with many factors in play. You have to have the right person at the right time with the right ideas."

TINA BROWN,
FORMER EDITOR OF
THE DEFUNCT *TALK*
MAGAZINE, 2002

TABLE 9.1
THE TOP 10 MAGAZINES (RANKED BY PAID U.S. CIRCULATION AND SINGLE-COPY SALES, 1972 vs. 2011)

Source: Magazine Publishers of America, http://www.magazine.org, 2011.

1972		2011	
Rank/Publication	Circulation	Rank/Publication	Circulation
1 *Reader's Digest*	17,825,661	1 *AARP The Magazine*	22,401,546
2 *TV Guide*	16,410,858	2 *AARP Bulletin*	22,204,197
3 *Woman's Day*	8,191,731	3 *Better Homes and Gardens*	7,633,372
4 *Better Homes and Gardens*	7,996,050	4 *Game Informer Magazine*	6,734,672
5 *Family Circle*	7,889,587	5 *Reader's Digest*	5,606,743
6 *McCall's*	7,516,960	6 *National Geographic*	4,463,196
7 *National Geographic*	7,260,179	7 *Good Housekeeping*	4,339,069
8 *Ladies' Home Journal*	7,014,251	8 *Woman's Day*	3,876,053
9 *Playboy*	6,400,573	9 *Family Circle*	3,846,672
10 *Good Housekeeping*	5,801,446	10 *People*	3,563,410

to the film company Lionsgate Entertainment for $255 million in 2009. As *TV Guide* fell out of favor, *Game Informer*–a magazine about digital games–become a top title as it chronicled the rise of another mass media industry.

Saturday Evening Post, Life, and Look Expire

Although *Reader's Digest* and women's supermarket magazines were not greatly affected by television, other general-interest magazines were. The *Saturday Evening Post* folded in 1969, *Look* in 1971, and *Life* in 1972. At the time, all three magazines were rated in the Top 10 in terms of paid circulation, and each had a readership that exceeded six million per issue. Why did these magazines fold? First, to maintain these high circulation figures, their publishers were selling the magazines for far less than the cost of production. For example, a subscription to *Life* cost a consumer twelve cents an issue, yet it cost the publisher more than forty cents per copy to make and mail.

Second, the national advertising revenue pie that helped make up the cost differences for *Life* and *Look* now had to be shared with network television–and magazines' slices were getting smaller. *Life*'s high pass-along readership meant that it had a larger audience than many prime-time TV shows. But it cost more to have a single full-page ad in *Life* than it did to buy a minute of ad time during evening television. National advertisers were often forced to choose between the two, and in the late 1960s and early 1970s television seemed a better buy to advertisers looking for the biggest audience.

Third, dramatic increases in postal rates had a particularly negative effect on oversized publications (those larger than the 8- by 10.5-inch standard). In the 1970s, postal rates increased by more than 400 percent for these magazines. The *Post* and *Life* cut their circulations drastically to save money. The *Post* went from producing 6.8 million to 3 million copies per issue; *Life*, which lost $30 million between 1968 and 1972, cut circulation from 8.5 million to 7 million. The economic rationale here was that limiting the number of copies would reduce production and postal costs, enabling the magazines to lower their ad rates to compete with network television. But in fact, with decreased circulation, these magazines became less attractive to advertisers trying to reach the largest general audience.

The general magazines that survived the competition for national ad dollars tended to be women's magazines, such as *Good Housekeeping*, *Better Homes and Gardens*, *Family Circle*, *Ladies' Home Journal*, and *Woman's Day*. These publications had smaller formats and depended

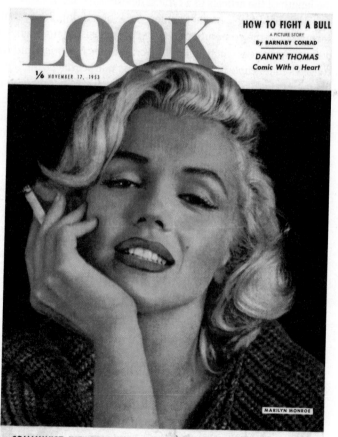

COMMUNIST INFILTRATION IN THE PROTESTANT CLERGY: TWO VIEWS

THE RISE AND FALL OF *LOOK*

With large pages, beautiful photographs, and compelling stories on celebrities like Marilyn Monroe, *Look* entertained millions of readers from 1937 to 1971, emphasizing photojournalism to compete with radio. By the late 1960s, however, TV lured away national advertisers, postal rates increased, and production costs rose, forcing *Look* to fold despite a readership of more than eight million.

PEOPLE STYLEWATCH capitalizes on its readers' desires to dress like their favorite celebrities. The magazine gives advice on fashion trends, shows affordable versions of designer pieces, and provides numerous photos of celebrities' clothing choices. And it's a hit. In 2009, when most magazines had a drop in circulation and ad pages, *People StyleWatch* had increases in both: 8.6 percent and 24 percent, respectively. Here, *StyleWatch* editors look over pages for an upcoming issue.

primarily on supermarket sales rather than on expensive mail-delivered subscriptions (like *Life* and *Look*). However, the most popular magazines, *TV Guide* and *Reader's Digest*, benefited not only from supermarket sales but also from their larger circulations (twice that of *Life*), their pocket size, and their small photo budgets. The failure of the *Saturday Evening Post*, *Look*, and *Life* as oversized general audience weeklies ushered in a new era of specialization.

People Puts Life Back into Magazines

In March 1974, Time Inc. launched *People*, the first successful mass market magazine to appear in decades. With an abundance of celebrity profiles and human-interest stories, *People* showed a profit in two years and reached a circulation of more than two million within five years. *People* now ranks first in revenue from advertising and circulation sales–more than $1.5 billion a year.

The success of *People* is instructive, particularly because only two years earlier television had helped kill *Life* by draining away national ad dollars. Instead of using a bulky oversized format and relying on subscriptions, *People* downsized and generated most of its circulation revenue from newsstand and supermarket sales. For content, it took its cue from our culture's fascination with celebrities. Supported by plenty of photos, its short articles are about one-third the length of the articles in a typical newsmagazine.

Although *People* has not achieved the broad popularity that *Life* once commanded, it does seem to defy the contemporary trend of specialized magazines aimed at narrow but well-defined audiences, such as *Tennis World, Game Informer,* and *Hispanic Business*. One argument suggests that *People* is not, in fact, a mass market magazine but a specialized publication targeting people with particular cultural interests: a fascination with music, TV, and movie stars. If *People* is viewed as a specialty magazine, its financial success makes much more sense. It also helps explain the host of magazines that try to emulate it, including *Us Weekly, Entertainment Weekly, In Touch Weekly, Star,* and *OK! People* has even spawned its own spin-offs, including *People en Español* and *People StyleWatch*; the latter is a low-cost fashion magazine that began in 2007 and features celebrity styles at discount prices.

Convergence: Magazines Confront the Digital Age

Although the Internet was initially viewed as the death knell of print magazines, the industry now embraces it. The Internet has become the place where print magazines like *Time* and *Entertainment Weekly* can extend their reach, where some magazines like *FHM* and *Elle Girl* can survive when their print version ends, or where online magazines like *Salon, Slate,* and *Wonderwall* can exist exclusively.

Magazines Move Online

Given the costs of paper, printing, and postage, creating magazine companion Web sites is a popular method for expanding the reach of consumer magazines. For example, *Wired* magazine has a print circulation of about 830,000. Online, Wired.com gets an average of 15.3 million unique visitors per month. Between 2006 and 2011, the number of consumer magazine Web sites grew by 30 percent, to more than 7,000.[8]

The Web also gives magazines unlimited space, which is at a premium in their printed versions, and the opportunity to do things that print can't do. Many online magazines now include blogs, original video and audio podcasts, social networks, games, virtual fitting rooms, and other interactive components that could never work in print. For example, PopularMechanics.com has added interactive 3-D models for do-it-yourself projects, so that a reader can go over plans to make an Adirondack chair, examining joints and parts from every angle. Other magazines offer printable coupons on their sites or, like *Redbook* and *GQ*, offer "snap" advertising coupons, in which the reader snaps a photo of a designated image in the print edition with his or her cell phone and sends the photo to the magazine for a coupon or promotional sample. In July 2009, *Popular Science* created perhaps the most ambitious print-digital hybrid project at the time. That issue asked readers to go to www.popsci.com/imagination and hold the print cover of the magazine to their computer WebCam to generate a 3-D image of windmills projecting from the cover (and to see the name of the sponsor, General Electric). The 3-D approach (called "augmented reality" advertising, or AR) has caught on. *GQ* has featured 3-D athletes in Calvin Klein underwear, and automotive magazines are using AR to bring car models to life.

WONDERWALL, launched in 2009 by MSN.com and media production company BermanBraun, is now a leading Internet entertainment magazine, with more than ten million unique visitors per month. The site has spawned three online spin-offs—*Wonderwall Latino*; *BTLWY*, a "powerwall" site of political celebrities that BermanBraun co-produces with MSNBC; and *Glo*, a style and beauty magazine produced with major magazine publisher Hachette Filipacchi Media.

Paperless: Magazines Embrace Digital Content

Webzines such as *Salon* and *Slate*, which are magazines that appear exclusively online, were pioneers in making the Web a legitimate site for breaking news and discussing culture and politics. *Salon* was founded in 1995 by five former reporters from the *San Francisco Examiner* who wanted to break from the traditions of newspaper publishing and build "a different kind of newsroom" to create well-developed stories and commentary. With the help of positive word-of-mouth comments, *Salon* is now the leading online magazine, claiming over 7.6 million unique monthly visitors in 2012. Its main online competitor, *Slate*, founded in 1996 and now owned by the Washington Post Company, draws about 6.8 million unique monthly visitors.

Other online-only magazines have tried to reinvent the idea of a magazine, instead of just adapting the print product to the Web. For example, MSN's *Wonderwall* (wonderwall.msn.com) uses a layout that is only possible in a digital magazine. Visitors are met by a vertical "wall" of more than sixty celebrity photographs, each linking to a story. *Lonny* (www.lonnymag.com), an interior design magazine, enables readers to flip through digital pages and then click through on items (such as pillows, chairs, fabrics) for purchase. As magazines create apps for smartphones and touchscreen tablets, editorial content is even more tightly woven with advertising. Readers can now, for example, read *Entertainment Weekly*'s top music recommendations on their iPhone or iPad and then click through to buy a song or album on iTunes. *Entertainment Weekly*, owned by Time Warner, then gets a cut of the sale it generated for iTunes, and the reader gets music almost instantly. (See "Tracking Technology: The New 'Touch' of Magazines" on page 330.)

The Domination of Specialization

The general trend away from mass market publications and toward specialty magazines coincided with radio's move to specialized formats in the 1950s. With the rise of television, magazines ultimately reacted the same way radio and movies did: They adapted. Radio

SPECIALIZED MAGAZINES target a wide range of interests from mainstream sports to hobbies like making model airplanes. Some of the more successful specialized magazines include *AARP The Magazine, Sports Illustrated,* and *National Geographic.*

The most popular sports and leisure magazine is *Sports Illustrated*, which took its name from a failed 1935 publication. Launched in 1954 by Henry Luce's Time Inc., *Sports Illustrated* was initially aimed at well-educated, middle-class men. It has become the most successful general sports magazine in history, covering everything from major-league sports and mountain climbing to foxhunting and snorkeling. Although frequently criticized for its immensely profitable but exploitative yearly swimsuit edition, *Sports Illustrated* also has done major investigative pieces—for example, on racketeering in boxing and on land conservation. Its circulation held steady at 3.2 million in 2012. *Sports Illustrated* competes directly with *ESPN The Magazine* and indirectly with dozens of leisure and niche sports magazine competitors like *Golf Digest, Outside,* and *Pro Football Weekly*.

Another popular magazine type that fits loosely into the leisure category includes magazines devoted to music—everything from hip-hop's *The Source* to country's *Country Weekly*. The all-time circulation champ in this category is *Rolling Stone*, started in 1967 as an irreverent, left-wing political and cultural magazine by twenty-one-year-old Jann Wenner. Once considered an alternative magazine, by 1982 *Rolling Stone* had paddled into the mainstream with a circulation approaching 800,000; by 2012, it had a circulation of more than 1.4 million. Many fans of the early *Rolling Stone*, however, disappointed with its move to increase circulation and reflect mainstream consumer values, turned to less high-gloss alternatives such as *Spin*.

Founded in 1888 by Boston lawyer Gardiner Green Hubbard and his famous son-in-law, Alexander Graham Bell, *National Geographic* promoted "humanized geography" and helped pioneer color photography in 1910. It was also the first publication to publish both undersea and aerial color photographs. In addition, many of *National Geographic*'s nature and culture specials on television, which began in 1965, rank among the most popular programs in the history of public television. *National Geographic*'s popularity grew slowly and steadily throughout the twentieth century, reaching 1 million in circulation in 1935 and 10 million in the 1970s. In the late 1990s, its circulation of paid subscriptions slipped to under 9 million. Other media ventures (for example, a cable channel and atlases) provided new revenue as circulation for the magazine continued to slide, falling to 4.2 million in 2012 (but with 3 million in international distribution). Despite its falling circulation, *National Geographic* is often recognized as one of the country's best magazines for its reporting and photojournalism. Today, *National Geographic* competes with other travel and geography magazines like *Discover, Smithsonian, Travel & Leisure, Condé Nast Traveler*, and its own *National Geographic Traveler*.

Magazines for the Ages

In the age of specialization, magazines have further delineated readers along ever-narrowing age lines, appealing more and more to very young and to older readers, groups often ignored by mainstream television.

The first children's magazines appeared in New England in the late 1700s. Ever since, magazines such as *Youth's Companion, Boy's Life* (the Boy Scouts' national publication since 1912), *Highlights for Children*, and *Ranger Rick* have successfully targeted preschool and elementary-school children. The ad-free and subscription-only *Highlights for Children* topped the children's magazine category in 2012, with a circulation of more than two million.

In the popular arena, the leading female teen magazines have shown substantial growth; the top magazine for thirteen- to nineteen-year-olds is *Seventeen*, with a circulation of two million in 2012. Several established magazines responded to the growing popularity of the teen market by introducing specialized editions, such as *Teen Vogue* and *Girl's Life*. (For a critical take on women's fashion magazines, see "Media Literacy and the Critical Process: Uncovering American Beauty" on page 334.)

Targeting young men in their twenties, *Maxim*, launched in 1997, was one of the fastest-growing magazines of the late 1990s, leveling off with a circulation of 2.5 million by 2005. *Maxim*'s covers boast the magazine's obsession with "sex, sports, beer, gadgets, clothes, fitness," a content mix that helped it eclipse rivals like *GQ* and *Esquire*. But by 2007, the lad fad had worn off, and *Maxim* closed its U.K. edition and downsized its U.S. staff.

In targeting audiences by age, the most dramatic success has come from magazines aimed at readers over age fifty, America's fastest-growing age segment. These publications have tried to meet the cultural interests of older Americans, who historically have not been prominently featured in mainstream consumer culture. The American Association of Retired Persons (AARP) and its magazine, *AARP The Magazine*, were founded in 1958 by retired California teacher Ethel Percy Andrus. Subscriptions to the bimonthly *AARP The Magazine* and the monthly *AARP Bulletin* come free when someone joins AARP and pays the modest membership fee ($16 in 2012). By the early 1980s, *AARP The Magazine*'s circulation approached seven million. However, with the AARP signing up thirty thousand new members each week by the late 1980s, both *AARP The Magazine* and the newsletter overtook *TV Guide* and *Reader's Digest* as the top circulated magazines. By 2012, both had circulations of nearly twenty-two million, far surpassing the circulations of all other magazines. Article topics in the magazine cover a range of lifestyle, travel, money, health, and entertainment issues, such as sex at age fifty-plus, secrets for spectacular vacations, and how poker can give you a sharper mind.

Elite Magazines

Although long in existence, *elite magazines* grew in popularity during the age of specialization. Elite magazines are characterized by their combination of literature, criticism, humor, and journalism and by their appeal to highly educated audiences, often living in urban areas. Among the numerous elite publications that grew in stature during the twentieth century were the *Atlantic Monthly, Vanity Fair*, and *Harper's*.

However, the most widely circulated elite magazine is the *New Yorker*. Launched in 1925 by Harold Ross, the *New Yorker* became the first city magazine aimed at a national upscale audience. Over the years, the *New Yorker* featured many of the twentieth century's most prominent biographers, writers, reporters, and humorists, including A. J. Liebling, Dorothy Parker, Lillian Ross, John Updike, E. B. White, and Garrison Keillor, as well as James Thurber's cartoons

" 'Secrets of Your Sex Drive,' 'Ten Ways to Look 10 Pounds Thinner' and 'Follow Your Dream—Find the Perfect Job Now.' Sound like the cover of *Cosmopolitan* magazine? Or maybe *Men's Health*? Think again. Those stories lead the latest issue of *AARP The Magazine*, which isn't just for grandma and grandpa anymore."

WASHINGTON TIMES, 2007

"Every magazine has its own architecture. *National Geographic* is a Greek revival temple. *TV Guide* is a fruit stand. The *New Yorker* is a men's hat store. The *Atlantic* is a church (Congregational)."

ROGER ROSENBLATT, *NEW REPUBLIC,* 1989

Media Literacy and the Critical Process

Uncovering American Beauty

How does the United States' leading fashion magazine define "beauty"? One way to explore this question is by critically analyzing the covers of *Cosmopolitan*.

1 DESCRIPTION. If you review a number of *Cosmopolitan* covers, you'll notice that they typically feature a body shot of a female model surrounded by blaring headlines often featuring the words *Hot* and *Sex* to usher a reader inside the magazine. The cover model is dressed provocatively and is positioned against a solid-color background. She looks confident. Everything about the cover is loud and brassy.

2 ANALYSIS. Looking at the covers over the last decade, and then the decade before it, what are some significant patterns? One thing you'll notice is that all of these models look incredibly alike, particularly when it comes to race: There is a disproportionate number of white cover models. But you'll notice that things are improving somewhat in this regard; *Cosmo* has used several Hispanic and African American cover models in recent years, but still they are few and far between. However, there is an even more consistent pattern regarding body type. Of cover model Hilary Duff, *Cosmo* said, "with long honey-colored locks, a smokin' bod, and killer confidence, Hilary's looking every bit the hot Hollywood starlet." In *Cosmo*-speak, "smokin' bod" means ultrathin (sometimes made even more so with digital modifications).

3 INTERPRETATION. What does this mean? Although *Cosmo* doesn't provide height and weight figures for its models, it's likely that it's selling an unhealthy body weight (in fact, photos can be digitally altered to make the models look even more thin). In its guidelines for the fashion industry, the Academy for Eating Disorders suggests "for women and men over the age of 18, adoption of a minimum body mass index threshold of 18.5 kg/m^2 (e.g., a female model who is 5'9" [1.75 m] must weigh more than 126 pounds [57.3 kg]), which recognizes that weight below this is considered underweight by the World Health Organization."[1]

4 EVALUATION. *Cosmopolitan* uses thin cover models as aspirational objects for its readers—that is, as women its readers would like to look like. Thus, these cover models become the image of what a "terrific" body is for its readers, who—by *Cosmopolitan*'s own account—are women age eighteen to twenty-four. *Cosmo* also notes that it's been the best-selling women's magazine in college bookstores for twenty-five years. But that target audience also happens to be the one most susceptible to body issues. As the Academy for Eating Disorders notes, "at any given time 10 percent or more of late adolescent and adult women report symptoms of eating disorders."[2]

5 ENGAGEMENT. Contact *Cosmo*'s editor in chief, Joanna Coles, and request representation of healthy body types on the magazine's covers. You can contact her and the editorial department via e-mail (cosmo_letters@hearst.com), telephone (212-649-3570), or U.S. mail: Joanna Coles, Editor, *Cosmopolitan*, 224 West 57th Street, New York, NY 10019. Your voice can be effective: In 2012, a thirteen-year-old girl started a petition on change.org and successfully got *Seventeen* to respond to the way it Photoshops images of models.

---

and Ogden Nash's poetry. It introduced some of the finest literary journalism of the twentieth century, devoting an entire issue to John Hersey's *Hiroshima* and serializing Truman Capote's *In Cold Blood*. By the mid-1960s, the *New Yorker*'s circulation hovered around 500,000; by 2012, its circulation stayed steady at 1 million.

Minority-Targeted Magazines

Minority-targeted magazines, like newspapers, have existed since before the Civil War, including the African American antislavery magazines *Emancipator, Liberator,* and *Reformer*. One of the most influential early African American magazines, the *Crisis*, was founded by W. E. B. Du Bois in 1910 and is the official magazine of the National Association for the Advancement of Colored People (NAACP).

In the modern age, the major magazine publisher for African Americans has been John H. Johnson, a former Chicago insurance salesman, who started *Negro Digest* in 1942 on $500 borrowed against his mother's furniture. By 1945, with a circulation of more than 100,000, the

Digest's profits enabled Johnson and a small group of editors to start *Ebony*, a picture-text magazine modeled on *Life* but serving black readers. The Johnson Publishing Company also successfully introduced *Jet*, a pocket-size supermarket magazine, in 1951. By 2012, *Jet*'s circulation was 700,000, while *Ebony*'s circulation was 1.2 million. *Essence*, the first major magazine geared toward African American women, debuted in 1969, and by 2012 it had a circulation of over 1 million.

Other minority groups also have magazines aimed at their own interests. The *Advocate*, founded in 1967 as a twelve-page newsletter, was the first major magazine to address issues of interest to gay men and lesbians, and it has in ensuing years published some of the best journalism about antigay violence, policy issues affecting the LGBT community, and AIDS–topics often not well covered by the mainstream press. *Out* is the top gay style magazine. Both are owned by Here Media, which also owns Here Networks and several LGBT Web sites.

With increases in Hispanic populations and immigration, magazines appealing to Spanish-speaking readers have developed rapidly since the 1980s. In 1983, the De Armas Spanish Magazine Network began distributing Spanish-language versions of mainstream American magazines, including *Cosmopolitan en Español*; *Harper's Bazaar en Español*; and *Ring*, the prominent boxing magazine. The bilingual *Latina* magazine was started with the help of Essence Communications in 1996, while recent magazine launches include *ESPN Deportes* and *Sports Illustrated en Español*. The new magazines target the most upwardly mobile segments of the growing American Hispanic population, which numbered more than fifty million–about 16.3 percent of the U.S. population–by 2012. Today, *People en Español*, *Latina*, and *Glamour en Español* rank as the top three Hispanic magazines by ad revenue.

Although national magazines aimed at other minority groups were slow to arrive, there are magazines now that target virtually every race, culture, and ethnicity, including *Asian Week*, *Native Peoples*, *Tikkun*, and many more.

Supermarket Tabloids

With headlines like "Sex Secrets of a Russian Spy," "Extraterrestrials Follow the Teachings of Oprah Winfrey," and "Al Qaeda Breeding Killer Mosquitoes," **supermarket tabloids** push the limits of both decency and credibility. Although they are published on newsprint, the Audit Bureau of Circulations, which checks newspaper and magazine circulation figures to determine advertising rates, counts weekly tabloids as magazines. Tabloid history can be traced to newspapers' use of graphics and pictorial layouts in the 1860s and 1870s, but the modern U.S. tabloid began with the founding of the *National Enquirer* by William Randolph Hearst in 1926. The *Enquirer* struggled until it was purchased in 1952 by Generoso Pope, who originally intended to use it to "fight for the rights of man" and "human decency and dignity."[9] In the interest of profit, though, Pope settled on the "gore formula" to transform the paper's anemic weekly circulation of seven thousand: "I noticed how auto accidents drew crowds and I decided that if it was blood that interested people, I'd give it to them."[10]

By the mid-1960s, the *Enquirer*'s circulation had jumped to over one million through the publication of bizarre human-interest stories, gruesome murder tales, violent accident accounts, unexplained phenomena stories, and malicious celebrity gossip. By 1974, the magazine's weekly

LATINA, launched in 1996, has become the largest magazine targeted to Hispanic women in the United States. It counts a readership of three million bilingual, bicultural women and is also the top Hispanic magazine in advertising pages.

"Inevitably, fashion advertisers that prop up the glossies will, like everyone else, increasingly migrate to Web and mobile interactive advertising."

ADVERTISING AGE,
2006

circulation topped four million. Its popularity inspired other tabloids like *Globe* (founded in 1954) and *Star*, founded by News Corp. in 1974, and the adoption of a tabloid style by general-interest magazines such as *People* and *Us Weekly*. Today, tabloid magazine sales are down from their peak in the 1980s, but they continue to be popular. American Media in Boca Raton, Florida, owns several magazines, including two key supermarket tabloids: *Star* and *National Enquirer*.

The Organization and Economics of Magazines

Given the great diversity in magazine content and ownership, it is hard to offer a common profile of a successful magazine. However large or small, online or in print, most magazines deal with the same basic functions: production, content, ads, and sales. In this section, we discuss how magazines operate, the ownership structure behind major magazines, and how smaller publications fulfill niche areas that even specialized magazines do not reach.

Magazine Departments and Duties

Unlike a broadcast station or a daily newspaper, a small newsletter or magazine can begin cheaply via computer-based **desktop publishing**, which enables an aspiring publisher-editor to write, design, lay out, and print or post online a modest publication. For larger operations, however, the work is divided into departments.

Editorial and Production

The lifeblood of a magazine is the *editorial department*, which produces its content, excluding advertisements. Like newspapers, most magazines have a chain of command that begins with a publisher and extends to the editor in chief, the managing editor, and a variety of subeditors. These subeditors oversee such editorial functions as photography, illustrations, reporting and writing, copyediting, layout, and print and multimedia design. Magazine writers generally include contributing staff writers, who are specialists in certain fields, and freelance writers, nonstaff professionals who are assigned to cover particular stories or a region of the country. Many magazines, especially those with small budgets, also rely on well-written unsolicited manuscripts to fill their pages. Most commercial magazines, however, reject more than 95 percent of unsolicited pieces.

Despite the rise of inexpensive desktop publishing, most large commercial magazines still operate several departments, which employ hundreds of people. The *production and technology department* maintains the computer and printing hardware necessary for mass market production. Because magazines are printed weekly, monthly, or bimonthly, it is not economically practical for most magazine publishers to maintain expensive print facilities. As with *USA Today*, many national magazines digitally transport magazine copy to various regional printing sites for the insertion of local ads and for faster distribution.

Advertising and Sales

The advertising and sales department of a magazine secures clients, arranges promotions, and places ads. Like radio stations, network television stations, and basic cable television stations, consumer magazines are heavily reliant on advertising revenue. The more successful the magazine, the more it can charge for advertisement space. Magazines provide their advertisers with rate cards, which indicate how much they charge for a certain amount of advertising space on a page. A top-rated consumer magazine might charge $350,000 for a full-page color ad and $103,000 for a third of a page, black-and-white ad. However, in today's competitive world, most rate cards are not very meaningful: Almost all magazines offer 25 to 50 percent rate discounts to advertisers.[11] Although fashion and general-interest magazines carry a higher percentage of ads than do political or literary magazines, the average magazine contains about 50 percent ad copy and 50 percent editorial material, a figure that has remained fairly constant for the past twenty-five years.

The traditional display ad has been the staple of magazine advertising for more than a century. As magazines move to tablet editions, the options for ad formats has grown immensely. For example, Condé Nast magazines offer static display ads with a link for its editions on the iPad, Kindle Fire, Nook, and Galaxy Tab. But they offer almost thirty other premium ad types, which can include audio, video, tap and reveal, and panoramic views. A single issue static page ad in tablet editions of titles like *GQ, Wired, Vanity Fair,* the *New Yorker,* and *Vogue* would cost $5,000. A premium ad with effects such as animation or a slide show costs $25,000, while a premium plus ad with effects like a virtual tour or full interactivity costs $45,000. (The cost per ad is discounted with purchases of multiple issues.)

A few contemporary magazines, such as *Highlights for Children*, have decided not to carry ads and rely solely on subscriptions and newsstand sales instead. To protect the integrity of their various tests and product comparisons, *Consumer Reports* and *Cook's Illustrated* carry no advertising. To strengthen its editorial independence, *Ms.* magazine abandoned ads in 1990 after years of pressure from the food, cosmetics, and fashion industries to feature recipes and more complementary copy.

Some advertisers and companies have canceled ads when a magazine featured an unflattering or critical article about a company or an industry.[12] In some instances, this practice has put enormous pressure on editors not to offend advertisers. The cozy relationships between some advertisers and magazines have led to a dramatic decline in investigative reporting, once central to popular magazines during the muckraking era.

As television advertising siphoned off national ad revenues in the 1950s, magazines began introducing different editions of their magazines to attract advertisers. **Regional editions** are national magazines whose content is tailored to the interests of different geographic areas. For example, *Sports Illustrated* often prints five different regional versions of its College Football Preview and March Madness Preview editions, picturing regional stars on each of the five covers. In **split-run editions**, the editorial content remains the same, but the magazine includes a few pages of ads purchased by local or regional companies. Most editions of *Time* and *Sports Illustrated,* for example, contain a number of pages reserved for regional ads. **Demographic editions**, meanwhile, are editions of magazines targeted at particular groups of consumers. In this case, market researchers identify subscribers primarily by occupation, class, and zip code. *Time* magazine, for example, developed special editions of its magazine for top management, high-income zip-code areas, and ultrahigh-income professional/managerial households. Demographic editions guarantee advertisers a particular magazine audience, one that enables them to pay lower rates for their ads because the ads will be run only in a limited number of copies of the magazine. The magazine can then compete with advertising in regional television or cable markets and in newspaper supplements. Because of the flexibility of special editions, new sources of income opened up for national magazines. Ultimately, these marketing strategies permitted the massive growth of magazines in the face of predictions that television would cripple the magazine industry.

Circulation and Distribution

The circulation and distribution department of a magazine monitors single-copy and subscription sales. Toward the end of the general-interest magazine era in 1950, newsstand sales

"If you don't acknowledge your magazine's advertisers, you don't have a magazine."

ANNA WINTOUR, EDITOR OF *VOGUE*, 2000

"So . . . the creative challenge, especially when you work for a bridal magazine, is how do we keep this material fresh? How do we keep it relevant? How do we, you know, get the reader excited, keep ourselves excited?"

DIANE FORDEN, EDITOR IN CHIEF, *BRIDAL GUIDE* MAGAZINE, 2004

Alternative Voices

Only eighty-four of the twenty thousand American magazines have circulations that top a million, so most alternative magazines struggle to satisfy small but loyal groups of readers. At any given time, there are over two thousand alternative magazines in circulation, with many failing and others starting up every month.

Alternative magazines have historically defined themselves in terms of politics–published either by the Left (the *Progressive, In These Times,* the *Nation*) or the Right (the *National Review, American Spectator, Insight*). However, what constitutes an alternative magazine has broadened over time to include just about any publication considered "outside the mainstream," ranging from environmental magazines to alternative lifestyle magazines to punk-zines–the magazine world's answer to punk rock. (**Zines,** pronounced "zeens," is a term used to describe self-published magazines.) *Utne Reader,* widely regarded as "the *Reader's Digest* of alternative magazines," has defined *alternative* as any sort of "thinking that doesn't reinvent the status quo, that broadens issues you might see on TV or in the daily paper."

Occasionally, alternative magazines have become marginally mainstream. For example, during the conservative Reagan era in the 1980s, William F. Buckley's *National Review* saw its circulation swell to more than 100,000–enormous by alternative standards. By 2012, the magazine continued to be the leading conservative publication, with a circulation of 150,000. On the Left, *Mother Jones* (named after labor organizer Mary Harris Jones), which champions muckraking and investigative journalism, had a circulation of 240,000 in 2012.

Most alternative magazines, however, are content to swim outside the mainstream. These are the small magazines that typically include diverse political, cultural, religious, international, and environmental subject matter, such as *Against the Current, BadAzz MoFo, Buddhadharma, Home Education Magazine, Jewish Currents, Small Farmer's Journal,* and *Humor Times.*

Magazines in a Democratic Society

Like other mass media, magazines are a major part of the cluttered media landscape. To keep pace, the magazine industry has become fast-paced and high-risk. Of the seven hundred to one thousand new magazines that start up each year, fewer than two hundred will survive longer than a year.

As an industry, magazine publishing–like advertising and public relations–has played a central role in transforming the United States from a producer society to a consumer society. Since the 1950s, though, individual magazines have not had the powerful national voice they once possessed, uniting separate communities around important issues such as abolition and suffrage. Today, with so many specialized magazines appealing to distinct groups of consumers, magazines play a much-diminished role in creating a sense of national identity.

Contemporary commercial magazines provide essential information about politics, society, and culture, thus helping us think about ourselves as participants in a democracy. Unfortunately, however, these magazines have often identified their readers as consumers first and citizens second. With magazines growing increasingly dependent on advertising,

THE *DAILY BEAST* is an online venture started by former magazine editor Tina Brown (*Tatler, Vanity Fair,* the *New Yorker, Talk*) and IAC Chairman Barry Diller. The *Beast* aims to "curate" news for readers and provide original reporting and opinion. In 2010, the *Daily Beast* merged with *Newsweek* with Brown as the editor in chief of both. However, the move failed to save the print edition of *Newsweek,* which published its final print issue in 2012. The publication will continue online and maintain its connection to the *Daily Beast.*

and some of them (such as shopping magazines like *Lucky*) being primarily *about* the advertising, controversial content sometimes has difficulty finding its way into print. More and more, magazines define their readers merely as viewers of displayed products and purchasers of material goods.

At the same time, magazines have arguably had more freedom than other media to encourage and participate in democratic debates. More magazine voices circulate in the marketplace than do broadcast or cable television channels. Moreover, many new magazines still play an important role in uniting dispersed groups of readers, often giving cultural minorities or newly arrived immigrants or alternative groups a sense of membership in a broader community. In addition, because magazines are distributed weekly, monthly, or bimonthly, they are less restricted by the deadline pressures experienced by newspaper publishers or radio and television broadcasters. Good magazines can usually offer more analysis of and insight into society than other media outlets can. In the midst of today's swirl of images, magazines and their advertisements certainly contribute to the commotion. But good magazines also maintain our connection to words, sustaining their vital role in an increasingly electronic and digital culture. ▶

CHAPTER REVIEW

COMMON THREADS

One of the Common Threads discussed in Chapter 1 is about the commercial nature of the mass media. The magazine industry is an unusual example of this. Big media corporations control some of the most popular magazines, and commercialism runs deep in many consumer magazines. At the same time, magazines are one of the most democratic mass media. How can that be?

There are more than twenty thousand magazine titles in the United States. But the largest and most profitable magazines are typically owned by some of the biggest media corporations. Time Warner, for example, counts *People, Time, Sports Illustrated, InStyle, FORTUNE, Southern Living*, and *Real Simple* among its holdings. Even niche magazines that seem small are often controlled by chains. Supermarket tabloids like *Star* and the *National Enquirer* are owned by Florida-based American Media, which also publishes *Shape, Muscle & Fitness, Men's Fitness, Fit Pregnancy*, and *Flex*.

High-revenue magazines, especially those focusing on fashion, fitness, and lifestyle, can also shamelessly break down the firewall between the editorial and business departments. "Fluff" story copy serves as a promotional background for cosmetic, clothing, and gadget advertisements. Many titles in the new generation of online and tablet magazines further break down that firewall—with a single click on a story or image, readers are linked to an e-commerce site where they can purchase the item they clicked on.

Digital retouching makes every model and celebrity thinner or more muscular, and always blemish-free. This altered view of their "perfection" becomes our ever-hopeful aspiration, spurring us to purchase the advertised products.

Yet the huge number of magazine titles—more than the number of radio stations, TV stations, cable networks, or yearly Hollywood releases—means that magazines span a huge range of activities and thought. Each magazine sustains a community—although some may think of readers more as consumers, while others view them as citizens—and several hundred new launches each year bring new voices to the marketplace and search for their own community to serve.

So there is the glitzy, commercial world of the big magazine industry with *Time*'s Person of the Year, the latest *Cosmo* girl, and the band on the cover of *Rolling Stone*. But many smaller magazines—like the *Georgia Review, Edutopia*, and *E–The Environmental Magazine*—account for the majority of magazine titles and the broad, democratic spectrum of communities that are their readers.

KEY TERMS

The definitions for the terms listed below can be found in the glossary at the end of the book. The page numbers listed with the terms indicate where the term is highlighted in the chapter.

magazine, 316
muckrakers, 321
general-interest magazines, 322
photojournalism, 322
pass-along readership, 323

Webzines, 329
supermarket tabloids, 335
desktop publishing, 336
regional editions, 337
split-run editions, 337

demographic editions, 337
evergreen subscriptions, 338
magalogs, 339
zines, 340

REVIEW QUESTIONS

The Early History of Magazines

1. Why did magazines develop later than newspapers in the American colonies?

2. Why did most of the earliest magazines have so much trouble staying financially solvent?

3. How did magazines become national in scope?

The Development of Modern American Magazines

4. How did magazines position women in the new consumer economy at the turn of the twentieth century?

5. What role did magazines play in social reform at the turn of the twentieth century?

6. When and why did general-interest magazines become so popular?

7. Why did some of the major general-interest magazines fail in the twentieth century?

8. What are the advantages of magazines moving to digital formats?

The Domination of Specialization

9. What triggered the move toward magazine specialization?

10. What are the differences between regional and demographic editions?

11. What are the most useful ways to categorize the magazine industry? Why?

The Organization and Economics of Magazines

12. What are the four main departments at a typical consumer magazine?

13. How do digital editions of magazines change the format of magazine advertising?

14. What are some of the models for digital distribution of magazines?

15. What are the major magazine chains, and what is their impact on the mass media industry in general?

Magazines in a Democratic Society

16. How do magazines serve a democratic society?

17. How does advertising affect what gets published in the editorial side of magazines?

QUESTIONING THE MEDIA

1. What role did magazines play in America's political and social shift from being colonies of Great Britain to becoming an independent nation?

2. Why is the muckraking spirit—so important in popular magazines at the turn of the twentieth century—generally missing from magazines today?

3. If you were the marketing director of your favorite magazine, how would you increase circulation through the use of digital editions?

4. Think of stories, ideas, and images (illustrations and photos) that did not appear in mainstream magazines. Why do you think this is so? (Use the Internet, Lexis-Nexis, or the library to compare your list with Project Censored, an annual list of the year's most under-reported stories.)

5. Discuss whether your favorite magazines define you primarily as a consumer or as a citizen. Do you think magazines have a responsibility to educate their readers as both? What can they do to promote responsible citizenship?

6. Do you think touchscreen tablet editions will be a successful format for magazines? Why or why not?

ADDITIONAL VIDEOS

Visit the Ⓒ VideoCentral: Mass Communication *section at* bedfordstmartins.com/mediaculture *for additional exclusive videos related to the issues discussed in Chapter 9.*

The History of Books from Papyrus to Paperbacks

Before books, or writing in general, oral cultures passed on information and values through the wisdom and memories of a community's elders or tribal storytellers. Sometimes these rich traditions were lost. Print culture and the book, however, gave future generations different and often more enduring records of authors' words.

Ever since the ancient Babylonians and Egyptians began experimenting with alphabets some five thousand years ago, people have found ways to preserve their written symbols. These first alphabets mark the development stage for books. Initially, pictorial symbols and letters were drawn on wood strips or pressed with a stylus into clay tablets, and tied or stacked together to form the first "books." As early as 2400 B.C.E., the Egyptians wrote on **papyrus** (from which the word *paper* is derived), made from plant reeds found along the Nile River. They rolled these writings in scrolls, much as builders do today with blueprints. This method was adopted by the Greeks in 650 B.C.E. and by the Romans (who imported papyrus from Egypt) in 300 B.C.E. Gradually, **parchment**–treated animal skin–replaced papyrus in Europe. Parchment was stronger, smoother, more durable, and less expensive because it did not have to be imported from Egypt.

At about the same time the Egyptians started using papyrus, the Babylonians recorded business transactions, government records, favorite stories, and local history on small tablets of clay. Around 1000 B.C.E., the Chinese also began creating booklike objects, using strips of wood and bamboo tied together in bundles. Although the Chinese began making paper from cotton and linen around 105 C.E., paper did not replace parchment in Europe until the thirteenth century because of questionable durability.

▼ **Books and the Power of Print**

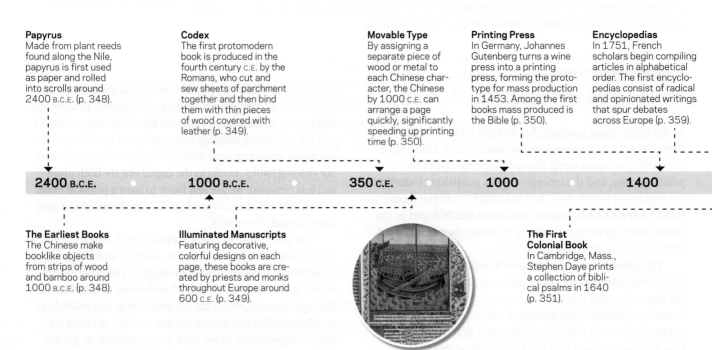

Papyrus
Made from plant reeds found along the Nile, papyrus is first used as paper and rolled into scrolls around 2400 B.C.E. (p. 348).

Codex
The first protomodern book is produced in the fourth century C.E. by the Romans, who cut and sew sheets of parchment together and then bind them with thin pieces of wood covered with leather (p. 349).

Movable Type
By assigning a separate piece of wood or metal to each Chinese character, the Chinese by 1000 C.E. can arrange a page quickly, significantly speeding up printing time (p. 350).

Printing Press
In Germany, Johannes Gutenberg turns a wine press into a printing press, forming the prototype for mass production in 1453. Among the first books mass produced is the Bible (p. 350).

Encyclopedias
In 1751, French scholars begin compiling articles in alphabetical order. The first encyclopedias consist of radical and opinionated writings that spur debates across Europe (p. 359).

2400 B.C.E.   **1000** B.C.E.   **350** C.E.   **1000**   **1400**

The Earliest Books
The Chinese make booklike objects from strips of wood and bamboo around 1000 B.C.E. (p. 348).

Illuminated Manuscripts
Featuring decorative, colorful designs on each page, these books are created by priests and monks throughout Europe around 600 C.E. (p. 349).

The First Colonial Book
In Cambridge, Mass., Stephen Daye prints a collection of biblical psalms in 1640 (p. 351).

The first protomodern book was probably produced in the fourth century by the Romans, who created the **codex**, a type of book made of sheets of parchment and sewn together along the edge, then bound with thin pieces of wood and covered with leather. Whereas scrolls had to be wound, unwound, and rewound, a codex could be opened to any page, and its configuration allowed writing on both sides of a page.

The Development of Manuscript Culture

During the Middle Ages (400-1500 C.E.), the Christian clergy strongly influenced what is known as **manuscript culture**, a period in which books were painstakingly lettered, decorated, and bound by hand. This period also marks the entrepreneurial stage in the evolution of books. During this time, priests and monks advanced the art of bookmaking; in many ways, they may be considered the earliest professional editors. Known as *scribes*, they transcribed most of the existing philosophical tracts and religious texts of the period, especially versions of the Bible. Through tedious and painstaking work, scribes became the chief caretakers of recorded history and culture, promoting ideas they favored and censoring ideas that were out of line with contemporary Christian thought.

Many books from the Middle Ages were **illuminated manuscripts**. These books featured decorative, colorful designs and illustrations on each page, often made for churches or wealthy clients. Their covers were made from leather, and some were embedded with precious gems or trimmed with gold and silver. During this period, scribes developed rules of punctuation, making distinctions between small and capital letters, and placing space between words to make reading easier. (Older Roman writing used all capital letters, and the words ran together on a page, making reading a torturous experience.) Hundreds of illuminated manuscripts still survive today in the rare book collections of museums and libraries.

> "All good books are alike in that they are truer than if they had really happened and after you are finished reading one you will feel that all that happened . . . belongs to you: the good and the bad, the ecstasy, the remorse and sorrow, the people and the places and how the weather was."
>
> ERNEST HEMINGWAY, *ESQUIRE* MAGAZINE, 1934

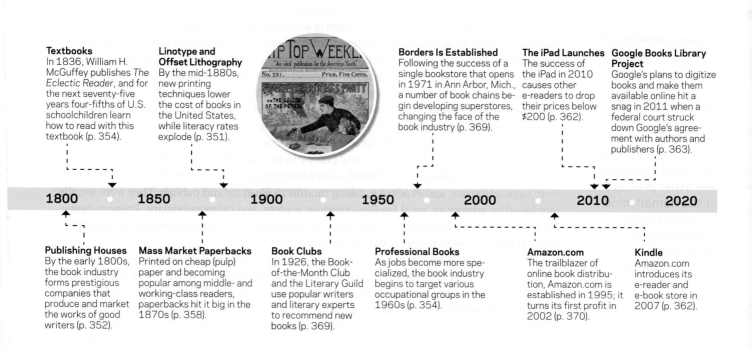

Textbooks
In 1836, William H. McGuffey publishes *The Eclectic Reader*, and for the next seventy-five years four-fifths of U.S. schoolchildren learn how to read with this textbook (p. 354).

Linotype and Offset Lithography
By the mid-1880s, new printing techniques lower the cost of books in the United States, while literacy rates explode (p. 351).

Borders Is Established
Following the success of a single bookstore that opens in 1971 in Ann Arbor, Mich., a number of book chains begin developing superstores, changing the face of the book industry (p. 369).

The iPad Launches
The success of the iPad in 2010 causes other e-readers to drop their prices below $200 (p. 362).

Google Books Library Project
Google's plans to digitize books and make them available online hit a snag in 2011 when a federal court struck down Google's agreement with authors and publishers (p. 363).

1800 1850 1900 1950 2000 2010 2020

Publishing Houses
By the early 1800s, the book industry forms prestigious companies that produce and market the works of good writers (p. 352).

Mass Market Paperbacks
Printed on cheap (pulp) paper and becoming popular among middle- and working-class readers, paperbacks hit it big in the 1870s (p. 358).

Book Clubs
In 1926, the Book-of-the-Month Club and the Literary Guild use popular writers and literary experts to recommend new books (p. 369).

Professional Books
As jobs become more specialized, the book industry begins to target various occupational groups in the 1960s (p. 354).

Amazon.com
The trailblazer of online book distribution, Amazon.com is established in 1995; it turns its first profit in 2002 (p. 370).

Kindle
Amazon.com introduces its e-reader and e-book store in 2007 (p. 362).

As an alternative, some enterprising students have developed Web sites to trade, resell, and rent textbooks. Other students have turned to online purchasing, either through e-commerce sites like Amazon.com, BarnesandNoble.com, and eBay.com, or through college textbook sellers like eCampus.com and textbooks.com, or through book renters like Chegg.com.

Mass Market Paperbacks

Unlike the larger-size trade paperbacks, which are sold mostly in bookstores, **mass market paperbacks** are sold on racks in drugstores, supermarkets, and airports as well as in bookstores. Contemporary mass market paperbacks—often the work of blockbuster authors such as Stephen King, Nora Roberts, Patricia Cornwell, and John Grisham—represent a large segment of the industry in terms of units sold, but because the books are low priced (under $10), they generate less revenue than trade books. Moreover, mass market paperbacks have experienced declining sales in recent years because bookstore chains prefer to display and promote the more expensive trade paperback and hardbound books, and e-books are becoming more popular for travelers.

Paperbacks became popular in the 1870s, mostly with middle- and working-class readers. This phenomenon sparked fear and outrage among those in the professional and educated classes, many of whom thought that reading cheap westerns and crime novels might ruin civilization. Some of the earliest paperbacks ripped off foreign writers, who were unprotected by copyright law and did not receive royalties for the books they sold in the United States. This changed with the International Copyright Law of 1891, which mandated that any work by any author could not be reproduced without the author's permission.

The popularity of paperbacks hit a major peak in 1939 with the establishment of Pocket Books by Robert de Graff. Revolutionizing the paperback industry, Pocket Books lowered the standard book price of fifty or seventy-five cents to twenty-five cents. To accomplish this, de Graff cut bookstore discounts from 30 to 20 percent, the book distributor's share fell from 46 to 36 percent of the cover price, and author royalty rates went from 10 to 4 percent. In its first three weeks, Pocket Books sold 100,000 books in New York City alone. Among its first titles was *Wake Up and Live* by Dorothea Brande, a 1936 best-seller on self-improvement that ignited an early wave of self-help books. Pocket Books also published *The Murder of Roger Ackroyd* by Agatha Christie; *Enough Rope*, a collection of poems by Dorothy Parker; and *Five Great Tragedies* by Shakespeare. Pocket Books' success spawned a series of imitators, including Dell, Fawcett, and Bantam Books.[8]

A major innovation of mass market paperback publishers was the **instant book**, a marketing strategy that involved publishing a topical book quickly after a major event occurred. Pocket Books produced the first instant book, *Franklin Delano Roosevelt: A Memorial*, six days after FDR's death in 1945. Similar to made-for-TV movies and television programs that capitalize on contemporary events, instant books enabled the industry to better compete with newspapers and magazines. Such books, however, like their TV counterparts, have been accused of circulating shoddy writing, exploiting tragedies, and avoiding in-depth analysis and historical perspective. Instant books have also made government reports into best-sellers. In 1964, Bantam published *The Report of the Warren Commission on the Assassination of President Kennedy*. After receiving the 385,000-word report on a Friday afternoon, Bantam staffers immediately began editing the Warren Report, and the book was produced within a week, ultimately selling over 1.6 million copies. Today, instant books continue to capitalize on contemporary events, including Hurricane Katrina in 2005, the inauguration of Barack Obama in 2009, and the wedding of Prince William and Kate Middleton in 2011.

Religious Books

The best-selling book of all time is the Bible, in all its diverse versions. Over the years, the success of Bible sales has created a large industry for religious books. After World War II, sales of religious books soared. Historians attribute the sales boom to economic growth and a nation seeking peace and security while facing the threat of "godless communism" and the Soviet Union.[9] By the 1960s, though, the scene had changed dramatically. The impact of the Civil Rights struggle, the Vietnam War, the sexual revolution, and the youth rebellion against authority led to declines in formal church membership. Not surprisingly, sales of some types of religious books dropped as well. To compete, many religious-book publishers extended their offerings to include serious secular titles on such topics as war and peace, race, poverty, gender, and civic responsibility.

Throughout this period of change, the publication of fundamentalist and evangelical literature remained steady. It then expanded rapidly during the 1980s, when the Republican Party began making political overtures to conservative groups and prominent TV evangelists. After a record year in 2004 (twenty-one thousand new titles), there has been a slight decline in the religious-book category. However, it continues to be an important part of the book industry, especially during turbulent social times.

Reference Books

Another major division of the book industry–**reference books**–includes dictionaries, encyclopedias, atlases, almanacs, and a number of substantial volumes directly related to particular professions or trades, such as legal casebooks and medical manuals.

The two most common reference books are encyclopedias and dictionaries. The idea of developing encyclopedic writings to document the extent of human knowledge is attributed to the Greek philosopher Aristotle. The Roman citizen Pliny the Elder (23-79 C.E.) wrote the oldest reference work still in existence, *Historia Naturalis*, detailing thousands of facts about animals, minerals, and plants. But it wasn't until the early 1700s that the compilers of encyclopedias began organizing articles in alphabetical order and relying on specialists to contribute essays in their areas of interest. Between 1751 and 1771, a group of French scholars produced the first multiple-volume set of encyclopedias.

The oldest English-language encyclopedia still in production, the *Encyclopaedia Britannica*, was first published in Scotland in 1768. U.S. encyclopedias followed, including *Encyclopedia Americana* (1829), *The World Book Encyclopedia* (1917), and *Compton's Pictured Encyclopedia* (1922). *Encyclopaedia Britannica* produced its first U.S. edition in 1908. This best-selling encyclopedia's sales dwindled in the 1990s due to competition from electronic encyclopedias (like Microsoft's *Encarta*), and it went digital too. *Encyclopaedia Britannica*, *Encarta*, and *The World Book Encyclopedia* are now the leading online and CD-based encyclopedias, although even they struggle today as young researchers increasingly rely on search engines such as Google or online resources like Wikipedia to find information (though many critics consider these sources inferior in quality).

Dictionaries have also accounted for a large portion of reference sales. The earliest dictionaries were produced by ancient scholars attempting to document specialized and rare words. During the manuscript period in the Middle Ages, however, European scribes and monks began creating glossaries and dictionaries to help people understand Latin. In 1604, a British schoolmaster prepared the first English dictionary. In 1755, Samuel Johnson produced the *Dictionary of the English Language*. Describing rather than prescribing word usage, Johnson was among the first to understand that language changes–that words and usage cannot be fixed for all time. In the United States in 1828, Noah Webster, using Johnson's work as a model, published the *American Dictionary of the English Language*, differentiating between British and American usages and simplifying spelling (for example, *colour* became *color* and *musick* became *music*). As with encyclopedias, dictionaries have moved mostly to online formats since the 1990s, and they struggle to compete with free online or built-in word-processing software dictionaries.

"Wikipedia, or any free information resources, challenge reference publishers to be better than free. . . . It isn't enough for a publisher to simply provide information, we have to add value."

TOM RUSSELL, RANDOM HOUSE REFERENCE PUBLISHER, 2007

University Press Books

The smallest division in the book industry is the nonprofit **university press**, which publishes scholarly works for small groups of readers interested in intellectually specialized areas such as literary theory and criticism, history of art movements, contemporary philosophy, and the like. Professors often try to secure book contracts from reputable university presses to increase their chances for *tenure*, a lifetime teaching contract. Some university presses are very small, producing as few as ten titles a year. The largest–the University of Chicago Press–regularly publishes more than two hundred titles a year. One of the oldest and most prestigious presses is Harvard University Press, formally founded in 1913 but claiming roots that go back to 1640, when Stephen Daye published the first colonial book in a small shop located behind the house of Harvard's president.

University presses have not traditionally faced pressure to produce commercially viable books, preferring to encourage books about highly specialized topics by innovative thinkers. In fact, most university presses routinely lose money and are subsidized by their university. Even when they publish more commercially accessible titles, the lack of large marketing budgets prevents them from reaching mass audiences. While large commercial trade houses are often criticized for publishing only blockbuster books, university presses often suffer the opposite criticism–that they produce mostly obscure books that only a handful of scholars read. To offset costs and increase revenue, some presses are trying to form alliances with commercial houses to help promote and produce academic books that have wider appeal.

Trends and Issues in Book Publishing

Ever since Harriet Beecher Stowe's abolitionist novel *Uncle Tom's Cabin* sold fifteen thousand copies in fifteen days back in 1852 (and three million total copies prior to the Civil War), many American publishers have stalked the *best-seller*, or blockbuster (just like in the movie business). While most authors are professional writers, the book industry also reaches out to famous media figures, who may pen a best-selling book (Ellen DeGeneres, Jerry Seinfeld, Bill Clinton) or a commercial failure (Whoopi Goldberg, Jay Leno). Other ways publishers attempt to ensure popular success involve acquiring the rights to license popular film and television programs or experimenting with formats like audio and e-books. In addition to selling new books, other industry issues include the preservation of older books and the history of banned books and censorship.

Influences of Television and Film

There are two major facets in the relationship among books, television, and film: how TV can help sell books and how books serve as ideas for TV shows and movies. Through TV exposure, books by or about talk-show hosts, actors, and politicians such as Stephen Colbert, Julie Andrews, Barack Obama, and Hillary Clinton sell millions of copies–enormous sales in a business where 100,000 in sales constitutes remarkable success. In national polls conducted from the 1980s through today, nearly 30 percent of respondents said they had read a book after seeing the story or a promotion on television.

One of the most influential forces in promoting books on TV was Oprah Winfrey. Even before the development of Oprah's Book Club in 1996, Oprah's afternoon talk show had become a major power broker in selling books. In 1993, for example, Holocaust survivor and Nobel Prize recipient Elie Wiesel appeared on *Oprah*. Afterward, his 1960 memoir, *Night*, which had been issued as a Bantam paperback in 1982, returned to the best-seller lists. In 1996, novelist Toni Morrison's nineteen-year-old book *Song of Solomon* became a paperback best-seller after Morrison appeared on *Oprah*. In 1998, after Winfrey brought Morrison's *Beloved* to movie screens, the book version was back on the best-seller lists. Each Oprah's Book Club selection became an immediate best-seller, generating tremendous excitement within the book industry. *The Oprah Winfrey Show* ended in 2011.

The film industry gets many of its story ideas from books, which results in enormous movie rights revenues for the book industry and its authors. Nicholas Sparks's *The Lucky One* (2008), Yann Martel's *Life of Pi* (2001), and J. R. R. Tolkein's *The Hobbit* (1937), for instance, became highly successful motion pictures in 2012. But the most profitable movie successes for the book industry in recent years emerged from fantasy works. J. K. Rowling's best-selling Harry Potter books have become hugely popular movies, as has Peter Jackson's film trilogy of J. R. R. Tolkien's enduringly popular *Lord of the Rings* (first published in the 1950s). The *Twilight* movie series has created a huge surge in sales of Stephanie Meyer's four-book saga, a success repeated by Suzanne Collins's *The Hunger Games*, which had the first movie in a planned series of four debut in 2012. Books have also inspired popular television programs, including *Game of Thrones* on HBO, *Dexter* on Showtime, *Gossip Girl* on CW, and *Pretty Little Liars* on ABC Family. In each case, the television shows boosted the sales of the original books, too. Journalist H. G. Bissinger's *Friday Night Lights: A Town, a Team, and a Dream* (1990), chronicling the story of a West Texas high school football team, inspired a 2004 film and then a 2006-2011 television series. The movie and television versions then spawned special editions of the book and frequent reprintings as the book became a classic sports account.

Audio Books

Another major development in publishing has been the merger of sound recording with publishing. *Audio books*–also known as talking books or books on tape–generally feature actors or authors reading entire works or abridged versions of popular fiction and nonfiction trade books. Indispensable to many sightless readers and older readers whose vision is diminished, audio books are also popular among regular readers who do a lot of commuter driving or who want to listen to a book at home while doing something else–like exercising. The number of audio books borrowed from libraries soared in the 1990s and early 2000s, and small bookstore chains developed to cater to the audio book niche. Audio books are now readily available on the Internet for downloading to iPods and other portable devices. Four hundred-plus new audio books are available annually.

Convergence: Books in the Digital Age

In 1971, Michael Hart, a student computer operator at the University of Illinois, typed up the text of the U.S. Declaration of Independence, and thus, the idea of the **e-book**–a digital book read on a computer or a digital reading device–was born. Hart soon founded Project

THE GREAT GATSBY, the classic American novel by F. Scott Fitzgerald, has been filmed several times, including a silent film in 1926 and a version with Robert Redford in 1974. The newest adaptation, directed by Baz Luhrmann and starring Tobey Maguire, Carey Mulligan, and Leonardo DiCaprio, arrived in 2012.

"Over 1,250 books, novels, short stories, and plays . . . have been released as feature-length films in the United States, in English, since 1980."

MID-CONTINENT PUBLIC LIBRARY, "BASED ON THE BOOK" DATABASE, 2011

"It is exciting to
contemplate a
future where the
cultural heritage
of our country is
available at your
fingertips."

DAVID FERRIERO,
ARCHIVIST OF THE
UNITED STATES OF
AMERICA, 2011

"But a digital *public
library* is quite a
different thing
than what Google
has undertaken
with its attempts
to digitize every
book ever printed.
After all, a digital
library won't be
just about storing
content, but it will
be about making
that content
accessible."

AUDREY WATTERS,
READWRITEWEB.COM,
2011

Gutenberg, which now offers more than forty thousand public domain books (older texts with expired copyrights) for free at www.gutenberg.org. Yet the idea of *commercial e-books*–putting copyrighted books like current best-sellers in digital form–took a lot longer to gain traction.

Print Books Move Online

Early portable reading devices from RCA and Sony in the 1990s were criticized for being too heavy, too expensive, or too difficult to read, while their e-book titles were scarce and had little cost advantage over full-price hardcover books. It is no surprise that these e-readers and e-books didn't catch on. Then in 2007, Amazon.com, the largest online bookseller, developed an e-reader (the Kindle) and an e-book store that seemed inspired by Apple's music industry-changing iPod and iTunes. The first Kindle had an easy-on-the-eyes electronic paper display, held more than two hundred books, and did something no other device could do before: wirelessly download e-books from Amazon's online bookstore. Moreover, most Kindle e-books sold for $9.99, less than half the price of most new hardcovers. This time, e-books caught on quickly, and Amazon couldn't make Kindles fast enough to keep up with demand. (To learn more about the controversy over e-book pricing, see "Tracking Technology–Paper Trail: Did Publishers and Apple Collude against Amazon?" on p. 364.)

Amazon has continued to refine its e-reader, and in 2011 it introduced the Kindle Fire, a color touchscreen tablet with Web browsing, access to all the media on Amazon, and the Amazon Appstore. The Kindle devices are the best-selling products ever on Amazon. Of course, the Kindle is no longer the only portable reading device on the market. Apps have transformed the iPod Touch, iPhone, and other smartphones into e-readers. In 2010, Apple introduced the iPad, a color touchscreen tablet that quickly outsold the Kindle. The immediate initial success of the iPad (introduced at a starting price of $499 and up), which sold three million units in less than three months, spurred other e-readers to drop their prices below $200. Before Amazon's Kindle Fire, other devices–like the Barnes & Noble Nook–have mimicked the iPad by adding color, e-mail, and an app store.

By 2012, e-books became the best-selling adult fiction book format in the United States (in terms of revenue), accounting for 15 percent of all books sold. Projections indicate that the figure could increase to 50 percent of the market by 2015.[10] But perhaps the best indicator that e-books are here to stay is that the *New York Times* launched a new weekly e-book best-seller list in February 2011. As the market grows rapidly, several companies are vying to be the biggest seller of e-books. Apple's iBookstore serves the iPad, iPod, and iPhone exclusively. Amazon and Barnes & Noble sell e-books for their readers but also have apps for other devices so that, for example, an iPad user could buy e-books from their stores. Google started its own e-book store (now Google Play) that enables customers to access its cloud-based e-books anywhere via any device, a feature that Amazon and Apple also now have.

The Future of E-Books

E-books are demonstrating how digital technology can help the oldest mass medium adapt and survive. Distributors, publishers, and bookstores also use digital technology to print books on demand, reviving books that would otherwise go out of print and avoiding the inconveniences of carrying unsold books. But perhaps the most exciting part of e-books is their potential for reimagining what a book can be. Computers or tablet touchscreens such as an iPad can host e-books with embedded video, hyperlinks, and dynamic content, enabling, for example, a professor to reorganize, add, or delete content of an e-textbook to tailor it to the needs of a specific class. Children's books may also never be the same. An *Alice in Wonderland* e-book developed for the iPad uses the device's motion and touchscreen technologies to make "the pop-up book of the 21st-century." Such developments are changing the reading experience: "users don't just flip the 'pages' of the e-book–they're meant to shake it, turn it, twist it, jiggle it, and watch the characters and settings in the book react."[11] E-books have also made the distribution of long-form journalism and novellas easier with products like the inexpensive Kindle Singles.

Preserving and Digitizing Books

Another recent trend in the book industry involves the preservation of older books, especially those from the nineteenth century printed on acid-based paper, which gradually deteriorates. At the turn of the twentieth century, research initiated by libraries concerned with losing valuable older collections provided evidence that acid-based paper would eventually turn brittle and self-destruct. The paper industry, however, did not respond, so in the 1970s leading libraries began developing techniques to halt any further deterioration (although this process could not restore books to their original state). Finally, by the early 1990s, motivated almost entirely by economics rather than by the cultural value of books, the paper industry began producing acid-free paper. Libraries and book conservationists, however, still had to focus attention on older, at-risk books. Some institutions began photocopying original books onto acid-free paper and made the copies available to the public. Libraries then stored the originals, which were treated to halt further wear.

Another way to preserve books is through digital imaging. The most extensive digitization project, the Google Books Library Project, which began in 2004, features partnerships with the New York Public Library and about twenty major university research libraries—including Harvard, Michigan, Oxford, and Stanford—to scan millions of books and make them available online. The Authors Guild and the Association of American Publishers initially sued Google for digitizing copyrighted books without permission. Google argued that displaying only a limited portion of the books was legal under "fair use" rules. Both sides forged an agreement in 2008 with Google, authors, and publishers sharing the revenue. But in 2011, a federal court struck down the agreement, arguing that it gave Google too much power to profit from millions of books for which Google didn't first obtain copyright permission. An alternative group, dissatisfied by the Google Books Library Project restricting its scanned book content from use by other commercial search services, started a nonprofit service in 2007. The Open Content Alliance is working with the Boston Public Library, several New England university libraries, Amazon, Microsoft, and Yahoo! to digitize millions of books with expired copyrights and make them freely available on the Internet Archive's Open Library. In 2010, they joined other libraries to plan what would be called the Digital Public Library of America.

Censorship and Banned Books

Over time, the wide circulation of books gave many ordinary people the same opportunities to learn that were once available to only a privileged few. However, as societies discovered the power associated with knowledge and the printed word, books were subjected to a variety of censors. Imposed by various rulers and groups intent on maintaining their authority, the censorship of books often prevented people from learning about the rituals and moral standards of other cultures. Political censors sought to banish "dangerous" books that promoted

▲

E-BOOKS have opened up many new possibilities for children's books and are even going so far as to redefine how a book looks and acts. The classic *Alice in Wonderland* has been reimagined into a fully interactive experience. You can tilt your iPad to make Alice grow bigger or smaller, and shake your iPad to make the Mad Hatter even madder.

Finally, because e-books make publishing and distribution costs low, **e-publishing** has enabled authors to sidestep traditional publishers. A new breed of large Internet-based publishing houses, such as Xlibris, iUniverse, Hillcrest Media, Amazon's CreateSpace, and AuthorSolutions, design and distribute books for a comparatively small price for aspiring authors who want to self-publish a title, which can even be formatted for the Kindle or iPad. Although sales are typically low for such books, the low overhead costs allow higher royalty rates for the authors and lower retail prices for readers.

Sometimes self-published books make it to the best-seller lists. British writer E. L. James's blockbuster erotic novel *Fifty Shades of Grey* was first written as fan fiction, posted to a busy *Twilight* fan forum beginning in 2009, where thousands read and commented on it. In 2012, Vintage bought the rights to *The Fifty Shades* trilogy for more than $1 million. Amanda Hocking, a writer in her mid-twenties from Minnesota, wrote several paranormal romance e-books that attracted attention from several publishers, and she signed a seven-figure advance contract with St. Martin's Press.[18] Some traditional publishers are considering the straight-to-e-book route themselves. Little, Brown & Company released Pete Hamill's *They Are Us* in digital format only.

Books and the Future of Democracy

As we enter the digital age, the book-reading habits of children and adults have become a social concern. After all, books have played an important role not only in spreading the idea of democracy but also in connecting us to new ideas beyond our local experience. The impact of our oldest mass medium—the book—remains immense. Without the development of printing presses and books, the idea of democracy would be hard to imagine. From the impact of Harriet Beecher Stowe's *Uncle Tom's Cabin*, which helped bring an end to slavery in the 1860s, to Rachel Carson's *Silent Spring*, which led to reforms in the pesticide industry in the 1960s, books have made a difference. They have told us things that we wanted—and needed—to know, and inspired us to action. And quite suddenly, Americans are reading more again. In a sharp turnaround from a decade earlier, a 2009 National Endowment for the Arts (NEA) study, *Reading on the Rise*, reported that "for the first time in the history of the survey—conducted five times since 1982—the overall rate at which adults read literature (novels and short stories, plays, or poems) rose by seven percent." Interestingly, the most rapid increase in literary reading was in young adults age eighteen to twenty-four, with significant increases among Hispanic and African American populations, and with fiction accounting for the new growth in all adult literary readers. The NEA surmised that millions of parents, teachers, librarians, and community leaders who endorsed reading and reading programs spurred the increase in reading. The survey found that America is basically divided in half: About 50 percent of Americans can be considered readers, and about 50 percent are nonreaders. Moreover, the NEA report noted

GOOD READS is a "social cataloging" site that merges the sometimes solitary act of reading with social media. Users can keep track of books they've read, write reviews, and recommend titles to others.

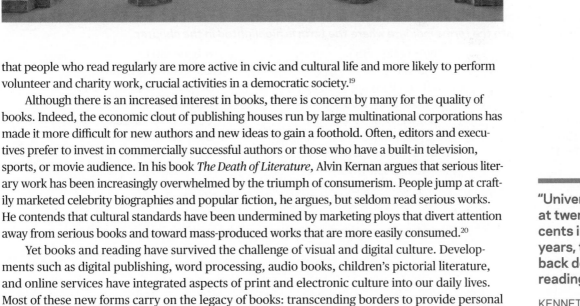

CARNEGIE LIBRARIES
The Carnegie Library of Pittsburgh was first opened in 1895 with a $1 million donation from Andrew Carnegie (at the time it was called Main Library). In total, eight branches were built in Pittsburgh as "Carnegie Libraries."

that people who read regularly are more active in civic and cultural life and more likely to perform volunteer and charity work, crucial activities in a democratic society.[19]

Although there is an increased interest in books, there is concern by many for the quality of books. Indeed, the economic clout of publishing houses run by large multinational corporations has made it more difficult for new authors and new ideas to gain a foothold. Often, editors and executives prefer to invest in commercially successful authors or those who have a built-in television, sports, or movie audience. In his book *The Death of Literature*, Alvin Kernan argues that serious literary work has been increasingly overwhelmed by the triumph of consumerism. People jump at craftily marketed celebrity biographies and popular fiction, he argues, but seldom read serious works. He contends that cultural standards have been undermined by marketing ploys that divert attention away from serious books and toward mass-produced works that are more easily consumed.[20]

Yet books and reading have survived the challenge of visual and digital culture. Developments such as digital publishing, word processing, audio books, children's pictorial literature, and online services have integrated aspects of print and electronic culture into our daily lives. Most of these new forms carry on the legacy of books: transcending borders to provide personal stories, world history, and general knowledge to all who can read.

Since the early days of the printing press, books have helped us to understand ideas and customs outside our own experiences. For democracy to work well, we must read. When we examine other cultures through books, we discover not only who we are and what we value but also who others are and what our common ties might be. ▶

"Universally priced at twenty-five cents in its early years, the paperback democratized reading in America."

KENNETH DAVIS,
TWO-BIT CULTURE, 1984

CHAPTER REVIEW

COMMON THREADS

One of the Common Threads discussed in Chapter 1 is about the commercial nature of the mass media convergence. Books have been products of a publishing industry in the United States at least since the early 1800s, but with the advent of digital technologies, the structure of the publishing industry is either evolving or dying. Is that a good or bad thing for the future of books?

Since the popularization of Gutenberg's printing press, there has always been some kind of gatekeeper in the publishing industry. Initially, it was religious institutions (e.g., determining what would constitute the books of the Bible), then intellectuals, educators, and—with the development of publishing houses in the early 1800s—a fully formed commercial publishing industry.

Now, with the digital turn in publishing, anyone can be an author. Clay Shirky, a digital theorist at New York University, argues that this completely undercuts the work of publishers. "Publishing is going away," Shirky says. "Because the word 'publishing' means a cadre of professionals who are taking on the incredible difficulty and complexity and expense of making something public. That's not a job anymore. That's a button. There's a button that says

'publish,' and when you press it, it's done."[21] Indeed, self-publishing is already a huge part of what the industry has become. As the *New York Times* noted, "Nearly 350,000 new print titles were published in 2011, and 150,000 to 200,000 of them were produced by self-publishing companies."[22] (Table 10.1 lists about 177,000 books published in 2011, so nearly that many more books were self-published in the same year.)

More books in circulation is great for democracy, for the inclusion of more voices. But is there still value to the acquisition, editing, and marketing of books that publishers do? Are these traditional gatekeepers worth keeping around? Is it a legitimate concern that the quality of book content will suffer without publishers to find, develop, and promote the work of the best authors?

KEY TERMS

The definitions for the terms listed below can be found in the glossary at the end of the book. The page numbers listed with the terms indicate where the term is highlighted in the chapter.

papyrus, 348
parchment, 348
codex, 349
manuscript culture, 349
illuminated manuscripts, 349
block printing, 350
printing press, 350
vellum, 350
paperback books, 351
dime novels, 351

pulp fiction, 351
linotype, 351
offset lithography, 351
trade books, 353
professional books, 354
textbooks, 354
mass market paperbacks, 358
instant book, 358
reference books, 359
university press, 360

e-book, 361
book challenge, 365
acquisitions editors, 367
subsidiary rights, 367
developmental editor, 368
copy editors, 368
design managers, 368
e-publishing, 372

For review quizzes, chapter summaries, links to media-related Web sites, and more, go to bedfordstmartins.com/mediaculture.

REVIEW QUESTIONS

The History of Books from Papyrus to Paperbacks

1. What distinguishes the manuscript culture of the Middle Ages from the oral and print eras in communication?

2. Why was the printing press such an important and revolutionary invention?

3. Why were books particularly important to women readers during the early periods of American history?

Modern Publishing and the Book Industry

4. Why did publishing houses develop?

5. Why is the trade book segment one of the most lucrative parts of the book industry?

6. What are the major issues that affect textbook publishing?

7. What has undermined the sales of printed and CD encyclopedias?

8. What is the relationship between the book and movie industries?

9. Why did the Kindle succeed in the e-book market where other devices had failed?

Trends and Issues in Book Publishing

10. In what ways have e-books reimagined what a book can be?

11. What are the major issues in the debate over digitizing millions of books for Web search engines?

12. What's the difference between a book that is challenged and one that is banned?

The Organization and Ownership of the Book Industry

13. What are the current ownership patterns in the book industry? How do they affect the kinds of books that are published?

14. What are the general divisions within a typical publishing house?

15. What was the impact of the growth of book superstores on the rest of the bookstore industry?

16. How have online bookstores and e-books affected bookstores and the publishing industry?

17. What are the concerns over Amazon's powerful role in determining book pricing and having its own publishing divisions?

18. What is Andrew Carnegie's legacy in regard to libraries in the United States and elsewhere?

Books and the Future of Democracy

19. Why is an increasing interest in reading a signal for improved democratic life?

QUESTIONING THE MEDIA

1. As books shift to being digital, what advantages of the bound-book format are we sacrificing?

2. Given the digital turn in the book industry, if you were to self-publish a book, what strategies would you take in marketing and distribution to help an audience find it?

3. Imagine that you are on a committee that oversees book choices for a high school library in your town. What policies do you think should guide the committee's selection of controversial books?

4. Why do you think the availability of television and cable hasn't substantially decreased the number of new book titles available each year? What do books offer that television doesn't?

5. Would you read a book on a) a computer, b) a phone, or c) a tablet? Why or why not?

ADDITIONAL VIDEOS

Visit the Ⓥ VideoCentral: Mass Communication *section at* bedfordstmartins.com/mediaculture *for additional exclusive videos related to Chapter 10, including:*

- TURNING THE PAGE: BOOKS GO DIGITAL
  Authors discuss how e-books are changing both how books are consumed and how they are written.

PART 4

The Business of Mass Media

The digital turn has brought about a shift in the locus of power in the mass media. For decades, the mass media have been dominated by giant corporations—such as Comcast (NBC Universal), Disney, Time Warner, News Corp., and CBS—that created the music, television, movies, and publications we consumed. Now a new digital market has grown up around them, displacing the way traditional mass media businesses operate, changing how advertising and public relations work, and breaking down the barriers of entry to startup media companies:

- **Changes in the structure of media economics.** The legacy media conglomerates have long been accustomed to competing in a media environment of their own making. The music, movie, television, radio, magazine, newspaper, and book industries were populated by the content of their vast subsidiaries—Universal music, Disney television channels, Warner Bros. movies, Time Inc. magazines, and the like. In just a few short years, these traditional media companies have lost some of their power due to the rise of major digital companies like Apple, Amazon, Google, Microsoft, and Facebook. These digital corporations are the new media conglomerates, despite not owning major content creation companies. They control the devices and platforms that people use to access all of their media, thus controlling which media people consume. Traditional media companies now find themselves in a position where they have to work with these companies (even if they balk at the 30-percent cut that Apple takes, for example) or risk losing their audience. It's a contentious but mutually beneficial relationship; the digital companies need the content companies and vice versa. This is not a new story, though: Block booking in the early film industry, battles between broadcast and cable, and disputes between record labels and radio illustrate the ongoing struggles of rival media powers.

- **The new digital ecosystem for advertising and public relations.** Professional media communicators are negotiating new terrain in the digital age, too. Not only are they figuring out what kinds of advertising or PR campaigns work best in the age of social media and mobile devices, they also are dealing with an age in which it's much more difficult to control the flow of information and the framing of a story. This new environment can be good and bad. The good is that it doesn't take a lot of money to get your message out there, but the bad is that every PR gaffe or crisis is magnified. Similarly, digital media can identify audiences with greater precision (our Google searches and Facebook "likes" give away a lot about us), but they also make containing communications far more difficult. Everyone on the Internet is a potential customer, but also a potential public critic.

- **Democracy and the redistribution of power.** The digital turn has allowed for more voices, more companies, and more creative startups, reversing many earlier concerns of mass media conglomerates. Now, the entry to being a content creator is much easier: It's simple to get songs listed in the iTunes store, books placed in the Amazon catalog, and videos posted to YouTube. With information more available, it's also easier for citizens to actively respond to messages formerly controlled by advertising and public relations. Social media have unleashed an army of fact-checking critics who push for more transparent communication.

The Big Five Digital Companies

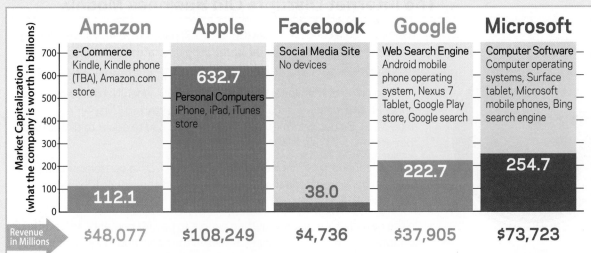

	Amazon	Apple	Facebook	Google	Microsoft
	e-Commerce		Social Media Site	Web Search Engine	Computer Software
	Kindle, Kindle phone (TBA), Amazon.com store	Personal Computers iPhone, iPad, iTunes store	No devices	Android mobile phone operating system, Nexus 7 Tablet, Google Play store, Google search	Computer operating systems, Surface tablet, Microsoft mobile phones, Bing search engine
Market Cap	112.1	632.7	38.0	222.7	254.7
Revenue in Millions	$48,077	$108,249	$4,736	$37,905	$73,723

Market Capitalization (what the company is worth in billions)

In 2012, as Apple's stock price soared, it became the most highly valued company in U.S. history–worth (by September) $632.7 billion. The stock price suggests that investors think Apple will continue to make money for a long time to come. How do Apple and its competitors make their money, and what are their contributions to the digital economy?

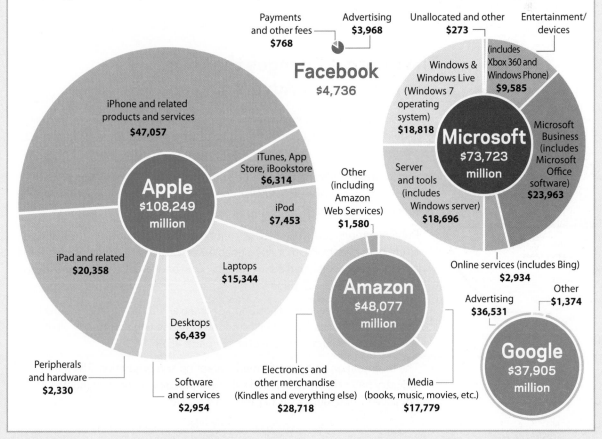

Facebook $4,736
- Payments and other fees $768
- Advertising $3,968

Apple $108,249 million
- iPhone and related products and services $47,057
- iTunes, App Store, iBookstore $6,314
- iPod $7,453
- Laptops $15,344
- Desktops $6,439
- Software and services $2,954
- Peripherals and hardware $2,330
- iPad and related $20,358

Amazon $48,077 million
- Other (including Amazon Web Services) $1,580
- Electronics and other merchandise (Kindles and everything else) $28,718
- Media (books, music, movies, etc.) $17,779

Microsoft $73,723 million
- Windows & Windows Live (Windows 7 operating system) $18,818
- Unallocated and other $273
- Entertainment/devices (includes Xbox 360 and Windows Phone) $9,585
- Microsoft Business (includes Microsoft Office software) $23,963
- Server and tools (includes Windows server) $18,696
- Online services (includes Bing) $2,934

Google $37,905 million
- Advertising $36,531
- Other $1,374

1 Consider your own media consumption. How many of these digital corporations do you interact with in a typical week? In what ways? Are those corporations and their products and services indispensable to your daily life?

See Notes for list of sources.

2 Can you imagine a scenario where one or more of these five corporations might not exist in five or ten years? What could go wrong that would turn people away from the company?

The Internet Disrupts Old Business Models

- The "old" media conglomerates (Chapter 13, pages 456–457) are learning to coexist with the "new" digital media conglomerates (Chapter 2, pages 62–66).

- The beginning of the digital turn arrived in 1999, when Napster was launched and massive illegal music file sharing started (Chapter 4, page 127). Since that time, every industry has had to adapt to digital media formats.

- Internet connectivity has moved digital gaming from a console- or computer-based experience to one that can be networked and mobile (Chapter 3, pages 85–88).

- In the new digital economy, getting people to pay for content can be difficult (Chapter 13, page 467). Pricing battles in the book industry (Chapter 10, page 362) and difficulty in getting people to pay for news (Chapter 8, pages 305–306) are some of the most significant upheavals in the industry.

The Internet Changes the Form and Function of Advertising and PR

- As more people carry smartphones, tablets, and other devices, advertising is quickly moving into mobile media, to reach us where we are (Chapter 11, pages 396–398).

- The Internet has transformed a longtime staple of public relations—the paper press release—into a collection of "remixable" multimedia elements (Chapter 12, pages 437–438).

- Public relations professionals have embraced social media for their ability to connect clients in a more personable way with their audiences. Yet, PR is careful about social media's immediacy: One bad tweet can turn viral almost instantly (Chapter 12, page 438).

- The low-budget search ads of Google have transformed that company into the largest advertising firm in the country—Google makes nearly all of its revenue from search ads (Chapter 13, page 469).

- The Internet has also transformed marketing and promotion. The movie industry has utilized social media campaigns to build interest months in advance of film releases (Chapter 7, page 266).

The Dark Side of Advertising and PR in the Digital Age

- The digital turn has made mass media so easy to access, we forget that the price is often turning over information about ourselves. Data mining cashes in on our personal information, often without our clear consent (Chapter 2, page 66).

- It's not always clear if someone advertising on social media is genuinely recommending a product, or is paid by a company to do so (Chapter 12, page 438).

- Digital advertising in video games (Chapter 3, page 97), television (Chapter 6, page 227), and movies (Chapter 7, page 264) generates greater revenue for media companies, but changes the narrative and experience of our media content.

- Is the tradeoff of greater access to digital media content worth the increasing invasion of our privacy (Extended Case Study, page 577)?

For more on Internet users creating their own content, watch the "User-Generated Content" video on *VideoCentral: Mass Communication* **at bedfordstmartins.com/mediaculture.**

Advertising and Commercial Culture

The year 2010 marked a significant moment for the future of advertising. First, Internet advertising revenue, fueled by continuing strong growth, surpassed newspaper advertising revenue. In just a decade, the Internet had become one of the major advertising media, with more than $26 billion in advertising revenue. Second, mobile advertising had grown big enough to gain the attention of the advertising industry. Although mobile advertising across North America only accounted for about $700 million in revenue in 2011, some of the largest media companies in the world made huge investments to bring many more ads to smartphone and tablet screens. These kinds of ads were estimated to rake in more than $5 billion in North America by 2015.[1] Within ten years, mobile advertising is likely to follow the trend set by Internet advertising. "Dollars always follow eyeballs," a media forecaster told the *Wall Street Journal*,[2] predicting that it was a matter of time before mobile became the next major advertising medium.

In this case, the "eyeballs" are on mobile media—smartphones and tablets. The two dominant players in this market are Google, with its Android platform, and Apple, with its line of iPhones, iPods, and iPads. Both companies have made significant investments in mobile advertising. Google, already the biggest advertising company in the world (95 percent of its $29.3 billion in revenue in 2010 came from Internet advertising), bought AdMob, a company that serves ads to mobile screens, for $750 million in 2010. With so many mobile phone and tablet devices from companies such as HTC, Samsung, LG, and Motorola using the Android platform, there is a ready network of devices available for Google's mobile advertising.

Meanwhile, Apple, an innovator in touchscreen devices, also purchased a mobile advertising firm, Quattro Wireless, for $275 million in early 2010. In April 2010, Apple unveiled its own mobile advertising platform, iAd, and soon after, Apple decided to shutter Quattro Wireless in order to focus all of its energies on developing iAd. By 2011, Apple regularly offered ads to iPhone and iPod Touch users that combine video and multimedia. Because Apple believes that most mobile-device customers are using apps, rather than surfing the Web or running Internet searches, the ads appear within the apps, and users don't need to exit the app in order to interact with the ad.

In December 2010, Apple debuted the iAd on the iPad—for the Disney blockbuster *Tron Legacy*. It featured nearly ten minutes of video, images from the film, a theater locator, and the option to preview and purchase the soundtrack—in fact, the ad almost functioned as an app itself. As Steve Jobs, Apple's late CEO, said, "iAd offers advertisers the emotion of TV with the interactivity of the web, and offers users a new way to explore ads without being hijacked out of their favorite apps."[3]

Mobile advertising is still in its infancy, but the competition for the attention of smartphone and tablet users will be intense, and is "the latest round in the new epic struggle between Apple and Google," according to *PCWorld* magazine.[4] These days, the two corporations are less about computers and search engines, and more about creating platforms to reach millions of consumers and tap into the multibillion-dollar advertising industry.

> "[With mobile ad campaigns] interactions, shares, 'likes,' texts, calls, stores located, apps downloaded, views, coupon redemptions, and impressions, are all possible success metrics—and nearly everything is measurable."
>
> INTERACTIVE ADVERTISING BUREAU, MARCH 2011

▲ *TODAY, ADVERTISEMENTS ARE EVERYWHERE AND IN EVERY MEDIA FORM.* Ads take up more than half the space in most daily newspapers and consumer magazines. They are inserted into trade books and textbooks. They clutter Web sites on the Internet. They fill our mailboxes and wallpaper the buses we ride. Dotting the nation's highways, billboards promote fast-food and hotel chains, while neon signs announce the names of stores along major streets and strip malls. Ads are even found in the restrooms of malls, restaurants, and bars.

At local theaters and on DVDs, ads now precede the latest Hollywood movie trailers. Corporate sponsors spend millions for **product placement**: buying spaces for particular goods to appear in a TV show, movie, or music video. Ads are part of a deejay's morning patter, and ads routinely interrupt our favorite TV and cable programs. In 2012, nearly 16 minutes and 20 seconds of each hour of prime-time network television carried commercials, program promos, and public service announcements–an increase from 13 minutes an hour in 1992. In addition, each hour of prime-time network TV carried about 11 minutes of product placements.[5] This means that about 26 minutes of each hour (or 43 percent) include some sort of paid sponsorship. According to the Food Marketing Institute, the typical supermarket's shelves are filled with thirty thousand to fifty thousand different brand-name packages, all functioning like miniature billboards. By some research estimates, the average American comes into contact with five thousand forms of advertising each day.[6]

Advertising comes in many forms, from classified ads to business-to-business ads, providing detailed information on specific products. However, in this chapter we concentrate on the more conspicuous advertisements that shape product images and brand-name identities. Because so much consumer advertising intrudes into daily life, ads are often viewed in a negative light. Although business managers agree that advertising is the foundation of a healthy media economy–far preferable to government-controlled media–audiences routinely complain about how many ads they are forced to endure, and they increasingly find ways to avoid them, like zipping through television ads with TiVo and blocking pop-up ads with Web browsers. In response, market researchers routinely weigh consumers' tolerance–how long an ad or how many ads they are willing to tolerate to get "free" media content. Without consumer advertisements, however, mass communication industries would cease to function in their present forms. Advertising is the economic glue that holds most media industries together.

In this chapter, we will:

- Examine the historical development of advertising–an industry that helped transform numerous nations into consumer societies
- Look at the first U.S. ad agencies; early advertisements; and the emergence of packaging, trademarks, and brand-name recognition
- Consider the growth of advertising in the last century, such as the increasing influence of ad agencies and the shift to a more visually oriented culture
- Outline the key persuasive techniques used in consumer advertising
- Investigate ads as a form of commercial speech, and discuss the measures aimed at regulating advertising
- Look at political advertising and its impact on democracy

It's increasingly rare to find spaces in our society that don't contain advertising. As you read this chapter, think about your own exposure to advertising. What are some things you like or admire about advertising? For example, are there particular ad campaigns that give you

THE "GOT MILK?" advertising campaign was originally designed by Goodby, Silverstein & Partners for the California Milk Processor Board in 1993. Since 1998, the National Milk Processor Board has licensed the "got milk?" slogan for its celebrity milk mustache ads like this one.

enormous pleasure? How and when do ads annoy you? Can you think of any ways you intentionally avoid advertising? For more questions to help you understand the role of advertising in our lives, see "Questioning the Media" in the Chapter Review.

Early Developments in American Advertising

Advertising has existed since 3000 B.C.E., when shop owners in ancient Babylon hung outdoor signs carved in stone and wood so that customers could spot their stores. Merchants in early Egyptian society hired town criers to walk through the streets, announcing the arrival of ships and listing the goods on board. Archaeologists searching Pompeii, the ancient Italian city destroyed when Mount Vesuvius erupted in 79 C.E., found advertising messages painted on walls. By 900 C.E., many European cities featured town criers who not only called out the news of the day but also directed customers to various stores.

Other early media ads were on handbills, posters, and broadsides (long, newsprint-quality posters). English booksellers printed brochures and bills announcing new publications as early as the 1470s, when posters advertising religious books were tacked on to church doors. In 1622, print ads imitating the oral style of criers appeared in the first English newspapers. Announcing land deals and ship cargoes, the first newspaper ads in colonial America ran in the *Boston News-Letter* in 1704.

To distinguish their approach from the commercialism of newspapers, early magazines refused to carry advertisements. By the mid-1800s, though, most magazines contained ads and most publishers started magazines hoping to earn advertising dollars. About 80 percent of

> "You can tell the ideals of a nation by its advertisements."
>
> NORMAN DOUGLAS, *SOUTH WIND*, 1917

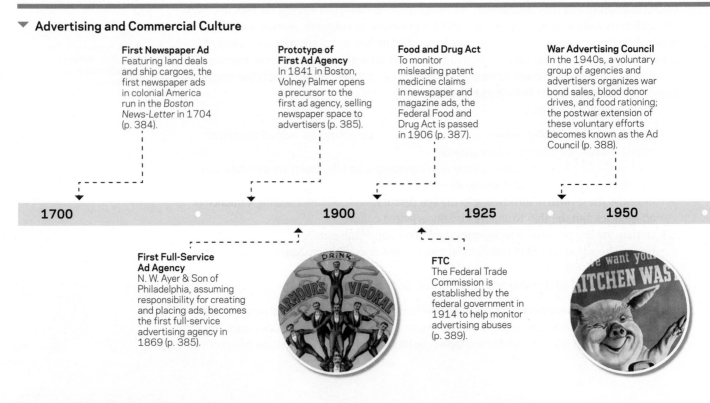

▼ **Advertising and Commercial Culture**

First Newspaper Ad
Featuring land deals and ship cargoes, the first newspaper ads in colonial America run in the *Boston News-Letter* in 1704 (p. 384).

Prototype of First Ad Agency
In 1841 in Boston, Volney Palmer opens a precursor to the first ad agency, selling newspaper space to advertisers (p. 385).

Food and Drug Act
To monitor misleading patent medicine claims in newspaper and magazine ads, the Federal Food and Drug Act is passed in 1906 (p. 387).

War Advertising Council
In the 1940s, a voluntary group of agencies and advertisers organizes war bond sales, blood donor drives, and food rationing; the postwar extension of these voluntary efforts becomes known as the Ad Council (p. 388).

| 1700 | 1900 | 1925 | 1950 |

First Full-Service Ad Agency
N. W. Ayer & Son of Philadelphia, assuming responsibility for creating and placing ads, becomes the first full-service advertising agency in 1869 (p. 385).

FTC
The Federal Trade Commission is established by the federal government in 1914 to help monitor advertising abuses (p. 389).

these early advertisements covered three subjects: land sales, transportation announcements (stagecoach and ship schedules), and "runaways" (ads placed by farm and plantation owners whose slaves had fled).

The First Advertising Agencies

Until the 1830s, little need existed for elaborate advertising, as few goods and products were even available for sale. Before the Industrial Revolution, 90 percent of Americans lived in isolated areas and produced most of their own tools, clothes, and food. The minimal advertising that did exist usually featured local merchants selling goods and services in their own communities. In the United States, national advertising, which initially focused on patent medicines, didn't start in earnest until the 1850s, when railroads linking the East Coast to the Mississippi River Valley began carrying newspapers, handbills, and broadsides–as well as national consumer goods–across the country.

The first American advertising agencies were newspaper **space brokers**, individuals who purchased space in newspapers and sold it to various merchants. Newspapers, accustomed to a 25 percent nonpayment rate from advertisers, welcomed the space brokers, who paid upfront. Brokers usually received discounts of 15 to 30 percent but sold the space to advertisers at the going rate. In 1841, Volney Palmer opened a prototype of the first ad agency in Boston; for a 25 percent commission from newspaper publishers, he sold space to advertisers.

Advertising in the 1800s

The first full-service modern ad agency, N. W. Ayer & Son, worked primarily for advertisers and product companies rather than for newspapers. Opening in 1869 in Philadelphia, the agency helped create, write, produce, and place ads in selected newspapers and magazines. The traditional payment structure at this time had the agency collecting a fee from its advertising client for each ad placed; the fee covered the price that each media outlet charged for placement of

> "The American apparatus of advertising is something unique in history[;] . . . it is like a grotesque, smirking gargoyle set at the very top of America's sky-scraping adventure in acquisition ad infinitum."
>
> JAMES RORTY,
> *OUR MASTER'S VOICE*,
> 1934

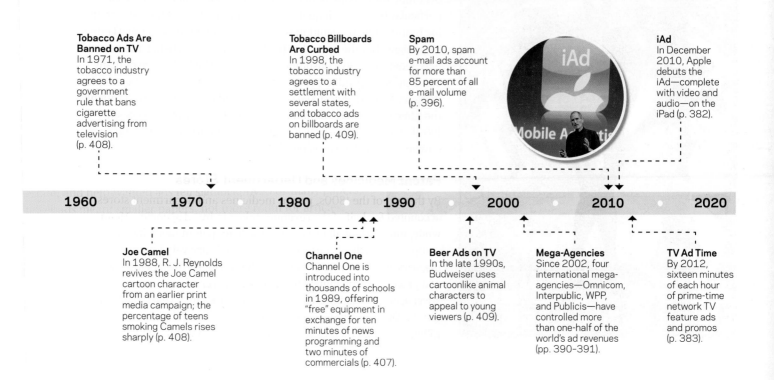

Tobacco Ads Are Banned on TV
In 1971, the tobacco industry agrees to a government rule that bans cigarette advertising from television (p. 408).

Tobacco Billboards Are Curbed
In 1998, the tobacco industry agrees to a settlement with several states, and tobacco ads on billboards are banned (p. 409).

Spam
By 2010, spam e-mail ads account for more than 85 percent of all e-mail volume (p. 396).

iAd
In December 2010, Apple debuts the iAd—complete with video and audio—on the iPad (p. 382).

1960   1970   1980   1990   2000   2010   2020

Joe Camel
In 1988, R. J. Reynolds revives the Joe Camel cartoon character from an earlier print media campaign; the percentage of teens smoking Camels rises sharply (p. 408).

Channel One
Channel One is introduced into thousands of schools in 1989, offering "free" equipment in exchange for ten minutes of news programming and two minutes of commercials (p. 407).

Beer Ads on TV
In the late 1990s, Budweiser uses cartoonlike animal characters to appeal to young viewers (p. 409).

Mega-Agencies
Since 2002, four international mega-agencies—Omnicom, Interpublic, WPP, and Publicis—have controlled more than one-half of the world's ad revenues (pp. 390-391).

TV Ad Time
By 2012, sixteen minutes of each hour of prime-time network TV feature ads and promos (p. 383).

sells itself as "the real thing," and the cosmetics industry offers synthetic products that promise to make women look "natural." The adjectives *real* and *natural* saturate American ads, yet almost always describe processed or synthetic goods. "Green" marketing has a similar problem, as it is associated with goods and services that aren't always environmentally friendly.

Philip Morris's Marlboro brand has used the association principle to completely transform its product image. In the 1920s, Marlboro began as a fashionable women's cigarette. Back then, the company's ads equated smoking with a sense of freedom, attempting to appeal to women who had just won the right to vote. Marlboro, though, did poorly as a women's product, and new campaigns in the 1950s and 1960s transformed the brand into a man's cigarette. Powerful images of active, rugged men dominated the ads. Often, Marlboro associated its product with nature: an image of a lone cowboy roping a calf, building a fence, or riding over a snow-covered landscape. In 2012, the branding consultancy BrandZ (a division of WPP) named Marlboro the world's seventh "most global brand," having an estimated worth of $73.9 billion. (Apple, IBM, Google, McDonald's, and Microsoft were the Top 5 rated brands.)

Disassociation as an Advertising Strategy

As a response to corporate mergers and public skepticism toward impersonal and large companies, a *disassociation corollary* emerged in advertising. The nation's largest winery, Gallo, pioneered the idea in the 1980s by establishing a dummy corporation, Bartles & Jaymes, to sell jug wine and wine coolers, thereby avoiding the use of the Gallo corporate image in ads and on its bottles. The ads featured Frank and Ed, two low-key, grandfatherly types, as "co-owners" and ad spokesmen. On the one hand, the ad was "a way to connect with younger consumers who yearn for products that are handmade, quirky, and authentic."[20] On the other hand, this technique, by concealing the Gallo tie-in, also allowed the wine giant to disassociate from the negative publicity of the 1970s—a period when labor leader Cesar Chavez organized migrant workers in a long boycott of Gallo.

In the 1990s, General Motors used the disassociation strategy. Reeling from a declining corporate reputation, GM tried to package the Saturn as "a small-town enterprise, run by folks not terribly unlike Frank and Ed" who provide caring, personal service.[21] In 2009, however, GM shut down its struggling Saturn brand during the economic recession. As an ad strategy, disassociation often links new brands in a product line to eccentric or simple regional places rather than to images conjured up by big cities and multinational conglomerates.

Advertising as Myth and Story

Another way to understand ads is to use **myth analysis**, which provides insights into how ads work at a general cultural level. Here, the term *myth* does not refer simply to an untrue story or outright falsehood. Rather, myths help us to define people, organizations, and social norms. According to myth analysis, most ads are narratives with stories to tell and social conflicts to resolve. Three common mythical elements are found in many types of ads:

1. Ads incorporate myths in mini-story form, featuring characters, settings, and plots.
2. Most stories in ads involve conflicts, pitting one set of characters or social values against another.
3. Such conflicts are negotiated or resolved by the end of the ad, usually by applying or purchasing a product. In advertising, the product and those who use it often emerge as the heroes of the story.

Even though the stories that ads tell are usually compressed into thirty seconds or onto a single page, they still include the traditional elements of narrative. For instance, many SUV ads ask us to imagine ourselves driving out into the raw, untamed wilderness, to a quiet, natural place that only, say, a Jeep can reach. The audience implicitly understands that the SUV can somehow, almost magically, take us out of our fast-paced, freeway-wrapped urban world plagued with long commutes, traffic jams, and automobile exhaust. This implied conflict between the natural world and the manufactured world is apparently resolved by the image of the SUV in a natural setting. Although SUVs typically clog our urban and suburban highways, get low gas mileage, and create tons of air pollution particulates, the ads ignore those facts. Instead, they offer an alternative story about the wonders of nature, and the SUV amazingly becomes the vehicle that negotiates the conflict between city/suburban blight and the unspoiled wilderness.

somehow, almost magically, take us out of our fast-paced, freeway-wrapped urban world plagued with long commutes, traffic jams, and automobile exhaust. This implied conflict between the natural world and the manufactured world is apparently resolved by the image of the SUV in a natural setting. Although SUVs typically clog our urban and suburban highways, get low gas mileage, and create tons of air pollution particulates, the ads ignore those facts. Instead, they offer an alternative story about the wonders of nature, and the SUV amazingly becomes the vehicle that negotiates the conflict between city/suburban blight and the unspoiled wilderness.

Most advertisers do not expect consumers to accept without question the stories or associations they make in ads; they do not "make the mistake of asking for belief."[22] Instead, ads are most effective when they create attitudes and reinforce values. Then they operate like popular fiction, encouraging us to suspend our disbelief. Although most of us realize that ads create a fictional world, we often get caught up in their stories and myths. Indeed, ads often work because the stories offer comfort about our deepest desires and conflicts—between men and women, nature and technology, tradition and change, the real and the artificial. Most contemporary consumer advertising does not provide much useful information about products. Instead, it tries to reassure us that through the use of familiar brand names, everyday tensions and problems can be managed (see "Media Literacy and the Critical Process: The Branded You" on page 405).

Product Placement

Product companies and ad agencies have become adept in recent years at *product placement*: strategically placing ads or buying space—in movies, TV shows, comic books, and most recently video games, blogs, and music videos—so products appear as part of a story's set environment (see "Examining Ethics: Brand Integration, Everywhere" on page 404). For example, in 2009, Starbucks became a naming sponsor of MSNBC's show *Morning Joe*—which now includes "Brewed by Starbucks" in its logo. In 2011, *Transformers: Dark Side of the Moon* had the most product placements of any film that year with sixty-nine, including deals with and references to NASA, Fox News, Apple, Mercedes-Benz, Ferrari, Nokia, Adidas, Nike, and Starbucks.

For many critics, product placement has gotten out of hand. What started out as subtle appearances in realistic settings—like Reese's Pieces in the 1982 movie *E.T.*—has turned into Coca-Cola being almost an honorary "cast member" on Fox's *American Idol* set. The practice is now so pronounced that it was a subject of Hollywood parody in the 2006 film *Talladega Nights: The Ballad of Ricky Bobby*, starring Will Ferrell.

In 2005, watchdog organization Commercial Alert asked both the FTC and the FCC to mandate that consumers be warned about product placement on television. The FTC rejected the petition, whereas the FCC proposed product placement rules but had not approved them by 2012. In contrast, the European Union recently approved product placement for television but requires programs to alert viewers of such paid placements. In Britain, for example, the letter "P" must appear in the corner of the screen at commercial breaks and at the beginning and end of a show to signal product placements.[23]

PRODUCT PLACEMENT in movies and television is more prevalent than ever. Reality shows have used particularly prominent placement, as when Subway promotes its image as a health-conscious fast food by appearing on the weight-loss competition series *The Biggest Loser*.

"The level of integration on- and off-screen in *Talladega Nights* is unprecedented. I can't remember ever seeing this much product placement displayed, from the commercials to the trailers for the film to the publicity and press events. It's pretty incredible, and it's pretty unheard of . . . a new and great thing for the brands involved."

AARON GORDON, MARKETING EXECUTIVE, 2006

before they turned eighteen) and tobacco money (tobacco companies make $1.8 billion from underage sales), and urges site visitors to organize the facts in their own customized folders. By 2007, with its jarring messages and cross-media platform, the "Truth" anti-tobacco campaign was recognized by 80 percent of teens and was ranked in the Top 10 "most memorable teen brands."[37]

Advertising, Politics, and Democracy

Advertising as a profession came of age in the twentieth century, facilitating the shift of U.S. society from production-oriented small-town values to consumer-oriented urban lifestyles. With its ability to create consumers, advertising became the central economic support system for our mass media industries. Through its seemingly endless supply of pervasive and persuasive strategies, advertising today saturates the cultural landscape. Products now blend in as props or even as "characters" in TV shows and movies. In addition, almost every national consumer product now has its own Web site to market itself to a global audience 365 days a year. With today's digital technology, ad images can be made to appear in places where they don't really exist. For example, advertisements can be superimposed on the backstop wall behind the batter during a nationally televised baseball broadcast. Viewers at home see the ads, but fans at the game do not.

Advertising's ubiquity, especially in the age of social media, raises serious questions about our privacy and the ease with which companies can gather data on our consumer habits. But an even more serious issue is the influence of ads on our lives as democratic citizens. With fewer and fewer large media conglomerates controlling advertising and commercial speech, what is the effect on free speech and political debate? In the future, how easy will it be to get heard in a marketplace where only a few large companies control access to that space?

Advertising's Role in Politics

Since the 1950s, political consultants have been imitating market-research and advertising techniques to sell their candidates, giving rise to **political advertising**, the use of ad techniques to promote a candidate's image and persuade the public to adopt a particular viewpoint. In the early days of television, politicians running for major offices either bought or were offered half-hour blocks of time to discuss their views and the issues of the day. As advertising time became more valuable, however, local stations and the networks became reluctant to give away time in large chunks. Gradually, TV managers began selling thirty-second spots to political campaigns, just as they sold time to product advertisers.

During the 1992 and 1996 presidential campaigns, third-party candidate Ross Perot restored the use of the half-hour time block when he ran political infomercials on cable and the networks. Barack Obama also ran a half-hour infomercial in 2008, and in the 2012 presidential race, both major candidates and various political organizations supporting them ran many online infomercials that were much longer than the standard thirty- to sixty-second TV spot. However, only very wealthy or well-funded candidates can afford such promotional strategies, and television does not usually provide free airtime to politicians. Questions about political ads continue to be asked: Can serious information on political issues be conveyed in thirty-second spots? Do repeated attack ads, which assault another candidate's character, so undermine citizens' confidence in the electoral process that they stop voting?[38] And how does a democratic

"Corporations put ads on fruit, ads all over the schools, ads on cars, ads on clothes. The only place you can't find ads is where they belong: on politicians."

MOLLY IVINS, SYNDICATED COLUMNIST, 2000

society ensure that alternative political voices, which are not well financed or commercially viable, still receive a hearing?

Although broadcasters use the public's airwaves, they have long opposed providing free time for political campaigns and issues, since political advertising is big business for television stations. TV broadcasters earned $400 million in 1996 and took in more than $1.5 billion from political ads during the presidential and congressional elections in 2004. In the historic 2008 election, more than $2.6 billion was spent on advertising by all presidential candidates and interest groups. In 2012 (with a total of $6 billion spent on all elections), more than $1.1 billion alone went to local broadcast TV stations in the twelve most highly contested states, with local cable raking in another $200 million in those states.[39]

The Future of Advertising

Although commercialism—through packaging both products and politicians—has generated cultural feedback that is often critical of advertising's pervasiveness, the growth of the industry has not diminished. Ads continue to fascinate. Many consumers buy magazines or watch the Super Bowl just for the advertisements. Adolescents decorate their rooms with their favorite ads and identify with the images certain products convey. In 2011, $144 billion was spent on U.S. advertising—up just about 1 percent over 2010.

A number of factors have made possible advertising's largely unchecked growth. Many Americans tolerate advertising as a "necessary evil" for maintaining the economy, but many dismiss advertising as not believable and trivial. As a result, unwilling to downplay its centrality to global culture, many citizens do not think advertising is significant enough to monitor or reform. Such attitudes have ensured advertising's pervasiveness and suggest the need to escalate our critical vigilance.

As individuals and as a society, we have developed an uneasy relationship with advertising. Favorite ads and commercial jingles remain part of our cultural world for a lifetime, but we detest irritating and repetitive commercials. We realize that without ads many mass media would need to reinvent themselves. At the same time, we should remain critical of what advertising has come to represent: the overemphasis on commercial acquisitions and images of material success, and the disparity between those who can afford to live comfortably in a commercialized society and those who cannot. ▶

"Mass advertising flourished in the world of mass media. Not because it was part of God's Natural Order, but because the two were mutually sustaining."

BOB GARFIELD,
ADVERTISING AGE,
2007

CHAPTER REVIEW

COMMON THREADS

One of the Common Threads discussed in Chapter 1 is the commercial nature of the mass media. The U.S. media system, due to policy choices made in the early mid-twentieth century, is built largely on a system of commercial sponsorship. This acceptance was based on a sense that media content and sponsors should remain independent of each other. In other words, sponsors and product companies should not control and create media content. Today, is that line between media content and advertising shifting—or completely disappearing?

Although media consumers have not always been comfortable with advertising, they developed a resigned acceptance of it because it "pays the bills" of the media system. Yet media consumers have their limits. Moments in which sponsors stepped over the usual borders of advertising into the realm of media content—including the TV quiz show and radio payola scandals, complimentary newspaper reports about advertisers' businesses, product placement in TV or movies, and now "Sponsored Stories" on Facebook—have generated the greatest legal and ethical debates about advertising.

Still, as advertising has become more pervasive and consumers more discriminating, ad practitioners have searched for ways to weave their work more seamlessly into the cultural fabric. Products now blend in as props or even as "characters" in TV shows and movies. Search engines deliver "paid" placements along with regular search results. Product placements are woven into video games. Advertising messages can also be the subject of viral videos—and consumers do the work of distributing the message.

Among the more intriguing efforts to become enmeshed in the culture are the ads that exploit, distort, or transform the political and cultural meanings of popular music. When Nike used the Beatles' song "Revolution" (1968) to promote Nike shoes in 1987 ("Nike Air is not a shoe . . . it's a revolution," the ad said), many music fans were outraged to hear the Beatles' music being used for the first time to sell products.

That was more than twenty-five years ago. These days, having a popular song used in a TV commercial is considered a good career move—even better than radio airplay. Similarly, while product placement in TV and movies was hotly debated in the 1980s and 1990s, the explosive growth of paid placements in video games hardly raises an eyebrow today. Even the lessons of the quiz show scandals, which forced advertisers out of TV program production in the late 1950s, are forgotten or ignored today as advertisers have been warmly invited to help develop TV programs.

Are we as a society giving up on trying to set limits on the never-ending onslaught of advertising? Are we weary of trying to keep advertising out of media production? How do we feel about the growing encroachment of ads into social networks like Facebook and Twitter? Why do we now seem less concerned about the integration of advertising into the core of media culture?

KEY TERMS

The definitions for the terms listed below can be found in the glossary at the end of the book. The page numbers listed with the terms indicate where the term is highlighted in the chapter.

product placement, 383
space brokers, 385
subliminal advertising, 389
slogan, 389
mega-agencies, 390
boutique agencies, 390
market research, 392
demographics, 392
psychographics, 392
focus groups, 392

Values and Lifestyles (VALS), 392
storyboard, 394
viral marketing, 394
media buyers, 394
saturation advertising, 395
account executives, 395
account reviews, 396
interstitials, 396
spam, 396
famous-person testimonial, 399

plain-folks pitch, 399
snob-appeal approach, 400
bandwagon effect, 400
hidden-fear appeal, 400
irritation advertising, 400
association principle, 400
myth analysis, 402
commercial speech, 405
political advertising, 414

REVIEW QUESTIONS

Early Developments in American Advertising

1. Whom did the first ad agents serve?

2. How did packaging and trademarks influence advertising?

3. Explain why patent medicines and department stores figured so prominently in advertising in the late 1800s.

4. What role did advertising play in transforming America into a consumer society?

The Shape of U.S. Advertising Today

5. What influences did visual culture exert on advertising?

6. What are the differences between boutique agencies and mega-agencies?

7. What are the major divisions at most ad agencies? What is the function of each department?

8. What are the advantages of Internet and mobile advertising over traditional media like newspapers and television?

Persuasive Techniques in Contemporary Advertising

9. How do the common persuasive techniques used in advertising work?

10. How does the association principle work, and why is it an effective way to analyze advertising?

11. What is the disassociation corollary?

12. What is product placement? Cite examples.

Commercial Speech and Regulating Advertising

13. What is commercial speech?

14. What are four serious contemporary issues regarding health and advertising? Why is each issue controversial?

15. What is the difference between puffery and deception in advertising? How can the FTC regulate deceptive ads?

Advertising, Politics, and Democracy

16. What are some of the major issues involving political advertising?

17. What role does advertising play in a democratic society?

QUESTIONING THE MEDIA

1. What is your earliest recollection of watching a television commercial? Do you think the ad had a significant influence on you?

2. Why are so many people critical of advertising?

3. If you were (or are) a parent, what strategies would you use to explain an objectionable ad to your child or teenager? Use an example.

4. Should advertising aimed at children be regulated? Support your response.

5. Should tobacco or alcohol advertising be prohibited? Why or why not? How would you deal with First Amendment issues regarding controversial ads?

6. Would you be in favor of regular advertising on public television and radio as a means of financial support for these media? Explain your answer.

7. Is advertising at odds with the ideals of democracy? Why or why not?

ADDITIONAL VIDEOS

Visit the ⓥ VideoCentral: Mass Communication *section at* bedfordstmartins.com/mediaculture *for additional exclusive videos related to Chapter 11, including:*

- BLURRING THE LINES: MARKETING PROGRAMS ACROSS PLATFORMS
  An executive for MTV New Media explores how recent television programs blur the line between scripted and reality shows—and how MTV markets online to reach today's younger viewers.

12

Public Relations and Framing the Message

In the mid-1950s, the blue jeans industry was in deep trouble. After hitting a postwar peak in 1953, jeans sales began to slide. The durable one-hundred-year-old denim product had become associated with rock and roll and teenage troublemakers. Popular movies, especially *The Wild One* and *Blackboard Jungle*, featured emotionally disturbed, blue jeans–wearing "young toughs" terrorizing adult authority figures. A Broadway play about juvenile delinquency was even titled *Blue Denim*. The worst was yet to come, however. In 1957, the public school system in Buffalo, New York, banned the wearing of blue jeans for all high school students. Formerly associated with farmers, factory workers, and an adult work ethic, jeans had become a reverse fashion statement for teenagers—something many adults could not abide.

THE DELINQUENT IN JEANS
Marlon Brando in
The Wild One (1953)

In response to the crisis, the denim industry waged a public relations (PR) campaign to eradicate the delinquency label and rejuvenate denim's image. In 1956, the nation's top blue jeans manufacturers formed the national Denim Council "to put schoolchildren back in blue jeans through a concerted national public relations, advertising, and promotional effort."[1] First the council targeted teens, but its promotional efforts were unsuccessful. The manufacturers soon realized that the problem was not with the teens but with the parents, administrators, teachers, and school boards. It was the adults who felt threatened by a fashion trend that seemed to promote disrespect through casualness. In response, the council hired a public relations firm to turn the image of blue jeans around. Over the next five years, the firm did just that.

The public relations team determined that mothers were refusing to outfit their children in jeans because of the product's association with delinquency.

To change this perception among women, the team encouraged fashion designers to update denim's image by producing new women's sportswear styles made from the fabric. Media outlets and fashion editors were soon inundated with news releases about the "new look" of durable denim.

The PR team next enlisted sportswear designers to provide new designs for both men's and women's work and utility clothes, long the backbone of denim sales. Targeting business reporters as well as fashion editors, the team transformed the redesign effort into a story that appealed to writers in both areas. They also planned retail store promotions nationwide, including "jean queen" beauty contests, and advanced positive denim stories in men's publications.

The team's major PR coup, however, involved an association with the newly formed national Peace Corps. The brainchild of the Kennedy administration, the Peace Corps encouraged young people to serve their country by working with people from developing nations.

Envisioning the Peace Corps as the flip side of delinquency, the Denim Council saw its opening. In 1961, it agreed to outfit the first group of two hundred corps volunteers in denim. As a result of all these PR efforts, by 1963 manufacturers were flooded with orders, and sales of jeans and other denim goods were way up. The delinquency tag disappeared, and jeans gradually became associated with a more casual, though not antisocial, dress ethic.

BLUE JEANS successfully reinvented their image and were (and still are) worn by volunteers who work for the Peace Corps.

▲ *THE BLUE JEANS STORY ILLUSTRATES A MAJOR DIFFERENCE* between advertising and public relations: Advertising is controlled publicity that a company or an individual buys; public relations attempts to secure favorable media publicity (which is more difficult to control) to promote a company or client. The transformation of denim in the public's eye was primarily achieved not by purchasing advertising but by restyling denim's image through friendly relations with reporters, who subsequently wrote stories associating the fabric with a casual, dedicated, youthful America.

Public relations (PR) covers a wide array of practices, such as shaping the public image of a politician or celebrity, establishing or repairing communication between consumers and companies, and promoting government agencies and actions, especially during wartime. Broadly defined, **public relations** refers to the total communication strategy conducted by a person, a government, or an organization attempting to reach and persuade an audience to adopt a point of view.[2] While public relations may sound very similar to advertising, which also seeks to persuade audiences, it is a different skill in a variety of ways. Advertising uses simple and fixed messages (e.g., "our appliance is the most efficient and affordable") that are transmitted directly to the public through the purchase of ads. Public relations involves more complex messages that may evolve over time (e.g., a political campaign or a long-term strategy to dispel unfavorable reports about "fatty processed foods") and may be transmitted to the public indirectly, often through the news media.

The social and cultural impact of public relations has been immense. In its infancy, PR helped convince many American businesses of the value of nurturing the public, who became purchasers rather than producers of their own goods after the Industrial Revolution. PR set the tone for the corporate image-building that characterized the economic environment of the twentieth century and for the battles of organizations taking sides in today's environmental, energy, and labor issues. Perhaps PR's most significant effect, however, has been on the political process, where individuals and organizations–on both the Right and the Left–hire spin doctors to shape their media images.

In this chapter, we will:

- Study the impact of public relations and the historical conditions that affected its development as a modern profession
- Look at nineteenth-century press agents and the role that railroad and utility companies played in developing corporate PR
- Consider the rise of modern PR, particularly the influences of former reporters Ivy Lee and Edward Bernays
- Explore the major practices and specialties of public relations
- Examine the reasons for the long-standing antagonism between journalists and members of the PR profession, and the social responsibilities of public relations in a democracy

As you read through this chapter, think about what knowledge you might already have about what public relations practitioners do, given that PR is an immensely powerful media industry and yet remains largely invisible. Can you think of a company or an organization, either national (like BP) or local (like your university or college), that might have engaged the help of a public relations team to handle a crisis? What did they do to make the public trust the organization more? When you see political campaign coverage, are you sometimes aware of the "spin doctors" who are responsible for making sure their candidate says or does the "right thing" at the "right time" so they can foster the most favorable public image that will gain the candidate the most votes? For more questions to help you understand the role of public relations in our lives, see "Questioning the Media" in the Chapter Review.

"An image . . . is not simply a trademark, a design, a slogan, or an easily remembered picture. It is a studiously crafted personality profile of an individual, institution, corporation, product, or service."

DANIEL BOORSTIN,
THE IMAGE, 1961

that were later adopted by books, radio programs, and Hollywood films about the American West. Along with Barnum, they were among the first to use **publicity**–a type of PR communication that uses various media messages to spread information about a person, corporation, issue, or policy–to elevate entertainment culture to an international level.

Big Business and Press Agents

As P. T. Barnum, Buffalo Bill, and John Burke demonstrated, utilizing the press brought with it an enormous power to sway the public and to generate business. So it is not surprising that during the 1800s America's largest industrial companies, particularly the railroads, also employed press agents to win favor in the court of public opinion.

The railroads began to use press agents to help them obtain federal funds. Initially, local businesses raised funds to finance the spread of rail service. Around 1850, however, the railroads began pushing for federal subsidies, complaining that local fund-raising efforts took too long. For example, Illinois Central was one of the first companies to use government *lobbyists* (people who try to influence the voting of lawmakers) to argue that railroad service between the North and the South was in the public interest and would ease tensions, unite the two regions, and prevent a war.

The railroad press agents successfully gained government support by developing some of the earliest publicity tactics. Their first strategy was simply to buy favorable news stories about rail travel from newspapers through direct bribes. Another practice was to engage in *deadheading*–giving reporters free rail passes with the tacit understanding that they would write glowing reports about rail travel. Eventually, wealthy railroads received the federal subsidies they wanted and increased their profits, while the American public shouldered much of the financial burden of rail expansion.

Having obtained construction subsidies, the larger rail companies turned their attention to bigger game–persuading the government to control rates and reduce competition, especially from smaller, aggressive regional lines. Railroad lobbyists argued that federal support would lead to improved service and guaranteed quality because the government would be keeping a close watch. These lobbying efforts, accompanied by favorable publicity, led to passage of the Interstate Commerce Act in 1881 authorizing railroads "to revamp their freight classification, raise rates, and eliminate fare reduction."[4] Historians have argued that, ironically, the PR campaign's success actually led to the decline of the railroads: Artificially maintained higher rates and burdensome government regulations forced smaller firms out of business and eventually drove many customers to other modes of transportation.

Along with the railroads, utility companies such as Chicago Edison and AT&T also used PR strategies in the late 1800s to derail competition and eventually attain monopoly status. In fact, AT&T's PR and lobbying efforts were so effective that they eliminated all telephone competition–with the government's blessing–until the 1980s. In addition to buying the votes of key lawmakers, the utilities hired third-party editorial services, which would send favorable articles about utilities to newspapers, assigned company managers to become leaders in community groups, produced ghostwritten articles (often using the names of prominent leaders and members of women's social groups, who were flattered to see their names in print), and influenced textbook authors to write histories favorable to the utilities.[5] The tactics of the 1880s and 1890s, however, would haunt public relations as it struggled to become a respected profession.

The Birth of Modern Public Relations

By the early 1900s, reporters and muckraking journalists began investigating the promotional practices behind many companies. As an informed citizenry paid more attention, it became more difficult for large firms to fool the press and mislead the public. With the rise of the middle class, increasing literacy among the working classes, and the spread of information through

"For setting forth of virtues (actual or alleged) of presidents, general managers, or directors, $2 per line. . . . Epic poems, containing descriptions of scenery, dining cars, etc., will be published at special rates."

CHICAGO NEWS REPORTER'S FICTIONAL RATES FOR THE BRIBES OFFERED TO JOURNALISTS FOR FAVORABLE RAILROAD COVERAGE, LATE 1880s

print media, democratic ideals began to threaten the established order of business and politics—and the elite groups who managed them. Two pioneers of public relations—Ivy Lee and Edward Bernays—emerged in this atmosphere to popularize an approach that emphasized shaping the interpretation of facts and "engineering consent."

Ivy Ledbetter Lee

Most nineteenth-century corporations and manufacturers cared little about public sentiment. By the early 1900s, though, executives realized that their companies could sell more products if they were associated with positive public images and values. Into this public space stepped Ivy Ledbetter Lee, considered one of the founders of modern public relations. Lee understood that the public's attitude toward big corporations had changed. He counseled his corporate clients that honesty and directness were better PR devices than the deceptive practices of the 1800s, which had fostered suspicion and an anti-big-business sentiment.

A minister's son, an economics student at Princeton University, and a former reporter, Lee opened one of the first PR firms in the early 1900s with George Park. Lee quit the firm in 1906 to work for the Pennsylvania Railroad, which, following a rail accident, hired him to help downplay unfavorable publicity. Lee's advice, however, was that Penn Railroad admit its mistake, vow to do better, and let newspapers in on the story. These suggestions ran counter to the then-standard practice of hiring press agents to manipulate the media, yet Lee argued that an open relationship between business and the press would lead to a more favorable public image. In the end, Penn and subsequent clients, notably John D. Rockefeller, adopted Lee's successful strategies.

By the 1880s, Rockefeller controlled 90 percent of the nation's oil industry and suffered from periodic image problems, particularly after Ida Tarbell's powerful muckraking series about the ruthless business tactics practiced by Rockefeller and his Standard Oil Company appeared in *McClure's Magazine* in 1904. The Rockefeller and Standard Oil reputations reached a low point in April 1914 when tactics to stop union organizing erupted in tragedy at a coal company in Ludlow, Colorado. During a violent strike, fifty-three workers and their family members, including thirteen women and children, died.

"Since crowds do not reason, they can only be organized and stimulated through symbols and phrases."

IVY LEE, 1917

Lee was hired to contain the damaging publicity fallout. He immediately distributed a series of "fact" sheets to the press, telling the corporate side of the story and discrediting the tactics of the United Mine Workers, who organized the strike. As he had done for Penn Railroad, Lee also brought in the press and staged photo opportunities. John D. Rockefeller Jr., who now ran the company, donned overalls and a miner's helmet and posed with the families of workers and union leaders. This was probably the first use of a PR campaign in a labor-management dispute. Over the years, Lee completely transformed the wealthy family's image, urging the discreet Rockefellers to publicize their charitable work. To improve his image, the senior Rockefeller took to handing out dimes to children wherever he went–a strategic ritual that historians attribute to Lee.

Called "Poison Ivy" by critics within the press and corporate foes, Lee had a complex understanding of facts. For Lee, facts were elusive and malleable, begging to be forged and shaped. In the Ludlow case, for instance, Lee noted that the women and children who died while retreating from the charging company-backed militia had overturned a stove, which caught fire and caused their deaths. His PR fact sheet implied that they had, in part, been victims of their own carelessness.

Edward Bernays

The nephew of Sigmund Freud, former reporter Edward Bernays inherited the public relations mantle from Ivy Lee. Beginning in 1919 when he opened his own office, Bernays was the first person to apply the findings of psychology and sociology to public relations, referring to himself as a "public relations counselor" rather than a "publicity agent." Over the years, Bernays's client list included General Electric, the American Tobacco Company, General Motors, *Good Housekeeping* and *Time* magazines, Procter & Gamble, RCA, the government of India, the city of Vienna, and President Coolidge.

Bernays also worked for the Committee on Public Information (CPI) during World War I, developing propaganda that supported America's entry into that conflict and promoting the image of President Woodrow Wilson as a peacemaker. Both efforts were among the first full-scale governmental attempts to mobilize public opinion. In addition, Bernays made key contributions to public relations education, teaching the first class called "public relations"–at New York University in 1923–and writing the field's first textbook, *Crystallizing Public Opinion*. For many years, his definition of PR was the standard: "Public relations is the attempt, by information, persuasion, and adjustment, to engineer public support for an activity, cause, movement, or institution."[6]

In the 1920s, Bernays was hired by the American Tobacco Company to develop a campaign to make smoking more publicly acceptable for women (similar campaigns are under way today in countries like China). Among other strategies, Bernays staged an event: placing women smokers in New York's 1929 Easter parade. He labeled cigarettes "torches of freedom" and encouraged women to smoke as a symbol of their newly acquired suffrage and independence from men. He also asked the women he placed in the parade to contact newspaper and newsreel companies in advance–to announce their symbolic protest. The campaign received plenty of free publicity from newspapers and magazines. Within weeks of the parade, men-only smoking rooms in New York theaters began opening up to women.

Through much of his writing, Bernays suggested that emerging freedoms threatened the established hierarchical order. He thought it was important for experts and leaders to control the direction of American society: "The duty of the higher strata of society–the cultivated, the learned, the expert, the intellectual–is therefore clear. They must inject moral and spiritual motives into public opinion."[7] For the cultural elite to maintain order and control, they would have to win the consent of the larger public. As a result, he termed the shaping of public opinion through PR as the "engineering of consent." Like Ivy Lee, Bernays thought that public opinion was malleable and not always rational: In the hands of the right experts, leaders, and PR counselors, public opinion could be shaped into forms people could rally behind.[8] However,

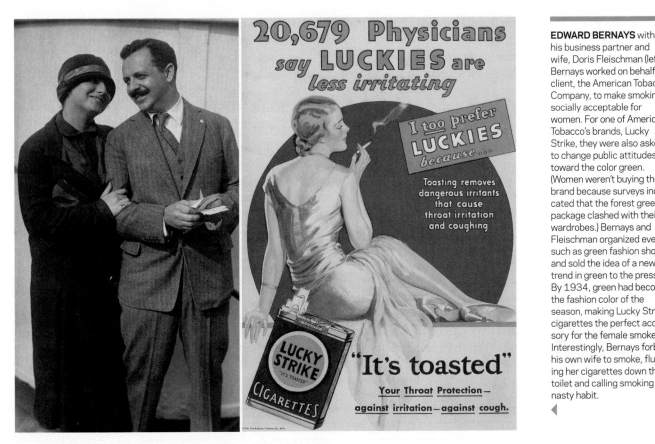

EDWARD BERNAYS with his business partner and wife, Doris Fleischman (left). Bernays worked on behalf of a client, the American Tobacco Company, to make smoking socially acceptable for women. For one of American Tobacco's brands, Lucky Strike, they were also asked to change public attitudes toward the color green. (Women weren't buying the brand because surveys indicated that the forest green package clashed with their wardrobes.) Bernays and Fleischman organized events such as green fashion shows and sold the idea of a new trend in green to the press. By 1934, green had become the fashion color of the season, making Lucky Strike cigarettes the perfect accessory for the female smoker. Interestingly, Bernays forbade his own wife to smoke, flushing her cigarettes down the toilet and calling smoking a nasty habit.

journalists like Walter Lippmann, who wrote the famous book *Public Opinion* in 1922, worried that PR professionals with hidden agendas, rather than journalists with professional detachment, held too much power over American public opinion.

Throughout Bernays's most active years, his business partner and later his wife, Doris Fleischman, worked with him on many of his campaigns as a researcher and coauthor. Beginning in the 1920s, she was one of the first women to work in public relations, and she introduced PR to America's most powerful leaders through a pamphlet she edited called *Contact*. Because she opened up the profession to women from its inception, PR emerged as one of the few professions—apart from teaching and nursing—accessible to women who chose to work outside the home at that time. Today, women outnumber men by more than three to one in the profession.

The Practice of Public Relations

Today, there are more than seven thousand PR firms in the United States, plus thousands of additional PR departments within corporate, government, and nonprofit organizations.[9] Since the 1980s, the formal study of public relations has grown significantly at colleges and universities. By 2011, the Public Relations Student Society of America (PRSSA) had more than ten thousand members and 322 chapters in colleges and universities. As certified PR programs have expanded (often requiring courses or a minor in journalism), the profession has relied less and less on its traditional practice of recruiting journalists for its workforce. At the same time, new courses in professional ethics and issues management have expanded the responsibility of future practitioners. In this section, we discuss the differences between public relations agencies and in-house PR services and the various practices involved in performing PR.

Approaches to Organized Public Relations

The Public Relations Society of America (PRSA) offers this simple and useful definition of PR: "Public relations helps an organization and its publics adapt mutually to each other." To carry out this mutual communication process, the PR industry uses two approaches. First, there are independent PR agencies whose sole job is to provide clients with PR services. Second, most companies, which may or may not also hire the independent PR firms, maintain their own in-house PR staffs to handle routine tasks, such as writing press releases, managing various media requests, staging special events, and dealing with internal and external publics.

Many large PR firms are owned by, or are affiliated with, multinational communications holding companies like WPP, Omnicom, and Interpublic (see Figure 12.1). Two of the largest PR agencies, Burson-Marsteller and Hill & Knowlton, generated part of the $16.05 billion in PR revenue for their parent corporation, the WPP Group, in 2012. Founded in 1953, Burson-Marsteller has 155 offices and affiliate partners in 108 countries and lists Facebook, IKEA, Coca-Cola, Sony, and the United Arab Emirates among its clients. Hill & Knowlton, founded in 1927, has 84 offices in 46 countries and includes Johnson & Johnson, Nestlé, Proctor & Gamble, Starbucks, Splenda, Florida Healthcare, and Latvia on its client list. Most independent PR firms are smaller and are operated locally or regionally. New York-based Edelman, the largest independent firm, is an

FIGURE 12.1

THE TOP 4 HOLDING FIRMS, WITH PUBLIC RELATIONS SUBSIDIARIES, 2012 (BY WORLDWIDE REVENUE IN U.S. DOLLARS)

Source: "Agency Family Trees, 2012," Advertising Age, April 30, 2012.

Note: Revenue represents total company income including PR agencies.

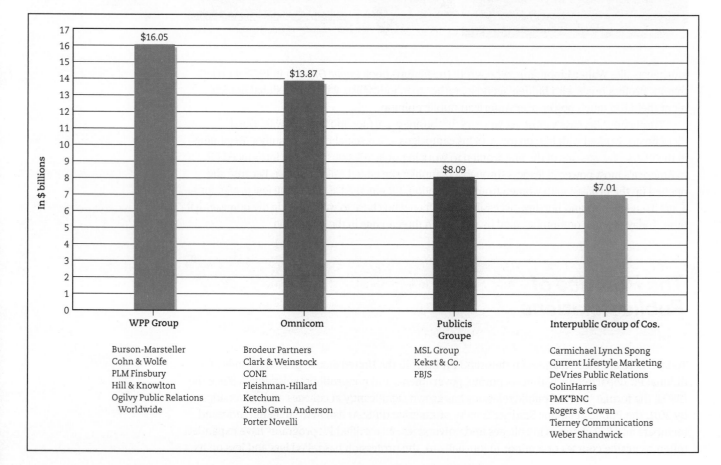

exception, with global operations and clients like Ben & Jerry's, Bank of America, General Electric, Hewlett-Packard, Samsung, and Unilever/Dove.

In contrast to these external agencies, most PR work is done in-house at companies and organizations. Although America's largest companies typically retain external PR firms, almost every company involved in the manufacturing and service industries has an in-house PR department. Such departments are also a vital part of many professional organizations, such as the American Medical Association, the AFL-CIO, and the National Association of Broadcasters, as well as large nonprofit organizations, such as the American Cancer Society, the Arthritis Foundation, and most universities and colleges.

Performing Public Relations

Public relations, like advertising, pays careful attention to the needs of its clients–politicians, small businesses, industries, and nonprofit organizations– and to the perspectives of its targeted audiences: consumers and the general public, company employees, shareholders, media organizations, government agencies, and community and industry leaders. To do so, PR involves providing a multitude of services, including publicity, communication, public affairs, issues management, government relations, financial PR, community relations, industry relations, minority relations, advertising, press agentry, promotion, media relations, social networking, and propaganda. This last service, **propaganda**, is communication strategically placed, either as advertising or as publicity, to gain public support for a special issue, program, or policy, such as a nation's war effort.

In addition, PR personnel (both PR technicians, who handle daily short-term activities, and PR managers, who counsel clients and manage activities over the long term) produce employee newsletters, manage client trade shows and conferences, conduct historical tours, appear on news programs, organize damage control after negative publicity, analyze complex issues and trends that may affect a client's future, manage Twitter accounts, and much more. Basic among these activities, however, are formulating a message through research, conveying the message through various channels, sustaining public support through community and consumer relations, and maintaining client interests through government relations.

Research: Formulating the Message

Before anything else begins, one of the most essential practices in the PR profession is doing research. Just as advertising is driven today by demographic and psychographic research, PR uses similar strategies to project messages to appropriate audiences. Because it has historically been difficult to determine why particular PR campaigns succeed or fail, research has become the key ingredient in PR forecasting. Like advertising, PR makes use of mail, telephone, and Internet surveys and focus group interviews–as well as social media analytic tools such as BlogPulse, Trendrr, or Twitalyzer–to get a fix on an audience's perceptions of an issue, policy, program, or client's image.

WORLD WAR II was a time when the U.S. government used propaganda and other PR strategies to drum up support for the war. One of the more iconic posters at the time asked women to join the workforce.

"It was the astounding success of propaganda during the war which opened the eyes of the intelligent few in all departments of life to the possibilities of regimenting the public mind."

EDWARD BERNAYS, *PROPAGANDA*, 1928

MESSAGE FORMULATION
Appealing to the eighteen- to twenty-four-year-old target age group, the interactive Web site for the Department of Defense's *"That Guy!"* anti-binge-drinking campaign uses humorous terms like "Sloberus SweaToomuch" and "Drunkus Obnoxious" to describe the stages of intoxication.

Research also helps PR firms focus the campaign message. For example, in 2006 the Department of Defense hired the PR firm Fleishman-Hillard International Communications to help combat the rising rates of binge drinking among junior enlisted military personnel. The firm first verified its target audience by researching the problem, finding from the Department of Defense's triennial Health Related Behaviors Survey that eighteen- to twenty-four-year-old servicemen had the highest rates of binge drinking. It then conducted focus groups to refine the tone of its anti-drinking message, and developed and tested its Web site for usability. The finalized campaign concept and message–"Don't Be *That Guy!"*–has been successful: It has shifted binge drinkers' attitudes toward less harmful drinking behaviors through a Web site (www .thatguy.com) and multimedia campaign that combines humorous videos, games, and cartoons with useful resources. By 2012, the campaign had been implemented in over eight hundred military locations across twenty-three countries and the award-winning Web site had been viewed by approximately 1.3 million visitors.[10]

Conveying the Message

One of the chief day-to-day functions in public relations is creating and distributing PR messages for the news media or the public. There are several possible message forms, including press releases, VNRs, and various online options.

Press releases, or news releases, are announcements written in the style of news reports that give new information about an individual, a company, or an organization and pitch a story idea to the news media. In issuing press releases, PR agents hope that their client information will be picked up by the news media and transformed into news reports. Through press releases, PR firms manage the flow of information, controlling which media get what material in which order. (A PR agent may even reward a cooperative reporter by strategically releasing information.) News editors and broadcasters sort through hundreds of releases daily to determine which ones contain the most original ideas or are the most current. Most large media institutions rewrite and double-check the releases, but small media companies often use them verbatim because of limited editorial resources. Usually, the more closely a press release resembles actual news copy, the more likely it is to be used. (See Figure 12.2.)

Since the introduction of portable video equipment in the 1970s, PR agencies and departments have also been issuing **video news releases (VNRs)**–thirty- to ninety-second visual press releases designed to mimic the style of a broadcast news report. Although networks and large TV news stations do not usually broadcast VNRs, news stations in small TV markets regularly use material from VNRs. On occasion, news stations have been criticized for using video footage from a VNR without acknowledging the source. In 2005, the FCC mandated that broadcast stations and cable operators must disclose the source of the VNRs that they air. As with press releases, VNRs give PR firms some control over what constitutes "news" and a chance to influence what the general public thinks about an issue, a program, or a policy.

The equivalent of VNRs for nonprofits are **public service announcements (PSAs)**: fifteen- to sixty-second audio or video reports that promote government programs,

Office of University Relations   University of **Northern Iowa**

3/25/11
FOR IMMEDIATE RELEASE

Contact:
James O'Connor, Office of University Relations, 319-273-2751, james.oconnor@uni.edu

Note to editors/news directors: *Media coverage is welcome. All members of the media -- reporters, photographers, videographers -- wishing to cover the May 7 commencement, must request a special media credential. Information about credentials can be found online at http://www.uni.edu/commencement/media-information.*

UNI announces new plans for spring commencement
First lady Michelle Obama to deliver commencement address

CEDAR FALLS, Iowa – The University of Northern Iowa is pleased to announce that first lady Michelle Obama will speak at UNI's spring commencement ceremony at 11 a.m., Saturday, May 7, in the UNI-Dome. The university will consolidate three ceremonies into one to provide all graduates the opportunity to be addressed by the first lady.

"We are pleased to host the first lady, someone whose commitment to service, children and healthy communities, reflects UNI's commitment to serve our community, our state and our nation," said UNI President Ben Allen. "We welcome this opportunity for our students to hear the first lady's inspiring story of how higher education impacted her life and her passion for service."

Approximately 1,900 students who will complete their degrees this semester are eligible to participate in the ceremony. "We apologize for any inconvenience this change in schedule may cause," said Allen.

All graduating students participating in the commencement ceremony will be allotted eight tickets for guests. Tickets are free, but all guests must have a ticket. All commencement seats will be general admission. Graduating students must order and pick up their tickets between April 4 and April 20. Tickets are subject to availability.

UNI staff and faculty not participating in the ceremony, and all other UNI students, can receive up to two tickets and can order tickets April 21 through 22. Beginning April 25, any remaining tickets will be made available to the general public. Orders will be limited to a maximum of two tickets and are subject to availability.

Tickets can be ordered by phone at 319-273-4TIX, or they can be picked up in person at any UNItix location. No online orders will be taken. Students, faculty and staff must present their UNI I.D. More details about commencement, the ticket-ordering process, UNI-Dome access and the day's ...nent ceremony will be

888 • www.uni.edu/ur

spring commissioning adets will be commissioned as

State Edition | The Des Moines Register

OBAMA TO SPEAK AT UNI GRADUATION

A Quad Cities teacher sent the request. The president is busy, but the first lady can do it.

By THOMAS BEAUMONT
tbeaumont@dmreg.com

First lady Michelle Obama plans to give the commencement speech at the University of Northern Iowa on May 7, the White House said Friday, thanks to a proud Bettendorf mother's letter to the White House.

Ann Geneva, a veteran Quad Cities kindergarten teacher, wrote President

Michelle Obama will speak at the May 7 ceremony.

from UNI, she told The Des Moines Register. Obama won Iowa's 2008 Democratic presidential caucuses, which launched him on his way to the nomination. Geneva voted for president. She said she simply thought a speech from him to her son's class would be inspiring.

"I think that the speeches he gives are heartfelt and inspiring," Geneva said. "So many young people going out into the world to find work need that inspiration."

For months, Geneva heard nothing. Then came a December voice-mail message at home with word that the White House had received the letter. On March 10,

Geneva had just put away her groceries after a trip to Walmart the following Friday when the phone rang. It was the first lady's office, calling to say that Michelle Obama would speak at her son's graduation.

"It was one of those things where you're standing there and you're thinking, 'Is this really happening?'" she said.

It is, and the Geneva family, including Adam's father, Allan, and two brothers, Alex and Andrew, plan to

---

educational projects, volunteer agencies, or social reform. As part of their requirement to serve the public interest, broadcasters have been encouraged to carry free PSAs. Since the deregulation of broadcasting began in the 1980s, however, there has been less pressure and no minimum obligation for TV and radio stations to air PSAs. When PSAs do run, they are frequently scheduled between midnight and 6 a.m., a less commercially valuable time slot.

Today, the Internet is an essential avenue for transmitting PR messages. Companies upload or e-mail press releases, press kits, and VNRs for targeted groups. Social media has also transformed traditional PR communications. For example, a social media press release pulls together "remixable" multimedia elements such as text, graphics, video, podcasts, and hyperlinks, giving journalists ample material to develop their own stories. (See "Case Study: Social Media Transform the Press Release," on page 432.)

FIGURE 12.2

DIFFERENCES BETWEEN A PRESS RELEASE AND A NEWS STORY

News reports can be heavily dependent on public relations for story ideas and content. At right above is a press release written by the Office of University Relations at University of Northern Iowa about First Lady Michelle Obama speaking at the 2011 spring commencement ceremony. The other two images show the Web and print news articles inspired by the release.

CASE STUDY

Social Media Transform the Press Release

More than a century ago, Ivy Lee began the now-standard practice of issuing press releases directly to newspapers when he responded to a rail accident for his client, the Pennsylvania Railroad Company. Lee delivered official releases to newspapers, detailing Pennsylvania Railroad's commitment to the rescue efforts and deflecting criticism, noting that "the equipment of the train was entirely new, having been in service but a few weeks, and is believed to have been perfect in every particular."[1]

Lee's direct approach worked, as the release was carried in full in newspapers like the *New York Times*. By reaching out to the press and opening the channels of communication, Lee was able to help his client escape complete blame for the accident, thus reducing the railroad's liability and preserving its profits and reputation.

Today, the press release continues in much the same century-old form: a statement on behalf of the client's interests, written in news style, and sent directly to the press. But the news media have since drastically changed. Along with print newspapers, broadcast media have become part of the press; more recently, all news forms have merged online, with a host of new Web-based news sites and mobile apps. With the changes in the news media comes a new form of the press release—the social media release. The PR industry recognizes that not only is the American public turning to the Internet for its news but journalists are growing more comfortable with researching their articles online, interviewing their subjects via e-mail, and using a variety of media in their stories—from text and hyperlinks to video and audio.

SHIFT Communications, a Boston-based independent public relations firm, offered a popular template for a social media press release in 2006 (and released version 1.5 in 2008).[2] The firm suggested social media release contains a headline and contact information, like the old press release, but puts the narrative in bullet points and includes embedded Web links to photos, videos, podcasts, pre-approved quotes, trackbacks to blogs linking to related news, and RSS feed links for updates—in short, an online newsroom to aid a multimedia journalist and bolster the information typically provided in a traditional press release. According to Todd S. DeFren of SHIFT Communications, "The Social Media Press Release merely amplifies prospective source materials; it does not replace a well-crafted, customized pitch nor replace the need to provide basic, factual news to the media."[3]

But as the news release adapts to social media, another public relations professional, Gary Shankman of Help a Reporter Out (HARO), cautions against public relations becoming too enamored of social media and sites like Facebook, Twitter, and YouTube. In his blog entry titled "Why I Will Never, Ever Hire a 'Social Media Expert,'" Shankman argues that social media are just tools and not a substitute for transparency, relevance, and good writing. "Social media, by itself, will not help you," Shankman writes. "We're making the same mistakes that we made during the DotCom era, where everyone thought that just adding the term .com to your corporate logo made you instantly credible. It didn't."[4]

The social media press release isn't the only format that's available for public relations professionals these days. Corporate communications consultant Dominic Jones endorses simplicity for today's press release: a twenty-five-word summary and a linked headline that takes readers to the client's Web site. "The single purpose of news releases today should be to get people to link to the details on our websites," Jones says. "To do that, we only need to convince them that it's worth their while to click the link."[5]

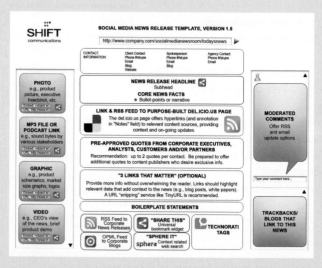

Media Relations

PR managers specializing in media relations promote a client or an organization by securing publicity or favorable coverage in the news media. This often requires an in-house PR person to speak on behalf of an organization or to direct reporters to experts who can provide information. Media-relations specialists also perform damage control or crisis management when negative publicity occurs. Occasionally, in times of crisis—such as a scandal at a university or a safety recall by a car manufacturer—a PR spokesperson might be designated as the only source of information available to news media. Although journalists often resent being cut off from higher administrative levels and leaders, the institution or company wants to ensure that rumors and inaccurate stories do not circulate in the media. In these situations, a game often develops between PR specialists and the media in which reporters attempt to circumvent the spokesperson and induce a knowledgeable insider to talk off the record, providing background details without being named directly as a source.

LADY GAGA established the nonprofit Born This Way Foundation (BTWF) in 2011 to help address childhood bullying and to inspire young people to serve their communities. The organization has incorporated various media elements into its campaign, including a blog and online public service announcements.

PR agents who specialize in media relations also recommend advertising to their clients when it seems appropriate. Unlike publicity, which is sometimes outside a PR agency's control, paid advertising may help to focus a complex issue or a client's image. Publicity, however, carries the aura of legitimate news and thus has more credibility than advertising. In addition, media specialists cultivate associations with editors, reporters, freelance writers, and broadcast news directors to ensure that press releases or VNRs are favorably received. (See "Examining Ethics: What Does It Mean to Be Green?" on page 434.)

Special Events and Pseudo-Events

Another public relations practice involves coordinating *special events* to raise the profile of corporate, organizational, or government clients. Since 1967, for instance, the city of Milwaukee has run Summerfest, a ten-day music and food festival that attracts about a million people each year and now bills itself as "The World's Largest Music Festival." As the festival's popularity grew, various companies sought to become sponsors of the event. Today, Milwaukee's Miller Brewing Company sponsors one of the music festival's stages, which carries the Miller name and promotes Miller Lite as the "official beer" of the festival. Briggs & Stratton and Harley Davidson are also among the local companies that sponsor stages at the event. In this way, all three companies receive favorable publicity by showing a commitment to the city in which their corporate headquarters are located.[11]

More typical of special-events publicity is a corporate sponsor aligning itself with a cause or an organization that has positive stature among the general public. For example, John Hancock Financial has been the primary sponsor of the Boston Marathon since 1986 and funds the race's prize money. The company's corporate communications department also serves as the PR office for the race, operating the pressroom and creating the marathon's media guide and other press materials. Eighteen other sponsors, including Adidas, Gatorade, PowerBar, and JetBlue Airways, also pay to affiliate themselves with the Boston Marathon. At the local level, companies often sponsor a community parade or a charitable fund-raising activity.

In contrast to a special event, a **pseudo-event** is any circumstance created for the sole purpose of gaining coverage in the media. Historian Daniel Boorstin coined the term in his

What Does It Mean to Be Green?

Back in the 1930s, public relations pioneer Edward Bernays labored behind the scenes to make green a more fashionable color. Why? Bernays was working to change women's attitudes toward the forest green packaging of his client Lucky Strike's cigarettes so women would smoke them.

Today, public relations professionals are openly working on behalf of clients to promote a different kind of "green"—environmentally sustainable practices. The idea of green practices goes back at least as far as the very first Earth Day, April 22, 1970, which marked the beginnings of the modern environmental movement. The term "green" as a synonym for being environmentally conscious was inspired by Greenpeace, the international environmental conservation organization founded in 1971, and by the similar political ideology that gained roots in Europe and Australia in the 1970s that prized ecological practices, participatory democracy, nonviolence, and social justice.

TIMBERLAND'S "green" practices include a nutritional label to show customers the environmental impact of each pair of shoes.

▼

Corporations in the United States and elsewhere began adapting to the changing culture, integrating environmental claims into their marketing and public relations. But it wasn't always clear what constituted "green." In 1992, the Federal Trade Commission first issued its "Green Guides," guidelines to ensure that environmental marketing practices don't run afoul of its prohibition against unfair or deceptive acts or practices, sometimes called "greenwashing." As concern about global warming has grown in recent years, green marketing and public relations now extend into nearly every part of business and industry: product packaging (buzzwords include *recyclable*, *biodegradable*, *compostable*, *refillable*, *sustainable*, and *renewable*), buildings and textiles, renewable energy certificates and carbon offsets (funding projects to reduce greenhouse gas emissions in one place to offset carbon emissions produced elsewhere), labor conditions, and fair trade.

Although there have been plenty of companies that make claims of "green" products and services, only some have infused environmentally sustainable practices throughout their corporate culture. In the United States, the New Hampshire–based footwear and clothing company Timberland has been a model for green practices and PR. In 2008, Timberland released a short- and long-term plan for corporate social responsibility performance covering the areas of energy,

product, workplace, and service that represent the company's material impacts. Timberland's plan is particularly noteworthy in that it reports its key corporate social responsibility indicators quarterly (not just once a year) and encourages a two-way dialogue with its stakeholders using social media platforms. Most recently, Timberland unveiled its Earthkeepers 2.0 boot, which uses the plastic from one-and-a-half recycled water bottles in each boot.

Ultimately, green PR requires a global outlook, as sustainability responds to issues of an increasingly small planet. There are now more than 8,700 corporations in 130 nations belonging to the United Nations Global Compact, a strategic policy initiative launched in 2000 for businesses to align their operations and strategies with ten universally accepted principles in human rights, labor, environment, and anticorruption. Still, the move toward sustainable business practices has a long way to go, as there are more than 6 million business firms in the United States alone.

The good news for sustainability and green public relations is that executives around the world are embracing the concept. A study by the UN Global Compact in 2011 revealed that 93 percent of 766 CEOs surveyed believe that sustainability will be "important" or "very important" to the future success of their company.[1]

To help organizations make progress on sustainability practices, a number of public relations firms specializing in corporate responsibility and sustainability have sprung up, including Interraction and CSG in the United States and Futerra in the United Kingdom. ◢

influential book *The Image* when pointing out the key contributions of PR and advertising in the twentieth century. Typical pseudo-events are press conferences, TV and radio talk show appearances, or any other staged activity aimed at drawing public attention and media coverage. The success of such events depends on the participation of clients, sometimes on paid performers, and especially on the media's attention to the event. In business, pseudo-events extend back at least as far as P. T. Barnum's publicity stunts, such as parading Jumbo the Elephant across the Brooklyn Bridge in the 1880s. In politics, Theodore Roosevelt's administration set up the first White House pressroom and held the first presidential press conferences in the early 1900s. By the 2000s, presidential pseudo-events involved a multimillion-dollar White House Communications Office. One of the most successful pseudo-events in recent years was the April 2011 Frito-Lay Flavor Kitchen, an outdoor test kitchen staged on a billboard platform two stories above Times Square in New York to promote the natural ingredients in the company's snack products. The promotion pushed Frito-Lay to over 2 million "likes" on Facebook and registered more than 375 million media impressions.

As powerful companies, savvy politicians, and activist groups became aware of the media's susceptibility to pseudo-events, these activities proliferated. For example, to get free publicity, companies began staging press conferences to announce new product lines. During the 1960s, antiwar and Civil Rights protesters began their events only when the news media were assembled. One anecdote from that era aptly illustrates the principle of a pseudo-event: A reporter asked a student leader about the starting time for a particular protest; the student responded, "When can you get here?" Today, politicians running for office are particularly adept at scheduling press conferences and interviews to take advantage of TV's appetite for live remote feeds and breaking news.

Community and Consumer Relations

Another responsibility of PR is to sustain goodwill between an agency's clients and the public. The public is often seen as two distinct audiences: communities and consumers.

Companies have learned that sustaining close ties with their communities and neighbors not only enhances their image and attracts potential customers but also promotes the idea that the companies are good citizens. As a result, PR firms encourage companies to participate in community activities such as hosting plant tours and open houses, making donations to national and local charities, and participating in town events like parades and festivals. In addition, more progressive companies may also get involved in unemployment and job-retraining programs, or donate equipment and workers to urban revitalization projects such as Habitat for Humanity.

In terms of consumer relations, PR has become much more sophisticated since 1965, when Ralph Nader's groundbreaking book, *Unsafe at Any Speed*, revealed safety problems concerning the Chevrolet Corvair. Not only did Nader's book prompt the discontinuance of the Corvair line; it also lit the fuse that ignited a vibrant consumer movement. After the success of Nader's book, along with a growing public concern over corporate mergers and their lack of accountability to the public, consumers became less willing to readily accept the claims of corporations. As a result of the consumer movement, many newspapers and TV stations

JP MORGAN organizes the JPMorgan Chase Corporate Challenge each year, a series of road races that raise money for several not-for-profit organizations around the world. Taking place in twelve major cities, including New York, Frankfurt, and Shanghai, the JPMorgan Chase-owned-and-operated races also allow financial firm JP Morgan to gain valuable publicity.

hired consumer reporters to track down the sources of customer complaints and embarrass companies by putting them in the media spotlight. Public relations specialists responded by encouraging companies to pay more attention to customers, establish product service and safety guarantees, and ensure that all calls and mail from customers were answered promptly. Today, PR professionals routinely advise clients that satisfied customers mean not only repeat business but also new business, based on a strong word-of-mouth reputation about a company's behavior and image.

Government Relations and Lobbying

While sustaining good relations with the public is a priority, so is maintaining connections with government agencies that have some say in how companies operate in a particular community, state, or nation. Both PR firms and the PR divisions within major corporations are especially interested in making sure that government regulation neither becomes burdensome nor reduces their control over their businesses.

Government PR specialists monitor new and existing legislation, create opportunities to ensure favorable publicity, and write press releases and direct-mail letters to persuade the public about the pros and cons of new regulations. In many industries, government relations has developed into **lobbying**: the process of attempting to influence lawmakers to support and vote for an organization's or industry's best interests. In seeking favorable legislation, some lobbyists contact government officials on a daily basis. In Washington, D.C., alone, there are about thirteen thousand registered lobbyists—and thousands more government-relations workers who aren't required to register under federal disclosure rules. Lobbying expenditures targeting the federal government rose above $3.3 billion in 2011, up from $1.64 billion ten years earlier.[12] (See Figure 12.3.)

Lobbying can often lead to ethical problems, as in the case of earmarks and astroturf lobbying. *Earmarks* are specific spending directives that are slipped into bills to accommodate the interests of lobbyists and are often the result of political favors or outright bribes. In 2006, lobbyist Jack Abramoff (dubbed "The Man Who Bought Washington" in *Time*) and several of his associates were convicted of corruption related to earmarks, leading to the resignation of leading House members and a decline in the use of earmarks.

Astroturf lobbying is phony grassroots public-affairs campaigns engineered by public relations firms. PR firms deploy massive phone banks and computerized mailing lists to drum up

> "I get in a lot of trouble if I'm quoted, especially if the quotes are accurate."
>
> A CONGRESSIONAL STAFF PERSON, EXPLAINING TO THE *WALL STREET JOURNAL* WHY HE CAN SPEAK ONLY "OFF THE RECORD," 1999

FIGURE 12.3

TOTAL LOBBYING SPENDING AND NUMBER OF LOBBYISTS (2000–2012)

Note: Figures on this page are calculations by the Center for Responsive Politics based on data from the Senate Office of Public Records, through August 14, 2012.

*The number of unique, registered lobbyists who have actively lobbied.

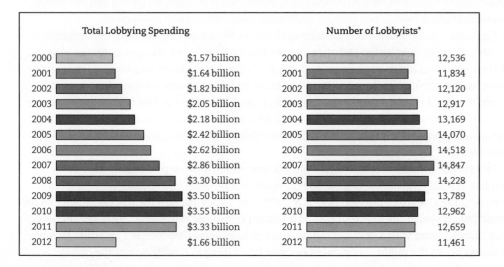

Total Lobbying Spending		Number of Lobbyists*	
2000	$1.57 billion	2000	12,536
2001	$1.64 billion	2001	11,834
2002	$1.82 billion	2002	12,120
2003	$2.05 billion	2003	12,917
2004	$2.18 billion	2004	13,169
2005	$2.42 billion	2005	14,070
2006	$2.62 billion	2006	14,518
2007	$2.86 billion	2007	14,847
2008	$3.30 billion	2008	14,228
2009	$3.50 billion	2009	13,789
2010	$3.55 billion	2010	12,962
2011	$3.33 billion	2011	12,659
2012	$1.66 billion	2012	11,461

support and create the impression that millions of citizens back their client's side of an issue. For instance, the Center for Consumer Freedom (CCF), an organization that appears to serve the interests of consumers, is actually a creation of the Washington, D.C.-based PR firm Berman & Co. and is funded by the restaurant, food, alcohol, and tobacco industries. According to Sourcewatch.org, which tracks astroturf lobbying, "Anyone who criticizes tobacco, alcohol, fatty foods or soda pop is likely to come under attack from CCF."

Public relations firms do not always work for the interests of corporations, however. They also work for other clients, including consumer groups, labor unions, professional groups, religious organizations, and even foreign governments. In 2005, for example, the California Center for Public Health Advocacy, a nonpartisan, nonprofit organization, hired Brown-Miller Communications, a small California PR firm, to rally support for landmark legislation that would ban junk food and soda sales in the state's public schools. Brown-Miller helped state legislators see obesity not as a personal choice issue but as a public policy issue, cultivated the editorial support of newspapers to compel legislators to sponsor the bills, and ultimately succeeded in getting a bill passed.

Presidential administrations also use public relations—with varying degrees of success—to support their policies. From 2002 to 2008, the Bush administration's Defense Department operated a "Pentagon Pundit" program, secretly cultivating more than seventy retired military officers to appear on radio and television talk shows and shape public opinion about the Bush agenda. In 2008, the *New York Times* exposed the unethical program and its story earned a Pulitzer Prize.[13] The Obama administration pledged to be more transparent. In 2010, the *Columbia Journalism Review* lauded the administration for "significant progress on transparency and access issues" but gave them poor grades on state secrets, online data, and background briefings.[14]

Public Relations Adapts to the Internet Age

Historically, public relations practitioners have tried to earn news media coverage (as opposed to buying advertising) to communicate their clients' messages to the public. While that is still true, the Internet, with its instant accessibility, offers public relations professionals a number of new routes for communicating with publics.

A company or organization's Web site has become the home base of public relations efforts. Companies and organizations can upload and maintain their media kits (including press releases, VNRs, images, executive bios, and organizational profiles), giving the traditional news media access to the information at any time. And because everyone can access these corporate Web sites, the barriers between the organization and the groups that PR professionals ultimately want to reach are broken down.

The Web also enables PR professionals to have their clients interact with audiences on a more personal, direct basis through social media tools like Facebook, Twitter, Wikipedia, and blogs. Now people can be "friends" and "followers" of companies and organizations. Corporate executives can share their professional and personal observations and seem downright chummy through a blog (e.g., Whole Foods Market's blog by CEO John Mackey). Executives, celebrities, and politicians can seem more accessible and personable through a Twitter feed. But social media's immediacy can also be a problem, especially for those who send messages into the public sphere without considering the ramifications. Several athletes in the 2012 London Olympics, for example, suffered for tweeting their unedited thoughts, including a Greek track athlete who was kicked off the team for her racist joke and a Swiss soccer player who was sent home early after he tweeted a slur about the Korean team that just defeated his.[15]

> "We're proud of the work we do for Saudi Arabia. It's a very challenging assignment."
>
> MIKE PETRUZZELLO, QORVIS COMMUNICATIONS

Media Literacy and the Critical Process

The Invisible Hand of PR

John Stauber, founder of the industry watchdog *PR Watch*, has described the PR industry as "a huge, invisible industry . . . that's really only available to wealthy individuals, large multinational corporations, politicians and government agencies."[1] How true is this? Is the PR industry so invisible?

1 DESCRIPTION. Test the so-called invisibility of the PR industry by seeing how often, and in what way, PR firms are discussed in the print media. Using LexisNexis, search U.S. newspapers–over the last six months–for any mention of three prominent PR firms: Weber Shandwick, Fleishman-Hillard, and Burson-Marsteller.

2 ANALYSIS. What patterns emerge from the search? Possible patterns may have to do with personnel: Someone was hired or fired. (These articles may be extremely brief, with only a quick mention of the firms.) Or these personnel-related articles may reveal connections between politicians or corporations and the PR industry. What about specific PR campaigns or articles that quote "experts" who work for Weber Shandwick, Fleishman-Hillard, or Burson-Marsteller?

3 INTERPRETATION. What do these patterns tell you about how the PR industry is covered by the news media? Was the coverage favorable? Was it critical or analytical? Did you learn anything about how the industry operates? Is the industry itself, its influencing strategies, and its wide reach across the globe visible in your search?

4 EVALUATION. PR firms–such as the three major firms in this search–have enormous power when it comes to influencing the public image of corporations, government bodies, and public policy initiatives in the United States and abroad. PR firms also have enormous influence over news content. Yet the U.S. media are silent on this influence. Public relations firms aren't likely to reveal their power, but should journalism be more forthcoming about its role as a publicity vehicle for PR?

5 ENGAGEMENT. Visit the Center for Media and Democracy's Web site (prwatch.org) and begin to learn about the unseen operations of the public relations industry. (You can also read SpinWatch.org.uk for similar critical analyses of PR in the United Kingdom.) Follow the CMD's Twitter feed. Read some of the organization's books, join forum discussions, or attend a *PR Watch* event. Visit the organization's wiki site, Source Watch (sourcewatch.org), and, if you can, do some research of your own on PR and contribute an entry.

---

a candidate's media image. In one example, former president Richard Nixon, who resigned from office in 1974 to avoid impeachment hearings regarding his role in the Watergate scandal, hired Hill & Knowlton to restore his postpresidency image. Through the firm's guidance, Nixon's writings, mostly on international politics, began appearing in Sunday op-ed pages. Nixon himself started showing up on television news programs like *Nightline* and spoke frequently before such groups as the American Newspaper Publishers Association and the Economic Club of New York. In 1984, after a media blitz by Nixon's PR handlers, the *New York Times* announced, "After a decade, Nixon is gaining favor," and *USA Today* trumpeted, "Richard Nixon is back." Before his death in 1994, Nixon, who never publicly apologized for his role in Watergate, saw a large portion of his public image shift from that of an arrogant, disgraced politician to that of a revered elder statesman.[25] Many media critics have charged that the press did not counterbalance this PR campaign and treated Nixon too reverently.

In terms of its immediate impact on democracy, the information crush delivered by public relations is at its height during national election campaigns. In 2008, some of the behind-the-scenes work of PR in presidential campaigns was revealed. First, Mark Penn, the chief strategist of Hillary Clinton's campaign to be the Democratic nominee, became a news story himself when he resigned from her campaign over a conflict of interest. Penn worked for Clinton while he maintained his position as chief executive of Burson-Marsteller, where he lobbied on behalf of Colombia for a trade treaty opposed by Clinton. Second, Scott McClellan, President George W.

Bush's press secretary from 2003 to 2006, disclosed in his 2008 book that the White House had a "carefully orchestrated campaign to shape and manipulate sources of public approval" and decided to "turn away from honesty and candor" in the lead-up to and during the Iraq war.[26] Both instances illustrate the centrality of public relations—and the temptation of stepping over ethical boundaries—in shaping politicians.

Though public relations often provides political information and story ideas, the PR profession bears only part of the responsibility for "spun" news; after all, it is the job of a PR agency to get favorable news coverage for the individual or group it represents. PR professionals police their own ranks for unethical or irresponsible practices, but the news media should also monitor the public relations industry, as they do other government and business activities. Journalism itself also needs to institute changes that will make it less dependent on PR and more conscious of how its own practices play into the hands of spin strategies. A positive example of change on this front is that many major newspapers and news networks now offer regular critiques of the facts and falsehoods contained in political advertising. This media vigilance should be on behalf of citizens, who are entitled to robust, well-rounded debates on important social and political issues.

Like advertising and other forms of commercial speech, PR campaigns that result in free media exposure raise a number of questions regarding democracy and the expression of ideas. Large companies and PR agencies, like well-financed politicians, have money to invest to figure out how to obtain favorable publicity. The question is not how to prevent that but how to ensure that other voices, less well financed and less commercial, also receive an adequate hearing. To that end, journalists need to become less willing conduits in the distribution of publicity. PR agencies, for their part, need to show clients that participating in the democratic process as responsible citizens can serve them well and enhance their image. ▶

"In politics, image [has] replaced action."

RANDALL ROTHENBERG, *WHERE THE SUCKERS MOON*, 1994

CHAPTER REVIEW

COMMON THREADS

One of the Common Threads in Chapter 1 is about the role that media play in democracy. One key ethical contradiction that can emerge in PR is that (according to the PRSA Code of Ethics) PR should be honest and accurate in disclosing information while at the same time being loyal and faithful to clients and their requests for confidentiality and privacy. In this case, how does the general public know when public communications are the work of paid advocacy, particularly when public relations play such a strong role in U.S. politics?

Public relations practitioners who are members of the Public Relations Society of America (PRSA) are obligated to follow the PRSA's Code of Ethics, which asks its members to sign the pledge: "To conduct myself professionally, with truth, accuracy, fairness, and responsibility to the public."

Yet the Code is not enforceable, and many public relations professionals simply ignore the PRSA. For example, only 14 of PR giant Burson-Marsteller's 2,200 worldwide employees are PRSA members.[27] Most lobbyists in Washington have to register with the House and Senate, so there is some public record of their activities to influence politics. Conversely, public relations professionals working to influence the political process don't have to register, so unless they act with the highest ethical standards and disclose what they are doing and who their clients are, they operate in relative secrecy.

According to National Public Radio (NPR), public relations professionals in Washington, D.C., work to engineer public opinion in advance of lobbying efforts to influence legislation. As NPR reported, "For PR folks, conditioning the legislative landscape means trying to shape public perception. So their primary target is journalists like Lyndsey Layton, who writes for *The Washington Post*. She says she gets about a dozen emails or phone calls in a day."[28]

Less ethical work includes assembling phony "astroturf" front groups to engage in communication campaigns to influence legislators, spreading unfounded rumors about an opposing side, and entertaining government officials in violation of government reporting requirements—all things the PRSA Code prohibits. Yet these are all-too-frequent practices in the realm of political public relations.

PRSA CEO Rosanna Fiske decries this kind of unethical behavior in her profession. "It's not that ethical public relations equals good public relations," Fiske says. "It is, however, that those who do not practice ethical public relations affect all of us, regardless of the environment in which we work, and the causes we represent."[29]

KEY TERMS

The definitions for the terms listed below can be found in the glossary at the end of the book. The page numbers listed with the terms indicate where the term is highlighted in the chapter.

public relations, 421
press agents, 422
publicity, 424
propaganda, 429

press releases, 430
video news releases (VNRs), 430
public service announcements
(PSAs), 430

pseudo-event, 433
lobbying, 436
astroturf lobbying, 436
flack, 440

REVIEW QUESTIONS

Early Developments in Public Relations

1. What did people like P. T. Barnum and Buffalo Bill Cody contribute to the development of modern public relations in the twentieth century?

2. How did railroads and utility companies give the early forms of corporate public relations a bad name?

3. What contributions did Ivy Lee make toward the development of modern PR?

4. How did Edward Bernays affect public relations?

The Practice of Public Relations

5. What are two approaches to organizing a PR firm?

6. What are press releases, and why are they important to reporters?

7. What is the difference between a VNR and a PSA?

8. What is a pseudo-event? How does it relate to the manufacturing of news?

9. What special events might a PR firm sponsor to build stronger ties to its community?

10. Why have research and lobbying become increasingly important to the practice of PR?

11. How does the Internet change the way in which public relations communicates with an organization's many publics?

12. What are some socially responsible strategies that a PR specialist can use during a crisis to help a client manage unfavorable publicity?

Tensions between Public Relations and the Press

13. Explain the historical background of the antagonism between journalism and public relations.

14. How did PR change old relationships between journalists and their sources?

15. In what ways is conventional news like public relations?

16. How does journalism as a profession contribute to its own manipulation at the hands of competent PR practitioners?

Public Relations and Democracy

17. In what ways does the profession of public relations serve the process of election campaigns? In what ways can it impede election campaigns?

QUESTIONING THE MEDIA

1. What do you think of when you hear the term *public relations*? What images come to mind? Where did these impressions come from?

2. What might a college or university do to improve public relations with homeowners on the edge of a campus who have to deal with noisy student parties and a shortage of parking spaces?

3. What steps can reporters and editors take to monitor PR agents who manipulate the news media?

4. Overall, are social media platforms a good thing for practicing public relations, or do they present more problems than they are worth?

5. Considering the *Exxon Valdez*, BP, and Tylenol cases cited in this chapter, what are some key things an organization can do to respond effectively once a crisis hits?

ADDITIONAL VIDEOS

Visit the ⊚ VideoCentral: Mass Communication *section at bedfordstmartins.com/mediaculture for additional exclusive videos related to Chapter 12, including:*

- FILLING THE HOLES: VIDEO NEWS RELEASES
  Television and PR experts explain the increasing use of video news releases as networks continue to cut costs.

- GOING VIRAL: POLITICAL CAMPAIGNS AND VIDEO
  Online video has changed political campaigning forever. In this video, Peggy Miles of Intervox Communications discusses how politicians use the Internet to reach out to voters.

But after its customer base fell from a high of 27 million in 2003 to under 4 million subscribers in 2011—a drop of 86 percent—AOL got back into the content game. In 2011 it paid $315 million to acquire the *Huffington Post*, a company that, according to the *New York Times*, "is a master of finding stories across the Web, stripping them to their essence and placing well-created headlines on them that rise to the top of search engine results, guaranteeing a strong audience."[1] The *Huffington Post* itself had already shifted into content creation, moving from merely aggregating news reports to hiring its own reporters and analysts to produce original stories.

Cable TV—for many years just a distributor of old network reruns and Hollywood movies—has also gotten into the business of telling stories over the last few years, creating award-winning programs like *The Sopranos*, *Mad Men*, *Dexter*, and *The Closer*. More recent media distributors entering the content creation business are Google and Netflix. Although Google claims that it is merely an aggregator or organizer of information and stories, it bought YouTube in 2006 for $1.6 billion and turned it into "a network for a postbroadcast world." *New York Times* business analyst David Carr points out that "YouTube's home page, which used to be a user-generated free-for-all, now has a clear hierarchy of channels, with an array of topics—'Entertainment,' 'News and Politics' and 'Sports'—that doesn't look that different from the menu guide on my cable set-top box."[2] And in 2011, Google, behaving like a cable or satellite TV company, started a subscription service called One Pass, which allows "consumers to buy professionally produced news and information across the Web with a single click."[3]

Netflix, like cable TV in the early days, made its mark distributing old TV shows and Hollywood films—by sending DVDs through the mail and, later, by shifting its distribution system to streaming old TV programs and movies. But in 2011 it announced its entry into the story creation game, acquiring the rights to *House of Cards*, an original one-hour "political drama" starring Kevin Spacey. Just like a traditional TV network would, Netflix ordered twenty-six episodes of its new TV series for 2012.[4] The company also ordered ten new episodes of the cult comedy series *Arrested Development*.

In the end, compelling narratives are what attract people to media—whether in the form of books or blogs, magazines or movies, TV shows or talk radio. People make sense of their experiences and articulate their values through narratives. And so "the story" of media economics today is—as it has always been—the telling and selling of stories.

"Google has been spending a lot of time and some significant money trying to help traditional media businesses stay in business, in part because Google does not want its search engines to crawl across a wasteland of machine-generated info-spam and amateur content with limited allure."

DAVID CARR, *NEW YORK TIMES*, 2011

over the last two decades have made our modern world very distinct from that of earlier generations–at least in economic terms. What's at the heart of this "Brave New Media World" is a media landscape that has been forever altered by the emergence of the Internet and a "changing of the guard" from traditional media giants like News Corp. and Time Warner to new digital giants like Amazon, Apple, Facebook, Google, and Microsoft. As the Google and Netflix ventures demonstrate, the Internet is marked by shifting and unpredictable terrain. In usurping the classified ads of newspapers and altering distribution for music, movies, and TV programs, the Internet has forced almost all media businesses to rethink not only the content they provide but the entire economic structure within which our capitalist media system operates.

In this chapter, we examine the economic impact of business strategies on various media. We will:

- Explore the issues and tensions that are a part of the current media economy
- Examine the rise of the Information Age, distinguished by flexible, specialized, and global markets
- Investigate the breakdown of economic borders, focusing on media consolidation, corporate mergers, synergy, deregulation, and the emergence of an economic global village
- Address ethical and social issues in media economics, investigating the limits of antitrust laws, the concept of consumer control, and the threat of cultural imperialism
- Examine the rise of new digital media conglomerates
- Consider the impact of media consolidation on democracy and on the diversity of the marketplace

As you read through this chapter, think about the different media you use on a daily basis. What media products or content did you consume over the past week? Do you know who owns them? How important is it to know this? Do you consume popular culture or read news from other countries? Why or why not? For more questions to help you understand the role of media economics in our lives, see "Questioning the Media" in the Chapter Review.

Analyzing the Media Economy

Given the sprawling scope of the mass media, the study of their economic conditions poses a number of complicated questions. For example, does the government need to play a stronger role in determining who owns the mass media and what kinds of media products are manufactured? Or should the government step back and let competition and market forces dictate what happens to mass media industries? Should citizen groups play a larger part in demanding that media organizations help maintain the quality of social and cultural life? Does the influence of American popular culture worldwide smother or encourage the growth of democracy and local cultures? Does the increasing concentration of economic power in the hands of several international corporations too severely restrict the number of players and voices in the media?

Answers to such questions span the economic and social spectrums. On the one hand, critics express concerns about the increasing power and reach of large media conglomerates. On the other hand, many free-market advocates maintain that as long as these structures ensure efficient operation and generous profits, they measure up as quality media organizations. In order to probe these issues fully, we need to understand key economic concepts across two broad areas: media structure and media performance.[5]

OPRAH WINFREY has built a remarkable media empire over the course of her long career. From book publishing to filmmaking and television, where she got her start, Oprah has established an expansive sphere of influence. Yet after launching cable TV network *OWN* in 2011, an acronym named for Winfrey herself, the modern-day media mogul has faced multiple challenges, including lackluster ratings and employee layoffs.

The Structure of the Media Industry

In most media industries, three common structures characterize the economics of the business: monopoly, oligopoly, and limited competition.

A **monopoly** occurs when a single firm dominates production and distribution in a particular industry, either nationally or locally. For example, at the national level, AT&T ran a rare government-approved-and-regulated monopoly–the telephone business–for more than a hundred years until its breakup in the mid-1980s. In a suit brought by the Justice Department and twenty states, software giant Microsoft was accused of monopolistic practices for controlling more than 80 percent of computer operating systems worldwide and was ordered to split into two separate companies. Microsoft, however, appealed and in 2002 agreed to a court settlement that imposed restrictions only on its business dealings with personal computer makers but left the company intact.

On the local level, monopoly situations have been more plentiful, occurring in any city that has only one newspaper or one cable company. While the federal government has encouraged owner diversity since the 1970s by prohibiting a newspaper from operating a broadcast or cable company in the same city, many individual local media monopolies have been purchased by national and international firms. For instance, Cox Communications has acquired nearly thirty cable monopoly systems–including those in San Diego, Oklahoma City, and Cleveland–clustered in seventeen states and serving more than six million customers. Likewise, in the newspaper business, chain operators like Gannett own hundreds of newspapers, most of which constitute a newspaper monopoly in their communities.

▼ Media Economics and the Global Marketplace

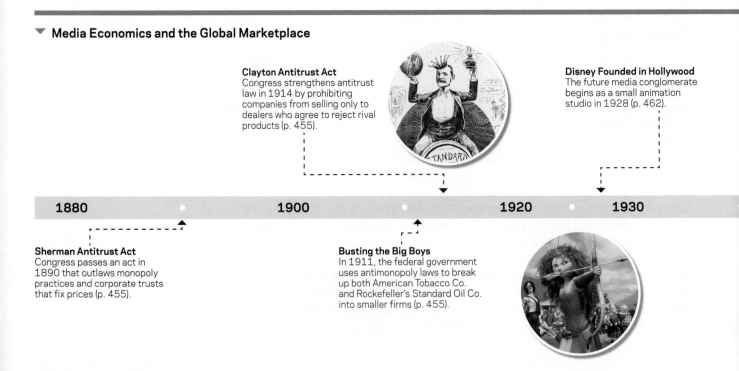

Clayton Antitrust Act
Congress strengthens antitrust law in 1914 by prohibiting companies from selling only to dealers who agree to reject rival products (p. 455).

Disney Founded in Hollywood
The future media conglomerate begins as a small animation studio in 1928 (p. 462).

| 1880 | 1900 | 1920 | 1930 |

Sherman Antitrust Act
Congress passes an act in 1890 that outlaws monopoly practices and corporate trusts that fix prices (p. 455).

Busting the Big Boys
In 1911, the federal government uses antimonopoly laws to break up both American Tobacco Co. and Rockefeller's Standard Oil Co. into smaller firms (p. 455).

In an **oligopoly**, just a few firms dominate an industry. For example, the book-publishing and feature-film businesses are both oligopolies. Each has five or six major players that control the majority of the production and distribution in the industry. The production and distribution of the world's music is basically controlled by just four international corporations–Warner Music (United States), Sony (Japan), Universal (France), and EMI (Great Britain). (In 2011, Universal announced it was purchasing EMI's record music division. If the sale gains regulatory approval, only three major music corporations will remain.) Usually conducting business only in response to one another, such companies face little economic competition from small independent firms. Oligopolies often add new ideas and product lines by purchasing successful independent companies.

Sometimes called *monopolistic competition*, **limited competition** characterizes a media market with many producers and sellers but only a few products within a particular category.[6] For instance, hundreds of independently owned radio stations operate in the United States. Most of these commercial stations, however, feature a limited number of formats–such as country, classic rock, or contemporary hits. Because commercial broadcast radio is now a difficult market to enter–requiring an FCC license and major capital investment–most stations play only one of the few formats that attract sizable audiences. Under these circumstances, fans of blues, alternative country, or classical music may not be able to find a radio station that matches their interests. Given the high start-up costs of launching a commercial business in any media industry, companies offering alternative products are becoming rare in the twenty-first century.

The Performance of Media Organizations

In analyzing the behavior and performance of media companies, economists pay attention to a number of elements–from how media make money to how they set prices and live up to society's expectations. In addition, many corporations now adapt their practices to new Internet standards. For example, most large regional newspapers from 2009 to 2011 had lost a high percentage of classified ad revenue to Internet companies and were adjusting to the losses by downsizing staffs; printing on fewer days of the week; and in some cases declaring bankruptcy, closing down, or moving to an online-only edition.

> "Communities across America are suffering through a crisis that could leave a dramatically diminished version of democracy in its wake.... In a nutshell, media corporations, after running journalism into the ground, have determined that news gathering and reporting are not profit-making propositions. So they're jumping ship."
>
> JOHN NICHOLS AND ROBERT McCHESNEY, *THE NATION*, 2009

Celler-Kefauver Act
In 1950, corporate mergers and joint ventures that reduce competition are limited (p. 455).

Disney Buys ABC
The 1995 deal is approved despite concerns that ABC News will pull its punches in coverage of Disney's empire (p. 457).

EchoStar-DirecTV Merger Blocked
The FCC moves to block a deal in 2002 that would have created a Direct Broadcast Satellite (DBS) monopoly (p. 472).

AOL buys the *Huffington Post*
Looking to expand in content creation, AOL acquires the *Huffington Post* for $315 million in 2011 (p. 457).

1950 **1970** **1990** **2010** **2020**

GATT Established
The General Agreement on Tariffs and Trade is established in 1947, opening an era of increasing globalization. The NAFTA agreement in 1994 and the WTO in 1995 further encourage trade and the export of certain jobs (p. 462).

GE Buys NBC
The 1985 merger sets off a wave of media consolidation (p. 457).

AOL Merges with Time Warner
Time Warner, already the largest media corporation, becomes even larger in 2001 with the addition of AOL, the largest Internet service provider (p. 457).

from the mid-1980s breakup of the AT&T telephone monopoly), into the cable TV business. In addition, cable operators regained the right to freely raise their rates and were authorized to compete in the local telephone business. At the time, some economists thought the new competition would lower consumer prices. Others predicted more mergers and an oligopoly in which a few mega-corporations would control most of the wires entering a home and dictate pricing.

As it turned out, part of each prediction occurred. The price of basic cable service more than doubled between 1996 and 2011, from $24.48 to $57.46 per month.[10] At the same time, the cost of a monthly telephone landline increased only about 20 percent, in part because a growing percentage of households replaced their landlines with mobile phones. Increasingly, companies like Comcast and AT&T try to corner all of the key communications systems by "bundling" multiple services—including digital cable television, high-speed Internet, home telephone, and wireless.

Deregulation Continues Today

Since the 1980s, a spirit of deregulation and special exemptions has guided communication legislation. For example, in 1995, despite complaints from NBC, Rupert Murdoch's Australian company News Corp. received a special dispensation from the FCC and Congress allowing the firm to continue owning and operating the Fox network and a number of local TV stations. The Murdoch decision ran counter to government decisions made after World War I. At that time, the government feared outside owners and thus limited foreign investment in U.S. broadcast operations to 20 percent. To make things easier, Murdoch became a U.S. citizen, and in 2004 News Corp. moved its headquarters to the United States, where the company was doing about 80 percent of its business.

FCC rules were further relaxed in late 2007, when the agency modified the newspaper-broadcast cross-ownership rule, allowing a company located in a Top 20 market to own one TV station and one newspaper as long as there were at least eight TV stations in the market. Previously, a company could not own a newspaper and a broadcast outlet—either a TV or radio station—in the same market (although if a media company had such cross-ownership prior to the early 1970s, the FCC usually granted waivers to let it stand). Murdoch had already been granted a permanent waiver from the FCC to own the *New York Post* and the New York TV station WNYW. So the FCC actually restructured the cross-ownership rule to accommodate News Corp. (In 2006, when News Corp. bought the New York-based *Wall Street Journal*, the FCC declared that the *Journal* was a national newspaper, not a local one that fell under the cross-ownership rule.) In 2011, the FCC voted to allow the same company to own a TV station and a newspaper in a Top 20 market. But in 2012, the Supreme Court let a lower court ruling stand that blocked the FCC's deregulation of cross-ownership, so the rules still exist.

The deregulation movement favored by administrations from Reagan through Clinton to George W. Bush returned media economics to nineteenth-century principles, which suggested that markets can take care of themselves with little government intervention. In this context, one of the ironies in broadcast history is that more than eighty years ago commercial radio broadcasters demanded government regulation to control technical interference and amateur competition. By the mid-1990s, however, the original reasons given for regulation no longer applied. With new cable channels, DBS, and the Internet, broadcasting was no longer considered a scarce resource—once a major rationale for regulation as well as government funding of noncommercial and educational stations.

Media Powerhouses: Consolidation, Partnerships, and Mergers

The antitrust laws of the twentieth century, despite their strength, have been unevenly applied, especially in terms of the media. When International Telephone & Telegraph (ITT) tried to acquire ABC in the 1960s, loud protests and government investigations sank the deal. But in the

"Big is bad if it stifles competition . . . but big is good if it produces quality programs."

MICHAEL EISNER,
THEN-CEO,
DISNEY, 1995

"It's a small world, after all."

THEME SONG,
DISNEY THEME PARKS

mid-1980s, as the Justice Department broke up AT&T's century-old monopoly–creating telephone competition–the government at the same time was also authorizing a number of mass media mergers that consolidated power in the hands of a few large companies. For example, when General Electric purchased RCA/NBC in the 1980s, the FTC, the FCC, and the Justice Department found few problems. Then, in 1996, computer giant Microsoft partnered with NBC to create a CNN alternative, MSNBC: a twenty-four-hour news channel available on both cable and the Internet.

In 1995, Disney acquired ABC for $19 billion. To ensure its rank as the world's largest media conglomerate, Time Warner countered and bought Turner Broadcasting in 1995 for $7.5 billion. In 2001, AOL acquired Time Warner for $106 billion–the largest media merger in history at the time. For a time the company was called AOL Time Warner. However, when the online giant saw its subscription service decline in the face of new high-speed broadband services from cable firms, the company went back to the Time Warner name and spun off AOL in 2009. Time Warner's failed venture in the volatile world of the Internet proved disastrous. The companies together were valued at $350 billion in 2000 but only at $50 billion in 2010. After suffering losses of over $700 million in 2010, AOL in 2011 bought the *Huffington Post,* a popular news and analysis Web site, for $315 million in an attempt to reverse its decline.

Also in 2001, the federal government approved a $72 billion deal uniting AT&T's cable division with Comcast, creating a cable company twice the size of its nearest competitor. (AT&T quickly left the merger, selling its cable holdings to Comcast for $47 billion late in 2001.) In 2009, Comcast struck a deal with GE to purchase a majority stake in NBC Universal, stirring up antitrust complaints from some consumer groups. In 2010, Congress began hearings on whether uniting a major cable company and a major broadcasting network under a single owner would decrease healthy competition between cable and broadcast TV and would hurt consumers. In 2011, the FCC approved the deal. In 2012, Comcast, as NBC's new owner, bought out Microsoft's share of MSNBC.

Until the 1980s, antitrust rules attempted to ensure diversity of ownership among competing businesses. Sometimes this happened, as in the breakup of AT&T, and sometimes it did not, as in the cases of local newspaper and cable monopolies and the mergers listed above. What has

Media Literacy and the Critical Process

1 DESCRIPTION. Using international box office revenue listings (www.boxofficemojo.com/intl is a good place to start), compare the recent weekly box office rankings of the United States to those of five other countries. (Your sample could extend across several continents or focus on a specific region, like Southeast Asia.) Limit yourself to the top ten or fifteen films in box office rank. Note where each film is produced (some films are joint productions of studios from two or more countries), and put your results in a table for comparison.

2 ANALYSIS. What patterns emerged in each country's box office rankings? What percentage of films came from the United States? What percentage of films were domestic productions in each country? What percentage of films came from countries other than the United States? In the United States, what percentage of top films originated with studios from other countries?

3 INTERPRETATION. So what do your discoveries mean? Can you make an argument for or against the existence of cultural imperialism by the United States? Are there film industries from other countries that dominate movie theaters in their region of the world? How would you critique the reverse of cultural imperialism, wherein international films from other countries rarely break into the Top 10 box office list? Does this happen in any countries you sampled?

4 EVALUATION. Given your interpretation, is cultural dominance by one country a good thing or a bad thing? Consider the potential advantages of creating a "global village" of shared popular culture versus the potential disadvantages of cultural imperialism. Also, is there any potential harm in a country's box office Top 10 list being filled by domestic productions and rarely having international films featured?

5 ENGAGEMENT. Contact your local movie theater (or the headquarters of the chain that owns it). Ask them how they decide which films to screen. If they don't show many international films, ask them why not. Be ready to provide a list of three to five international films released in the United States (see the full list of current U.S. releases at www.boxofficemojo.com) that haven't yet been screened in your theater.

Cultural Imperialism and Movies

In the 1920s, the U.S. film industry became the leader of the worldwide film business. The images and stories of American films are well known in nearly every corner of the earth. But with major film production centers in places like India, China, Hong Kong, Japan, South Korea, Mexico, the United Kingdom, Germany, France, Russia, and Nigeria, how much do U.S. films dominate international markets today? Conversely, how often do international films get much attention in the United States?

---

are still uncertain whether this type of Internet exposure actually works as a form of promotion for their content, drawing in new viewers and readers. In addition, these companies are unsure of how to take the next step–getting people who are accustomed to free online content to pay. Some categories of media content do better than others. For example, a 2012 Nielsen survey found that "tablet owners aren't opposed to paying for the media they really want." In the United States, 62 percent of tablet owners had paid for downloading music, while 58 percent paid for books, 51 percent for movies, 41 percent for TV shows and magazines, 27 percent for streaming radio, 22 percent for sports, and only 19 percent for news.[23]

The Rise of the New Digital Media Conglomerates

The digital turn marks a shift in the media environment from the legacy media powerhouses like Time Warner and Disney to the new digital media conglomerates. Five companies reign larger than others in digital media: Amazon, Apple, Facebook, Google, and Microsoft. Each has become powerful for different reasons. Amazon's entrée is that it has grown into the largest e-commerce site in the world. In recent years, Amazon has begun shifting from delivering physical products (e.g., bound books) to distributing digital products (e.g., e-books and downloadable music, movies, television shows, and more), on its digital devices (Kindles). Apple's strength has been creating the technology and the infrastructure to bring any media content to users' fingertips. When many traditional media companies didn't have the means to distribute content online easily, Apple developed the shiny devices (the iPod, iPhone, and iPad) and easy-to-use systems (the iTunes store) to do it, immediately transforming the media industries. Today, Apple has a hand in every media industry, as it offers the premiere platforms of the digital turn. In 2012, Apple became the most valuable company in the world, with shares worth $625.3 billion.

Facebook's strength has been its ability to become central to communication and social media. As Facebook's number of users approached one billion worldwide in 2012, the company still struggled to fully leverage those users (and the massive amounts of data they share about themselves) into advertising sales, particularly as its users move to accessing Facebook via mobile phones. Unlike the other four digital companies, Facebook lacks hardware devices to access the Internet and digital media. Google, which draws its huge numbers of users through its search function, has much more successfully translated those users (and the information provided by their search terms) into an advertising business worth more than $42 billion a year. Google is also moving into the same digital media distribution business that Apple and Amazon offer, via its Android phone operating system and its Nexus 7 tablet. Microsoft, one of the wealthiest digital companies in the world, is making the transition from being the top software company (a business that is slowly in decline) to competing in the digital media world with its Bing search engine and devices like its successful Xbox game console and its new Surface tablet. Microsoft also owns Yammer, a business social network, and holds a small ownership share in Facebook.

Given how technologically adept these five digital corporations have proven to be, they still need to provide compelling narratives to attract people (to repeat a point from the beginning of the chapter). All five companies are weak in this regard, as they rely on other companies' media narratives (e.g., the sounds, images, words, and pictures) or the stories that their own users provide (as in Facebook posts or YouTube videos). The history of mass communication suggests that it is the content—the narratives—that are enduring, while the devices and distribution systems are not.

The Digital Age Favors Small, Flexible Startup Companies

All of the leading digital companies of today were once small startups that emerged at important junctures of the digital age. The earliest, Microsoft and Apple, were established in the mid-1970s, with the rise of the personal computer. Amazon began in 1995 with the popularization of the Web and the beginnings of e-commerce. Google was established in 1998, as search engines became the best way of navigating the Web. And Facebook, starting in 2004, proved to be the best social media site to emerge in the 2000s. For each success story, though, hundreds of other firms failed or flamed out quickly (e.g., MySpace).

Today, the juncture in the digital era is the growing importance of social media and mobile devices. Like in the earlier periods, the strategy for startup companies is to find a niche market, connect with consumers, and then get big fast, swallowing up or overwhelming competitors. Instagram, Foursquare, Twitter, and Zynga are recent examples of this. The successful startups then take two paths—either be acquired by a larger company (e.g., Google buying YouTube, Facebook buying Instagram) or go it alone and try to get even bigger (e.g., Twitter). Either way, success might not last long, especially in an age when people's interests can move on very quickly.

Such diversification promotes oligopolies in which a few behemoth companies control most media production and distribution. This kind of economic arrangement makes it difficult for products offered outside an oligopoly to compete in the marketplace. For instance, in broadcast TV, the few networks that control prime time–all of them now owned by or in league with film studios–offer programs that are selected from known production companies that the networks either contract with regularly or own outright. Thus, even with a very good program or series idea, an independent production company–especially one that operates outside Los Angeles or New York–has a very difficult time entering the national TV market. The film giants even prefer buying from each other before dealing with independents. So, for example, in 2009 CBS sold syndication rights for its popular crime show *The Mentalist* to the TNT cable channel for over $2 million per episode. And for years, CBS's *Without a Trace* and NBC's *Law and Order* were both running in syndication on cable's TNT channel, owned by Time Warner, which also co-owns the CW network with CBS.

Local Monopolies

Because antitrust laws aim to curb national monopolies, most media monopolies today operate locally. For instance, although Gannett owns ninety daily newspapers, it controls less than 10 percent of daily U.S. newspaper circulation. Nonetheless, almost all Gannett papers are monopolies–that is, they are the only papers in their respective towns. Virtually every cable company has been granted monopoly status in its local community; these firms alone often decide which channels are made available and what rates are charged.

Furthermore, antitrust laws have no teeth globally. Although international copyright laws offer some protection to musicians and writers, no international antitrust rules exist to pro-hibit transnational companies from buying up as many media companies as they can afford. Still, as legal scholar Harry First points out, antitrust concerns are "alive and well and living in Europe."[25] For example, when Sony and Bertelsmann's BMG unit joined their music businesses, only the European Union (EU) raised questions about the merger on behalf of the independent labels and musicians worried about the oligopoly structure of the music business. The EU has frequently reviewed the merger, starting in 2004, but decided in late 2008 to withdraw its opposition.

Occasionally, independent voices raise issues that aid the Justice Department and the FTC in their antitrust cases. For example, when EchoStar (now the DISH Network) proposed to purchase DirecTV in 2001, a number of rural, consumer, and Latino organizations spoke out against the merger for several reasons. Latino organizations opposed the merger because in many U.S. markets, Direct Broadcast Satellite (DBS) service offers the only available Spanish-language television programming. The merger would have left the United States with just one major DBS company and created a virtual monopoly for EchoStar, which had fewer Spanish-language offerings than DirecTV. In 2002, the FCC declined to approve the merger, saying it would not serve the public interest, convenience, and necessity.

In 2011, AT&T moved to acquire T-Mobile, another wireless telecom giant (with more than thirty-three million customers), for $39 billion. The Justice Department opposed the merger on antitrust grounds (media watchdog groups said it would have left the country with just three major mobile phone companies, giving consumers far fewer options), leading AT&T to eventu-ally scrap the deal.

The Fallout from a Free Market

Since the wave of media mergers began with gusto in the 1980s, a number of consumer critics have pointed to the lack of public debate surrounding the tightening oligopoly structure of international media. Economists and media critics have traced the causes and history of this void to two major issues: a reluctance to criticize capitalism and the debate over how much control consumers have in the marketplace.

Equating Free Markets with Democracy

In the 1920s and 1930s, commercial radio executives, many of whom befriended FCC members, succeeded in portraying themselves as operating in the public interest while labeling their non-commercial radio counterparts in education, labor, or religion as mere voices of propaganda. In these early debates, corporate interests succeeded in aligning the political ideas of democracy, misleadingly, with the economic structures of capitalism.

Throughout the Cold War period in the 1950s and 1960s, it became increasingly difficult to criticize capitalism, which had become a synonym for democracy in many circles. In this context, any criticism of capitalism became an attack on the free marketplace. This, in turn, appeared to be a criticism of free speech because the business community often sees its right to operate in a free marketplace as an extension of its right to buy commercial speech in the form of advertising. As longtime CBS chief William Paley told a group of educators in 1937: "He who attacks the fundamentals of the American system" of commercial broadcasting "attacks democracy itself."[26]

Broadcast historian Robert McChesney, discussing the rise of commercial radio during the 1930s, has noted that leaders like Paley "equated capitalism with the free and equal market-place, the free and equal marketplace with democracy, and democracy with 'Americanism.'"[27] The collapse of the former Soviet Union's communist economy in the 1990s is often portrayed as a triumph for democracy. As we now realize, however, it was primarily a victory for capitalism and free-market economies.

Consumer Choice vs. Consumer Control

As many economists point out, capitalism is not structured democratically but arranged vertically, with powerful corporate leaders at the top and hourly wage workers at the bottom. But democracy, in principle, is built on a more horizontal model in which each individual has an equal opportunity to have his or her voice heard and vote counted. In discussing free markets, economists distinguish between similar types of consumer power: *consumer control* over marketplace goods and freedom of *consumer choice*: "The former requires that consumers participate in deciding what is to be offered; the latter is satisfied if [consumers are] free to select among the options chosen for them by producers."[28] Most Americans and the citizens of other economically developed nations clearly have *consumer choice*: options among a range of media products. Yet consumers and even media employees have limited *consumer control*: power in deciding what kinds of media get created and circulated.

One promising development concerns the role of independent and alternative producers, artists, writers, and publishers. Despite the movement toward economic consolidation, the fringes of media industries still offer a diversity of opinions, ideas, and alternative products. In fact, when independent companies become even marginally popular, they are often pursued by large companies that seek to make them subsidiaries. For example, alternative music often taps into social concerns that are not normally discussed in the recording industry's corporate boardrooms. Moreover, business leaders "at the top" depend on independent ideas "from below" to generate new product lines. A number of transnational corporations encourage the development of local artists–talented individuals who might have the capacity to transcend the regional or national level and become the next global phenomenon.

> "[AOL Time Warner] turned into one of the biggest corporate disasters in U.S. history: America Online's business collapsed, synergies failed to materialize, the company missed its financial targets, and the stock price plunged."
>
> *WALL STREET JOURNAL*, 2003

> "What they were really looking forward to was creating the biggest shopping mall in the world."
>
> BEN BAGDIKIAN, AUTHOR OF *THE MEDIA MONOPOLY*, ON THE AOL-TIME WARNER MERGER, 2000

CULTURAL IMPERIALISM
Ever since Hollywood gained an edge in film production and distribution during World War I, U.S. movies have dominated the box office in Europe, in some years accounting for more than 80 percent of the revenues taken in by European theaters.

Cultural Imperialism

The influence of American popular culture has created considerable debate in international circles. On the one hand, the notion of freedom that is associated with innovation and rebellion in American culture has been embraced internationally. The global spread of and access to media have made it harder for political leaders to secretly repress dissident groups because police and state activity (such as the torture of illegally detained citizens) can now be documented digitally and easily dispatched by satellite, the Internet, and cell phones around the world.

On the other hand, American media are shaping the cultures and identities of other nations. American styles in fashion and food, as well as media fare, dominate the global market—a process known as **cultural imperialism**. Today, many international observers contend that the idea of consumer control or input is even more remote in countries inundated by American movies, music, television, and images of beauty. For example, consumer product giant Unilever sells Dove soap with its "Campaign for Real Beauty" in the United States, but markets Fair & Lovely products—a skin-lightening line—to poor women in India.

Although many indigenous forms of media culture—such as Brazil's *telenovela* (a TV soap opera), Jamaica's reggae, and Japan's anime—are extremely popular, U.S. dominance in producing and distributing mass media puts a severe burden on countries attempting to produce their own cultural products. For example, American TV producers have generally recouped their production costs by the time their TV shows are exported. This enables American distributors to offer these programs to other countries at bargain rates, undercutting local production companies that are trying to create original programs.

Defenders of American popular culture argue that because some aspects of our culture challenge authority, national boundaries, and outmoded traditions, they create an arena in which citizens can raise questions. Supporters also argue that a universal popular culture creates a *global village* and fosters communication across national boundaries.

Critics, however, believe that although American popular culture often contains protests against social wrongs, such protests "can be turned into consumer products and lose their bite. Protest itself becomes something to sell."[29] The harshest critics have also argued that American cultural imperialism both hampers the development of native cultures and negatively influences teenagers, who abandon their own rituals to adopt American tastes. The exportation of U.S. entertainment media is sometimes viewed as "cultural dumping" because it discourages the development of original local products and value systems.

Perhaps the greatest concern regarding a global village is the cultural disconnection for people whose standards of living are not routinely portrayed in contemporary media. About two-thirds of the world's population cannot afford most of the products advertised on American, Japanese, and European television. Yet more and more of the world's populations are able to glimpse consumer abundance and middle-class values through television, magazines, and the Internet.

As early as the 1950s, media managers feared political fallout–"the revolution of rising expectations"–in that ads and products would raise the hopes of poor people but not keep pace with their actual living conditions.[30] Furthermore, the conspicuousness of consumer culture makes it difficult for many of us to imagine other ways of living that are not heavily dependent on the mass media and brand-name products.

The Media Marketplace and Democracy

In the midst of today's major global transformations of economies, cultures, and societies, the best way to monitor the impact of transnational economies is through vigorous news attention and lively public discussion. Clearly, however, this process is hampered. Starting in the 1990s, for example, news organizations, concerned about the bottom line, severely cut back the number of reporters assigned to cover international developments. This occurred–especially after 9/11–just as global news became more critical than ever to an informed citizenry.

We live in a society in which often-superficial or surface consumer concerns, stock market quotes, and profit aspirations, rather than broader social issues, increasingly dominate the media agenda. In response, critics have posed some key questions: As consumers, do we care who owns the media as long as most of us have a broad selection of products? Do we care who owns the media as long as multiple voices *seem* to exist in the market?

The Effects of Media Consolidation on Democracy

Merged and multinational media corporations will continue to control more aspects of production and distribution. Of pressing concern is the impact of mergers on news operations, particularly the influence of large corporations on their news subsidiaries. These companies have the capacity to use major news resources to promote their products and determine national coverage.

Because of the growing consolidation of mass media, it has become increasingly difficult to sustain a public debate on economic issues. From a democratic perspective, the relationship of our mass media system to politics has been highly dysfunctional. Politicians in Washington, D.C., have regularly accepted millions of dollars in contributions from large media conglomerates and their lobbying groups to finance their campaigns. This changed in 2008 when the Obama campaign raised much of its financing from small donors. Still, corporations got a big boost from the Supreme Court in early 2010 in the *Citizens United* case. In a five-to-four vote, the court "ruled that the government may not ban political spending by corporations in candidate elections."[31] Justice Anthony Kennedy, writing for the

THE PRESIDENT AND COFOUNDER of Free Press, a national nonpartisan organization dedicated to media reform, Robert McChesney is one of the foremost scholars of media economics in the United States. He is also the host of *Media Matters*, a radio call-in show that discusses the relationship between politics and media. Notable guests on the show have included Seymour Hersh, Amy Goodman, Gore Vidal, and Lawrence Lessig. McChesney (left) most recently published *The Death and Life of American Journalism* (2010) with John Nichols (right).

majority, said, "If the First Amendment has any force, it prohibits Congress from fining or jailing citizens, or associations of citizens, for simply engaging in political speech." The ruling overturned two decades of precedents that had limited direct corporate spending on campaigns, including the Bipartisan Campaign Reform Act of 2002 (often called McCain-Feingold after the senators who sponsored the bill), which placed restrictions on buying TV and radio campaign ads.

As unfettered corporate political contributions count as "political speech," some corporations are experiencing backlash (or praise) once their customers discover their political positions. For example, in 2012 fast food outlet Chick-fil-A's charitable foundation "was revealed to be funneling millions to groups that oppose gay marriage and, until recently, promoted gay 'cure' therapies," resulting in a firestorm of criticism, but also a wave of support from others, the *Daily Beast* reported. In the same year, Amazon founder and CEO Jeff Bezos and his wife donated $2.5 million of their own money to support a same-sex marriage referendum in Washington State, gaining praise and criticism from some Amazon customers.[32]

Politicians have often turned to local television stations, spending record amounts during each election period to get their political ads on the air. In 2004, local TV stations reaped an estimated $1.6 billion from political advertising during the election season. The 2008 election season broke another record, with $2.2 billion going to broadcast TV. But although broadcasters have been happy to take political ad money, they have been poor public citizens in covering their regional U.S. congressional candidates. According to a Lear Center Local News Study,

the amount of time given to presidential news coverage [in 2004] was in most cases roughly equivalent to the amount of presidential advertising time, even in markets where the presidential race was competitive. By contrast, in races for the U.S. Senate, ads outnumbered news by as much as seventeen-to-one, and in U.S. House races by as much as seven-to-one.[33]

In 2010, TV stations took in $2.5 billion during a midterm congressional election—another record. With even more unregulated campaign contributions, spending for the 2012 presidential and congressional races totaled almost $6 billion.[34]

The Media Reform Movement

Robert McChesney and John Nichols described the state of concern about the gathering consolidation of mainstream media power: "'Media Reform' has become a catch-all phrase to describe the broad goals of a movement that says consolidated ownership of broadcast and cable media, chain ownership of newspapers, and telephone and cable-company colonization of the Internet pose a threat not just to the culture of the Republic but to democracy itself."[35] While our current era has spawned numerous grassroots organizations that challenge media to do a better job for the sake of democracy, there has not been a large outcry from the general public for the kinds of concerns described by McChesney and Nichols. There is a reason for that. One key paradox of the Information Age is that for such economic discussions to be meaningful and democratic, they must be carried out in the popular media as well as in educational settings. Yet public debates and disclosures about the structure and ownership of the media are often not in the best economic interests of media owners.

Still, in some places, local groups and consumer movements are trying to address media issues that affect individual and community life. Such movements—like the National Conference for Media Reform—are usually united by geographic ties, common political backgrounds,

"The top management of the networks, with a few notable exceptions, has been trained in advertising, research, or show business. But by the nature of the corporate structure, they also make the final and crucial decisions having to do with news and public affairs. Frequently they have neither the time nor the competence to do this."

EDWARD R. MURROW, BROADCAST NEWS PIONEER, 1958

or shared concerns about the state of the media. The Internet has also made it possible for media reform groups to form globally, uniting around such issues as contesting censorship or monitoring the activities of multinational corporations. The movement was also largely responsible for the success of preserving "network neutrality," which prevents Internet service providers from censoring or penalizing particular Web sites and online services (see Chapter 2).

With this reform victory, and the 2008-09 economic crisis, perhaps we are more ready than ever to question some of the hierarchical and undemocratic arrangements of what McChesney, Nichols, and other reform critics call "Big Media." Even in the face of so many media mergers, the general public today seems open to such examinations, which might improve the global economy, improve worker conditions, and also serve the public good. By better understanding media economics, we can make a contribution to critiquing media organizations and evaluating their impact on democracy. ▷

CHAPTER REVIEW

COMMON THREADS

One of the Common Threads discussed in Chapter 1 is about the commercial nature of the mass media. In thinking about media ownership regulations, it is important to consider how the media wield their influence.

During the 2000 presidential election, two marginal candidates, Pat Buchanan on the Right, and Ralph Nader on the Left, shared a common view that both major party candidates largely ignored. Buchanan and Nader warned of the increasing power of corporations to influence the economy and our democracy. In fact, between 2000 and 2012, total spending on lobbying in the nation's capital grew from $1.57 billion to more than $3 billion.[36] (See Chapter 12 for more on lobbyists.)

These warnings generally have gone unnoticed and unreported by mainstream media, whose reporters, editors, and pundits often work for the giant media corporations that not only are well represented by Washington lobbyists but also give millions of dollars in campaign contributions to the major parties to influence legislation that governs media ownership and commercial speech.

Fast-forward to 2012. As politicians spoke of transparency and truth-telling, their campaign funding process had few of those characteristics. In the aftermath of the U.S. Supreme Court's *Citizens United* (2010) decision, new Super PACS (Political Action Committees) formed that can channel unlimited funds into political races as long as they don't officially "coordinate" with the political campaigns. With his own Super PAC (named "Americans for a Better Tomorrow, Tomorrow") comedian Stephen Colbert has satirized the lax standards of Super PAC rules that enable hundreds of millions of dollars to be channeled into politics while obscuring disclosure of the contributors' identities. By December 2012, Super PACs had spent more than $644 million on the 2012 election cycle (mostly in negative attack ads), with the majority of contributions coming from a few dozen elite ultra-wealthy donors. For example, Las Vegas casino magnate Sheldon Adelson and his wife donated in excess of $54 million to candidates and Super PACs in the 2012 election cycle.[37] The huge influx of money was a boon for media advertising profits.

What both Buchanan and Nader argued in 2000 was that corporate influence is a bipartisan concern that we share in common and that all of us in a democracy need to be vigilant about how powerful and influential corporations become. This is especially true for the media companies that report the news and distribute many of our cultural stories. As media-literate consumers, we need to demand that the media serve as watchdogs over the economy and our democratic values. And when they fall down on the job, we need to demand accountability (through alternative media channels or the Internet), especially from those mainstream media—radio, television, and cable—that are licensed to operate in the public interest.

KEY TERMS

The definitions for the terms listed below can be found in the glossary at the end of the book. The page numbers listed with the terms indicate where the term is highlighted in the chapter.

monopoly, 452
oligopoly, 453
limited competition, 453

direct payment, 454
indirect payment, 454
economies of scale, 454

hegemony, 459
synergy, 462
cultural imperialism, 474

REVIEW QUESTIONS

Analyzing the Media Economy

1. How are the three basic structures of mass media organizations—monopoly, oligopoly, and limited competition—different from one another?

2. What are the differences between direct and indirect payments for media products?

3. What are some of society's key expectations of its media organizations?

The Transition to an Information Economy

4. Why has the federal government emphasized deregulation at a time when so many media companies are growing so large?

5. How have media mergers changed the economics of mass media?

Specialization, Global Markets, and Convergence

6. How do global and specialized markets factor into the new media economy? How are regular workers affected?

7. Using Disney as an example, what is the role of synergy in the current climate of media mergers?

8. Why have Amazon, Apple, Facebook, Google, and Microsoft emerged as the leading corporations of the digital era?

Social Issues in Media Economics

9. What are the differences between freedom of consumer choice and consumer control?

10. What is cultural imperialism, and what does it have to do with the United States?

The Media Marketplace and Democracy

11. What do critics and activists fear most about the concentration of media ownership? How do media managers and executives respond to these fears?

12. What are some promising signs regarding the relationship between media economics and democracy?

QUESTIONING THE MEDIA

1. Why are consumers more likely to pay to download some digital content, like music and books, and less likely to pay for other content, like sports and news?

2. Why are narratives—media content—crucial to the success of a media corporation?

3. How does the concentration of media ownership limit the number of voices in the marketplace? Do we need rules limiting media ownership?

4. Is there such a thing as a global village? What does this concept mean to you?

ADDITIONAL VIDEOS

Visit the ⊙ VideoCentral: Mass Communication **section at bedfordstmartins.com/mediaculture** **for additional exclusive videos related to Chapter 13, including:**

- THE MONEY BEHIND THE MEDIA
  Producers, advertisers, and advocates discuss how ownership systems and profits shape media production.

PART 5
Democratic Expression and the Mass Media

The freedom and openness of the Internet is a double-edged sword. In a digital world overloaded with data and news, it has become much easier to obtain information. With so many people paying attention to the details of everyday life, it is also easier to uncover wrongdoing by business and government, and even to hold these institutions to higher levels of transparency. The news media are helping to do this, but the digital turn and online outlets—particularly Facebook, Twitter, and YouTube—have provided new methods that allow ordinary citizens and nonprofit groups to do some of the work once performed by investigative journalists. The lack of centralized control over the Internet also means that people have been able to use digital technologies and our interconnectedness as a way to be heard and to effect change. Both the Arab Spring uprisings in the Middle East and the Occupy Wall Street movement serve as examples.

At the same time, though, this ease of getting information has led to more situations of ethically gray practices. For example, "hacktivists" like WikiLeaks and Anonymous have raised issues regarding whether some government and business documents should remain secret—to protect national security, the volatile economic markets, or vulnerable diplomats or other individuals at work in difficult areas of the world—or if all information should be made available to the public at all times. The fragmented and accessible nature of the Internet has led to concerns about how to best police the online world and control its overwhelming array of voices and traffic. For example, parents remain concerned about their kids accessing pornography and violent media on the Internet, and governments and corporations alike are still figuring out how to regulate piracy and copyright issues involving the Internet. In fact, two congressional anti-piracy bills, the House's Stop Online Piracy Act (SOPA) and the Senate's Protect Intellectual Property Act (PIPA) were under consideration in early 2012. The proposed bills were intended to protect against copyright violations and intellectual property theft, but many Web sites and everyday users opposed the legislation as violating the open spirit of the Internet. Wikipedia, Reddit, Mozilla, WordPress, and MoveOn.org, among many others, participated in a massive twenty-four-hour Internet blackout. The bills were withdrawn as a result of the protests. Later bipartisan legislation, the Online Protection and Enforcement of Digital Trade Act, sponsored by a Republican congressman and a Democratic senator, proposed a compromise bill that would fight piracy but protect Internet access and openness. We may be seeing similar compromises in the years ahead as we continue to explore how powerful mass media fit into a democracy.

Social News Media

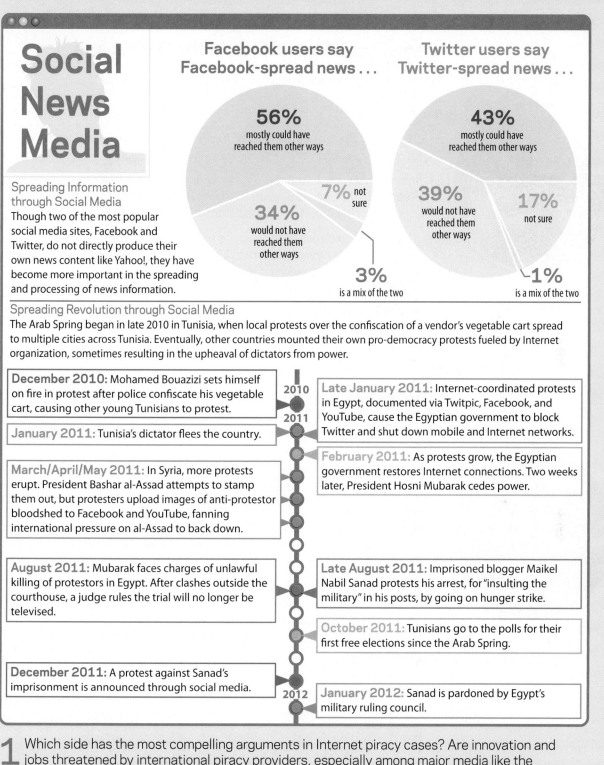

Facebook users say Facebook-spread news . . .

56% mostly could have reached them other ways

7% not sure

34% would not have reached them other ways

3% is a mix of the two

Twitter users say Twitter-spread news . . .

43% mostly could have reached them other ways

39% would not have reached them other ways

17% not sure

1% is a mix of the two

Spreading Information through Social Media

Though two of the most popular social media sites, Facebook and Twitter, do not directly produce their own news content like Yahoo!, they have become more important in the spreading and processing of news information.

Spreading Revolution through Social Media

The Arab Spring began in late 2010 in Tunisia, when local protests over the confiscation of a vendor's vegetable cart spread to multiple cities across Tunisia. Eventually, other countries mounted their own pro-democracy protests fueled by Internet organization, sometimes resulting in the upheaval of dictators from power.

December 2010: Mohamed Bouazizi sets himself on fire in protest after police confiscate his vegetable cart, causing other young Tunisians to protest.

January 2011: Tunisia's dictator flees the country.

March/April/May 2011: In Syria, more protests erupt. President Bashar al-Assad attempts to stamp them out, but protesters upload images of anti-protestor bloodshed to Facebook and YouTube, fanning international pressure on al-Assad to back down.

August 2011: Mubarak faces charges of unlawful killing of protestors in Egypt. After clashes outside the courthouse, a judge rules the trial will no longer be televised.

December 2011: A protest against Sanad's imprisonment is announced through social media.

2010
2011
2012

Late January 2011: Internet-coordinated protests in Egypt, documented via Twitpic, Facebook, and YouTube, cause the Egyptian government to block Twitter and shut down mobile and Internet networks.

February 2011: As protests grow, the Egyptian government restores Internet connections. Two weeks later, President Hosni Mubarak cedes power.

Late August 2011: Imprisoned blogger Maikel Nabil Sanad protests his arrest, for "insulting the military" in his posts, by going on hunger strike.

October 2011: Tunisians go to the polls for their first free elections since the Arab Spring.

January 2012: Sanad is pardoned by Egypt's military ruling council.

1 Which side has the most compelling arguments in Internet piracy cases? Are innovation and jobs threatened by international piracy providers, especially among major media like the Hollywood movie industry or the music recording business? Or is piracy the price we pay in a free and open society where the Internet is one of the major illustrations of our nation's free expression?

2 Are social networks like Facebook and Twitter—which can often spur protests and facilitate change—enough to actually overthrow a repressive government? What can you learn from current research about what is now going on in the countries that were affected by Arab Spring uprisings in early 2011?

See Notes for list of sources.

Democratic Expression in the Digital Age

Though debates continue about how open and free the Internet should be, society and culture have experienced many positive effects of a relatively open Internet.

- The United States has a history of free expression and free press going back to our First Amendment (Chapter 16, pages 549–550).

- In some ways, the Internet is a mass medium best-suited for true unlimited free speech (Chapter 16, page 570), and, as such, fighting for net neutrality has become an important cause (Chapter 2, pages 71–72).

- This freedom includes giving voice to those not necessarily in power, as with the Arab Spring protests (Chapter 2, pages 54–55), the rise of blogging and the way it connects to citizen journalism (Chapter 8, pages 307–308), and our newfound ability to communicate with big corporations via social media (Chapter 13, page 469).

The Issues and Gray Areas of the Digital Age

Still, several concerns about the ease of spreading information on the Internet remain in the digital age.

- Violent and sexual content is easier to distribute and access online (Chapter 2, page 69), especially when users can make and distribute their own inappropriate content (Chapter 16, page 570).

- Internet privacy, or lack thereof, can exacerbate the issue of journalists' need to get a story first and fastest—sometimes disregarding ethics (Chapter 14, page 494).

- While the Internet gives us the opportunity to demand and receive further transparency from our government and corporations, there are ethical gray areas involving dissemination of information via groups like WikiLeaks (Chapter 14, page 514) and hacktivist groups like Anonymous (Chapter 2, pages 56–57).

Regulating an Open and Free Internet

As such, questions arise about how we might go about regulating the Internet, if at all.

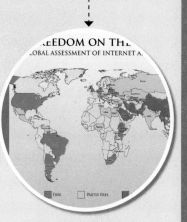

- Recent attempts to regulate the Internet, like the SOPA and PIPA bills proposed in early 2012, have been met with criticism—and protest from some of the highest-profile sites on the Web (Chapter 16, page 572).

- Many of the regulations like SOPA and PIPA address (or call into question) copyright law. Piracy has affected many of the mass media, particularly the music industry, which has been forced to reevaluate its business model due to widespread downloading (Chapter 4, pages 149-150).

- Though piracy is often referred to using the blanket term *illegal downloading*, copyright law has many uneven and unclear rules regarding sampling sounds, images, video, and text (Chapter 16, Examining Ethics box, page 571).

- Other media industries have regulated themselves as a result of media effects research (Chapter 15, pages 526-528), like the digital gaming industry (Chapter 3, page 103) and the film industry (Chapter 7, page 259). But such efforts may not matter in the age of the Internet, when users can consume virtually any content at virtually any time (Chapter 16, page 557).

- Proponents of Net neutrality believe that every Web site and user have the right to the same Internet speed and access, while corporations would prefer to offer faster, higher-priority connections to clients who pay more—or preferential service for content providers who pay more (Chapter 2, pages 71-72).

> ▶ **For more on Internet users creating their own content, watch the "User-Generated Content" video on** *VideoCentral: Mass Communication* **at bedfordstmartins.com/mediaculture.**

14

The Culture of Journalism

Values, Ethics, and Democracy

In 1887, a young reporter left her job at the *Pittsburgh Dispatch* to seek her fortune in New York City. Only twenty-three years old, Elizabeth "Pink" Cochrane had grown tired of writing for the society pages and answering letters to the editor. She wanted to be on the front page. But at that time, it was considered "unladylike" for women journalists to use their real names, so the *Dispatch* editors, borrowing from a Stephen Foster song, had dubbed her "Nellie Bly."

After four months of persistent job-hunting and freelance writing, Nellie Bly earned a tryout at Joseph Pulitzer's *New York World*, the nation's biggest paper. Her assignment: to investigate the deplorable conditions at the Women's Lunatic Asylum on Blackwell's Island. Her method: to get herself declared mad and committed to the asylum. After practicing the look of a disheveled lunatic in front of mirrors, wandering city streets unwashed and seemingly dazed, and terrifying her fellow boarders in a New York rooming house by acting crazy, she succeeded in convincing doctors and officials to commit her. Other New York newspapers reported her incarceration, speculating on the identity of this "mysterious waif," this "pretty crazy girl" with the "wild, hunted look in her eyes."[1]

Her two-part story appeared in October 1887 and caused a sensation. She was the first reporter to pull off such a stunt. In the days before objective journalism, Nellie Bly's dramatic first-person accounts documented harsh cold baths ("three buckets of water over my head—ice cold water—into my eyes, my ears, my nose and my mouth"); attendants who abused and taunted patients; and newly arrived immigrant women, completely sane, who were committed to this "rat trap" simply because no one could understand them. After the exposé, Bly was famous. Pulitzer gave her a permanent job, and New York City committed $1 million toward improving its asylums.

Within a year, Nellie Bly had exposed a variety of shady scam artists, corrupt politicians and lobbyists, and unscrupulous business practices. Posing as an "unwed mother" with an unwanted child, she uncovered an outfit trafficking in newborn babies. And disguised as a sinner in need of reform, she revealed the appalling conditions at a home for "unfortunate women." A lifetime champion of women and the poor, Nellie Bly pioneered what was then called *detective* or *stunt* journalism. Her work inspired the twentieth-century practice of investigative journalism—from Ida Tarbell's exposés of oil corporations in the early 1900s

to the 2011 Pulitzer Prize for investigative reporting, awarded to Paige St. John of the *Sarasota Herald-Tribune* for her work on "the weaknesses in the murky property-insurance system vital to Florida homeowners, providing handy data to assess insurer reliability and stirring regulatory action."[2]

Such journalism can be dangerous. Working for Dublin's *Sunday Independent*, Veronica Guerin was the first reporter to cover in depth Ireland's escalating organized crime and drug problem. In 1995, a man forced his way into her home and shot her in the thigh. After the assault, she wrote about the incident, vowing to continue her reporting despite her fears. She was also punched in the face by the suspected head of Ireland's gang world, who threatened to hurt Guerin's son and kill her if she wrote about the crime boss. She kept writing. In December 1995, she flew to New York to receive the International Press Freedom Award from the Committee to Protect Journalists.

When Guerin returned to Dublin, she began writing stories naming gang members suspected of masterminding drug-related crimes and a string of eleven unsolved contract murders. In June 1996, while stopped in her car at a Dublin intersection, she was shot five times by two hired killers. Ireland and the world's journalists mourned Veronica Guerin's death. Later, the Irish government created laws that allowed judges to deny bail to dangerous suspects and opened a bureau to confiscate money and property from suspected drug criminals and gang members.

◢ *JOURNALISM IS THE ONLY MEDIA ENTERPRISE* that democracy absolutely requires—and it is the only media practice and business that is specifically mentioned and protected by the U.S. Constitution. However, with the major decline in traditional news audiences, the collapse of many newspapers, and the rise of twenty-four-hour cable news channels and Internet news blogs, mainstream journalism is searching for new business models and better ways to connect with the public.

In this chapter, we examine the changing news landscape and definitions of journalism. We will:

- Explore the values underlying news and ethical problems confronting journalists
- Investigate the shift from more neutral news models to partisan cable and online news
- Study the legacy of print-news conventions and rituals
- Investigate the impact of television and the Internet on news
- Consider contemporary controversial developments in journalism and democracy—specifically, the public journalism movement and satirical forms of news

As you read this chapter, think about how often you look at the news in a typical day. What are some of the recent events or issues you remember reading about in the news? Where is the first place you go to find information about a news event or issue? If you start with a search engine, what newspapers or news organizations do you usually end up looking at? Do you prefer opinion blogs over news organizations for your information? Why or why not? Do you pay for news—either by buying a newspaper or news magazine or by going online? For more questions to help you understand the role of journalism in our lives, see "Questioning the Media" in the Chapter Review.

> "A journalist is the lookout on the bridge of the ship of state. He peers through the fog and storm to give warnings of dangers ahead. . . . He is there to watch over the safety and the welfare of the people who trust him."
>
> JOSEPH PULITZER, 1904

Modern Journalism in the Information Age

In modern America, serious journalism has sought to provide information that enables citizens to make intelligent decisions. Today, this guiding principle faces serious threats. Why? First, we may just be producing too much information. According to social critic Neil Postman, as a result of developments in media technology, society has developed an "information glut" that transforms news and information into "a form of garbage."[3] Postman believed that scientists, technicians, managers, and journalists merely pile up mountains of new data, which add to the problems and anxieties of everyday life. As a result, too much unchecked data—especially on the Internet—and too little thoughtful discussion emanate from too many channels of communication.

A second, related problem suggests that the amount of data the media now provide has questionable impact on improving public and political life. Many people feel cut off from our major institutions, including journalism. As a result, some citizens are looking to take part in public conversations and civic debates—to renew a democracy in which many voices participate. For example, one benefit of the controversial *Bush v. Gore* 2000 post-presidential election story was the way its legal and political complications engaged the citizenry at a much deeper level than the predictable, staged campaigns themselves did.

> "When watchdogs, bird dogs, and bull dogs morph into lap dogs, lazy dogs, or yellow dogs, the nation is in trouble."
>
> TED STANNARD, FORMER UPI REPORTER

What Is News?

In a 1963 staff memo, NBC news president Reuven Frank outlined the narrative strategies integral to all news: "Every news story should . . . display the attributes of fiction, of drama. It should have structure and conflict, problem and denouement, rising and falling action,

"DEEP THROAT"
The major symbol of twentieth-century investigative journalism, Carl Bernstein and Bob Woodward's (above right) coverage of the Watergate scandal for the *Washington Post* helped topple the Nixon White House. In *All the President's Men*, the newsmen's book about their investigation, a major character is Deep Throat, the key unidentified source for much of Woodward's reporting. Deep Throat's identity was protected by the two reporters for more than thirty years. Then in summer 2005 he revealed himself as Mark Felt (above), the former No. 2 official in the FBI during the Nixon administration. (Felt died in 2008.)

a beginning, a middle, and an end."[4] Despite Frank's candid insights, many journalists today are uncomfortable thinking of themselves as storytellers. Instead, they tend to describe themselves mainly as information-gatherers.

News is defined here as the process of gathering information and making narrative reports—edited by individuals for news organizations—that offer selected frames of reference; within those frames, news helps the public make sense of important events, political issues, cultural trends, prominent people, and unusual happenings in everyday life.

Characteristics of News

Over time, a set of conventional criteria for determining **newsworthiness**—information most worthy of transformation into news stories—has evolved. Journalists are taught to select and develop news stories relying on one or more of these criteria: timeliness, proximity, conflict, prominence, human interest, consequence, usefulness, novelty, and deviance.[5]

Most issues and events that journalists select as news are *timely* or *new*. Reporters, for example, cover speeches, meetings, crimes, and court cases that have just happened. In addition, most of these events have to occur close by, or in *proximity* to, readers and viewers. Although local TV news and papers offer some national and international news, readers and viewers expect to find the bulk of news devoted to their own towns and communities.

Most news stories are narratives and thus contain a healthy dose of *conflict*—a key ingredient in narrative writing. In developing news narratives, reporters are encouraged to seek contentious quotes from those with opposing views. For example, stories on presidential elections almost always feature the most dramatic opposing Republican and Democratic positions. And many stories in the aftermath of the terrorist attacks of September 11, 2001, pitted the values of other cultures against those of Western culture—for example, Islam vs. Christianity or premodern traditional values vs. contemporary consumerism.

Reader and viewer surveys indicate that most people identify more closely with an individual than with an abstract issue. Therefore, the news media tend to report stories that feature *prominent*, powerful, or influential people. Because these individuals often play a role in shaping the rules and values of a community, journalists have traditionally been responsible for keeping a watchful eye on them and relying on them for quotes.

But reporters also look for the *human-interest* story: extraordinary incidents that happen to "ordinary" people. In fact, reporters often relate a story about a complicated issue (such as unemployment, war, tax rates, health care, or homelessness) by illustrating its impact on one "average" person, family, or town.

Two other criteria for newsworthiness are *consequence* and *usefulness*. Stories about isolated or bizarre crimes, even though they might be new, near, or notorious, often have little impact on our daily lives. To balance these kinds of stories, many editors and reporters believe that some news must also be of consequence to a majority of readers or viewers. For example, stories about issues or events that affect a family's income or change a community's laws have consequence. Likewise, many people look for stories with a practical use: hints on buying a used car or choosing a college, strategies for training a pet or removing a stain.

Finally, news is often about the *novel* and the *deviant*. When events happen that are outside the routine of daily life, such as a seven-year-old girl trying to pilot a plane across the country or an ex-celebrity involved in a drug deal, the news media are there. Reporters also cover events that appear to deviate from social norms, including murders, rapes, fatal car crashes, fires, political scandals, and gang activities. For example, as the war in Iraq escalated, any suicide bombing in the Middle East represented the kind of novel and deviant behavior that qualified as major news.

Values in American Journalism

Although newsworthiness criteria are a useful way to define news, they do not reveal much about the cultural aspects of news. News is both a product and a process. It is both the morning paper or evening newscast and a set of subtle values and shifting rituals that have been adapted to historical and social circumstances, such as the partisan press ideals of the 1700s or the informational standards of the twentieth century.

For example, in 1841, Horace Greeley described the newly founded *New York Tribune* as "a journal removed alike from servile partisanship on the one hand and from gagged, mincing neutrality on the other."[6] Greeley feared that too much neutrality would make reporters into wimps who stood for nothing. Yet the neutrality Greeley warned against is today a major value of conventional journalism, with mainstream reporters assuming they are acting as detached and all-seeing observers of social experience.

Neutrality Boosts Credibility . . . and Sales

As former journalism professor and reporter David Eason notes: "Reporters . . . have no special method for determining the truth of a situation nor a special language for reporting their findings. They make sense of events by telling stories about them."[7]

Even though journalists transform events into stories, they generally believe that they are–or should be–neutral observers who present facts without passing judgment on them. Conventions such as the inverted-pyramid news lead, the careful attribution of sources, the minimal use of adverbs and adjectives, and a detached third-person point of view all help reporters perform their work in an apparently neutral way.

Like lawyers, therapists, and other professionals, many modern journalists believe that their credibility derives from personal detachment. Yet the roots of this view reside in less noble territory. Jon Katz, media critic and former CBS News producer, discusses the history of the neutral pose:

The idea of respectable detachment wasn't conceived as a moral principle so much as a marketing device. Once newspapers began to mass market themselves in the mid-1880s, . . . publishers ceased being working, opinionated journalists. They mutated instead into businessmen eager to reach the broadest number of readers and antagonize the fewest. . . . Objectivity works well for publishers, protecting the status quo and keeping journalism's voice militantly moderate.[8]

"The 'information' the modern media provide leaves people feeling useless not because it's so bleak but because it's so trivial. It doesn't inform at all; it only bombards with random data bits, faux trends, and surveys that reinforce preconceptions."

SUSAN FALUDI,
THE NATION, 1996

"Real news is bad news—bad news about somebody, or bad news for somebody."

MARSHALL McLUHAN,
UNDERSTANDING MEDIA, 1964

OCCUPY WALL STREET
On September 17, 2011, a group of protestors gathered in Zuccotti Park in New York's financial district and officially launched the Occupy Wall Street protest movement. Their slogan, "We are the 99 percent," addressed the growing income disparity in the United States, furthering the idea that the nation's wealth is unfairly concentrated among the top-earning 1 percent. Although forced out of Zuccotti Park on November 15, 2011, the movement's efforts resonated with people across the country and around the world. By the end of 2011, Occupy protests had spread to over 951 cities in eighty-two countries.

To reach as many people as possible across a wide spectrum, publishers and editors realized as early as the 1840s that softening their partisanship might boost sales.

Partisanship Trumps Neutrality . . . Especially Online and On Cable

Since the rise of cable and the Internet, today's media marketplace offers a fragmented world where appealing to the widest audience no longer makes the best economic sense. More options than ever exist, with newspaper readers and TV viewers embracing cable news, social networks, blogs, and Twitter. The old "mass" audience has morphed into smaller niche audiences who embrace particular hobbies, storytelling, and politics. News media outlets that hope to survive no longer appeal to mass audiences but to interest groups—from sports fans and history buffs to conservatives or liberals. So, mimicking the news business of the eighteenth century, partisanship has become good business. For the news media today, muting political leanings to reach a mass audience makes no sense when such an audience no longer exists in the way it once did, especially as in the days when only three major TV networks offered evening news for one-half hour, once a day. Instead, news media now make money by targeting and catering to niche groups on a 24/7 news cycle.

In such a marketplace, we see the decline of a more neutral journalistic model that promoted fact-gathering, documents, and expertise, and that held up "objectivity" as the ideal for news practice. Rising in its place is a new era of partisan news—what Bill Kovach and Tom Rosenstiel call a "journalism of assertion"—marked partly by a return to journalism's colonial roots and partly by the downsizing of the "journalism of verification" that kept watch over our central institutions.[9] This transition is symbolized by the rise of the cable news pundit on Fox News or MSNBC as a kind of "expert" with more standing than verified facts, authentic documents, and actual experts. Today, the new partisan fervor found in news, both online and on cable, has been a major catalyst for the nation's intense political and ideological divide.

Other Cultural Values in Journalism

Even the neutral journalism model, which most reporters and editors still aspire to, remains a selective and uneven process. Reporters and editors turn some events into reports and discard many others. This process is governed by a deeper set of subjective beliefs that are not neutral. Sociologist Herbert Gans, who studied the newsroom cultures of CBS, NBC, *Newsweek*, and *Time* in the 1970s, generalized that several basic "enduring values" have been shared by most American reporters and editors. The most prominent of these values, which persist to this day, are ethnocentrism, responsible capitalism, small-town pastoralism, and individualism.[10]

By **ethnocentrism** Gans means that, in most news reporting, especially foreign coverage, reporters judge other countries and cultures on the basis of how "they live up to or imitate American practices and values." Critics outside the United States, for instance, point out that CNN's international news channels portray world events and cultures primarily from an American point of view rather than through some neutral, global lens.

Gans also identified **responsible capitalism** as an underlying value, contending that journalists sometimes naïvely assume that businesspeople compete with one another not primarily to maximize profits but "to create increased prosperity for all." Gans points out that although most reporters and editors condemn monopolies, "there is little implicit or explicit criticism of the oligopolistic nature of much of today's economy."[11] In fact, during the major economic recession of 2008-09, many journalists did not fully understand the debt incurred by media oligopolies and other financial conditions that led to the bankruptcies and shutdowns of numerous newspapers during this difficult time.

Another value that Gans found was the romanticization of **small-town pastoralism**: favoring the small over the large and the rural over the urban. Many journalists equate small-town life with innocence and harbor suspicions of cities, their governments, and urban experiences. Consequently, stories about rustic communities with crime or drug problems have often been framed as if the purity of country life had been contaminated by "mean" big-city values.

Finally, **individualism**, according to Gans, remains the most prominent value underpinning daily journalism. Many idealistic reporters are attracted to this profession because it rewards the rugged tenacity needed to confront and expose corruption. Beyond this, individuals who overcome personal adversity are the subjects of many enterprising news stories.

Often, however, journalism that focuses on personal triumphs fails to explain how large organizations and institutions work or fail. Many conventional reporters and editors are unwilling or unsure of how to tackle the problems raised by institutional decay. In addition, because they value their own individualism and are accustomed to working alone, many journalists dislike cooperating on team projects or participating in forums in which community members discuss their own interests and alternative definitions of news.[12]

Facts, Values, and Bias

Traditionally, reporters have aligned facts with an objective position and values with subjective feelings.[13] Within this context, news reports offer readers and viewers details, data, and description. It then becomes the citizen's responsibility to judge and take a stand about the social problems represented by the news. Given these assumptions, reporters are responsible only for adhering to the tradition of the trade—"getting the facts." As a result, many reporters view themselves as neutral "channels" of information rather than selective storytellers or citizens actively involved in public life.

Still, most public surveys have shown that while journalists may work hard to stay neutral, the addition of partisan cable channels such as Fox News and MSNBC has undermined reporters who try to report fairly. So while conservatives tend to see the media as liberally biased, liberals tend to see the media as favoring conservative positions. (See "Case Study: Bias in the News" on page 492.) But political bias is complicated. During the early years of Barack Obama's presidency, many pundits on the political Right argued that Obama got much more favorable media coverage than did former president George W. Bush. But left-wing politicians and critics maintained that the right-wing media—especially news analysts associated with conservative talk radio and Fox's cable channel—rarely reported evenhandedly on Obama, painting him as a "socialist" or as "anti-American."

According to Evan Thomas of *Newsweek* magazine, "the suspicion of press bias" comes from two assumptions or beliefs that the public holds about news media: "The first is that reporters are out to get their subjects. The second is that the press is too close to its subjects."[14] Thomas argues that the "press's real bias is for conflict." He says that mainstream editors and reporters traditionally value scandals, "preferably sexual," and "have a weakness for war, the ultimate conflict." Thomas claims that in the end journalists "are looking for narratives that reveal something of character. It is the human drama that most compels our attention."[15]

"Your obligation, as an independent news organization, is to verify the material, to supply context, to exercise responsible judgment about what to publish and what not to publish and to make sense of it."

BILL KELLER, FORMER EXECUTIVE EDITOR, *NEW YORK TIMES*, 2011, WRITING ABOUT USING MATERIAL FROM WIKILEAKS

CASE STUDY

Bias in the News

All news is biased. News, after all, is primarily selective storytelling, not objective science. Editors choose certain events to cover and ignore others; reporters choose particular words or images to use and reject others. The news is also biased in favor of storytelling, drama, and conflict; in favor of telling "two sides of a story"; in favor of powerful and well-connected sources; and in favor of practices that serve journalists' space and time limits.

In terms of overt political bias, a 2010 Pew study reported that 81 percent of Republicans polled said they "completely" or "mostly agree" that "most news sources today are biased in their coverage"; for Democrats in this study, the figure was 64 percent and for independents, 76 percent.[1] Since the late 1960s, public perception says that mainstream news media operate mostly with a liberal bias. A June 2006 Harris Poll found 38 percent of adults surveyed detected a liberal bias in news coverage while 25 percent sensed a conservative bias (31 percent were "not sure" and 5 percent said there was "no bias").[2] This would seem to be supported by a 2004 Pew Research Center survey that found that 34 percent of national journalists self-identify as liberal, 7 percent as conservative, and 54 percent as moderate.[3]

Given primary dictionary definitions of *liberal* (adj., "favorable to progress or reform, as in political or religious affairs")

and *conservative* (adj., "disposed to preserve existing conditions, institutions, etc., or to restore traditional ones, and to limit change"), it is not surprising that a high percentage of liberals and moderates gravitate to mainstream journalism.[4] A profession that honors documenting change, checking power, and reporting wrongdoing would attract fewer conservatives, who are predisposed to "limit change." As sociologist Herbert Gans demonstrated in *Deciding What's News*, most reporters are socialized into a set of work rituals—especially getting the story first and telling it from "both sides" to achieve a kind of balance.[5] In fact, this commitment to political "balance" mandates that if journalists interview someone on the Left, they must also interview someone on the Right. Ultimately, such balancing acts require reporters to take middle-of-the-road or moderate positions.

Still, the "liberal bias" narrative persists. In 2001, Bernard Goldberg, a former producer at CBS News, wrote *Bias*. Using anecdotes from his days at CBS, he maintained that national news slanted to the Left.[6] In 2003, Eric Alterman, a columnist for the *Nation*, countered with *What Liberal Media?* Alterman admitted that mainstream news media do reflect more liberal views on social issues, but argued that they had become more conservative on politics and economics—displayed in their support

for deregulated media and concentrated ownership.[7] Alterman says the liberal bias tale persists because conservatives keep repeating it in the major media. Conservative voices have been so successful that one study in *Communication Research* reported "a fourfold increase over the past dozen years in the number of Americans telling pollsters that they discerned a liberal bias in the news. But a review of the media's actual ideological content, collected and coded over a 12-year period, offered no corroboration whatever for this view."[8] However, a 2010 study in the *Harvard International Journal of Press/Politics* reported that both Democratic and Republican leaders are able "to influence perceptions of bias" by attacking the news media.[9]

Since journalists are primarily storytellers, and not scientists, searching for liberal or conservative bias should not be the main focus of our criticism. Under time and space constraints, most journalists serve the routine practices of their profession, which calls on them to moderate their own political agendas. News reports, then, are always "biased," given human imperfection in storytelling and in communicating through the lens of language, images, and institutional values. Fully critiquing news stories depends, then, on whether they are fair, represent an issue's complexity, provide verification and documentation, represent multiple views, and serve democracy. ◢

IS THERE A BIAS IN REPORTING THE NEWS?

	Completely agree	Mostly agree	Mostly disagree	Completely disagree
Republicans	33%	48%	12%	12%
Democrats	14%	50%	24%	6%
Independents	23%	53%	14%	5%

Note: Margin of error is +/- 2 percentage points.
Source: PRC Internet & American Life Project and PRC Project for Excellence in Journalism Online News Survey, December 28, 2009–January 18, 2010.

Ethics and the News Media

A profound ethical dilemma that national journalists occasionally face, especially in the aftermath of 9/11, is: When is it right to protect government secrets, and when should those secrets be revealed to the public? How must editors weigh such decisions when national security bumps up against citizens' need for information?

In 2006, Dean Baquet, then editor of the *Los Angeles Times*, and Bill Keller, executive editor of the *New York Times*, wrestled with these questions in a coauthored editorial:

> *Finally, we weigh the merits of publishing against the risks of publishing. There is no magic formula. . . . We make our best judgment.*
>
> *When we come down on the side of publishing, of course, everyone hears about it. Few people are aware when we decide to hold an article. But each of us, in the past few years, has had the experience of withholding or delaying articles when the administration convinces us that the risk of publication outweighed the benefits. . . .*
>
> *We understand that honorable people may disagree . . . to publish or not to publish. But making those decisions is a responsibility that falls to editors, a corollary to the great gift of our independence. It is not a responsibility we take lightly. And it is not one we can surrender to the government.*[16]

What makes the predicament of these national editors so tricky is that in the war against terrorism, some politicians claimed that one value terrorists truly hate is "our freedom"; yet what is more integral to liberty than the freedom of an independent press—so independent that for more than two hundred years U.S. courts have protected the news media's right to criticize our political leaders and, within boundaries, reveal government secrets?

Ethical Predicaments

What is the moral and social responsibility of journalists, not only for the stories they report but also for the actual events or issues they are shaping for millions of people? Wrestling with such media ethics involves determining the moral response to a situation through critical reasoning. Although national security issues raise problems for a few of our largest news organizations, the most frequent ethical dilemmas encountered in most newsrooms across the United States involve intentional deception, privacy invasions, and conflicts of interest.

Deploying Deception

Ever since Nellie Bly faked insanity to get inside an asylum in the 1880s, investigative journalists have used deception to get stories. Today, journalists continue to use disguises and assume false identities to gather information on social transgressions. Beyond legal considerations, though, a key ethical question comes into play: Does the end justify the means? For example, can a newspaper or TV newsmagazine use deceptive ploys to go undercover and expose a suspected fraudulent clinic that promises miracle cures at a high cost? Are news professionals justified in posing as clients desperate for a cure?

In terms of ethics, there are at least two major positions and multiple variations. First, *absolutist ethics* suggests that a moral society has laws and codes, including honesty, that everyone must live by. This means citizens, including members of the news media, should tell the truth at all times and in all cases. In other words, the ends (exposing a phony clinic) never justify the means (using deception to get the story). An editor who is an absolutist would cover this story by asking a reporter to find victims who have been ripped off by the clinic, telling the story through their eyes. At the other end of the spectrum is *situational ethics*, which promotes ethical decisions on a case-by-case basis. If a greater public good could be served by using deceit, journalists and editors who believe in situational ethics would sanction deception as a practice.

Should a journalist withhold information about his or her professional identity to get a quote or a story from an interview subject? Many sources and witnesses are reluctant to talk with journalists, especially about a sensitive subject that might jeopardize a job or hurt another person's reputation. Journalists know they can sometimes obtain information by posing as someone other than a journalist, such as a curious student or a concerned citizen.

Most newsrooms frown on such deception. In particular situations, though, such a practice might be condoned if reporters and their editors believed that the public needed the information. The ethics code adopted by the Society of Professional Journalists (SPJ) is fairly silent on issues of deception. The code "requires journalists to perform with intelligence, objectivity, accuracy, and fairness," but it also says that "truth is our ultimate goal." (See Figure 14.1, "SPJ Code of Ethics," on page 495.)

Invading Privacy

To achieve "the truth" or to "get the facts," journalists routinely straddle a line between "the public's right to know" and a person's right to privacy. For example, journalists may be sent to hospitals to gather quotes from victims who have been injured. Often there is very little the public might gain from such information, but journalists worry that if they don't get the quote, a competitor might. In these instances, have the news media responsibly weighed the protection of individual privacy against the public's right to know? Although the latter is not constitutionally guaranteed, journalists invoke the public's right to know as justification for many types of stories.

One infamous example is the recent phone hacking scandal involving News Corp.'s now-shuttered U.K. newspaper, *News of the World*. In 2011, the *Guardian* reported that *News of the World* reporters had hired a private investigator to hack into the voice mail of thirteen-year-old murder victim Milly Dowler and had deleted some messages. Although there had been past allegations of reporters from *News of the World* hacking into the private voice mails of the British royal family, government officials, and celebrities, this revelation on the extent of *News of the World*'s phone hacking activities caused a huge scandal and led to the arrests and resignations of several senior executives. Today, in the digital age, when reporters can gain access to private e-mail messages, Twitter accounts, and Facebook pages as well as voice mail, such practices raise serious questions about how far a reporter should go to get information.

In the case of privacy issues, media companies and journalists should always ask the ethical questions: What public good is being served here? What significant public knowledge will be gained through the exploitation of a tragic private moment? Although journalism's code of ethics says, "The news media must guard against invading a person's right to privacy," this clashes with another part of the code: "The public's right to know of events of public importance and interest is the overriding mission of the mass media."[17] When these two ethical standards collide, should journalists err on the side of the public's right to know?

Conflict of Interest

Journalism's code of ethics also warns reporters and editors not to place themselves in positions that produce a **conflict of interest**–that is, any situation in which journalists may stand to benefit personally from stories they produce. "Gifts, favors, free travel, special treatment or

FIGURE 14.1

SOCIETY OF PROFESSIONAL JOURNALISTS' CODE OF ETHICS

Source: Society of Professional Journalists (SPJ).

▼

Code of Ethics

Preamble

Members of the Society of Professional Journalists believe that public enlightenment is the forerunner of justice and the foundation of democracy. The duty of the journalist is to further those ends by seeking truth and providing a fair and comprehensive account of events and issues. Conscientious journalists from all media and specialties strive to serve the public with thoroughness and honesty. Professional integrity is the cornerstone of a journalist's credibility.

Members of the Society share a dedication to ethical behavior and adopt this code to declare the Society's principles and standards of practice.

Seek Truth and Report It

Journalists should be honest, fair and courageous in gathering, reporting and interpreting information.

Journalists should:

■ Test the accuracy of information from all sources and exercise care to avoid inadvertent error. Deliberate distortion is never permissible.

■ Diligently seek out subjects of news stories to give them the opportunity to respond to allegations of wrongdoing.

■ Identify sources whenever feasible. The public is entitled to as much information as possible on sources' reliability.

■ Always question sources' motives before promising anonymity. Clarify conditions attached to any promise made in exchange for information. Keep promises.

■ Make certain that headlines, news teases and promotional material, photos, video, audio, graphics, sound bites and quotations do not misrepresent. They should not oversimplify or highlight incidents out of context.

■ Never distort the content of news photos or video. Image enhancement for technical clarity is always permissible. Label montages and photo illustrations.

■ Avoid misleading re-enactments or staged news events. If re-enactment is necessary to tell a story, label it.

■ Avoid undercover or other surreptitious methods of gathering information except when traditional open methods will not yield information vital to the public. Use of such methods should be explained as part of the story.

■ Never plagiarize.

■ Tell the story of the diversity and magnitude of the human experience boldly, even when it is unpopular to do so.

■ Examine their own cultural values and avoid imposing those values on others.

■ Avoid stereotyping by race, gender, age, religion, ethnicity, geography, sexual orientation, disability, physical appearance or social status.

■ Support the open exchange of views, even views they find repugnant.

■ Give voice to the voiceless; official and unofficial sources of information can be equally valid.

■ Distinguish between advocacy and news reporting. Analysis and commentary should be labeled and not misrepresent fact or context.

■ Distinguish news from advertising and shun hybrids that blur the lines between the two.

■ Recognize a special obligation to ensure that the public's business is conducted in the open and that government records are open to inspection.

Minimize Harm

Ethical journalists treat sources, subjects and colleagues as human beings deserving of respect.

Journalists should:

■ Show compassion for those who may be affected adversely by news coverage. Use special sensitivity when dealing with children and inexperienced sources or subjects.

■ Be sensitive when seeking or using interviews or photographs of those affected by tragedy or grief.

■ Recognize that gathering and reporting information may cause harm or discomfort. Pursuit of the news is not a license for arrogance.

■ Recognize that private people have a greater right to control information about themselves than do public officials and others who seek power, influence or attention. Only an overriding public need can justify intrusion into anyone's privacy.

■ Show good taste. Avoid pandering to lurid curiosity.

■ Be cautious about identifying juvenile suspects or victims of sex crimes.

■ Be judicious about naming criminal suspects before the formal filing of charges.

■ Balance a criminal suspect's fair trial rights with the public's right to be informed.

Act Independently

Journalists should be free of obligation to any interest other than the public's right to know.

Journalists should:

■ Avoid conflicts of interest, real or perceived.

■ Remain free of associations and activities that may compromise integrity or damage credibility.

■ Refuse gifts, favors, free travel and special treatment, and shun secondary employment, political involvement, public office and service in community organizations if they compromise journalistic integrity.

■ Disclose unavoidable conflicts.

■ Be vigilant and courageous about holding those with power accountable.

■ Deny favored treatment to advertisers and special interests and resist their pressure to influence news coverage.

■ Be wary of sources offering information for favors or money; avoid bidding for news.

Be Accountable

Journalists are accountable to their readers, listeners, viewers and each other.

Journalists should:

■ Clarify and explain news coverage and invite dialogue with the public over journalistic conduct.

■ Encourage the public to voice grievances against the news media.

■ Admit mistakes and correct them promptly.

■ Expose unethical practices of journalists and the news media.

■ Abide by the same high standards to which they hold others.

FAREED ZAKARIA, *Time* magazine editor-at-large and host of CNN's *GPS*, was briefly suspended from both *Time* and CNN in August 2012 when media blogs accused him of plagiarizing scholar Jill Lepore's essay on gun control in one of his columns. Reinstated after both *Time* and CNN found no evidence of plagiarism, Zakaria has apologized for his "terrible mistake," which he explains came as a result of mixing up different notes from different sources. Zakaria's scandal underscores the potential consequences of one ethical lapse, even for journalists as high-profile as Zakaria.

"In the era of YouTube, Twitter and 24-hour cable news, nobody is safe."

VAN JONES, FORMER SPECIAL ADVISOR TO THE OBAMA ADMINIS-TRATION ON ENVIRON-MENTAL JOBS, WHO WAS FORCED TO RESIGN IN 2009 BECAUSE OF HIS PAST CRITICISMS OF REPUBLICAN LEADERS THAT SURFACED ON TALK RADIO AND TV

privileges," the code states, "can compromise the integrity of journalists and their employers. Nothing of value should be accepted."[18] Although small newspapers with limited resources and poorly paid reporters might accept such "freebies" as game tickets for their sportswriters and free meals for their restaurant critics, this practice does increase the likelihood of a conflict of interest that produces favorable or uncritical coverage.

On a broader level, ethical guidelines at many news outlets attempt to protect journalists from compromising positions. For instance, in most cities, U.S. journalists do not actively participate in politics or support social causes. Some journalists will not reveal their political affiliations, and some even decline to vote.

For these journalists, the rationale behind their decisions is straightforward: Journalists should not place themselves in a situation in which they might have to report on the misdeeds of an organization or a political party to which they belong. If a journalist has a tie to any group, and that group is later suspected of involvement in shady or criminal activity, the reporter's ability to report on that group would be compromised—along with the credibility of the news outlet for which he or she works. Conversely, other journalists believe that not actively participating in politics or social causes means abandoning their civic obligations. They believe that fairness in their reporting, not total detachment from civic life, is their primary obligation.

In the digital age, conflict of interest cases surrounding opinion blogging have grown more complicated, especially when those opinion blogs run under the banner of traditional news media. For example, in 2010 David Weigel, whom the *Washington Post* hired to blog about the conservative movement, was forced to resign after private e-mails and listserv messages were exposed in which he had used inflammatory rhetoric to vent about well-known conservatives like Matt Drudge, Ron Paul, and Rush Limbaugh. A *Post* editor commented at the time, "We can't have any tolerance for the perception that people are conflicted or bring a bias to their work. . . . There's abundant room on our Web site for a wide range of viewpoints, and we should be transparent about everybody's viewpoint."[19] Critics afterward noted that mainstream news media sites should make clear to their readers whether the bloggers are actually opinion writers or professional journalists trying to write fairly on subjects about which they may not agree. In this case, Weigel's credibility regarding his ability to blog fairly about right-wing politicians and pundits was compromised when his personal exchanges ridiculing conservatives came to light. This case illustrates the increasingly blurry line between the old journalism of verification and the new journalism of assertion.

Resolving Ethical Problems

When a journalist is criticized for ethical lapses or questionable reporting tactics, a typical response might be "I'm just doing my job" or "I was just getting the facts." Such explanations are troubling, though, because in responding this way, reporters are transferring personal responsibility for the story to a set of institutional rituals.

There are, of course, ethical alternatives to self-justifications such as "I'm just doing my job" that force journalists to think through complex issues. With the crush of deadlines and daily duties, most media professionals deal with ethical situations only on a case-by-case basis as issues arise. However, examining major ethical models and theories provides a common strategy for addressing ethics on a general rather than a situational basis. The most well-known ethical standard, the Judeo-Christian command to "love your neighbor as yourself," provides one foundation for constructing ethical guidelines. Although we cannot address all major moral codes here, a few key precepts can guide us.

Aristotle, Kant, Bentham, and Mill

The Greek philosopher Aristotle offered an early ethical concept, the "golden mean"–a guideline for seeking balance between competing positions. For Aristotle, this was a desirable middle ground between extreme positions, usually with one regarded as deficient, and the other excessive. For example, Aristotle saw ambition as the balance between sloth and greed.

Another ethical principle entails the "categorical imperative," developed by German philosopher Immanuel Kant (1724-1804). This idea maintains that a society must adhere to moral codes that are universal and unconditional, applicable in all situations at all times. For example, the Golden Rule ("Do unto others as you would have them do unto you") is articulated in one form or another in most of the world's major religious and philosophical traditions, and operates as an absolute moral principle. The First Amendment, which prevents Congress from abridging free speech and other rights, could be considered an example of an unconditional national law.

British philosophers Jeremy Bentham (1748-1832) and John Stuart Mill (1806-1873) promoted an ethical principle derived from "the greatest good for the greatest number," directing us "to distribute a good consequence to more people rather than to fewer, whenever we have a choice."[20]

Developing Ethical Policy

Arriving at ethical decisions involves several steps. These include laying out the case; pinpointing the key issues; identifying involved parties, their intents, and their competing values; studying ethical models; presenting strategies and options; and formulating a decision.

One area that requires ethics is covering the private lives of people who unintentionally have become prominent in the news. Consider Richard Jewell, the Atlanta security guard who, for eighty-eight days, was the FBI's prime suspect in the city park bombing at the 1996 Olympics. The FBI never charged Jewell with a crime, and he later successfully sued several news organizations for libel. The news media competed to be the first to report important developments in the case, and with the battle for newspaper circulation and broadcast ratings adding fuel to a complex situation, editors were reluctant to back away from the story once it began circulating.

At least two key ethical questions emerged: (1) Should the news media have named Jewell as a suspect even though he was never charged with a crime? (2) Should the media have camped out daily in front of his mother's house in an attempt to interview him and his mother? The Jewell case pitted the media's right to tell stories and earn profits against a person's right to be left alone.

Working through the various ethical stages, journalists formulate policies grounded in overarching moral principles.[21] Should reporters, for instance, follow the Golden Rule and be willing to treat themselves, their families, or their friends the way they treated the Jewells? Or should they invoke Aristotle's "golden mean" and seek moral virtue between extreme positions?

In Richard Jewell's situation, journalists could have developed guidelines to balance Jewell's interests and the news media's. For example, in addition to apologizing for using Jewell's name in early accounts, reporters might have called off their stakeout and allowed Jewell to set interview times at a neutral site, where he could talk with a small pool of journalists designated to relay information to other media outlets.

"We should have the public interest and not the bottom line at heart, or else all we can do is wait for a time when sex doesn't sell."

SUSAN UNGARO, EDITOR, *FAMILY CIRCLE*, ON MEDIA COVERAGE OF THE CLINTON-LEWINSKY SCANDAL, 1998

Reporting Rituals and the Legacy of Print Journalism

Unfamiliar with being questioned themselves, many reporters are uncomfortable discussing their personal values or their strategies for getting stories. Nevertheless, a stock of rituals, derived from basic American values, underlie the practice of reporting. These include focusing on the present, relying on experts, balancing story conflict, and acting as adversaries toward leaders and institutions.

Focusing on the Present

In the 1840s, when the telegraph first enabled news to crisscross America instantly, modern journalism was born. To complement the new technical advances, editors called for a focus on the immediacy of the present. Modern front-page print journalism began to de-emphasize political analysis and historical context, accenting instead the new and the now.

As a result, the profession began drawing criticism for failing to offer historical, political, and social analyses. This criticism continues today. For example, urban drug stories heavily dominated print and network news during the 1986 and 1988 election years. Such stories, however, virtually disappeared from the news by 1992, although the nation's serious drug and addiction problems had not diminished.[22] For many editors and reporters at the time, drug stories became "yesterday's news."

Modern journalism tends to reject "old news" for whatever new event or idea that disrupts today's routines. During the 1996 elections, when statistics revealed that drug use among middle-class high school students was rising, reporters latched on to new versions of the drug story, but their reports made only limited references to the 1980s. And although drug problems and addiction rates did not diminish in subsequent years, these topics were virtually ignored by journalists during national elections from 2000 to 2012. Indeed, given the space and time constraints of current news practices, reporters seldom link stories to the past or to the ebb and flow of history. (To analyze current news stories, see "Media Literacy and the Critical Process: Telling Stories and Covering Disaster" on page 499.)

Getting a Good Story

Early in the 1980s, the Janet Cooke hoax demonstrated the difference between the mere telling of a good story and the social responsibility to tell the truth.[23] Cooke, a former *Washington Post* reporter, was fired for fabricating an investigative report for which she initially won a Pulitzer Prize. (It was later revoked.) She had created a cast of characters, featuring a mother who contributed to the heroin addiction of her eight-year-old son.

At the time the hoax was exposed, Chicago columnist Mike Royko criticized conventional journalism for allowing narrative conventions–getting a good story–to trump journalism's responsibility to the daily lives it documents: "There's something more important than a story here. This eight-year-old kid is being murdered. The editors should have said forget the story, find the kid. . . . People in any other profession would have gone right to the police."[24] Had editors at the *Post* demanded such help, Cooke's hoax would not have gone as far as it did.

According to Don Hewitt, the creator and longtime executive producer of *60 Minutes*, "There's a very simple formula if you're in Hollywood, Broadway, opera, publishing, broadcasting, newspapering. It's four very simple words–tell me a story."[25] For most journalists, the bottom line is "Get the story"–an edict that overrides most other concerns. It is the standard against which many reporters measure themselves and their profession.

Media Literacy and the Critical Process

1 DESCRIPTION. Find print and broadcast news versions of the *same* disaster story (use LexisNexis if available). Make copies of each story, and note the pictures chosen to tell the story.

2 ANALYSIS. Find patterns in the coverage. How are the stories treated differently in print and on television? Are there similarities in the words chosen or images used? What kinds of experience are depicted? Who are the sources the reporters use to verify their information?

3 INTERPRETATION. What do these patterns suggest? Can you make any interpretations or arguments based on the kinds of disaster covered, sources used, areas covered, or words/images chosen? How are the stories told in relation to their importance to the entire community or nation? How complex are the stories?

Telling Stories and Covering Disaster

Covering difficult stories—such as natural disasters like Hurricane Sandy in 2012—may present challenges to journalists about how to frame their coverage. The opening sections, or leads, of news stories can vary depending on the source—whether it is print, broadcast, or online news—or even the editorial style of the news organization (e.g., some story leads are straightforward; some are very dramatic). And, although modern journalists claim objectivity as a goal, it is unlikely that a profession in the storytelling business can approximate any sort of scientific objectivity. The best journalists can do is be fair, reporting and telling stories to their communities and nation by explaining the complicated and tragic experiences they convert into words or pictures. To explore this type of coverage, try this exercise with examples from recent disaster coverage of a regional or national event.

4 EVALUATION. Which stories are the strongest? Why? Which are the weakest? Why? Make a judgment on how well these disaster stories serve your interests as a citizen and the interests of the larger community or nation.

5 ENGAGEMENT. In an e-mail or letter to the editor, report your findings to relevant editors and TV news directors. Make suggestions for improved coverage and cite strong stories that you admired. How did they respond?

Getting a Story First

In a discussion on public television about the press coverage of a fatal airline crash in Milwaukee in the 1980s, a news photographer was asked to discuss his role in covering the tragedy. Rather than take up the poignant, heartbreaking aspects of witnessing the aftermath of such an event, the excited photographer launched into a dramatic recounting of how he had slipped behind police barricades to snap the first grim photos, which later appeared in the *Milwaukee Journal*. As part of their socialization into the profession, reporters often learn to evade authority figures to secure a story ahead of the competition.

The photographer's recollection points to the important role journalism plays in calling public attention to serious events and issues. Yet he also talked about the news-gathering process as a game that journalists play. It's now routine for local television stations, 24/7 cable news, and newspapers to run self-promotions about how they beat competitors to a story. In addition, during political elections, local television stations and networks project winners in particular races and often hype their projections when they are able to forecast results before the competition does. This practice led to the fiasco in November 2000 when the major networks and cable news services badly flubbed their predictions regarding the outcome of voting in Florida during the presidential election.

JONAH LEHRER had built an impressive career as a best-selling author and staff writer for the *New Yorker* and *Wired* magazine when in 2012 it was discovered he had recycled his own work, an act of "self-plagiarism," on multiple different occasions. It was also discovered that his 2012 book *Imagine: How Creativity Works* contained several fabricated quotes, many of which were incorrectly attributed to Bob Dylan.

Journalistic *scoops* and exclusive stories attempt to portray reporters in a heroic light: They have won a race for facts, which they have gathered and presented ahead of their rivals. It is not always clear, though, how the public is better served by a journalist's claim to have gotten a story first. In some ways, the 24/7 cable news, the Internet, and bloggers have intensified the race for getting a story first. With a fragmented audience and more media competing for news, the mainstream news often feels more pressure to lure an audience with exclusive, and sometimes sensational, stories. Although readers and viewers might value the aggressiveness of reporters, the earliest reports are not necessarily better, more accurate, or as complete as stories written later with more context and perspective.

For example, in summer 2010 a firestorm erupted around the abrupt dismissal of Shirley Sherrod, a Georgia-based African American official with the U.S. Department of Agriculture, over a short clip of a speech posted by the late right-wing blogger Andrew Breitbart on his Web site BigGovernment .com. His clip implied that Sherrod had once discriminated against a white farm family who had sought her help when their farm was about to be foreclosed. FoxNews.com picked up the clip, and soon it was all over cable TV, where Sherrod and the Obama administration were denounced as "reverse racists." The secretary of agriculture, Tom Vilsack, demanded and got Sherrod's resignation. However, once reporters started digging deeper into the story and CNN ran an interview with the white farmers that Sherrod had actually helped, it was revealed that the 2½-minute clip had been re-edited and taken out of context from a 43-minute speech Sherrod had given at an NAACP event. In the speech, Sherrod talked about the discrimination that both poor white and black farmers had faced, and about rising above her own past. (Her father had been murdered forty-five years earlier, and an all-white Georgia grand jury did not indict the accused white farmer despite testimony from three witnesses.) Conservative pundits apologized, Glenn Beck demanded that Sherrod be rehired, and Tom Vilsack offered her a new job (which she ultimately declined).[26]

This kind of scoop behavior, which becomes viral in the digital age, demonstrates pack or **herd journalism,** which occurs when reporters stake out a house, chase celebrities in packs, or follow a story in such herds that the entire profession comes under attack for invading people's privacy, exploiting their personal problems, or just plain getting the story wrong.

Relying on Experts

Another ritual of modern print journalism—relying on outside sources—has made reporters heavily dependent on experts. Reporters, though often experts themselves in certain areas by virtue of having covered them over time, are not typically allowed to display their expertise overtly. Instead, they must seek outside authorities to give credibility to seemingly neutral reports. *What* daily reporters know is generally subordinate to *who* they know.

During the early 1900s, progressive politicians and leaders of opinion such as President Woodrow Wilson and columnist Walter Lippmann believed in the cultivation of strong ties among national reporters, government officials, scientists, business managers, and researchers. They wanted journalists supplied with expertise across a variety of areas. Today, the widening gap between those with expertise and those without it has created a need for public mediators. Reporters have assumed this role as surrogates who represent both leaders' and readers' interests. With their access to experts, reporters transform specialized and insider knowledge into the everyday commonsense language of news stories.

Reporters also frequently use experts to create narrative conflict by pitting a series of quotes against one another, or on occasion use experts to support a particular position. In addition, the use of experts enables journalists to distance themselves from daily experience; they are able to attribute the responsibility for the events or issues reported in a story to those who are quoted.

To use experts, journalists must make direct contact with a source–by phone or e-mail or in person. Journalists do not, however, heavily cite the work of other writers; that would violate reporters' desire not only to get a story first but to get it on their own. Telephone calls and face-to-face interviews, rather than extensively researched interpretations, are the stuff of daily journalism.

Newsweek's Jonathan Alter once called expert sources the "usual suspects." Alter contended that "the impression conveyed is of a world that contains only a handful of knowledgeable people. . . . Their public exposure is a result not only of their own abilities, but of deadlines and a failure of imagination on the part of the press."[27]

In addition, expert sources have historically been predominantly white and male. Fairness and Accuracy in Reporting (FAIR) conducted a major study of the 14,632 sources used during 2001 on evening news programs on ABC, CBS, and NBC. FAIR found that only 15 percent of sources were women–and 52 percent of these women represented "average citizens" or "non-experts." By contrast, of the male sources, 86 percent were cast in "authoritative" or "expert" roles. Among "U.S. sources" where race could be determined, the study found that white sources "made up 92 percent of the total, blacks 7 percent, Latinos and Arab-Americans 0.6 percent each, and Asian Americans 0.2 percent."[28] (At that time, the 2000 census reported the U.S. population stood at 69 percent white, 13 percent Hispanic, 12 percent black, and 4 percent Asian.)" So as mainstream journalists increased their reliance on a small pool of experts, they probably alienated many viewers, who may have felt excluded from participation in day-to-day social and political life.

A 2005 study by the Pew Project for Excellence in Journalism found similar results. The study looked at forty-five different news outlets over a twenty-day period, including newspapers, nightly network newscasts and morning shows, cable news programs, and Web news sites. Newspapers, the study found, "were the most likely of the media studied to cite at least one female source . . . (41% of stories)," while cable news "was the least likely medium to cite a female source (19% of stories)." The study also found that in "every [news] topic category, the majority of stories cited at least one male source," but "the only topic category where women crossed the 50% threshold was lifestyle stories." The study found that women were least likely to be cited in stories on foreign affairs, while sports sections of newspapers also "stood out in particular as a male bastion," with only 14 percent citing a female source.[29]

By 2012, the evidence again suggested little improvement. In fact, a study from the 4th Estate showed that over a six-month period during the 2012 election, men were "much more likely to be quoted on their subjective insight in newspapers and on television." This held true even on stories specifically dealing with women's issues. The 4th Estate study showed that "in front page articles about the 2012 election that mention[ed] abortion or birth control, men [were] 4 to 7 times more likely to be cited than women." The study concluded by noting that such a "gender gap undermines the media's credibility."[30]

By the late 1990s, many journalists were criticized for blurring the line between remaining neutral and being an expert. The boom in twenty-four-hour cable news programs at this time led to a news vacuum that eventually was filled with talk shows and interviews with journalists willing to give their views. During events with intense media coverage, such as the 2000 through 2012 presidential elections, 9/11, and the Iraq war, many print journalists appeared several times a day on cable programs acting as experts on the story, sometimes providing factual information but mostly offering opinion and speculation.

Some editors even encourage their reporters to go on these shows for marketing reasons. Today, many big city newspapers have office space set aside for reporters to use for cable, TV,

> "I made a special effort to come on the show today because I have . . . mentioned this show as being bad . . . as it's hurting America."
>
> JON STEWART, ON CNN'S *CROSSFIRE*, 2004

and Internet interviews. Critics contend that these practices erode the credibility of the profession by blending journalism with celebrity culture and commercialism. Daniel Schorr, who worked as a journalist for seventy years (he died in 2010), resigned from CNN when the cable network asked him to be a commentator during the 1984 Republican National Convention along with former Texas governor John Connally. Schorr believed that it was improper to mix a journalist and a politician in this way, but the idea seems innocent by today's blurred standards. As columnist David Carr pointed out in the *New York Times* in 2010, "Where there was once a pretty bright line between journalist and political operative, there is now a kind of continuum, with politicians becoming media providers in their own right, and pundits, entertainers and journalists often driving political discussions."[31]

Balancing Story Conflict

For most journalists, *balance* means presenting all sides of an issue without appearing to favor any one position. The quest for balance presents problems for journalists. On the one hand, time and space constraints do not always permit representing *all* sides; in practice this value has often been reduced to "telling *both* sides of a story." In recounting news stories as two-sided dramas, reporters often misrepresent the complexity of social issues. The abortion controversy, for example, is often treated as a story that pits two extreme positions (staunchly pro-life vs. resolutely pro-choice) against each other. Yet people whose views fall somewhere between these positions are seldom represented (studies show this group actually represents the majority of Americans). In this manner, "balance" becomes a narrative device to generate story conflict.

On the other hand, although many journalists claim to be detached, they often stake out a moderate or middle-of-the-road position between the two sides represented in a story. In claiming neutrality and inviting readers to share their detached point of view, journalists offer a distant, third-person, all-knowing point of view (a narrative device that many novelists use as well), enhancing the impression of neutrality by making the reporter appear value-free (or valueless).

The claim for balanced stories, like the claim for neutrality, disguises journalism's narrative functions. After all, when reporters choose quotes for a story, these are usually the most dramatic or conflict-oriented words that emerge from an interview, press conference, or public meeting. Choosing quotes sometimes has more to do with enhancing drama than with being fair, documenting an event, or establishing neutrality.

The balance claim has also served the financial interests of modern news organizations that stake out the middle ground. William Greider, a former *Washington Post* editor, makes the tie between good business and balanced news: "If you're going to be a mass circulation journal, that means you're going to be talking simultaneously to lots of groups that have opposing views. So you've got to modulate your voice and pretend to be talking to all of them."[32]

Acting as Adversaries

The value that many journalists take the most pride in is their adversarial relationship with the prominent leaders and major institutions they cover. The prime narrative frame for portraying this relationship is sometimes called a *gotcha story*, which refers to the moment when, through questioning, the reporter nabs "the bad guy" or wrongdoer.

This narrative strategy—part of the *tough questioning style* of some reporters—is frequently used in political reporting. Many journalists assume that leaders are hiding something and that the reporter's main job is to ferret out the truth through tenacious fact-gathering and "gotcha" questions. An extension of the search for balance, this stance locates the reporter in the middle, between "them" and "us," between political leaders and the people they represent.

Critics of the tough question style of reporting argue that, while it can reveal significant information, when overused it fosters a cynicism among journalists that actually harms the democratic process. Although journalists need to guard against becoming too cozy with their political sources, they sometimes go to the other extreme. By constantly searching for what politicians may be hiding, some reporters may miss other issues or other key stories.

When journalists employ the gotcha model to cover news, being tough often becomes an end in itself. Thus reporters believe they have done their job just by roughing up an interview subject or by answering the limited "What is going on here?" question. Yet the Pulitzer Prize, the highest award honoring journalism, often goes to the reporter who asks ethically charged and open-ended questions, such as "Why is this going on?" and "What ought to be done about it?"

Journalism in the Age of TV and the Internet

The rules and rituals governing American journalism began shifting in the 1950s. At the time, former radio reporter John Daly hosted the CBS network game show *What's My Line?* When he began moonlighting as the evening TV news anchor on ABC, the network blurred the entertainment and information border, foreshadowing what was to come.

In the early days, the most influential and respected television news program was CBS's *See It Now.* Coproduced by Fred Friendly and Edward R. Murrow, *See It Now* practiced a kind of TV journalism lodged somewhere between the neutral and narrative traditions. Generally regarded as "the first and definitive" news documentary on American television, *See It Now* sought "to report in depth—to tell and show the American audience what was happening in the world using film as a narrative tool."[33] Murrow worked as both the program's anchor and its main reporter, introducing the investigative model of journalism to television—a model that programs like *60 Minutes*, *20/20*, and *Dateline* would imitate. Later, of course, Internet news gathering and reporting would further alter journalism.

Differences between Print, TV, and Internet News

Although TV news reporters share many values, beliefs, and conventions with their print counterparts, television transformed journalism in a number of ways. First, broadcast news is driven by its technology. If a camera crew and news van are dispatched to a remote location for a live broadcast, reporters are expected to justify the expense by developing a story, even if nothing significant is occurring. For instance, when a national political candidate does not arrive at the local airport in time for an interview on the evening news, the reporter may cover a flight delay instead. Print reporters, in contrast, slide their notebooks or laptops back into their bags and report on a story when it occurs. However, with print reporters now posting regular online updates to their stories, they offer the same immediacy that live television news does. In fact, in most newsrooms today, the online version of a story is often posted before the newspaper or TV version appears.

Second, while print editors cut stories to fit the physical space around ads, TV news directors have to time stories to fit between commercials. Despite the fact that a much higher percentage of space is devoted to print ads (about 60 percent at most dailies), TV ads (which take up less than 25 percent of a typical thirty-minute news program) generally seem more intrusive to viewers, perhaps because TV ads take up time rather than space. The Internet has "solved" these old space and time problems by freeing stories from those constraints online.

Third, while modern print journalists are expected to be detached, TV news derives its credibility from live, on-the-spot reporting; believable imagery; and viewers' trust in the reporters

> "It's the job of journalists to make complicated things interesting. The shame of American journalism is that [PBS's] *Frontline*, with its limited resources, has been doing infinitely better, more thoughtful, more creative reporting on places like Afghanistan or Rwanda than the richest networks in the world. If it is a glory for *Frontline*, it is a shame for those big networks and the [people] at the top of the corporate structure who run them."
>
> DAVID HALBERSTAM, JOURNALIST, OCTOBER 2001

ANN CURRY announced her resignation as co-anchor of the *Today* show in June 2012 after just one year on the job. Rumors swirled that network executives at NBC had been planning her departure for months, potentially pinning the show's low ratings on Curry's on-air personality. Meanwhile gossip columnists buzzed that Curry was forced out due to the way she dressed and her refusal to cover her gray hair. Now an NBC News national and international correspondent and *Today* anchor at large, Curry has a strong fan base that has rallied behind her in the wake of what some maintain was an unfair, potentially discriminatory dismissal from *Today*.

and anchors. In fact, since the early 1970s most annual polls have indicated that the majority of viewers find television news a more credible resource than print news. Viewers tend to feel a personal regard for the local and national anchors who appear each evening on TV sets in their living rooms. In fact, in Pew Research Center's 2012 news credibility and believability study (which still does not rate online news sources like *Politico* or *Huffington Post*), the three top news outlets with the highest "positive" rating from those polled were "local TV news" (65 percent), *60 Minutes* (64 percent), and ABC News (59 percent). By comparison, Fox News was tied with the *New York Times* and *USA Today* as the only organizations in the study to have higher negative than positive ratings—all at just 49 percent positive. The highest rated newspaper in the study was the *Wall Street Journal* with a 58 percent positive rating, while the "daily newspaper you know best" scored a 57 percent positive rating.[34]

By the mid-1970s, the public's fascination with the Watergate scandal, combined with the improved quality of TV journalism, helped local news departments realize profits. In an effort to retain high ratings, stations began hiring consultants, who advised news directors to invest in national prepackaged formats, such as Action News or Eyewitness News. Traveling the country, viewers noticed similar theme music and opening graphic visuals from market to market. Consultants also suggested that stations lead their newscasts with *crime blocks:* a group of TV stories that recount the worst local criminal transgressions of the day. A cynical slogan soon developed in the industry: "If it bleeds, it leads." This crime-block practice continues today at most local TV news stations.

Few stations around the country have responded to viewers and critics who complain about the overemphasis on crime. (In reality, FBI statistics reveal that crime and murder rates have fallen or leveled off in most major urban areas since the 1990s.) In 1996, the news director at KVUE-TV in Austin, Texas, created a new set of criteria that had to be met for news reports to qualify as responsible crime stories. She asked that her reporters answer the following questions: Do citizens or officials need to take action? Is there an immediate threat to safety? Is there a threat to children? Does the crime have significant community impact? Does the story lend itself to a crime prevention effort? With KVUE's new standards, the station eliminated many routine crime stories. Instead, the station provided a context for understanding crime rather than a mindless running tally of the crimes committed each day.[35]

Pretty-Face and Happy-Talk Culture

In the early 1970s at a Milwaukee TV station, consultants advised the station's news director that the evening anchor looked too old. The anchor, who showed a bit of gray, was replaced and went on to serve as the station's editorial director. He was thirty-two years old at the time. In the late 1970s, a reporter at the same station was fired because of a "weight problem," although that was not given as the official reason. Earlier that year, she had given birth to her first child. In 1983, Christine Craft, a former Kansas City television news anchor, was awarded $500,000 in damages in a sex discrimination suit against station KMBC (she eventually lost the monetary award when the station appealed). She had been fired because consultants believed she was too old, too unattractive, and not deferential enough to men.

Such stories are rampant in the annals of TV news. They have helped create a stereotype of the half-witted but physically attractive news anchor, reinforced by popular culture images (from Ted Baxter on TV's *Mary Tyler Moore Show* to Ron Burgundy in the film *Anchorman*). Although the situation has improved slightly, national news consultants set the agenda for what local reporters should cover (lots of crime) as well as how they should look and sound (young, attractive, pleasant, and with no regional accent). Essentially, news consultants–also known as *news doctors*–have advised stations to replicate the predominant male and female advertising images of the 1960s and 1970s in modern local TV news.

Another strategy favored by news consultants is *happy talk:* the ad-libbed or scripted banter that goes on among local news anchors, reporters, meteorologists, and sports reporters before and after news reports. During the 1970s, consultants often recommended such chatter to create a more relaxed feeling on the news set and to foster the illusion of conversational intimacy with viewers. Some also believed that happy talk would counter much of that era's "bad news," which included coverage of urban riots and the Vietnam War. A strategy still used today, happy talk often appears forced and may create awkward transitions, especially when anchors transition to reports on events that are sad or tragic.

Sound Bitten

Beginning in the 1980s, the term **sound bite** became part of the public lexicon. The TV equivalent of a quote in print news, a sound bite is the part of a broadcast news report in which an expert, a celebrity, a victim, or a person-in-the-street responds to some aspect of an event or issue. With increasing demands for more commercial time, there is less time for interview subjects to explain their views, and sound bites have become the focus of intense criticism. Studies revealed that during political campaigns the typical sound bite from candidates had shrunk from an average duration of forty to fifty seconds in the 1950s and 1960s to fewer than eight seconds by the late 1990s. With shorter comments from interview subjects, TV news sometimes seems like dueling sound bites, with reporters creating dramatic tension by editing competing viewpoints together as if interviewees had actually been in the same location speaking to one another. Of course, print news also pits one quote against another in a story, even though the actual interview subjects may never have met. Once again, these reporting techniques, also at work in online journalism, are evidence of the profession's reliance on storytelling devices to replicate or create conflict.

Pundits, "Talking Heads," and Politics

The transformation of TV news by cable–with the arrival of CNN in 1980–led to dramatic changes in TV news delivery at the national level. Prior to cable news (and the Internet), most people tuned to their local and national news late in the afternoon or evening on a typical weekday, with each program lasting just thirty minutes. But today, the 24/7 news cycle means that we can get TV news anytime, day or night, and constant new content has led to major changes in what is considered news. Because it is expensive to dispatch reporters to document stories or maintain foreign news bureaus to cover international issues, the much less expensive "talking head" pundit has become a standard for cable news channels. Such a programming strategy requires few resources beyond the studio and a few guests.

Today's main cable channels have built their evening programs along partisan lines and follow the model of journalism as opinion and assertion: Fox News goes right with pundit stars like Bill O'Reilly and Sean Hannity; MSNBC leans left with

ANDERSON COOPER has been the primary anchor of *Anderson Cooper 360°* since 2003. Although the program is mainly taped and broadcast from his New York City studio, and typically features reports of the day's main news stories with added analyses from experts, Cooper is one of the few "talking heads" who still reports live fairly often from the field for major news stories. Most recently and notably, he has done extensive coverage of the 2010 BP oil spill in the Gulf of Mexico (below), the February 2011 uprisings in Egypt, and the devastating earthquake in Japan in 2011.
▼

VideoCentral ◎
Mass Communication
bedfordstmartins.com
/mediaculture

**The Contemporary
Journalist: Pundit or
Reporter?**
Journalists discuss whether
the 24/7 news cycle encourages reporters to offer
opinions more than facts.
Discussion: What might
be the reasons reporters
should give opinions, and
what might be the reasons
why they shouldn't?

Rachel Maddow and Lawrence O'Donnell; and CNN stakes out the middle with hosts that try to strike a more neutral pose like Anderson Cooper. Although CNN does much more original reporting than Fox News and MSNBC (Cooper often reports live from the scene of events), the originator of cable news lost 35 percent of its total audience in spring 2012 alone. During this time period, CNN averaged 470,000 total viewers each evening, while MSNBC averaged 817,000 total viewers, down 12 percent from 2011. Fox News continued to lead the cable prime-time news wars, averaging 2.15 million viewers per night, about the same as in 2011.[36]

Today's cable and Internet audiences seem to prefer partisan "talking heads" over tradi-tional reporting. This suggests that in today's fragmented media marketplace, going after niche audiences along political lines is smart business—although not necessarily good journalism. What should concern us today is the jettisoning of good journalism—anchored in reporting and verification—that uses reporters to document stories and interview key sources. In its place, on cable and online, are highly partisan pundits who may have strong opinions and charisma but who may not have all their facts straight.

Convergence Enhances and Changes Journalism

For mainstream print and TV reporters and editors, online news has added new dimensions to journalism. Both print and TV news can continually update breaking stories online, and many reporters now post their online stories first and then work on traditional versions. This means that readers and viewers no longer have to wait until the next day for the morning paper or for the lo-cal evening newscast for important stories. To enhance the online reports, which do not have the time or space constraints of television or print, newspaper reporters increasingly are required to provide video or audio for their stories. This might allow readers and viewers to see full interviews rather than just selected print quotes in the paper or short sound bites on the TV report.

However, online news comes with a special set of problems. Print reporters, for example, can do e-mail interviews rather than leaving the office to question a subject in person. Many editors discourage this practice because they think relying on e-mail gives interviewees the chance to control and shape their answers. While some might argue that this provides more thoughtful answers, journalists say it takes the elements of surprise and spontaneity out of the traditional news interview, during which a subject might accidentally reveal information—something less likely to occur in an online setting.

Another problem for journalists, ironically, is the wide-ranging resources of the Internet. This includes access to versions of stories from other papers or broadcast stations. The mountain of information available on the Internet has made it all too easy for journalists to—unwittingly or intentionally—copy other journalists' work. In addition, access to databases and other informa-tional sites can keep reporters at their computers rather than out tracking down new kinds of information, cultivating sources, and staying in touch with their communities.

Most notable, however, for journalists in the digital age are the demands that convergence has made on their reporting and writing. Print journalists at newspapers (and magazines) are expected to carry digital cameras so they can post video along with the print versions of their stories. TV reporters are expected to write print-style news reports for their station's Web site to supplement the streaming video of their original TV stories. And both print and TV reporters are often expected to post the Internet versions of their stories first, before the versions they do for the morning paper or the six o'clock news. Increasingly, journalists today are also expected to tweet and blog.

The Power of Visual Language

The shift from a print-dominated culture to an electronic-digital culture requires that we look carefully at differences among various approaches to journalism. For example, the visual language of TV news and the Internet often captures events more powerfully than words. Over the past fifty years, television news has dramatized America's key events. Civil Rights activists, for instance, acknowledge that the movement benefited enormously from televised news that documented the plight of southern blacks in the 1960s. The news footage of southern police officers turning powerful water hoses on peaceful Civil Rights demonstrators or the news images of "white only" and "colored only" signs in hotels and restaurants created a context for understanding the disparity between black and white in the 1950s and 1960s.

Other enduring TV images are also embedded in the collective memory of many Americans: the Kennedy and King assassinations in the 1960s; the turmoil of Watergate in the 1970s; the first space shuttle disaster and the Chinese student uprisings in the 1980s; the Oklahoma City federal building bombing in the 1990s; the terrorist attacks on the Pentagon and World Trade Center in 2001; Hurricane Katrina in 2005; the historic 2008 election of President Obama; the Arab Spring uprisings in 2011; and in 2012 the brutal murders of twenty schoolchildren and six adults in Newtown, Connecticut. During these critical events, TV news has been a cultural reference point marking the strengths and weaknesses of our world. (See "Global Village: Why Isn't Al Jazeera English on More U.S. TV Systems?" on page 509 for more on global news access in the digital age.)

Today, the Internet, for good or bad, functions as a repository for news images and video, allowing us to catch up on stories we may have missed or to be overexposed to controversial (or trivial) clips. In 2010, as Donald Trump toyed briefly with running for president in 2012, he resurrected an old accusation, suggesting that the president was born in Kenya, not in Hawaii. This story spread across the Internet—on Twitter, blogs, and Internet forums—and traditional news outlets also covered the "controversy," even doing stories about *not* covering completely unfounded rumors. Trump gained popularity among right-wing voters and became a front-runner in GOP polls. In late April 2011, President Obama released his long-form birth certificate, putting an end to what he called "silliness," and marveling at "the degree to which this [story] just kept on going."[37]

NEWS IN THE DIGITAL AGE
Today, more and more journalists use Twitter in addition to performing their regular reporting duties. Muck Rack collects journalists' tweets in one place, making it easier than ever to access breaking news and real-time, one-line reporting.

Alternative Models: Public Journalism and "Fake" News

In 1990, Poland was experiencing growing pains as it shifted from a state-controlled economic system to a more open market economy. The country's leading newspaper, *Gazeta Wyborcza*, the first noncommunist newspaper to appear in Eastern Europe since the 1940s, was also undergoing challenges. Based in Warsaw with a circulation of about 350,000 at the time, *Gazeta Wyborcza* had to report on and explain the new economy and the new crime wave that accompanied it. Especially troubling to the news staff and Polish citizens were gangs that robbed

VideoCentral ◎
Mass Communication
bedfordstmartins.com
/mediaculture

Fake News/Real News: A Fine Line
The editor of the *Onion* describes how the publication critiques "real" news media. **Discussion:** How many of your news sources might be considered "fake" news versus traditional news, and how do you decide which sources to consult?

American and Western European tourists at railway stations, sometimes assaulting them in the process. The stolen goods would then pass to an outer circle, whose members transferred the goods to still another exterior ring of thieves. Even if the police caught the inner circle members, the loot usually disappeared.

These developments triggered heated discussions in the newsroom. A small group of young reporters, some of whom had recently worked in the United States, argued that the best way to cover the story was to describe the new crime wave and relay the facts to readers in a neutral manner. Another group, many of whom were older and more experienced, felt that the paper should take an advocacy stance and condemn the criminals through interpretive columns on the front page. The older guard won this particular debate, and more interpretive pieces appeared.[38]

This story illustrates the two competing models that have influenced American and European journalism since the early 1900s. The first—the *informational* or *modern model*—emphasizes describing events and issues from a seemingly neutral point of view. The second—a more *partisan* or *European model*—stresses analyzing occurrences and advocating remedies from an acknowledged point of view.

In most American newspapers today, the informational model dominates the front page, while the partisan model remains confined to the editorial pages and an occasional front-page piece. However, alternative models of news—from the serious to the satirical—have emerged to challenge modern journalistic ideals.

The Public Journalism Movement

From the late 1980s through the 1990s, a number of papers experimented with ways to involve readers more actively in the news process. These experiments surfaced primarily at midsize daily papers, including the *Charlotte Observer*, the *Wichita Eagle*, the *Virginian-Pilot*, and the *Minneapolis Star Tribune*. Davis "Buzz" Merritt, editor and vice president of the *Wichita Eagle* at the time, defined key aspects of **public journalism**:

- It moves beyond the limited mission of "telling the news" to a broader mission of helping public life go well, and acts out that imperative. . . .
- It moves from detachment to being a fair-minded participant in public life. . . .
- It moves beyond only describing what is "going wrong" to imagining what "going right" would be like. . . .
- It moves from seeing people as consumers—as readers or nonreaders, as bystanders to be informed—to seeing them as a public, as potential actors in arriving at democratic solutions to public problems.[39]

CITIZEN JOURNALISM
One way technology has allowed citizens to become involved in the reporting of news is through cell phone photos and videos uploaded online. Witnesses can now pass on what they have captured to major mainstream news sources, like CNN's iReports or onto their own blogs and Web sites.

Public journalism is best imagined as a conversational model for news practice. Modern journalism had drawn a distinct line between reporter detachment and community involvement; public journalism—driven by citizen forums, community conversations, and even talk shows—obscured this line.

In the 1990s—before the full impact of the Internet—public journalism served as a response to the many citizens who felt alienated from participating in public life in a meaningful way. This alienation arose, in part, from viewers who watched passively as the political process seemed to play out in the news and on TV between the

Why Isn't Al Jazeera English on More U.S. TV Systems?

I n early May 2011, the day after U.S. Navy Seals killed al-Qaeda's symbolic leader Osama bin Laden in a Pakistani suburb, Marwan Bishara wrote an analysis for Aljazeera.net— the Web site for Al Jazeera English, a news service based in Washington, D.C., with headquarters in Doha, Qatar. Bishara said that "for the Muslim world, bin Laden [had] already been made irrelevant by the Arab Spring that underlined the meaning of people's power through peaceful means." Bishara also reminded his readers "that bin Laden's al-Qaeda and its affiliates [had] killed far more Arabs and Muslims than they did Westerners."[1] He concluded that with bin Laden's death, the United States had even less of a reason to continue fighting in Afghanistan, a view shared by the majority of Americans in most 2011 polls.

This analysis from Al Jazeera English (AJE, formerly Al Jazeera International) was not much different from mainstream U.S. news opinion on cable shows and in newspaper editorials. Yet Fox News commentator Bill O'Reilly still labeled Al Jazeera "anti-American,"[2] even though its English reporting staff is represented by journalists from fifty different nations, including the United States. Still, many Americans seemed to disagree with O'Reilly—Al Jazeera's Web site got 1.6 million hits in the United States during the early days of

Egypt's uprising against their once entrenched dictator. [3]

In 2006 when AJE began, the conservative media watchdog group Accuracy in Media (AIM) reported in a poll that 53 percent of Americans were opposed to the English language version of Al Jazeera. At the time, AIM circulated a video titled "Terror Television" that linked the Arab Al Jazeera service (AJE's parent company) to "the perpetrators of 9/11 and the old Saddam Hussein dictatorship" in Iraq.[4] This video, coupled with the fact that Al Jazeera received and broadcast bin Laden's videotape messages after 9/11, contributed to the idea of Al Jazeera as "bin Laden's station" in many people's minds.

Today the main Al Jazeera Arabic network, which began in 1996, reaches 220 million TV households in more than a hundred countries and runs news bureaus in sixty-five countries (compared to CNN's thirty-three).[5] But as late as January 2013, AJE was available on cable or satellite systems in the United States in only a handful of cities, including Burlington, Vermont; Toledo, Ohio; Washington, D.C.; and New York City. (AJE started a campaign in 2011 to get carried on more U.S. cable and satellite systems.) This lack of access to Arab and Middle

East news led Stephen Colbert on Comedy Central's *The Colbert Report* to question Al Jazeera's Cairo correspondent on why the network couldn't get on U.S. TV systems when there was clearly room for "17 Showtimes and a channel for pets."[6]

In an increasingly interconnected world in which the Middle East plays an ever-growing role, most U.S. citizens have no cable or satellite access to the world's main Arab news service, likely because TV executives fear backlash if they offer an Arab news service on their systems. First Amendment scholar and Columbia University president Lee Bollinger has in fact called on the FCC to "use its authority to expand access to foreign news bureaus." Failing to do so, Bollinger argues, "threatens to put America's understanding of the world at a significant disadvantage relative to other countries."[7]

"I think we should be careful—I mean we shouldn't think that [the journalist's] role is to release the Arab people from oppression. But I think we should also . . . have our eyes open to capture any event that could be the start of the end of any dictator in the Arab world."

—Mohammed Krichen, Tunisian-born Al Jazeera news anchor, 2011

party operatives and media pundits. Public journalism was a way to involve both the public and journalists more centrally in civic and political life. Editors and reporters interested in addressing citizen alienation–and reporter cynicism–began devising ways to engage people as conversational partners in determining the news. In an effort to draw the public into discussions about community priorities, these journalists began sponsoring citizen forums, where readers would have a voice in shaping aspects of the news that directly affected them.

An Early Public Journalism Project

Although isolated citizen projects and reader forums are sprinkled throughout the history of journalism, the public journalism movement began in earnest in 1987 in Columbus, Georgia. The city was suffering from a depressed economy, an alienated citizenry, and an entrenched leadership. In response, a team of reporters from the *Columbus Ledger-Enquirer* surveyed and talked with community leaders and other citizens about the future of the city. The paper then published an eight-part series based on the findings.

When the provocative series evoked little public response, the paper's leadership realized there was no mechanism or forum for continuing the public discussions about the issues raised in the series. Consequently, the paper created such a forum by organizing a town meeting, and helped create a new civic organization to tackle issues such as racial tension and teenage antisocial behavior.

The Columbus project generated public discussion, involved more people in the news process, and eased race and class tensions by bringing various groups together in public conversations. In the newsroom, the *Ledger-Enquirer* tried to reposition the place of journalists in politics: "Instead of standing outside the political community and reporting on its pathologies, they took up residence within its borders."[40]

Criticizing Public Journalism

By 2000, more than a hundred newspapers, many teamed with local television and public radio stations, had practiced some form of public journalism. Yet many critics remained skeptical of the experiment, raising a number of concerns including the weakening of four journalistic hallmarks: editorial control, credibility, balance, and diverse views.[41]

First, some editors and reporters argued that public journalism was co-opted by the marketing department, merely pandering to what readers wanted and taking editorial control away from newsrooms. They believed that focus group samples and consumer research–tools of marketing, not journalism–blurred the boundary between the editorial and business functions of a paper. Some journalists also feared that as they became more active in the community, they may have been perceived as community boosters rather than as community watchdogs.

Second, critics worried that public journalism compromised the profession's credibility, which many believe derives from detachment. They argued that public journalism turned reporters into participants rather than observers. However, as the *Wichita Eagle*'s editor Davis Merritt pointed out, professionals who have credibility "share some basic values about life, some common ground about common good." Yet many journalists have insisted they "don't share values with anyone; that [they] are value-neutral."[42] Merritt argued that, as a result, modern journalism actually has little credibility with the public, which the Pew Research Center's annual credibility surveys bear out.

Third, critics also contended that public journalism undermined "balance" and the both-sides-of-a-story convention by constantly seeking common ground and community consensus; therefore, it ran the risk of dulling the rough edges of democratic speech. Public journalists countered that they were trying to set aside more room for centrist positions. Such positions were often representative of many in the community but were missing in the mainstream news, which has been more interested in the extremist views that make for a more dramatic story.

Fourth, many traditional reporters asserted that public journalism, which they considered merely a marketing tool, had not addressed the changing economic structure of the news business.

> "The idea is to frame stories from the citizen's view, rather than inserting man-in-the-street quotes into a frame dominated by professionals."
>
> JAY ROSEN, NYU, 1995

With more news outlets in the hands of fewer owners, both public journalists and traditional reporters needed to raise tough questions about the disappearance of competing daily papers and newsroom staff cutbacks at local monopoly newspapers. Facing little competition, in 2010 and 2011 newspapers continued to cut reporting staffs and expensive investigative projects, reduced the space for news, or converted to online-only operations. While such trends temporarily helped profits and satisfied stockholders, they limited the range of stories told and views represented in a community.

"Fake" News and Satiric Journalism

For many young people, it is especially disturbing that two wealthy, established political parties–beholden to special interests and their lobbyists–control the nation's government. After all, 98 percent of congressional incumbents get reelected each year–not always because they've done a good job but often because they've made promises and done favors for the lobbyists and interests that helped get them elected in the first place.

Why shouldn't people, then, be cynical about politics? It is this cynicism that has drawn increasingly larger audiences to "fake" news shows like *The Daily Show with Jon Stewart* and *The Colbert Report* on cable's Comedy Central. Following in the tradition of *Saturday Night Live* (*SNL*), which began in 1975, news satires tell their audiences something that seems truthful about politicians and how they try to manipulate media and public opinion. But most important, these shows use humor to critique the news media and our political system. *SNL*'s sketches on GOP vice presidential candidate Sarah Palin in 2008 drew large audiences and shaped the way younger viewers thought about the election.

The Colbert Report satirizes cable "star" news hosts, particularly Fox's Bill O'Reilly and MSNBC's Chris Matthews, and the bombastic opinion-assertion culture promoted by their programs. In critiquing the limits of news stories and politics, *The Daily Show*, "anchored" by Stewart, parodies the narrative conventions of evening news programs: the clipped eight-second "sound bite" that limits meaning and the formulaic shot of the TV news "stand up," which depicts reporters "on location," attempting to establish credibility by revealing that they were really there.

On *The Daily Show*, a cast of fake reporters are digitally superimposed in front of exotic foreign locales, Washington, D.C., or other U.S. locations. In a 2004 exchange with "political correspondent" Rob Corddry, Stewart asked him for his opinion about presidential campaign tactics. "My opinion? I don't have opinions," Corddry answered. "I'm a reporter, Jon. My job is to spend half the time repeating what one side says, and half the time repeating the other. Little thing called objectivity; might want to look it up."

NEWS AS SATIRE
Political satirists Jon Stewart and Stephen Colbert have welcomed a variety of political leaders and celebrity guests to their respective news shows, *The Daily Show with Jon Stewart* and *The Colbert Report*, throughout their time on-air. In 2012, Stewart interviewed President Obama for the sixth time, while Colbert welcomed First Lady Michelle Obama to his show a few months before the election. Here Stewart is shown interviewing Navy Admiral Mike Mullen, while Colbert is pictured with John Grunsfeld, Associate Administrator for NASA's Science Mission Directorate.

As news court jester, Stewart exposes the melodrama of TV news that nightly depicts the world in various stages of disorder while offering the stalwart, comforting presence of celebrity-anchors overseeing it all from their high-tech command centers. Even before CBS's usually neutral and aloof Walter Cronkite signed off the evening news with "And that's the way it is," network news anchors tried to offer a sense of order through the reassurance of their individual personalities.

Yet even as a fake anchor, Stewart displays a much greater range of emotion—a range that may match our own—than we get from our detached "hard news" anchors: more amazement, irony, outrage, laughter, and skepticism. For example, during his program's coverage of the 2012 presidential election, he would frequently show genuine irritation or even outrage—coupled with irony and humor—whenever a politician or political ad presented information that was untrue or misleading.

While Stewart often mocks the formulas that real TV news programs have long used, he also presents an informative and insightful look at current events and the way "traditional" media cover them. For example, he exposes hypocrisy by juxtaposing what a politician said recently in the news with the opposite position articulated by the same politician months or years earlier. Indeed, many Americans have admitted that they watch satires such as *The Daily Show* not only to be entertained but also to stay current with what's going on in the world. In fact, a prominent Pew Research Center study in 2007 found that people who watched these satiric shows were more often "better informed" than most other news consumers, usually because these viewers tended to get their news from multiple sources and a cross-section of news media.[43]

Although the world has changed, local TV news story formulas (except for splashy opening graphics and Doppler weather radar) have gone virtually unaltered since the 1970s, when *SNL*'s "Weekend Update" first started making fun of TV news. Newscasts still limit reporters' stories to two minutes or less and promote stylish anchors, a "sports guy," and a certified meteorologist as familiar personalities whom we invite into our homes each evening. Now that a generation of viewers has been raised on the TV satire and political cynicism of "Weekend Update," David Letterman, Jimmy Fallon, Conan O'Brien, *The Daily Show*, and *The Colbert Report*, the slick, formulaic packaging of political ads and the canned, cautious sound bites offered in news packages are simply not so persuasive.

Journalism needs to break free from tired formulas—especially in TV news—and reimagine better ways to tell stories. In fictional TV, storytelling has evolved over time, becoming increasingly complex. Although the Internet and 24/7 cable have introduced new models of journalism and commentary, why has TV news remained virtually unchanged over the past forty years? Are there no new ways to report the news? Maybe audiences would value news that matches the complicated storytelling that surrounds them in everything from TV dramas to interactive video games to their own conversations. We should demand news story forms that better represent the complexity of our world.

> "There's no journalist today, real or fake, who is more significant for people 18 to 25."
>
> SETH SIEGEL, ADVERTISING AND BRANDING CONSULTANT, TALKING ABOUT JON STEWART

Democracy and Reimagining Journalism's Role

Journalism is central to democracy: Both citizens and the media must have access to the information that we need to make important decisions. As this chapter illustrates, however, this is a complicated idea. For example, in the aftermath of 9/11, some government officials claimed that reporters or columnists who raised questions about fighting terrorism, invading Iraq, or developing secret government programs were being unpatriotic. Yet the basic principles of democracy require citizens and the media to question our leaders and government. Isn't this, after all, what the American Revolution was all about? (See "Examining Ethics: WikiLeaks, Secret Documents, and Good Journalism?" on page 514.)

Conventional journalists will fight ferociously for the principles that underpin journalism's basic tenets—questioning government, freedom of the press, the public's right to know, and two sides to every story. These are mostly worthy ideals, but they do have limitations. These tenets, for example, generally do not acknowledge any moral or ethical duty for journalists to improve the quality of daily life. Rather, conventional journalism values its news-gathering capabilities and the well-constructed news narrative, leaving the improvement of civic life to political groups, nonprofit organizations, business philanthropists, individual citizens, and practitioners of Internet activism.

Social Responsibility

Although reporters have traditionally thought of themselves first and foremost as observers and recorders, some journalists have acknowledged a social responsibility. Among them was James Agee in the 1930s. In his book *Let Us Now Praise Famous Men*, which was accompanied by the Depression-era photography of Walker Evans, Agee regarded conventional journalism as dishonest, partly because the act of observing intruded on people and turned them into story characters that newspapers and magazines exploited for profit.

Agee also worried that readers would retreat into the comfort of his writing—his narrative—instead of confronting what for many families was the horror of the Great Depression. For Agee, the question of responsibility extended not only to journalism and to himself but to the readers of his stories as well: "The reader is no less centrally involved than the authors and those of whom they tell."[44] Agee's self-conscious analysis provides insights into journalism's hidden agendas and the responsibility of all citizens to make public life better.

Deliberative Democracy

According to advocates of public journalism, when reporters are chiefly concerned with maintaining their antagonistic relationship to politics and are less willing to improve political discourse, news and democracy suffer. *Washington Post* columnist David Broder thinks that national journalists like him—through rising salaries, prestige, and formal education—have distanced themselves "from the people that we are writing for and have become much, much closer to people we are writing about."[45] Broder believes that journalists need to become activists, not for a particular party but for the political process and in the interest of re-energizing public life. For those who advocate for public journalism, this might also involve mainstream media spearheading voter registration drives or setting up pressrooms or news bureaus in public libraries or shopping malls, where people converge in large numbers.

Public journalism offers people models for how to deliberate in forums, and then it covers those deliberations. This kind of community journalism aims to reinvigorate a *deliberative democracy* in which citizen groups, local government, and the news media together work more actively to shape social, economic, and political agendas. In a more deliberative democracy, a large segment of the community discusses public life and social policy before advising or electing officials who represent the community's interests.

In 1989, the historian Christopher Lasch argued that "the job of the press is to encourage debate, not to supply the public with information."[46] Although he overstated his case—journalism does both and more—Lasch made a cogent point about how conventional journalism had lost its bearings. Adrift in data, mainstream journalism had lost touch with its partisan roots. The early

> "If I can convince you of anything, it is to buck the current system. Remember anew that you are a public servant and your business is protecting the public from harm. Even if those doing harm also pay your salary."
>
> DAN RATHER, IN HIS ACCEPTANCE SPEECH AT A COMMITTEE TO PROTECT JOURNALISTS EVENT, NOVEMBER 2011

> "Neither journalism nor public life will move forward until we actually rethink, redescribe, and reinterpret what journalism is; not the science of information of our culture but its poetry and conversation."
>
> JAMES CAREY, KETTERING REVIEW, 1992

WikiLeaks, Secret Documents, and Good Journalism?

Since its inception in 2006, the controversial Web site WikiLeaks has released millions of documents—from revelations of toxic dumps in Africa to 250,000 U.S. State Department diplomatic cables and video footage of a U.S. airstrike in Baghdad that killed civilians. WikiLeaks's main spokesperson and self-identified "editor-in-chief," Julian Assange, an Australian online activist, has been called everything from a staunch free-speech advocate to a "hi-tech terrorist" (by U.S. Vice President Joe Biden). Certainly, government leaders around the world have faced embarrassment from the site's many document dumps and secrecy breaches.

In June 2010 WikiLeaks offered 500,000-plus documents, called the "War Logs," to three mainstream print outlets—the *Guardian* in the United Kingdom, the German magazine *Der Spiegel*, and the *New York Times*. These documents were mainly U.S. military and state department dispatches and internal memos related to the Afghan and Iraq wars—what Bill Keller, then executive editor of the *New York Times*, called a "huge breach of secrecy" for those running the wars. Keller described working with WikiLeaks as an adventure that "combined the cloak-and-dagger intrigue of handling a vast secret archive with the more mundane feat of sorting, search-

ing and understanding a mountain of data."[1] Indeed, one of the first major stories the *Times* wrote, based on the War Logs project, reported on "Pakistan's ambiguous role as an American ally."[2] Then just a few months later, Osama bin Laden was found hiding in the middle of a Pakistani suburb.

WikiLeaks presents a number of ethical dilemmas and concerns for journalists and citizens. News critic and journalism professor Jay Rosen has called WikiLeaks "the world's first stateless news organization."[3] But is WikiLeaks actually doing journalism—and therefore entitled to First Amendment protections? Or is it merely an important "news source, news provider, content host, [or] whistleblower," exposing things that governments would rather keep secret?[4] And should *any* document or material obtained by WikiLeaks be released for public scrutiny, or should some kinds of documents and materials be withheld?

Examining Ethics Activity

As a class or in smaller groups, consider the ethical concerns laid out above.

Following the ethical template outlined on page 19 in Chapter 1, begin by researching the topic, finding as much information and analysis as possible. Read Bill Keller's *New York Times Magazine* piece or his longer 2011 *Times* report, "Open Secrets: WikiLeaks, War and American Diplomacy" (www.nytimes.com/opensecrets). See also Nikki Usher's work for Harvard's Nieman Journalism Lab and Jay Rosen's blog, *PressThink*. Consider also journalism criticism and news study sites such as the *Columbia Journalism Review*, the Pew Research Center, and the First Amendment Center. Watch Julian Assange's interview on CBS's *60 Minutes* from January 2011.

Next, based on your research and informed analysis, decide whether WikiLeaks is a legitimate form of journalism and whether there should be newsroom policies that restrict the release of some kinds of documents for a news organization in partnership with a resource like WikiLeaks (such as the "War Logs" project described above). Create an outline for such policies.

"In media history up to now, the press is free to report on what the powerful wish to keep secret because the laws of a given nation protect it. But Wikileaks is able to report on what the powerful wish to keep secret because the logic of the Internet permits it. . . . Just as the Internet has no terrestrial address or central office, neither does Wikileaks."

—Jay Rosen, *PressThink*, 2010

mission of journalism—to advocate opinions and encourage public debate—has been relegated to alternative magazines, the editorial pages, news blogs, and cable news channels starring allegedly elite reporters. Tellingly, Lasch connected the gradual decline in voter participation, which began in the 1920s, to more professionalized conduct on the part of journalists. With a modern, supposedly "objective" press, he contended, the public increasingly began to defer to the "more professional" news media to watch over civic life on its behalf.

As the advocates of public journalism acknowledged, people had grown used to letting their representatives think and act for them. More community-oriented journalism and other civic projects offer citizens an opportunity to deliberate and to influence their leaders. This may include broadening the story models and frames they use to recount experiences; paying more attention to the historical and economic contexts of these stories; doing more investigative reports that analyze both news conventions and social issues; taking more responsibility for their news narratives; participating more fully in the public life of their communities; admitting to their cultural biases and occasional mistakes; and ensuring that the verification model of reporting is not overwhelmed by the new journalism of assertion.

Arguing that for too long journalism has defined its role only in negative terms, news scholar Jay Rosen notes: "To be adversarial, critical, to ask tough questions, to expose scandal and wrongdoing . . . these are necessary tasks, even noble tasks, but they are negative tasks." In addition, he suggests, journalism should assert itself as a positive force, not merely as a watchdog or as a neutral information conduit to readers but as "a support system for public life."[47] ▶

CHAPTER REVIEW

COMMON THREADS

One of the Common Threads discussed in Chapter 1 is about the role that media play in a democracy. Today, one of the major concerns is the proliferation of news sources. How well is our society being served by this trend—especially on cable and the Internet—compared with the time when just a few major news media sources dominated journalism?

Historians, media critics, citizens, and even many politicians argue that a strong democracy is only possible with a strong, healthy, skeptical press. In the "old days," a few legacy or traditional media—key national newspapers, three major networks, and three newsmagazines—provided most of the journalistic common ground for discussing major issues confronting U.S. society.

In today's online and 24/7 cable world, though, the legacy or mainstream media have ceded some of their power and many of their fact-checking duties to new media forms, especially in the blogosphere. As discussed in this chapter and in Chapter 8, this loss is partly economic, driven by severe cutbacks in newsroom staffs due to substantial losses in advertising (which has gone to the Internet), and partly because bloggers, 24/7 cable news media, and news satire shows like *The Daily Show* and *The Colbert Report* are fact-checking the media as well as reporting stories that used to be the domain of professional news organizations.

The case before us then goes something like this: In the "old days," the major news media provided us with major news narratives to share, discuss, and argue about. But in today's explosion of news and information, that common ground has eroded or is shifting. Instead, today we often rely only on those media sources that match our comfort level, cultural values, or political affiliations; increasingly these are blog sites, radio talk shows, or cable channels. Sometimes these opinion channels and sites are not supported with the careful fact-gathering and verification that has long been a pillar of the best kinds of journalism.

So in today's media environment, how severely have technological and cultural transformations undermined the "common ground" function of mainstream media? And, are these changes ultimately good or bad for democracy?

KEY TERMS

The definitions for the terms listed below can be found in the glossary at the end of the book. The page numbers listed with the terms indicate where the term is highlighted in the chapter.

news, 488
newsworthiness, 488
ethnocentrism, 490
responsible capitalism, 490

small-town pastoralism, 491
individualism, 491
conflict of interest, 494
herd journalism, 500

sound bite, 505
public journalism, 508

REVIEW QUESTIONS

Modern Journalism in the Information Age

1. What are the drawbacks of the informational model of journalism?

2. What is news?

3. Explain the values shift in journalism today from a more detached or neutral model to a more partisan or assertion model.

Ethics and the News Media

4. How do issues such as deception and privacy present ethical problems for journalists?

5. Why is getting a story first important to reporters?

6. What are the connections between so-called neutral journalism and economics?

Reporting Rituals and the Legacy of Print Journalism

7. Why have reporters become so dependent on experts?

8. Why do many conventional journalists (and citizens) believe firmly in the idea that there are two sides to every story?

Journalism in the Age of TV and the Internet

9. How is credibility established in TV news as compared with print journalism?

10. With regard to TV news, what are sound bites and happy talk?

11. What roles are pundits now playing in 24/7 cable news?

12. In what ways has the Internet influenced traditional forms of journalism?

Alternative Models: Public Journalism and "Fake" News

13. What is public journalism? In what ways is it believed to make journalism better?

14. What are the major criticisms of the public journalism movement, and why do the mainstream national media have concerns about public journalism?

15. What role do satirical news programs like The Daily Show and The Colbert Report play in the world of journalism?

Democracy and Reimagining Journalism's Role

16. What is deliberative democracy, and what does it have to do with journalism?

QUESTIONING THE MEDIA

1. What are your main criticisms of the state of news today? In your opinion, what are the news media doing well?

2. If you were a reporter or an editor, would you quit voting in order to demonstrate your ability to be neutral? Why or why not?

3. Is the trend toward opinion-based partisan news programs on cable and the Internet a good thing or bad thing for democracy?

4. Is there political bias in front-page news stories? If so, cite examples.

5. How would you go about formulating an ethical policy with regard to using deceptive means to get a story?

6. For a reporter, what are the dangers of both detachment from and involvement in public life?

7. Do satirical news programs make us more cynical about politics and less inclined to vote? Why or why not?

8. What steps would you take to make journalism work better in a democracy?

ADDITIONAL VIDEOS

Visit the Ⓒ VideoCentral: Mass Communication section at bedfordstmartins.com/mediaculture for additional exclusive videos related to Chapter 14, including:

- JOURNALISM ETHICS: WHAT NEWS IS FIT TO PRINT? Journalism and legal scholars discuss the ethical considerations inherent to the news industry.

- THE OBJECTIVITY MYTH
Pulitzer Prize–winning journalist Clarence Page and the Onion editor Joe Randazzo explore how objectivity began in journalism and how reporter biases may nonetheless influence news stories.

- SHIELD LAWS AND NONTRADITIONAL JOURNALISTS Reporters and media critics explain what shield laws are and how they apply to both professional and citizen journalists.

In 1995, an eighteen-year-old woman and her boyfriend went on a killing spree in Louisiana after reportedly watching Oliver Stone's 1994 film *Natural Born Killers* more than twenty times. The family of one of the victims filed a lawsuit against Stone and Time Warner, charging that the film—starring Juliette Lewis and Woody Harrelson as a demented, celebrity-craving young couple on a murderous rampage—irresponsibly incited real-life violence. Stone and Time Warner argued that the lawsuit should be dismissed on the grounds of free speech, and the case was finally thrown out in 2001. There was no evidence, according to the judge, that Stone had intended to incite violence.

In 1999, two heavily armed students wearing trench coats attacked Columbine High School in Littleton, Colorado. They planted as many as fifty bombs and murdered twelve fellow students and a teacher before killing themselves. In the wake of this tragedy, many people blamed the mass media, speculating that the killers had immersed themselves in the dark lyrics of shock rocker Marilyn Manson and were desensitized to violence by "first-person-shooter" video games such as *Doom*.

In April 2007, a student massacred thirty-two people on the Virginia Tech campus before killing himself. Gunman Seung-Hui Cho was mentally disturbed and praised "martyrs like Eric and Dylan," the infamous Columbine killers. But Cho's rampage included a twist: During the attack, he sent a package of letters, videos, and photos of himself to NBC News. The images and ramblings of his "multimedia manifesto" became a major part of the news story (as did ethical questions about the news media broadcasting clips of his videos) while the country tried to make sense of the tragedy.

Yet another tragic shooting occurred in 2012 in Aurora, Colorado, at a midnight screening of *The Dark Knight Rises*. A shooter opened fire in the darkened theater, killing twelve people and injuring fifty-eight. The gunman was identified as James Holmes, a twenty-four-year-old wearing a gas mask and trench coat, and carrying several semiautomatic firearms. Holmes repeatedly identified himself as "The Joker" to police.

Each of these events has renewed long-standing cultural debates over the suggestive power of music, visual imagery, and screen violence. Since the emergence of popular music, movies, television, and video games as influential mass media, the relationship between make-believe stories and real-life imitation has drawn a great deal of attention. Concerns have been raised not only by parents, teachers, and politicians but also by several generations of mass communication researchers.

▲

"The relationship between make-believe stories and real-life imitation has drawn a great deal of attention."

◢ *AS THESE TRAGIC TALES OF VIOLENCE ILLUSTRATE,* many believe that media have a powerful effect on individuals and society. This belief has led media researchers to focus most of their efforts on two types of research: media effects research and cultural studies research.

Media effects research attempts to understand, explain, and predict the effects of mass media on individuals and society. The main goal of this type of research is to uncover whether there is a connection between aggressive behavior and violence in the media, particularly in children and teens. In the late 1960s, government leaders–reacting to the social upheavals of that decade–first set aside $1 million to examine this potential connection. Since that time, thousands of studies have told us what most teachers and parents believe instinctively: Violent scenes on television and in movies stimulate aggressive behavior in children and teens– especially young boys.

The other major area of mass media research is **cultural studies**. This research approach focuses on how people make meaning, apprehend reality, articulate values, and order experience through their use of cultural symbols. Cultural studies scholars also examine the way status quo groups in society, particularly corporate and political elites, use media to circulate their messages and sustain their interests. This research has attempted to make daily cultural experience the focus of media studies, keying on the subtle intersections among mass communication, history, politics, and economics.

In this chapter, we will:

- Examine the evolution of media research over time
- Focus on the two major strains of media research, investigating the strengths and limitations of each
- Conclude with a discussion of how media research interacts with democratic ideals

As you get a sense of media effects and cultural studies research, think of some research questions of your own. Consider your own Internet habits. How do the number of hours you spend online every day, the types of online content you view, and your motivations for where you spend your time online shape your everyday behavior? Also, think about the ways your gender, race, sexuality, or class plays into other media you consume–like the movies and television you watch and the music you like. For more questions to help you understand the effects of media in our lives, see "Questioning the Media" in the Chapter Review.

Early Media Research Methods

In the early days of the United States, philosophical and historical writings tried to explain the nature of news and print media. For instance, the French political philosopher Alexis de Tocqueville, author of *Democracy in America,* noted differences between French and American newspapers in the early 1830s:

In France the space allotted to commercial advertisements is very limited, and . . . the essential part of the journal is the discussion of the politics of the day. In America three quarters of the enormous sheet are filled with advertisements and the remainder is frequently occupied by political intelligence or trivial anecdotes; it is only from time to time that one finds a corner devoted to the passionate discussions like those which the journalists of France every day give to their readers.[1]

"The pictures inside the heads of these human beings, the pictures of themselves, of others, of their needs, purposes, and relationships, are their public opinions."

WALTER LIPPMANN,
PUBLIC OPINION, 1922

During most of the nineteenth century, media analysis was based on moral and political arguments, as noted in the de Tocqueville quote.[2]

More scientific approaches to mass media research did not begin to develop until the late 1920s and 1930s. In 1920, Walter Lippmann's *Liberty and the News* called on journalists to operate more like scientific researchers in gathering and analyzing factual material. Lippmann's next book, *Public Opinion* (1922), was the first to apply the principles of psychology to journalism. Considered by many academics to be "the founding book in American media studies,"[3] it led to an expanded understanding of the effects of the media, emphasizing data collection and numerical measurement. According to media historian Daniel Czitrom, by the 1930s "an aggressively empirical spirit, stressing new and increasingly sophisticated research techniques, characterized the study of modern communication in America."[4] Czitrom traces four trends between 1930 and 1960 that contributed to the rise of modern media research: propaganda analysis, public opinion research, social psychology studies, and marketing research.

Propaganda Analysis

After World War I, some media researchers began studying how governments used propaganda to advance the war effort. They found that during the war, governments routinely relied on propaganda divisions to spread "information" to the public. Though propaganda was considered a positive force for mobilizing public opinion during the war, researchers after the war labeled propaganda negatively, calling it "partisan appeal based on half-truths and devious manipulation of communication channels."[5] Harold Lasswell's important 1927 study *Propaganda Technique in the World War* focused on propaganda in the media, defining propaganda as "the control of opinion by significant symbols, . . . by stories, rumors, reports, pictures and other forms of social communication."[6] **Propaganda analysis** thus became a major early focus of mass media research.

Public Opinion Research

Researchers soon went beyond the study of war propaganda and began to focus on more general concerns about how the mass media filtered information and shaped public attitudes. In the face of growing media influence, Walter Lippmann distrusted the public's ability to function as knowledgeable citizens as well as journalism's ability to help the public separate truth from lies. In promoting the place of the expert in modern life, Lippmann celebrated the social scientist as part of a new expert class that could best make "unseen facts intelligible to those who have to make decisions."[7]

Today, social scientists conduct *public opinion research* or citizen surveys; these have become especially influential during political elections. On the upside, public opinion research on diverse populations has provided insights into citizen behavior and social differences, especially during election periods or following major national events. For example, a 2012 *Wall Street Journal*/NBC News poll confirmed what several other reputable polls reported: a majority of Americans favor same-sex marriage. Since 1988, when more than 70 percent of Americans opposed same-sex marriage, the balance has been gradually shifting toward support. This shift has accelerated since 2009.[8]

On the downside, journalism has become increasingly dependent on polls, particularly for political insight. Some critics argue that this heavy reliance on measured public opinion has begun to adversely affect the active political involvement of American citizens. Many people do not vote because they have seen or read poll projections and have decided that their votes will not make a difference. Furthermore, some critics of incessant polling argue that the public is just passively responding to surveys that mainly measure opinions on topics of interest to business, government, academics, and the mainstream news media. A final problem is the pervasive use of unreliable **pseudo-polls**, typically call-in, online, or person-in-the-street polls that the news media use to address a "question of the day." The National Council of Public Opinion Polls notes that "unscientific pseudo-polls are widespread and sometimes entertaining, if always quite meaningless," and discourages news media from conducting them.[9]

Social Psychology Studies

While opinion polls measure public attitudes, *social psychology studies* measure the behavior and cognition of individuals. The most influential early social psychology study, the Payne Fund Studies, encompassed a series of thirteen research projects conducted by social psychologists between 1929 and 1932. Named after the private philanthropic organization that funded the research, the Payne Fund Studies were a response to a growing national concern about the effects of motion pictures, which had become a particularly popular pastime for young people in the 1920s. These studies, which were later used by some politicians to attack the movie industry, linked frequent movie attendance to juvenile delinquency, promiscuity, and other antisocial behaviors, arguing that movies took "emotional possession" of young filmgoers.[10]

In one of the Payne studies, for example, children and teenagers were wired with "electrodes" and "galvanometers," mechanisms that detected any heightened response via the

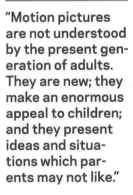

"Motion pictures are not understood by the present generation of adults. They are new; they make an enormous appeal to children; and they present ideas and situations which parents may not like."

MOTION PICTURES AND THE SOCIAL ATTITUDES OF CHILDREN: A PAYNE FUND STUDY, 1933

SOCIAL AND PSYCHOLOGICAL EFFECTS OF MEDIA Concerns about film violence are not new. This 1930 movie, *Little Caesar*, follows the career of gangster Rico Bandello (played by Edward G. Robinson, shown), who kills his way to the top of the crime establishment and gets the girl as well. The Motion Picture Production Code, which was established a few years after this movie's release, reined in sexual themes and profane language, set restrictions on film violence, and attempted to prevent audiences from sympathizing with bad guys like Rico.

◀

FIGURE 15.1

TV PARENTAL GUIDELINES

The TV industry continues to study its self-imposed rating categories, promising to fine-tune them to ensure that the government keeps its distance. These standards are one example of a policy that was shaped in part by media research. Since the 1960s, research has attempted to demonstrate links between violent TV images and increased levels of aggression among children and adolescents.

Source: TV Parental Guidelines Monitoring Board, http://www.tvguidelines.org, accessed December 30, 2012.

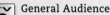

The following categories apply to programs designed solely for children:

All Children
This program is designed to be appropriate for all children. Whether animated or live-action, the themes and elements in this program are specifically designed for a very young audience, including children from ages 2–6. This program is not expected to frighten young children.

Directed to Older Children — Fantasy Violence
*For those programs where fantasy violence may be more intense or more combative than other programs in this category, such programs will be designated **TV-Y7-FV**.*

Directed to Older Children
This program is designed for children age 7 and above. It may be more appropriate for children who have acquired the developmental skills needed to distinguish between make-believe and reality. Themes and elements in this program may include mild fantasy violence or comedic violence, or may frighten children under the age of 7. Therefore, parents may wish to consider the suitability of this program for their very young children.

The following categories apply to programs designed for the entire audience:

General Audience
Most parents would find this program suitable for all ages. Although this rating does not signify a program designed specifically for children, most parents may let younger children watch this program unattended. It contains little or no violence, no strong language and little or no sexual dialogue or situations.

Parental Guidance Suggested
This program contains material that parents may find unsuitable for younger children. Many parents may want to watch it with their younger children. The theme itself may call for parental guidance and/or the program may contain one or more of the following: some suggestive dialogue (D), infrequent coarse language (L), some sexual situations (S), or moderate violence (V).

Parents Strongly Cautioned
This program contains some material that many parents would find unsuitable for children under 14 years of age. Parents are strongly urged to exercise greater care in monitoring this program and are cautioned against letting children under the age of 14 watch unattended. This program may contain one or more of the following: intensely suggestive dialogue (D), strong coarse language (L), intense sexual situations (S), or intense violence (V).

Mature Audiences Only
This program is specifically designed to be viewed by adults and therefore may be unsuitable for children under 17. This program may contain one or more of the following: crude indecent language (L), explicit sexual activity (S), or graphic violence (V).

subject's skin. The researchers interpreted changes in the skin as evidence of emotional arousal. In retrospect, the findings hardly seem surprising: The youngest subjects in the group had the strongest reaction to violent or tragic movie scenes, while the teenage subjects reacted most strongly to scenes with romantic and sexual content. The researchers concluded that films could be dangerous for young children and might foster sexual promiscuity among teenagers. The conclusions of this and other Payne Fund Studies contributed to the establishment of the film industry's production code, which tamed movie content from the 1930s through the 1950s (see Chapter 16). As forerunners of today's TV violence and aggression research, the Payne Fund Studies became the model for media research. (See Figure 15.1 for one example of a contemporary policy that has developed from media research. Also see "Case Study: The Effects of TV in a Post-TV World" on page 525.)

Marketing Research

A fourth influential area of early media research, *marketing research,* developed when advertisers and product companies began conducting surveys on consumer buying habits in the 1920s. The emergence of commercial radio led to the first ratings systems that measured how many people were listening on a given night. By the 1930s, radio networks, advertisers, large stations, and advertising agencies all subscribed to ratings services. However, compared with print media, whose circulation departments kept careful track of customers' names and addresses, radio listeners were more difficult to trace. This problem precipitated the development of

The Effects of TV in a Post-TV World

Since TV's emergence as a mass medium, there has been persistent concern about the effects of violence, sex, and indecent language seen in television programs. The U.S. Congress had its first hearings on the matter of television content in 1952 and has held hearings in every subsequent decade.

In its coverage of congressional hearings on TV violence in 1983, the *New York Times* accurately captured the nature of these recurring public hearings: "Over the years, the principals change but the roles remain the same: social scientists ready to prove that television does indeed improperly influence its viewers, and network representatives, some of them also social scientists, who insist that there is absolutely nothing to worry about."[1]

One of the central focuses of the TV debate has been television's effect on children. In 1975, the major

---

FOX'S *GLEE*, about the trials and tribulations of a high school singing club and its alumni, caught the ire of the PTC for its depiction of sexuality and religious irreverence.

▼

broadcast networks (then ABC, CBS, and NBC) bowed to congressional and FCC pressure and agreed to a "family hour" of programming in the first hour of prime-time television (8–9 P.M. Eastern, or 7–8 P.M. Central). Shows such as *Happy Days*, *The Cosby Show*, and *Little House on the Prairie* flourished in that time slot. By 1989, Fox had arrived as a fourth major network, and successfully counterprogrammed in family hour with dysfunctional family shows like *Married . . . With Children*.

The most prominent watchdog monitoring prime-time network television's violence, sex, and indecent language has been the Parents Television Council (PTC), formed in 1995. The lobbying group's primary mission is to "promote and restore responsibility and decency to the entertainment industry in answer to America's demand for positive, family-oriented television programming. The PTC does this by fostering changes in TV programming to make the early hours of prime time family-friendly and suitable for viewers of all ages."[2] The PTC (through its Web campaign) played a leading role in inundating the FCC with complaints and getting the FCC to approve a steep increase in its fines for broadcast indecency.

Yet, for the ongoing concerns of parent groups and Congress, it's worth asking: What are the effects of TV in what researchers now call a "post-TV" world? In just the past few years, digital video recorders have become common, and services like Hulu, YouTube, Netflix, iTunes, and on-demand cable viewing mean that viewers can access TV programming of all types at any time of the day. Although

Americans are watching more television than ever before, it's increasingly time-shifted programming. How should we consider the possible harmful effects of prime-time network television given that most American families are no longer watching during the appointed broadcast network prime-time hours? Does the American public care about such media effects in this post-TV world?

These days, the Parents Television Council still releases their weekly "Family Guide to Prime Time Television" on their Web site. A sample of their guide from September 2012, for example, listed no shows as "family-friendly," while Fox's hit program *Glee* earned a red light designation because it "may include gratuitous sex, explicit dialogue, violent content, or obscene language."[3] Of one episode, a PTC spokesperson said, "The gist of the show was lap dances with students are cool, the celibacy club is not, and when it's presented in that way, it really cheapens whatever discussion there is about consequence and responsibility."[4]

Of course, as television viewers move away from broadcast networks and increasingly watch programming from multiple sources on a range of devices, the PTC's traditional concern about prime-time network viewing can seem outdated. In 2012, the PTC announced it was giving its seal of approval to the Inspiration Network cable channel "for programming that embraces time-honored values."[5] The channel's lineup featured shows like *The Waltons; Dr. Quinn, Medicine Woman; Little House on the Prairie;* and *Happy Days*—all shows from an era decades before our post-TV world. ◢

increasingly sophisticated marketing research methods to determine consumer preferences and media use, such as direct-mail diaries, television meters, phone surveys, telemarketing, and Internet tracking. In many instances, product companies looking for participation in their surveys paid consumers nominal amounts of money to take part in these studies.

Research on Media Effects

As concern about public opinion, propaganda, and the impact of the media merged with the growth of journalism and mass communication departments in colleges and universities, media researchers looked more and more to behavioral science as the basis of their research. Between 1930 and 1970, "Who says what to whom with what effect?" became the key question "defining the scope and problems of American communications research."[11] In addressing this question specifically, media effects researchers asked follow-up questions such as this: If children watch a lot of TV cartoons (stimulus or cause), will this repeated act influence their behavior toward their peers (response or effect)? For most of the twentieth century, media researchers and news reporters used different methods to answer similar sets of questions—who, what, when, and where—about our daily experiences. (See "Media Literacy and the Critical Process: Wedding Media and the Meaning of the Perfect Wedding Day" on page 531.)

Early Theories of Media Effects

A major goal of scientific research is to develop theories or laws that can consistently explain or predict human behavior. The varied impacts of the mass media and the diverse ways in which people make popular culture, however, tend to defy predictable rules. Historical, economic, and political factors influence media industries, making it difficult to develop systematic theories that explain communication. Researchers developed a number of small theories, or models, that help explain individual behavior rather than the impact of the media on large populations. But before these small theories began to emerge in the 1970s, mass media research followed several other models. Developing between the 1930s and the 1970s, these major approaches included the hypodermic-needle, minimal-effects, and uses and gratifications models.

The Hypodermic-Needle Model

One of the earliest media theories attributed powerful effects to the mass media. A number of intellectuals and academics were fearful of the influence and popularity of film and radio in the 1920s and 1930s. Some social psychologists and sociologists who arrived in the United States after fleeing Germany and Nazism in the 1930s had watched Hitler use radio, film, and print media as propaganda tools. They worried that the popular media in America also had a strong hold over vulnerable audiences. This concept of powerful media affecting weak audiences has been labeled the **hypodermic-needle model**, sometimes also called the *magic bullet theory* or the *direct effects model*. It suggests that the media shoot their potent effects directly into unsuspecting victims.

   One of the earliest challenges to this theory involved a study of Orson Welles's legendary October 30, 1938, radio broadcast of *War of the Worlds*, which presented H. G. Wells's Martian invasion novel in the form of a news report and frightened millions of listeners who didn't realize it was fictional (see Chapter 5). In a 1940 book-length study of the broadcast, *The Invasion from Mars: A Study in the Psychology of Panic*, radio researcher Hadley Cantril argued

that contrary to expectations according to the hypodermic-needle model, not all listeners thought the radio program was a real news report. Instead, Cantril, after conducting personal interviews and a nationwide survey of listeners and analyzing newspaper reports and listener mail to CBS Radio and the FCC, noted that although some did believe it to be real (mostly those who missed the disclaimer at the beginning of the broadcast), the majority reacted out of collective panic, not out of a gullible belief in anything transmitted through the media. Although the hypodermic-needle model over the years has been disproved by social scientists, many people still attribute direct effects to the mass media, particularly in the case of children.

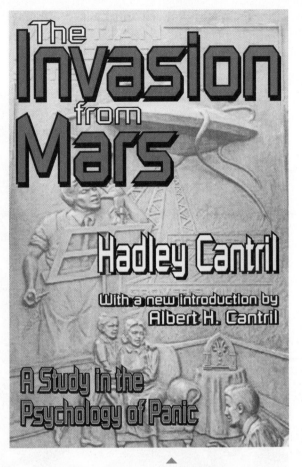

The Minimal-Effects Model

Cantril's research helped to lay the groundwork for the **minimal-effects model**, or *limited model*. With the rise of empirical research techniques, social scientists began discovering and demonstrating that media alone cannot cause people to change their attitudes and behaviors. Based on tightly controlled experiments and surveys, researchers argued that people generally engage in **selective exposure** and **selective retention** with regard to the media. That is, people expose themselves to the media messages that are most familiar to them, and they retain the messages that confirm the values and attitudes they already hold. Minimal-effects researchers have argued that in most cases mass media reinforce existing behaviors and attitudes rather than change them. The findings from the first comprehensive study of children and television–by Wilbur Schramm, Jack Lyle, and Edwin Parker in the late 1950s–best capture the minimal-effects theory:

For some children, under some conditions, some television is harmful. For other children under the same conditions, or for the same children under other conditions, it may be beneficial. For most children, under most conditions, most television is probably neither particularly harmful nor particularly beneficial.[12]

In addition, Joseph Klapper's important 1960 research study, *The Effects of Mass Communication*, found that the mass media only influenced individuals who did not already hold strong views on an issue and that the media had a greater impact on poor and uneducated audiences. Solidifying the minimal-effects argument, Klapper concluded that strong media effects occur largely at an individual level and do not appear to have large-scale, measurable, and direct effects on society as a whole.[13]

The minimal-effects theory furthered the study of the relationship between the media and human behavior, but it still assumed that audiences were passive and were acted upon by the media. Schramm, Lyle, and Parker suggested that there were problems with the position they had taken on effects:

In a sense the term "effect" is misleading because it suggests that television "does something" to children. The connotation is that television is the actor, the children are acted upon. Children are thus made to seem relatively inert; television, relatively active. Children are sitting victims; television bites them. Nothing can be further from the fact. It is the children who are most active in this relationship. It is they who use television, rather than television that uses them.[14]

Indeed, as the authors observed, numerous studies have concluded that viewers–especially young children–are often *actively* engaged in using media.

MEDIA EFFECTS?
In *The Invasion from Mars: A Study in the Psychology of Panic*, Hadley Cantril (1906–1969) argued against the hypodermic-needle model as an explanation for the panic that broke out after the *War of the Worlds* radio broadcast. A lifelong social researcher, Cantril also did a lot of work in public opinion research, even working with the government during World War II.

"If we're a nation possessed of a murderous imagination, we didn't start the bloodletting. Look at Shakespeare, colossus of the Western canon. His plays are written in blood."

SCOT LEHIGH,
BOSTON GLOBE, 2000

USES AND GRATIFICATIONS
In 1952, audience members at the Paramount Theater in Hollywood donned 3-D glasses for the opening night screening of *Bwana Devil,* the first full-length color 3-D film. The uses and gratifications model of research investigates the appeal of mass media, such as going out to the movies.

The Uses and Gratifications Model

A response to the minimal-effects theory, the **uses and gratifications model** was proposed to contest the notion of a passive media audience. Under this model, researchers—usually using in-depth interviews to supplement survey questionnaires—studied the ways in which people used the media to satisfy various emotional or intellectual needs. Instead of asking, "What effects do the media have on us?" researchers asked, "Why do we use the media?" Asking the *why* question enabled media researchers to develop inventories cataloguing how people employed the media to fulfill their needs. For example, researchers noted that some individuals used the media to see authority figures elevated or toppled, to seek a sense of community and connectedness, to fulfill a need for drama and stories, and to confirm moral or spiritual values.[15]

Although the uses and gratifications model addressed the *functions* of the mass media for individuals, it did not address important questions related to the impact of the media on society. Once researchers had accumulated substantial inventories of the uses and functions of media, they often did not move in new directions. Consequently, uses and gratifications never became a dominant or enduring theory in media research.

Conducting Media Effects Research

Media research generally comes from the private or public sector—each type with distinguishing features. *Private research*, sometimes called *proprietary research*, is generally conducted for a business, a corporation, or even a political campaign. It is usually applied research in the sense that the information it uncovers typically addresses some real-life problem or need. *Public research*, in contrast, usually takes place in academic and government settings. It involves information that is often more *theoretical* than applied; it tries to clarify, explain, or predict the effects of mass media rather than to address a consumer problem.

Most media research today focuses on the effects of the media in such areas as learning, attitudes, aggression, and voting habits. This research employs the **scientific method**, a blueprint long used by scientists and scholars to study phenomena in systematic stages. The steps in the scientific method include:

1. identifying the research problem
2. reviewing existing research and theories related to the problem
3. developing working hypotheses or predictions about what the study might find
4. determining an appropriate method or research design
5. collecting information or relevant data
6. analyzing results to see if the hypotheses have been verified
7. interpreting the implications of the study to determine whether they explain or predict the problem

The scientific method relies on *objectivity* (eliminating bias and judgments on the part of researchers); *reliability* (getting the same answers or outcomes from a study or measure during repeated testing); and *validity* (demonstrating that a study actually measures what it claims to measure).

In scientific studies, researchers pose one or more **hypotheses**: tentative general statements that predict the influence of an *independent variable* on a *dependent variable*. For example, a researcher might hypothesize that frequent TV viewing among adolescents (independent variable) causes poor academic performance (dependent variable). Or, another researcher might hypothesize that playing first-person-shooter video games (independent variable) is associated with aggression in children (dependent variable).

Broadly speaking, the methods for studying media effects on audiences have taken two forms–experiments and survey research. To supplement these approaches, researchers also use content analysis to count and document specific messages that circulate in mass media.

Experiments

Like all studies that use the scientific method, **experiments** in media research isolate some aspect of content; suggest a hypothesis; and manipulate variables to discover a particular medium's impact on attitude, emotion, or behavior. To test whether a hypothesis is true, researchers expose an *experimental group*–the group under study–to a selected media program or text. To ensure valid results, researchers also use a *control group*, which serves as a basis for comparison; this group is not exposed to the selected media content. Subjects are picked for each group through **random assignment**, which simply means that each subject has an equal chance of being placed in either group. Random assignment ensures that the independent variables researchers want to control are distributed to both groups in the same way.

For instance, to test the effects of violent films on pre-adolescent boys, a research study might take a group of ten-year-olds and randomly assign them to two groups. Researchers expose the experimental group to a violent action movie that the control group does not see. Later, both groups are exposed to a staged fight between two other boys so that the researchers can observe how each group responds to an actual physical confrontation. Researchers then determine whether or not there is a statistically measurable difference between the two groups' responses to the fight. For example, perhaps the control subjects tried to break up the fight but the experimental subjects did not. Because the groups were randomly selected and the only measurable difference between them was the viewing of the movie, researchers may conclude that under these conditions the violent film caused a different behavior. (See the "Bobo doll" experiment photos on page 532.)

When experiments carefully account for independent variables through random assignment, they generally work well to substantiate direct cause-effect hypotheses. Such research takes place both in laboratory settings and in field settings, where people can be observed using the media in their everyday environments. In field experiments, however, it is more difficult for researchers to control variables. In lab settings, researchers have more control, but other problems may occur. For example, when subjects are removed from the environments in which they regularly use the media, they may act differently–often with fewer inhibitions–than they would in their everyday surroundings.

Experiments have other limitations as well. One, they are not generalizable to a larger population; they cannot tell us whether cause-effect results can be duplicated outside of the laboratory. Two, most academic experiments today are performed on college students, who are convenient subjects for research but are not representative of the general public. Finally, while most experiments are fairly good at predicting short-term media effects under controlled conditions, they do not predict how subjects will behave months or years later in the real world.

Survey Research

In the simplest terms, **survey research** is the collecting and measuring of data taken from a group of respondents. Using random sampling techniques that give each potential subject an equal chance to be included in the survey, this research method draws on much larger populations than those used in experimental studies. Surveys may be conducted through direct mail,

"Theories abound, examples multiply, but convincing facts that specific media content is reliably associated with particular effects have proved quite elusive."

GUY CUMBERBATCH, *A MEASURE OF UNCERTAINTY*, 1989

"Writing survey questions and gathering data are easy; writing good questions and collecting useful data are not."

MICHAEL SINGLETARY, *MASS COMMUNICATION RESEARCH*, 1994

personal interviews, telephone calls, e-mail, and Web sites, enabling survey researchers to accumulate large amounts of information by surveying diverse cross sections of people. These data help to examine demographic factors such as educational background, income level, race, ethnicity, gender, age, sexual orientation, and political affiliations, along with questions directly related to the survey topic.

Two other benefits of surveys are that they are usually generalizable to the larger society and that they enable researchers to investigate populations in long-term studies. For example, survey research can measure subjects when they are ten, twenty, and thirty years old to track changes in how frequently they watch television and what kinds of programs they prefer at different ages. In addition, large government and academic survey databases are now widely available and contribute to the development of more long-range or **longitudinal studies**, which make it possible for social scientists to compare new studies with those conducted years earlier.

Like experiments, surveys have several drawbacks. First, survey investigators cannot account for all the variables that might affect media use; therefore, they cannot show cause-effect relationships. Survey research can, however, reveal **correlations**—or associations—between two variables. For example, a random questionnaire survey of ten-year-old boys might demonstrate that a correlation exists between aggressive behavior and watching violent TV programs. Such a correlation, however, does not explain what is the cause and what is the effect—that is, do violent TV programs cause aggression, or are more aggressive ten-year-old boys simply drawn to violent television? Second, the validity of survey questions is a chronic problem for survey practitioners. Surveys are only as good as the wording of their questions and the answer choices they present. For example, as NPR reported, "[I]f you ask people whether they support or oppose the death penalty for murderers, about two-thirds of Americans say they support it. If you ask whether people prefer that murderers get the death penalty or life in prison without parole, then you get a 50-50 split."[16]

Content Analysis

Over the years, researchers recognized that experiments and surveys focused on general topics (violence) while ignoring the effects of specific media messages (gun violence, fistfights, etc.). As a corrective, researchers developed a method known as **content analysis** to study these messages. Such analysis is a systematic method of coding and measuring media content.

Although content analysis was first used during World War II for radio, more recent studies have focused on television, film, and the Internet. Probably the most influential content analysis studies were conducted by George Gerbner and his colleagues at the University of Pennsylvania. Beginning in the late 1960s, they coded and counted acts of violence on network television. Combined with surveys, their annual "violence profiles" showed that heavy watchers of television, ranging from children to retired Americans, tend to overestimate the amount of violence that exists in the actual world.[17]

The limits of content analysis, however, have been well documented. First, this technique does not measure the effects of the messages on audiences, nor does it explain how those messages are presented. For example, a content analysis sponsored by the Kaiser Family Foundation that examined more than eleven hundred television shows found that 70 percent featured sexual content.[18] But the study didn't explain how viewers interpreted the content or the context of the messages.

Second, problems of definition occur in content analysis. For instance, in the case of coding and counting acts of violence, how do researchers distinguish slapstick cartoon aggression from the violent murders or rapes in an evening police drama? Critics point out that such varied depictions may have diverse and subtle effects on viewers that are not differentiated by content analysis. Finally, critics point out that as content analysis grew to be a primary tool in media research, it sometimes pushed to the sidelines other ways of thinking about television and media

Media Literacy and the Critical Process

1 DESCRIPTION. Select three or four bridal media and compare. Possible choices include magazines such as *Brides*, *Bridal Guide*, *Modern Bride*, and *Martha Stewart Weddings*; reality TV shows like *My Fair Wedding*, *Bridezillas*, *Say Yes to the Dress*, *My Big Fat American Gypsy Wedding*, and *Four Weddings*; Web sites like the Knot, Southern Bride, and Project Wedding; and games like *My Fantasy Wedding*, *Wedding Dash*, and *Imagine Wedding Designer*.

2 ANALYSIS. What patterns do you find in the wedding media? (Consider what isn't depicted as well.) Are there limited ways in which femininity is defined? Do men have an equal role in the planning of wedding events? Are weddings depicted as something just for heterosexuals? Do the wedding media presume that weddings are first-time experiences for the couple getting married? What seem to be the standards in terms of consumption–the expense, size, and number of things to buy and rent to make a "perfect" day?

3 INTERPRETATION. What do the wedding media seem to say

Wedding Media and the Meaning of the Perfect Wedding Day

According to media researcher Erika Engstrom, the bridal industry in the United States generates $50 to $70 billion annually, with more than two million marriages a year.[1] Supporting that massive industry are books, magazines, Web sites, reality TV shows, and digital games (in addition to fictional accounts in movies and music) that promote the idea of what a wedding should be. As these media outlets suggest what a "perfect wedding" is, what values are wrapped up in their wedding narratives?

about what it is to be a woman or a man on her or his wedding day? What do the gender roles of the wedding suggest about the appropriate gender roles in married life after the wedding? What do the wedding media infer about the appropriate level of consumption? In other words, for all of the interpretation, consider the role of wedding media in constructing *hegemony*: in their depiction of what makes a perfect wedding, do the media stories work to get us to accept the dominant cultural values relating to things like gender relations and consumerism?

4 EVALUATION. Come to a judgment about the wedding media analyzed. Are they good or bad on cer-

tain dimensions? Do they promote gender equality? Do they promote marriage equality (i.e., gay marriage)? Do they offer alternatives to having a "perfect" day without buying all of the trappings of so many weddings?

5 ENGAGEMENT. Talk to friends about what weddings are supposed to celebrate, and if an alternative conception of a wedding would be a better way of celebrating a union of two people. (In real life, if there is discomfort in talking about alternative ways to celebrate a wedding, that's probably the pressure of hegemony. Why is that pressure so strong?) Share your criticisms and ideas on wedding Web sites as well.

content. Broad questions concerning the media as a popular art form, as a measure of culture, as a democratic influence, or as a force for social control are difficult to address through strict measurement techniques. Critics of content analysis, in fact, have objected to the kind of social science that reduces culture to acts of counting. Such criticism has addressed the tendency by some researchers to favor measurement accuracy over intellectual discipline and inquiry.[19]

Contemporary Media Effects Theories

By the 1960s, the first departments of mass communication began graduating Ph.D.-level researchers schooled in experiment and survey research techniques, as well as content analysis. These researchers began documenting consistent patterns in mass communication and developing new theories. Five of the most influential contemporary theories that help explain media effects are social learning theory, agenda-setting, the cultivation effect, the spiral of silence, and the third-person effect.

Social Learning Theory

Some of the most well-known studies that suggest a link between the mass media and behavior are the "Bobo doll" experiments, conducted on children by psychologist Albert Bandura and his colleagues at Stanford University in the 1960s. Bandura concluded that the experiments demonstrated a link between violent media programs, such as those on television, and aggressive behavior. Bandura developed **social learning theory** as a four-step process: *attention* (the subject must attend to the media and witness the aggressive behavior), *retention* (the subject must retain the memory for later retrieval), *motor reproduction* (the subject must be able to physically imitate the behavior), and *motivation* (there must be a social reward or reinforcement to encourage modeling of the behavior).

Supporters of social learning theory often cite real-life imitations of media aggression (see the beginning of the chapter) as evidence of social learning theory at work. Yet critics note that many studies conclude just the opposite–that there is no link between media content and aggression. For example, millions of people have watched episodes of *CSI* and *The Sopranos* without subsequently exhibiting aggressive behavior. As critics point out, social learning theory simply makes television, film, and other media scapegoats for larger social problems relating to violence. Others suggest that experiencing media depictions of aggression can actually help viewers let off steam peacefully through a catharsis effect.

Agenda-Setting

A key phenomenon posited by contemporary media effects researchers is **agenda-setting**: the idea that when the mass media focus their attention on particular events or issues, they determine– that is, set the agenda for–the major topics of discussion for individuals and society. Essentially, agenda-setting researchers have argued that the mass media do not so much tell us what to think as *what to think about*. Traceable to Walter Lippmann's notion in the early 1920s that the media "create pictures in our heads," the first investigations into agenda-setting began in the 1970s.[20]

Over the years, agenda-setting research has demonstrated that the more stories the news media do on a particular subject, the more importance audiences attach to that subject. For instance, when the media seriously began to cover ecology issues after the first Earth Day in 1970, a much higher percentage of the population began listing the environment as a primary social concern in surveys. When *Jaws* became a blockbuster in 1975, the news media started featuring more shark attack stories; even landlocked people in the Midwest began ranking sharks as a major problem, despite the rarity of such incidents worldwide. More recently, extensive news coverage about the documentary *An Inconvenient Truth* and its companion best-selling book in 2006 sparked the highest-ever public concern about global warming, according to national surveys. But in the following years the public's sense of urgency faltered somewhat as stories about the economy and other topics dominated the news agenda.

The Cultivation Effect

Another mass media phenomenon—the **cultivation effect**—suggests that heavy viewing of television leads individuals to perceive the world in ways that are consistent with television portrayals. This area of media effects research has pushed researchers past a focus on how the media affects individual behavior and toward a focus on larger ideas about the impact on perception.

The major research in this area grew from the attempts of George Gerbner and his colleagues to make generalizations about the impact of televised violence. The cultivation effect suggests that the more time individuals spend viewing television and absorbing its viewpoints, the more likely their views of social reality will be "cultivated" by the images and portrayals they see on television.[21] For example, Gerbner's studies concluded that although fewer than 1 percent of Americans are victims of violent crime in any single year, people who watch a lot of television tend to overestimate this percentage. Such exaggerated perceptions, Gerbner and his colleagues argued, are part of a "mean world" syndrome, in which viewers with heavy, long-term exposure to television violence are more likely to believe that the external world is a mean and dangerous place.

According to the cultivation effect, media messages interact in complicated ways with personal, social, political, and cultural factors; they are one of a number of important factors in determining individual behavior and defining social values. Some critics have charged that cultivation research has provided limited evidence to support its findings. In addition, some have argued that the cultivation effects recorded by Gerbner's studies have been so minimal as to be benign and that, when compared side-by-side, the perceptions of heavy television viewers and nonviewers in terms of the "mean world" syndrome are virtually identical.

The Spiral of Silence

Developed by German communication theorist Elisabeth Noelle-Neumann in the 1970s and 1980s, the **spiral of silence** theory links the mass media, social psychology, and the formation of public opinion. The theory proposes that those who believe that their views on controversial issues are in the minority will keep their views to themselves—that is, become silent—for fear of social isolation, which diminishes or even silences alternative perspectives. The theory is based on social psychology studies, such as the classic conformity research studies of Solomon Asch in 1951. In Asch's study on the effects of group pressure, he demonstrated that a test subject is more likely to give clearly wrong answers to questions about line lengths if all other people in

MALI
The West African nation of Mali has been in the midst of a political crisis since its northern region was seized by rebel forces in 2012. One of the most devastating outcomes of the country's political strife is the recruitment of child soldiers, as desperate, poor families often give up their children to rebels in exchange for food and money. Despite the devastation in Mali, many feel the international response to Mali's crisis has been woefully inadequate and the mass media's coverage equally insufficient.

the room unanimously state an incorrect answer. Noelle-Neumann argued that mass media, particularly television, can exacerbate this effect by communicating real or presumed majority opinions widely and quickly.

According to the theory, the mass media can help create a false, overrated majority; that is, a true majority of people holding a certain position can grow silent when they sense an opposing majority in the media. One criticism of the theory is that some people may not fall into a spiral of silence because they don't monitor the media, or they mistakenly perceive that more people hold their position than really do. Noelle-Neumann acknowledges that in many cases, "hard-core" nonconformists exist and remain vocal even in the face of social isolation and can ultimately prevail in changing public opinion.[22]

The Third-Person Effect

Identified in a 1983 study by W. Phillips Davison, the **third-person effect** theory suggests that people believe others are more affected by media messages than they are themselves.[23] In other words, it proposes the idea that "we" can escape the worst effects of media while still worrying about people who are younger, less educated, more impressionable, or otherwise less capable of guarding against media influence.

Under this theory, we might fear that other people will, for example, take tabloid newspapers seriously, imitate violent movies, or get addicted to the Internet, while dismissing the idea that any of those things could happen to us. It has been argued that the third-person effect is instrumental in censorship, as it would allow censors to assume immunity to the negative effects of any supposedly dangerous media they must examine.

Evaluating Research on Media Effects

The mainstream models of media research have made valuable contributions to our understanding of the mass media, submitting content and audiences to rigorous testing. This wealth of research exists partly because funding for studies on the effects of the media on young people remains popular among politicians and has drawn ready government support since the 1960s. Media critic Richard Rhodes argues that media effects research is inconsistent and often flawed but continues to resonate with politicians and parents because it offers an easy-to-blame social cause for real-world violence.[24]

Funding restricts the scope of some media effects and survey research, particularly if the government, business, or other administrative agendas do not align with researchers' interests. Other limits also exist, including the inability to address how media affect communities and social institutions. Because most media research operates best in examining media and individual behavior, fewer research studies explore media's impact on community and social life. Some research has begun to address these deficits and also to turn more attention to the increasing impact of media technology on international communication.

Cultural Approaches to Media Research

During the rise of modern media research, approaches with a stronger historical and interpretive edge developed as well, often in direct opposition to the scientific models. In the late 1930s, some social scientists began to warn about the limits of "gathering data" and "charting trends," particularly when these kinds of research projects served only advertisers and media organizations and tended to be narrowly focused on individual behavior, ignoring questions like "Where are institutions taking us?" and "Where do we want them to take us?"[25]

In the United States in the 1960s, an important body of research–loosely labeled *cultural studies*–arose to challenge mainstream media effects theories. Since that time, cultural studies research has focused on how people make meaning, understand reality, and order experience by using cultural symbols that appear in the media. This research has attempted to make everyday culture the centerpiece of media studies, focusing on how subtly mass communication shapes and is shaped by history, politics, and economics. Other cultural studies work examines the relationships between elite individuals and groups in government and politics and how media play a role in sustaining the authority of elites and, occasionally, in challenging their power.

Early Developments in Cultural Studies Research

In Europe, media studies have always favored interpretive rather than scientific approaches; in other words, researchers there have approached the media as if they were literary or cultural critics rather than experimental or survey researchers. These approaches were built on the writings of political philosophers such as Karl Marx and Antonio Gramsci, who investigated how mass media support existing hierarchies in society. They examined how popular culture and sports distract people from redressing social injustices, and they addressed the subordinate status of particular social groups, something emerging media effects researchers were seldom doing.

In the United States, early criticism of media effects research came from the Frankfurt School, a group of European researchers who emigrated from Germany to America to escape Nazi persecution in the 1930s. Under the leadership of Max Horkheimer, T. W. Adorno, and Leo Lowenthal, this group pointed to at least three inadequacies of traditional scientific approaches to media research, arguing that they (1) reduced large "cultural questions" to measurable and "verifiable categories"; (2) depended on "an atmosphere of rigidly enforced neutrality"; and (3) refused to place "the phenomena of modern life" in a "historical and moral context."[26] The researchers of the Frankfurt School did not completely reject the usefulness of measuring and counting data. They contended, however, that historical and cultural approaches were also necessary to focus critical attention on the long-range effects of the mass media on audiences.

Since the time of the Frankfurt School, criticisms of the media effects tradition and its methods have continued, with calls for more interpretive studies of the rituals of mass communication. Academics who have embraced a cultural approach to media research try to understand how media and culture are tied to the actual patterns of communication in daily life. For example, in the 1970s, Stuart Hall and his colleagues studied the British print media and the police, who were dealing with an apparent rise in crime and mugging incidents. Arguing that the close relationship between the news and the police created a form of urban surveillance, the authors of *Policing the Crisis* demonstrated that the mugging phenomenon was exacerbated, and in part created, by the key institutions assigned the social tasks of controlling crime and reporting on it.[27]

Conducting Cultural Studies Research

Cultural research focuses on the investigation of daily experience, especially on issues of race, gender, class, and sexuality, and on the unequal arrangements of power and status in contemporary society. Such research emphasizes how some social and cultural groups have been marginalized and ignored throughout history. Consequently, cultural studies have attempted to recover lost or silenced voices, particularly among African American; Native American; Asian and Asian American; Arabic; Latino; Appalachian; lesbian, gay, bisexual, and transgender (LGBT); immigrant; and women's cultures. The major analytical approaches in cultural studies research today are textual analysis, audience studies, and political economy studies.

"When people say to you, 'of course that's so, isn't it?' that 'of course' is the most ideological moment, because that's the moment at which you're least aware that you are using a particular framework."

STUART HALL, CULTURAL THEORIST, 1983

Textual Analysis

In cultural studies research, **textual analysis** highlights the close reading and interpretation of cultural messages, including those found in books, movies, and TV programs. It is the equivalent of measurement methods like experiments and surveys and content analysis. While media effects research approaches media messages with the tools of modern science–replicability, objectivity, and data–textual analysis looks at rituals, narratives, and meaning. One type of textual analysis is *framing research*, which looks at recurring media story structures, particularly in news stories. Media sociologist Todd Gitlin defines media frames as "persistent patterns of cognition, interpretation, and presentation, of selection, emphasis, and exclusion, by which symbol-handlers routinely organize discourse, whether verbal or visual."[28] (For more on framing research, see "Case Study: Labor Gets Framed" on page 537.)

Although textual analysis has a long and rich history in film and literary studies, it became significant to media in 1974 when Horace Newcomb's book *TV: The Most Popular Art* became the first serious academic book to analyze television shows. Newcomb studied why certain TV programs and formats became popular, especially comedies, westerns, mysteries, soap operas, news reports, and sports programs. Newcomb took television programs seriously, examining patterns in the most popular programs at the time, such as the *Beverly Hillbillies*, *Bewitched*, and *Dragnet,* which traditional researchers had usually snubbed or ignored. Trained as a literary scholar, Newcomb argued that content analysis and other social science approaches to popular media often ignored artistic traditions and social context. For Newcomb, "the task for the student of the popular arts is to find a technique through which many different qualities of the work–aesthetic, social, psychological–may be explored" and to discover "why certain formulas . . . are popular in American television."[29]

Before Newcomb's work, textual analysis generally focused only on "important" or highly regarded works of art–debates, films, poems, and books. But by the end of the 1970s a new generation of media studies scholars, who had grown up on television and rock and roll, began to study less elite forms of culture. They extended the concept of what a "text" is to include architecture, fashion, tabloid magazines, pop icons like Madonna, rock music, hip-hop, soap operas and telenovelas, movies, cockfights, shopping malls, reality TV, Martha Stewart, and professional wrestling–trying to make sense of the most taken-for-granted aspects of everyday media culture. Often the study of these seemingly minor elements of popular culture provides insight into broader meanings within our society. By shifting the focus to daily popular culture artifacts, cultural studies succeeded in focusing scholarly attention not just on significant presidents, important religious leaders, prominent political speeches, or military battles but on the more ordinary ways that "normal" people organize experience and understand their daily lives.

Audience Studies

Cultural studies research that focuses on how people use and interpret cultural content is called **audience studies**, or *reader-response research*. Audience studies differs from textual analysis because the subject being researched is the audience for the text, not the text itself. For example, in *Reading the Romance: Women, Patriarchy, and Popular Literature,* Janice Radway studied a group of midwestern women who were fans of romance novels. Using her training in literary criticism and employing interviews and questionnaires, Radway investigated the meaning of romance novels to the women. She argued that reading romance novels functions as personal time for some women, whose complex family and work lives leave them very little time for themselves. The study also suggested that these particular romance-novel fans identified with the active, independent qualities of the romantic heroines they most admired. As a cultural study, Radway's work did not claim to be scientific, and her findings are not generalizable to all women. Rather, Radway was interested in investigating and interpreting the relationship between reading popular fiction and ordinary life.[30]

CASE STUDY

Labor Gets Framed

Labor union membership in the United States dropped from a high of 34.7 percent of the workforce in 1954 to about 11.8 percent (6.9 percent in the private sector) by 2012. In a world where economic and social forces increasingly separate the "haves" from the "have-nots" and popular media such as entertainment television and film rarely address labor issues, the news media remain one of the few places to find stories about the decline in labor unions and the working class.

Could the way in which news stories frame labor unions have an impact on how people in the United States understand them?

Analyzing the frames of news stories—that is, the ways in which journalists present them—is one form of textual analysis. Unfortunately, if one looks at how the news media frame their reports about labor unions, one has to conclude that news coverage of labor is not at all good.

UNION PROTESTS
In 2011, thousands of Wisconsin teachers staged "sickouts" to protest the passing of a bill that would take away public employees' collective-bargaining rights.

In a major study,[1] hundreds of network television news (ABC, CBS, and NBC) and national newspaper (*New York Times* and *USA Today*) reports involving labor over a ten-year period were analyzed to get a sense of how such stories are framed.

An interesting pattern emerged. Instead of discovering a straightforward bias against labor, the study found that news stories frame labor in a way that selects the consumer perspective (as opposed to a citizen or worker perspective). That is, labor unions aren't portrayed as inherently bad, but any kind of collective action by workers, communities, and even consumers that upsets the American consumer economy and its business leaders and entrepreneurs is framed as a bad thing.

The classic example is the strike story. Even though less than 2 percent of all contract negotiations result in strikes, news stories seem to show union members regularly wielding picket signs. The real stars of strike stories, though, are the inconvenienced consumers—sour-faced people who are livid about missed flights, late package delivery, or canceled ball games. And usually the reports don't explain why a strike is occurring; viewers and readers mainly learn that the hallowed American consumer is upset and if those darned workers would just be a little more agreeable, then none of this inconvenience would have happened.

The frame carries an interesting underlying assumption: If collective action is bad, then economic intervention by citizens should happen only at the individual level (e.g., quit or "vote with your pocketbook" if you don't like something). Of course, individual action would preempt collective action on the part of organizations such as labor unions, which, as organized groups, hold the promise of offering more democratic and broader solutions to problems that affect not one but many workers.

Corporate news that appears in many newspaper business sections frames labor stories in ways that are in harmony with the media corporations' own economic priorities. But such stories need to do so without giving the appearance of bias, which would undermine their credibility. So they frame these stories from the perspective of the consumer. In recent years, in stories about government workers in states like Wisconsin, Ohio, and Michigan, the narratives are the same, and the consumer perspective becomes the taxpayer perspective.

With such framing, the news media's stories undercut a legal institution—labor unions—that might serve as a useful remedy for millions of American workers who want independent representation in their workplace. In fact, national surveys have shown that the majority of American workers would like a stronger voice in their workplaces but have negative opinions about unions, so they aren't likely to consider joining them.[2]

And that's the disconnect that the framing study illustrates: People want independent workplace representation, but—according to the news—labor unions and similar forms of collective action are hardly a viable option. ◢

"I take culture ... and the analysis of it to be therefore not an experimental science in search of law but an interpretive one in search of meaning."

CLIFFORD GEERTZ,
CULTURAL
ANTHROPOLOGIST,
1973

PUBLIC SPHERE
Conversations in eighteenth-century English coffeehouses (like the one shown) inspired Jürgen Habermas's public-sphere theory. However, Habermas expressed concerns that the mass media could weaken the public sphere by allowing people to become passive consumers of the information that the media distributes instead of entering into debates with one another about what is best for society. What do you think of such concerns? Has the proliferation of political cable shows, Internet bloggers, and other mediated forums decreased serious public debate, or has it just shifted the conversation to places besides coffeehouses?

Radway's influential cultural research used a variety of interpretive methods, including literary analysis, interviews, and questionnaires. Most important, these studies helped define culture in broad terms, as being made up of both the *products* a society fashions and the *processes* that forge those products.

Political Economy Studies

A focus on the production of popular culture and the forces behind it is the topic of **political economy studies**, which specifically examine interconnections among economic interests, political power, and how that power is used. Among the major concerns of political economy studies is the increasing conglomeration of media ownership. The increasing concentration of ownership means that the production of media content is being controlled by fewer and fewer organizations, investing those companies with more and more power. Moreover, the domination of public discourse by for-profit corporations may mean that the bottom line for all public communication and popular culture is money, not democratic expression.

Political economy studies work best when combined with textual analysis and audience studies, which provide context for understanding the cultural content of a media product, its production process, and how the audience responds. For example, a major media corporation may, for commercial reasons, create a film and market it through a number of venues (political economy), but the film's meaning or popularity makes sense only within the historical and narrative contexts of the culture (textual analysis), and it may be interpreted by various audiences in ways both anticipated and unexpected (audience studies).

Cultural Studies' Theoretical Perspectives

Developed as an alternative to the predictive theories of social science research (e.g., if X happens, the result will be Y), cultural studies research on media is informed by more general perspectives about how the mass media interact with the world. Two foundational concepts in cultural studies research are (1) the public sphere, and (2) the idea of communication as culture.

The Public Sphere

The idea of the **public sphere**, defined as a space for critical public debate, was first advanced by German philosopher Jürgen Habermas in 1962.[31] Habermas, a professor of philosophy, studied late-seventeenth-century and eighteenth-century England and France, and he found those societies to be increasingly influenced by free trade and the rise of the printing press. At that

historical moment, an emerging middle class began to gather to discuss public life in coffeehouses, meeting halls, and pubs and to debate the ideas of novels and other publications in literary salons and clubs. In doing so, this group (which did not yet include women, peasants, the working classes, and other minority groups) began to build a society beyond the control of aristocrats, royalty, and religious elites. The outcome of such critical public debate led to support for the right to assembly, free speech, and a free press.

Habermas's research is useful to cultural studies researchers when they consider how democratic societies and the mass media operate today. For Habermas, a democratic society should always work to create the most favorable communication situation possible–a public sphere. Basically, without an open communication system, there can be no democratically functioning society. This fundamental notion is the basis for some arguments on why an open, accessible mass media system is essential. However, Habermas warned that the mass media could also be an enemy of democracy, cautioning modern societies to beware of "the manipulative deployment of media power to procure mass loyalty, consumer demand, and 'compliance' with systematic imperatives" of those in power.[32]

Communication as Culture

As Habermas considered the relationship between communication and democracy, media historian James Carey considered the relationship between communication and culture. Carey rejected the "transmission" view of communication–that is, that a message goes simply from sender to receiver. Carey argued that communication is more of a cultural ritual; he famously defined communication as "a symbolic process whereby reality is produced, maintained, repaired, and transformed."[33] Thus communication creates our reality and maintains that reality in the stories we tell ourselves. For example, think about novels, movies, and other stories, representations, and symbols that explicitly or tacitly supported discrimination against African Americans in the United States prior to the Civil Rights movement. When events occur that question reality (like protests and sit-ins in the 1950s and 1960s), communication may repair the culture with adjusted narratives or symbols, or it may completely transform the culture with new dominant symbols. Indeed, analysis of media culture in the 1960s and afterward (including books, movies, TV, and music) suggests a U.S. culture undergoing repair and transformation.

Carey's ritual view of communication leads cultural studies researchers to consider communication's symbolic process as culture itself. Everything that defines our culture–our language, food, clothing, architecture, mass media content, and the like–is a form of symbolic communication that signifies shared (but often still contested) beliefs about culture at a point in historical time. From this viewpoint, then, cultural studies is tightly linked with communication studies.

CULTURAL STUDIES researchers are interested in the production, meaning, and audience response to a wide range of elements within communication culture, including the meaning of the recent trend of "dark" subject matter in young adult novels like the *Twilight* series by Stephanie Meyer, *The Hunger Games* by Suzanne Collins, or *Wintergirls* by Laurie Halse Anderson. As such books are made into movies, researchers may also study the cultural fascination with actors who appear in them (like Robert Pattinson, a star of the *Twilight* films, shown here).

Evaluating Cultural Studies Research

In opposition to media effects research, cultural studies research involves interpreting written and visual "texts" or artifacts as symbolic representations that contain cultural, historical, and political meaning. For example, the wave of police and crime TV shows that appeared in the mid-1960s can be interpreted as a cultural response to concerns and fears people had about urban unrest and income disparity. Audiences were drawn to the heroes of these dramas, who often exerted control over forces that, among society in general, seemed out of control. Similarly, people today who participate in radio talk shows, Internet forums, and TV reality shows can be viewed, in part, as responding to feeling disconnected from economic success or political power. Taking part in these forums represents a popular culture avenue for engaging with media in ways that are usually reserved for professional actors or for the rich, famous, and powerful. As James Carey put it, the cultural approach, unlike media effects research, which is grounded in the social sciences, "does not seek to explain human behavior, but to understand it. . . . It does not attempt to predict human behavior, but to diagnose human meanings."[34] In other words, a cultural approach does not provide explanations for laws that govern how mass media behave. Rather, it offers interpretations of the stories, messages, and meanings that circulate throughout our culture.

One of the main strengths of cultural studies research is the freedom it affords to broadly interpret the impact of the mass media. Because cultural work is not bound by the precise control of variables, researchers can more easily examine the ties between media messages and the broader social, economic, and political world. For example, media effects research on politics has generally concentrated on election polls and voting patterns, while cultural research has broadened the discussion to examine class, gender, and cultural differences among voters and the various uses of power by individuals and institutions in authority. Following Horace Newcomb's work, cultural investigators have expanded the study of media content beyond "serious" works. They have studied many popular forms, including music, movies, and prime-time television.

Just as media effects research has its limits, so does cultural studies research. Sometimes cultural studies have focused exclusively on the meanings of media programs or "texts," ignoring their effect on audiences. Some cultural studies, however, have tried to address this deficiency by incorporating audience studies. Both media effects and cultural studies researchers today have begun to look at the limitations of their work more closely, borrowing ideas from one another to better assess the complexity of the media's meaning and impact.

Media Research and Democracy

> "In quantum gravity, as we shall see, the space-time manifold ceases to exist as an objective reality; geometry becomes relational and contextual; and the foundational conceptual categories of prior science—among them, existence itself—become problematized and relativized. This conceptual revolution, I will argue, has profound implications for the content of a future postmodern and liberatory science."
>
> FROM ALAN SOKAL'S PUBLISHED JARGON-RIDDLED HOAX, 1996

One charge frequently leveled at academic studies is that they fail to address the everyday problems of life; they often seem to have little practical application. The growth of mass media departments in colleges and universities has led to an increase in specialized jargon, which tends to alienate and exclude nonacademics. Although media research has built a growing knowledge base and dramatically advanced what we know about the effect of mass media on individuals and societies, the academic world has paid a price. That is, the larger public has often been excluded from access to the research process even though cultural research tends to identify with marginalized groups. The scholarship is self-defeating if its complexity removes it from the daily experience of the groups it addresses. Researchers themselves have even found it difficult to speak to one another across disciplines because of discipline-specific language used to analyze and report findings. For example, understanding the elaborate statistical analyses used to document media effects requires special training.

In some cultural research, the language used is often incomprehensible to students and to other audiences who use the mass media. A famous hoax in 1996 pointed out just how inaccessible some academic jargon can be. Alan Sokal, a New York University physics professor, submitted an impenetrable article, "Transgressing the Boundaries: Toward a Transformative Hermeneutics of Quantum Gravity," to a special issue of the academic journal *Social Text* devoted to science and postmodernism. As he had expected, the article–a hoax designed to point out how dense academic jargon can sometimes mask sloppy thinking–was published. According to the journal's editor, about six reviewers had read the article but didn't suspect that it was phony. A public debate ensued after Sokal revealed his hoax. Sokal said he worries that jargon and intellectual fads cause academics to lose contact with the real world and "undermine the prospect for progressive social critique."[35]

In addition, increasing specialization in the 1970s began isolating many researchers from life outside of the university. Academics were locked away in their "ivory towers," concerned with seemingly obscure matters to which the general public couldn't relate. Academics across many fields, however, began responding to this isolation and became increasingly active in political and cultural life in the 1980s and 1990s. For example, literary scholar Henry Louis Gates Jr. began writing essays for *Time* and the *New Yorker* magazines. Linguist Noam Chomsky has written for decades about excessive government and media power; he was also the subject of an award-winning documentary, *Manufacturing Consent: Noam Chomsky and the Media.* Essayist and cultural critic Barbara Ehrenreich has written often about labor and economic issues in magazines such as *Time* and the *Nation.* In her 2008 book *This Land Is Their Land: Reports from a Divided Nation,* she investigates incidents of poverty among recent college graduates, undocumented workers, and Iraq war military families, documenting the wide divide between rich and poor. Georgetown University sociology professor Michael Eric Dyson, author of the book *April 4, 1968: Martin Luther King, Jr.'s Death and How It Changed America,* made frequent appearances on network and cable news channels during the 2008 presidential campaign to speak on the issues of race and the meaning of Barack Obama's historic candidacy. Melissa Harris-Perry, a political science professor at Tulane, writes about race, class, and politics for the *Nation,* and also hosts a news and opinion show for MSNBC.

In recent years, public intellectuals have also encouraged discussion about media production in a digital world. Harvard law professor Lawrence Lessig has been a leading advocate of efforts to rewrite the nation's copyright laws to enable noncommercial "amateur culture" to flourish on the Internet. American University's Pat Aufderheide, longtime media critic for the alternative magazine *In These Times,* worked with independent filmmakers to develop the *Documentary Filmmakers' Statement of Best Practices in Fair Use,* which calls for documentary filmmakers to have reasonable access to copyrighted material for their work.

Like public journalists, public intellectuals based on campuses help carry on the conversations of society and culture, actively circulating the most important new ideas of the day and serving as models for how to participate in public life. ▶

PUBLIC INTELLECTUALS
Melissa Harris-Perry writes about race, class, and politics for the *Nation,* and also hosts a weekend news and opinion show for MSNBC. Her most recent book is *Sister Citizen: Shame, Stereotypes, and Black Women in America.*

"My idea of a good time is using jargon and citing authorities."

MATT GROENING,
SCHOOL IS HELL, 1987

CHAPTER REVIEW

COMMON THREADS

One of the Common Threads discussed in Chapter 1 is about the commercial nature of the mass media. In controversies about media content, how much of what society finds troubling in the mass media is due more to the commercial nature of the media than to any intrinsic quality of the media themselves?

For some media critics, such as former advertising executive Jerry Mander in his popular book *Four Arguments for the Elimination of Television* (1978), the problems of the mass media (in his case, television) are inherent in the technology of the medium (e.g., the hypnotic lure of a light-emitting screen) and can't be fixed or reformed. Other researchers focus primarily on the effects of media on individual behavior.

But how much of what critics dislike about television and other mass media—including violence, indecency, immorality, inadequate journalism, and unfair representations of people and issues—derives from the way in which the mass media are organized in our culture rather than from anything about the technologies themselves or their effects on behavior? In other words, are many criticisms of television and other mass media merely masking what should be broader criticisms of capitalism?

One of the keys to accurately analyzing television and the other mass media is to tease apart the effects of a capitalist economy (which organizes media industries and relies on advertising, corporate underwriting, and other forms of sponsorship to profit from them) from the effects of the actual medium (television, movies, the Internet, radio, newspapers, etc.). If our media system wasn't commercial in nature—wasn't controlled by large corporations—would the same "effects" exist? Would the content change? Would different kinds of movies fill theaters? Would radio play the same music? What would the news be about? Would search engines generate other results?

Basically, would society be learning other things if the mass media were organized in a noncommercial way? Would noncommercial mass media set the same kind of political agenda, or would they cultivate a different kind of reality? What would the spiral of silence theory look like in a noncommercial media system?

Perhaps noncommercial mass media would have their own problems. Indeed, there may be effects that can't be unhitched from the technology of a mass medium, no matter what the economy is. But it's worth considering whether any effects are due to the economic system that brings the content to us. If we determine that the commercial nature of the media is a source of negative effects, then we should also reconsider our policy solutions for trying to deal with those effects.

KEY TERMS

The definitions for the terms listed below can be found in the glossary at the end of the book.
The page numbers listed with the terms indicate where the term is highlighted in the chapter.

media effects research, 521
cultural studies, 521
propaganda analysis, 522
pseudo-polls, 523
hypodermic-needle model, 526
minimal-effects model, 527
selective exposure, 527
selective retention, 527
uses and gratifications model, 528

scientific method, 528
hypotheses, 529
experiments, 529
random assignment, 529
survey research, 529
longitudinal studies, 530
correlations, 530
content analysis, 530
social learning theory, 532

agenda-setting, 532
cultivation effect, 533
spiral of silence, 533
third-person effect, 534
textual analysis, 536
audience studies, 536
political economy studies, 538
public sphere, 538

REVIEW QUESTIONS

Early Media Research Methods

1. What were the earliest types of media studies, and why weren't they more scientific?

2. What were the major influences that led to scientific media research?

Research on Media Effects

3. What are the differences between experiments and surveys as media research strategies?

4. What is content analysis, and why is it significant?

5. What are the differences between the hypodermic-needle model and the minimal-effects model in the history of media research?

6. What are the main ideas behind social learning theory, agenda-setting, the cultivation effect, the spiral of silence, and the third-person effect?

7. What are some strengths and limitations of modern media research?

Cultural Approaches to Media Research

8. Why did cultural studies develop in opposition to media effects research?

9. What are the features of cultural studies?

10. How is textual analysis different from content analysis?

11. What are some of the strengths and limitations of cultural research?

Media Research and Democracy

12. What is a major criticism about specialization in academic research at universities?

13. How have public intellectuals contributed to society's debates about the mass media? Give examples.

QUESTIONING THE MEDIA

1. Think about instances in which the mass media have been blamed for a social problem. Could there be another, more accurate cause (an underlying variable) of that problem?

2. One charge leveled against a lot of media research—both the effects and the cultural models—is that it has very little impact on changing our media institutions. Do you agree or disagree, and why?

3. Do you have a major concern about media in society that hasn't been, but should be, addressed by research? Explain your answer.

4. Can you think of a media issue on which researchers from different fields at a university could team up to study together? Explain.

ADDITIONAL VIDEOS

Visit the ⓒ VideoCentral: Mass Communication *section at bedfordstmartins.com/mediaculture for additional exclusive videos related to Chapter 15.*

In 2012, the annual State of the First Amendment national survey found that 63 percent of respondents said that corporations or unions should not be able to spend unlimited amounts to oppose or support a candidate, while 30 percent said, yes, they should be able to spend whatever they want (7 percent were undecided).[1] While the Supreme Court decision ran counter to public opinion, many advocates on the political Right and some on the Left offered that the amendment—which says "Congress shall make no law . . . abridging the freedom of speech"—means what it says. Whereas many who support *Citizens United* make a free-market argument that individuals and corporations in a free country should be able to spend their money on whatever they want, traditional First Amendment supporters like Gene Policinski of the First Amendment Center argue that the "good intentions" behind the idea of limiting campaign spending "don't justify ignoring a basic concept that the Supreme Court majority pointed out in its ruling: Nothing in the First Amendment provides for 'more or less' free-speech protection depending on who is speaking." In criticizing attempts by Congress to restore campaign finance limits, Policinski asks this question in his defense of *Citizens United*: "Do we really want Congress to have the power to exclude certain groups from participating in political speech?"[2]

Was the direction of the 2012 presidential campaign overly determined by those who had money to buy those ads that many Americans used to make decisions in a national election? This is not yet totally clear, since many variables underpin choices that individual voters make. Still, those with limited means are at a clear disadvantage compared to those who have money when it comes to buying expensive commercial speech in the form of TV ads during a presidential campaign. Some critics and many political scientists also attribute low percentages in voter registration and turnout in some states and regions to a feeling or sense that money, more than ever in an age of *Citizens United*, controls politics, parties, and policies. They further argue that it is virtually impossible for a third-party candidate to compete against a two-party system because so much money is needed to fund and sustain a far-flung national campaign, usually fought out in a handful of states where the outcome is in doubt. In July 2012, the state senate in California voted for a resolution urging the U.S. Congress to restore campaign-finance laws. One California lawmaker who supported the resolution argued, "If Congress doesn't act, our electoral process will be more dominated by millionaires and billionaires and their concerns will drown out the voice of common Americans."[3]

▲

"[W]e need a constitutional amendment to reset our campaign finance system and to re-establish that principle that democracy means rule by the people, not giant corporations."

ROBERT WEISSMAN, PRESIDENT OF PUBLIC CITIZEN ADVOCACY GROUP, 2012

◤ **THE CULTURAL AND POLITICAL STRUGGLES OVER WHAT CONSTITUTES** *"FREE SPEECH"* or "free expression" have defined American democracy. In 1989, when Supreme Court Justice William Brennan Jr. was asked to comment on his favorite part of the Constitution, he replied, "The First Amendment, I expect. Its enforcement gives us this society. The other provisions of the Constitution really only embellish it." Of all the issues that involve the mass media and popular culture, none is more central—or explosive—than freedom of expression and the First Amendment. Our nation's historical development can often be traced to how much or how little we tolerated speech during particular periods.

The current era is as volatile a time as ever for free speech issues. Contemporary free speech debates include copyright issues, hate-speech codes on college and university campuses, explicit lyrics in music, violent images in film and television, the swapping of media files on the Internet, and the right of the press to publish government secrets.

In this chapter, we will:

- Examine free expression issues, focusing on the implications of the First Amendment for a variety of mass media
- Investigate the models of expression, the origins of free expression, and the First Amendment
- Examine the prohibition of censorship and how the First Amendment has been challenged and limited throughout U.S. history
- Focus on the impact of gag orders, shield laws, the use of cameras in the courtroom, and some of the clashes between the First Amendment and the Sixth Amendment
- Review the social and political pressures that gave rise to early censorship boards and the current film ratings system
- Discuss First Amendment issues in broadcasting, considering why it has been treated differently from print media
- Explore the newest frontier in free expression—the Internet

One of the most important laws relating to the media is the First Amendment (see the marginal quote on this page for its full text). While you've surely heard about its protections, do you know how or why it was put in place? Have you ever known someone who had to fight to express an idea—for example, was anyone in your high school ever sent home for wearing a certain T-shirt or hat that school officials deemed "offensive"? Have you ever felt that your access to some media content was restricted or censored? What were the circumstances, and how did you respond? For more questions to help you understand the role of freedom of expression in our lives, see "Questioning the Media" in the Chapter Review.

> **"Congress shall make no law respecting an establishment of religion, or prohibiting the free exercise thereof; or abridging the freedom of speech, or of the press; or the right of the people peaceably to assemble, and to petition the Government for a redress of grievances."**
>
> FIRST AMENDMENT, U.S. CONSTITUTION, 1791

The Origins of Free Expression and a Free Press

When students from other cultures attend school in the United States, many are astounded by the number of books, news articles, editorials, cartoons, films, TV shows, and Web sites that make fun of U.S. presidents, the military, and the police. Many countries' governments throughout history have jailed, even killed, their citizens for such speech "violations." For instance, between 1992 and July 2012, more than 900 international journalists were killed in the line of duty, often because someone disagreed with what they wrote or reported.[4] In the United States, however, we have generally taken for granted our right to criticize and poke fun at the

JOURNALISTS IN IRAQ
During the Iraq war, journalists were embedded with troops to provide "frontline" coverage. The freedom the U.S. press had to report on the war came at a cost. According to the Committee to Protect Journalists, 225 journalists and media workers were killed in Iraq between 2003 and 2011 as a result of hostile actions.

government and other authority figures. Moreover, many of us are unaware of the ideas that underpin our freedoms and don't realize the extent to which those freedoms surpass those in most other countries.

In fact, a 2011 survey related that forty-seven nations allow virtually no freedom of the press, with those governments exercising tight control over the news media and even intimidating, jailing, and executing journalists.[5]

Models of Expression

Since the mid-1950s, four conventional models for speech and journalism have been used to categorize the widely differing ideas underlying free expression.[6] These models include the authoritarian, communist, libertarian, and social responsibility concepts. They are distinguished by the levels of freedom permitted and by the attitudes of the ruling and political classes toward the freedoms granted to the average citizen. Today, given the diversity among nations, the experimentation of journalists, and the collapse of many communist press systems, these categories are no longer as relevant. Nevertheless, they offer a good point of departure for discussing the press and democracy.

The **authoritarian model** developed at about the time the printing press first arrived in sixteenth-century England. Its advocates held that the general public, largely illiterate in those days, needed guidance from an elite, educated ruling class. Government criticism and public dissent were not tolerated, especially if such speech undermined "the common good"–an ideal that elites and rulers defined and controlled. Censorship was also frequent, and the government issued printing licenses primarily to publishers who were sympathetic to government and ruling-class agendas.

Today, many authoritarian systems operate in developing countries throughout Asia, Latin America, and Africa, where journalism often joins with government and business to foster economic growth, minimize political dissent, and promote social stability, believing too much speech freedom would undermine the delicate stability of their social infrastructures. In these societies, criticizing government programs may be viewed as an obstacle to keeping the peace, and both reporters and citizens may be punished if they question leaders and the status quo too fiercely.

In the authoritarian model, the news is controlled by private enterprise. But under the **communist or state model**, the press is controlled by the government because state leaders believe the press should serve the goals of the state. Although some government criticism is tolerated under this model, ideas that challenge the basic premises of state authority are not. Although state media systems were in decline throughout the 1990s, there are still a few countries using this model, including Myanmar (Burma), China, Cuba, and North Korea.

The **social responsibility model** characterizes the ideals of mainstream journalism in the United States. The concepts and assumptions behind this model were outlined in 1947 by the Hutchins Commission, which was formed to examine the increasing influence of the press. The commission's report called for the development of press watchdog groups because the mass media had grown too powerful and needed to become more socially responsible. Key recommendations encouraged comprehensive news reports that put issues and events in context; more news forums for the exchange of ideas; better coverage of society's range of economic classes and social groups; and stronger overviews of our nation's social values, ideals, and goals.

A socially responsible press is usually privately owned (although the government technically operates the broadcast media in most European democracies). In this model, the press functions as a **Fourth Estate**–that is, as an unofficial branch of government that monitors the legislative, judicial, and executive branches for abuses of power. In theory, private ownership keeps the news media independent of government. Thus they are better able to watch over the system on behalf of citizens. Under this model, the press supplies information to citizens so that they can make informed decisions regarding political and social issues.

The flip side of the state and authoritarian models and a more radical extension of the social responsibility model, the **libertarian model** encourages vigorous government criticism and supports the highest degree of individual and press freedoms. Under a libertarian model, no restrictions would be placed on the mass media or on individual speech. Libertarians tolerate the expression of everything, from publishing pornography to advocating anarchy. In North America and Europe, many alternative newspapers and magazines operate on such a model. Placing a great deal of trust in citizens' ability to distinguish truth from fabrication, libertarians maintain that speaking out with absolute freedom is the best way to fight injustice and arrive at the truth.

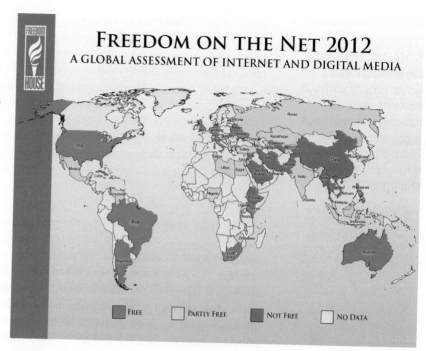

FREEDOM ON THE NET 2012
A GLOBAL ASSESSMENT OF INTERNET AND DIGITAL MEDIA

FREE　PARTLY FREE　NOT FREE　NO DATA

PRESS FREEDOM
The international human rights organization Freedom House comparatively assesses political rights and civil liberties in 194 of the world's countries and territories. Among the nations counted as not entirely free are China, Cuba, Iraq, Iran, Pakistan, North Korea, Russia, and Libya.

The First Amendment of the U.S. Constitution

To understand the development of free expression in the United States, we must first understand how the idea for a free press came about. In various European countries throughout the 1600s, in order to monitor—and punish, if necessary—the speech of editors and writers, governments controlled the circulation of ideas through the press by requiring printers to obtain licenses from them. However, in 1644, English poet John Milton, author of *Paradise Lost*, published his essay *Areopagitica*, which opposed government licenses for printers and defended a free press. Milton argued that all sorts of ideas, even false ones, should be allowed to circulate freely in a democratic society, because eventually the truth would emerge. In 1695, England stopped licensing newspapers, and most of Europe followed. In many democracies today, publishing a newspaper, magazine, or newsletter remains one of the few public or service enterprises that requires no license.

Less than a hundred years later, the writers of the U.S. Constitution were ambivalent about the freedom of the press. In fact, the Constitution as originally ratified in 1788 didn't include a guarantee of freedom of the press. Constitutional framer Alexander Hamilton thought it impractical to attempt to define "liberty of the press," and that whatever declarations might be added to the Constitution, its security would ultimately depend on public opinion. At that time, though, nine of the original thirteen states had charters defending the freedom of the press, and the states pushed to have federal guarantees of free speech and press approved at the first session of the new Congress. The Bill of Rights, which contained the first ten amendments to the Constitution, was adopted in 1791.

The commitment to freedom of the press, however, was not resolute. In 1798, the Federalist Party, which controlled the presidency and Congress, passed the Sedition Act to silence opposition to an anticipated war against France. Led by President John Adams, the Federalists

> "Were it left to me to decide whether we should have a government without newspapers, or newspapers without a government, I should not hesitate a moment to prefer the latter."
>
> THOMAS JEFFERSON, ON THE BRUTAL PRESS COVERAGE OF HIM BY OPPOSITION PARTY NEWSPAPERS, 1787

believed that defamatory articles by the opposition Democratic-Republican Party might stir up discontent against the government and undermine its authority. Over the next three years, twenty-five individuals were arrested and ten were convicted under the act, which was also used to prosecute anti-Federalist newspapers. After failing to curb opposition, the Sedition Act expired in 1801 during Thomas Jefferson's presidency. Jefferson, a Democratic-Republican who had challenged the act's constitutionality, pardoned all defendants convicted under it.[7] Ironically, the Sedition Act, the first major attempt to constrain the First Amendment, became the defining act in solidifying American support behind the notion of a free press. As journalism historian Michael Schudson explained, "Only in the wake of the Sedition Act did Americans boldly embrace a free press as a necessary bulwark of a liberal civil order."[8]

Censorship as Prior Restraint

In the United States, the First Amendment has theoretically prohibited censorship. Over time, Supreme Court decisions have defined censorship as **prior restraint**. This means that courts and governments cannot block any publication or speech before it actually occurs, on the principle that a law has not been broken until an illegal act has been committed. In 1931, for example, the Supreme Court determined in *Near v. Minnesota* that a Minneapolis newspaper could not be stopped from publishing "scandalous and defamatory" material about police and law officials whom they felt were negligent in arresting and punishing local gangsters.[9] However, the Court left open the idea that the news media could be ordered to halt publication in exceptional cases. During a declared war, for instance, if a U.S. court judged that the publication of an article would threaten national security, such expression could be restrained prior to its printing. In fact, during World War I the U.S. Navy seized all wireless radio transmitters. This was done to ensure control over critical information about weather conditions and troop movements that might inadvertently aid the enemy. In the 1970s, though, the Pentagon Papers decision and the *Progressive* magazine case tested important concepts underlying prior restraint.

The Pentagon Papers Case

In 1971, with the Vietnam War still in progress, Daniel Ellsberg, a former Defense Department employee, stole a copy of the forty-seven-volume report "History of U.S. Decision-Making Process on Vietnam Policy." A thorough study of U.S. involvement in Vietnam since World War II, the report was classified by the government as top secret. Ellsberg and a friend leaked the study—nicknamed the Pentagon Papers—to the *New York Times* and the *Washington Post*. In June 1971, the *Times* began publishing articles based on the study. To block any further publications, the Nixon administration applied for and received a federal court injunction against the *Times*, arguing that the publication of these documents posed "a clear and present danger" to national security.

A lower U.S. district court supported the newspaper's right to publish, but the government's appeal put the case before the Supreme Court less than three weeks after the first article was published. In a six-to-three vote, the Court sided with the newspaper. Justice Hugo Black, in his majority opinion, attacked the government's attempt to suppress publication: "Both the history and language of the First Amendment support the view that the press must be left free to publish news, whatever the source, without censorship, injunctions, or prior restraints."[10] (See "Media Literacy and the Critical Process: Who Knows the First Amendment?" on page 552.)

The *Progressive* Magazine Case

The issue of prior restraint for national security surfaced again in 1979, when an injunction was issued to block publication of the *Progressive*, a national left-wing magazine, in which the editors planned to publish an article entitled "The H-Bomb Secret: How We Got It, Why We're Telling It." The dispute began when the editor of the magazine sent a draft to the Department of Energy to verify technical portions of the article. Believing that the article contained sensitive data that

might damage U.S. efforts to halt the proliferation of nuclear weapons, the Energy Department asked the magazine not to publish it. When the magazine said it would proceed anyway, the government sued the *Progressive* and asked a federal district court to block publication.

Judge Robert Warren sought to balance the *Progressive*'s First Amendment rights against the government's claim that the article would spread dangerous information and undermine national security. In an unprecedented action, Warren sided with the government, deciding that "a mistake in ruling against the United States could pave the way for thermonuclear annihilation for us all. In that event, our right to life is extinguished and the right to publish becomes moot."[11] During appeals and further litigation, several other publications, including the *Milwaukee Sentinel* and *Scientific American*, published their own articles related to the H-bomb, getting much of their information from publications already in circulation. None of these articles, including the one eventually published in the *Progressive*–after the government dropped the case during an appeal–contained the precise technical details needed to actually design a nuclear weapon, nor did they provide information on where to obtain the sensitive ingredients.

Even though the article was eventually published, Warren's decision stands as the first time in American history that a prior-restraint order imposed in the name of national security actually stopped the initial publication of a controversial news report.

Unprotected Forms of Expression

Despite the First Amendment's provision that "Congress shall make no law" restricting speech, the federal government has made a number of laws that do just that, especially concerning false or misleading advertising, expressions that intentionally threaten public safety, and certain speech restrictions during times of war or other national security concerns.

Beyond the federal government, state laws and local ordinances have on occasion curbed expression, and over the years the court system has determined that some kinds of expression do not merit protection under the Constitution, including seditious expression, copyright infringement, libel, obscenity, privacy rights, and expression that interferes with the Sixth Amendment.

Seditious Expression

For more than a century after the Sedition Act of 1798, Congress passed no laws prohibiting dissenting opinion. But by the twentieth century the sentiments of the Sedition Act reappeared in times of war. For instance, the Espionage Acts of 1917 and 1918, which were enforced during

PRIOR RESTRAINT
In 1971, Daniel Ellsberg surrendered to government prosecutors in Boston. Ellsberg was a former Pentagon researcher who turned against America's military policy in Vietnam and leaked information to the press. He was charged with unauthorized possession of top-secret federal documents. Later called the Pentagon Papers, the documents contained evidence on the military's bungled handling of the Vietnam War. In 1973, an exasperated federal judge dismissed the case when illegal government-sponsored wiretaps of Ellsberg's psychoanalyst came to light during the Watergate scandal.

Media Literacy and the Critical Process

1 DESCRIPTION. Working alone or in small groups, find eight to ten people you know from two different age groups: (1) from your peers and friends or younger siblings; (2) from your parents' and/or grandparents' generations. (Do not choose students from your class.) Interview your subjects individually, either in person, by phone, or by e-mail, and ask them this question: If Congress were considering the following law–then offer the First Amendment (see page 547), but don't tell them what it is–would they approve? Then ask them to respond to the following series of questions, adding any other questions that you think would be appropriate:

1. Do you agree or disagree with the freedoms? Explain.
2. Which do you support, and which do you think are excessive or provide too much freedom?
3. Ask them if they recognize the law. Note how many identify it as the First Amendment to the U.S. Constitution and how many do not. Note the percentage from each age group.
4. Optional: Ask if your respondents are willing to share their political leanings–

Who Knows the First Amendment?

Enacted in 1791, the First Amendment supports not just press and speech freedoms but also religious freedom and the right of people to protest and to "petition the government for a redress of grievances." It also says that "Congress shall make no law" abridging or prohibiting these five freedoms. To investigate some critics' complaint that many citizens don't exactly know the protections offered in the First Amendment, conduct your own survey. Discuss with friends, family, or colleagues what they know or think about the First Amendment.

Republican, Democrat, Independent, not sure, disaffected, apathetic, or other. Record their answers.

2 ANALYSIS. What patterns emerge in the answers from the two groups? Are their answers similar or different? How? Note any differences in the answers based on gender, level of education, or occupation.

3 INTERPRETATION. What do these patterns mean? Are your interview subjects supportive or unsupportive of the First Amendment? What are their reasons?

4 EVALUATION. How do your interviewees judge the freedoms? In general, what did your interview subjects know about the First Amendment? What impresses you about your subjects' answers? Do you find anything alarming or troubling in their answers?

5 ENGAGEMENT. Research free expression and locate any national studies that are similar to this assignment. Then, check the recent national surveys on attitudes toward the First Amendment at either www.freedomforum.org or www.firstamendmentcenter.org. Based on your research, educate others. Do a presentation in class or at your college or university about the First Amendment.

World Wars I and II, made it a federal crime to disrupt the nation's war effort, authorizing severe punishment for seditious statements.

In the landmark *Schenck v. United States* (1919) appeal case during World War I, the Supreme Court upheld the conviction of a Socialist Party leader, Charles T. Schenck, for distributing leaflets urging American men to protest the draft, in violation of the recently passed Espionage Act. In upholding the conviction, Justice Oliver Wendell Holmes wrote two of the more famous interpretations and phrases in the First Amendment's legal history:

But the character of every act depends upon the circumstances in which it is done. The most stringent protection of free speech would not protect a man in falsely shouting fire in a theater and causing a panic.

The question in every case is whether the words used are used in such circumstances and are of such a nature as to create a clear and present danger that they will bring about the substantive evils that Congress has a right to prevent.

In supporting Schenck's sentence—a ten-year prison term—Holmes noted that the Socialist leaflets were entitled to First Amendment protection, but only during times of peace. In establishing the "clear and present danger" criterion for expression, the Supreme Court demonstrated the limits of the First Amendment.

And in 2010, after WikiLeaks released thousands of confidential U.S. embassy cables into the public domain, the U.S. Justice Department contemplated charging the Web site's founder Julian Assange with violating the 1917 Espionage Act. One U.S. senator insisted that "[Assange] be prosecuted to the fullest extent of the law. And if that becomes a problem, we need to change the law."[12] Although most legal experts considered this a weak case, the incident demonstrated that some politicians still want to curtail political dissent guaranteed by the First Amendment. As of 2012, no journalist had ever been successfully prosecuted under the 1917 act.

Copyright Infringement

Appropriating a writer's or an artist's words or music without consent or payment is also a form of expression that is not protected as speech. A **copyright** legally protects the rights of authors and producers to their published or unpublished writing, music, lyrics, TV programs, movies, or graphic art designs. When Congress passed the first Copyright Act in 1790, it gave authors the right to control their published works for fourteen years, with the opportunity for a renewal for another fourteen years. After the end of the copyright period, the work enters the **public domain**, which gives the public free access to the work. The idea was that a period of copyright control would give authors financial incentive to create original works, and that the public domain gives others incentive to create derivative works.

Over the years, as artists lived longer, and more important, as corporate copyright owners became more common, copyright periods were extended by Congress. In 1976, Congress extended the copyright period to the life of the author plus fifty years, or seventy-five years for a corporate copyright owner. In 1998 (as copyrights on works such as Disney's Mickey Mouse were set to expire), Congress again extended the copyright period for twenty additional years. As Stanford law professor Lawrence Lessig observed, this was the eleventh time in forty years that the terms for copyright had been extended.[13] (See "Examining Ethics: A Generation of Copyright Criminals?" on page 571.)

Corporate owners have millions of dollars to gain by keeping their properties out of the public domain. Disney, a major lobbyist for the 1998 extension, would have lost its copyright to Mickey Mouse in 2004, but now continues to earn millions on its movies, T-shirts, and Mickey Mouse watches through 2024. Warner/Chappell Music, which owns the copyright to the popular "Happy Birthday to You" song, will keep generating money on the song at least through 2030, and even longer if corporations successfully pressure Congress for another extension.

Today, nearly every innovation in digital culture creates new questions about copyright law. For example, is a video mash-up that samples copyrighted sounds and images a copyright violation or a creative accomplishment protected under the concept of *fair use* (the same standard that enables students to legally quote attributed

THE LIMITS OF COPYRIGHT The iconic album art for the Velvet Underground's 1967 debut, a banana print designed by artist Andy Warhol, has been a subject of controversy in recent years as a copyright dispute between the Andy Warhol Foundation for the Visual Arts and the rock band has continued to flourish. The most recent disagreement occurred when the Warhol Foundation, which has previously accused the Velvet Underground of violating their claim to the print, announced plans to license the banana design for iPhone cases. Accusing the foundation of copyright violation, the band filed a copyright claim to the design, which a federal judge later dismissed.

text from other works in their research papers)? Is it fair use for a blog to quote an entire newspaper article, as long as it has a link and an attribution? Should news aggregators like Google News and Yahoo! News pay something to financially strapped newspapers when they link to their articles? One of the laws that tips the debates toward stricter enforcement of copyright is the Digital Millennium Copyright Act of 1998, which outlaws any action or technology that circumvents copyright protection systems. In other words, it may be illegal to merely create or distribute technology that enables someone to make illegal copies of digital content, such as a music file or a DVD.

LIBEL AND THE MEDIA
This is the 1960 *New York Times* advertisement that triggered one of the most influential and important libel cases in U.S. history.

Libel

The biggest legal worry that haunts editors and publishers is the issue of libel, a form of expression that, unlike political expression, is not protected as free speech under the First Amendment. **Libel** refers to defamation of character in written or broadcast form; libel is different from **slander**, which is spoken language that defames a person's character. Inherited from British common law, libel is generally defined as a false statement that holds a person up to public ridicule, contempt, or hatred or injures a person's business or occupation. Examples of libelous statements include falsely accusing someone of professional dishonesty or incompetence (such as medical malpractice); falsely accusing a person of a crime (such as drug dealing); falsely stating that someone is mentally ill or engages in unacceptable behavior (such as public drunkenness); or falsely accusing a person of associating with a disreputable organization or cause (such as the Mafia or a neo-Nazi military group).

Since 1964, the *New York Times v. Sullivan* case has served as the standard for libel law. The case stems from a 1960 full-page advertisement placed in the *New York Times* by the Committee to Defend Martin Luther King and the Struggle for Freedom in the South. Without naming names, the ad criticized the law-enforcement tactics used in southern cities–including Montgomery, Alabama–to break up Civil Rights demonstrations. The ad condemned "southern violators of the Constitution" bent on destroying King and the movement. Taking exception, the city commissioner of Montgomery, L. B. Sullivan, sued the *Times* for libel, claiming the ad defamed him indirectly. Although Alabama civil courts awarded Sullivan $500,000, the newspaper's lawyers appealed to the Supreme Court, which unanimously reversed the ruling, holding that Alabama libel law violated the *Times*' First Amendment rights.[14]

As part of the *Sullivan* decision, the Supreme Court asked future civil courts to distinguish whether plaintiffs in libel cases are public officials or private individuals. Citizens with more "ordinary" jobs, such as city sanitation employees, undercover police informants, nurses, or unknown actors, are normally classified as private individuals. Private individuals have to prove (1) that the public statement about them was false; (2) that damages or actual injury occurred (such as the loss of a job, harm to reputation, public humiliation, or mental anguish); and (3) that the publisher or broadcaster was negligent in failing to determine the truthfulness of the statement.

There are two categories of public figures: (1) public celebrities (movie or sports stars) or people who "occupy positions of such pervasive power and influence that they are deemed public figures for all purposes" (such as presidents, senators, mayors, etc.), and (2) individuals who have thrown themselves–usually voluntarily but sometimes involuntarily–into the middle of "a significant public controversy," such as a lawyer defending a prominent client, an advocate for an antismoking ordinance, or a labor union activist.

Public officials also have to prove falsehood, damages, negligence, and **actual malice** on the part of the news medium; actual malice means that the reporter or editor knew the statement was false and printed or broadcast it anyway, or acted with a reckless disregard for the truth. Because actual malice against a public official is hard to prove, it is difficult for public figures to win libel suits. The *Sullivan* decision allowed news operations to aggressively pursue legitimate news stories without fear of continuous litigation. However, the mere threat of a libel suit still scares off many in the news media. Plaintiffs may also belong to one of many vague classification categories, such as public high school teachers, police officers, and court-appointed attorneys. Individuals from these professions end up as public or private citizens depending on a particular court's ruling.

Defenses against Libel Charges

Since the 1730s, the best defense against libel in American courts has been the truth. In most cases, if libel defendants can demonstrate that they printed or broadcast statements that were essentially true, such evidence usually bars plaintiffs from recovering any damages–even if their reputations were harmed.

In addition, there are other defenses against libel. Prosecutors, for example, who would otherwise be vulnerable to being accused of libel, are granted *absolute privilege* in a court of law so that they are not prevented from making accusatory statements toward defendants. The reporters who print or broadcast statements made in court are also protected against libel; they are granted conditional or **qualified privilege**, allowing them to report judicial or legislative proceedings even though the public statements being reported may be libelous.

Another defense against libel is the rule of **opinion and fair comment**. Generally, libel applies only to intentional misstatements of factual information rather than opinion, and therefore opinions are protected from libel. However, because the line between fact and opinion is often hazy, lawyers advise journalists first to set forth the facts on which a viewpoint is based and then to state their opinion based on those facts. In other words, journalists should make it clear that a statement of opinion is a criticism and not an allegation of fact.

One of the most famous tests of opinion and fair comment occurred in 1983 when Larry Flynt, publisher of *Hustler* magazine, published a spoof of a Campari advertisement depicting conservative minister and political activist Jerry Falwell as a drunk and as having had sexual relations with his mother. In fine print at the bottom of the page, a disclaimer read: "Ad parody–not to be taken seriously." Often a target of Flynt's irreverence and questionable taste, Falwell sued for libel, asking for $45 million in damages. In the verdict, the jury rejected the libel suit but found that Flynt had intentionally caused Falwell emotional distress,

"You cannot hold us to the same [libel] standards as a newscast or you kill talk radio. If we had to qualify everything we said, talk radio would cease to exist."

LIONEL, WABC TALK-RADIO MORNING HOST, 1999

LIBEL AND OBSCENITY
Prior to his 1984 libel trial, *Hustler* magazine publisher Larry Flynt was also convicted of pandering obscenity. Here, Flynt answers questions from newsmen on February 9, 1977, as he is led to jail.

awarding Falwell $200,000. The case drew enormous media attention and raised concerns about the erosion of the media's right to free speech. However, Flynt's lawyers appealed, and in 1988 the Supreme Court unanimously overturned the verdict. Although the Court did not condone the *Hustler* spoof, the justices did say that the magazine was entitled to constitutional protection. In affirming *Hustler*'s speech rights, the Court suggested that even though parodies and insults of public figures might indeed cause emotional pain, denying the right to publish them and awarding damages for emotional reasons would violate the spirit of the First Amendment.[15]

Libel laws also protect satire, comedy, and opinions expressed in reviews of books, plays, movies, and restaurants. Such laws may not, however, protect malicious statements in which plaintiffs can prove that defendants used their free-speech rights to mount a damaging personal attack.

Obscenity

For most of this nation's history, legislators have argued that **obscenity** does not constitute a legitimate form of expression protected by the First Amendment. The problem, however, is that little agreement has existed on how to define an obscene work. In the 1860s, a court could judge an entire book obscene if it contained a single passage believed capable of "corrupting" a person. In fact, throughout the 1800s certain government authorities outside the courts—especially U.S. post office and customs officials—held the power to censor or destroy material they deemed obscene.

This began to change in the 1930s during the trial involving the celebrated novel *Ulysses* by Irish writer James Joyce. Portions of *Ulysses* had been serialized in the early 1920s in an American magazine, *Little Review*, copies of which were later seized and burned by postal officials. The publishers of the magazine were fined $50 and nearly sent to prison. Because of the four-letter words contained in the novel and the book-burning and fining incidents, British and American publishing houses backed away from the book, and in 1928 the U.S. Customs Office officially banned *Ulysses* as an obscene work. Ultimately, however, Random House agreed to publish the work in the United States if it was declared "legal." Finally,

> "I shall not today attempt to define [obscenity]. . . . And perhaps I never could succeed in intelligibly doing so. But I know it when I see it."
>
> SUPREME COURT JUSTICE POTTER STEWART, 1964

in 1933 a U.S. judge ruled that an important literary work such as *Ulysses* was a legitimate, protected form of expression, even if portions of the book were deemed objectionable by segments of the population.

In a landmark 1957 case, *Roth v. United States*, the Supreme Court offered this test of obscenity: whether to an "average person," applying "contemporary standards," the major thrust or theme of the material "taken as a whole" appealed to "prurient interest" (in other words, was intended to "incite lust"). By the 1960s, based on *Roth*, expression was not obscene if only a small part of the work lacked "redeeming social value."

The current legal definition of obscenity derives from the 1973 *Miller v. California* case, which stated that to qualify as obscenity, the material must meet three criteria: (1) the average person, applying contemporary community standards, would find that the material as a whole appeals to prurient interest; (2) the material depicts or describes sexual conduct in a patently offensive way; and (3) the material, as a whole, lacks serious literary, artistic, political, or scientific value. The *Miller* decision contained two important ideas not present in *Roth*. First, it acknowledged that different communities and regions of the country have different values and standards with which to judge obscenity. Second, it required that a work be judged *as a whole*, so that publishers could not use the loophole of inserting a political essay or literary poem into pornographic materials to demonstrate in court that their publications contained redeeming features.

Since the *Miller* decision, courts have granted great latitude to printed and visual obscenity. By the 1990s, major prosecutions had become rare—aimed mostly at child pornography—as the legal system accepted the concept that a free and democratic society must tolerate even repulsive kinds of speech. Most battles over obscenity are now online, where the global reach of the Internet has eclipsed the concept of community standards. The most recent incarnation of the Child Online Protection Act—originally passed in 1998 to make it illegal to post "material that is harmful to minors"— was found unconstitutional in 2007 because it would infringe on the right to free speech on the Internet. In response to an online sexual predator case, in 2010 Massachusetts passed a law to protect children from obscene material on computers and the Internet. But a number of publishers and free speech groups argued that the law was too broad and would harm legitimate speech on the Internet. A new complication in defining pornography has emerged with cases of "sexting," in which minors produce and send sexually graphic images of themselves via cell phones or the Internet. (See "Case Study: Is 'Sexting' Pornography?" on page 558.)

The Right to Privacy

Whereas libel laws safeguard a person's character and reputation, the right to privacy protects an individual's peace of mind and personal feelings. In the simplest terms, the **right to privacy** addresses a person's right to be left alone, without his or her name, image, or daily activities becoming public property. Invasions of privacy occur in different situations, the most common of which are intrusion into someone's personal space via unauthorized tape recording, photographing, wiretapping, and the like; making available to the public personal records such as health and phone records; disclosing personal information such as religion, sexual activities, or personal activities; and the unauthorized appropriation of someone's image

PAPARAZZI
Prince William and Catherine, Duchess of Cambridge, have been an object of ongoing fascination since marrying in 2011. The media frenzy surrounding the royal couple came to a head when the French tabloid *Closer* published images of what appears to be the Duchess sunbathing topless while on vacation, prompting the royal family to press criminal charges against the publication. The British royal family is sadly all too familiar with the paparazzi, with Prince William's mother, Diana, Princess of Wales, dying in a car accident after being chased by paparazzi in 1997.

CASE STUDY

Is "Sexting" Pornography?

According to U.S. federal and state laws, when someone produces, transmits, or possesses images with graphic sexual depictions of minors, it is considered child pornography. Digital media have made the circulation of child pornography even more pervasive, according to a 2006 study on child pornography on the Internet. About one thousand people are arrested each year in the United States for child pornography, and they have few distinguishing characteristics other than being "likely to be white, male, and between the ages of 26 and 40."[1]

Now a new social practice has challenged the common wisdom of what is obscenity and who are child pornographers: What happens when the people who produce, transmit, and possess images with graphic sexual depictions of minors are minors themselves?

The practice in question is "sexting," the sending or receiving of sexual images via mobile phone text messages or via the Internet. Sexting occupies a gray area of obscenity law—yes, these are images of minors; but no, they don't fit the intent of child pornography laws, which are designed to stop the exploitation of children by adults.

While such messages are usually meant to be completely personal, technology makes it otherwise. "All control over the image is lost—it can be forwarded repeatedly all over the school, town, state, country and world," says Steven M. Dettelbach, U.S. attorney for the Northern District of Ohio.[2] And given the endless archives of the Internet, such images never really go away but can be accessed by anyone with enough skills to find them.

A recent national survey found that 15 percent of teens ages twelve to seventeen say they have received sexually suggestive nude or nearly nude images of someone they know via text messaging. Another 4 percent of teens ages twelve to seventeen say they have sent sexually suggestive nude or nearly nude images of themselves via text messaging. The rates are even higher for teens at age seventeen—8 percent have sent such images, and 30 percent have received them.[3]

Some recent cases illustrate how young people engaging in sexting have gotten caught up in a legal system designed to punish pedophiles. In 2008, as a high school senior, Florida resident Phillip Alpert, then eighteen, sent nude images of his sixteen-year-old girlfriend to friends after they got in an argument. He was convicted of child pornography and is required to be registered as a sex offender for the next twenty-five years. In Iowa, eighteen-year-old Jorge Canal Jr. was also convicted as a sex offender after sending a photo of his genitals to a fourteen-year-old girl—a friend who asked him to send the photo as a joke. Her parents found the photo and pressed charges. In 2009, three Pennsylvania girls took seminude pictures of themselves and sent the photos to three boys. All six minors were charged with child pornography. A judge later halted the charges in the interest of freedom of speech and parental rights. In all of these cases, and others like them, technology and social trends challenged the status quo beliefs on obscenity laws and the media. How can the courts adequately apply laws *written before the invention of the Internet* to such "digital crimes"? Although some state legislatures don't approve of sexting, they also don't think it should carry heavy penalties. Vermont, Nebraska, and Utah have already changed their laws to downgrade the punishment for sexting. Other states, including Connecticut, Florida, New York, and Ohio, are also considering adjustments to their child pornography laws so that teens with poor judgment aren't treated like pedophiles. How do *you* think sexting should be handled with current child pornography and obscenity laws? ◢

▲

"What's more disturbing—that teens are texting each other naked pictures of themselves, or that it could get them branded as sex offenders for life?"

— Tracy Clark-Flory, Salon.com, 2009

or name for advertising or other commercial purposes. In general, the news media have been granted wide protections under the First Amendment to do their work. For instance, the names and pictures of both private individuals and public figures can usually be used without their consent in most news stories. Additionally, if private citizens become part of public controversies and subsequent news stories, the courts have usually allowed the news media to treat them like public figures (i.e., record their quotes and use their images without the individuals' permission). The courts have even ruled that accurate reports of criminal and court records, including the identification of rape victims, do not normally constitute privacy invasions. Nevertheless, most newspapers and broadcast outlets use their own internal guidelines and ethical codes to protect the privacy of victims and defendants, especially in cases involving rape and child abuse.

Public figures have received some legal relief as many local municipalities and states have passed "anti-paparazzi" laws that protect individuals from unwarranted scrutiny and surveillance of personal activities on private property or outside public forums. Some courts have ruled that photographers must keep a certain distance away from celebrities, although powerful zoom lens technology usually overcomes this obstacle. However, every year brings a few stories of a Hollywood actor or sports figure punching a tabloid photographer or TV cameraman who got too close. And in 2004, the Supreme Court ruled—as an exception to the Freedom of Information Act—that families of prominent figures who have died have the right to object to the release of autopsy photos, so that the images may not be exploited.

A number of laws also protect the privacy of regular citizens. For example, the Privacy Act of 1974 protects individuals' records from public disclosure unless individuals give written consent. The Electronic Communications Privacy Act of 1986 extended the law to computer-stored data and the Internet, although subsequent court decisions ruled that employees have no privacy rights in electronic communications conducted on their employer's equipment. The USA PATRIOT Act of 2001, however, weakened the earlier laws and gave the federal government more latitude in searching private citizens' records and intercepting electronic communications without a court order.

First Amendment vs. Sixth Amendment

Over the years, First Amendment protections of speech and the press have often clashed with the Sixth Amendment, which guarantees an accused individual in "all criminal prosecutions . . . the right to a speedy and public trial, by an impartial jury." In 1954, for example, the Sam Sheppard case garnered enormous nationwide publicity and became the inspiration for the TV show and film *The Fugitive*. Featuring lurid details about the murder of Sheppard's wife, the press editorialized in favor of Sheppard's quick arrest; some papers even pronounced him guilty. A prominent and wealthy osteopath, Sheppard was convicted of the murder, but twelve years later Sheppard's new lawyer, F. Lee Bailey, argued before the Supreme Court that his client had not received a fair trial because of prejudicial publicity in the press. The Court overturned the conviction and freed Sheppard.

Gag Orders and Shield Laws

A major criticism of recent criminal cases concerns the ways in which lawyers use the news media to comment publicly on cases that are pending or are in trial. After the Sheppard reversal in the 1960s, the Supreme Court introduced safeguards that judges could employ to ensure fair trials in heavily publicized cases. These included sequestering juries (Sheppard's jury was not sequestered), moving cases to other jurisdictions, limiting the number of reporters, and placing restrictions, or **gag orders**, on lawyers and witnesses. In some countries, courts have issued

"[Jailed *New York Times* reporter Judith Miller] does not believe, nor do we, that reporters are above the law, but instead holds that the work of journalists must be independent and free from government control if they are to effectively serve as government watchdogs."

REPORTERS COMMITTEE FOR FREEDOM OF THE PRESS, 2005

gag orders to prohibit the press from releasing information or giving commentary that might prejudice jury selection or cause an unfair trial. In the United States, however, especially since a Supreme Court review in 1976, gag orders have been struck down as a prior-restraint violation of the First Amendment.

In opposition to gag rules, **shield laws** have favored the First Amendment rights of reporters, protecting them from having to reveal their sources for controversial information used in news stories. The news media have argued that protecting the confidentiality of key sources maintains a reporter's credibility, protects a source from possible retaliation, and serves the public interest by providing information that citizens might not otherwise receive. In the 1960s, when the First Amendment rights of reporters clashed with Sixth Amendment fair-trial concerns, judges usually favored the Sixth Amendment arguments. In 1972, a New Jersey journalist became the first reporter jailed for contempt of court for refusing to identify sources in a probe of the Newark housing authority. After this case, a number of legal measures emerged to protect the news media. Thirty-five states and the District of Columbia now have some type of shield law, and several other states have some shield law protection through legal precedent. There is no federal shield law in the United States, though, leaving journalists exposed to subpoenas from federal prosecutors and courts.

Cameras in the Courtroom

The debates over limiting intrusive electronic broadcast equipment and photographers in the courtroom actually date to the sensationalized coverage of the Bruno Hauptmann trial in the mid-1930s. Hauptmann was convicted and executed for the kidnap-murder of the nineteen-month-old son of Anne and Charles Lindbergh (the aviation hero who made the first solo flight across the Atlantic Ocean in 1927). During the trial, Hauptmann and his attorney complained that the circus atmosphere fueled by the presence of radio and flash cameras prejudiced the jury and turned the public against him.

After the trial, the American Bar Association amended its professional ethics code, Canon 35, stating that electronic equipment in the courtroom detracted "from the essential dignity of the proceedings." Calling for a ban on photographers and radio equipment, the association believed that if such elements were not banned, lawyers would begin playing to audiences and negatively alter the judicial process. For years after the Hauptmann trial, almost every state banned photographic, radio, and TV equipment from courtrooms.

As broadcast equipment became more portable and less obtrusive, however, and as television became the major news source for most Americans, courts gradually reevaluated their bans on broadcast equipment. In fact, in the early 1980s the Supreme Court ruled that the presence of TV equipment did not make it impossible for a fair trial to occur, leaving it up to each state to implement its own system. The ruling opened the door for the debut of Court TV (now truTV) in 1991 and the televised O.J. Simpson trial of 1994 (the most publicized case in history). All states today allow television coverage of cases, although most states place certain restrictions on coverage of courtrooms, often leaving it up to the discretion of the presiding judge. While U.S. federal courts now allow limited TV coverage of their trials, the Supreme Court continues to ban TV from its proceedings, but in 2000 the Court broke its anti-radio rule by permitting delayed radio broadcasts of the hearings on the Florida vote recount case that determined the winner of the 2000 presidential election.

As libel law and the growing acceptance of courtroom cameras indicate, the legal process has generally, though not always, tried to ensure that print and other news media are able to cover public issues broadly without fear of reprisals.

MEDIA IN THE COURTROOM
Photographers surround aviator Charles A. Lindbergh (without hat) as he leaves the courthouse in Flemington, N.J., during the trial in 1935 of Bruno Hauptmann on charges of kidnapping and murdering Lindbergh's infant son.

◀

Film and the First Amendment

When the First Amendment was ratified in 1791, even the most enlightened leaders of our nation could not have predicted the coming of visual media such as film and television. Consequently, new communication technologies have not always received the same kinds of protection under the First Amendment as those granted to speech or print media like newspapers, magazines, and books. Movies, in existence since the late 1890s, only earned legal speech protection after a 1952 Supreme Court decision. Prior to that, social and political pressures led to both censorship and self-censorship in the movie industry.

CENSORSHIP
A native of Galveston, Texas, Jack Johnson (1878–1946) was the first black heavyweight boxing champion, from 1908 to 1914. His stunning victory over white champion Jim Jeffries (who had earlier refused to fight black boxers) in 1910 resulted in race riots across the country and led to a ban on the interstate transportation of boxing films. A 2005 Ken Burns documentary, *Unforgivable Blackness*, chronicles Johnson's life.

Social and Political Pressures on the Movies

During the early part of the twentieth century, movies rose in popularity among European immigrants and others from modest socio-economic groups. This, in turn, spurred the formation of censorship groups, which believed that the movies would undermine morality. During this time, according to media historian Douglas Gomery, criticism of movies converged on four areas: "the effects on children, the potential health problems, the negative influences on morals and manners, and the lack of a proper role for educational and religious institutions in the development of movies."[16]

Public pressure on movies came both from conservatives, who saw them as a potential threat to the authority of traditional institutions, and from progressives, who worried that children and adults were more attracted to movie houses than to social organizations and urban education centers. As a result, civic leaders publicly escalated their pressure, organizing local *review boards* that screened movies for their communities. In 1907, the Chicago City Council created an ordinance that gave the police authority to issue permits for the exhibition of movies. By 1920, more than ninety cities in the United States had some type of movie censorship board made up of vice squad officers, politicians, or citizens. By 1923, twenty-two states had established such boards.

Meanwhile, social pressure began to translate into law as politicians, wanting to please their constituencies, began to legislate against films. Support mounted for a federal censorship bill. When Jack Johnson won the heavyweight championship in 1908, boxing films became the target of the first federal censorship law aimed at the motion-picture industry. In 1912, the government outlawed the transportation of boxing movies across state lines. The laws against boxing films, however, had more to do with Johnson's race than with concern over violence in movies. The first black heavyweight champion, he was perceived as a threat to some in the white community.

The first Supreme Court decision regarding film's protection under the First Amendment was handed down in 1915 and went against the movie industry. In *Mutual v. Ohio*, the Mutual Film Company of Detroit sued the state of Ohio, whose review board had censored a number of the distributor's films. On appeal, the case arrived at the Supreme Court, which unanimously ruled that motion pictures were not a form of speech but "a business pure and simple" and, like a circus, merely a "spectacle" for entertainment with "a special capacity for evil." This ruling would stand as a precedent for thirty-seven years, although a movement to create a national censorship board failed.

Self-Regulation in the Movie Industry

As the film industry expanded after World War I, the impact of public pressure and review boards began to affect movie studios and executives who wanted to ensure control over their economic well-being. In the early 1920s, a series of scandals rocked Hollywood: actress Mary

Pickford's divorce and quick marriage to actor Douglas Fairbanks; director William Desmond Taylor's unsolved murder; and actor Wallace Reid's death from a drug overdose. But the most sensational scandal involved aspiring actress Virginia Rappe, who died a few days after a wild party in a San Francisco hotel hosted by popular silent-film comedian Fatty Arbuckle. After Rappe's death, the comedian was indicted for rape and manslaughter, in a case that was sensationalized in the press. Although two hung juries could not reach a verdict, Arbuckle's career was ruined. Censorship boards across the country banned his films. Even though he was acquitted at his third trial in 1922, the movie industry tried to send a signal about the kinds of values and lifestyles it would tolerate: Arbuckle was banned from acting in Hollywood. He later resurfaced to direct several films under the name Will B. Goode.

In response to the scandals, particularly the first Arbuckle trial, the movie industry formed the Motion Picture Producers and Distributors of America (MPPDA) and hired as its president Will Hays, a former Republican National Committee chair. Also known as the Hays Office, the MPPDA attempted to smooth out problems between the public and the industry. Hays black-listed promising actors or movie extras with even minor police records. He also developed an MPPDA public relations division, which stopped a national movement for a federal law censoring movies.

The Motion Picture Production Code

During the 1930s, the movie business faced a new round of challenges. First, various conservative and religious groups–including the influential Catholic Legion of Decency–increased their scrutiny of the industry. Second, deteriorating economic conditions during the Great Depression forced the industry to tighten self-regulation in order to maintain profits and keep harmful public pressure at bay. In 1927, the Hays Office had developed a list of "Don'ts and Be Carefuls" to steer producers and directors away from questionable sexual, moral, and social themes. Nevertheless, pressure for a more formal and sweeping code mounted. As a result, in the early 1930s the Hays Office established the Motion Picture Production Code, whose overseers were charged with officially stamping Hollywood films with a moral seal of approval.

The code laid out its mission in its first general principle: "No picture shall be produced which will lower the moral standards of those who see it. Hence the sympathy of the audience shall never be thrown to the side of crime, wrong-doing, evil or sin." The code dictated how producers and directors should handle "methods of crime," "repellent subjects," and "sex hygiene." A section on profanity outlawed a long list of phrases and topics, including "toilet gags" and "traveling salesmen and farmer's daughter jokes." Under "scenes of passion," the code dictated that "excessive and lustful kissing, lustful embraces, suggestive postures and gestures are not to be shown," and it required that "passion should be treated in such a manner as not to stimulate the lower and baser emotions." The section on religion revealed the influences of a Jesuit priest and a Catholic publisher, who helped write the code: "No film or episode may throw ridicule on any religious faith," and "ministers of religion . . . should not be used as comic characters or as villains."

Adopted by 95 percent of the industry, the code influenced nearly every commercial movie made between the mid-1930s and the early 1950s. It also gave the industry a relative degree of freedom, enabling the major studios to remain independent of outside regulation. When television arrived, however, competition from the new family medium forced movie producers to explore more adult subjects.

The *Miracle* Case

In 1952, the Supreme Court heard the *Miracle* case–officially *Burstyn v. Wilson*–named after Roberto Rossellini's film *Il Miracolo* (*The Miracle*). The movie's distributor sued the head of

"No approval by the Production Code Administration shall be given to the use of . . . *damn* [or] *hell* (excepting when the use of said last two words shall be essential and required for portrayal, in proper historical context, of any scene or dialogue based upon historical fact or folklore, or for the presentation in proper literary context of a Biblical, or other religious quotation, or a quotation from a literary work provided that no such use shall be permitted which is intrinsically objectionable or offends good taste)."

MOTION PICTURE PRODUCTION CODE, 1934

the New York Film Licensing Board for banning the film. A few New York City religious and political leaders considered the 1948 Italian film sacrilegious and pressured the film board for the ban. In the film, an unmarried peasant girl is impregnated by a scheming vagrant who tells her that he is St. Joseph and she has conceived the baby Jesus. The importers of the film argued that censoring it constituted illegal prior restraint under the First Amendment. Because such an action could not be imposed on a print version of the same story, the film's distributor argued that the same freedom should apply to the film. The Supreme Court agreed, declaring movies "a significant medium for the communication of ideas." The decision granted films the same constitutional protections as those enjoyed by the print media and other forms of speech. Even more important, the decision rendered most activities of film review boards unconstitutional, because these boards had been engaged in prior restraint. Although a few local boards survived into the 1990s to handle complaints about obscenity, most of them had disbanded by the early 1970s.

The MPAA Ratings System

"An NC-17 rating is seen as box-office suicide by the film industry.... In the 20 years since its inception, NC-17 has been unable to shed its smutty image."

RACHEL SCOTT, THE *GUARDIAN*, 2010

The current voluntary movie rating system—the model for the advisory labels for music, television, and video games—developed in the late 1960s after discontent again mounted over movie content, spurred on by such films as 1965's *The Pawnbroker*, which contained brief female nudity, and 1966's *Who's Afraid of Virginia Woolf?*, which featured a level of profanity and sexual frankness that had not been seen before in a major studio film. In 1966, the movie industry hired Jack Valenti to run the MPAA (the Motion Picture Association of America, formerly the MPPDA), and in 1968 he established an industry board to rate movies. Eventually, G, PG, R, and X ratings emerged as guideposts for the suitability of films for various age groups. In 1984, prompted by the releases of *Gremlins* and *Indiana Jones and the Temple of Doom*, the MPAA added the PG-13 rating and sandwiched it between PG and R to distinguish slightly higher levels of violence or adult themes in movies that might otherwise qualify as PG-rated films (see Table 16.1).

The MPAA copyrighted all ratings designations as trademarks, except for the X rating, which was gradually appropriated as a promotional tool by the pornographic film industry. In fact, between 1972 and 1989 the MPAA stopped issuing the X rating. In 1990, however, based on protests from filmmakers over movies with adult sexual themes that they did not consider pornographic, the industry copyrighted the NC-17 rating—no children age seventeen or under. In 1995, *Showgirls* became the first movie to intentionally seek an NC-17 to demonstrate that the rating was commercially viable. However, many theater chains refused to carry NC-17 movies, fearing economic sanctions and boycotts by their customers or religious groups. Many newspapers also refused to carry ads for NC-17 films. Panned by the critics, *Showgirls* flopped at the box office. Since then, the NC-17 rating has not proved commercially

TABLE 16.1

THE VOLUNTARY MOVIE RATING SYSTEM

Source: Motion Picture Association of America, "What Do the Ratings Mean?," http://www .mpaa.org/FlmRat_Ratings.asp, accessed May 1, 2009.

▶

Rating	Description
G	**General Audiences:** All ages admitted; contains nothing that would offend parents when viewed by their children.
PG	**Parental Guidance Suggested:** Parents urged to give "parental guidance" as it may contain some material not suitable for young children.
PG-13	**Parents Strongly Cautioned:** Parents should be cautious because some content may be inappropriate for children under the age of 13.
R	**Restricted:** The film contains some adult material. Parents/guardians are urged to learn more about it before taking children under the age of 17 with them.
NC-17	**No one 17 and under admitted:** Adult content. Children are not admitted.

viable, and distributors avoid releasing films with the rating, preferring to label such films "unrated" or to cut the film to earn an R rating, as happened with *Clerks* (1994), *Eyes Wide Shut* (1999), *Brüno* (2009), and *Blue Valentine* (2010). Today, there is mounting protest against the MPAA, which many argue is essentially a censorship board that limits the First Amendment rights of filmmakers.

Expression in the Media: Print, Broadcast, and Online

During the Cold War, a vigorous campaign led by Joseph McCarthy, an ultraconservative senator from Wisconsin, tried to rid both government and the media of so-called communist subversives who were allegedly challenging the American way of life. In 1950, a publication called *Red Channels: The Report of Communist Influence in Radio and Television* aimed "to show how the Communists have been able to carry out their plan of infiltration of the radio and television industry." *Red Channels*, inspired by McCarthy and produced by a group of former FBI agents, named 151 performers, writers, and musicians who were "sympathetic" to communist or left-wing causes. Among those named were Leonard Bernstein, Will Geer, Dashiell Hammett, Lillian Hellman, Lena Horne, Burgess Meredith, Arthur Miller, Dorothy Parker, Pete Seeger, Irwin Shaw, and Orson Welles. For a time, all were banned from working in television and radio even though no one on the list was ever charged with a crime.[17]

Although the First Amendment protects an individual's right to hold controversial political views, network executives either sympathized with the anticommunist movement or feared losing ad revenue. At any rate, the networks did not stand up to the communist witch-hunters. In order to work, a blacklisted or "suspected" performer required the support of the program's sponsor. Though *I Love Lucy*'s Lucille Ball, who in sympathy with her father once registered to vote as a communist in the 1930s, retained Philip Morris's sponsorship of her popular program, other performers were not as fortunate. Although no evidence was ever introduced to show how entertainment programs circulated communist propaganda, by the early 1950s the TV networks were asking actors and other workers to sign loyalty oaths denouncing communism—a low point for the First Amendment.

The communist witch-hunts demonstrated key differences between print and broadcast protection under the First Amendment. On the one hand, licenses

RED CHANNELS, a 215-page report published by American Business Consultants (a group of former FBI agents) in 1950, placed 151 prominent writers, directors, and performers from radio, movies, and television on a blacklist, many of them simply for sympathizing with left-wing democratic causes. Although no one on the list was ever charged with a crime, many of the talented individuals targeted by *Red Channels* did not work in their professions for years thereafter.

for printers and publishers have been outlawed since the eighteenth century. On the other hand, in the late 1920s commercial broadcasters themselves asked the federal government to step in and regulate the airwaves. At that time, they wanted the government to clear up technical problems, channel noise, noncommercial competition, and amateur interference. Ever since, most broadcasters have been trying to free themselves from the government intrusion they once demanded.

The FCC Regulates Broadcasting

> "It is the right of the viewers and listeners, not the right of the broadcasters, which is paramount."
>
> SUPREME COURT DECISION IN *RED LION BROADCASTING CO. V. FCC*, 395 U.S. 367, JUNE 9, 1969

Drawing on the argument that limited broadcast signals constitute a scarce national resource, the Communications Act of 1934 mandated that radio broadcasters operate in "the public interest, convenience, and necessity." Since the 1980s, however, with cable and, later, DBS increasing channel capacity, station managers have lobbied to own their airwave assignments. Although the 1996 Telecommunications Act did not grant such ownership, stations continue to challenge the "public interest" statute. They argue that because the government is not allowed to dictate content in newspapers, it should not be allowed to control broadcasting via licenses or mandate any broadcast programming.

Two cases—*Red Lion Broadcasting Co. v. FCC* (1969) and *Miami Herald Publishing Co. v. Tornillo* (1974)—demonstrate the historic legal differences between broadcast and print. The *Red Lion* case began when WGCB, a small-town radio station in Red Lion, Pennsylvania, refused to give airtime to Fred Cook, author of a book that criticized Barry Goldwater, the Republican Party's presidential candidate in 1964. A conservative radio preacher and Goldwater fan, the Reverend Billy James Hargis, verbally attacked Cook on-air. Cook asked for response time from the two hundred stations that carried the Hargis attack. Most stations complied, granting Cook free reply time. But WGCB offered only to sell Cook time. He appealed to the FCC, which ordered the station to give Cook free time. The station refused, claiming that its First Amendment rights granted it control over its program content. On appeal, the Supreme Court sided with the FCC, deciding that whenever a broadcaster's rights conflict with the public interest, the public interest must prevail. In interpreting broadcasting as different from print, the Supreme Court upheld the 1934 Communications Act by reaffirming that broadcasters' responsibilities to program in the public interest may outweigh their right to program whatever they want.

> "A responsible press is an undoubtedly desirable goal, but press responsibility is not mandated by the Constitution and like many other virtues it cannot be legislated."
>
> SUPREME COURT DECISION IN *MIAMI HERALD PUBLISHING CO. V. TORNILLO*, 418 U.S. 241, JUNE 25, 1974

In contrast, five years later, in *Miami Herald Publishing Co. v. Tornillo*, the Supreme Court sided with the newspaper. A political candidate, Pat Tornillo Jr., requested space to reply to an editorial opposing his candidacy. Previously, Florida had a right-to-reply law, which permitted a candidate to respond, in print, to editorial criticisms from newspapers. Counter to the *Red Lion* decision, the Court in this case struck down the Florida state law as unconstitutional. The Court argued that mandating that a newspaper give a candidate space to reply violated the paper's First Amendment rights to control what it chose to publish. The two decisions demonstrate that the unlicensed print media receive protections under the First Amendment that have not always been available to licensed broadcast media.

Dirty Words, Indecent Speech, and Hefty Fines

In theory, communication law prevents the government from censoring broadcast content. Accordingly, the government may not interfere with programs or engage in prior restraint, although it may punish broadcasters for **indecency** or profanity after the fact. Over the years, a handful of radio stations have had their licenses suspended or denied after an unfavorable FCC review of past programming records. Concerns over indecent broadcast programming began in 1937 when NBC was scolded by the FCC for running a sketch featuring comic actress Mae West

INDECENT SPEECH
The sexual innuendo of an "Adam and Eve" radio sketch between sultry film star Mae West and dummy Charlie McCarthy (voiced by ventriloquist Edgar Bergen) on a Sunday evening in December 1937 enraged many listeners of Bergen's program. The networks banned West from further radio appearances for what was considered indecent speech.

on ventriloquist Edgar Bergen's network program. West had the following conversation with Bergen's famous wooden dummy, Charlie McCarthy:

WEST: *That's all right. I like a man that takes his time. Why don't you come home with me? I'll let you play in my woodpile . . . you're all wood and a yard long. . . .*
CHARLIE: *Oh, Mae, don't, don't . . . don't be so rough. To me love is peace and quiet.*
WEST: *That ain't love—that's sleep.*[18]

After the sketch, West did not perform on radio for years. Ever since, the FCC has periodically fined or reprimanded stations for indecent programming, especially during times when children might be listening.

AMERICAN DAD! has topped the Parents Television Council's "Worst TV Show of the Week" list numerous times since premiering in 2005. The PTC, which collects indecency complaints via its Web site and directs them to the Federal Communications Commission (FCC), evaluates shows based on occurrences of gratuitous sex, explicit dialogue, violent content, or obscene language. From *Family Guy* creator Seth MacFarlane, *American Dad!* continues to make the PTC's list in its eighth season on air.

In the 1960s, *topless radio* featured deejays and callers discussing intimate sexual subjects in the middle of the afternoon. The government curbed the practice in 1973, when the chairman of the FCC denounced topless radio as "a new breed of air pollution . . . with the suggestive, coaxing, pear-shaped tones of the smut-hustling host."[19] After an FCC investigation, a couple of stations lost their licenses, some were fined, and topless radio was temporarily over. It reemerged in the 1980s, this time with doctors and therapists—instead of deejays—offering intimate counsel over the airwaves.

The current precedent for regulating broadcast indecency stems from a complaint to the FCC in 1973. In the middle of the afternoon, WBAI, a nonprofit Pacifica network station in New York, aired George Carlin's famous comedy sketch about the seven dirty words that could not be uttered by broadcasters. A father, riding in a car with his fifteen-year-old son, heard the program and complained to the FCC, which sent WBAI a letter of reprimand. Although no fine was issued, the station appealed on principle and won its case in court. The FCC, however, appealed to the Supreme Court. Although no court had legally defined indecency (and still hasn't), the Supreme Court's unexpected ruling in the 1978 *FCC v. Pacifica Foundation* case sided with the FCC and upheld the agency's authority to require broadcasters to air adult programming at times when children are not likely to be listening. The Court ruled that so-called indecent programming, though not in violation of federal obscenity laws, was a nuisance and could be restricted to late-evening hours. As a result, the FCC banned indecent programs from most stations between 6:00 A.M. and 10:00 P.M. In 1990, the FCC tried to ban such programs entirely. Although a federal court ruled this move unconstitutional, it still upheld the time restrictions intended to protect children.

This ruling provides the rationale for the indecency fines that the FCC has frequently leveled against programs and stations that have carried indecent programming during daytime and evening hours. While Howard Stern and his various bosses held the early record for racking up millions in FCC indecency fines in the 1990s—before Stern moved to unregulated satellite radio—the largest-ever fine was for $3.6 million, leveled in 2006 against 111 TV stations that broadcast a 2004 episode of the popular CBS program *Without a Trace* that depicted teenage characters taking part in a sexual orgy.

After the FCC later fined broadcasters for several instances of "fleeting expletives" during live TV shows, the four major networks sued the FCC on grounds that their First Amendment rights had been violated. In its fining flurry, the FCC was partly responding to organized campaigns aimed at Howard Stern's vulgarity and at the Janet Jackson exposed-breast incident during the 2004 Super Bowl half-time show. In 2006, Congress substantially increased the FCC's maximum allowable fine to $325,000 per incident of indecency—meaning that one fleeting expletive in a live entertainment, news, or sports program could cost millions of dollars in fines, as it is repeated on affiliate stations across the country. But in 2010, a federal appeals court rejected the FCC's policy against fleeting expletives, arguing that it was constitutionally vague and had a chilling effect on free speech "because broadcasters have no way of knowing what the FCC will find offensive."[20]

Political Broadcasts and Equal Opportunity

In addition to indecency rules, another law that the print media do not encounter is **Section 315** of the 1934 Communications Act, which mandates that, during elections, broadcast stations must provide equal opportunities and response time for qualified political candidates. In other words, if broadcasters give or sell time to one candidate, they must give or sell the same opportunity to others. Local broadcasters and networks have fought this law for years, complaining that it has required them to give marginal third-party candidates with little hope for success equal airtime in political discussions. Broadcasters claim that because no similar rule applies to newspapers or magazines, the law violates their First Amendment right to control content. In fact, because of this rule, many stations avoid all political programming, ironically reversing the rule's original intention. The TV networks managed to get the law amended in 1959 to exempt newscasts, press conferences, and other events—such as political debates—that qualify as news. For instance, if a senator running for office appears in a news story, opposing candidates cannot invoke Section 315 and demand free time. The FCC has subsequently ruled that interview portions of programs like the *700 Club* and *TMZ* also count as news.

Due to Section 315, many stations from the late 1960s through the 1980s refused to air movies starring Ronald Reagan. Because his film appearances did not count as bona fide news stories, politicians opposing Reagan as a presidential candidate could demand free time in markets that ran old Reagan movies. For the same reason, in 2003, TV stations in California banned the broadcast of Arnold Schwarzenegger movies when he became a candidate for governor, and dozens of stations nationwide preempted an episode of *Saturday Night Live* that was hosted by Al Sharpton, a Democratic presidential candidate.

However, supporters of the equal opportunity law argue that it has provided forums for lesser-known candidates representing views counter to those of the Democratic and Republican parties. They further note that one of the few ways for alternative candidates to circulate their messages widely is to buy political ads, thus limiting serious outside contenders to wealthy candidates, such as Ross Perot, Steve Forbes, or members of the Bush or Clinton families.

The Demise of the Fairness Doctrine

Considered an important corollary to Section 315, the **Fairness Doctrine** was to controversial issues what Section 315 is to political speech. Initiated in 1949, this FCC rule required stations (1) to air and engage in controversial-issue programs that affected their communities, and (2) to provide competing points of view when offering such programming. Antismoking activist John Banzhaf ingeniously invoked the Fairness Doctrine to force cigarette advertising off television in 1971. When the FCC mandated antismoking public service announcements to counter "controversial" smoking commercials, tobacco companies decided not to challenge an outright ban rather than tolerate a flood of antismoking spots authorized by the Fairness Doctrine.

Over the years, broadcasters argued that mandating opposing views every time a program covered a controversial issue was a burden not required of the print media, and that it forced many of them to refrain from airing controversial issues. As a result, the Fairness Doctrine ended with little public debate in 1987 after a federal court ruled that it was merely a regulation rather than an extension of Section 315 law.

Since 1987, however, periodic support for reviving the Fairness Doctrine has surfaced. Its supporters argue that broadcasting is fundamentally different from—and more pervasive than—print media, requiring greater accountability to the public. Although many broadcasters disagree, supporters of fairness rules insist that as long as broadcasters are licensed as

"There is no doubt about the unique impact of radio and television. But this fact alone does not justify government regulation. In fact, quite the contrary. We should recall that the printed press was the only medium of mass communication in the early days of the republic— and yet this did not deter our predecessors from passing the First Amendment to prohibit abridgement of its freedoms."

CHIEF JUDGE DAVID BAZELON, U.S. COURT OF APPEALS, 1972

VideoCentral ◎
Mass Communication
bedfordstmartins.com
/mediaculture

Bloggers and Legal Rights
Legal and journalism scholars discuss the legal rights and responsibilities of bloggers.
Discussion: What are some of the advantages and disadvantages of the audience turning to blogs, rather than traditional sources, for news?

public trustees of the airwaves–unlike newspaper or magazine publishers–legal precedent permits the courts and the FCC to demand responsible content and behavior from radio and TV stations.

Communication Policy and the Internet

Many have looked to the Internet as the one true venue for unlimited free speech under the First Amendment because it is not regulated by the government, it is not subject to the Communications Act of 1934, and little has been done in regard to self-regulation. Its current global expansion is comparable to that of the early days of broadcasting, when economic and technological growth outstripped law and regulation. At that time, noncommercial experiments by amateurs and engineering students provided a testing ground that commercial interests later exploited for profit. In much the same way, amateurs, students, and various interest groups have explored and extended the communication possibilities of the Internet. They have experimented so successfully that commercial vendors have raced to buy up pieces of the Internet since the 1990s.

Public conversations about the Internet have not typically revolved around ownership. Instead, the debates have focused on First Amendment issues such as civility and pornography. Not unlike the public's concern over television's sexual and violent images, the scrutiny of the Internet is mainly about harmful images and information online, not about who controls it and for what purposes. However, as we watch the rapid expansion of the Internet, an important question confronts us: Will the Internet continue to develop as a democratic medium? By 2011, the answer to that question was still unclear. In late 2010, the FCC created net neutrality rules for wired (cable and DSL) broadband providers, requiring that they provide the same access to all Internet services and content. Yet, these new rules exempted wireless (mobile phone) broadband providers, enabling them to block Web services as they wish. Early in 2011, the U.S. House of Representatives moved to overturn the FCC net neutrality regulations. But in November 2011, the U.S. Senate voted to keep in place federal net neutrality rules and to preserve open Internet access. Nonetheless, the battle continues, and its eventual outcome will determine whether the broadband Internet connections will be defined as an *essential utility* to which everyone has access and for which rates are controlled (like water or electricity), or an *information service* for which Internet service providers can charge as much as they wish (as with cable TV).

Critics and observers hope that a vigorous debate about ownership will develop–a debate that will go beyond First Amendment issues. The promise of the Internet as a democratic forum encourages the formation of all sorts of regional, national, and global interest groups. In fact, many global movements use the Internet to fight political forms of censorship. Human Rights Watch, for example, encourages free-expression advocates to use blogs "for disseminating information about, and ending, human rights abuses around the world."[21] Where oppressive regimes have tried to monitor and control Internet communication, Human Rights Watch suggests bloggers post anonymously to safeguard their identity. Just as fax machines, satellites, and home videos helped expedite and document the fall of totalitarian regimes in Eastern Europe in the late 1980s, the Internet helps spread the word and activate social change today.

> "The FCC's only goal here is to make sure that the Internet we know and love does not become corrupted and altered by a small number of large corporations controlling the last free and open distribution channel we have in this country."
>
> U.S. SEN. AL FRANKEN (D-MN), 2011

HOW the F.C.C. LOGS IN to the INTERNET...

NET NEUTRALITY

A Generation of Copyright Criminals?

As a student reading this book, you have probably already composed plenty of research papers, and quoted, with attribution, from various printed sources. This is a routine practice, and you are within the legal bounds of *fair use* of the sources you sampled. The concept of fair use has existed in U.S. case law for more than 150 years.

But, what if you are composing a song, or creating a video, and you decide to sample bits of music or a clip of film? Under current law, you have little protection and may be subject to a lawsuit from the recording or motion picture industry alleging copyright infringement.

DJ GIRL TALK mixes his beats with samples from other artists to create new music.

As inexpensive digital technology became available, artists began sampling sounds and images, much like scholars and writers might sample texts. In the late 1980s, University of Iowa communication studies professor Kembrew McLeod explains, sampling "was a creative window that had been forced open by hip-hop artists," but "by the early 1990s, the free experimentation was over. . . . [E]veryone had to pay for the sounds that they sampled or risk getting sued."[1] The cost for most acts was far too prohibitive. Fees to use snippets of copyrighted sounds in the Beastie Boys' 1989 sample-rich *Paul's Boutique* recording cost $250,000.[2] Today, a recording based on creative mash-ups of samples probably couldn't even be made, as some copyright owners demand up to $50,000 for sampling just a few seconds of their song.

Nevertheless, some artists are still trying. Pittsburgh-based mash-up DJ Girl Talk (Gregg Gillis) has no problem performing his sample-heavy music, where he remixes a dozen or more samples on his laptop with some of his own beats to create a new song. Copyright royalties are covered for his live public performances, since many venues already have public performance agreements with copyright management agencies BMI, ASCAP, and SESAC. (These are the same agencies that collect fees from restaurants and radio stations for publicly performed music.) But—and this is one of the many inconsistencies in copyright law—if Gillis wants to make a recording of his music, the cost of the copyright royalty payments (should they even be granted by the copyright holder) would exceed the revenue generated by the CD. If he doesn't get copyright permission for the samples used, he risks hundreds of thousands of dollars in penalties.

Despite the threat of lawsuits, Gillis and an independent label—appropriately named Illegal Art—released the acclaimed *Night Ripper* album in 2006 and *Feed the Animals* (which uses 322 samples) in 2008. In defending the recording against potential lawsuits, Gillis and his label argue that they are protected from copyright infringement by the fair use exemption, which allows for *transformative use*—creating new work from bits of copyrighted work.[3]

The uneven and unclear rules for the use of sound, images, video, and text have become one of the most contentious issues of today's digital culture. As digital media make it easier than ever to create and re-create cultural content, copyright law has yet to catch up with these new forms of expression.

"There's no way to kill this technology. You can only criminalize its use," Harvard Law professor and Internet activist Lawrence Lessig notes. "If this is a crime, we have a whole generation of criminals."[4]

The First Amendment and Democracy

For most of our nation's history, citizens have counted on journalism to monitor abuses in government and business. During the muckraking period, writers like Upton Sinclair, Ida Tarbell, and Sinclair Lewis made strong contributions in reporting corporate expansion and social change. Unfortunately, however, news stories about business issues today are usually reduced to consumer affairs reporting. In other words, when a labor strike or a factory recall is covered, the reporter mainly tries to answer the question "How do these events affect consumers?" Although this is an important news angle, discussions about media ownership or labor management ethics are not part of the news that journalists typically report. Similarly, when companies announce mergers, reporters do not routinely question the economic wisdom or social impact of such changes but instead focus on how consumers will be affected.

At one level, journalists have been compromised by the ongoing frenzy of media mergers involving newspapers, TV stations, radio stations, and Internet corporations. As Bill Kovach, former curator of Harvard's Nieman Foundation for Journalism, pointed out, "This rush to merge mainly entertainment organizations that have news operations with companies deeply involved in doing business with the government raises ominous questions about the future of watchdog journalism."[22] In other words, how can journalists adequately cover and lead discussions on issues of media ownership? The very companies they work for are the prime buyers and sellers of major news-media outlets.

As a result, it is becoming increasingly important that the civic role of watchdog be shared by both citizens and journalists. Citizen action groups like Free Press, the Media Access Project, and the Center for Digital Democracy have worked to bring media ownership issues into the

> "One thing is clear: media reform will not be realized until politicians add it to their list of issues like the environment, education, the economy, and health care."
>
> ROBERT McCHESNEY, FREEPRESS.NET, 2004

SOPA ACT
On January 18, 2012, Wikipedia participated in a protest against the Stop Online Piracy Act (SOPA) by blacking out its landing page for an entire twenty-four hours and posting the message "Imagine a World Without Free Knowledge." SOPA, proposed by the U.S. House of Representatives in 2011 to expand the government's ability to protect copyrighted intellectual property online, threatens services like Wikipedia that rely on a free and open Internet.

mainstream. However, it is important to remember that the First Amendment protects not only the news media's free-speech rights but also the rights of all of us to speak out. Mounting concerns over who can afford access to the media go to the heart of free expression. As we struggle to determine the future of converging print, electronic, and digital media and to strengthen the democratic spirit underlying media technology, we need to stay engaged in spirited public debates about media ownership and control, about the differences between commercial speech and free expression. As citizens, we need to pay attention to who is included and excluded from opportunities not only to buy products but also to speak out and shape the cultural landscape. To accomplish this, we need to challenge our journalists and our leaders. More important, we need to challenge ourselves to become watchdogs–critical consumers and engaged citizens– who learn from the past, care about the present, and map mass media's future. ▶

CHAPTER REVIEW

COMMON THREADS

One of the Common Threads discussed in Chapter 1 is about the role that media play in a democracy. Is a free media system necessary for democracy to exist, or must democracy first be established to enable a media system to operate freely? What do the mass media do to enhance or secure democracy?

In 1787, as the Constitution was being formed, Thomas Jefferson famously said, "were it left to me to decide whether we should have a government without newspapers, or newspapers without a government, I should not hesitate a moment to prefer the latter." Jefferson supported the notion of a free press and free speech. He stood against the Sedition Act, which penalized free speech, and did not support its renewal when he became president in 1801.

Nevertheless, as president, Jefferson had to withstand the vitriol and allegations of a partisan press. In 1807, near the end of his second term, Jefferson's idealism about the press had cooled, as he remarked, "The man who never looks into a newspaper is better informed than he who reads them, inasmuch as he who knows nothing is nearer the truth than he whose mind is filled with falsehoods and errors."

Today, we contend with mass media that extend far beyond newspapers—a media system that is among the biggest and most powerful institutions in the country. Unfortunately, it is also a media system that too often envisions us as consumers of capitalism, not citizens of a democracy. Media sociologist Herbert Gans argues that the media alone can't guarantee a democracy.[23] "Despite much disingenuous talk about citizen empowerment by politicians and merchandisers, citizens have never had much clout. Countries as big as America operate largely through organizations," Gans explains.

But in a country as big as America, the media constitute one of those critical organizations that can help or hurt us in creating a more economically and politically democratic society. At their worst, the media can distract or misinform us with falsehoods and errors. But at their Jeffersonian best, the media can shed light on the issues, tell meaningful stories, and foster the discussions that can help a citizens' democracy flourish.

KEY TERMS

The definitions for the terms listed below can be found in the glossary at the end of the book. The page numbers listed with the terms indicate where the term is highlighted in the chapter.

authoritarian model, 548
communist or state model, 548
social responsibility model, 548
Fourth Estate, 548
libertarian model, 549
prior restraint, 550
copyright, 553

public domain, 553
libel, 554
slander, 554
actual malice, 555
qualified privilege, 555
opinion and fair comment, 555
obscenity, 556

right to privacy, 557
gag orders, 559
shield laws, 560
indecency, 566
Section 315, 569
Fairness Doctrine, 569

REVIEW QUESTIONS

The Origins of Free Expression and a Free Press

1. Explain the various models of the news media that exist under different political systems.

2. What is the basic philosophical concept that underlies America's notion of free expression?

3. What happened with the passage of the Sedition Act of 1798, and what was its relevance to the United States' new First Amendment?

4. How has censorship been defined historically?

5. What is the public domain, and why is it an important element in American culture?

6. Why is the case of *New York Times v. Sullivan* so significant in First Amendment history?

7. What does a public figure have to do to win a libel case? What are the main defenses that a newspaper can use to thwart a charge of libel?

8. What is the legal significance of the *Falwell v. Flynt* case?

9. How has the Internet changed battles over what constitutes obscenity?

10. What issues are at stake when First Amendment and Sixth Amendment concerns clash?

Film and the First Amendment

11. Why were films not constitutionally protected as a form of speech until 1952?

12. Why did film review boards develop, and why did they eventually disband?

13. How did both the Motion Picture Production Code and the current movie rating system come into being?

Expression in the Media: Print, Broadcast, and Online

14. The government and the courts view print and broadcasting as different forms of expression. What are the major differences?

15. What's the difference between obscenity and indecency?

16. What is the significance of Section 315 of the Communications Act of 1934?

17. Why didn't broadcasters like the Fairness Doctrine?

The First Amendment and Democracy

18. What are the similarities and differences between the debates over broadcast ownership in the 1920s and Internet ownership today?

19. Why is the future of watchdog journalism in jeopardy?

QUESTIONING THE MEDIA

1. Have you ever had an experience in which you thought personal or public expression went too far and should be curbed? Explain. How might you remedy this situation?

2. If you owned a community newspaper and had to formulate a policy for your editors about which letters from readers could appear in a limited space on your editorial page, what kinds of letters would you eliminate and why? Would you be acting as a censor in this situation? Why or why not?

3. The writer A. J. Liebling once said that freedom of the press belonged only to those who owned one. Explain why you agree or disagree.

4. Should the United States have a federal shield law to protect reporters?

5. What do you think of the current movie rating system? Should it be changed? Why or why not?

6. Should the Fairness Doctrine be revived? Why or why not?

7. Should corporations, unions, and rich individuals be able to contribute any amount of money they want to support particular candidates and pay for TV ads? Why or why not?

ADDITIONAL VIDEOS

Visit the ▣ VideoCentral: Mass Communication **section at bedfordstmartins.com/mediaculture for additional exclusive videos related to Chapter 16, including:**

- THE FIRST AMENDMENT AND STUDENT SPEECH
  Legal and newspaper professionals explain how student newspapers are protected by the First Amendment.

- FREEDOM OF INFORMATION
  Ken Bunting, executive director of the National Freedom of Information Coalition, explains the importance of government transparency and accountability, particularly in an age of digital communication.

- Facebook users upload 300 million images each day.[2]
- Twitter users send 340 million tweets each day.[3]
- More than 6 billion text messages are sent each day (more than 2 trillion per year).[4]
- 144.8 billion e-mails are sent every day.[5]
- 72 hours of video are uploaded to YouTube every minute.[6]

Yet we probably don't know what exactly we *did agree to* when we signed up for Facebook, Twitter, e-mail service, mobile phone service, or a Google, Amazon, Apple, or LinkedIn account. Is there an invasion of privacy that we did not consent to (or at least did not knowingly consent to)? What happens when corporations have our data?

Since 1995, the U.S. Federal Trade Commission (FTC) has studied privacy on the Web, and developed rules and guidelines for fair information practices online. The FTC has called on businesses to make "privacy the 'default setting' for commercial data practices and giving consumers greater control over the collection and use of their personal data through simplified choices and increased transparency." The FTC argues that fair practices on consumer privacy will "enhance trust and stimulate commerce."[7]

Even so, progress on industry self-regulation toward that goal has been slow, as the temptation to use consumer data for more immediate commercial purposes is high. West Virginia Senator John D. Rockefeller IV noted, "In my experience, corporations are unlikely to regulate themselves out of profits."[8] In fact, although the FTC has long called for Web sites to make no data collection the default setting unless customers "opt in," most sites make automatic data collection the default, and consumers must navigate through menus to find out how to opt out.

A number of recent cases have called other privacy matters to the foreground. For example, the FTC obtained court orders against Google, Facebook, Twitter, and MySpace to require the companies to obtain their customers' consent before changing their data privacy practices and to adopt stronger privacy standards. Auditors will monitor compliance at each company for twenty years.[9]

Since that agreement with the FTC, Facebook has also agreed with the California Attorney General's office that all apps in the Facebook App Center would include written privacy policies. The agreement will likely benefit Facebook app users beyond California, too. Illinois passed, and several other states are developing, legislation to prohibit employers from demanding social media passwords of applicants and employees so they can screen their profiles. (Amazingly, this has happened. Some colleges and universities have also demanded the same information from NCAA athletes.) The laws also prohibit retaliation if the applicants or employees decline to provide passwords. Employers can still look at publicly available profiles.[10]

With each new technological innovation, there is an opportunity to gather more information on consumers, and to exploit it for profit. In the fall of 2012, the European Union ruled that Facebook could not use facial recognition software for "tag suggestions," as its users did not consent to having their identities used that way. The *New York Times* zeroed in on Facebook's business and ethical dilemma: "Facebook is under pressure from Wall Street to profit from its vast trove of data, including pictures, and also from regulators worldwide over the use of personal information."[11] Facebook is certain to move on to its next idea for using its vast trove of data.

◢ THUS, SECURING INFORMATION PRIVACY REMAINS AN ENORMOUS PROBLEM.

As consumers, we self-disclose our words and images, but often we have little idea what happens to them next. For this case, we will critically analyze the heart of the ethical dilemma: the privacy agreements that digital sites and apps make with us.

As detailed in Chapter 1, a media-literate perspective involves mastering five overlapping critical stages that build on each other: (1) *description*: paying close attention, taking notes, and researching the subject under study; (2) *analysis*: discovering and focusing on significant patterns that emerge from the description stage; (3) *interpretation*: asking and answering the "What does that mean?" and "So what?" questions about your findings; (4) *evaluation*: arriving at a judgment about whether the content is good, bad, poor, or mediocre, which involves subordinating one's personal views to the critical assessment resulting from the first three stages; and (5) *engagement*: taking some action that connects our critical interpretations and evaluations with our responsibility to question the privacy practices of digital companies.

Step 1: Description

For the description phase, you will need to research and take notes on two or three privacy statements. If you are like us, privacy statements are probably the last thing you would want to read. But reading them can be empowering, since it's the only way you'll find out how companies will use your personal information and data.

Here's how we'll do it. The White House released a Consumer Privacy Bill of Rights in 2012 as general principles that all organizations should adopt for fair information practice.[12] We'll apply the seven standards from that bill as a checklist to describe privacy statements.

- Individual Control: Consumers have a right to exercise control over what personal data companies collect from them and how they are used. (Do consumers have complete control over their entire personal profile, and can they easily limit or withdraw consent to use that data? If you close your account, do they eliminate all of your information?)
- Transparency: Consumers have a right to easily understandable and accessible information about privacy and security practices. (Is the policy in plain, understandable language? Do they share your information with other parties?)
- Respect for Context: Consumers have a right to expect that companies will collect, use, and disclose personal data in ways that are consistent with the context in which consumers provide the data. (For example, do they provide greater protections for children and teenagers?)
- Security: Consumers have a right to secure and responsible handling of personal data. (Does the company make clear its policy for making your account data safe from accidental disclosure or hacker attacks?)

GENE SPERLING, director of the National Economic Council in the Obama administration, has helped spearhead an online consumer privacy initiative since his appointment in 2011. When the White House introduced the Consumer Privacy Bill of Rights in February 2012, Sperling explained the bill would help give people more control over how their personal data are used online and would also require companies to post coherent and accessible privacy and security policies on their sites.

- Access and Accuracy: Consumers have a right to access and correct personal data in usable formats, in a manner that is appropriate to the sensitivity of the data and the risk of adverse consequences to consumers if the data are inaccurate. (Do customers have a right to access all of their data and correct their records if they are wrong?)
- Focused Collection: Consumers have a right to reasonable limits on the personal data that companies collect and retain. (Does the company collect only necessary information, and does it dispose of, or de-identify, personal data when they are no longer needed?)
- Accountability: Consumers have a right to have personal data handled by companies with appropriate measures in place to assure they adhere to the Consumer Privacy Bill of Rights. (Does the company train employees to correctly handle personal data, perform regular audits, and monitor third-party users of the data?)

There are a number of places you might look to find privacy statements. The easiest way is to do a search of the company name and the word "privacy"–for example, "Google privacy," which takes one to http://www.google.com/policies/privacy/. (Other companies you might check include Amazon, Apple, AT&T, Facebook, Hulu, Microsoft, Netflix, Pandora, Pinterest, Tumblr, Twitter, Verizon, Yahoo!, and Zynga.)

GOOGLE STREET VIEW was investigated by the FCC in 2012 after Google revealed its Street View cars had unintentionally collected confidential information about people's online activity on public Wi-Fi networks. Although the FCC cleared Google of charges that it had illegally collected Wi-Fi data, several countries have limited Google Street View activity due to privacy concerns, and some, like the Czech Republic, have banned it altogether.

Step 2: Analysis

In the second stage of the critical process, analysis, you will isolate patterns that emerged from these statements and that call for closer attention. For example:

- Which companies require that users must opt out if they don't want to receive marketing communications?
- Which companies explain their policy on cookies and other tracking technologies?
- Which companies share their customers' information with other subsidiaries of their large corporation?
- Which companies explicitly state that their customer information is a business asset, so if they are part of a business merger or acquisition, their personal information may be sold to the new company? Which companies don't address this scenario?
- Which companies state they may collect users' geo-location by tracking their mobile devices?
- Which companies explain why they need the data they gather on customers? (For example, if they need a users' birthday or gender, do they explain why?)
- Which companies have a statement about information for children 13 years and younger? Which don't say anything about young customers?

- Which privacy statements are written in clear language? Which were difficult to decipher?
- Which companies explain what will happen to your information if you close down your account?

Step 3: Interpretation

In the interpretation stage, you will determine the larger meanings of the patterns you have analyzed. The most difficult stage in criticism, interpretation demands an answer to the questions "So what?" and "What does this all mean?" For example, after analyzing the privacy statements, what might the similarities and differences say about these companies' fundamental dilemma in treating customer information as both a business asset to be monetized and as the private information of real people to be carefully protected?

Does the privacy statement read like a dry legal document for the company, to ward off potential lawsuits? Or does the policy appear to be a genuine attempt at communicating with consumers? (Keep in mind that nice design isn't everything, and can be deceiving. It is possible that a privacy policy could be badly designed, but offer more protections than one that has a friendly design, but doesn't provide strong privacy protections to users.) Do you feel more concerned or less worried about the state of personal data after reviewing the privacy statements? Ultimately, for each company's privacy statement you analyzed, does the company seem to be more focused on profiting from personal information (and then obscuring what they actually do), or does the company seem to have made a legitimate effort to bring a useful service to consumers and take responsibility for their personal information?

If you looked at the privacy statements of Facebook, Google, Twitter, or MySpace, did the fact that the FTC is monitoring them seem to have an effect on their privacy policies being better than others?

MICHEL MORGANELLA
Kicked off the Swiss Olympic soccer team for tweeting a racial slur aimed at his South Korean opponent, Morganella was the second athlete to be disqualified from the London Olympics for making racist comments on Twitter, following triple jumper Voula Papachristou. Morganella and Papachristou's actions highlight the reality that when we post online, our thoughts and ideas become a public matter that may endure forever.

Step 4: Evaluation

The evaluation stage of the critical process is about making informed judgments. Building on description, analysis, and interpretation, you can better evaluate the fair information practices of digital corporations.

Consider each privacy statement, and judge whether they offered fair information practices that balanced their need for customer information against the rights of customers. Did they meet, exceed, or fall short of the general objective of the FTC for privacy to be the "default setting" and for simplified choices and increased transparency for consumers?

Overall, to return to our initial question, is the convenience of our digital ecosystem worth the increasing invasion of our privacy? Is it possible to truly control our privacy within Facebook, Twitter, and other companies, even if we agree to their terms? Does privacy really matter, or should we just "get over it"?

Step 5: Engagement

> "Thoughts transposed into type are in effect published, and publication removes the expression of those thoughts from the intimate and personal sphere."
>
> MARSHALL MCLUHAN, *COUNTERBLAST*, 1969

The fifth stage of the critical process—engagement—encourages you to take action, adding your own voice to the process of shaping our culture and environment.

For every company that has a privacy statement, there should also be the opportunity for feedback. If you see something that conflicts with standard privacy protections (e.g., what data are collected and why; how they will be used and how long they will be maintained, as well as your rights to control access and use of your information), you should seriously consider whether you want to do business with that Web site. If a Web site does not live up to its privacy policy, contact the company and let it know. Also, if you consider the matter to be serious you should take your concerns directly to the FTC and file a consumer complaint. Groups such as the Electronic Privacy Information Center (epic.org)

ELECTRONIC PRIVACY INFORMATION CENTER
Founded in 1994 to bring attention to emerging privacy concerns in the information age, EPIC is dedicated to educating the general public about ways they can protect themselves from self-invasion of privacy. EPIC also publishes the award-winning *EPIC Alert* every two weeks, an online newsletter containing information about current privacy and civil liberty issues.

and the Electronic Frontier Foundation (EFF) are helpful resources in learning more about current privacy issues and your rights as a consumer.

At a higher level, consider corresponding with agencies like the FTC. The FTC received only about 450 public comments as it worked toward its 2012 recommendations on consumer privacy. That's a lot for an FTC proposal, but surprisingly low for such an important global issue. You can comment publicly through an online form for any policy the FTC develops. Be inspired by the public comments made by others on the FTC Web site, at http://ftc.gov/os /publiccomments.shtm.

> "[Facebook is the] world's largest privately held database of face prints—without the explicit consent of its users."
>
> U.S. SEN. AL FRANKEN (D-MN), 2012

Notes

1 Mass Communication: A Critical Approach

1. On 2012 federal election costs, see for examples Nicholas Confessore and Jess Bidgood, "Conservative Megadonors Get Little for Their Money," *International Herald Tribune*, November 9, 2012, sec. News, p. 7; "The $6 Billion Election," *Intelligencer Journal/New Era* (Lancaster, PA), November 9, 2012, p. A12.; and Luke Rosiak, "Campaign-Funding Floodgates Burst Open in 2012," *Washington Times*, November 7, 2012, p. A7.

2. Jeremy Peters, "73,000 Political Ads Test Even a City of Excess," *New York Times*, October 16, 2012, p. A1.

3. Wesley Hester and Olympia Meola, "Ad Frenzy," *Richmond Times Dispatch*, August 19, 2012; and Brian Steinberg, "Surviving the Political Ad Deluge," *Advertising Age*, October 16, 2012, p. 14.

4. Steinberg, *Advertising Age*, p. 14.

5. See Wolff, *USA Today*, p. 1.

6. See "Mad Money: TV Ads in the 2012 Presidential Campaign," *Washington Post*, http://www.washingtonpost.com/wp-srv/special /politics/track-presidential-campaign-ads, accessed November 12, 2012.

7. For exit poll data, see "Building Blocks of Re-Election," *New York Times*, November 11, 2012, sec. Sunday Review, p. 7.

8. See "18-29-Year-Old Voters Propel Obama to Victory," *PR Newswire*, November 5, 2008; and Graham Richardson, "Connected to Voters Who Count," *The Australian*, November 9, 2012, sec. Features, p. 14.

9. Neil Postman, *Amusing Ourselves to Death: Public Discourse in the Age of Show Business* (New York: Penguin Books, 1985), 19.

10. James W. Carey, *Communication as Culture: Essays on Media and Society* (Boston: Unwin Hyman, 1989), 203.

11. Postman, *Amusing Ourselves to Death*, 65. See also Elizabeth Eisenstein, *The Printing Press as an Agent of Change*, 2 vols. (Cambridge: Cambridge University Press, 1979).

12. James Fallows, "How to Save the News," *Atlantic*, June 2010, http://www.theatlantic.com/magazine/archive/2010/06/how-to-save -the-news/8095/.

13. "Generation M²: Media in the Lives of 8-to-18-Year-Olds," A Kaiser Family Foundation Study, p. 2, accessed May 24, 2010, http://www.kff .org/entmedia/upload/8010.pdf.

14. Jefferson Graham, "For TV Networks, Social Is Hugely Important," *USA Today*, May 3, 2012, http://www.usatoday.com/tech/columnist /talkingtech/story/2012-05-02/social-media-tv/54705524/1.

15. Jerome Bruner, *Making Stories: Law, Literature, Life* (New York: Farrar, Straus & Giroux, 2002), 8.

16. Roger Rosenblatt, "I Am Writing Blindly," *Time*, November 6, 2000, p. 142.

17. See Plato, *The Republic*, Book II, 377B.

18. For a historical discussion of culture, see Lawrence Levine, *Highbrow/Lowbrow: The Emergence of Cultural Hierarchy in America* (Cambridge, Mass.: Harvard University Press, 1988).

19. For an example of this critical position, see Allan Bloom, *The Closing of the American Mind: How Higher Education Has Failed Democracy and Impoverished the Souls of Today's Students* (New York: Simon & Schuster, 1987).

20. For overviews of this position, see Postman, *Amusing Ourselves to Death*; and Stuart Ewen, *Captains of Consciousness: Advertising and the Social Roots of the Consumer Culture* (New York: McGraw-Hill, 1976).

21. See Carey, *Communication as Culture*.

22. Walter Lippmann, *Public Opinion* (New York: Free Press, 1922), 11, 19, 246-247.

23. For more on this idea, see Cecelia Tichi, *Electronic Hearth: Creating an American Television Culture* (New York: Oxford University Press, 1991), 187-188.

24. See Jon Katz, "Rock, Rap and Movies Bring You the News," *Rolling Stone*, March 5, 1992, p. 33.

◢ EXAMINING ETHICS   Covering War, p. 18

1. Bill Carter, "Some Stations to Block 'Nightline' War Tribute," *New York Times*, April 30, 2004, p. A13.

2. For reference and guidance on media ethics, see Clifford Christians, Mark Fackler, and Kim Rotzoll, *Media Ethics: Cases and Moral Reasoning*, 4th ed. (White Plains, N.Y.: Longman, 1995); and Thomas H. Bivins, "A Worksheet for Ethics Instruction and Exercises in Reason," *Journalism Educator* (Summer 1993): 4-16.

◢ CASE STUDY   The Sleeper Curve, p. 22

1. Steven Johnson, *Everything Bad Is Good for You: How Today's Popular Culture Is Actually Making Us Smarter* (New York: Riverhead Books, 2005). See book's subtitle.

2. Neil Postman, *Amusing Ourselves to Death: Public Discourse in the Age of Show Business* (New York: Penguin Books, 1985).

3. Ibid., 3-4.

4. Ibid., 129-131.

5. Steven Johnson, "Watching TV Makes You Smarter," *New York Times Magazine*, April 24, 2005, 55ff. Article adapted from Johnson's book *Everything Bad Is Good for You*. All subsequent quotations are from this article.

◢ GLOBAL VILLAGE   Bedouins, Camels, Transistors, and Coke, p. 34

1. Václav Havel, "A Time for Transcendence," *Utne Reader*, January/ February 1995, p. 53.

2. Dan Rather, "The Threat to Foreign News," *Newsweek*, July 17, 1989, p. 9.

Part 1 Opener

Infographic source: http://web.pewinternet.org/Reports/2011/Cell-Phones/Key-Findings.aspx

2 The Internet, Digital Media, and Media Convergence

1. Linda Smith, "Technology Puts Bite on Rescue Dogs," *Hobart Mercury* (Australia), December 2, 2008, p. 3.

2. Kathryn Zickuhr and Aaron Smith, "Digital Differences," Pew Internet & American Life Project, April 13, 2012, http://pewinternet .org/Reports/2012/Digital-differences.aspx.

3. David Landis, "World Wide Web Helps Untangle Internet's Labyrinth," *USA Today*, August 3, 1994, p. D10.

4. "Trend Data (Adults)," Pew Internet & American Life Project, April 2012, http://www.pewinternet.org/Static-Pages/Trend-Data -%28Adults%29/Home-Broadband-Adoption.aspx.

5. Peter H. Lewis, "The Computer Always Beeps Twice," *New York Times*, April 28, 1994, p. 1.

6. Ibid.

7. Jodi Wilgoren, "As Snow Shuts Schools, Computer Users Boot Up," *New York Times*, January 15, 1999, p. B5.

8. "comScore Releases May 2012 U.S. Search Engine Rankings," comScore, June 13, 2012, http://www.comscore.com/Press_Events /Press_Releases/2012/6/comScore_Releases_May_2012_U.S._Search_ Engine_Rankings.

9. Lawrence Lessig, *Remix: Making Art and Commerce Thrive in the Hybrid Economy* (New York: Penguin, 2009).

10. Amanda Lenhart, Mary Madden, Alexandra Rankin Macgill, and Aaron Smith, "Teens and Social Media," Pew Internet & American Life Project, December 19, 2007, http://www.pewinternet.org/Reports /2007/Teens-and-Social-Media.aspx.

11. Jessica Clark, "Public Media 2.0: Dynamic, Engaged Publics," Center for Social Media, February 2009, http://www.centerforsocialmedia .org/future-public-media/documents/white-papers/public-media -20-dynamic-engaged-publics.

12. Heidi Cohen, "30 Social Media Definitions," May 9, 2011, http:// heidicohen.com/social-media-definition/.

13. Andreas Kaplan and Michael Haenlein, "Users of the World, Unite! The Challenges and Opportunities of Social Media," *Business Horizons* (2010): 53, 59-68.

14. SmartDataCollective, "Farewell to BlogPulse," January 14, 2012, http://smartdatacollective.com/node/44748.

15. "Twitter Turns Six," *Twitter Blog*, March 21, 2012, http://blog.twitter .com/2012/03/twitter-turns-six.html.

16. Peter J. Schuyten, "The Computer Entering Home," *New York Times*, December 6, 1978, p. D4.

17. Jon Fingas, "comScore: Android Tips the 51% Mark in US Share, iPhone Nips Its Heels with 31%," *Engadget*, May 1, 2012, http://www.engadget .com/2012/05/01/comscore-us-smartphone-share-march-2012/.

18. "Select Your Widget–Search Widget," Twitter, accessed June 4, 2012, https://twitter.com/about/resources/widgets.

19. Chris Anderson and Michael Wolff, "The Web Is Dead. Long Live the Internet," *Wired*, August 17, 2010, http://www.wired.com/magazine /2010/08/ff_webrip. Also see Charles Arthur, "Walled Gardens Look Rosy for Facebook, Apple–and Would-Be Censors," *Guardian*, April 17, 2012, http://www.guardian.co.uk/technology/2012/apr/17/walled-gardens -facebook-apple-censors.

20. Arthur, "Walled Gardens."

21. Tim Berners-Lee, James Hendler, and Ora Lassila, "The Semantic Web," *Scientific American*, May 17, 2001.

22. Ibid.

23. Farhad Manjoo, "The Great Tech War of 2012: Apple, Facebook, Google, and Amazon Battle for the Future of the Innovation Economy," *Fast Company*, October 19, 2011, http://www.fastcompany.com /magazine/160/tech-wars-2012-amazon-apple-google-facebook.

24. Jessica E. Vascellaro and Amir Efrati, "Apple and Google Expand Their Battle to Mobile Maps," *Wall Street Journal*, June 4, 2012, http://online.wsj .com/article/SB10001424052702304543904577398502695522974.html.

25. "Facebook Inc.," *New York Times*, accessed June 1, 2012, http://topics .nytimes.com/top/news/business/companies/facebook_inc/index.html.

26. Wayne Friedman, "Location-Based Ads Hit $6B by 2015," *Media Daily News*, June 27, 2011, http://www.mediapost.com/publications /article/153133/location-based-ads-hit-6b-by-2015.html#axzz2LZB5LCm6.

27. Mark Zuckerberg, "Our Commitment to the Facebook Community," *The Facebook Blog*, November 29, 2011, http://blog.facebook.com/blog .php?post=10150378701937131.

28. See Federal Trade Commission, *Privacy Online: Fair Information Practices in the Electronic Marketplace*, May 2000, http://www.ftc.gov /reports/privacy2000.pdf.

29. American Library Association, "CIPA Questions and Answers," July 16, 2003, http://www.ala.org/ala/washoff/woissues/civilliberties /cipaweb/adviceresources/CIPAQA.pdf.

30. Kathryn Zickuhr and Aaron Smith, "Digital Differences," Pew Internet & American Life Project, April 13, 2012, http://pewinternet .org/Reports/2012/Digital-differences/Overview.aspx.

31. Ibid.

32. John Horrigan, "Wireless Internet Use," Pew Internet & American Life Project, July 22, 2009, http://www.pewinternet.org/Reports/2009 /12-Wireless-Internet-Use.aspx?r=1.

33. ClickZ, "Stats-Web Worldwide," http://www.clickz.com/showPage .html?page=stats/web_worldwide.

34. Federal Communications Commission, "In the Matter of Preserving the Open Internet Broadband Industry Practices," Report and Order FCC 10-201, December 23, 2010, http://www.fcc.gov/Daily_Releases /Daily_Business/2010/db1223/FCC-10-201A1.pdf.

35. Brewster Kahle, quoted in Katie Hafner, "Libraries Shun Deals to Place Books on the Web," *New York Times*, October 22, 2008, http:// www.nytimes.com/2007/10/22/technology/22library.html.

36. David Bollier, "Saving the Information Commons," Remarks to American Library Association Convention, Atlanta, June 15, 2002, http://www.lita.org/ala/acrlbucket/copyrightcommitt /copyrightcommitteepiratesbollier.cfm.

37. Douglas Gomery, "In Search of the Cybermarket," *Wilson Quarterly* (Summer 1994): 10.

◢ EXAMINING ETHICS   The "Anonymous" Hackers of the Internet, p. 56

1. Matt Liebowitz, "Anonymous Targets Monsanto Again in Latest Data Dump," MSNBC, March 2, 2012, http://www.msnbc.msn.com/id /46606307/ns/technology_and_science-security/t/anonymous-targets -monsanto-again-latest-data-dump/#.UBFr216chs8.

2. Chris Landers, "Serious Business: Anonymous Takes On Scientology (and Doesn't Afraid of Anything)." *Baltimore City Paper*, April 2, 2008, http://www2.citypaper.com/columns/story.asp?id=15543.

3. Somini Sengupta, "Arrests Sow Mistrust inside a Clan of Hackers," *New York Times*, March 6, 2010, http://www.nytimes.com/2012/03/07 /technology/lulzsec-hacking-suspects-are-arrested.html.

4. David Sanger, "Obama Order Sped Up Wave of Cyberattacks against Iran," *New York Times*, June 1, 2012, http://www.nytimes.com/2012/06 /01/world/middleeast/obama-ordered-wave-of-cyberattacks-against -iran.html.

WHAT GOOGLE OWNS   What Does This Mean?, p. 64

1. Google, Inc., "Google Announces Fourth Quarter and Fiscal Year 2011 Results," January 19, 2012, http://investor.google.com/earnings/2011 /Q4_google_earnings.html.

2. Google, Inc., "2012 Financial Tables," accessed June 14, 2012, http://investor.google.com/financial/tables.html.

3. "Google, Inc.," *New York Times*, August 23, 2012, http://topics.nytimes .com/top/news/business/companies/google_inc/index.html.

4. Meghan Kelly, "96 Percent of Google's Revenue Is Advertising, Who Buys It?" infographic, *VentureBeat*, January 29, 2012, http://venturebeat .com/2012/01/29/google-advertising/.

5. Ibid.

6. Roger Cheng, "Google Says 850K Android Devices Activated Each Day," CNET, February 27, 2012, http://reviews.cnet.com/8301-13970_7 -57385635-78/google-says-850k-android-devices-activated-each-day/.

7. Ben Parr, "The Google Revenue Equation, and Why Google's Building Chrome OS," Mashable, July 11, 2009, http://mashable.com/2009/07/11 /google-equation/.

8. NASDAQ, "GOOG: Stock Quote & Summary Data," http://quotes .nasdaq.com/asp/SummaryQuote.asp?symbol=GOOG&selected=GOOG.

9. Anne VanderMey, "Inside Google's Recruiting Machine," CNNMoney, February 24, 2012, http://tech.fortune.cnn.com/2012/02/24/google -recruiting/.

◢ GLOBAL VILLAGE   Designed in California, Assembled in China, p. 65

1. Charles Duhigg and Keith Bradsher, "How the U.S. Lost Out on iPhone Work," New York Times, January 21, 2012, http://www.nytimes.com /2012/01/22/business/apple-america-and-a-squeezed-middle-class.html.

2. Ibid. See also Charles Duhigg and David Barboza, "In China, Human Costs Are Built into an iPad," New York Times, January 25, 2012, http:// www.nytimes.com/2012/01/26/business/ieconomy-apples-ipad-and -the-human-costs-for-workers-in-china.html.

3. Bill Weir, "A Trip to the iFactory: 'Nightline' Gets an Unprecedented Glimpse inside Apple's Chinese Core," ABC News, February 20, 2012, http:// abcnews.go.com/International/trip-ifactory-nightline-unprecedented -glimpse-inside-apples-chinese/story?id=15748745#.T9AQTu2PfpA.

4. Barbara Demick and David Sarno, "Firm Shaken by Suicides," Los Angeles Times, May 26, 2010, http://articles.latimes.com/2010/may/26 /world/la-fg-china-suicides-20100526.

5. Fair Labor Association, "Fair Labor Association Secures Commitment to Limit Workers' Hours, Protect Pay at Apple's Largest Supplier," March 29, 2012, http://www.fairlabor.org/blog/entry/fair-labor-association -secures-commitment-limit-workers-hours-protect-pay-apples-largest.

3 Digital Gaming and the Media Playground

1. World of Warcraft, "Beginner's Guide: What Is World of Warcraft," accessed June 17, 2012, http://us.battle.net/wow/en/game/guide/.

2. Medievaldragon, "World of Warcraft: Mists of Pandaria–Fact Sheet," March 19, 2012, http://www.blizzplanet.com/blog/comments/world-of -warcraft-mists-of-pandaria-fact-sheet.

3. "Global Industry Analysts Predicts Gaming Market to Reach $91 Billion by 2015," VG24/7, June 29, 2009, http://www.vg247.com/2009 /06/23/global-industry-analysts-predicts-gaming-market-to-reach -91-billion-by-2015/.

4. Erkki Huhtamo, "Slots of Fun, Slots of Trouble: An Archaeology of Arcade Gaming," in Joost Raessens and Jeffrey Goldstein, eds., Handbook of Computer Game Studies (Cambridge, Mass.: MIT, 2005), 10.

5. Ibid., 9–10.

6. Seth Porges, "11 Things You Didn't Know about Pinball History," Popular Mechanics, http://www.popularmechanics.com/technology /gadgets/toys/4328211-new#fbIndex.

7. David Winter, "Magnavox Odyssey," accessed June 20, 2012, http:// www.pong-story.com/odyssey.htm.

8. "December 2011 NPD U.S. Console Sales Charts," January 13, 2012, http://gamerinvestments.com/video-game-stocks/index.php/2012/01 /13/december-2011-npd-u-s-console-sales-charts/.

9. Jeff Cade, "The Real Money of Fantasy Sports," MSN Money, April 3, 2012, http://money.msn.com/personal-finance/the-real-money-of-fantasy-sports .aspx.

10. David M. Ewalt, "Microsoft Xbox Is Winning the Living Room War. Here's Why," Forbes, June 4, 2012, http://www.forbes.com/sites/davidewalt/2012 /06/04/microsoft-xbox-is-winning-the-living-room-war-heres-why/.

11. iPhone sales calculated from Apple's quarterly sales, from Q3 2007 to Q2 2012. See also Sam Costello, "What Are iPad Sales All Time?" About.com, April 2012, http://ipod.about.com/od/ipadmodelsandterms /f/ipad-sales-to-date.htm; and "App Store Metrics," June 18, 2012, http://148apps.biz/app-store-metrics/?mpage=appcount.

12. Sam Anderson, "Just One More Game . . . Angry Birds, Farmville and Other Hyperaddictive 'Stupid Games,'" New York Times, April 4, 2012, http://www.nytimes.com/2012/04/08/magazine/angry-birds-farmville -and-other-hyperaddictive-stupid-games.html.

13. Dan Graziano, "Diablo III Becomes the Fastest-Selling PC Game of All Time," BGR, May 23, 2012, http://www.bgr.com/2012/05/23/diablo -iii-sales-pc-game-record/.

14. Editorial: "Final Eclipse of Conversation?" Milwaukee Journal, December 19, 1981, p. 12.

15. Pierre Lévy, Collective Intelligence: Mankind's Emerging World in Cyberspace (New York: Basic Books, 1997), xxviii.

16. World of Warcraft, "Beginner's Guide, Chapter III: Playing Together," accessed June 23, 2012, http://us.battle.net/wow/en/game/guide /playing-together.

17. GameSpot Fuse, accessed June 23, 2012, http://fuse.gamespot.com/.

18. Entertainment Software Association, "In-Game Advertising," accessed June 26, 2012, http://www.theesa.com/games-improving -what-matters/advertising.asp.

19. Ibid.

20. Douglas A. Gentile, et al., "Pathological Video Game Use among Youths: A Two-Year Longitudinal Study," Pediatrics 127, no. 2 (2011), doi:10.1542/peds.2010-1353.

21. Michelle L. Brandt, "Video Games Activate Reward Regions of Brain in Men More than Women, Stanford Study Finds," Stanford School of Medicine, February 4, 2008, http://med.stanford.edu/news_releases /2008/february/videobrain.html.

22. Andrew Salmon, "Couple: Internet Gaming Addiction Led to Baby's Death," CNN, April 1, 2010, http://articles.cnn.com/2010-04-01/world /korea.parents.starved.baby_1_gaming-addiction-internet-gaming -gaming-industry?_s=PM:WORLD.

23. Jason Epstein, "10 of the Most Delightfully Violent Video Games of All Time," Guyism.com, February 13, 2012, http://guyism.com/tech /gadgets/10-of-the-most-violent-video-games-of-all-time.html.

24. Patrick Markey and Charlotte N. Markey, "Vulnerability to Violent Video Games: A Review and Integration of Personality Research," Review of General Psychology 14(2) (2010): 82–91.

25. National Center for Women & Information Technology, "NCWIT Factsheet," accessed June 26, 2012, http://www.ncwit.org/sites/default /files/resources/ncwitfactsheet.pdf. Also see Tasneen Raja, "The Rise of the Brogrammer," Mother Jones, July/August 2012, p. 8.

26. Daniel Engber, "How Do Video Games Get Rated?" Slate.com, July 15, 2005, http://www.slate.com/articles/news_and_politics/explainer /2005/07/how_do_video_games_get_rated.html.

27. Janna Anderson and Lee Rainie, "The Future of Gamification," Pew Internet & American Life Project, May 18, 2012, http://pewinternet.org /Reports/2012/Future-of-Gamification/Overview.aspx.

28. Entertainment Software Association, "Essential Facts about the Computer and Video Game Industry 2012," June 5, 2012, http://www.theesa.com/newsroom/release_detail.asp?releaseID=174.

29. John Markoff, "COMPANY NEWS; Sony Starts a Division to Sell Game Machines," *New York Times*, May 19, 1994, http://www.nytimes.com/1994/05/19/business/company-news-sony-starts-a-division-to-sell-game-machines.html.

30. Business Wire, "Nintendo 64 Sold Out; Company Pushes for More Product; Frenzied Consumers Demand to Buy before Product Officially Launches," October 2, 1996, http://findarticles.com/p/articles/mi_mOEIN/is_1996_Oct_2/ai_18745127/.

31. "Tired of Waiting for Prices to Fall, Consumers Are Returning to Video Games," *New York Times*, January 26, 1998, http://www.nytimes.com/1998/01/26/business/tired-of-waiting-for-prices-to-fall-consumers-are-returning-to-video-games.html.

32. John Markoff, "Microsoft's Game Plan; Xbox to Go Head to Head with Sony," *New York Times*, September 4, 2000, http://www.nytimes.com/2000/09/04/business/microsoft-s-game-plan-xbox-to-go-head-to-head-with-sony.html.

33. Craig Glenday, ed., "Hardware History II." *Guinness World Records Gamer's Edition 2008* (London: Guinness World Records, 2008), 27.

34. Blizzard Entertainment, "Mission Statement," accessed July 7, 2012, http://us.blizzard.com/en-us/company/about/mission.html.

35. Alex Pham, "Star Wars: The Old Republic–The Costliest Game of All Time?" *Los Angeles Times,* January 20, 2012, http://latimesblogs.latimes.com/entertainmentnewsbuzz/2012/01/star-wars-old-republic-cost.html

36. See AppData, accessed June 30, 2012, http://www.appdata.com/devs/10-zynga.

37. Matt Brian, "Rovio's Angry Birds Titles Hit 1 Billion Cumulative Downloads," *Next Web*, May 9, 2012, http://thenextweb.com/mobile/2012/05/09/rovios-angry-birds-titles-hit-1-billion-cumulative-downloads/.

38. Rob Waugh, "Star Wars Epic Uses the Force–and $100M–to Take on World of Warcraft," *Mail Online*, December 20, 2011, http://www.dailymail.co.uk/sciencetech/article-2076105/Star-Wars-epic-takes-4-billion-titan-online-gaming-World-Warcraft.html.

39. "John Madden Net Worth," *Celebrity Networth,* accessed July 5, 2012, http://www.celebritynetworth.com/richest-athletes/nfl/john-madden-net-worth/.

40. Robert Purchese, "Modern Warfare 3 Day 1 Shipments 'Largest in History,'" Eurogamer.net, November 9, 2011, http://www.eurogamer.net/articles/2011-11-09-modern-warfare-3-day-1-shipments-largest-in-history. See also Tom Ivan, "Modern Warfare 3 Sets 5 Day Entertainment Sales Record," *CVG*, November 17, 2011, http://www.computerandvideogames.com/326425/modern-warfare-3-sets-5-day-entertainment-sales-record/.

41. Ian Hamilton, "Blizzard's World of Warcraft Revenue Down," *Orange County Register*, November 8, 2010, http://ocunwired.ocregister.com/2010/11/08/blizzards-world-of-warcraft-revenue-down/.

42. See GameStop, "About GameStop," accessed June 29, 2012, http://news.gamestop.com/about_us.

43. Tyler Nagata, "Nearly 50% of GameStop's Profits Come from Pre-Owned Sales," *GamesRadar,* November 19, 2010, http://www.gamesradar.com/nearly-50-of-gamestops-profits-come-from-pre-owned-sales/.

44. "Steam: Valve's Ingenious Digital Store," infographic, *Daily Infographic,* February 24, 2012, http://dailyinfographic.com/steam-valves-ingenious-digital-store-infographic.

45. Matthew Sabatini, "Google Play (Android Market) vs Apple App Store–2012," *Android Authority,* April 24, 2012, http://www.androidauthority.com/google-play-vs-apple-app-store-2012-76566/.

46. Jeff Beer, "Rise of Mobile Gaming Surprises Big Video-Game Developers," *Canadian Business*, April 2, 2012, p. 30.

47. Aaron Leitko, "Kickstarter.com Helps Video Game Developers Reboot Old Titles," *Washington Post*, May 25, 2012, http://www.washingtonpost.com/lifestyle/style/kickstartercom-helps-video-game-developers-reboot-old-titles/2012/05/25/gJQAMeFipU_story.html.

48. Evan Narcisse, "Supreme Court: 'Video Games Qualify for First Amendment Protection,'" *Time*, June 27, 2011, http://techland.time.com/2011/06/27/supreme-court-video-games-qualify-for-first-amendment-protection/.

49. Entertainment Software Association, "Essential Facts about the Computer and Video Game Industry 2012," June 5, 2012, http://www.theesa.com/newsroom/release_detail.asp?releaseID=174.

50. Charlie Jane Anders, "*Prometheus* Writer Jon Spaihts on How to Create a Great Space Movie," *io9*, May 10, 2012, http://io9.com/5909279/prometheus-writer-jon-spaihts-on-how-to-create-a-great-space-movie.

51. Ray Muzyka, "To *Mass Effect 3* players, from Dr. Ray Muzyka, Co-Founder of BioWare," March 21, 2012, http://blog.bioware.com/2012/03/21/4108/.

◢ **GLOBAL VILLAGE   South Korea's Gaming Obsession, p. 100**

1. Chico Harlan, "S. Korean Gamers Now Have Plenty to Cheer About," *Washington Post*, August 17, 2010, p. A8, http://www.washingtonpost.com/wp-dyn/content/article/2010/08/16/AR2010081602506.html.

2. Seth Schiesel, "Land of the Video Geek," *New York Times*, October 8, 2006, www.nytimes.com/2006/10/08/arts/08schi.html.

3. Brett Staebell, "BoxeR in Brief," *Escapist*, April 6, 2010, http://www.escapistmagazine.com/articles/view/issues/issue_248/7378-BoxeR-in-Brief.

4. "Tournaments, Live Broadcasts Herald Rise of E-Sports," *Korea Times*, February 8, 2012, http://www.koreatimes.co.kr/www/news/art/2012/05/201_104371.html.

5. Schiesel, "Land of the Video Geek."

6. Ibid.

7. Harlan, "S. Korean Gamers."

8. Carolyn Sun, "South Korea Is the Most-Wired Country in the World–and Online Games Are the New Drug of Choice for Its Youth," *Newsweek*, International Edition, October 24, 2011.

◢ **Media Literacy and the Critical Process   First-Person Shooter Games: Misogyny as Entertainment?, p. 102**

1. Seth Schiesel, "Way Down Deep in the Wild, Wild West," *New York Times*, May 16, 2010, http://www.nytimes.com/2010/05/17/arts/television/17dead.html.

2. The Red Dragon, "Red Dead Redemption Coolest Achievement Ever–Dastardly Tutorial," May 19, 2010, http://www.youtube.com/watch?v=Vmtdvpp9dMc&feature=related.

3. Tracy Clark-Flory, "Grand Theft Misogyny," Salon.com, May 3, 2008, http://www.salon.com/life/broadsheet/2008/05/03/gta.

4. Matt Cabral, "A History of GTA and How It Helped Shape Red Dead Redemption," *PCWorld Australia*, July 13, 2010, http://www.pcworld.idg.com.au/article/352981/history_gta_how_it_helped_shape_red_dead_redemption/.

WHAT MICROSOFT OWNS   What Does This Mean?, p. 106

1. "Financial Highlights," *Microsoft Corporation Annual Report 2011,* http://www.microsoft.com/investor/reports/ar11/financial_highlights/index.html.

2. "Research and Development," *Microsoft Corporation Annual Report 2011,* http://www.microsoft.com/investor/reports/ar11/financial_review/research_development.html.

3. "Employees," *Microsoft Corporation Annual Report 2011,* http://www.microsoft.com/investor/reports/ar11/financial_review/employees.html.

4. Nick Bilton, "Xbox Gives Microsoft a Head Start in the Battle for Every Screen," *New York Times,* June 3, 2012, http://bits.blogs.nytimes.com/2012/06/03/xbox-gives-microsoft-a-head-start-in-the-battle-for-every-screen/.

5. "2012 USA Yearly Chart," VG Chartz, http://www.vgchartz.com/yearly/2012/USA/.

6. Bilton, "Xbox Gives Microsoft a Head Start."

7. David Murphy, "Microsoft Unveils New Xbox LIVE Statistics–Average Gamerscore: 11,286," PCMag.com, March 12, 2011, http://www.pcmag.com/article2/0,2817,2381862,00.asp.

8. Douglas McIntyre, "America's 10 Largest Web Sites," NBCnews.com, March 25, 2012, http://bottomline.msnbc.msn.com/_news/2012/03/25/10760486-americas-10-largest-websites.

Part 2 Opener

Infographic sources:

http://blog.nielsen.com/nielsenwire/online_mobile/cross-platform-report-how-we-watch-from-screen-to-screen/

http://techcrunch.com/2012/01/08/how-people-watch-tv-online/

http://blog.nielsen.com/nielsenwire/mediauniverse/

http://techcrunch.com/2012/01/12/hulus-2011-revenue-grew-60-percent-to-420m-will-invest-500m-in-new-content-this-year/

http://blog.nielsen.com/nielsenwire/online_mobile/what-netflix-and-hulu-users-are-watching-and-how/

http://www.ifpi.org/content/library/DMR2012_key_facts_and_figures.pdf

http://www.ifpi.org/content/library/DMR2011.pdf

http://techland.time.com/2011/04/12/study-more-people-watch-music-on-youtube-than-download-it/

http://www.statisticbrain.com/pandora-radio-statistics/

http://www.statista.com/statistics/190989/active-users-of-music-streaming-service-pandora-since-2009/

4 Sound Recording and Popular Music

1. Thom Yorke, "David Byrne and Thom Yorke on the Real Value of Music," *Wired,* December 18, 2007, http://www.wired.com/entertainment/music/magazine/16-01/ff_yorke.

2. Greg Kot, "1.2 Million Downloads Reported for Radiohead's 'In Rainbows,' a Collection of Chilling Love Songs," ChicagoTribune.com, October 12, 2007, http://leisureblogs.chicagotribune.com/turn_it_up/2007/10/12-million-down.html.

3. Andrew Lipsman, "Radiohead Redux," ComScore, February 12, 2008, http://www.comscore.com/mt/mt-search.cgi?tag=Radiohead&blog_id=2.

4. ComScore, "For Radiohead Fans, Does 'Free' + 'Download' = 'Freeload'?"

November 5, 2007, http://www.comscore.com/press/release.asp?press=1883.

5. Glenn Peoples, "Singer Amanda Palmer Raises Record-Breaking $379K in Almost Two Days via Kickstarter," *Hollywood Reporter,* May 3, 2012, http://www.hollywoodreporter.com/news/amanda-palmer-kickstarter-new-album-319893.

6. "Amanda Palmer: The New Record, Art Book, and Tour," April 30, 2012, http://www.kickstarter.com/projects/amandapalmer/amanda-palmer-the-new-record-art-book-and-tour.

7. First Sounds, http://www.firstsounds.org/.

8. Thomas Edison, quoted in Marshall McLuhan, *Understanding Media* (New York: McGraw-Hill, 1964), 276.

9. Mark Coleman, *Playback: From the Victrola to MP3* (Cambridge, Mass.: Da Capo Press, 2003).

10. Shawn Fanning, quoted in Steven Levy, "The Noisy War over Napster," *Newsweek,* June 5, 2000, p. 46.

11. Ethan Smith, "Limewire Found to Infringe Copyrights," *Wall Street Journal,* May 12, 2010, http://online.wsj.com/article/SB10001424052748704247904575240572654422514.html.

12. See Bruce Tucker, "'Tell Tchaikovsky the News': Postmodernism, Popular Culture and the Emergence of Rock 'n' Roll," *Black Music Research Journal* 9(2) (Fall 1989): 280.

13. Robert Palmer, *Deep Blues: A Musical and Cultural History of the Mississippi Delta* (New York: Penguin, 1982), 15.

14. LeRoi Jones, *Blues People* (New York: Morrow Quill, 1963), 168.

15. Mick Jagger, quoted in Jann S. Wenner, "Jagger Remembers," *Rolling Stone,* December 14, 1995, p. 66.

16. Little Richard, quoted in Charles White, *The Life and Times of Little Richard: The Quasar of Rock* (New York: Harmony Books, 1984), 65-66.

17. Quoted in Dave Marsh and James Bernard, *The New Book of Rock Lists* (New York: Fireside, 1994), 15.

18. Tucker, "'Tell Tchaikovsky the News,'" 287.

19. See Gerri Hershey, *Nowhere to Run: The Story of Soul Music* (New York: Penguin Books, 1984).

20. Ken Tucker, quoted in Ward, Stokes, and Tucker, *Rock of Ages: The Rolling Stone History of Rock and Roll* (New York: Simon & Schuster, 1986), 521.

21. Stephen Thomas Erlewine, "Nirvana," in Michael Erlewine, ed., *All Music Guide: The Best CDs, Albums, & Tapes,* 2nd ed. (San Francisco: Miller Freeman Books, 1994), 233.

22. See RIAA, "2011 Year-End Shipment Statistics," http://riaa.org/keystatistics.php?content_selector=2008-2009-U.S-Shipment-Numbers; and IFPI; "Digital Music Report 2012," www.ifpi.org/content/library/DMR2012.pdf.

23. Ed Christman, "iTunes On Top, Again," Retail Track, *Billboard,* May 12, 2012, 8.

24. Alex Pham, "The Black Keys Black Out Spotify, MOG, Rdio and Rhapsody," *Los Angeles Times,* December 7, 2011, http://latimesblogs.latimes.com/music_blog/2011/12/the-black-keys-latest-album-el-camino-is-out-everywhere-except-on-spotify-rdio-and-rhapsody-the-bands-decision-fi.html.

25. Alex Pham, "Nielsen: No Evidence of On-Demand Music Streams Hurting Download Sales," *Los Angeles Times,* March 14, 2012, http://latimesblogs.latimes.com/entertainmentnewsbuzz/2012/03/nielsen-on-demand-streams-download-sales.html.

26. International Federation of the Phonographic Industry, "Digital Music Report 2012," www.ifpi.org/content/library/DMR2012.pdf.

27. Estimates for "Dividing the Profits" are based on data from Steve Knopper, "The New Economics of the Music Industry," *Rolling Stone*, October 25, 2011, http://www.rollingstone.com/music/news/the-new-economics-of-the-music-industry-20111025.

28. Jeff Leeds, "The Net Is a Boon for Indie Labels," *New York Times*, December 27, 2005, p. E1.

29. Courtney Harding, "Owl City Soars from Parents' Basement to Chart Peak," *Reuters*, January 22, 2010, http://www.reuters.com/article/2010/01/23/industry-us-owlcity-idUSTRE60M0EH20100123.

30. Nat Hentoff, "Many Dreams Fueled Long Development of U.S. Music," *Milwaukee Journal*/United Press International, February 26, 1978, p. 2.

WHAT APPLE OWNS   What Does This Mean?, p. 146

1. Henry Blodget, "15 Amazing Facts about Apple," *Business Insider*, October 28, 2010, http://www.businessinsider.com/15-amazing-facts-about-apple-2010-10. See also, Stephanie Buck, "Apple by the Numbers," infographic, *Mashable*, http://mashable.com/2012/05/22/apple-by-the-numbers-infographic/.

2. David Segal, "Apple's Retail Army, Long on Loyalty but Short on Pay," *New York Times*, June 23, 2012, http://www.nytimes.com/2012/06/24/business/apple-store-workers-loyal-but-short-on-pay.html.

3. Economix Editors, "The iEconomy: How Much Do Foxconn Workers Make?" *New York Times*, February 24, 2012, http://economix.blogs.nytimes.com/2012/02/24/the-ieconomy-how-much-do-foxconn-workers-make/.

4. Donald Melanson, "Apple: 16 Billion iTunes Songs Downloaded, 300 Million iPods Sold," *Engadget*, October 4, 2011, http://www.engadget.com/2011/10/04/apple-16-billion-itunes-songs-downloaded-300-million-ipods-sol/.

5. Charles Cooper, "Apple's Cook: 172 million 'Post-PC' Devices in the Last Year," *CNET*, March 7, 2012, http://news.cnet.com/8301-13579_3-57392567-37/apples-cook-172-million-post-pc-devices-in-the-last-year/.

6. Chris Velazco, "Android and iOS Still Lead in Smartphone Market Share, but the Race for Third Rages On," TechCrunch, July 12, 2012, http://techcrunch.com/2012/07/12/android-and-ios-still-lead-in-smartphone-market-share-but-the-race-for-third-rages-on/. See also Nick Wingfield and Nick Bilton, "As Tablet Race Heats Up, Apple May Try Smaller Device," *New York Times*, July 15, 2012, http://www.nytimes.com/2012/07/16/technology/apple-may-meet-tablet-competition-with-smaller-ipad.html.

7. Apple Press Info, "Apple's App Store Downloads Top 25 Billion," Apple.com, March 5, 2012, http://www.apple.com/pr/library/2012/03/05/Apples-App-Store-Downloads-Top-25-Billion.html.

8. Buck, "Apple by the Numbers."

⑤ Popular Radio and the Origins of Broadcasting

1. Tom Lewis, *Empire of the Air: The Men Who Made Radio* (New York: HarperCollins, 1991), 181.

2. Captain Linwood S. Howeth, USN (Retired), *History of Communications-Electronics in the United States Navy* (Washington, D.C.: Government Printing Office, 1963), http://earlyradiohistory.us/1963hw.htm.

3. Margaret Cheney, *Tesla: Man out of Time* (New York: Touchstone, 2001).

4. William J. Broad, "Tesla, a Bizarre Genius, Regains Aura of Greatness," *New York Times*, August 28, 1984, http://query.nytimes.com/gst/fullpage.html?res=9400E4DD1038F93BA1575BC0A962948260&sec=health&spon=&partner=permalink&exprod=permalink.

5. Michael Pupin, "Objections Entered to Court's Decision," *New York Times*, June 10, 1934, E5.

6. Lewis, *Empire of the Air*, 73.

7. For a full discussion of early broadcast history and the formation of RCA, see Eric Barnouw, *Tube of Plenty* (New York: Oxford University Press, 1982); Susan Douglas, *Inventing American Broadcasting, 1899-1922* (Baltimore: Johns Hopkins University Press, 1987); and Christopher Sterling and John Kitross, *Stay Tuned: A Concise History of American Broadcasting* (Belmont, Calif.: Wadsworth, 1990).

8. See Jefferson Cowie, *Capital Moves: RCA's Seventy-Year Quest for Cheap Labor* (New York: New Press, 2001).

9. Robert W. McChesney, *Telecommunications, Mass Media & Democracy: The Battle for Control of U.S. Broadcasting, 1928-1935* (New York: Oxford University Press, 1994).

10. Michele Hilmes, *Radio Voices: American Broadcasting, 1922-1952* (Minneapolis: University of Minnesota Press, 1997).

11. "Amos 'n' Andy Show," Museum of Broadcast Communications, http://www.museum.tv/archives/etv/A/htmlA/amosnandy/amosnandy.htm.

12. Arbitron, "Radio Today: How America Listens to Radio," 2011 ed., http://www.arbitron.com/home/radiotoday.htm.

13. Arbitron, "The Infinite Dial 2010: Digital Platforms and the Future of Radio," June 4, 2010, www.arbitron.com.

14. Ed Christman, "RIAA, Pandora, NARAS, NAB Square Off on Capitol Hill," Billboard.biz, June 7, 2012, http://www.billboard.biz/bbbiz/industry/legal-and-management/riaa-pandora-naras-nab-square-off-on-capitol-1007257152.story.

15. Ibid.

16. National Association of Broadcasters, "Equipping Mobile Phones with Broadcast Radio Capability for Emergency Preparedness Additional Resources," accessed July 22, 2012, http://www.nab.org/advocacy/issueResources.asp?id=2354&issueID=1082.

17. Radio Advertising Bureau, *Why Radio Fact Sheets*, 2012, http://www.rab.com/whyradio/RadioFacts.cfm.

18. Radio Advertising Bureau, "Radio Revenue Trends," accessed July 22, 2012, http://www.rab.com/public/pr/yearly.cfm.

19. Federal Communications Commission, "Broadcast Station Totals," June 30, 2012, http://www.fcc.gov/document/broadcast-station-totals-june-30-2012.

20. Peter DiCola, "False Premises, False Promises: A Quantitative History of Ownership Consolidation in the Radio Industry," Future of Music Coalition, December 13, 2006, http://futureofmusic.org/article/research/false-premises-false-promises.

21. "Statement of FCC Chairman William E. Kennard on Low Power FM Radio Initiative," March 27, 2000, http://www.fcc.gov/Speeches/Kennard/Statements/2000/stwek024.html.

PAST-PRESENT-FUTURE   Radio, p. 157

1. Kathleen Miles, "Pandora Is Number One Radio Station in LA, According to Surprising New Report," *Huffington Post*, April 25, 2012, http://www.huffingtonpost.com/2012/04/25/pandora-number-one-la_n_1453185.html.

◢ **GLOBAL VILLAGE   Radio Mogadishu, p. 182**

1. Reporters Without Borders, "Radio Journalist Slain by Gunmen in Mogadishu," May 5, 2010, http://en.rsf.org/somalie-radio-journalist-slain-by-gunmen-05-05-2010,37392.html.

2. Mohammed Ibrahim, "Somali Radio Stations Halt Music," *New York Times*, April 13, 2010, http://www.nytimes.com/2010/04/14/world/africa/14somalia.html.

3. Jeffrey Gettleman, "A Guiding Voice amid the Ruins of a Capital City," *New York Times*, March 29, 2010, http://www.nytimes.com/2010/03/30/world/africa/30mogadishu.html.

4. Patrick Jackson, "Somali Anger at Threat to Music," *BBC*, April 7, 2010, http://news.bbc.co.uk/2/hi/africa/8604830.stm.

WHAT CLEAR CHANNEL OWNS What Does This Mean?, p. 188

1. All data, unless noted otherwise, obtained from the Clear Channel Communications, Inc., 2011 form 10-K annual report to the Securities and Exchange Commission.
2. "Company Backgrounder," Premiere Networks, accessed August 18, 2012, http://premiereradio.com/pages/corporate/about.html.
3. "Welcome to Katz," Katz Media Group, accessed August 18, 2012, http://www.katz-media.com/.

6 Television and Cable: The Power of Visual Culture

1. Amanda Kondology, "'ABC World News with Diane Sawyer' Closes Total Viewing Gap with 'NBC Nightly News' by 3%," *TV by the Numbers*, June 5, 2012, http://tvbythenumbers.zap2it.com/2012/06/05/abc-world-news-with-diane-sawyer-closes-total-viewing-gap-with-nbc-nightly-news-by-3/136864/.
2. John Seabrook, "Streaming Dreams: YouTube Turns Pro," *New Yorker*, January 16, 2012, http://www.newyorker.com/reporting/2012/01/16/120116fa_fact_seabrook.
3. See Austin Carr, "Netflix Spending up to $100,000 per Episode of Primetime TV," *Fast Company*, December 2, 2010, http://www.fastcompany.com/1706933/netflix-spending-up-to-100000-per-episode-of-primetime-tv.
4. Michael Liedtke, "Netflix Q1 2012: Millions of New Subscribers Added," *Huffington Post*, April 23, 2012, http://www.huffingtonpost.com/2012/04/23/netflix-q1-2012_n_1447123.html.
5. See Edmund Lee, "Netflix CEO Reed Hastings: We Won't Compete with Cable TV," *Advertising Age*, May 4, 2011, http://adage.com/article/mediaworks/netflix-ceo-reed-hastings-compete-cable-tv/227364/.
6. See Sam Schechner, "Comcast Takes Aim at Netflix," *Wall Street Journal*, February 22, 2012, http://online.wsj.com/article/SB10001424052970204909104577237321153043092.html.
7. Richard Huff, "TV and Web Are Hot Ratings Couple," *Daily News* [New York], March 20, 2010, TV sec., p. 62.
8. See "Online Video Usage Up 45%," *NielsenWire*, February 11, 2011, http://blog.nielsen.com/nielsenwire/online_mobile/january-2011-online-video-usage-up-45/.
9. J. Fred MacDonald, *One Nation under Television: The Rise and Decline of Network TV* (Chicago: Nelson-Hall Publishers, 1994), 70.
10. Edgar Bergen, quoted in MacDonald, *One Nation under Television*, 78.
11. See Horace Newcomb, *TV: The Most Popular Art* (Garden City, N.Y.: Anchor Books, 1974), 31, 39.
12. Ibid., 35.
13. Association of Public Television Stations (APTS), "Congress Provides Critical Funding Increases to Public Broadcasting for FY2010," December 15, 2009, http://www.apts.org/news/FY2010Funding.cfm.
14. See Elizabeth Jensen, "PBS Plans Promotional Breaks within Programs," *New York Times*, May 31, 2011, http://www.nytimes.com/2011/05/39/business/media/31adco.html.
15. See Charles McGrath, "Is PBS Still Necessary?" *New York Times*, February 17, 2008, sec. 2, pp. 1, 23.
16. John Boland quoted in Katy June-Friesen, "Surge of Channels . . . Depress PBS Ratings," *Current.org*, December 8, 2008, http://www.current.org/audience/aud0822pbs.shtml.
17. MacDonald, *One Nation under Television*, 181.

18. United States v. Midwest Video Corp., 440 U.S. 689 (1979).
19. Federal Communications Commission, "Report on Cable Industry Prices," January 16, 2009, http://hraunfoss.fcc.gov/edocs_public/attachmatch/DA-09-53A1.pdf.
20. National Cable and Telecommunication Association, "Operating Metrics," accessed July 12, 2012, http://www.ncta.com/StatsGroup/OperatingMetric.aspx.
21. See Jack Loechner, "TV Advertising Most Influential," *MediaPost, Research Brief*, March 23, 2011, http://www.mediapost.com/publications/article/147033/#axzz2LZB5LCm6.
22. Bill Carter, "Cable TV, the Home of High Drama," *New York Times*, April 5, 2010, pp. B1, B3.
23. Stuart Elliott, "How to Value Ratings with DVR Delay," *New York Times*, February 13, 2006, p. C15.
24. See Josef Adalian, "The 2011-12 TV Season: What We Watched and What We Skipped," Vulture.com, June 21, 2012, www.vulture.com/2012/06/201112-tv-season-by-the-numbers.html.
25. William J. Ray, "Private Enterprise, Privileged Enterprise, or Free Enterprise," accessed February 21, 2012, http://www.glasgow-ky.com/papers/#PrivateEnterprise.
26. Ibid.

PAST-PRESENT-FUTURE Television, p. 195

1. Bill Carter, "As Talent Flees to Cable, Networks Fight Back," *New York Times*, May 13, 2012, http://www.nytimes.com/2012/05/14/business/media/as-talent-flees-to-cable-networks-fight-back.html.

◢ **CASE STUDY** ESPN: Sports and Stories, p. 204

1. See Linda Haugsted, "ESPN's First-Place Finish," *Multichannel News*, March 3, 2008, p. 21.

WHAT NEWS CORP. OWNS What Does This Mean?, p. 232

1. News Corp., *Annual Report 2011*, http://www.newscorp.com.
2. "Fox Takes Season's Adults 18-49 Ratings Title; CBS Tops Viewership," TV by the Numbers, May 24, 2011, http://tvbythenumbers.zap2it.com/2011/05/24/fox-takes-seasons-adults-18-49-ratings-title-cbs-tops-viewership/93788/.
3. Brian Steinberg, "'American Idol,' NFL Duke It Out for Priciest TV Spot," *AdAge*, October 24, 2011, http://adage.com/article/media/chart-american-idol-nfl-duke-priciest-tv-spot/230547/.
4. Brian Stelter, "News Corporation Sells MySpace for $35 Million," *Media Decoder, New York Times*, June 29, 2011, http://mediadecoder.blogs.nytimes.com/2011/06/29/news-corp-sells-myspace-to-specific-media-for-35-million/.

7 Movies and the Impact of Images

1. Roger Ebert, "Citizen Kane (1941)," May 24, 1998, http://rogerebert.suntimes.com/apps/pbcs.dll/article?AID=/19980524/reviews08/401010334/1023.
2. Roger Ebert, "Avatar," December 11, 2009, http://rogerebert.suntimes.com/apps/pbcs.dll/article?AID=/20091211/REVIEWS/912119998.
3. John Cawelti, *Adventure, Mystery, and Romance: Formula Stories as Art and Popular Culture* (Chicago: University of Chicago Press, 1976), 35.
4. See Charles Musser, *The Emergence of Cinema: The American Screen to 1907* (New York: Scribner's, 1991).
5. Douglas Gomery, *Shared Pleasures: A History of Movie Presentation in the United States* (Madison: University of Wisconsin Press, 1992), 18.
6. Douglas Gomery, *Movie History: A Survey* (Belmont, Calif.: Wadsworth, 1991), 167.

7. See Cawelti, *Adventure, Mystery, and Romance,* 80-98.

8. See Barbara Koenig Quart, *Women Directors: The Emergence of a New Cinema* (New York: Praeger, 1988).

9. See Gomery, *Shared Pleasures,* 171-180.

10. Ismail Merchant, "Kitschy as Ever, Hollywood Is Branching Out," *New York Times,* November 22, 1998, sec. 2, pp. 15, 30.

11. See Eric Barnouw, *Tube of Plenty: The Evolution of American Television,* rev. ed. (New York: Oxford University Press, 1982), 108-109.

12. See Douglas Gomery, "Who Killed Hollywood?" *Wilson Quarterly* (Summer 1991): 106-112.

13. Motion Picture Association of America, "Theatrical Market Statistics U.S./Canada," 2011, http://www.mpaa.org/resources.

14. Mike Snider, "Blu-ray Grows, but DVD Slide Nips Home Video Sales," *USA Today,* January 9, 2012, http://www.usatoday.com/tech/news/story/2012-01-10/blu-ray-sales-2011/52473310/1.

15. Motion Picture Association of America, "Theatrical Market Statistics 2011."

16. Jeff Gammage, "Digital or Diet: Theaters Scramble for Pricey New Projectors," *Philadelphia Inquirer,* January 13, 2013, p. A01.

17. Julianne Pepitone, "Americans Now Watch More Online Movies than DVDs," *CNN/Money,* March 22, 2012, http://money.cnn.com/2012/03/22/technology/streaming-movie-sales/index.htm.

18. Jake Coyle, "Clicking through the Wild West of Video-on-Demand," *Associated Press,* March 29, 2012, http://www.businessweek.com/ap/2012-03/D9TQAOI00.htm.

19. Brooks Barnes, "How 'Hunger Games' Built Up Must-See Fever," *New York Times,* March 18, 2012, http://www.nytimes.com/2012/03/19/business/media/how-hunger-games-built-up-must-see-fever.html.

20. David S. Cohen, "Academy to Preserve Digital Content," *Variety,* August 3, 2007, http://www.variety.com/article/VR1117969687.html.

21. David Thorburn, "Television as an Aesthetic Medium," *Critical Studies in Mass Communication* (June 1987): 168.

◢ CASE STUDY Breaking through Hollywood's Race Barrier, p. 252

1. Douglas Gomery, *Shared Pleasures: A History of Movie Presentation in the United States* (Madison: University of Wisconsin Press, 1992), 155-170.

2. Felicia R. Lee, "To Blacks, Precious Is 'Demeaned' or 'Angelic,'" *New York Times,* November 20, 2009, http://www.nytimes.com/2009/11/21/movies/21precious.html. Also see Mary Mitchell, "Precious Little Patience for Blaxploitation; Degradation of Black Folks Not My Idea of Entertainment," *Chicago Sun-Times,* December 17, 2009, p. 12.

WHAT DISNEY OWNS What Does This Mean?, p. 266

1. All data were obtained from the Walt Disney Company Annual Report, 2011, http://thewaltdisneycompany.com/investors/financial-information/annual-report; Walt Disney Company 2011 Form 10-K, Annual Report to the Securities and Exchange Commission.

Part 3 Opener

Infographic sources:

http://www.infographicsshowcase.com/the-influential-power-of-print-infographic/

http://www.journalism.org/analysis_report/tablet/

Jenkins Group:

http://libraries.pewinternet.org/2012/04/04/the-rise-of-e-reading/

http://stateofthemedia.org/2012/digital-news-gains-audience-but-loses-more-ground-in-chase-for-revenue/digital-by-the-numbers/

http://www.economistgroup.com/leanback/new-business-models/12-stats-that-matter-to-digital-publishing/

http://www.adweek.com/news/press/digital-circ-still-tiny-142570

http://accessabc.wordpress.com/2012/08/07/the-top-25-u-s-consumer-magazines-for-the-first-half-of-2012/

8 Newspapers: The Rise and Decline of Modern Journalism

1. See Jeremy Peters and Brian Stelter, "News Corporation Introduces the Daily, a Digital-Only Newspaper," *New York Times,* February 2, 2011, http://www.nytimes.com/2011/02/03/business/media/03daily.html.

2. Murdoch quoted in Damon Kiesow, "First Issue of the *Daily* Reveals Magazine Look, Tabloid Feel & iPad Interactivity," Poynter Institute, February 2, 2011, http://www.poynter.org/latest-news/media-lab/mobile-media/117383/first-issue-of-the-daily-reveals-magazine-look-tabloid-feel-ipad-interactivity.

3. Ibid.

4. See Adam Gabbatt, "*The Daily* Tablet Newspaper's Future in Doubt after Huge First Year Losses," *Guardian,* July 13, 2012, http://www.guardian.co.uk/world/2012/jul/13/the-daily-future-doubt-losses.

5. Joshua Benton, "Who Is the *Daily* Trying to Reach?" Nieman Journalism Lab, February 2011, http://www.niemanlab.org/2011/02/who-is-the-daily-trying-to-reach.

6. Pew Research Center's Project for Excellence in Journalism, *State of the News Media 2012: Executive Summary,* accessed August 15, 2012, http://www.journalism.org.

7. See Kay Mills, *A Place in the News: From the Women's Pages to the Front Page* (New York: Dodd, Mead, 1988).

8. Piers Brendon, *The Life and Death of the Press Barons* (New York: Atheneum, 1983), 136.

9. William Randolph Hearst, quoted in Brendon, *The Life and Death of the Press Barons,* 134.

10. Michael Schudson, *Discovering the News: A Social History of American Newspapers* (New York: Basic Books, 1978), 23.

11. See David T. Z. Mindich, "Edwin M. Stanton, the Inverted Pyramid, and Information Control," *Journalism Monographs* 140 (August 1993).

12. John C. Merrill, "Objectivity: An Attitude," in Merrill and Ralph L. Lowenstein, eds., *Media, Messages and Men* (New York: David McKay, 1971), 240.

13. Roy Peter Clark, "A New Shape for the News," *Washington Journalism Review* (March 1984): 47.

14. Curtis D. MacDougall, *The Press and Its Problems* (Dubuque: William C. Brown, 1964), 143, 189.

15. See Edwin Emery, *The Press and America: An Interpretative History of the Mass Media,* 3rd ed. (Englewood Cliffs, N.J.: Prentice-Hall, 1972), 562.

16. Walter Lippmann, *Liberty and the News* (New York: Harcourt, Brace and Howe, 1920), 92.

17. Tom Wolfe, quoted in Leonard W. Robinson, "The New Journalism: A Panel Discussion," in Ronald Weber, ed., *The Reporter as Artist: A Look at the New Journalism Controversy* (New York: Hastings House, 1974), 67. See also Tom Wolfe and E. E. Johnson, eds., *The New Journalism* (New York: Harper & Row, 1973).

18. Tom Wicker, *On Press* (New York: Viking, 1978), 3-5.

19. Jack Newfield, "The 'Truth' about Objectivity and the New Journalism," in Charles C. Flippen, ed., *Liberating the Media* (Washington, D.C.: Acropolis Books, 1973), 63-64.

20. Abramson, quoted in Nat Ives, "Abramson and Keller, NYT's Incoming and Outgoing Top Editors, Talk Challenges and Changes," June 2, 2011, http://adage.com/article/mediaworks/q-a-york-times-jill-abramson-bill-keller/227928/.

21. See Newspaper Association of America, April 25, 2006, http://www.naa.org. For updates, see also Pew Research Center's Project for Excellence in Journalism, *State of the News Media 2009*, http://www.journalism.org. See also Richard Pérez-Peña, "Newspaper Circulation Falls by More than 10%," *New York Times*, October 27, 2009, p. B3.

22. See Sreenath Sreenivasan, "As Mainstream Papers Struggle, the Ethnic Press Is Thriving," *New York Times*, July 22, 1996, p. C7.

23. "Ethnic: Summary Essay," *State of the News Media 2010*, Pew Research Center's Project for Excellence in Journalism, accessed June 8, 2010, http://www.stateofthemedia.org/2010/ethnic_summary_essay.php.

24. Ibid.

25. See Barbara K. Henritze, *Bibliographic Checklist of American Newspapers* (Baltimore: Clearfield, 2009).

26. April Turner, "Black Journalists Ranks Cut by Nearly 1,000 in Past Decade," National Association of Black Journalists newsletter, April 4, 2012, http://www.nabj.org/news/88558.

27. Pamela Newkirk, "The Not-So-Great Migration," *Columbia Journalism Review*, May-June 2011, http://www.cjr.org/feature/the_not-so-great_migration.php.

28. Turner, "Black Journalists Ranks Cut by Nearly 1,000 in Past Decade."

29. Special thanks to Mary Lamonica and her students at New Mexico State University.

30. Pew Research Center's Project for Excellence in Journalism, *State of the News Media 2010*, http://www.stateofthenewsmedia.org/2010/.

31. See "Table O," American Society of News Editors 2011 Newsroom Census.

32. Pew Research Center's Project for Excellence in Journalism, *State of the News Media 2010*, http://www.stateofthenewsmedia.org/2010/. See also United States Census 2010.

33. Wil Cruz, "The New *New Yorker*: Ethnic Media Fill the Void," *Newsday*, June 26, 2002, p. A25.

34. See Chinese Media Guide, "About *Chinese Daily News*," http://www.chineseadvertisingagencies.com/mediaguide/Chinese-Daily-News.html.

35. American Society of News Editors, "Newsroom up Slightly, Minority Numbers Plunge for Third Straight Year," ASNE newsletter, April 7, 2011, http://www.asne.org/Aricle_View/articleid/1788.

36. Pew Research Center Publications, "The New Face of Washington's Press Corps," February 11, 2009, http://pewresearch.org/pubs/1115/washington-press-corps-study.

37. "Decline in Newsroom Jobs Slows," American Society of News Editors, accessed June 8, 2010, http://www.asne.org.

38. Rick Edmonds, "ASNE Newsroom Census Total Reflects Decline in Traditional Journalism Jobs," Poynter.org, May 6, 2011, http://www.poynter.org/latest-news/business-news/the-biz-blog/130184.

39. Mallary Jean Tenore, "New ASNE Figures Show Percentage of Minorities in Newspaper Newsrooms Continue to Decline," Poynter.org, April 4, 2012, http://www.poynter.org/latest-news/mediwire/169006.

40. See Mac Ryan, "Amid Industry Cuts, Warren Buffett Says He Is Looking to Buy More Newspapers," Forbes.com, May 24, 2012, http://www.forbes.com/sites/ryanmac/2012/05/24; and Christine Haughney, "Newspaper Work, with Warren Buffett as Boss," *New York Times*, June 17, 2012, http://www.nytimes.com/2012/06/18/business/media.

41. See Philip Meyer, "Learning to Love Lower Profits," *American Journalism Review* (December 1995): 40-44.

42. "Newspapers: Summary Essay," *State of the News Media 2010*.

43. Pew Research Center's Project for Excellence in Journalism, *State of the News Media 2012*, http://www.stateofthenewsmedia.org/2012/.

44. World Association of Newspapers, "Newspaper Circulation Grows Despite Economic Downturn," May 27, 2009, http://www.wan-press.org/article18148.html.

45. World Association of Newspapers, accessed June 16, 2010, http://www.wan-press.org.

46. "Newspapers: Summary Essay," *State of the News Media 2010*.

47. Ibid.

48. "Anyone with a Modem Can Report on the World," Liberty Round Table Library Essays, June 2, 1998, address before the National Press Club, http://www.libertyroundtable.org/library/essay.drudge.html.

49. Joshua Micah Marshall, quoted in Noam Cohen, "Blogger, Sans Pajamas, Rakes Muck and a Prize," *New York Times*, February 25, 2008, http://www.nytimes.com.

50. Richard Pérez-Peña, "Newspaper Ad Revenue Could Fall as Much as 30%," *New York Times*, April 15, 2009, p. B3.

51. See "Gannett Newspapers and Yahoo Create Local Advertising Partnership," Chicago Press Release Services, July 19, 2010, http://chicagopressrelease.com/technology/gannett-newspapers-and-yahoo; Evan Hessel, "Yahoo!'s Dangerous Newspaper Deal?" Forbes.com, June 6, 2009, http://www.forbes.com/2009/06/22/advertising-newspapers-internet-business-media-yahoo; and Kate Kaye, "Media General Expands Yahoo Partnership to TV-Only Markets," Clickz Marketing News, June 11, 2010, http://www.clickz.com/clickz/news/1721928/media-general-xpands-yahoo-partnership.

52. D. M. Levine, "Small Papers Lead the Way on Paywall," *Adweek*, June 3, 2011, http://www.adweek.com/news/press/small-papers-lead-the-way.

53. Seth Fiegerman, "*New York Times* Digital Subscription Growth Slows Ad Revenue Decline," Mashable, accessed February 7, 2013, http://www.mashable.com/2013/02/07/new-york-times-digital-subscibers-2.

54. "Newspapers: Building Digital Revenues Proves Painfully Slow," Pew Research Center's Project for Excellence in Journalism, *State of the News Media 2012*, http://stateofthemedia.org/2012/newspapers-building-digital-revenues-proves-painfully-slow/.

55. Leonard Downie and Michael Schudson, "The Reconstruction of American Journalism," Columbia Journalism Report, October 20, 2009, pp. 77-91. See either http://www.columbiajournalismreport.org or http://www.cjr.org for the full report. All quoted material below is from the report. See also Leonard Downie Jr. and Michael Schudson, "Finding a New Model for News Reporting," *Washington Post*, October 19, 2009, http://www.washingtonpost.com.

56. Brian Deagon, "You, Reporting Live: Citizen Journalism Relies on Audience; Now, Everyone's a Stringer . . . ," *Investor's Business Daily*, March 31, 2008, p. A4.

57. "Special Report: Community Journalism," *The State of the News Media 2010*, accessed July 2, 2010, http://www.stateofthemedia.org/2010/specialreports_community_journalism.php.

58. Committee to Protect Journalists, accessed August 2012, http://www.cpj.org/killed/.

59. Marc Santora and Bill Carter, "War in Iraq Becomes the Deadliest Assignment for Journalists in Modern Times," *New York Times*, May 30, 2006, p. A10.

60. See Matthew Ingram, "What Will Save AOL: *Huffington Post* or Patch?" Gigaom, June 9, 2011, http://www.gigaom.com/2011/06/09/which-will-save-aol-huffington-post-or-patch.

61. John Carroll, "News War, Part 3," *Frontline*, PBS, February 27, 2007, http://www.pbs.org/wgbh/pages/frontline/newswar/etc/script3.html.

◢ CASE STUDY   Alternative Journalism: Dorothy Day and I. F. Stone, p. 297

1. I. F. Stone, quoted in Jack Lule, "I. F. Stone: Professional Excellence in Raising Hell," *QS News* (Summer 1989): 3.

WHAT GANNETT OWNS   What Does This Mean?, p. 302

1. Gannett Company Annual Report, 2010, accessed July 15, 2011, http://phx.corporate-ir.net/External.File?item=UGFyZW50SUQ9NDE5MTAOfENoaWxkSUQ9NDMyMjc5fFR5cGU9MQ==&t=1, p. 1.

2. Ibid, p. 4.

3. Ibid, p. 7.

4. Ibid, p. 3.

⑨ **Magazines in the Age of Specialization**

1. Jennifer Benjamin, "How Cosmo Changed the World," accessed August 13, 2012, http://www.cosmopolitan.com/magazine/about-us_how-cosmo-changed-the-world.

2. Sammye Johnson, "Promoting Easy Sex without the Intimacy: *Maxim* and *Cosmopolitan* Cover Lines and Cover Images," in Mary-Lou Galician and Debra L. Merskin, eds., *Critical Thinking about Sex, Love, and Romance in the Mass Media* (Mahwah, N.J.: Erlbaum, 2007), 55-74.

3. Karen S. H. Roggenkamp, "'Dignified Sensationalism': Elizabeth Bisland, *Cosmopolitan*, and Trips around the World," paper presented at "Writing the Journey: A Conference on American, British, and Anglophone Writers and Writing," University of Pennsylvania, June 10-13, 1999, http://faculty.tamu-commerce.edu/kroggenkamp/bisland.html.

4. John Tebbel and Mary Ellen Zuckerman, *The Magazine in America, 1741-1990* (New York: Oxford University Press, 1991), 116.

5. See Theodore Peterson, *Magazines in the Twentieth Century* (Urbana: University of Illinois Press, 1964), 5.

6. See Richard Ohmann, *Selling Culture: Magazines, Markets, and Class at the Turn of the Century* (New York: Verso, 1996).

7. See Peterson, *Magazines*, 5.

8. Magazine Publishers of America, "The Number of Magazine Web Sites Has Increased 30%" *Magazine Media Factbook 2011-12*, http://www.magazine.org/advertising/magazine-media-factbook/.

9. Generoso Pope, quoted in William H. Taft, *American Magazines for the 1980s* (New York: Hastings House, 1982), 226-227.

10. See S. Elizabeth Bird, *For Enquiring Minds: A Cultural Study of Supermarket Tabloids* (Knoxville: University of Tennessee Press, 1992), 24.

11. See Robin Pogrebin, "The Number of Ad Pages Does Not Make the Magazine," *New York Times*, August 26, 1996, p. C1.

12. See Gloria Steinem, "Sex, Lies and Advertising," *Ms.* (July-August 1990): 18-28.

13. Jason Pontin "Why Publishers Don't Like Apps," *Technology Review*, May 7, 2012, http://www.technologyreview.com/news/427785/why-publishers-dont-like-apps/.

◢ PAST-PRESENT-FUTURE   Magazines, p. 315

1. Christine Haughney, "Women's Magazines Lead Overall Decline in Newsstand Sales," *New York Times*, August 7, 2012, http://mediadecoder.blog.nytimes.com/2012/08/07/womens-magazines-lead-overall-decline-in-newsstand-sales/.

2. Katerina-Eva Matsa, Jane Sasseen, and Amy Mitchell, "Magazines: Are Hopes for Tablets Overdone?" *State of the News Media 2012*, Pew Research Center's Project for Excellence in Journalism, http://stateofthemedia.org/2012/magazines-are-hopes-for-tablets-overdone/.

◢ CASE STUDY   The Evolution of Photojournalism, p. 324

1. Carrie Melgao, "Ralph Lauren Model Filippa Hamilton: I Was Fired Because I Was Too Fat!" *New York Daily News*, October 14, 2009, http://www.nydailynews.com/lifestyle/fashion/2009/10/14/2009-10-14_model_fired_for_being_too_fat.html#ixzzOriJa9skc.

2. Ken Harris, quoted in Jesse Epstein, "Sex, Lies, and Photoshop," *New York Times*, March 8, 2009, http://video.nytimes.com/video/2009/03/09/opinion/1194838469575/sex-lies-and-photoshop.html.

◢ TRACKING TECHNOLOGY   The New "Touch" of Magazines, p. 330

1. Steve Smith, "Zinio Brings Digital Newsstand to iPhone," *MinOnline*, January 12, 2010, http://www.minonline.com/news/Zinio-Brings-Digital-Newsstand-to-iPhone_13188.html.

2. Chris Anderson, "The Wired Tablet App: A Video Demonstration," *Wired.com*, accessed July 2, 2010, http://www.wired.com/epicenter/2010/02/the-wired-ipad-app-a-video-demonstration/.

3. Steve Meyers, "Wenner: Publishers' Rush to iPad Is 'Sheer Insanity and Insecurity and Fear,'" Poynter.org, May 30, 2011, http://www.poynter.org/latest-news/romenesko/134162/wenner-publishers-rush-to-ipad-is-sheer-insanity-and-inscurity-and-fear/.

4. Katerina-Eva Matsa, Jane Sasseen, and Amy Mitchell, "Magazines: Are Hopes for Tablets Overdone?" *State of the News Media 2012*, Pew Research Center's Project for Excellence in Journalism, http://stateofthemedia.org/2012/magazines-are-hopes-for-tablets-overdone/.

5. Jared Keller, "Will Digital Reading Entirely Replace Print?" *Atlantic*, June 24, 2011, http://www.theatlantic.com/technology/archive/2011/06/will-digital-reading-entirely-replace-print/240967.

◢ Media Literacy and the Critical Process   Uncovering American Beauty, p. 334

1. Academy for Eating Disorders, "Academy for Eating Disorders Guidelines for the Fashion Industry," http://www.aedweb.org/public/fashion_guidelines.cfm.

2. Ibid.

WHAT TIME WARNER OWNS   What Does This Mean?, p. 340

1. Time Warner 2011 Annual Report, http://ir.timewarner.com/phoenix.zhtml?c=70972&p=irol-reportsannual, p. 57.

2. Time Inc., "Highlights," accessed August 14, 2012, http://www.timewarner.com/our-content/time-inc/.

3. Time Inc., "Core Statistics," January 2012, http://www.timewarner.com/our-content/time-inc/.

4. Time Inc., "About Us, Core Statistics," accessed July 7, 2010, http://www.timeinc.com/aboutus/.

5. Time Warner, "The Entertainment Leader," April 25, 2012, http://www.timewarner.com/our-content/warner-bros-entertainment/.

6. Ibid.

7. Time Warner, "It's HBO," May 1, 2012, http://www.timewarner.com/our-content/home-box-office/.

8. Time Warner, "Warner Bros. Anti-Piracy Operations," accessed August 14, 2012, http://www.warnerbros.com/studio/divisions/home-entertainment/anti-piracy-operations.html.

10 Books and the Power of Print

1. Josh Hyatt, "Read 'Em and Beep; Electronic Books Coming to a Screen Near You," *Boston Globe*, September 6, 1992, p. 61.

2. Eric Holder, "Attorney General Eric Holder Speaks at the E-Books Press Conference," U.S. Department of Justice, April 22, 2011, http://www.justice.gov/iso/opa/ag/speeches/2012/ag-speech-1204111.html.

3. Claire Cain Miller and Julie Bosman, "E-Books Outsell Print Books at Amazon," *New York Times,* May 19, 2011, http://www.nytimes.com/2011/05/20/technology/20amazon.html.

4. See Elizabeth Eisenstein, *The Printing Press as an Agent of Change* (Cambridge: Cambridge University Press, 1980).

5. See Quentin Reynolds, *The Fiction Factory: From Pulp Row to Quality Street* (New York: Street & Smith/Random House, 1955), 72-74.

6. For a comprehensive historical overview of the publishing industry and the rise of publishing houses, see John A. Tebbel, *A History of Book Publishing in the United States*, 4 vols. (New York: R. R. Bowker, 1972-1981).

7. National Association of College Stores, "Higher Education Retail Market Facts & Figures 2012," http://www.nacs.org/research/Industry Statistics/higheredfactsfigures.aspx.

8. For a historical overview of paperbacks, see Kenneth Davis, *Two-Bit Culture: The Paperbacking of America* (Boston: Houghton Mifflin, 1984).

9. See John P. Dessauer, *Book Publishing: What It Is, What It Does* (New York: R. R. Bowker, 1974), 48.

10. Alison Flood, "Ebook Sales Pass Another Milestone," *Guardian,* April 15, 2011, http://www.guardian.co.uk/books/2011/apr/15/ebook-sales-milestone. See also Laura Hazard Owen, "New Data Provides Deeper Profile of Typical E-Book 'Power Buyer,'" moconews.net, May 23, 2011, http://paidcontent.org./2011/05/23/419-new-data-provides-deeper-profile-of-typical-e-book-power-buyer.

11. "Alice in Wonderland iPad App Reinvents Reading (Video)," *Huffington Post*, April 14, 2010, http://www.huffingtonpost.com/2010/04/14/alice-in-wonderland-ipad_n_537122.html.

12. Bibb Porter, "In Publishing, Bigger Is Better," *New York Times*, March 31, 1998, p. A27.

13. Randy Kennedy, "Cash Up Front," *New York Times,* June 5, 2005, http://nytimes.com/2005/06/05/books/review/05KENN01.html.

14. Jim Milliot, "Tracking the Transition: Bookstats," *Publishers Weekly,* August 12, 2011, http://www.publishersweekly.com/pw/by-topic/industry-news/financial-reporting/article/48348-tracking-the-transition-bookstats.html.

15. Stephanie Clifford and Julie Bosman, "Publishers Look beyond Bookstores," *New York Times*, February 27, 2011, http://www.nytimes.com/2011/02/28/business/28bookstores.html.

16. Motoko Rich and Brad Stone, "Publisher Wins Fight with Amazon over E-Books," *New York Times*, February 1, 2010, p. B1.

17. Steve Wasserman, "The Amazon Effect," *Nation*, May 29, 2012, http://www.thenation.com/article/168125/amazon-effect#.

18. Neal Pollack, "The Case for Self-Publishing," *New York Times*, May 20, 2011, http://www.nytimes.com/2011/05/22/books/review/the-case-for-self-publishing.html. Also see "An Epic Tale of How It All Happened," Amanda Hocking's Blog, August 27, 2010, http://amandahocking.blogspot.com/2010/08/epic-tale-of-how-it-all-happened.html.

19. National Endowment for the Arts, *Reading on the Rise*, January 12, 2009, http://www.arts.gov/research/ReadingonRise.pdf.

20. Alvin Kernan, *The Death of Literature* (New Haven: Yale University Press, 1990).

21. "How We Will Read: Clay Shirky," Findings.com, April 5, 2012, http://blog.findings.com/post/20527246081/how-we-will-read-clay-shirky.

22. Alan Finder, "The Joys and Hazards of Self-Publishing on the Web," *New York Times*, August 15, 2012, http://www.nytimes.com/2012/08/16/technology/personaltech/ins-and-outs-of-publishing-your-book-via-the-web.html.

WHAT AMAZON OWNS   What Does This Mean?, p. 372

1. Amazon.com, "Company Facts, Q2 2012," http://phx.corporate-ir.net/phoenix.zhtml?c=176060&p=irol-factSheet.

2. Amazon.com Inc., Annual Report, 2011, http://www.annualreports.com/Company/1755.

3. Leena Rao, "Amazon: We Sold over 4 Million Kindle Devices This Month; Gifting of E-Books Up 175 Percent," TechCrunch, December 29, 2011, http://techcrunch.com/2011/12/29/amazon-we-sold-over-4-million-kindle-devices-this-month-gifting-of-e-books-up-175-percent/.

4. Amazon.com, Inc. Annual Report, 2011.

5. Ibid.

6. Stephanie Clifford, "Amazon Leaps into High End of the Fashion Pool," *New York Times,* May 7, 2012, http://www.nytimes.com/2012/05/08/business/amazon-plans-its-next-conquest-your-closet.html.

7. "Amazon.com, Inc.," Business Day, *New York Times*, July 26, 2012, http://topics.nytimes.com/top/news/business/companies/amazon_inc/index.html.

Part 4 Opener

Infographic sources:

http://google.client.shareholder.com/investorkit.cfm

http://investor.apple.com/sec.cfm#filings

http://phx.corporate-ir.net/phoenix.zhtml?c=97664&p=irol-reportsannual

http://www.microsoft.com/investor/SEC/default.aspx

http://investor.fb.com/

11 Advertising and Commercial Culture

1. "Mobile Advertising Stats . . . ," mobiThinking.com, June 22, 2011, http://www.mobithinking.com/blog/mobile-advertising-statistics-2011.

2. See Nat Worden, "Web Advertising Eclipsed Newspapers in 2010," *Wall Street Journal*, April 14, 2011, http://online.wsj.com/article/SB10001424052748703551304576261092386405686.html#ixzz1Ov1Xih57.

3. Apple Inc., "Apple to Debut iAds on July 1," June 7, 2010, http://www.apple.com/pr/library/2010/06/07iads.html.

4. David Coursey, "Report: Apple Buying Mobile Ad Company for $275 Million," *PCWorld*, January 5, 2010, http://www.pcworld.com

/businesscenter/article/185884/report_apple_buying_mobile_ad_company_for_275_million.html.

5. Teresa F. Lindeman, "Product Placement Nation: Advertisers Pushing the Boundaries to Bring in More Bucks," *Pittsburgh Post-Gazette*, May 13, 2011, http://www.post-gazette.com/pg/11133/1146175-28-0.stm.

6. Caitlin A. Johnson, "Cutting through Advertising Clutter," *CBS Sunday Morning*, September 16, 2006, http://www.cbsnews.com /stories/2006/09/17/sunday/main2015684.shtml.

7. For a written and pictorial history of early advertising, see Charles Goodrum and Helen Dalrymple, *Advertising in America: The First 200 Years* (New York: Harry N. Abrams, 1990), 31.

8. Michael Schudson, *Advertising: The Uneasy Persuasion* (New York: Basic Books, 1984), 164.

9. Lauren Goode, "Internet Is Set to Overtake Newspapers in Ad Revenue," *Wall Street Journal*, June 15, 2010, http://blogs.wsj.com/digits/2010/06/15 /internet-is-set-to-overtake-newspapers-in-ad-revenue/.

10. "X-Ray Films Hits Target's Bull's-Eye," *Shoot Magazine*, February 6, 2004.

11. Andrew McMains and Noreen O'Leary, "GM Shifts Chevy Biz to Publicis from C-E," *Adweek*, April 23, 2010, http://www.adweek.com /aw/content_display/news/account-activity/e3i091074075f7ed276cf 510b1df8dddbcd.

12. Bettina Fabos, "The Commercialized Web: Challenges for Libraries and Democracy," *Library Trends* 53, no. 4 (Spring 2005): 519-523.

13. Noreen O'Leary, "GroupM: Global Web Ad Spend Up 16 Percent in 2011," *Adweek*, April 9, 2012, http://www.adweek.com/news/advertising -branding/groupmglobal-web-ad-spend-16-percent.

14. Ibid.

15. See Erick Schonfeld, "Cowen: Google's Mobile Ad Revenue Could Surge to $5.8 Million in 2012," TechCrunch, January 21, 2012, http:// techcrunch.com/2012/01/21/cowen-googles-mobile-ad-revenues-could -surge. See also ClickZ, "Facebook IPO Show Ad Revenue Increased 69% in 2011," Search Engine Watch, February 2, 2012.

16. Jack Neff, "Unilever to Double Digital Spending This Year," *Advertising Age*, June 25, 2010, http://adage.com/cannes2010/article?article_ id=144672.

17. Jon Gibs and Sean Bruich, "Advertising Effectiveness: Understanding the Value of a Social Media Impression," April 2010, http://www.iab.net /media/file/NielsenFacebookValueofSocialMediaImpressions.pdf.

18. See Somini Sengupta, "Like It or Not, His Face Is on Ad," *New York Times*, June 1, 2012, p. A1.

19. Leslie Savan, "Op Ad: Sneakers and Nothingness," *Village Voice*, April 2, 1991, p. 43.

20. See Mary Kuntz and Joseph Weber, "The New Hucksterism," *Business Week*, July 1, 1999, 79.

21. Ibid.

22. Schudson, *Advertising*, 210.

23. Eric Pfanner, "Your Brand on TV for a Fee, in Britain," *New York Times*, March 6, 2011, http://www.nytimes.com/2011/03/07/business /media/07iht-adco.html.

24. Vance Packard, *The Hidden Persuaders* (New York: Basic Books, 1957, 1978), 229.

25. See Eileen Dempsey, "Auld Lang Syne," *Columbus Dispatch*, December 28, 2000, p. 1G; John Reinan, "The End of the Good Old Days," *Minneapolis Star Tribune*, August 31, 2004, p. 1D.

26. See Schudson, *Advertising*, 36-43; Andrew Robertson, *The Lessons of Failure* (London: MacDonald, 1974).

27. Kim Campbell and Kent Davis-Packard, "How Ads Get Kids to Say, I Want It!" *Christian Science Monitor*, September 18, 2000, p. 1.

28. See Jay Mathews, "Channel One: Classroom Coup or a 'Sham'?" *Washington Post*, December 26, 1994, p. A1ff.

29. See Michael F. Jacobson and Laurie Ann Mazur, *Marketing Madness: A Survival Guide for a Consumer Society* (Boulder, Colo.: Westview Press, 1995), 29-31.

30. "Ads Beat News on School TVs," *Pittsburgh Post-Gazette*, March 6, 2006, p. A7.

31. Hilary Waldman, "Study Links Advertising, Youth Drinking," *Hartford Courant*, January 3, 2006, p. A1.

32. Alix Spigel, "Selling Sickness: How Drug Ads Changed Healthcare," National Public Radio, October 13, 2009, http://www.npr.org/templates /story/story.php?storyid=113675737.

33. Bruce Japsen, "Drug Makers Dial Down TV Advertising," *New York Times*, February 2, 2012, http://prescription.blogs.nytimes.com/2012 /02/02/drug-makers-dial-down-tv-advertising.

34. Jeffrey Godsick, quoted in T. L. Stanley, "Hollywood Continues Its Fast-Food Binge," AdWeek, June 6, 2009, http://www.adweek.com/news /advertising-branding/hollywood-continues-its-fast-food-binge-10597.

35. Douglas J. Wood, "Ad Issues to Watch for in '06," *Advertising Age*, December 19, 2005, p. 10.

36. Associated Press, "Two Ephedra Sellers Fined for False Ads," *Washington Post*, July 2, 2003, p. A7.

37. Beth Harskovits, "Corporate Profile: Legacy's Truth Finds Receptive Audience," *PR Week*, June 12, 2006, p. 9.

38. See Stephen Ansolabehere and Shanto Iyengar, *Going Negative: How Attack Ads Shrink and Polarize the Electorate* (New York: Free Press, 1996).

39. Katherine Q. Seelye, "About $2.6 Billion Spent on Political Ads in 2008," *New York Times*, December 2, 2008, http://thecaucus.blogs .nytimes.com/2008/12/02/about-26-billion-spent-on-political-ads -in-2008.

◢ **EXAMINING ETHICS** Brand Integration, Everywhere, p. 404

1. Kantar Media, "Kantar Media Reports U.S. Advertising Expenditures Increased 5.1% in the First Quarter of 2010," May 26, 2010, http://www .kantarmediana.com/news/05262010.htm.

2. "A Place for Everything: Product Placements These Days Go beyond Putting a Coke Can in the Background," *Media Week*, March 1, 2010, p. 12.

3. Stephanie Clifford, "Branding Comes Early in Filmmaking Process," *New York Times*, April 4, 2010, p. A1.

4. Writers Guild of America, West, "Product Integration," accessed September 8, 2010, http://www.wga.org/content/default.aspx?id=1405.

◢ **GLOBAL VILLAGE** Smoking Up the Global Market, p. 410

1. Peh Shing Huei, "7 Chinese Cities All Fired Up to Curb Smoking," *Straits Times*, January 23, 2010, p. 4.

2. "Women Now Main Target of Tobacco Firms," Chinadaily.com.cn, May 19, 2010, http://www.chinadaily.com.cn/china/2010-05/19 /content_9865347.htm.

3. Ibid.

4. National Institutes of Health, "Fact Sheet: Global Tobacco Research," October 2010, http://report.nib.gov/NIHfactsheets/View.FactSheet .aspx?csid-93.

12 Public Relations and Framing the Message

1. Matthew J. Culligan and Dolph Greene, *Getting Back to the Basics of Public Relations and Publicity* (New York: Crown Publishers, 1982), 90.

2. Ibid., 100.

3. See Stuart Ewen, *PR! A Social History of Spin* (New York: Basic Books, 1996).

4. Marvin N. Olasky, "The Development of Corporate Public Relations, 1850-1930," *Journalism Monographs* 102 (April 1987): 14.

5. Ibid., 15.

6. Edward Bernays, "The Theory and Practice of Public Relations: A Résumé," in E. L. Bernays, ed., *The Engineering of Consent* (Norman: University of Oklahoma Press, 1955), 3-25.

7. Edward Bernays, *Crystallizing Public Opinion* (New York: Horace Liveright, 1923), 217.

8. Michael Schudson, *Discovering the News: A Social History of American Newspapers* (New York: Basic Books, 1978), 136.

9. PRSA, "Industry Facts & Figures," accessed August 26, 2012, http://media.prsa.org/prsa+overview/industry+facts+figures/.

10. "Don't Be *That Guy*!" 2009, http://www.instituteforpr.org/files/uploads/That_Guy_JFGRA.pdf.

11. The lead author of this book, Richard Campbell, worked briefly as the assistant PR director for Milwaukee's Summerfest in the early 1980s.

12. OpenSecrets.org, "Lobbying Database," accessed August 26, 2012, http://opensecrets.org/lobby.

13. David Barstow, "Message Machine: Behind TV Analysis, Pentagon's Hidden Hand," *New York Times*, April 20, 2008, http://www.nytimes.com/2008/04/20/us/20generals.html.

14. Clint Hendler, "Report Card: Obama's Marks at Transparency U," *Columbia Journalism Review*, January 5, 2010, http://www.cjr.org/transparency/report_card.php.

15. Brian Proffitt, "Top Career-Destroying Twitter Gaffes: Olympic Edition," ReadWriteWeb, August 1, 2012, http://www.readwriteweb.com/archives/top-five-career-destroying-twitter-gaffes-olympic-edition.php.

16. Stanley Walker, "Playing the Deep Bassoons," *Harper's*, February 1932, 365.

17. Ibid., 370.

18. Ivy Lee, *Publicity* (New York: Industries Publishing, 1925), 21.

19. Schudson, *Discovering the News*, 136.

20. Ivy Lee, quoted in Ray Eldon Hiebert, *Courtier to the Crowd: The Story of Ivy Lee and the Development of Public Relations* (Ames: Iowa State University Press, 1966), 114.

21. See Walter Lippmann, *Public Opinion* (New York: Free Press, 1922, 1949), 221.

22. See Jonathan Tasini, "Lost in the Margins: Labor and the Media," *Extra!* (Summer 1992): 2-11.

23. PRWatch, "About Us," accessed August 26, 2012, http://www.prwatch.org/cmd.

24. John Stauber, "Corporate PR: A Threat to Journalism?" *Background Briefing: Radio National*, March 30, 1997, http://www.abc.net.au/rn/talks/bbing/stories/s10602.htm.

25. See Alicia Mundy, "Is the Press Any Match for Powerhouse PR?" in Ray Eldon Hiebert, ed., *Impact of Mass Media* (White Plains, N.Y.: Longman, 1995), 179-188.

26. Elisabeth Bumiller, "In Ex-Spokesman's Book, Harsh Words for Bush," *New York Times*, May 28, 2008, http://www.nytimes.com/2008/05/28/washington/28mcclellan.html.

27. Rosanna Fiske, "PR Pros: Haven't We Learned Anything about Disclosure?" PRSay, May 11, 2011, http://prsay.prsa.org/index.php/2011/05/11/pr-and-communications-pros-havent-we-learned-anything-about-disclosure/.

28. Elizabeth Blair, "Under the Radar, PR's Political Savvy," National Public Radio, May 19, 2011, http://www.npr.org/2011/05/19/136436263/under-the-radar-pr-s-political-savvy.

29. Fiske, "PR Pros."

◢ CASE STUDY   Social Media Transform the Press Release, p. 432

1. "Statement by Pennsylvania: Dead Not More than 57–Wreck's Cause a Mystery," *New York Times*, October 29, 1906, p. 2.

2. Todd DeFren, Shift Communications, "Social Media News Release Template, Version 1.5," April 18, 2008, http://www.pr-squared.com/index.php/2008/04/social_media_release_template.

3. Todd DeFren, Shift Communications, "SHIFT Communications Debuts First-Ever Template for 'Social Media Press Release,'" May 23, 2006, http://multivu.prnewswire.com/mnr/shift/24521/.

4. Peter Shankman, "Why I Will Never, Ever Hire a 'Social Media Expert,'" May 23, 2011, http://www.businessinsider.com/why-i-will-never-ever-hire-a-social-media-expert-2011-5.

5. Dominic Jones, "'Social Media' Wire Releases Are Bogus," *IR Web Report*, January 17, 2007, http://irwebreport.com/20070117/social-media-wire-releases-are-bogus/.

◢ EXAMINING ETHICS   What Does It Mean to Be Green?, p. 434

1. United Nations Global Compact, "A New Era of Sustainability," May 25, 2011, http://www.unglobalcompact.org/news/126-05-25-2011.

◢ Media Literacy and the Critical Process   The Invisible Hand of PR, p. 444

1. John Stauber, "Corporate PR: A Threat to Journalism?" *Background Briefing: Radio National*, March 30, 1997, http://www.abc.net.au/rn/talks/bbing/stories/s10602.htm.

13 Media Economics and the Global Marketplace

1. Verne G. Kopytoff, "AOL's Bet on Another Makeover," *New York Times*, February 7, 2011, http://www.nytimes.com/2011/02/08/technology/08aol.html.

2. David Carr, "The Evolving Mission of Google," *New York Times*, March 20, 2011, http://www.nytimes.com/2011/03/21/business/media/21carr.html.

3. Ibid.

4. Ben Fritz, "Netflix Confirms Deal to Offer Original Content," *Los Angeles Times*, March 19, 2011, http://www.articles.latimes.com/print/2011/mar/19/business/la-fi-ct-netflix-house-20110319.

5. For this section, the authors are indebted to the ideas and scholarship of Douglas Gomery, a media economist and historian, formerly from the University of Maryland.

6. Douglas Gomery, "The Centrality of Media Economics," in Mark R. Levy and Michael Gurevitch, eds., *Defining Media Studies* (New York: Oxford University Press, 1994), 202.

7. Ibid., 200.

8. Ibid., 203-204.

9. David Harvey, *The Condition of Postmodernity: An Enquiry into the Origins of Cultural Change* (Oxford: Basil Blackwell, 1989), 171.

8. M. D. Watts et al., "Elite Cues and Media Bias in Presidential Campaigns: Explaining Public Perceptions of a Liberal Press," *Communication Research* 26 (1999): 144-175.

9. See Glen R. Smith, "Politicians and the News Media: How Elite Attacks Influence Perceptions of Media Bias," *Harvard International Journal of Press/Politics* (July 1, 2010): 319-343.

◢ GLOBAL VILLAGE   Why Isn't Al Jazeera English on More U.S. TV Systems?, p. 509

1. Marwan Bishgara, "Analysis: Killing the Alibi," Aljazeera.net, May 2, 2011, http://www.english.aljazeera.net/indepth/opinion/2011/05/201152820164117366.html.

2. See Brian Stelter, "Al Jazeera English Finds an Audience," *New York Times*, January 31, 2011, http://www.nytimes.com/2011/02/01/world/middleeast/01jazeera.html.

3. Ibid.

4. See Accuracy in Media, "New Poll Says American People Oppose U.S. Launch of Al-Jazeera International," September 13, 2006, http://www.aim.org/press-release/new-poll-says-american-people-oppose-us-launch-of-al-jazeera-international/.

5. Sherry Ricchiardi, "The Al Jazeera Effect," *American Journalism Review*, March/April 2011, http://www.ajr.org/article_printable.asp?id=5077.

6. Michael Paterniti, "Inside Al Jazeera," *GQ*, June 2011, http://www.gq.com/newpolitics/newsmakers/201106/al-jazeera-english.

7. Lee Bollinger, "Al Jazeera Can Help U.S. Join Conversation," *Bloomberg Businessweek*, May 21, 2011, http://www.businessweek.com/news/2011-03-15/al-jazeera-can-help-u-s-join-conversation-lee-c-bollinger.html.

◢ EXAMINING ETHICS   WikiLeaks, Secret Documents, and Good Journalism?, p. 514

1. Bill Keller, "The Boy Who Kicked the Hornet's Nest," *New York Times Magazine*, January 30, 2011, pp. 33-34.

2. Ibid, p. 37.

3. Jay Rosen, "The Afghanistan War Logs Released by Wikileaks, the World's First Stateless News Organization," *PressThink*, July 26, 2010, http://www.pressthink.org/2010/07/the-afghanistan-war-logs-released-by-wikileaks-the-worlds-first-stateless-news-organization.

4. Nikki Usher, "Why WikiLeaks' Latest Document Dump Makes Everyone in Journalism–and the Public–a Winner," *Nieman Journalism Lab*, December 3, 2010, http://www.niemanlab.org/2010/12/why-wikileaks-latest-document-dump-makes-everyone-in-journalism-and-the-public-a-winner/.

15 Media Effects and Cultural Approaches to Research

1. Alexis de Tocqueville, *Democracy in America* (New York: Modern Library, 1835, 1840, 1945, 1981), 96-97.

2. Steve Fore, "Lost in Translation: The Social Uses of Mass Communications Research," *Afterimage*, no. 20 (April 1993): 10.

3. James Carey, *Communication as Culture: Essays on Media and Society* (Boston: Unwin Hyman, 1989), 75.

4. Daniel Czitrom, *Media and the American Mind: From Morse to McLuhan* (Chapel Hill: University of North Carolina Press, 1982), 122-125.

5. Ibid., 123.

6. Harold Lasswell, *Propaganda Technique in the World War* (New York: Alfred A. Knopf, 1927), 9.

7. Walter Lippmann, *Public Opinion* (New York: Macmillan, 1922), 18.

8. Tim Hanrahan, "WSJ/NBC Poll on Gay Marriage: 2012 vs. 2009 vs. 2004," *Washington Wire*, May 7, 2012, http://blogs.wsj.com/washwire/2012/05/07/wsjnbc-poll-on-gay-marriage-2012-vs-2009-vs-2004/.

9. Sheldon R. Gawiser and G. Evans Witt, "20 Questions a Journalist Should Ask about Poll Results," 2nd ed., http://www.ncpp.org/qajsa.htm.

10. See W. W. Charters, *Motion Pictures and Youth: A Summary* (New York: Macmillan, 1934); and Garth Jowett, *Film: The Democratic Art* (Boston: Little, Brown, 1976), 220-229.

11. Czitrom, *Media and the American Mind*, 132. See also Harold Lasswell, "The Structure and Function of Communication in Society," in Lyman Bryson, ed., *The Communication of Ideas* (New York: Harper and Brothers, 1948), 37-51.

12. Wilbur Schramm, Jack Lyle, and Edwin Parker, *Television in the Lives of Our Children* (Stanford, Calif.: Stanford University Press, 1961), 1.

13. See Joseph Klapper, *The Effects of Mass Communication* (New York: Free Press, 1960).

14. Schramm, Lyle, and Parker, *Television*, 1.

15. For an early overview of uses and gratifications, see Jay Blumler and Elihu Katz, *The Uses of Mass Communication* (Beverly Hills, Calif.: Sage, 1974).

16. National Public Radio, "Death-Penalty Option Varies Depending on Question," *Weekend Edition*, July 2, 2006.

17. See George Gerbner et al., "The Demonstration of Power: Violence Profile No. 10," *Journal of Communication* 29 no. 3 (1979): 177-196.

18. Kaiser Family Foundation, *Sex on TV 4* (Menlo Park, Calif.: Henry C. Kaiser Family Foundation, 2005).

19. Robert P. Snow, *Creating Media Culture* (Beverly Hills, Calif.: Sage, 1983), 47.

20. See Maxwell McCombs and Donald Shaw, "The Agenda-Setting Function of Mass Media," *Public Opinion Quarterly* 36 no. 2 (1972): 176-187.

21. See Nancy Signorielli and Michael Morgan, *Cultivation Analysis: New Directions in Media Effects Research* (Newbury Park, Calif.: Sage, 1990).

22. John Gastil, *Political Communication and Deliberation* (Beverly Hills, Calif.: Sage, 2008), 60.

23. W. Phillips Davison, "The Third-Person Effect in Communication," *Public Opinion Quarterly* 47 no. 1: 1-15. doi: 10.1086/268763.

24. Richard Rhodes, *The Media Violence Myth*, 2000, http://www.abffe.com/myth1.htm.

25. Robert Lynd, *Knowledge for What? The Place of Social Science in American Culture* (Princeton, N.J.: Princeton University Press, 1939), 120.

26. Czitrom, *Media and the American Mind,* 143; and Leo Lowenthal, "Historical Perspectives of Popular Culture," in Bernard Rosenberg and David White, eds., *Mass Culture: The Popular Arts in America* (Glencoe, Ill.: Free Press, 1957), 52.

27. See Stuart Hall et al., *Policing the Crisis: Mugging, the State, and Law and Order* (London: Macmillan, 1978).

28. Todd Gitlin, *The Whole World Is Watching* (Berkeley: University of California Press, 1980), 7.

29. Horace Newcomb, *TV: The Most Popular Art* (Garden City, N.Y.: Anchor Books, 1974), 19, 23.

30. See Janice Radway, *Reading the Romance: Women, Patriarchy, and Popular Literature* (Chapel Hill: University of North Carolina Press, 1984).

31. Jürgen Habermas, *The Structural Transformation of the Public Sphere* (Cambridge, Mass.: MIT Press, 1962/1994).

32. Craig Calhoun, ed., *Habermas and the Public Sphere* (Cambridge, Mass.: MIT Press, 1994), 452.

33. James W. Carey, *Communication as Culture* (New York: Routledge, 1989), 23.

34. James Carey, "Mass Communication Research and Cultural Studies: An American View," in James Curran, Michael Gurevitch, and Janet Woollacott, eds., *Mass Communication and Society* (London: Edward Arnold, 1977), 418, 421.

35. Alan Sokal, quoted in Scott Janny, "Postmodern Gravity Deconstructed, Slyly," *New York Times*, May 18, 1996, p. 1. See also The Editors of Lingua Franca, eds., *The Sokal Hoax: The Sham That Shook the Academy* (Lincoln, Neb.: Bison Press, 2000).

◢ CASE STUDY The Effects of TV in a Post-TV World, p. 525

1. Frank J. Prial, "Congressmen Hear Renewal of Debate over TV Violence," *New York Times*, April 16, 1983, http://www.nytimes.com/1983/04/16/arts/congressmen-hear-renewal-of-debate-over-tv-violence.html.

2. Parents Television Council, "What Is the PTC's Mission?" accessed May 15, 2011, http://www.parentstv.org/PTC/faqs/main.asp#What%20is%20the%20PTCs%20mission.

3. Parents Television Council, "Family Guide to Prime Time Television," accessed September 15, 2012, http://www.parentstv.org/PTC/familyguide/main.asp.

4. Lindsay Powers, "Parents Television Council Blasts Sex Episode of 'Glee' as 'Appalling,'" *Hollywood Reporter*, March 9, 2011, http://www.hollywoodreporter.com/news/parents-television-council-blasts-sex-166036.

5. Parents Television Council, "INSP Network Earns PTC Seal of Approval," May 23, 2012, http://www.parentstv.org/PTC/news/release/2012/0523.asp.

◢ Media Literacy and the Critical Process Wedding Media and the Meaning of the Perfect Wedding Day, p. 531

1. Erika Engstrom, *The Bride Factory: Mass Media Portrayals of Women and Weddings* (New York: Peter Lang, 2012).

◢ CASE STUDY Labor Gets Framed, p. 537

1. Christopher R. Martin, *Framed! Labor and the Corporate Media* (Ithaca, N.Y.: Cornell University Press, 2003).

2. Richard B. Freeman and Joel Rogers, *What Workers Want* (Ithaca, N.Y.: Cornell University Press, 1999).

16 Legal Controls and Freedom of Expression

1. First Amendment Center, "2012 Survey: Public Opposes Unlimited Campaign Spending," July 17, 2012, http://www.firstamendmentcenter.org/2012-survey-public-opposes-unlimited-campaign-spending.

2. Gene Policinski, "Amendment to Undo Citizens United Won't Do," First Amendment Center, September 21, 2011, http://www.firstamendmentcenter.org/amendment-to-undo-citizens-united-wont-do.

3. Common Dreams staff, "California Legislature Approves Resolution Opposing Citizens United Ruling," Common Dreams, July 6, 2012, http://www.pdacommunity.org/california/1892-california-legislature-approves-resolution-opposing-citizen-united-ruling.

4. Committee to Protect Journalists, "943 Journalists Killed since 1992," accessed October 10, 2012, http://www.cpj.org/killed/.

5. Freedom House, "Freedom in the World 2011: The Authoritarian Challenge to Democracy," January 13, 2011, http://freedomhouse.org/template.cfm?page=70&release=1310.

6. Fred Siebert, Theodore Peterson, and Wilbur Schramm, *Four Theories of the Press* (Urbana: University of Illinois Press, 1956).

7. See Douglas M. Fraleigh and Joseph S. Tuman, *Freedom of Speech in the Marketplace of Ideas* (New York: St. Martin's Press, 1997), 71-73.

8. Michael Schudson, *The Good Citizen: A History of American Civic Life* (Cambridge, Mass.: Harvard University Press, 1998), 77.

9. See Fraleigh and Tuman, *Freedom of Speech,* 125.

10. Hugo Black, quoted in "*New York Times Company v. U.S.*: 1971," in Edward W. Knappman, ed., *Great American Trials: From Salem Witchcraft to Rodney King* (Detroit: Visible Ink Press, 1994), 609.

11. Robert Warren, quoted in "*U.S. v. The Progressive*: 1979," in Knappman, ed., *Great American Trials,* 684.

12. Michael Lindenberger, "The U.S.'s Weak Legal Case against WikiLeaks," *Time*, December 9, 2010, http://www.time.com/time/nation/article/0,8599,2035994,00.html.

13. Lawrence Lessig, "Opening Plenary–Media at a Critical Juncture: Politics, Technology and Culture," National Conference on Media Reform, Minneapolis, Minnesota, June 7, 2008.

14. See Knappman, ed., *Great American Trials,* 517-519.

15. Ibid., 741-743.

16. Douglas Gomery, *Movie History: A Survey* (Belmont, Calif.: Wadsworth, 1991), 57.

17. See Eric Barnouw, *Tube of Plenty: The Evolution of American Television,* rev. ed. (New York: Oxford University Press, 1982), 118-130.

18. See "Dummy and Dame Arouse the Nation," *Broadcasting-Telecasting,* October 15, 1956, p. 258; and Lawrence Lichty and Malachi Topping, *American Broadcasting: A Source Book on the History of Radio and Television* (New York: Hastings House, 1975), 530.

19. Dean Burch, quoted in Peter Fornatale and Joshua Mills, *Radio in the Television Age* (Woodstock, N.Y.: Overlook Press, 1980), 85.

20. *Fox Television Stations, Inc. v. FCC*, No. 06-1760 (2nd Cir. 2010).

21. Human Rights Watch, "Become a Blogger for Human Rights," http://hrw.org/blogs.htm.

22. Bill Kovach, "Big Deals, with Journalism Thrown In," *New York Times,* August 3, 1995, p. A17.

23. Herbert J. Gans, *Democracy and the News* (Oxford: Oxford University Press, 2003), ix.

◢ CASE STUDY Is "Sexting" Pornography?, p. 558

1. Richard Wortley and Stephen Smallbone, "Child Pornography on the Internet," U.S. Department of Justice, May 2006, http://www.cops.usdoj.gov/files/ric/Publications/e04062000.pdf.

2. Steven Dettelbach, quoted in Tracy Russo, "'Sexting' Town Hall Meeting Held in Cleveland," *Justice Blog*, March 19, 2010, http://blogs.usdoj.gov/blog/archives/650.

3. Amanda Lenhart, "Teens and Sexting," Pew Internet & American Life Project, December 15, 2009, http://pewresearch.org/pubs/1440/teens-sexting-text-messages.

◢ EXAMINING ETHICS A Generation of Copyright Criminals?, p. 571

1. Kembrew McLeod, *Freedom of Expression®: Overzealous Copyright Bozos and Other Enemies of Creativity* (New York: Doubleday, 2005), 67-68.

2. Ibid.

3. Michael D. Ayers, "White Noise: Girl Talk," *Billboard,* June 14, 2008.

4. Lawrence Lessig, quoted in *Rip: A Remix Manifesto*, dir. Brett Gaylor, 2008.

Extended Case Study:
Our Digital World and the Self-invasion of Privacy, p. 577

1. Marshall McLuhan, *Counterblast* (New York: Harcourt, Brace & World, 1969), 103.
2. Somini Sengupta and Kevin J. O'Brien, "Facebook Can ID Faces, but Using Them Grows Tricky," *New York Times*, September 21, 2012, http://www.nytimes.com/2012/09/22/technology/facebook-backs-down-on-face-recognition-in-europe.html.
3. Twitter, "Twitter Stats," accessed September 23, 2012, https://business.twitter.com/en/basics/what-is-twitter/.
4. Michael O'Grady, "SMS Usage Remains Strong in the US: 6 Billion SMS Messages Are Sent Each Day," *Michael O'Grady's Blog*, June 19, 2012, http://blogs.forrester.com/michael_ogrady/12-06-19-sms_usage_remains_strong_in_the_us_6_billion_sms_messages_are_sent_each_day.
5. Mark Hachman, "Email Will Never Die: The Man Who Invented It Reveals Why," *Huffington Post*, September 6, 2012, http://www.huffingtonpost.com/2012/09/06/email-will-never-die_n_1860881.html.
6. YouTube, "Statistics," accessed September 23, 2012, http://www.youtube.com/t/press_statistics.
7. Federal Trade Commission, "Protecting Consumer Privacy in an Era of Rapid Change," March 2012, http://ftc.gov/os/2012/03/120326privacyreport.pdf.
8. Edward Wyatt, "F.T.C. and White House Push for Online Privacy Laws," *New York Times*, May 9, 2012, http://www.nytimes.com/2012/05/10/business/ftc-and-white-house-push-for-online-privacy-laws.html.
9. Julia Angwin, "Google, FTC Near Settlement on Privacy," *Wall Street Journal*, July 10, 2012, http://online.wsj.com/article/SB10001424052702303567704577517081178553046.html.
10. Jason Keyser, "Illinois Facebook Password Law Bars Employers from Asking for Social Media Logins," *Huffington Post*, August 1, 2012, http://www.huffingtonpost.com/2012/08/01/illinois-facebook-passwor_0_n_1730396.html.
11. Sengupta and O'Brien, "Facebook Can ID Faces."
12. The White House, "Consumer Data Privacy in a Networked World: A Framework for Protecting Privacy and Promoting Innovation in the Global Digital Economy," February 2012, http://www.whitehouse.gov/sites/default/files/privacy-final.pdf.

Glossary

A&R (artist & repertoire) agents talent scouts of the music business who discover, develop, and sometimes manage performers.

access channels in cable television, a tier of nonbroadcast channels dedicated to local education, government, and the public.

account executives in advertising, client liaisons responsible for bringing in new business and managing the accounts of established clients.

account reviews in advertising, the process of evaluating or reinvigorating an ad campaign, which results in either renewing the contract with the original ad agency or hiring a new agency.

acquisitions editors in the book industry, editors who seek out and sign authors to contracts.

action games games emphasizing combat-type situations that ask players to test their reflexes and to punch, slash, shoot, or throw as strategically and accurately as possible so as to strategically make their way through a series of levels.

actual malice in libel law, a reckless disregard for the truth, such as when a reporter or an editor knows that a statement is false and prints or airs it anyway.

adult contemporary (AC) one of the oldest and most popular radio music formats, typically featuring a mix of news, talk, oldies, and soft rock.

adventure games games requiring players to interact with individual characters and a sometimes hostile environment in order to solve puzzles.

advergames video games created for purely promotional purposes.

affiliate station a radio or TV station that, though independently owned, signs a contract to be part of a network and receives money to carry the network's programs; in exchange, the network reserves time slots, which it sells to national advertisers.

agenda-setting a media-research argument that says that when the mass media pay attention to particular events or issues, they determine–that is, set the agenda for–the major topics of discussion for individuals and society.

album-oriented rock (AOR) the radio music format that features album cuts from mainstream rock bands.

alternative rock nonmainstream rock music, which includes many types of experimental music and some forms of punk and grunge.

AM amplitude modulation; a type of radio and sound transmission that stresses the volume or height of radio waves.

analog in television, standard broadcast signals made of radio waves (replaced by digital standards in 2009).

analog recording a recording that is made by capturing the fluctuations of the original sound waves and storing those signals on records or cassettes as a continuous stream of magnetism–analogous to the actual sound.

analysis the second step in the critical process, it involves discovering significant patterns that emerge from the description stage.

anthology dramas a popular form of early TV programming that brought live dramatic theater to television; influenced by stage plays, anthologies offered new teleplays, casts, directors, writers, and sets from week to week.

arcade establishments that gather multiple coin-operated games together and can be considered newer versions of the penny arcade.

ARPAnet the original Internet, designed by the U.S. Defense Department's Advanced Research Projects Agency (ARPA).

association principle in advertising, a persuasive technique that associates a product with some cultural value or image that has a positive connotation but may have little connection to the actual product.

astroturf lobbying phony grassroots public affairs campaigns engineered by public relations firms; coined by U.S. Senator Lloyd Bentsen of Texas (it was named after AstroTurf, the artificial grass athletic field surface).

audience studies cultural studies research that focuses on how people use and interpret cultural content. Also known as reader-response research.

audiotape lightweight magnetized strands of ribbon that make possible sound editing and multiple-track mixing; instrumentals or vocals can be recorded at one location and later mixed onto a master recording in another studio.

authoritarian model a model for journalism and speech that tolerates little public dissent or criticism of government; it holds that the general public needs guidance from an elite and educated ruling class.

avatar a graphic interactive "character" situated within the world of a game, such as *World of Warcraft* or *Second Life*.

bandwagon effect an advertising strategy that incorporates exaggerated claims that everyone is using a particular product, so you should, too.

basic cable in cable programming, a tier of channels composed of local broadcast signals, nonbroadcast access channels (for local government, education, and general public use), a few regional PBS stations, and a variety of cable channels downlinked from communication satellites.

Big Five/Little Three from the late 1920s through the late 1940s, the major movie studios that were vertically integrated and that dominated the industry. The Big Five were Paramount, MGM, Warner Brothers, Twentieth Century Fox, and RKO. The Little Three were those studios that did not own theaters: Columbia, Universal, and United Artists.

Big Six the six major Hollywood studios that currently rule the commercial film business: Warner Brothers, Paramount, Twentieth Century Fox, Universal, Columbia Pictures, and Disney.

block booking an early tactic of movie studios to control exhibition, involving pressuring theater operators to accept marginal films with no stars in order to get access to films with the most popular stars.

blockbuster the type of big-budget special effects films that typically have summer or holiday release dates, heavy promotion, and lucrative merchandising tie-ins.

block printing a printing technique developed by early Chinese printers, who hand-carved characters and illustrations into a block of wood, applied ink to the block, and then printed copies on multiple sheets of paper.

bloggers people who post commentary on personal and political opinion-based Web sites.

blogs sites that contain articles in reverse chronological journal-like form, often with reader comments and links to other articles on the Web (from the term *Weblog*).

blues originally a kind of black folk music, this music emerged as a distinct category in the early 1900s; it was influenced by African American spirituals, ballads, and work songs in the rural South, and by urban guitar and vocal solos from the 1930s and 1940s.

book challenge a formal complaint to have a book removed from a public or school library's collection.

boutique agencies in advertising, small regional ad agencies that offer personalized services.

broadband data transmission over a fiber-optic cable–a signaling method that handles a wide range of frequencies.

broadcasting the transmission of radio waves or TV signals to a broad public audience.

browsers information-search services, such as Microsoft's Internet Explorer, Firefox, and Google Chrome, that offer detailed organizational maps to the Internet.

cartridge early physical form of video games that were played on consoles manufactured by companies like Nintendo, Sega, and Atari.

casual games games that have very simple rules and are usually quick to play, such as *Tetris* or *Angry Birds*.

CATV (community antenna television) an early cable system that originated where mountains or tall buildings blocked TV signals; because of early technical and regulatory limits, CATV contained only twelve channels.

celluloid a transparent and pliable film that can hold a coating of chemicals sensitive to light.

chapter show in television production, any situation comedy or dramatic program whose narrative structure includes self-contained stories that feature a problem, a series of conflicts, and a resolution from week to week (for contrast, see **serial program** and **episodic series**).

cinema verité French term for *truth film*, a documentary style that records fragments of everyday life unobtrusively; it often features a rough, grainy look and shaky, handheld camera work.

citizen journalism a grassroots movement wherein activist amateurs and concerned citizens, not professional journalists, use the Internet and blogs to disseminate news and information.

codex an early type of book in which paperlike sheets were cut and sewed together along an edge, then bound with thin pieces of wood and covered with leather.

collective intelligence the sharing of knowledge and ideas, particularly in the world of gaming.

commercial speech any print or broadcast expression for which a fee is charged to the organization or individual buying time or space in the mass media.

common carrier a communication or transportation business, such as a phone company or a taxi service, that is required by law to offer service on a first-come, first-served basis to whoever can pay the rate; such companies do not get involved in content.

communication the process of creating symbol systems that convey information and meaning (for example, language, Morse code, film, and computer codes).

Communications Act of 1934 the far-reaching act that established the Federal Communications Commission (FCC) and the federal regulatory structure for U.S. broadcasting.

communist or state model a model for journalism and speech that places control in the hands of an enlightened government, which speaks for ordinary citizens and workers in order to serve the common goals of the state.

compact discs (CDs) playback-only storage discs for music that incorporate pure and very precise digital techniques, thus eliminating noise during recording and editing sessions.

conflict of interest considered unethical, a compromising situation in which a journalist stands to benefit personally from the news report he or she produces.

conflict-oriented journalism found in metropolitan areas, newspapers that define news primarily as events, issues, or experiences that deviate from social norms; journalists see their role as observers who monitor their city's institutions and problems.

consensus narratives cultural products that become popular and command wide attention, providing shared cultural experiences.

consensus-oriented journalism found in small communities, newspapers that promote social and economic harmony by providing community calendars and meeting notices and carrying articles on local schools, social events, town government, property crimes, and zoning issues.

consoles devices people use specifically to play video games.

contemporary hit radio (CHR) originally called *Top 40 radio*, this radio format encompasses everything from hip-hop to children's songs; it appeals to many teens and young adults.

content analysis in social science research, a method for studying and coding media texts and programs.

content communities online communities that exist for the sharing of all types of content from text to photos and videos.

convergence the first definition involves the technological merging of media content across various platforms (see also **cross platform**). The second definition describes a business model that consolidates various media holdings under one corporate umbrella.

cookies information profiles about a user that are usually automatically accepted by a Web browser and stored on the user's own computer hard drive.

copy editors the people in magazine, newspaper, and book publishing who attend to specific problems in writing such as style, content, and length.

copyright the legal right of authors and producers to own and control the use of their published or unpublished writing, music, and lyrics; TV programs and movies; or graphic art designs.

Corporation for Public Broadcasting (CPB) a private, nonprofit corporation created by Congress in 1967 to funnel federal funds to nonprofit radio and public television.

correlations observed associations between two variables.

country claiming the largest number of radio stations in the United States, this radio format includes such subdivisions as old-time, progressive, country-rock, western swing, and country-gospel.

cover music songs recorded or performed by musicians who did not originally write or perform the music; in the 1950s, some white producers and artists capitalized on popular songs by black artists by "covering" them.

critical process the process whereby a media-literate person or student studying mass communication forms and practices employs the techniques of description, analysis, interpretation, evaluation, and engagement.

cross platform a particular business model that involves a consolidation of various media holdings—such as cable connection, phone service, television transmission, and Internet access—under one corporate umbrella (also known as **convergence**).

cultivation effect in media research, the idea that heavy television viewing leads individuals to perceive reality in ways that are consistent with the portrayals they see on television.

cultural imperialism the phenomenon of American media, fashion, and food dominating the global market and shaping the cultures and identities of other nations.

cultural studies in media research, the approaches that try to understand how the media and culture are tied to the actual patterns of communication used in daily life; these studies focus on how people make meanings, apprehend reality, and order experience through the use of stories and symbols.

culture the symbols of expression that individuals, groups, and societies use to make sense of daily life and to articulate their values; a process that delivers the values of a society through products or other meaning-making forms.

data mining the unethical gathering of data by online purveyors of content and merchandise.

deficit financing in television, the process whereby a TV production company leases its programs to a network for a license fee that is actually less than the cost of production; the company hopes to recoup this loss later in rerun syndication.

demographic editions national magazines whose advertising is tailored to subscribers and readers according to occupation, class, and zip-code address.

demographics in market research, the study of audiences or consumers by age, gender, occupation, ethnicity, education, and income.

description the first step in the critical process, it involves paying close attention, taking notes, and researching the cultural product to be studied.

design managers publishing industry personnel who work on the look of a book, making decisions about type style, paper, cover design, and layout.

desktop publishing a computer technology that enables an aspiring publisher/editor to inexpensively write, design, lay out, and even print a small newsletter or magazine.

development the process of designing, coding, scoring, and testing a game.

developmental editor in book publishing, the editor who provides authors with feedback, makes suggestions for improvements, and obtains advice from knowledgeable members of the academic community.

digital in television, the type of signals that are transmitted as binary code.

digital communication images, texts, and sounds that use pulses of electric current or flashes of laser light and are converted (or encoded) into electronic signals represented as varied combinations of binary numbers, ones and zeros; these signals are then reassembled (decoded) as a precise reproduction of a TV picture, a magazine article, or a telephone voice.

digital divide the socioeconomic disparity between those who do and those who do not have access to digital technology and media, such as the Internet.

digital recording music recorded and played back by laser beam rather than by needle or magnetic tape.

digital video the production format that is replacing celluloid film and revolutionizing filmmaking because the cameras are more portable and production costs are much less expensive.

dime novels sometimes identified as pulp fiction, these cheaply produced and low-priced novels were popular in the United States beginning in the 1860s.

direct broadcast satellite (DBS) a satellite-based service that for a monthly fee downlinks hundreds of satellite channels and services; DBS began distributing video programming directly to households in 1994.

direct payment in media economics, the payment of money, primarily by consumers, for a book, a music CD, a movie, an online computer service, or a cable TV subscription.

documentary a movie or TV news genre that documents reality by recording actual characters and settings.

domestic comedy a TV hybrid of the sitcom in which characters and settings are usually more important than complicated situations; it generally features a domestic problem or work issue that characters have to solve.

drive time in radio programming, the periods between 6 and 10 A.M. and 4 and 7 P.M., when people are commuting to and from work or school; these periods constitute the largest listening audiences of the day.

e-book a digital book read on a computer or electronic reading device.

e-commerce electronic commerce, or commercial activity, on the Web.

economies of scale the economic process of increasing production levels so as to reduce the overall cost per unit.

electromagnetic waves invisible electronic impulses similar to visible light; electricity, magnetism, light, broadcast signals, and heat are part of such waves, which radiate in space at the speed of light, about 186,000 miles per second.

electronic publishers communication businesses, such as broadcasters or cable TV companies, that are entitled to choose what channels or content to carry.

e-mail electronic mail messages sent over the Internet; developed by computer engineer Ray Tomlinson in 1971.

engagement the fifth step in the critical process, it involves actively working to create a media world that best serves democracy.

Entertainment Software Rating Board (ESRB) a self-regulating organization that assigns ratings to games based on six categories: EC (Early Childhood), E (Everyone), E 10+, T (Teens), M 17+, and AO (Adults Only 18+).

episodic series a narrative form well suited to television because the main characters appear every week, sets and locales remain the same, and technical crews stay with the program; episodic series feature new adventures each week, but a handful of characters emerge with whom viewers can regularly identify (for contrast, see **chapter show**).

e-publishing Internet-based publishing houses that design and distribute books for comparatively low prices for authors who want to self-publish a title.

ethnocentrism an underlying value held by many U.S. journalists and citizens, it involves judging other countries and cultures according to how they live up to or imitate American practices and ideals.

evaluation the fourth step in the critical process, it involves arriving at a judgment about whether a cultural product is good, bad, or mediocre; this requires subordinating one's personal taste to the critical assessment resulting from the first three stages (description, analysis, and interpretation).

evergreens in TV syndication, popular, lucrative, and enduring network reruns, such as the *Andy Griffith Show* or *I Love Lucy*.

evergreen subscriptions magazine subscriptions that automatically renew on the subscriber's credit card.

experiments in regard to the mass media, research that isolates some aspect of content, suggests a hypothesis, and manipulates variables to discover a particular medium's impact on attitudes, emotions, or behavior.

Fairness Doctrine repealed in 1987, this FCC rule required broadcast stations to both air and engage in controversial-issue programs that affected their communities and, when offering such programming, to provide competing points of view.

famous-person testimonial an advertising strategy that associates a product with the endorsement of a well-known person.

feature syndicates commercial outlets or brokers, such as United Features and King Features, that contract with newspapers to provide work from well-known political writers, editorial cartoonists, comic-strip artists, and self-help columnists.

Federal Communications Commission (FCC) an independent U.S. government agency charged with regulating interstate and international communications by radio, television, wire, satellite, cable, and the Internet.

Federal Radio Commission (FRC) a body established in 1927 to oversee radio licenses and negotiate channel problems.

feedback responses from receivers to the senders of messages.

fiber-optic cable thin glass bundles of fiber capable of transmitting along cable wires thousands of messages converted to shooting pulses of light; these bundles of fiber can carry broadcast channels, telephone signals, and all sorts of digital codes.

fin-syn (Financial Interest and Syndication Rules) FCC rules that prohibited the major networks from running their own syndication companies or from charging production companies additional fees after shows had completed their prime-time runs; most fin-syn rules were rescinded in the mid-1990s.

first-person shooter (FPS) games that allow players to feel like they are actually holding a weapon and to feel physically immersed in the drama.

first-run syndication in television, the process whereby new programs are specifically produced for sale in syndication markets rather than for network television.

flack a derogatory term that, in journalism, is sometimes applied to a public relations agent.

FM frequency modulation; a type of radio and sound transmission that offers static-less reception and greater fidelity and clarity than AM radio by accentuating the pitch or distance between radio waves.

focus groups a common research method in psychographic analysis in which moderators lead small-group discussions about a product or an issue, usually with six to twelve people.

folk music music performed by untrained musicians and passed down through oral traditions; it encompasses a wide range of music, from Appalachian fiddle tunes to the accordion-led zydeco of Louisiana.

folk-rock amplified folk music, often featuring politically overt lyrics; influenced by rock and roll.

format radio the concept of radio stations developing and playing specific styles (or formats) geared to listeners' age, race, or gender; in format radio, management, rather than deejays, controls programming choices.

Fourth Estate the notion that the press operates as an unofficial branch of government, monitoring the legislative, judicial, and executive branches for abuses of power.

fourth-screens technologies like smartphones, iPods, iPads, and mobile TV devices that are forcing major changes in consumer viewing habits and media content creation.

fringe time in television, the time slot either immediately before the evening's prime-time schedule (called *early fringe*) or immediately following the local evening news or the network's late-night talk shows (called *late fringe*).

gag orders legal restrictions prohibiting the press from releasing preliminary information that might prejudice jury selection.

gameplay the way in which a game's rules, rather than the graphics, sound, and narrative style, structure how players interact with a game.

gangster rap a style of rap music that depicts the hardships of urban life and sometimes glorifies the violent style of street gangs.

gatekeepers editors, producers, and other media managers who function as message filters, making decisions about what types of messages actually get produced for particular audiences.

general-interest magazines types of magazines that address a wide variety of topics and are aimed at a broad national audience.

genre a narrative category in which conventions regarding similar characters, scenes, structures, and themes recur in combination.

grunge rock music that takes the spirit of punk and infuses it with more attention to melody.

guilds or clans in gaming, coordinated, organized team-like groups that can either be small and easygoing or large and demanding.

HD radio a digital technology that enables AM and FM radio broadcasters to multicast two to three additional compressed digital signals within their traditional analog frequency.

hegemony the acceptance of the dominant values in a culture by those who are subordinate to those who hold economic and political power.

herd journalism a situation in which reporters stake out a house or follow a story in such large groups that the entire profession comes under attack for invading people's privacy or exploiting their personal tragedies.

hidden-fear appeal an advertising strategy that plays on a sense of insecurity, trying to persuade consumers that only a specific product can offer relief.

high culture a symbolic expression that has come to mean "good taste"; often supported by wealthy patrons and corporate donors, it is associated with fine art (such as ballet, the symphony, painting, and classical literature), which is available primarily in theaters or museums.

hip-hop music that combines spoken street dialect with cuts (or samples) from older records and bears the influences of social politics, male boasting, and comic lyrics carried forward from blues, R&B, soul, and rock and roll.

Hollywood Ten the nine screenwriters and one film director subpoenaed by the House Un-American Activities Committee (HUAC) who were sent to prison in the late 1940s for refusing to disclose their memberships or to identify communist sympathizers.

HTML (hypertext markup language) the written code that creates Web pages and links; a language all computers can read.

human-interest stories news accounts that focus on the trials and tribulations of the human condition, often featuring ordinary individuals facing extraordinary challenges.

hypodermic-needle model an early model in mass communication research that attempted to explain media effects by arguing that the media figuratively shoot their powerful effects into unsuspecting or weak audiences; sometimes called the *bullet theory* or *direct effects model*.

hypotheses in social science research, tentative general statements that predict a relationship between a dependent variable and an independent variable.

illuminated manuscripts books from the Middle Ages that featured decorative, colorful designs and illustrations on each page.

indecency an issue related to appropriate broadcast content; the government may punish broadcasters for indecency or profanity after the fact, and over the years a handful of radio stations have had their licenses suspended or denied over indecent programming.

indies independent music and film production houses that work outside industry oligopolies; they often produce less mainstream music and film.

indirect payment in media economics, the financial support of media products by advertisers, who pay for the quantity or quality of audience members that a particular medium attracts.

individualism an underlying value held by most U.S. journalists and citizens, it favors individual rights and responsibilities above group needs or institutional mandates.

in-game advertisements integrated, oftentimes subtle advertisements, such as as billboards, logos, or store-fronts in a game, that can either be static or dynamic.

instant book in the book industry, a marketing strategy that involves publishing a topical book quickly after a major event occurs.

instant messaging a Web feature that enables users to chat with buddies in real time via pop-up windows assigned to each conversation.

intellectual properties in gaming, the stories, characters, personalities, and music that require licensing agreements.

Internet the vast network of telephone and cable lines, wireless connections, and satellite systems designed to link and carry computer information worldwide.

Internet radio online radio stations that either "stream" simulcast versions of on-air radio broadcasts over the Web or are created exclusively for the Internet.

Internet service provider (ISP) a company that provides Internet access to homes and businesses for a fee.

interpretation the third step in the critical process, it asks and answers the "What does that mean?" and "So what?" questions about one's findings.

interpretive journalism a type of journalism that involves analyzing and explaining key issues or events and placing them in a broader historical or social context.

interstitials advertisements that pop up in a screen window as a user attempts to access a new Web page.

inverted-pyramid style a style of journalism in which news reports begin with the most dramatic or newsworthy information—answering *who*, *what*, *where*, and *when* (and less frequently *why* or *how*) questions at the top of the story—and then trail off with less significant details.

investigative journalism news reports that hunt out and expose corruption, particularly in business and government.

irritation advertising an advertising strategy that tries to create product-name recognition by being annoying or obnoxious.

jazz an improvisational and mostly instrumental musical form that absorbs and integrates a diverse body of musical styles, including African rhythms, blues, big band, and gospel.

joint operating agreement (JOA) in the newspaper industry, an economic arrangement, sanctioned by the government, that permits competing newspapers to operate separate editorial divisions while merging business and production operations.

kinescope before the days of videotape, a 1950s technique for preserving television broadcasts by using a film camera to record a live TV show off a studio monitor.

kinetograph an early movie camera developed by Thomas Edison's assistant in the 1890s.

kinetoscope an early film projection system that served as a kind of peep show in which viewers looked through a hole and saw images moving on a tiny plate.

leased channels in cable television, channels that allow citizens to buy time for producing programs or present-ing their own viewpoints.

libel in media law, the defamation of character in written expression.

libertarian model a model for journalism and speech that encourages vigorous government criticism and supports the highest degree of freedom for individual speech and news operations.

limited competition in media economics, a market with many producers and sellers but only a few differentiable products within a particular category; sometimes called *monopolistic competition*.

linotype a technology introduced in the nineteenth century that enabled printers to set type mechanically using a typewriter-style keyboard.

literary journalism news reports that adapt fictional storytelling techniques to nonfictional material; some-times called *new journalism*.

lobbying in governmental public relations, the process of attempting to influence the voting of lawmakers to support a client's or an organization's best interests.

longitudinal studies a term used for research studies that are conducted over long periods of time and often rely on large government and academic survey databases.

low culture a symbolic expression supposedly aligned with the questionable tastes of the "masses," who enjoy the commercial "junk" circulated by the mass media, such as soap operas, rock music, talk radio, comic books, and monster truck pulls.

low-power FM (LPFM) a new class of noncommercial radio stations approved by the FCC in 2000 to give voice to local groups lacking access to the public airwaves; the 10-watt and 100-watt stations broadcast to a small, community-based area.

magalog a combination of a glossy magazine and retail catalogue that is often used to market goods or services to customers or employees.

magazine a nondaily periodical that comprises a collection of articles, stories, and ads.

manuscript culture a period during the Middle Ages when priests and monks advanced the art of bookmaking.

market research in advertising and public relations agencies, the department that uses social science techniques to assess the behaviors and attitudes of consumers toward particular products before any ads are created.

mass communication the process of designing and delivering cultural messages and stories to diverse audiences through media channels as old as the book and as new as the Internet.

massively multiplayer online role-playing games (MMORPGs) role-playing games set in virtual fantasy worlds that require users to play through an avatar.

mass market paperbacks low-priced paperback books sold mostly on racks in drugstores, supermarkets, and airports, as well as in bookstores.

mass media the cultural industries–the channels of communication–that produce and distribute songs, novels, news, movies, online computer services, and other cultural products to a large number of people.

mass media channel newspapers, books, magazines, radio, movies, television, or the Internet.

media buyers in advertising, the individuals who choose and purchase the types of media that are best suited to carry a client's ads and reach the targeted audience.

media effects research the mainstream tradition in mass communication research, it attempts to understand, explain, and predict the impact–or effects–of the mass media on individuals and society.

media literacy an understanding of the mass communication process through the development of critical-thinking tools–description, analysis, interpretation, evaluation, engagement–that enable a person to become more engaged as a citizen and more discerning as a consumer of mass media products.

mega-agencies in advertising, large firms or holding companies that are formed by merging several individual agencies and that maintain worldwide regional offices; they provide both advertising and public relations services and operate in-house radio and TV production studios.

megaplexes movie theater facilities with fourteen or more screens.

messages the texts, images, and sounds transmitted from senders to receivers.

microprocessors miniature circuits that process and store electronic signals, integrating thousands of electronic components into thin strands of silicon along which binary codes travel.

minimal-effects model a mass communication research model based on tightly controlled experiments and survey findings; it argues that the mass media have limited effects on audiences, reinforcing existing behaviors and attitudes rather than changing them.

modding the most advanced form of **collective intelligence**; slang for modifying game software or hardware.

modern the term describing a historical era spanning the time from the rise of the Industrial Revolution in the eighteenth and nineteenth centuries to the present; its social values include celebrating the individual, believing in rational order, working efficiently, and rejecting tradition.

monopoly in media economics, an organizational structure that occurs when a single firm dominates production and distribution in a particular industry, either nationally or locally.

Morse code a system of sending electrical impulses from a transmitter through a cable to a reception point; developed by the American inventor Samuel Morse.

movie palaces ornate, lavish single-screen movie theaters that emerged in the 1910s in the United States.

MP3 short for MPEG-1 Layer 3, an advanced type of audio compression that reduces file size, enabling audio to be easily distributed over the Internet and to be digitally transmitted in real time.

muckrakers reporters who used a style of early-twentieth-century investigative journalism that emphasized a willingness to crawl around in society's muck to uncover a story.

multichannel video programming distributors (MVPDs) the cable industry's name for its largest revenue generators, including cable companies and DBS providers.

multiple-system operators (MSOs) large corporations that own numerous cable television systems.

multiplexes contemporary movie theaters that exhibit many movies at the same time on multiple screens.

must-carry rules rules established by the FCC requiring all cable operators to assign channels to and carry all local TV broadcasts on their systems, thereby ensuring that local network affiliates, independent stations (those not carrying network programs), and public television channels would benefit from cable's clearer reception.

myth analysis a strategy for critiquing advertising that provides insights into how ads work on a cultural level; according to this strategy, ads are narratives with stories to tell and social conflicts to resolve.

narrative the structure underlying most media products, it includes two components: the story (what happens to whom) and the discourse (how the story is told).

narrative films movies that tell a story, with dramatic action and conflict emerging mainly from individual characters.

narrowcasting any specialized electronic programming or media channel aimed at a target audience.

National Public Radio (NPR) noncommercial radio established in 1967 by the U.S. Congress to provide an alternative to commercial radio.

net neutrality the principle that every Web site and every user—whether a multinational corporation or you—has the right to the same Internet network speed and access.

network a broadcast process that links, through special phone lines or satellite transmissions, groups of radio or TV stations that share programming produced at a central location.

network era the period in television history, roughly from the mid-1950s to the late 1970s, that refers to the dominance of the Big Three networks—ABC, CBS, and NBC—over programming and prime-time viewing habits; the era began eroding with a decline in viewing and with the development of VCRs, cable, and new TV networks.

news the process of gathering information and making narrative reports—edited by individuals in a news organization—that create selected frames of reference and help the public make sense of prominent people, important events, and unusual happenings in everyday life.

newshole the space left over in a newspaper for news content after all the ads are placed.

newspaper chain a large company that owns several papers throughout the country.

newsreels weekly ten-minute magazine-style compilations of filmed news events from around the world organized in a sequence of short reports; prominent in movie theaters between the 1920s and the 1950s.

news/talk/information format the fastest-growing radio format in the 1990s, dominated by news programs or talk shows.

newsworthiness the often unstated criteria that journalists use to determine which events and issues should become news reports, including timeliness, proximity, conflict, prominence, human interest, consequence, usefulness, novelty, and deviance.

nickelodeons the first small makeshift movie theaters, which were often converted cigar stores, pawnshops, or restaurants redecorated to mimic vaudeville theaters.

ninjas game players who snatch loot out of turn and then leave a group, or **PUG**.

noobs game players who are clueless beginners.

O & Os TV stations "owned and operated" by networks.

objective journalism a modern style of journalism that distinguishes factual reports from opinion columns; reporters strive to remain neutral toward the issue or event they cover, searching out competing points of view among the sources for a story.

obscenity expression that is not protected as speech if these three legal tests are all met: (1) the average person, applying contemporary community standards, would find that the material as a whole appeals to prurient interest; (2) the material depicts or describes sexual conduct in a patently offensive way; (3) the material, as a whole, lacks serious literary, artistic, political, or scientific value.

off-network syndication in television, the process whereby older programs that no longer run during prime time are made available for reruns to local stations, cable operators, online services, and foreign markets.

offset lithography a technology that enabled books to be printed from photographic plates rather than metal casts, reducing the cost of color and illustrations and eventually permitting computers to perform typesetting.

oligopoly in media economics, an organizational structure in which a few firms control most of an industry's production and distribution resources.

online fantasy sports games in which players assemble teams and use actual sports results to determine scores in their online games. These games reach a mass audience, have a major social component, and take a managerial perspective on the game.

online piracy the illegal uploading, downloading, or streaming of copyrighted material, such as music or movies.

open-source software noncommercial software shared freely and developed collectively on the Internet.

opinion and fair comment a defense against libel that states that libel applies only to intentional misstatements of factual information rather than to statements of opinion.

opt-in or **opt-out policies** controversial Web site policies over personal data gathering: *opt-in* means Web sites must gain explicit permission from online consumers before the site can collect their personal data; *opt-out* means that Web sites can automatically collect personal data unless the consumer goes to the trouble of filling out a specific form to restrict the practice.

option time a business tactic, now illegal, whereby a radio network in the 1920s and 1930s paid an affiliate station a set fee per hour for an option to control programming and advertising on that station.

Pacifica Foundation a radio broadcasting foundation established in Berkeley, California, by journalist and World War II pacifist Lewis Hill; he established KPFA, the first nonprofit community radio station, in 1949.

paperback books books made with less expensive paper covers, introduced in the United States in the mid-1800s.

papyrus one of the first substances to hold written language and symbols; produced from plant reeds found along the Nile River.

Paramount decision the 1948 U.S. Supreme Court decision that ended vertical integration in the film industry by forcing the studios to divest themselves of their theaters.

parchment treated animal skin that replaced papyrus as an early pre-paper substance on which to document written language.

partisan press an early dominant style of American journalism distinguished by opinion newspapers, which generally argued one political point of view or pushed the plan of the particular party that subsidized the paper.

pass-along readership the total number of people who come into contact with a single copy of a magazine.

payola the unethical (but not always illegal) practice of record promoters paying deejays or radio programmers to favor particular songs over others.

pay-per-view (PPV) a cable-television service that allows customers to select a particular movie for a fee, or to pay $25 to $40 for a special one-time event.

paywall an online portal that charges consumers a fee for access to news content.

penny arcade the first thoroughly modern indoor playground, filled with coin-operated games.

penny papers (also *penny press*) refers to newspapers that, because of technological innovations in printing, were able to drop their price to one cent beginning in the 1830s, thereby making papers affordable to working and emerging middle classes and enabling newspapers to become a genuine mass medium.

phishing an Internet scam that begins with phony e-mail messages that appear to be from an official site and request that customers send their credit card numbers and other personal information to update the account.

photojournalism the use of photos to document events and people's lives.

pinball machine the most prominent mechanical game, in which players score points by manipulating the path of a metal ball on a playfield in a glass-covered case.

plain-folks pitch an advertising strategy that associates a product with simplicity and the common person.

podcasting a distribution method (coined from "iPod" and "broadcasting") that enables listeners to download audio program files from the Internet for playback on computers or digital music players.

political advertising the use of ad techniques to promote a candidate's image and persuade the public to adopt a particular viewpoint.

political economy studies an area of academic study that specifically examines interconnections among economic interests, political power, and how that power is used.

pop music popular music that appeals either to a wide cross section of the public or to sizable subdivisions within the larger public based on age, region, or ethnic background; the word *pop* has also been used as a label to distinguish popular music from classical music.

populism a political idea that tries to appeal to ordinary people by contrasting "the people" with "the elite."

portal an entry point to the Internet, such as a search engine.

postmodern the term describing a contemporary historical era spanning the 1960s to the present; its social values include opposing hierarchy, diversifying and recycling culture, questioning scientific reasoning, and embracing paradox.

premium channels in cable programming, a tier of channels that subscribers can order at an additional monthly fee over their basic cable service; these may include movie channels and interactive services.

press agent the earliest type of public relations practitioner, who seeks to advance a client's image through media exposure.

press releases in public relations, announcements–written in the style of news reports–that give new information about an individual, a company, or an organization and pitch a story idea to the news media.

prime time in television programming, the hours between 8 and 11 P.M. (or 7 and 10 P.M. in the Midwest), when networks have traditionally drawn their largest audiences and charged their highest advertising rates.

Prime Time Access Rule (PTAR) an FCC regulation that reduced networks' control of prime-time programming to encourage more local news and public-affairs programs, often between 6 and 7 P.M.

printing press a fifteenth-century invention whose movable metallic type technology spawned modern mass communication by creating the first method for mass production; it reduced the size and cost of books, made them the first mass medium affordable to less affluent people, and provided the impetus for the Industrial Revolution, assembly-line production, modern capitalism, and the rise of consumer culture.

prior restraint the legal definition of censorship in the United States; it prohibits courts and governments from blocking any publication or speech before it actually occurs.

product placement the advertising practice of strategically placing products in movies, TV shows, comic books, and video games so the products appear as part of a story's set environment.

professional books technical books that target various occupational groups and are not intended for the general consumer market.

Progressive Era a period of political and social reform that lasted from the 1890s to the 1920s.

progressive rock an alternative music format that developed as a backlash to the popularity of Top 40.

propaganda in advertising and public relations, a communication strategy that tries to manipulate public opinion to gain support for a special issue, program, or policy, such as a nation's war effort.

propaganda analysis the study of propaganda's effectiveness in influencing and mobilizing public opinion.

pseudo-events in public relations, circumstances or events created solely for the purpose of obtaining coverage in the media.

pseudo-polls typically call-in, online, or person-in-the-street nonscientific polls that the news media use to address a "question of the day."

psychographics in market research, the study of audience or consumer attitudes, beliefs, interests, and motivations.

Public Broadcasting Act of 1967 the act by the U.S. Congress that established the Corporation for Public Broadcasting, which oversees the Public Broadcasting Service (PBS) and National Public Radio (NPR).

Public Broadcasting Service (PBS) noncommercial television established in 1967 by the U.S. Congress to provide an alternative to commercial television.

public domain the end of the copyright period for a work, at which point the public may begin to access it for free.

publicity in public relations, the positive and negative messages that spread controlled and uncontrolled information about a person, a corporation, an issue, or a policy in various media.

public journalism a type of journalism, driven by citizen forums, that goes beyond telling the news to embrace a broader mission of improving the quality of public life; also called *civic journalism*.

public relations the total communication strategy conducted by a person, a government, or an organization attempting to reach and persuade its audiences to adopt a point of view.

public service announcements (PSAs) reports or announcements, carried free by radio and TV stations, that promote government programs, educational projects, voluntary agencies, or social reform.

public sphere those areas or arenas in social life–like the town square or coffee house–where people come together regularly to discuss social and cultural problems and try to influence politics; the public sphere is distinguished from governmental spheres where elected officials and other representatives conduct affairs of state.

PUGs in gaming, temporary teams usually assembled by match-making programs integrated into a game (short for "Pick-Up Groups").

pulp fiction a term used to describe many late-nineteenth-century popular paperbacks and dime novels, which were constructed of cheap machine-made pulp material.

punk rock rock music that challenges the orthodoxy and commercialism of the recording business; it is characterized by loud, unpolished qualities, a jackhammer beat, primal vocal screams, crude aggression, and defiant or comic lyrics.

qualified privilege a legal right allowing journalists to report judicial or legislative proceedings even though the public statements being reported may be libelous.

Radio Act of 1912 the first radio legislation passed by Congress, it addressed the problem of amateur radio operators cramming the airwaves.

Radio Act of 1927 the second radio legislation passed by Congress; in an attempt to restore order to the airwaves, the act stated that licensees did not own their channels but could license them if they operated to serve the "public interest, convenience, or necessity."

Radio Corporation of America (RCA) a company developed during World War I that was designed, with government approval, to pool radio patents; the formation of RCA gave the United States almost total control over the emerging mass medium of broadcasting.

radio waves a portion of the electromagnetic wave spectrum that was harnessed so that signals could be sent from a transmission point and obtained at a reception point.

random assignment a social science research method for assigning research subjects; it ensures that every subject has an equal chance of being placed in either the experimental group or the control group.

rating in TV audience measurement, a statistical estimate expressed as a percentage of households tuned to a program in the local or national market being sampled.

receivers the targets of messages crafted by senders.

reference books dictionaries, encyclopedias, atlases, and other reference manuals related to particular professions or trades.

regional editions national magazines whose content is tailored to the interests of different geographic areas.

rerun syndication in television, the process whereby programs that stay in a network's lineup long enough to build up a certain number of episodes (usually four seasons' worth) are sold, or syndicated, to hundreds of TV markets in the United States and abroad.

responsible capitalism an underlying value held by many U.S. journalists and citizens, it assumes that businesspeople should compete with one another not primarily to maximize profits but to increase prosperity for all.

retransmission fee the fee that cable providers pay to broadcast networks for the right to carry their channels.

rhythm and blues (or **R&B**) music that merges urban blues with big-band sounds.

right to privacy addresses a person's right to be left alone, without his or her name, image, or daily activities becoming public property.

rockabilly music that mixes bluegrass and country influences with those of black folk music and early amplified blues.

rock and roll music that merges the African American influences of urban blues, gospel, and R&B with the white influences of country, folk, and pop vocals.

role-playing games (RPGs) games that are typically set in a fantasy or sci-fi world in which each player (there can be multiple players in a game) chooses to play as a character that specializes in a particular skill set.

rotation in format radio programming, the practice of playing the most popular or best-selling songs many times throughout the day.

satellite radio pay radio services that deliver various radio formats nationally via satellite.

saturation advertising the strategy of inundating a variety of print and visual media with ads aimed at target audiences.

scientific method a widely used research method that studies phenomena in systematic stages; it includes identifying a research problem, reviewing existing research, developing working hypotheses, determining appropriate research design, collecting information, analyzing results to see if the hypotheses have been verified, and interpreting the implications of the study.

Section 315 part of the 1934 Communications Act; it mandates that during elections, broadcast stations must provide equal opportunities and response time for qualified political candidates.

selective exposure the phenomenon whereby audiences seek messages and meanings that correspond to their preexisting beliefs and values.

selective retention the phenomenon whereby audiences remember or retain messages and meanings that correspond to their preexisting beliefs and values.

senders the authors, producers, agencies, and organizations that transmit messages to receivers.

serial program a radio or TV program, such as a soap opera, that features continuing story lines from day to day or week to week (for contrast, see **chapter show**).

share in TV audience measurement, a statistical estimate of the percentage of homes tuned to a certain program, compared with those simply using their sets at the time of a sample.

shield laws laws protecting the confidentiality of key interview subjects and reporters' rights not to reveal the sources of controversial information used in news stories.

simulation games games that involve managing resources and planning worlds that are typically based in reality.

situation comedy a type of comedy series that features a recurring cast and set as well as several narrative scenes; each episode establishes a situation, complicates it, develops increasing confusion among its characters, and then resolves the complications.

sketch comedy short television comedy skits that are usually segments of TV variety shows; sometimes known as *vaudeo*, the marriage of vaudeville and video.

slander in law, spoken language that defames a person's character.

slogan in advertising, a catchy phrase that attempts to promote or sell a product by capturing its essence in words.

small-town pastoralism an underlying value held by many U.S. journalists and citizens, it favors the small over the large and the rural over the urban.

snob-appeal approach an advertising strategy that attempts to convince consumers that using a product will enable them to maintain or elevate their social station.

social learning theory a theory within media effects research that suggests a link between the mass media and behavior.

social media digital applications that allow people worldwide to have conversations, share common interests, and generate their own media content online.

social networking sites sites on which users can create content, share ideas, and interact with friends.

social responsibility model a model for journalism and speech, influenced by the libertarian model, that encourages the free flow of information to citizens so they can make wise decisions about political and often more social issues.

soul music that mixes gospel, blues, and urban and southern black styles with slower, more emotional, and melancholic lyrics.

sound bite in TV journalism, the equivalent of a quote in print; the part of a news report in which an expert, a celebrity, a victim, or a person on the street is interviewed about some aspect of an event or issue.

space brokers in the days before modern advertising, individuals who purchased space in newspapers and sold it to various merchants.

spam a computer term referring to unsolicited e-mail.

spiral of silence a theory that links the mass media, social psychology, and the formation of public opinion; the theory says that people who hold minority views on controversial issues tend to keep their views silent.

split-run editions editions of national magazines that tailor ads to different geographic areas.

spyware software with secretive codes that enable commercial firms to "spy" on users and gain access to their computers.

stereo the recording of two separate channels or tracks of sound.

storyboard in advertising, a blueprint or roughly drawn comic-strip version of a proposed advertisement.

strategy games games in which perspective is omniscient and the player must survey the entire "world" or playing field and make strategic decisions.

studio system an early film production system that constituted a sort of assembly-line process for moviemaking; major film studios controlled not only actors but also directors, editors, writers, and other employees, all of whom worked under exclusive contracts.

subliminal advertising a 1950s term that refers to hidden or disguised print and visual messages that allegedly register on the subconscious, creating false needs and seducing people into buying products.

subsidiary rights in the book industry, selling the rights to a book for use in other media forms, such as a mass market paperback, a CD-ROM, or the basis for a movie screenplay.

supermarket tabloids newspapers that feature bizarre human-interest stories, gruesome murder tales, violent accident accounts, unexplained phenomena stories, and malicious celebrity gossip.

superstations local independent TV stations, such as WTBS in Atlanta or WGN in Chicago, that have uplinked their signals onto a communication satellite to make themselves available nationwide.

survey research in social science research, a method of collecting and measuring data taken from a group of respondents.

syndication leasing TV stations or cable networks the exclusive right to air TV shows.

synergy in media economics, the promotion and sale of a product (and all its versions) throughout the various subsidiaries of a media conglomerate.

talkies movies with sound, beginning in 1927.

Telecommunications Act of 1996 the sweeping update of telecommunications law that led to a wave of media consolidation.

telegraph invented in the 1840s, it sent electrical impulses through a cable from a transmitter to a reception point, transmitting Morse code.

textbooks books made for the el-hi (elementary and high school) and college markets.

textual analysis in media research, a method for closely and critically examining and interpreting the meanings of culture, including architecture, fashion, books, movies, and TV programs.

third-person effect the theory that people believe others are more affected by media messages than they are themselves.

third screens the computer-type screens on which consumers can view television, movies, music, newspapers, and books.

time shifting the process whereby television viewers record shows and watch them later, when it is convenient for them.

Top 40 format the first radio format, in which stations played the forty most popular hits in a given week as measured by record sales.

trade books the most visible book industry segment, featuring hardbound and paperback books aimed at general readers and sold at bookstores and other retail outlets.

transistors invented by Bell Laboratories in 1947, these tiny pieces of technology, which receive and amplify radio signals, make portable radios possible.

trolls players who take pleasure in intentionally spoiling a gaming experience for others.

underground press radical newspapers, run on shoestring budgets, that question mainstream political policies and conventional values; the term usually refers to a journalism movement of the 1960s.

university press the segment of the book industry that publishes scholarly books in specialized areas.

urban contemporary one of radio's more popular formats, primarily targeting African American listeners in urban areas with dance, R&B, and hip-hop music.

uses and gratifications model a mass communication research model, usually employing in-depth interviews and survey questionnaires, that argues that people use the media to satisfy various emotional desires or intellectual needs.

Values and Lifestyles (VALS) a market-research strategy that divides consumers into types and measures psychological factors, including how consumers think and feel about products and how they achieve (or do not achieve) the lifestyles to which they aspire.

vellum a handmade paper made from treated animal skin, used in the Gutenberg Bibles.

vertical integration in media economics, the phenomenon of controlling a mass media industry at its three essential levels: production, distribution, and exhibition; the term is most frequently used in reference to the film industry.

video news releases (VNRs) in public relations, the visual counterparts to press releases; they pitch story ideas to the TV news media by mimicking the style of a broadcast news report.

video-on-demand (VOD) cable television technology that enables viewers to instantly order programming such as movies to be digitally delivered to their sets.

viral marketing short videos or other content that marketers hope will quickly gain widespread attention as users share it with friends online, or by word of mouth.

vitascope a large-screen movie projection system developed by Thomas Edison.

Webzine a magazine that publishes on the Internet.

wiki Web sites Web sites that are capable of being edited by any user; the most famous is Wikipedia.

wireless telegraphy the forerunner of radio, a form of voiceless point-to-point communication; it preceded the voice and sound transmissions of one-to-many mass communication that became known as broadcasting.

wireless telephony early experiments in wireless voice and music transmissions, which later developed into modern radio.

wire services commercial organizations, such as the Associated Press, that share news stories and information by relaying them around the country and the world, originally via telegraph and now via satellite transmission.

World Wide Web (WWW) a data-linking system for organizing and standardizing information on the Internet; the WWW enables computer-accessed information to associate with—or link to—other information, no matter where it is on the Internet.

yellow journalism a newspaper style or era that peaked in the 1890s, it emphasized high-interest stories, sensational crime news, large headlines, and serious reports that exposed corruption, particularly in business and government.

zines self-published magazines produced on personal computer programs or on the Internet.

Credits

Text Credits

16, Figure 1.1: "Daily Media Consumption by Platform, 2010 (8- to 18-Year-Olds)." The Henry J. Kaiser Family Foundation.
47, Figure 2.1: "Distributed Networks." Reprinted with the permission of Simon & Schuster, Inc. from WHERE WIZARDS STAY UP LATE: THE ORIGINS OF THE INTERNET by Katie Hafner and Matthew Lyon. Copyright © 1996 by Katie Hafner and Matthew Lyon. All rights reserved. **89, Case Study:** Butler, Isaac. "Thoughts on Video Game Narrative." Parabasis, March 30, 2011. Reprinted by permission of the author. **90, Figure 3.1:** "Top Video Game Genres by Units Sold, 2011." Entertainment Software Association. **107, Figure 3.2:** "Where the Money Goes on a $60 Video Game." Altered Gamer. **125, Figure 4.1:** "Annual Vinyl, Tape, CD, Mobile, and Digital Sales." Recording Industry Association of America.
143, Tracking Technology: Seabrook, John. "The Song Machine: The Hitmakers behind Rihanna." The New Yorker, March 26, 2012. Reprinted by permission of the author. **144, Figure 4.2:** "U.S. Market Share of the Major Labels in the Recording Industry, 2011." Nielsen SoundScan. **147, Figure 4.3:** Knopper, Steve. "Where the Money Goes: The New Economics of the Music Industry: How Artists Really Make Money in the Cloud—or Don't." Rolling Stone, October 25, 2011. **148, Case Study:** Lafraniere, Sharon. Adapted from "In the Jungle, the Unjust Jungle, a Small Victory," from The New York Times, March 26, 2006. Copyright © 2006 The New York Times. All rights reserved. Used by permission and protected by the Copyright Laws of the United States. The printing, copying, redistribution, or retransmission of this content without express written permission is prohibited. **160, Figure 5.1:** "The Electromagnetic Spectrum." NASA. **173, Figure 5.2:** Cheshire, David. "AM and FM Waves." Van Nostrand Reinhold (International) Professional & Reference. **174, Figure 5.3:** Radio Program Log for an Adult Contemporary (AC) Station. KCVM, Cedar Falls, IA.
176, Figure 5.4: "The Most Popular Radio Formats in the United States among Persons Age Twelve and Older." Arbitron. **177, Case Study:** Excerpted from "Host: The Origins of Talk Radio" by David Foster Wallace. Originally published in The Atlantic, April 2005, 66-68. Reprinted with permission of the Frederick Hill-Bonnie Nadell, Inc. Literary Agency, as agents for the author. **202, Figure 6.1:** "A Basic Cable Television System." Clear Creek Telephone & Television. **206, Figure 6.2:** "Prime-Time TV Audience, 1984-2009." Nielsen TV Ratings Data, 2010. The Nielsen Company. **208, Figure 6.3:** "The Cross Platform Report Q3 2011." The Nielsen Company. **210, Figure 6.4:** "A Look at the Top Genres over the Past Decade," from "Ten Years of Primetime: The Rise of Reality and Sports Programming," September 21, 2011. The Nielsen Company. **222, Figure 6.5:** "Prime-Time Network TV Pricing, 2011" by Brian Steinberg. **228, Tracking Technology:** "Streaming Dreams: YouTube Turns Pro" by John Seabrook. The New Yorker, January 16, 2012. Reprinted by permission of the author.
261, Figure 7.1: "Gross Revenues from Box-Office Sales, 1987-2011." Motion Picture Association of America, U.S. Market Statistics, 2011. **262, Table 7.1:** "The Top 10 All-Time Box-Office Champions." July 11, 2011. Reprinted with the permission of Box Office Guru, Inc. **264, Figure 7.2:** "Market Share of U.S. Film Studios and Distributors, 2011 (in $ Millions)." Box Office Mojo, Studio Market Share. **266, Figure 7.3:** "Online Movie Market Share Ranking in 2011." IHS Screen Digest, June 2012. **296, Figure 8.1:** "Selected Alternative Newspapers in the United States." Reprinted by permission of Association of Alternative Newsmedia. **303, Global Village:** Pfanner,

Eric. Excerpted from "How the German Newspaper Industry Stays Healthier than Its U.S. Counterpart." International Herald Tribune, May 17, 2010. Copyright © 2010 The New York Times. All rights reserved. Used by permission and protected by the Copyright Laws of the United States. The printing, copying, redistribution, or retransmission of this content without express written permission is prohibited. **305, Figure 8.2:** "Percentage Change in Ad Spending by Medium, 2011-2012." MediaLife Magazine, "Ad Spending Is Back on the Rise," accessed August 22, 2012. **339, Figure 9.1:** "Revenue Growth of Top Magazine Companies, 2008-2010." Advertising Age, Data Center, December 2011. **354, Figure 10.1:** "Estimated U.S. Book Revenue, 2010." Publishers Weekly, "Book Stats Publishing Categories Highlights." **355, Figure 10.2:** "Where the New Textbook Dollar Goes." © 2011 by the National Association of College Stores. **356, Case Study:** Rogers, Mark C. "Comic Books Blend Print and Visual Art." **364, Tracking Technology:** Auletta, Ken. "Paper Trail: Did Publishers and Apple Collude against Amazon?" © 2012 by Ken Auletta. Used by permission. All rights reserved.
366, Figure 10.3: "Banned and Challenged Books," American Library Association. **368, Figure 10.4:** Auletta, Ken. "How a Book's Revenue Is Divided." From The New Yorker, "Publish or Peril: Can the iPad Topple the Kindle and Save the Book Business?" April 26, 2010. **371, Figure 10.5:** Owen, Laura Hazard. "New Stats Show iPad Surging Again as Kindle Fire, Nook Tablet, Fall." Paidcontent.org. August 14, 2012. **390, Figure 11.1:** "Global Revenue for the World's Four Largest Agencies (in Billions of Dollars)." Advertising Age, Agency Family Trees 2012. Updated August 16, 2012. **391, Figure 11.2:** "U.S. Ad Spending Totals/Zenith Optimedia Forecasts through 2012." Advertising Age, June 20, 2011. **393, Figure 11.3:** "Types and Characteristics from the VALS Framework." Used with permission of Strategic Business Insights (SBI). **428, Figure 12.1:** "The Top 4 Holding Firms, with Public Relations Subsidiaries, 2012 (by Worldwide Revenue in U.S. Dollars)." Advertising Age, Agency Family Trees 2012. **436, Figure 12.3:** "Total Lobbying Spending and Number of Lobbyists (2000-2012)." Center for Responsive Politics, based on data from the Senate Office of Public Records, through August 14, 2012. **442, Table 12.1:** "Public Relations Society of America, Member Code of Ethics." Reprinted with permission of The Public Relations Society of America. **464, Case Study:** "Ownership of Full-Power Commercial Radio Stations." FCC Form 323 filings; U.S. Census Bureau; Free Press Research, 2007. **465, Case Study:** "Ownership of Full-Power Commercial TV Stations." FCC Form 323 filings; U.S. Census Bureau; Free Press Research, 2007. **492, Case Study:** "Is There a Bias in Reporting the News?" PRC Internet & American Life Project and PRC Project for Excelllence in Journalism Online News Survey. **495, Figure 14.1:** "Society of Professional Journalists' Code of Ethics." © Copyright Society of Professional Journalists. Reprinted with permission. **524, Figure 15.1:** "TV Parental Guidelines." TV Parental Guidelines Monitoring Board. Reprinted by permission.

Photo Credits

Key: Bettmann/Corbis = BT/CO; Getty Images = GI; Photofest = PF; The Everett Collection = EC

Praise spread, CO/BT; **xiii**, Ida Mae Astute/ABC via GI; **xiv**, Fred Paul/GI; **xv**, Johannes Eisele/AFP/GI; **xvi**, © Andy Sturmey/UPPA/ZUMApress.com; **xvii**, Tim Pannell/Corbis/Photolibrary; **xviii**, Prashant Gupta/© FX Network/courtesy EC; **xix**, Copyright ©

Index

Twitter
advertising on, 44, 398
journalists use of, 507
live-tweeting, 14, 60
media event tweets, 13-14, 60
media multitasking with, 13-14
as oral culture, 9
popularity of, 53
privacy audit by FTC, 578
public relations use of, 437
and self-disclosure, 578, 581
2001: A Space Odyssey, 202
Tylenol crisis, 423, 439

U2, 140
Ubisoft, 84, 96, 107
Ultrasurf, 55
UltraViolet, 265-66
Ulysses (Joyce), 366, 556-57
Uncharted, 90, 105
Uncle Tom's Cabin (Stowe), 353, 360
Undefeated, 254
underground press, 279, 296-97
Underwood, Carrie, 142
Unforgivable Blackness, 562
Ungaro, Susan, 497
Unilever, 397, 474
United Artists
history of, 245
in Little Three, 240, 247
United Features, 299
United Independent Broadcasters (UIB), 167
United Mine Workers, 425-26
United Nations Global Compact, 434
United Negro College Fund, 388
United Press International (UPI), 298
Universal
as current major studio, 264
GE purchase of, 265
in Little Three, 240, 247
market share (2011), 264
Universal Music Group
CDs, priced reduction, 454
EMI purchase plan, 453
market share (2011), 144
on music video revenues, 147, 149
as oligopoly, 453
payola settlement, 185
Polygram purchase by, 144
University of Chicago Press, 360
university press books, 359
Univision Communications
number of stations (2011), 186
Spanish-language radio, 187
Spanish-language television, 217

Univision Network, 217, 230
Univision Online, 187
Unsafe at Any Speed (Nader), 423, 435
Up, 97, 463
Updike, John, 333
Up in the Air, 404
Uptown cigarettes, 408
Uptown records, 144
urban contemporary music format, 178
Urban Outfitters, 369
USA Network, 194, 203
USA PATRIOT Act of 2001, 68, 557
USA Today
apps, use of, 302
circulation (2011 vs. 2012), 286, 305
color/format of, 289-90
daily circulation, size of, 302
digital copy, regional printing, 336
Gannett ownership of, 299
online format, 59
in post-modern era, 28
and reader credibility, 504
television as model for, 279, 289-90
USA Weekend, 301
U.S. Commerce Department, radio, early regulation, 164-65
U.S. Defense Department
Internet, development of, 46-48
public relations by, 430, 437
uses and gratifications model, 528
Usher, 142
Usher, Nikki, 514
U.S. Justice Department
AT&T/T-Mobile merger rejected by, 472
antitrust enforcement, 455
on Apple e-book price fixing, 346, 364, 370
network television, limiting control of, 218-19, 224
U.S. News & World Report, 323
USS Maine, 324
Us Weekly, 328, 330, 336
Utne Reader, 340
U-verse television service, 231

vacuum tube, wireless telephony, 161
Valens, Ritchie, 134
Valenti, Jack, 564
Vallée, Rudy, 129
values. *See* cultural values
Values and Lifestyles (VALS) system, 392-94

Valve Corporation, 95, 110
Vampire Diaries, 227
Vampire Weekend, 140
VandeHei, Jim, 302
Vanderbilt, Cornelius, 455
Van Doren, Charles, 200-201
Vanishing Lady, The, 243
Vanity Fair, 330, 333, 337, 339
Vann, Robert C., 294
Van Sant, Gus, 266
Van Zandt, Steve, 208
variables, research, 529
variety shows
radio shows, 169
television, 210-11
Varney, Christine A., 364
vaudeville, 129, 210-11
Veep, 23
vellum, 350
Velvet Underground, 139, 553
Verizon
as broadband ISP, 50
digital piracy activism, 127
FiOS television service, 231
net neutrality as issue, 71
subscribers, number of, 230
Verne, Jules, 314
Versus, 231
vertical integration, 245, 258, 265, 370
Vertigo, 250
Vevo, 120, 121, 150
VHS (Video Home System), 206-7, 241
Viacom
CBS purchased by, 230
film studios of, 264
independent films, end of, 256
market share (2011), 264
split of, 187
YouTube copyright infringement suit, 467
Victor Talking Machine Company, 12, 124, 166-67
Victrolas, 122, 124
video, streaming. *See* streaming video
videocassette recorders (VCRs), 206, 241, 260
video games
development of, 40, 80, 82-83
evolution of. *See* digital gaming
video news releases (VNRs), 423, 430
video-on-demand (VOD), 205
video rentals, 207, 253
video sharing services, 53. *See also* YouTube

Vietnam War
news coverage, 214
Pentagon Papers, 550-51
photojournalism, 325
protests, 139
reporter casualties, 308
television images, 14, 15
View, The, 35
Village People, 140
Village Voice, 279, 296
Vilsack, Tom, 500
Vimeo, 53, 56
violence and media
and digital gaming, 80, 90, 99, 103
examples of, 519-20
and movie ratings, 564
online dangerous information, 69
study of. *See* media effects research
television programs, 525
Vioxx ads, 411
viral marketing, 394
viral videos, 53-54, 405
Virginian-Pilot, 508
Virginia Tech campus shooting, 520
Virgin record stores, 145
virtual communities, for gamers. *See* digital game virtual communities
virtual game worlds. *See also* massively multiplayer online role-playing games (MMORPGs)
virtual social worlds, 54, 86-87, 106-7
VistaVision, 259
visual design, in advertising, 389-90
vitascope, 240, 243
Vivendi, 265
Vivendi Blizzard, 106
vocational texts, 355
Vogue, 314, 337, 339
Voice, The, 14, 60, 227
Voice of San Diego, 309
voice recognition
digital gaming interactivity, 81, 84, 87, 93, 103
Semantic Web application, 62
Volkswagen ads, 394, 395, 399
Volvo ads, 412
Vow, The, 250
Vudu, 265

WABC, 194
wage gap
Apple, 146
media companies, 459

More Media. Integrated.

bedfordstmartins.com/mediaculture

Throughout the new integrated media edition of *Media and Culture*, the book directs you to the *Media and Culture* companion Web site, where videos from *VideoCentral: Mass Communication* complement the material in the text. The book lists any further related videos under "Additional Videos" in the Chapter Review sections. Here is a quick list of all the videos featured in the book by chapter. For directions on how to access these videos online, please see instructions to the right.